The Eschatology of the Restoration of All Things

The dawning of the age of enlightenment

Mike Parsons

The Eschatology of the Restoration of All Things

Copyright © 2022 Mike Parsons,
Freedom Apostolic Ministries Ltd.

Cover Design: Jeremy Westcott.
Copyright © 2022 Jeremy Westcott,
Freedom Apostolic Ministries Ltd.

The right of Mike Parsons to be identified as the author of this work has been asserted by him in accordance with the Copyright, Designs and Patents Act 1988.

All rights reserved. No part of this publication may be reproduced or transmitted in any form or by any means, electronic or mechanical including photocopying, recording or any information storage or retrieval system, without prior permission in writing from the publishers.

First published in the United Kingdom in 2022 by
The Choir Press
in conjunction with
Freedom Apostolic Ministries Ltd.

ISBN 978-1-78963-335-1

Contents

Introduction v
1. My Eschatological Journey. 13
2. The Fruit of the Poisonous Tree. 23
3. Happy Eschatology. 49
4. The Second Coming is Raptureless, Tribulationless and Millenniumless. 125
5. Zionism and the Luciferian Agenda 261
6. Hebrew Roots Theology and Jewish Mysticism. 373
7. The Political and Religious Spirit and its Luciferian Babel Agenda. 431
8. The Hoodwinking of History. 461
9. Exposing the Great Deception. 497
10. The Revealing of the Sons of God. 539
11. Creative Sonship Responsibility 673
Appendices 785

Introduction

In my previous books, *My Journey Beyond Beyond* and *The Restoration of All Things – My continuing journey beyond beyond*, I shared my experiences and encounters concerning deeper intimacy and relationship with my heavenly Father. These revealed His true nature as love and therefore the restoration of all things as His agenda for creation. The books were written like a tapestry of my supernatural encounters to create a picture that eventually revealed the Father's true character, nature and essence as unconditional love.

In the first book, four threads were woven together to create a rich tapestry expressing the pure joy and delight of a child discovering true reality for the first time. This journey is full of surprising revelations and experiences which unveiled further dimensions and depths beyond beyond once again. My encounters took me deeper into the Father's loving heart, unveiling and revealing His Oracles for creation's restoration.

The second book wove further threads together to continue my journey that unveiled the purpose of the great shift in 2020, the oracles of the Father's heart, sonship in regards to restoration, the full scope of restoration, exploding the 'hell' myth, and universalism.

The conclusion I arrived at, having spent thousands of hours journaling my encounters with God who is Father, Son and Spirit – was that the restoration of all things is an inevitable consequence of who God is. That conclusion gives a context that enables us to look to the future with optimistic anticipation and expectation.

Father revealed to me that there are four streams of revelation that are flowing towards one another to become one mighty river of the restoration of all things. Those four streams of revelation that have directly contributed to my revealing of restoration journey are:

- Realised eschatology
- Mystical sonship
- Christian Universalism
- Energy frequency healing

Without the stream of realised or happy eschatology, there is no context for the expectation of the restoration of all things. That is why I am writing this book about eschatology, which I now know to be an oxymoron and a deception in itself.

Why is eschatology so important to my journey and the restoration of all things?

What is eschatology and why is it an oxymoron or self-contradictory word?

The word arises from the Greek *eschatos,* meaning 'last' and the suffix '-logy' meaning 'the study of', and first appeared in English around 1844. The Oxford English Dictionary defines eschatology as 'the part of theology concerned with death, judgment, and the final destiny of the soul and humankind'.

> eschatology (n.) 1834, from Latinized form of Greek eskhatos "last, furthest, uttermost, extreme, most remote" in time, space, degree (from PIE *eghs-ko-, suffixed form of *eghs "out;" see ex-) + -ology. In theology, the study of the four last things (death, judgment, heaven, hell).
> – Online Etymology Dictionary
>
> eschaton (n.) "divinely ordained climax of history," 1935, coined by Protestant theologian Charles Harold Dodd

INTRODUCTION

(1884-1973) from Greek eskhaton, neuter of eskhatos "last, furthest, uttermost."
– Online Etymology Dictionary

Eschatology / ɛskəˈtɒlədʒi is a part of theology concerned with the final events of history or the ultimate destiny of humanity. This concept is commonly referred to as the 'end of the world' or 'end times'.
– dbpedia: *About: Eschatology*

In common evangelical understanding, it would be a study of the 'end times' and half the Amazon rainforest has probably been cut down to make the paper for all the books written about the subject.

The end times in pop theology is looking to the future end of the world and time of the destruction of the heavens and the earth which ushers in the eternal state and the age to come in a new heaven and earth. Therein lies the paradox: how can there be an end if you believe in the restoration of all things? If, according to Isaiah 9:6, there is no end to the increase of God's government and peace, how can there be a final end? That is why eschatology is an oxymoron to anyone who believes in the restoration of all things.

For a Child will be born to us, a Son will be given to us;
And the government will rest on His shoulders;
And His name will be called Wonderful Counselor, Mighty God,
Eternal Father, Prince of Peace.
There will be no end to the increase of His government or of peace
On the throne of David and over his kingdom,
To establish it and to uphold it with justice and righteousness
From then on and forevermore.

INTRODUCTION

The zeal of the Lord of armies will accomplish this.
(Isaiah 9:6-7).

It is not only an oxymoron but also part of the great deception that has hoodwinked mankind since they followed the Luciferian agenda of the DIY tree of the knowledge of good and evil. That is the path that pursues humanistic knowledge in independence from God, which will always lead to deception because, as Jesus stated, the devil was a murderer and a liar from the beginning:

You are of your father the devil, and you want to do the desires of your father. He was a murderer from the beginning and does not stand in the truth because there is no truth in him. Whenever he tells a lie, he speaks from his own nature, because he is a liar and the father of lies. (John 8:44).

In chapter 9, I will attempt to weave all the threads together to expose what the Father called 'the great deception'. That deception is the Luciferian goal of establishing a counterfeit one-world government in one physical location, Jerusalem, where an elite group will rule over the subjugated, subhuman *goyim* (or Gentiles) under Noahide laws.

In the final two chapters, I will share my experiences of the revealing of the sons of God to answer creation's groaning for restoration.

I am writing this book primarily because in 2020 the Father told me several times to write it.

"Son, the eschatology of restoration is a book that must be written to warn and prepare the Joshua generation for their restoration mandate.

INTRODUCTION

"Son, do not waver, and trust that you are on the right path. So do not hold back: write the book that will reveal the eschatology of restoration so Our children can be free from religious and political deception.

"Son, you must take up this mandate and write the book *The Eschatology of the Restoration of All Things* that will expose the deceptions and reveal the Luciferian agendas behind them."

In the pursuit of the truth, my primary source is the Truth Himself, Jesus, who is the greatest fact-checker of them all. Before I go any further I want to share my rationale concerning evidential material and historical accuracy. I have researched many sources, some of which are contradictory: so which sources do I trust and believe and which do I not? I do not want to operate in confirmation bias so I have not just looked at the sources of information that I already know agrees with my position. I have looked at much material that contradicts both the premise of this book and my eschatological views to get a balance and uncover the truth.

My starting point is always what the Father or Jesus have said to me and what frequency that truth carries. If you spend enough time hanging out with the source of all truth you will find it easier to discern what has the frequency of truth and what does not. We have to train our senses by practice to discern what is true and that is best done in a relationship with the Truth that develops through encounters. Knowledge is not to be intellectually discerned, as that is just information, but it must be spiritually known by experience. We can then know something as a personal testimony and not just know about something as information. Only by engaging God directly can we know the truth by experience and be confident of what is, in fact, the truth.

I have found truth in sources that I do not overall agree with and I have found errors in those sources that I usually accept. So having done much research for this book, particularly regarding the historical records, I have quoted many sources, including Wikipedia and Encyclopaedia Britannica. The choice of those sources may raise a few eyebrows, but they make information easy to engage, unlike many academic articles that are often very technical and use language and terminology that is difficult to understand. So I used the sources that balance truth with ease of understanding when those sources carry the frequency of truth.

I have quoted from sources that I fundamentally disagree with on a philosophical and moral level because they contain elements of truth hidden within the mire of ideology. Therefore I may quote from sources without endorsing their ideology. There is truth hidden within many conspiracies that may obscure it to most people: that is why we discern the truth by the frequency it carries, not from its source.

I always seek the Father before committing anything to paper as His is the agenda behind this book, not my own. As a good friend, Jonathan Cavan (founder of the *Liebusters* ministry) often says, there is only truth and lies. There are no grey areas with God but amongst people the truth may be dismissed, hidden, obscured, or twisted; and there are often half-truths in amongst the downright lies of deliberate misinformation campaigns.

If there is a great conspiracy behind many historical events and an agenda that is hidden, and I believe there is, then trying to expose it is very difficult as those who control the financial

INTRODUCTION

and media systems can hide their agenda through influencing the historical records. Just because the history books or seminary required reading list present things as incontrovertible facts, that does not make that information the truth.

It is important that you take what I write and fact-check it yourself with the Truth but please attempt to do so with an open heart and mind or you may hear what you want to hear.

1. My Eschatological Journey.

My journey towards embracing the restoration of all things with passion was integrally entwined with my destiny on a long and winding road. My journey has taken me on a path where my eschatological understanding was not just deconstructed but destroyed and there was no renewed position of eschatology to look forward towards, just a backward view to realisation and completion of all biblical prophecy.

I was brought up in St. Ives, Cornwall, in England. St. Ives is a small historic fishing village (now a tourist destination) that had a long religious history going back to the fifth century when legend has it that it was established by the Irish missionary, Saint Ia.

As a child growing up in that place steeped in religion, one subject was predominant: eschatology. There were conferences and conventions each year which majored on that one issue and it was what most Christians that I knew liked to discuss at length. I was fascinated by the subject, drawn to the deception by the religious spirit operating behind it. I spent many hours in deep discussion in my teenage years and avidly devoured many books about the subject.

I was brought up in a Bible Christian Methodist chapel that was strongly evangelically influenced and focused heavily on the subject of eschatology. The Brethren movement was very strong in St. Ives (where there were three Brethren assemblies of different factions: open, closed and exclusive) and I would go on to join the Barnoon open brethren assembly (in pursuit of my now wife rather than any deep theological truth).

Little did I know at the time that the Brethren movement was the root of the poisonous tree of much false futurist eschatology that produced the poisoned fruit of rapture, cessationism, millennialism and Zionism, bound up in the doctrine of dispensationalism. I will include more detail on that subject in later chapters.

While in that Brethren assembly during the mid-1970s and early 1980s I was given a whole library of books relating to the roots of the Brethren movement and particularly the birth of its dispensational eschatology. I was very well educated in dispensational premillennialist rapture theology through the many conferences, books and radio Bible class teaching materials that were sent to me monthly.

In those days I could have probably told you what the third toe of the beast with ten heads represented, such was the major focus and topic of most Christian conversations. It was fascinatingly deceptive, drawing people into looking at current events in the newspapers and on the television for the 'signs of the times'. There were so many predictions about when the rapture would occur and what was leading to Armageddon and the 'Great Tribulation' that Christian people in our town were living in a constant state of fearful expectation.

This fear of being left behind when the rapture came was the focus of much gospel preaching and further exacerbated by films such as *A Thief in the Night* and *Some Said it Thundered*, although the latter was 'off' theologically as it implied that Christians would have to go through the tribulation and I believed in a pretribulation rapture. That belief was pure escapism, but who wants to go through a tribulation anyway?

I was brought up as a cessationist, where there was no awareness of the Holy Spirit as a reality in our lives and no concept of spiritual gifts operating. Those things were only for the early church dispensation and since we now had the Bible we did not have the evidence of spiritual gifts; they were childish things and no longer needed as we were now grown up and had the perfect Bible to guide and direct us. That was how my indoctrinated beliefs led me to think.

The ridiculousness of it all was summed up by my wife, brought up in a Brethren family, who recounted what she would do as a child. When she would come home from school and find no one at home, she would run into the street looking for a child to assuage her fear, as she knew that they would not be left behind.

This nonsense continued to be perpetuated by the pop theology of the hugely popular *Left Behind* fiction book series that was later made into a terrible film. This dangerous, demonic doctrine still infects so many people with fear – so much so that sadly one lady in the USA even killed her children so they would not have to go through the tribulation that is still being prophesied to occur. An eschatology that causes that is truly evil and needs to be completely eradicated from society.

Discovering the truth of the baptism of the Holy Spirit triggered the first of my many theological deconstructions, that of cessationism. My experience was completely at odds with the teaching I had received in the Brethren movement (which I was later to discover was the perpetrator of so much of the eschatological deception that I was living in).

My baptism in the Spirit in 1986 came with a challenge from God to understand 'the kingdom of God', which (as I was still a member of a Brethren assembly) was a challenge to my futurist, dispensationalist theology. If the Holy Spirit's gifts are for today, as I had experienced for myself, then what other lies did dispensationalism contain?

The second theological deconstruction was inevitably that of my eschatology and that process took place during the period 1986-1990, long before I had any idea of where this was all heading.

As I did not have any access to any study material outside of my stream of belief, I was led by the Father to seek His face concerning eschatology. That, in hindsight, was the Father's doing, as it meant that the revelation that I received was directly from Him and unfolded in stages as milestones over the next 35 years.

The fact that we are on a journey of discovery is very important to acknowledge, as it allows us to cross rivers that would be too wide but for the many stepping stones that enable us to discover the truth.

The initial eschatological revelation that the Father enabled me to receive challenged my view of the 'rapture,' 'tribulation' and 'millennium'.

I believed in a pretribulation rapture that would trigger a 7-year tribulation that would be the precursor to the second coming of Jesus, ushering in His literal 1000-year reign on earth in a Zionist-controlled Jerusalem, where there would be a third temple and re-instigation of animal sacrifices and the Law. I had it all figured out and I was so shocked to realise that I had been hoodwinked into believing a total deception.

The first of my stepping stones enabled me to embrace what I thought was the final truth, a position that was a manageable step from where I once stood. Without any outside influence, I was able to reject a pretribulation rapture, and the tribulation itself, and therefore a literal millennium. My theological stepping stone was based on what Jesus taught in Matthew 24 and Luke 21, that the tribulation occurred in the generation that followed Jesus' ascension; and there was no rapture, just believers who fled the destruction of Jerusalem as Jesus had warned them to.

I was later to discover that this was called a partial preterist view of the Bible, and was also a postmillennial view, and that many other people also believed the same, which was a comfort at the time.

Eschatology is the study of the 'end times' and this intermediary step was a step (even if it was a stretch) that I was able to take at that time on my journey. I was able to balance the fact that there was no rapture of the church, literal tribulation period or millennium (and therefore no literal antichrist or beast) with a literal second coming of Jesus, resurrection and judgment at a future date. The book of Revelation was written before 70 AD and all but the last few chapters referring to resurrection and judgment was already fulfilled in the past.

I stood on that stepping stone for many years, content that I understood the future: that it was hopeful and optimistic and the kingdom of God would fill the earth before Jesus would return and usher in the age to come.

It was not until the deconstruction of my theological belief in penal substitutionary atonement and eternal conscious torment in the literal fires of 'hell' that my eschatological deconstruction could continue as I took another step. As I stood on that stepping stone I could see the other side of the river, which was the full implication of the restoration of all things.

During my time standing on the partial preterist stone, I found several books written by David Chilton very helpful to stabilise my position. *Paradise Restored*, *The Great Tribulation* and *Days of Vengeance* are now available as free pdf downloads from the internet.

What I did not know at that time was that David Chilton was excommunicated from the partial preterist community before he died in 1986 because he was wrestling with what he finally concluded: that full preterism was the inevitable next eschatological step of the journey.

Once I had taken the step to the belief in the restoration of all things, a step fully explained in my last book, a realised non-eschatological step encompassing some aspects of full preterism was inevitable to be able to stay consistent and keep the integrity of the implications of what Jesus taught.

Today I stand on that non-eschatological ground that is happy and realised, with a mystical mixture of the earthly and the heavenly. I will explain this position in detail during the remainder of this book. Are there any further steps to be taken that will go further and bring even greater stability perhaps, as the journey of enlightenment continues?

As a simple holding explanation for those challenged or confused about their own beliefs, below is a basic understanding of the different eschatological positions concerning how to understand biblical prophecy and the 'millennium'.

> Those who hold to partial preterism believe that the prophecies in Daniel, Matthew 24, and Revelation (except

for the last two or three chapters) have already been fulfilled and were fulfilled no later than the first century AD. According to partial preterism, there is no rapture, and passages describing the tribulation and the Antichrist are actually referring to the destruction of Jerusalem in AD70 and the Roman emperor Titus. Partial preterists do believe in the return of Christ to earth and a future resurrection and judgment, but they do not teach a millennial kingdom or that Israel as a nation has a place in God's future plan. According to partial preterists, the Bible's references to "the last days" are speaking of the last days of the Old Jewish Covenant, not the last days of the earth itself...

The partial preterist viewpoint leads to a belief in Amillennialism (or Post-millennialism) and is associated with covenant theology. Of course, it rejects dispensationalism... While partial preterism is within the scope of orthodoxy, it is not the majority view among Christians today.
– Dick Lockhart, *Blogging Scripture HIS Way* blog).

The deception of the futurist fruit of the poisonous tree of dispensationalism has infiltrated much of the evangelical movement.

According to full preterism, all prophecy in the Bible is really history. The preterist interpretation of Scripture regards the book of Revelation as a symbolic picture of first-century conflicts, and therefore there are no longer any future biblical end times. The term preterism comes from the Latin praeter, meaning "past." Thus, preterism is the view that the biblical prophecies concerning the "end times" have already been fulfilled – in the past. Preterism is directly opposed to futurism, which sees the end-times prophecies as having a still-future fulfilment.

Preterism teaches the book of Revelation is fully fulfilled and that all the end-times prophecies of the New Testament were fulfilled in AD70 when the Romans attacked and destroyed Jerusalem. Preterism teaches that every event normally associated with the end times – Christ's second coming, the tribulation, the resurrection of the dead, the final judgment – has already happened. (In the case of the final judgment, it is still in the process of being fulfilled.) Jesus' return to earth was both a "spiritual" and physical return during the period of AD66 and AD70.

Preterism teaches that the Law was fulfilled in AD70 and God's covenant with Israel was ended. The "new heavens and the new earth" spoken of in Revelation 21:1 is, to the preterist, a description of the world under the New Covenant. Just as a Christian is made a "new creation" (2 Corinthians 5:17), so the world under the New Covenant is a "new earth."
– gotquestions.org/preterist

The mystical view is that we are the new heavens and the new earth where we are all mystically included and dwelling in God; and that God is indwelling the new wineskin temple that we now are. We are of the order of Melchizedek, kings and priests enthroned in heaven and oracles and legislators as gateways to manifest heaven on earth.

What of millennial beliefs? I do not personally believe that any eschatological or millennial view is the whole truth. Jesus is the Truth and there must be room for continued mystery on our journey to enlightenment. The mystical view in my opinion can keep both spiritual and physical and the heavenly and earthly in balance.

Some are so confused by the whole subject that they call themselves pan-millennialists (hoping that it will all 'pan out' in the end). That presupposes of course that there is an end and not just continual enlightenment in the possible ages to come.

> Premillennialists understand Christ's return to come before this millennial period. Postmillennialists and Amillennialists understand Christ's return to occur after the millennium. They differ in that Postmillennialists see the millennium as a physical reality on earth while Amillennialists see it as a spiritual reign in heaven.
>
> Amillennialism understands the Kingdom of God proclaimed by Jesus and his apostles to be synonymous with the millennial kingdom of Revelation 20:4-6. The kingdom of God is a present-day reality with Christ ruling from heaven. And it is a kingdom populated by all those who have given their lives to the lordship of Jesus.
> – Ed Jarrett (christianity.com)

I believe there is truth and balance in both perspectives if you see through a mystical lens.

Some full preterists believe that the millennium is a symbolic period fulfilled during the first generation following Jesus' ascension. My mystic view is that the sons of God of the order of Melchizedek are reigning both in heaven and on earth and that heaven will continue to manifest on earth until everything is restored to God's original purpose and intention and the kingdom of God has filled the earth. There will be no end to the increase of God's government and peace and this will continue until everything in the universe(s) and dimensions has been restored.

"What then?" is a question many will ask. The answers lie within the dark cloud of the mystery of God who is creative light and where we can dwell and learn to abide.

I found that as my eschatology changed in the 1980s, so too did my view of God; and that then led me to look at what would happen not just at the end of the world but beyond that. This opened up the possibility of a different result even if I was not prepared to go there at that point of my journey.

My journey continued along what I now see as an inevitable path towards restoration and paradise restored. Where will this journey lead us? I believe, from my conversations with the Father, towards a place where the mature sons of God become ascended fathers themselves – but that is another story yet to unfold.

2. The Fruit of the Poisonous Tree.

I was about a few thousand words into this chapter and I was wrestling with fact-checking things that I had repeated in conversation many times. Those things that I learned reading the old Brethren books were weighing heavily on me. How could I be sure that what I was writing about that had occurred nearly 200 years ago was the truth? There was so much conspiracy surrounding the Brethren and the Scofield Bible's influence on Zionism that it was as if I was wading through treacle. This was also the time when so many people seemed to be so deceived in the political mess of the 2020 US election and President Trump. Those poor souls were convinced that they were right and that it was not over yet, but even though very sincere that they had heard directly from God Himself that Trump would be re-elected and the deep state would be exposed, it was all deception. I did not want to be caught up in exposing a 'great conspiracy' that itself turned out to be a deception.

Then I had two encounters that made everything clear and brought me to the conclusion that I had a personal relationship with the Truth and therefore had access to the greatest fact-checking source of all. So I have included my journal entries for those two days in January 2021.

12th January 2021

"Son, there are many dark clouds and each has its purpose, as you have experienced for yourself, but there are more encounters that are a continuation of the processes that you are in. Some dark clouds express the processes of transformation that need to be outworked in isolation and mystery for them to be successful, as in your separation and reintegration of soul and spirit. Some are places of safety where the transformations can be away from the eyes of those who would hinder the process, as you have discovered in the restoration of the fallen ones. These are places and processes but the most significant is the dark cloud within the realm of perfection where you experience the creative light of Our being face to face.

"Son, now we invite you into the dark cloud of light within the created realm of eternity, as this process is key for the next stage of your maturity; but first you must encounter the fire stones."

As I reflected on this invitation, wondering what this stage could be, I set the desire of my heart on the fire stones. I stood before the throne of the Ancient of Days, where the Father gave me a large golden key and a scroll before beckoning me to sit next to Him on His left, which I thought was rather odd. As I sat there, three very powerful and imposing angels stood around me and I felt very encouraged, strengthened and emboldened. I looked at the scroll and it was a mandate for exposing the great deception and the key would open the way for the truth to come into the light.

Inspired, I got up and went to the fire stones, where the river of fire was flowing from the throne. I began walking down the 11 steps, remembering the last times when the last two steps were formed. I stood on the bottom step with the desire to engage the dark cloud burning within me. I felt such passionate love burning in my entire being, transforming me once again; so I embraced the fire and rejoiced in such passion. Suddenly I knew: as I stood there the enormity of the task that was ahead of me became very real and in focus. I felt passionate about the book but also knew I was incapable of writing it in my present state, even with the key and the scroll.

I ascended the steps one by one, very slowly, so that each one could have its transforming effect on me. Each step birthed a greater passion, almost painful in its intensity, which was another stage of ascension and part of this maturation process. With each step I felt stronger, yet more aware of my weaknesses, so I knew that I had to become more dependent on the revelation of intimacy that I would be entering into within the dark cloud invitation.

As I ascended and stood on the last step, another step formed before me; and as I stood on it there was a great surge of energy. This was energy at a level I had not experienced before in this way and form but it felt familiar. I was enveloped in the frequencies of sounds and light so breath-taking in their beauty that my whole being was spaghettified and swirled within the light, moving to the rhythm of the frequency.

I was and wasn't, all at the same time, as my whole being was charged with energy that I had never felt before. It was like I was continually blinking in and out of conscious time-based existence.

This process felt eternal, as if my whole existence was phasing, moving in and out of eternity, my being energised with each cycle as I moved in and out of God. I knew from my past limited experiences that I was encountering *perichoresis* at a very different level of truth and reality.

Then abruptly it ended and I ascended into the created realm of eternity, where I was standing before the dark cloud. I waited patiently, knowing that although I had an invitation to enter, I had to let all that had just happened sink in and do its work. The longer I waited, the more I knew that I would never be able to complete the mandate I had been given without what was to come.

Desire to the point of desperation grew within me yet my being was totally at rest. There was no striving: I was filled with love, joy and peace, totally content and satisfied like never before.

14th January 2021

I stood looking at the dark cloud, a cloud like none other I had seen or entered. It was intense but also seemed to be a living thing. I felt apprehensive as I watched it pulsating, swirling, shifting, like it was ready to engulf me.

"Son, you have your invitation. There is nothing to fear but this will bring greater changes than you could ever imagine or think."

So I took a step and the cloud moved towards me, engulfing me in complete darkness that went through every particle of my being. The deeper the darkness, the more intense the light was that filled my mind. It was as if I was totally cocooned in a darkness that was in reality the brightest light. My senses were heightened, my consciousness enlightened with a light so bright it matched the depth of darkness that I was in.

The darkness was the light, the very light of God that was truth itself; and then, one by one, I saw the darkness of deceptions overwhelmed by the pure, creative light of truth. All of the deception that I was wrestling with in writing the book was transformed by that light so I could see the truth of who and what was behind it.

I saw figuratively the tree of the knowledge of good and evil engulfed in the purest of light that exposed its agenda. I saw the great deception of 'I will' that has enslaved humanity; it was like a mass of living darkness, tendrils attached to all mankind and all we have made in independence. I saw the light of truth overwhelm each tendril of darkness until each one retracted and all that was left was one dark 'I' that itself was then consumed by the light.

My mind, a consciousness that had been shattered, splintered by the darkness like everyone else's, was being bathed in the most amazing light. Each lie, like a splinter I had learned to live with, was consumed by that healing light of pure truth and I knew that I knew that all I had been wrestling with was not a conspiracy theory but a conspiracy truth.

Mankind has been deceived into living a lie. An eschatological lie had been accepted as a truth that promotes the Luciferian agenda of one-world government who have made a name for themselves. That name, called many things - Babel, Egypt, Babylon, Greece, Rome, Britain, Russia, Germany, Spain, Israel, Zion – was now revealed as Lucifer.

I could see the depth of deception that could cause men to murder millions of innocent people to fulfil their objectives: Pharaoh, Stalin, the Zionist elite behind the holocaust, all willing to sacrifice millions slaughtered to hide the truth behind the great deception. The bright and morning star is the light that is the false sun and son, who has deceived mankind and most of Christianity into supporting his agenda to be worshipped as God.

I could see clearly now, so I did not have to water the deception down to make it more palatable or find it down for fear of the anti-Semitic accusations and reprisals. I heard the comforting voice of the Father gently say "Speak the truth that you now know in love to bring the great deception into the light."

The dark cloud receded, drawing back from me, leaving me exhausted but inspired. Now I knew I could write what I had been hesitant to write, in the knowledge of what I had seen. I proceeded with confidence that even if what I was writing could not be completely confirmed, or if it was included in some conspiratorial document, that I would know what frequency it carried, that of truth or lies; and that I could always check it out directly with Jesus, the Truth, and with the Spirit of Truth. I 'knew that I knew' that what the Father had mandated me to do, I was going to complete, however hard it got or whatever hindrances were thrown in my way.

'I wills'

So getting back to the matter in hand, where did it all go wrong?

How far back do you want to go? The fall of man in the garden, or even further, to the fall of an archangel who has many names? The great deception of course goes back to the Luciferian agenda of 'I will'.

The five 'I wills' of Satan, as revealed in Isaiah 14, give some background that will help us unveil the deception that has kept mankind in bondage to the Luciferian agenda. In Isaiah 14:13-14 are five phrases expressing the sinful desires of Lucifer. Each begins with 'I will' and reveals Satan's self-sufficiency and self-worship.

"How you have fallen from heaven,
O star of the morning, son of the dawn!
You have been cut down to the earth,

You who have weakened the nations!
"But you said in your heart,
'I will ascend to heaven;
I will raise my throne above the stars of God,
And I will sit on the mount of assembly
In the recesses of the north.
'I will ascend above the heights of the clouds;
I will make myself like the Most High.' (Isaiah 14:12-14).

- I will ascend to heaven,
- I will raise my throne above the stars of God;
- I will sit on the mount of assembly,
- I will ascend above the heights of the clouds,
- I will make myself like the Most High.

These statements reveal Satan's sinful nature, his rebellion, his disobedience, his self-sufficiency, his pride, his self-exaltation, and his all-encompassing pride and arrogance. For Satan, it's all about him, and nothing about God.

I want to share a conversation that the Father had with me while I was writing this chapter that will hopefully give a context to the many challenges to your ideologies that this book may create. This conversation took place on the 6th January 2021 during my daily engagement with the Father.

"Son, as you learn to abide in the realm of light, in a state of being, you will be able to discern that which does and that which does not resonate with Our heart of love and truth. The frequency of the light of love and truth will be a genuine reflection of that which represents Us; and that which is false, deceptive or not living will become more and more obvious.

"Time in intimacy with the light of Our glory will ensure the light of your glory is a true reflection of who We truly are and creation will be able to respond to your light and the sound frequency of your voice.

"In 2021 the spotlight of truth will shine brightly to expose the great deception of the Luciferian tree of the knowledge of good and evil agendas. The deception of independence, the cult of I, can be found embedded within the original 'I will' statements that defined the motive of the first rebellion.

"I is the same as 1 and there is no I in the word 'team'. And there can be no relationship with 1: that is why independence, division and separation are the tools of the religious and political spirit behind the Babel agenda of false unity seen in the statement 'we will make a name for ourselves'. Selfishness is the hallmark of the DIY tree agenda, 'I will' its cry, as doing and works are its modus operandi.

"Son, this is why so many of Our children and even some of those who know they are Our sons, are weary, burdened and live on the treadmill of independence. The call to all who are weary and heavy-laden to come to the light of truth and find rest in their true identity is still being made today.

"Son, rest is truly being and knowing the inclusion and acceptance of unfailing unconditional love and limitless grace. Being is being gentle and humble of heart and that is only to be found abiding within *I am that I am* in the true identity of being. The greatest deception has been fooling Our children to work for, by their own independent self-effort, what they already have and are as Our children.

"The religious spirit enslaves Our children through dead works of performance because they have lost their true identity and live as orphans even though they are already included in Our family. The political spirit offers the false family of nationalism, tribalism and denominating through division, which is falsely uniting under a banner of colour, race, ethnicity, birthplace, religion, social status, class or any other man-made category that divides.

"So many of Our children think they are uniting when they are actually dividing, just as they were deceived into doing at Babel. We mandated them to fill the earth as one family but they were deceived into making a name for themselves; and then, once they were dispersed, they falsely united, creating independent nations that would compete and fight for territory.

"The empire spirit is the Luciferian agenda behind all attempts to conquer to form one-world government under a false messiah figure. The latest and current version is the Talmudic Judaistic agenda behind the global control systems of economics, politics, corporations, media, entertainment, energy and pharmaceuticals that are the front of the religious and political spirit.

"All the ideologies that have been created from the tree of the knowledge of good and evil are inherently flawed; and that includes all forms of government: capitalism, communism, right, left and middle; and all forms of economics.

"The Kingdom of God is a relational covenantal system of mutual support and encouragement where everyone is part of one family and finds fulfilment in being who they were created to be. The world without the fall would be a very different place; and living in a garden, in harmony and oneness with creation, is very different from living in a city, dependent upon mankind's technology and ingenuity. The politicising of the prophetic movement to support conflicting ideologies is the work of the religious and political spirit and it has been exposed through the US presidential election as another deception that Our children and sons have fallen for.

"Son, the Kingdom of God is a government of love producing the fruit of righteousness, peace and joy so all can be blessed and fulfil their destiny. You are mandated to expose the great deception and the Luciferian agendas behind it so the sons of God can rule righteously in love, free from the infiltration of the religious and political spirit."

This book is an attempt to fulfil that mandate and I do not seek to offend; but the revealing of deception that leads to the deconstruction and renewal of our minds and beliefs can be a tough process, as I can personally testify. "Why me, Father?" is a thought I have often had (but it is one that I have never voiced, as I trust that the Father knows what He is doing).

I will go back to the true poisonous tree found in the garden when I look at the other aspects of the delusion and deception in which mankind has been living in later chapters. To look at why the majority of protestant believers have a futurist eschatological belief system, I will be looking back to the birth of the Brethren movement that planted the poisonous tree from which many are eating the fruit.

Plymouth Brethren

As I have stated previously, being part of that Brethren movement, I was heavily invested in futurist dispensationalist eschatology and it was not until I was baptised by the Holy Spirit that I was open enough to be able to hear the voices of Jesus as the Truth and of the Spirit of Truth. Being curious is a trait of which I was most certainly guilty and which the Holy Spirit used to get me to look at the history of the Brethren movement and the roots of its eschatology. Having access to many books written in the 1820s and 1830s that recorded Brethren history was very helpful in discovering the truth of the roots of much evangelical eschatology.

I met Martin Scott during the late 1990s when I was part of a regional leaders' group who embarked on a series of events across the South West region of the United Kingdom called 'Sowing Seeds for Revival'. These events were inspired by an optimistic view of the future that included revival (whatever that means) and, to a degree, restoration, as all the leaders involved were from what was known as the new church or restoration church movement.

The events were seeking for community transformation and I believe were some of my first steps on the road to the restoration of all things. My understanding of restoration was probably confined to the theological restoration that was embodied by the restoration movement of new churches that began to grow in the UK in the 1970s. This movement had two wings which Andrew Walker, in his book *Restoring the Kingdom*[1], classified as R1 and R2. R1 encompassed Harvestime (which later became Covenant Ministries International) churches, mostly in the Midlands, Wales and North of England, and New Frontiers International, Salt and Light, and Cornerstone churches in the South of England. R2 was formed of the Pioneer and Ichthus churches which were on the fringe. My understanding of what restoration truly means has obviously broadened significantly since those days to include all things.

These were exciting events where we would gather for a few days in a specific area seeking prophetic insight and revelation

---

[1] Dr Andrew Walker, *Restoring the Kingdom*, Eagle (1998).

in the mornings, practically looking to outwork that in the afternoons and spending the evenings together in conversation and debate.

Martin Scott was a prophetic voice who helped to facilitate these events in many places around the UK. Meeting and conversing with Martin inspired me to think outside the box and seek heavenly revelation. Our conversations about eschatology were particularly interesting in regards to believing in an optimistic outcome for creation.

I am indebted to Martin for his eschatological studies and his academic abilities and specifically his thesis on *The eschatology of the new church movement 1970 to 1996*[2] that helped me to catalogue my recollections of what I had read from those early Brethren writers. This thesis is still available to download free of charge on the internet. Martin has a 40-part podcast series specifically on the subject of eschatology still available at the time of writing[3].

There are many stepping stones produced by progressive revelation, which can take people across the divide from deception to truth from many starting points and by many different routes. I believe our relationship with the Spirit is vital if we are to cross the great divide to find the truth. If that relationship can be hindered then deception holds sway.

For the centuries of the dark ages, most were kept from the truth. When the authority that is birthed from intimacy with the Spirit was lost, men began looking to other sources for their understanding. As a result, many plain and precious

---

[2] Martin Scott, *The eschatology of the new church movement 1970 to 1996* – https://3generations.eu/ebooks/HCM_Eschatology.pdf
[3] Martin Scott, *Eschatology podcasts* https://3generations.eu/eschatology-podcasts

truths were lost or hidden beneath layers of manmade doctrine.

There were crucial points in history, for example, the council held in 325 AD in Nicaea. By this time Christianity had ceased to be an underground counter-cultural movement to become the state religion of the Roman Empire. The loss of intimacy with the Spirit of Truth created the inability of Christians to agree among themselves on basic points of doctrine.

To resolve differences, Emperor Constantine called together a group of Christian bishops to establish once and for all the official doctrines of the church.

Consensus did not come easily. Opinions on such basic subjects as the nature of God were diverse and deeply felt, and debate was often fierce. Decisions were not made by inspiration or revelation, but by majority vote, and some disagreeing factions split off and formed new churches. Similar doctrinal councils were held later, in A.D. 451, 787, and 1545, with similarly divisive results.

The beautiful simplicity of the truth of the good news of a loving God was under attack from an enemy that was even more destructive than all persecutions experienced by the early church from Rome or Judaism: the philosophical thinking and machinations of uninspired men. The truth became based more on popular opinion than on revelation. This period of time was called the Dark Ages. They were dark largely because the light of the true gospel of Jesus Christ had been lost. – churchofjesuschrist.org

Religious systems that focused on dead works and religious observance kept the truth hidden from most but the light of truth throughout history has always had a remnant who kept the light burning.

The restoration of various aspects of truth has occurred when brave men and women were willing to listen to the small, still voice of the Spirit within and challenge the status quo of the current orthodox positions. They were often called heretics and many were killed, burned at the stake by the religious systems to maintain their power bases.

> Then in 1517, the Spirit moved Martin Luther, a German priest who was disturbed at how far the church had strayed from the gospel as taught by Christ. His work led to a reformation, a movement that was taken up by such other visionaries as John Calvin, Huldrych Zwingli and John Wesley.
>
> I believe these reformers were inspired to create an environment in which God could restore lost truths and priesthood authority. – churchofjesuschrist.org

With each subsequent restoration of truth there were more outward and emotional manifestations of the Holy Spirit. These so-called excesses were an indication that the Spirit was doing a deeper work within the believer to unlock their true sonship.

The first great awakening began in the 1730s and went into the 1740s and was associated in the USA with Jonathan Edwards, and in the UK with John Wesley and George Whitfield. The second great awakening occurred in the late eighteenth century, lasting until the mid-nineteenth century. These movements were the birthing place of modern evangelicalism and many movements can be traced back to these times of spiritual awakening.

The awakenings often had spontaneous manifestations of the Holy Spirit and spirituality associated with them. Unfortunately alongside the good elements of restored truth, there were often also many deceptions and mixtures.

The scheme usually employed to stop such movements from continuing to embrace and release progressive revelation was that of denominationalism. Denominations were usually birthed out of division and soulish arguments around ownership and control of truth that resulted in the susceptibility to error. This tactic to keep the truth hidden was to sow tares with the wheat in the form of cults or sects that mixed and polluted the truth with error. It seems that whenever the Holy Spirit moves, man's deception follows, as the sources of revelation become a mixture of the two trees.

In that environment, there were many who, in seeking the truth, became dissatisfied with religion; and the two movements I want to focus on are those that became the originators of false futurist eschatology.

This denominating to defend the truth that had been revealed often opposed the next revelation that was to come. As a reaction to the protestant reformation of the 1500s, where Martin Luther identified the Roman Catholic Church with the Whore of Babylon and the Beast, in 1585 a Jesuit priest by the name of Francisco Ribera published a 500-page work that placed Daniel 9:24-27, Matthew 24, and Revelation 4-19 in the distant future. This was the foundation of many modern end-time views, but not until this material was rediscovered separately by Edward Irving (who would found the Apostolic Catholic Church) and John Nelson Darby (who would go on to found the Brethren movement).

The historical environment where the majority optimistic postmillennial view of eschatology was challenged and subverted by the more pessimistic premillennial view that had an escapist rapture added to it by Irving and Darby. That environment was catalysed by three wars that shook the optimistic perspective. The American revolutionary war of 1775 to 1783, the French revolutionary war of 1792 to 1802 and the Napoleonic wars of 1803 to 1815 destabilised the world and created the seedbed for the negative futurist eschatology of dispensationalism. Whenever there are wars or fearful world events the environment is ripe for pessimistic prophetic teachings to proliferate. From 1826 there were meetings in the home of Henry Drummond in Albury, Surrey, in which such pessimistic prophetic speculations thrived.

John Nelson Darby

This brings us to 1827–28 when in Dublin, Ireland, a group of Anglicans were the catalyst for the formation of the Brethren movement. Those taking part included Anthony Norris Groves, Edward Cronin, John Nelson Darby and John Gifford Bellett. They valued the principle of *sola scriptura* (scripture alone) above the direct inspiration of the Holy Spirit through gifts.

In December 1831 the first meetings in England were held in Plymouth and what became known as the Plymouth Brethren movement soon spread throughout the United Kingdom. Meanwhile, Darby's premillennial views were probably influenced by those he met at the prophetic conferences sponsored by Lady Powerscourt near Dublin in the early 1830s.

By 1845 the original Plymouth group had more than 1,000 people gathering and the term 'Darbyites' was also used for the more exclusive groups. It was in 1845 that the first of many disagreements occurred, eventually leading to splits and schisms. Darby had instituted a second meeting at Plymouth, which cut off from the other groups in 1848 to form the Exclusive Brethren, which itself subsequently split many times. In the small town where I lived there were three different Brethren assemblies and five different Methodist chapels.

Darby was probably influenced by Irving even though he would never admit it because of Irving's association with spiritual gifts. I read first-hand accounts from those who were involved in the Brethren history books I was bequeathed. Darby visited Exclusive assemblies in America seven times between 1862 and 1877, promoting the dispensational eschatology and belief systems he had developed[4]. When the Holy Spirit spontaneously began moving amongst those seeking truth, Edward Irving embraced that truth but Darby rejected spiritual gifts as demonic manifestations.

Doctrinally, Darby was the primary influence in expressing and propagating what came to be the distinctive ultra-literalist theology of the Brethren concerning the final days of history. A belief in cessationism became central to the system of eschatology that emerged, that of dispensationalism. Cessationism, the belief that all spiritual gifts have ended, again has its origin in division and reaction. The original formulation of cessationism arose in response to claims of healing and miracles in the Catholic Church. Rejection of the Holy Spirit and division over doctrine both, in my opinion, lead to the possibility of deception and demonic doctrinal

---

[4] Ernest R. Sandeen, *The Roots of Fundamentalism: British & American Millenarianism, 1800-1930*, University of Chicago Press (2008) pp. 70–79.

influence. Both are found in the foundations of futurist eschatology and all eschatology seems to be a very divisive subject, inciting strong negative emotions.

Dispensationalism

Darby and Brethrenism became the main proponents of dispensational theology and futurist eschatology and that cause was greatly helped by the production of the Scofield Reference Bible, one of the first to include commentary alongside the biblical texts.

The poisonous tree was planted and its fruit began to grow as, through the framework of dispensationalism, it espoused the doctrines of the rapture, a two-part premillennial second coming, a literal millennium reign of Jesus on earth, and the roots of Zionism where there were two distinct and separate peoples of God, the church (the heavenly people, who would be whisked away) and the earthly, Jewish, people of Israel.

Therefore we must consider what dispensationalism is and why it infiltrated and infected so much of evangelical eschatology.

Dispensationalism is a framework of thinking that is used to interpret the Bible and it has a strong connection to premillennialism. Dispensationalism has a very literal perspective of *sola scriptura*, believes that the Bible is inerrant and infallible and separates Israel and the Church into an earthly and a heavenly people of God. Dispensationalism breaks down biblical history into seven dispensations, or eras.

Most dispensationalists agree on these seven basic dispensations:

- Innocence (pre-Fall)

- Conscience (Fall to Noah)
- Government (Noah to Abraham)
- Promise (Abraham to Moses)
- Mosaic Law (Moses to Christ)
- Grace (current age)
- Millennial Kingdom (1,000-year earthly reign of Christ, yet to come).

Following the American Civil War, and with World Wars I and II looming, pessimism began to take hold of American (and to a degree, British) societies and so dispensationalism became more popular. It was heavily influenced by Zionism and therefore the year 1948, when the state of Israel was re-established, became a very significant date and time on the so-called 'prophetic clock'. Dispensationalists believed that according to Romans 11 there would be a worldwide revival before Israel was grafted back in. The establishment of Israel validated dispensationalism to many, but it also resulted in much wild speculation as to the date of the Second Coming and the doom and gloom of futurist theology. There was a proliferation of the 'end time' books by Hal Lindsey, Tim LaHaye and many others that I had devoured when I was caught up in this deception.

The Scofield Bible

The origin of the Scofield Bible and the agenda behind its infiltration of the majority of seminaries (especially in the USA) is an important subject to include here, as it is part of the great deception and reveals who is behind it. Cyrus Ingerson Scofield (1843-1921) was a lawyer and politician before his conversion (not that we should hold that against him). Below is part of a Wikipedia article for background purposes.

Scofield apprenticed in the law office of his brother-in-law and then worked in the St. Louis assessor's office before moving to Atchison, Kansas, in late 1869. In 1871, Scofield was elected to the Kansas House of Representatives, first from Atchison for one year and then from Nemaha County, for a second. In 1873 he worked for the election of John J. Ingalls as senator from Kansas, and when Ingalls won, the new senator had Scofield appointed U. S. District Attorney for Kansas – at 29, the youngest in the country. Nevertheless, that same year Scofield was forced to resign "under a cloud of scandal" because of questionable financial transactions, which may have included accepting bribes from railroads, stealing political contributions intended for Ingalls, and securing bank promissory notes by forging signatures. It is possible that Scofield was jailed on forgery charges, although there is no extant evidence in the public records.

Perhaps in part because of his self-confessed heavy drinking, Scofield abandoned his wife and two daughters during this period. Leontine Cerrè Scofield divorced him on grounds of desertion in 1883, and the same year Scofield married Hettie Hall von Wartz, with whom he eventually had a son.

According to Scofield, he was converted to evangelical Christianity through the testimony of a lawyer acquaintance. Certainly, by the late fall of 1879, Scofield was assisting in the St. Louis evangelistic campaign conducted by Dwight L. Moody, and he served as the secretary of the St. Louis YMCA. Significantly, Scofield came under the mentorship of James H. Brookes, pastor of Walnut Street Presbyterian Church, St. Louis, a prominent dispensationalist premillennialist...

As the author of the pamphlet "Rightly Dividing the Word of Truth" (1888), Scofield soon became a leader in dispensational premillennialism, a forerunner of twentieth-century Christian fundamentalism. Although, in theory, Scofield returned to his Dallas pastorate in 1903, his projected reference Bible consumed much of his energy, and he was also mostly either unwell or in Europe. When the Scofield Reference Bible was published in 1909, it quickly became the most influential statement of dispensational premillennialism...
– Wikipedia: *C. I. Scofield*

The *Scofield Reference Bible* was published by the Oxford University Press in 1909, followed by revised editions in 1917 and 1967. This deceptive work received worldwide recognition.

So what or who was behind the publishing of the Scofield Bible? What was the agenda of the eschatology of the Scofield Bible, which popularised the three most poisonous fruits of dispensationalism, those of a premillennial secret rapture, literal millennialism and Zionism? Who or what would benefit from the infiltration into Christianity of these insidious doctrines?

The answers to these questions are one key to understanding the Luciferian agenda of the tree of the knowledge of good and evil and uncovering the great deception that the world has been living in. Unfortunately, the answers and the truth are hidden under seemingly impenetrable layers of conspiracy and theories (ranging from the Illuminati and one-world government to global cabals and the deep state) that are designed to obscure the truth but actually hides the truth in plain sight. The fact that truths and lies are both labelled conspiracies makes it all the harder to unravel the great deception.

The following is from a letter by Dick Knolls published in *The Chronicle* in 2013 entitled *Scofield Bible Had a Big Effect on the United States*. The deception is being exposed and although many would call this a conspiracy theory I believe there is some truth behind it.

To the editor:

In today's marketplace, speaking the truth can be considered a revolutionary act and in some cases suicidal. That being said, as a minister of the Gospel, I'm commanded, by Scripture, to "expose the unfruitful works of darkness."

In his book, "The Rise of Israel: A History of a Revolutionary State," Jonathan R. Adleman describes the crucial support Israel receives from Christian fundamentalists as "totally fortuitous." However, the incredible career of C.I. Scofield, the man who wrote "the Bible of Fundamentalism" (dispensationalism), casts serious doubt on that assertion. "Totally fortuitous," hardly!

A brief history will explain why. As a young con artist in Kansas after the Civil War, Scofield tied in with a Jewish lawyer who was sent to Atchison, Kan., by the "Secret Six."

Pulling strings both in Kansas and with his compatriots back east, Ingalls assisted Scofield in gaining admission to the bar, and procured his appointment as the federal attorney for Kansas. These two became partners in a railroad scam, which led to Scofield serving time for criminal forgery.

Upon his release from prison, now as a professing "born again" Christian, Scofield deserted his first wife and two daughters and took as his mistress a young girl from the St. Louis Flower Mission. He later abandoned her for another woman, whom he eventually married.

Following his questionable connections to New York, he settled in at the Lotus Club, apparently funded by Samuel Untermayer, a Wall Street lawyer, who later became chairman of the American Jewish Committee, president of the American League of Jewish Patriots and chairman of the non-sectarian Anti-Nazi League.

Untermayer introduced Scofield to numerous key Zionists, both here and in Europe. These Zionists included Gompers, LaGuardia, Straus, Baruch and Schiff. These are the people who financed Scofield's research trips to Oxford and arranged the publication of his bible, which has dubious footnotes and heretical implications. Scofield's theology was most helpful in getting many fundamentalist Christians to back the international interest in one of Untermeyer's key projects – the Zionist movement.

It is impossible to overstate the influence of Scofield and his bible on 20th century Christians, as well as our nation. If there had been no Scofield bible, American presidents influenced by Christian Zionism, such as Harry Truman, Lyndon Johnson, Ronald Reagan and George W. Bush, would most likely have been less sympathetic to Israel's demands, and consequently more attentive to U.S. interests.

The Palestinians (who possess real Semitic DNA, unlike most professing Jews today) would have had a fair shake, rather than being dehumanized by the Talmudic Zionist Knesset and international Zionism.

I believe that had Scofield not been seduced up by his Zionist handlers, America would not be controlled by an international banking cabal, the Middle East would not be experiencing the numerous wars designed by the Zionist neo-cons who have been dictating American foreign policy, the church would not be supporting the Zionist Christian heresy and America would not be bankrupt and on a course of designed destruction.

Dick Knolls

I have never really been into conspiracies, viewing them as the purview of the cranks and fringe element who should have better and more productive things to do with their time. I will stick to sharing what the Father has told me directly and undisputable, referenced historical facts, although that is very difficult to do, so you can make up your own mind.

I contend that there was an agenda for the production of the Scofield Bible that was not a godly one. That agenda helped emasculate the authority of the church by creating a belief system that removed the responsibility of the church for their world and generation. There would be no need to care for the world or prepare and disciple future generations if the church was going to be raptured to heaven and escape the eventual destruction of the earth by fire. Many people did not bother with education because there was supposed to be an imminent return of Jesus. This gave rise to scientific and academic atheism as many Christians removed their influence from those spheres. Christians were not, and to a degree still are not, at the forefront of scientific discovery and green and world conservation issues. This is seen in many new fields of scientific discovery. For example, quantum physics: those scientists could not find a Christian or western philosophical worldview to fit the weird science of quantum physics so they turned to the east and a more impersonal spiritual force, often termed 'the universe' or 'the light'. Even the field of alternative medicine based on frequency was rejected by Christians and adopted by what is known as the New Age. There is much catching up to do and Christians are now beginning to embrace the truths that God is revealing, as seen with books such as *The Physics of Heaven*[5] and *Quantum Glory*[6] and the establishing of wellness centres embracing frequency healing technology.

This agenda diminished the authority that sons of God should have been administrating in the earth. It also prepared the way for the great deception that would cause the fundamentalist right of the church to support the Zionist agenda to establish the land of Israel. This agenda hides the true agenda: to establish an earthly messiah in the image of Lucifer, as expressed by Nimrod at Babel (which is a Talmudic Jewish agenda for a one-world government based in Jerusalem that would rule the inhuman Gentiles, who were only created to serve God's people, the Jews, under Noahide laws). Christian Zionists are deceived into supporting the Luciferian Zionist agenda for the one-world government in a millennial kingdom – though not through Jesus but an earthly messiah.

---

[5] Judy Franklin and Ellyn Davis (eds.), *The Physics of Heaven*, Destiny Image (2015).
[6] Phil Mason, *Quantum Glory: The Science of Heaven Invading Earth*, XP Publishing (2012).

The fruit of the poisonous tree is at the heart of dispensationalism, which strongly influenced evangelical eschatological theology, particularly in America and those countries influenced by American missionaries. This teaching, with a two-part coming of Jesus – one of a secret rapture of the church followed by a seven-year tribulation and the second 'Second Coming' of Jesus to establish an earthly millennial kingdom in Jerusalem for Israel – has deceived many into believing in a pessimistic futurist eschatology. It is high time for this infection to be eradicated from the minds of true believers so that they can take their place as sons of God, seated in heavenly places, administrating the government of God's Kingdom and peace through the restoration of all things.

I will expand on the themes of the great deception, rooted in the tree of the knowledge of good and evil but incarnated as the poisonous tree in modern history, in later chapters.

3. Happy Eschatology.

An optimistic, restored future

Why am I not pessimistic about the future?

Answer: because I believe in the restoration of all things and there is no room for pessimism within that hope.

Why do I not believe in eschatology but do believe in a very optimistic, restored future?

The answer lies in happy or realised eschatology: the reality that all prophecy in the Bible has already been fulfilled or realised in a past generation, as Jesus foretold. Now that position will no doubt cause many to raise an eyebrow as it is in total contradiction to what most of us have been taught or believed. I believe if we see and interpret the Bible through the lens of Jesus, the one who Himself is the fulfilment of all of the promises of God and the consummation of all the covenants of God, we will be able to discern the truth from the deception.

My understanding of the future moved from the very pessimistic view that I was brought up with to the more optimistic view that I now hold but that process was not in isolation. There were many beliefs, mindsets, paradigms and worldviews that were challenged, deconstructed and renewed as my face to face encounters with the Father became more intimate and He revealed His heart to me. My encounters in heaven and within my own spirit and heart created many opportunities for cognitive dissonance to occur and those experiences revealed just how much I was operating in confirmation bias. If I had continued to allow what I thought I already knew to be true to maintain my beliefs then I would still be living in the same deception that I am now seeking to expose. Instead I chose to trust my encounters with the Father, who continued to reveal how unconditionally loving, gracious and merciful He truly is, and that enabled Him to transform my understanding in so many areas of belief.

The deepening of my experiences of a loving Father meant that I could no longer believe what I was conditioned to by my religious upbringing. The greatest challenges initially concerned the nature of the work of the cross and judgment, which meant that I had honestly to face issues relating to the atonement and to 'hell' as punishment and eternal conscious torment. By focusing on what Jesus taught and demonstrated while here on the earth, as the incarnation and the express image of a loving heavenly Father, I was able to see that what He said about the destruction of Jerusalem in the coming generation and the fires of Gehenna (usually translated as 'hell') were about the same events.

The Father took me through a long process of deconstruction where His love challenged the foundational pillars of my belief systems. The pillar of evangelicalism held all the other eight pillars in their place, to create a coherent worldview that was confirmed by the principle of *sola scriptura*, the Bible alone. My face to face encounters with the Father, Son, and Spirit undermined and destroyed my trust in how the Bible is translated and my interpretation of it. In the past, whenever I read the Bible, it had always confirmed what I already believed and therefore my mind went unrenewed and the status quo of my religious programming remained in place.

No more. The first evil, demonic doctrine that the Father challenged was Penal Substitutionary Atonement, and as I looked at the assumptions it made about what the Bible was saying, I realised that I had been sold a total fabricated lie. This lie was the cornerstone of my belief systems. Once it was exposed and rejected, that brought about the collapse of all those associated doctrines such as hell being a place of eternal conscious torment, physical death being the end of choice, and the so-called biblical concepts of everlasting eternal judgment, 'eternal', and 'forever and ever' in the context of punishment and torment.

When that first domino fell, all the others collapsed, like some elaborate domino rally where my belief systems were all organised like a pattern of dominos, each connected to the previous and the next. Domino after domino fell as my mind was deconstructed but for quite a while I was tripping over the rubble of the collapsed pillars, unable to find solid ground on which to stand. This felt less than stable; I was uncomfortable with the uncertainty – what did I believe? – and only after I had experiences and testimonies that confirmed a more loving belief system did I feel more secure.

If we allow the Father to deconstruct our minds, a process we can resist, it will involve a religious deprogramming that will challenge many of our theology and doctrines. If we have face to face encounters that reveal the true nature of God they will inevitably create cognitive dissonance which we must embrace if we are to be transformed. Discovering the true reality of who God is by experience will change us and it inevitably changed how I saw the Bible and its role in my life. Hermeneutical frameworks influence our exegetical understanding of the Bible and therefore create belief systems that can limit the scope of our sonship and restoration. Our sonship is inextricably linked to creation's freedom and restoration, as Paul indicates in his letter to the Roman church:

The Spirit Himself testifies with our spirit that we are children of God, and if children, heirs also, heirs of God and fellow heirs with Christ, if indeed we suffer with Him so that we may also be glorified with Him...

For the anxious longing of the creation waits eagerly for the revealing of the sons of God. For the creation was subjected to futility, not willingly, but because of Him who subjected it, in hope that the creation itself also will be set free from its slavery to corruption into the freedom of the glory of the children of God. (Romans 8:16-17, 19-21).

What we believe will unavoidably hinder, restrict, limit or help in the process of the restoration of all things of which we have coheirship as sons. Some specific areas of doctrine and theology influence our thinking about the scope of what can be restored and our involvement in it. Many of the doctrines I was taught in the evangelical, Brethren and charismatic streams limited the scope of restoration.

If we take some time to reflect on the major influences on our lives, we will probably see some areas that may have predisposed us to hold particular views. Our initial religious upbringing or first church stream experiences may have been Protestant, Roman Catholic, or Orthodox; Reformed, Evangelical, Charismatic, Pentecostal or Trinitarian. If we were brought up in a Protestant setting, then was it a Calvinistic or Arminian environment, that of determinism or based on the concept of free will? How was the Bible used? Was it a literal or figurative interpretation? Was it reformed or evangelical and was it Pentecostal or Charismatic (as that in itself would affect how we might accept or mistrust experience)? What were the eschatological systems that we were exposed to? Dispensationalism, premillennial futurism, or perhaps Covenant theology, Amillennialism or Postmillennialism?

Many positions are paradoxical and therefore contradictory but all sides of these debates use the Bible to prove their position, creating confusion that we could do without. As I am writing this chapter, the conspiracies concerning the American election are raging, with so many believing that the election was stolen from Trump and that he is still president even though Biden has been inaugurated. Why are so many living in denial, clinging onto the hope that the so-called prophecies will still turn out to be true? Why are so many mystics who claim to have heavenly encounters promoting the wildest of conspiracies?

I believe the deception and delusions they believe are rooted in the fruit of the poisonous eschatological tree that inspires fear for the future. As one by one the latest predictions and conspiracies fail to materialise, the delusion gets stronger and the futurist prophets double down, refusing to concede their false prophecies. Those who behaved honourably by apologising for their errors have been vilified by those who once followed them, with vitriolic personal attacks. What turns usually sensible, loving believers into attack dogs, viciously going for the throats of those who have the temerity to back down?

I believe behind the deceptions and the vicious attacks are the political and religious spirit that thrives on creating division, conflict, enmity and strife amongst brothers and sisters in God's family.

I had determined to hold my peace, waiting for the inauguration on January 20th 2021, but with all the terrible personal attacks and delusion I decided to post a response on Facebook, calling for peace and reconciliation:

> I have kept silent on social media about this issue and I was going to remain so until after January 20th but in light of the horrendous posts from Christians inspiring hatred, making death threats against prophets who have repented and anyone that disagrees with their political views, I can remain silent no longer.
>
> I am shocked by the deception so many seem to be living in, even many in the mystic community.
>
> As one by one their hopes are being removed and their fears realised, they become more in denial and more desperate, clinging on to the hope of President Trump's re-election, believing more and more wild conspiracy theories and falling deeper into deception.
>
> It is time to wake up and get real.
>
> The Father spoke to me plainly in November before and following the election that President Trump would not be re-elected and I included those conversations in my *Vision Destiny 2021*[7] teaching series where I share my journals publically.
>
> I have no political skin in this game. I believe that both the left and right-wing of the bird politically flew straight out of the tree of the knowledge of good and evil.
>
> No political system is going to solve mankind's problem and no president or prime minister is going to be our saviour.

---

[7] Access this free series at eg.freedomarc.org/vision-destiny-2021

The only thing remaining after all the shaking of our manmade systems, including the political and religious ones, will be the Kingdom of God that will fill the earth.

I call for peace and reconciliation. There is no need to humiliate those who got it wrong because God is an unconditionally loving God with limitless grace and mercy.

Yes, there is a need for accountability if we publically make statements that turn out to be false but we should do that in a loving, respectful and honouring way. We have all got things wrong and will undoubtedly all do so again; so we will probably need the mercy and grace of our brothers and sisters to help us bear our burdens in the future.

We have all been deceived in our lives, believing things we do not now believe, and we are all still deceived in some areas of our lives (including myself); but there is no shame in that, as we are all on a journey of enlightenment, discovering progressively revealed truth.

I call for all my friends who have been embroiled in this deception, which is the work of the religious and political spirit agenda that Jesus warned us about, to take stock, go back to the Father with open hearts and minds and honestly ask Him to reveal the truth to you.

I do not expect anyone to believe me and I am prepared for the fallout from this post but please, please do not continue to go deeper into the deception of denial, but come into the realm of light surrounding the Father to receive true enlightenment.

For those of you who become angry at this post please ask yourself why, and what should be the appropriate response. Jesus, as Prince of Peace and not war, called for us to forgive those who seem to be our enemies and pray for them, not shoot them or put them to the sword.

Please let's treat each other with love, honour and respect as we are all children of God, and therefore brothers and sisters and part of His family, even if we disagree about issues and have different political or theological views.

I will remove any offensive or conspiracy orientated posts and any that incite violence.

Blessings - Mike Parsons

I will also share my encounter with the Father in January and my response to the political quagmire that caused a deep heart response.

20th January 2021

"Son, love, peace and joy are the hallmarks of Kingdom living and will continue to expand through and beyond Our sons to fill the earth and creation.

"Blessed (empowered to prosper and succeed) are the peacemakers, for they administrate the fundamentals of the Kingdom.

"Blessed are those who are gentle and humble in heart, for they know who We are and they know who they are and live in the rest of being. They see what We are doing from Our state of being - *I am that I am* - so all their doing can be from their state of being.

"Son, being free to know, see, be, do and go is the hallmark of a mature son who can live in and choose true reality.

"Son, see from the realm of light today what is occurring in, above and on the earth, and what We are doing, so you can be in full cooperation and collaboration with the light of truth that is radiating from Our face, which is a true manifestation of who We are."

Immediately I was aware of where I was standing and that I was being illuminated by the light of His countenance, being filled with the knowledge of God. I was also aware that I was brooding in the Cradle of Life within the heart and mind of the Father, His thoughts becoming my thoughts.

I saw the reality and truth of peace and resonated with the sound of many waters until I was the sound of His voice, amplified within the Chamber of Destiny, broadcast and connected in union within the mind of Christ.

I saw the living light of grace, the Quantum Lumens, activated within the Chamber of Creation and the light of peace began to stream out into creation. I heard and felt a deep sigh go forth into creation: "Peace, be still." It was heavy, thick, glorious: a blanket of peace descended over creation.

There will be no end to the increase of His government and peace through the sons of God as His peacemakers. I do not doubt that peace will triumph, through the Prince of Peace, who fully expresses the heart of God as love and light.

"Son, union will triumph over division, covenant will triumph over competition, peacemaking will triumph over warmongering, and family will triumph over tribalism. Have no doubt: love wins, because love is unconditional and never fails, never gives up, is faithful, consistent and eternal.

"I call to the sons of God to arise and shine love's light and truth into the darkness of deception."

I knew this to be the cry of the Father's heart and His deep desire for His children to come out of the darkness of the deception of the religious and political spirit.

> Now that the fat lady has truly sung, I implore all my friends and followers in Facebook-land to come out of denial and stop descending into madness.
>
> Now the 20th of January is here and the inauguration has taken place, please do not move on to the next date, March 4th, which is filled with expectation but is just another false hope. Please do not listen to the voice of the so-called prophets deluded by the political spirit and follow them into deeper deception.
>
> There is no emergency broadcast coming. No insurrection act is being signed. There will be no communication blackout, no military enforced world peace, no space force coming to your rescue, no global reset or "Nesara Gesara" economic reset freeing you from your debt.
>
> (National Economic Security and Recovery Act (NESARA) is a conspiracy theory developed from a set of proposed economic reforms for the United States suggested during the 1990s by Harvey Francis Barnard.)
>
> Please do not continue to follow the latest Q conspiracy into deeper deception as you will continue to be deluded and disappointed.
>
> I implore you to follow the light of truth out of the darkness of deception and seek first the kingdom of God and His righteousness.
>
> I believe all the things you have been looking for in the delusion of the political and religious spirit will come

about as the Kingdom of God fills the earth with God's glory and lovingkindness.

I believe the global cabals will be exposed and fall. I believe the swamp will indeed be drained. I believe in a brave new world as we transition into the next age of Aquarius.

I do not believe any of those things will be achieved through any system that has come from the tree of the knowledge of good and evil: it is all an elaborate deception and delusion.

No political, economic, corporate control system will ever establish the Kingdom of God on earth as it is in heaven.

Everything that can be shaken will be shaken and the only thing that will remain is God's kingdom, so please do not build your hopes and dreams on the shifting sands but the solid rock of the Prince of Peace.

There is no need to shame or humiliate anyone who has been deceived as we have all been there and no doubt we will all be there again.

So let's extend the hand of friendship for reconciliation to one another, whatever our political or religious opinion, and let's demonstrate love, grace and mercy to one another as the world is desperately looking for answers in this time of great shaking and uncertainty.

Let's seek first the kingdom together in the union of the new covenant as sons of God, seated in the heavenly places as priests and kings so we can be the oracles and legislators of the order of Melchizedek and the kingdom of God can fill the earth.

Encounters with the Truth

Our specific theological frameworks of eschatology and prophetic interpretation will influence our understanding and often create confirmationally-biased views that limit us. Those religious frameworks have the power to transform mild-mannered believers into raging bulls, charging into their self-created enemies.

In this age of fake news and misinformation, how do we know what is fact and what is fiction, what is true and what is the truth? The truth can change the facts as they are temporary and not permanent because the Truth, Jesus Himself, never changes; but there is one thing that is certain, that lies are always lies. Our problem today when it comes to discernment is that truth can be hidden under layers of lies and conspiracies.

We need face to face encounters with the Truth Himself in an intimate love relationship to reveal the truth. Below is the account of such an encounter I had while writing this chapter that gives me the confidence to continue this project to reveal the truth.

26th January 2021

"Son, receive all that We are releasing to you and embrace the transformation this will bring as change will be accelerated as the next age approaches."

I stood in the light, where I remembered my last engagement with the fire stones. As I contemplated what I had previously experienced, I saw twelve specific facets of the Father's face and further revelation began to flow until each facet released a burst of coloured light energy, filled with truth. I absorbed that truth into my being until I was pulsating with the frequency of each colour unified in my being. I became alive with limitless energy, glowing like a twelve-coloured rainbow, filled with the knowledge of the truth that previously I had no connection to; but it was not yet cognitive in my mind but hidden, waiting to be discovered. Now, when I experience information, I will be able to discern truth from lies, as the hidden knowledge is activated within me.

"Son, now the truth that has been imparted to you will enable you to be a cosmic fact-checker, as when you encounter information, you will discern by frequency vibration. There is so much disinformation being released to confuse and deflect so that the real truth is hidden behind the smoke and mirrors. You will be able to detect where grains of truth are obscured by mountains of lies and most people will dismiss and miss the truth. The conspiracies are created to keep people from the real truth by packaging truth within lies so that Our children will believe lies as the truth or reject the truth because it is hidden within lies.

"Son, now, armed with this ability to discern, you will be able to reveal the truth; but do not try to expose the lies, just allow the light of truth to do that itself. As you proclaim the truth, the light will shine brightly enough that its frequency will cause the alarm bells to ring within the minds of those who are open.

"More of Our children are awakening out of the slumber of deception that has dulled their ability to discern into a new day of revealed truth. The next age of enlightenment is coming with greater light as the end of this age passes in the transition that most will not be aware of, but the forerunners are awakening.

"Son, 'the dawning of the age of enlightenment' is the more positive way to describe the exposing of the great deception of the Luciferian agenda. You will never need to fear the darkness when you know you are light and that is what creation itself is looking for within the revealing of the sons of God. You can now accurately discern no truth, some truth and the truth within any type of written statement or audio or video teaching, testimony or account."

What is the basis for believing in an optimistic or better future, rather than an event that will rescue us from failure in our sonship mandate, where our big brother comes and saves the day? The answer is quite simple, even if it may be packaged in some complexities. It is the promise of the restoration of all things where the kingdom of God fills the earth and the glory of God covers the earth.

Therefore repent and return, so that your sins may be wiped away, in order that times of refreshing may come from the presence of the Lord; and that He may send Jesus, the Christ appointed for you, whom heaven must receive until the period of restoration of all things, about which God spoke by the mouths of His holy prophets from ancient times. (Acts 3:19-21 NASB).

Reform ye, therefore, and turn back, for your sins being blotted out, that times of refreshing may come from the presence of the Lord, and He may send Jesus Christ who before hath been preached to you, whom it behoveth heaven, indeed, to receive till times of a restitution of all things, of which God spake through the mouth of all His holy prophets from the age. (Acts 3:19-21 YLT).

The literal rendition (without any interpretation to make it easier to read) gives us the facts: that Jesus has been received into heaven at the resurrection and then the final ascension. Jesus remaining in heaven was until times of restitution or restoration of all things that have been prophesied. Amos states that in the old covenant God did nothing without revealing what He was doing through prophets:

*Certainly the Lord God does nothing
Unless He reveals His secret plan
To His servants the prophets.* (Amos 3:7).

It is important to see what the old covenant prophets said and what and when they were referring to and compare that with how Jesus interpreted what they said. We must also remember who their audience were and that all prophecies would have been for the future of that audience at that time but may well be (and I believe actually all are) in our past.

So what did God reveal to the prophets of the old covenant that would be part of this restoration process? The answer to that question is found in the accounts of the prophets in the Bible and hopefully within the pages of my last book. The issue that I want to address here in the light of our subject of eschatology is not so much what, but when. When did the period of restoration begin, or is it still in the future? The answer to that question is linked to when the kingdom of God was established on earth and to when Jesus came a second time: are those past or future? I will cover the specific issue of the second coming of Jesus in great detail in the next chapter, so here we will look at when the kingdom was established.

The Kingdom established

It is also vitally important to remember that Jesus was the fulfilment of the law and the prophets. Jesus, as the living word of God, consummated all of that which God inspired the prophets to speak or record:

"Do not presume that I came to abolish the Law or the Prophets; I did not come to abolish, but to fulfill. For truly I say to you, until heaven and earth pass away, not the smallest letter or stroke of a letter shall pass from the Law, until all is accomplished!" (Matthew 5:17-18).

"For all the Prophets and the Law prophesied until John. And if you are willing to accept it, John himself is Elijah who was to come." (Matthew 11:13-14).

And His disciples asked Him, "Why then do the scribes say that Elijah must come first?" And He answered and said, "Elijah is coming and will restore all things; but I say to you that Elijah already came, and they did not recognize him, but did to him whatever they wanted. So also the Son of Man is going to suffer at their hands." Then the disciples understood that He had spoken to them about John the Baptist. (Matthew 17:10-13).

Jesus linked the coming of John the Baptist to the end or fulfilment of the law and prophets and the transition from the old to the new covenant and the establishment of the period of the restoration of all things. John, figuratively Elijah, made way for the coming of Jesus to fulfil all of the law and prophets. When Jesus prophesied, He was not an old covenant prophet but the Word of God. He was the fulfilment of all that had been spoken and He clarified when all the prophecies would take place. Jesus, as the living Word of God, is the authoritative word on all prophecy. Jesus was the fulfilment of all God's promises and covenants, as all were consummated in Him:

For as many as the promises of God are, in Him they are yes; therefore through Him also is our Amen to the glory of God through us. Now He who establishes us with you in Christ and anointed us is God, who also sealed us and gave us the Spirit in our hearts as a pledge. (2 Corinthians 1:20-22 NASB).

For as many as are the promises of God, in Christ they are [all answered] "Yes." So through Him we say our "Amen" to the glory of God. (2 Corinthians 1:20 AMP).

In him the detail of every single promise of God is fulfilled; Jesus is God's yes to your entire well being. In our union with him the Amen that echoes in us gives evidence to his glorious intent through us. God himself authorizes our oneness with you in ¹Christ. He is our ¹anointing. (The word, *¹chrio* means to smear or rub with oil, to anoint). *His personal signet signature is the official stamp that sanctions the integrity of our ministry to you; this is the seal of the Spirit in our hearts.* (2 Corinthians 1:20-22 Mirror).

He made known to us the mystery of His will, according to His good pleasure which He set forth in Him, regarding His plan of the fullness of the times, to bring all things together in Christ, things in the heavens and things on the earth. (Ephesians 1:9-10).

Daniel used the analogy of a stone and a mountain in regards to the kingdom that would be established:

"You, O king, were watching and behold, there was a single great statue; that statue, which was large and of extraordinary radiance, was standing in front of you, and its appearance was awesome. The head of that statue was made of fine gold, its chest and its arms of silver, its belly and its thighs of bronze, its legs of iron, and its feet partly of iron and

partly of clay. You continued watching until a stone was broken off without hands, and it struck the statue on its feet of iron and clay, and crushed them. Then the iron, the clay, the bronze, the silver, and the gold were crushed to pieces all at the same time, and they were like chaff from the summer threshing floors; and the wind carried them away so that not a trace of them was found. But the stone that struck the statue became a great mountain and filled the entire earth...

"And in the days of those kings the God of heaven will set up a kingdom which will never be destroyed, and that kingdom will not be left for another people; it will crush and put an end to all these kingdoms, but it will itself endure forever. Just as you saw that a stone was broken off from the mountain without hands, and that it crushed the iron, the bronze, the clay, the silver, and the gold, the great God has made known to the king what will take place in the future; so the dream is certain and its interpretation is trustworthy." (Daniel 2:31-35, 44-45).

Jesus Himself used the same analogy and connected the rejection of the stone and coming of the kingdom with the end of the old covenant system that would occur in that generation. Jesus prophesied that this end would occur in the generation still living when he spoke; and that the kingdom would be taken from Israel and given to another people. The Apostles Paul and Peter later revealed who these people would be: the *ekklesia* Jesus would build, the continuation of the people of God, those of the faith of Abraham, the true Jews, those circumcised of heart and the true Israel of God. The temple would no longer be literal but figurative of the new wineskin of the *ekklesia* that He would establish, made up of living stones who were themselves temples of the Holy Spirit.

And coming to Him as to a living stone which has been rejected by people, but is choice and precious in the sight of God, you also, as living stones, are being built up as a spiritual house for a holy priesthood, to offer spiritual sacrifices that are acceptable to God through Jesus Christ. (1 Peter 2:4-5).

Jesus was the stone from Mount Zion that would become a great mountain which would fill the earth. Jesus, that stone, was rejected by the Jewish religious leaders while He was still on the earth. Jesus prophesied that those who rejected Him as the stone would be judged and the kingdom would be removed from their stewardship:

Jesus said to them, "Did you never read in the Scriptures, 'A stone which the builders rejected, this has become the chief cornerstone; this came about from the Lord, and it is marvelous in our eyes'? Therefore I say to you, the kingdom of God will be taken away from you and given to a people producing its fruit. And the one who falls on this stone will be broken to pieces; and on whomever it falls, it will crush him." (Matthew 21:42-44).

"Woe to you, scribes and Pharisees, hypocrites! For you build the tombs for the prophets and decorate the monuments of the righteous, and you say, 'If we had been living in the days of our fathers, we would not have been partners with them in shedding the blood of the prophets.' So you testify against yourselves, that you are sons of those who murdered the prophets. Fill up, then, the measure of the guilt of your fathers. You snakes, you offspring of vipers, how will you escape the sentence of hell [Gehenna]?

"Therefore, behold, I am sending you prophets and wise men and scribes; some of them you will kill and crucify, and some of them you will flog in your synagogues, and persecute from

city to city, so that upon you will fall the guilt of all the righteous blood shed on earth, from the blood of righteous Abel to the blood of Zechariah, the son of Berechiah, whom you murdered between the temple and the altar. Truly I say to you, all these things will come upon this generation.

"Jerusalem, Jerusalem, who kills the prophets and stones those who have been sent to her! How often I wanted to gather your children together, the way a hen gathers her chicks under her wings, and you were unwilling. Behold, your house is being left to you desolate!" (Matthew 23:29-38).

Jesus, quoting Daniel 9:27, placed Daniel's prophecy and the fulfilment of Daniel's 70 weeks in that current generation. Jesus Himself then prophesied that those events would be fulfilled in that generation with the final destruction of the temple that would signify the end of the old covenant (which, according to Hebrews 8:13, was fading away and would become obsolete).

"And he will confirm a covenant with the many for one week, but in the middle of the week he will put a stop to sacrifice and grain offering; and on the wing of abominations will come the one who makes desolate, until a complete destruction, one that is decreed, gushes forth on the one who makes desolate." (Daniel 9:27).

When He said, "A new covenant," He has made the first obsolete. But whatever is becoming obsolete and growing old is about to disappear. (Hebrews 8:13).

In Matthew 24, Jesus firmly placed all the events He prophesied as occurring in that generation:

"Therefore when you see the abomination of desolation which was spoken of through Daniel the prophet, standing in the holy

place - let the reader understand - then those who are in Judea must flee to the mountains." (Matthew 24:15-16).

"Truly I say to you, this generation will not pass away until all these things take place. Heaven and earth will pass away, but My words will not pass away." (Matthew 24:34-35).

Those events include the destruction of the temple:

Jesus left the temple area and was going on His way when His disciples came up to point out the temple buildings to Him. But He responded and said to them, "Do you not see all these things? Truly I say to you, not one stone here will be left upon another, which will not be torn down.

And as He was sitting on the Mount of Olives, the disciples came to Him privately, saying, "Tell us, when will these things happen, and what will be the sign of Your coming, and of the end of the age. (Matthew 24:1-3).

Firstly, they were asking about the signs of Jesus' presence, not '(second) coming': 'coming' is a mistranslation of the word *parousia* (which means presence). Secondly, they were asking about the end of the age, not the end of the world – another futurist mistranslation that some translations use, this time of the word *aionios*. What were those signs that would signify His presence and the soon-coming end of the age?

And Jesus answered and said to them, "See to it that no one misleads you. For many will come in My name, saying, 'I am the Christ,' and they will mislead many people. (Matthew 24: 4-5).

False messiahs: Matthew 24:4, 6, 24; Mark 13:5, 21-22; and Luke 21:3 all use the term *pseudochristos* for messianic pretenders. Theudas, Dositheos the Samaritan, Simon bar

Gioras and Menalem were among those who came claiming to be the Messiah at this time.

"And you will be hearing of wars and rumors of wars. See that you are not alarmed, for those things must take place, but that is not yet the end. For nation will rise against nation, and kingdom against kingdom, and there will be famines and earthquakes in various places. But all these things are merely the beginning of birth pains." (Matthew 24:6-8).

This period referred to in Matthew 24:4–31 covers the time known as the seventieth week of Daniel or more popularly the 'tribulation period'. Jesus is telling His disciples that when they see the beginning of the birth pangs they should flee. This period did mark the end of the old covenant system but more importantly the establishment of the new covenant wineskin. Birth is bringing forth something new and it is not focusing on the pregnancy: birth is the end of a pregnancy – and for many that would be a relief – but the joy of motherhood far outweighs the pain of childbirth. The signs that Jesus refers to must become the focus of the establishing of the kingdom and the beginning of the period of the restoration of all things: it is not about the end of the world.

Wars and rumours of wars occurred widely during this period, as recorded in the *Annals of Tacitus* (a Roman historian), covering the period from 14 AD to the death of Nero in 68 AD. These describe the tumult of the period with phrases such as 'disturbances in Germany', 'commotions in Africa', 'commotions in Thrace', 'insurrections in Gaul', 'intrigues among the Parthians', 'the war in Britain' and 'the war in Armenia'. Wars were fought from one end of the Roman Empire to the other. Within this description we can see further fulfilment: *"For nation will rise against nation and kingdom against kingdom".*

Famines and earthquakes also occurred during this period, as they have in all generations. Beginning with the book of Acts, we see that famines were prevalent in the period before Jerusalem's destruction in 70 AD. Contemporary historians such as Tacitus, Suetonius, and Josephus mention other famines during the period before 70 AD. There are many historical records of earthquakes that occurred before Jerusalem was destroyed in the first century. Three earthquakes are mentioned in the book of Acts before the destruction of Jerusalem in 70 AD. A particularly powerful quake shook Jerusalem in 67 AD and Tacitus mentions earthquakes in Crete, Rome, Apamea, Phrygia, Campania, Laodicea and Pompeii during the time just before Jerusalem's destruction.

"Then they will hand you over to tribulation and kill you, and you will be hated by all nations because of My name. And at that time many will fall away, and they will betray one another and hate one another. And many false prophets will rise up and mislead many people. And because lawlessness is increased, most people's love will become cold. (Matthew 24:9-12).

There is much evidence within the Bible itself, particularly in the book of Acts, confirming that these signs were contemporary to the present generation that Jesus spoke of.

"But the one who endures to the end is the one who will be saved." (Matthew 24:13).

This verse has been used to mean spiritual salvation for those who remain faithful but in reality it is talking about physical salvation from the destruction of Jerusalem that Jesus warned them to look out for.

This gospel of the kingdom shall be preached in the whole world as a testimony to all the nations, and then the end will come. (Matthew 24:14).

This is a sign that many are still looking for to ratify that Jesus can return. However, as multiple predictions about the date of Jesus' return have come and gone without fulfilment, many believe that this whole world preaching has already taken place. In fact, the following scriptures suggest that it took place soon after Jesus' ascension, perhaps even on the day of Pentecost:

Now there were Jews living in Jerusalem, devout men from every nation under heaven. (Acts 2:5).

... the gospel which has come to you, just as in all the world also it is constantly bearing fruit and increasing... (Colossians 1:5-6).

... the gospel that you have heard, which was proclaimed in all creation under heaven... (Colossians 1:23).

... because your faith is being proclaimed throughout the whole world. (Romans 1:8).

But I say, surely they have never heard, have they? Indeed they have; "Their voice has gone out into all the earth, and their words to the ends of the world." (Romans 10:18).

The phrase 'end of the age' means the close of a period of time (for example, an era or epoch). In this instance, it is referring to the Jewish age or dispensation which was about to come to an abrupt end. All those passages that speak of 'the end,' 'the end of the age,' or 'the ends of the ages,' refer to the same conclusion or consummation that was soon or about to take place. There was a clear expectation that these things were near and a warning to be ready and prepared for those of that generation.

Therefore when you see the abomination of desolation which was spoken of through Daniel the prophet, standing in the holy place - let the reader understand - then those who are in Judea must flee to the mountains. Whoever is on the housetop must not go down to get things out of his house. And whoever is in the field must not turn back to get his cloak. But woe to those women who are pregnant, and to those who are nursing babies in those days! Moreover, pray that when you flee, it will not be in the winter, or on a Sabbath. For then there will be a great tribulation, such as has not occurred since the beginning of the world until now, nor ever will again. And if those days had not been cut short, no life would have been saved; but for the sake of the elect those days will be cut short. (Matthew 24:15-22).

The sign of the abomination of desolation (or as Luke puts it, armies surrounding Jerusalem) was the sign that Jesus warned them about so they could flee and not die in the siege that was coming. It was not a sign of an impending 'rapture'.

But when you see Jerusalem surrounded by armies, then recognize that her desolation is near. Then those who are in Judea must flee to the mountains, and those who are in the midst of the city must leave, and those who are in the country must not enter the city; because these are days of vengeance so that all things which are written will be fulfilled. (Luke 21:20-22).

Every believer in Jerusalem who endured to the end knew to look for those signs; and they all fled to Pella, a mountain town, and were saved. Pella is known to be one of the earliest historical Christian sites. According to Josephus, no Christians died in the destruction of Jerusalem[8] but the dead bodies of 300,000 or more of those who did not believe were thrown into the fires of the literal Gehenna, a rubbish dump outside of Jerusalem.

Then if anyone says to you, 'Behold, here is the Christ,' or 'He is over here,' do not believe him. For false Christs and false prophets will arise and will provide great signs and wonders, so as to mislead, if possible, even the elect. Behold, I have told you in advance. So if they say to you, 'Behold, He is in the wilderness,' do not go out; or, 'Behold, He is in the inner rooms,' do not believe them. (Matthew 24:23-26).

Many of these 'false Christs' were inciting violence and rebellion, as referred to by Gamaliel:

"For, some time ago Theudas appeared, claiming to be somebody, and a group of about four hundred men joined him. But he was killed, and all who followed him were dispersed and came to nothing. After this man, Judas of Galilee appeared in the days of the census and drew away some people after him; he also perished, and all those who followed him were scattered." (Acts 5:36-37).

I will discuss the coming of the Son of Man (Matthew 24:27, 30-32) more fully in the next chapter.

But immediately after the tribulation of those days the sun will be darkened, and the moon will not give its light, and the stars

---

[8] Josephus: The Complete Works
https://ccel.org/ccel/josephus/complete/complete.iii.vii.ix.html

will fall from the sky, and the powers of the heavens will be shaken. (Matthew 24:29).

'And it shall be in the last days,' God says...
'And I will grant wonders in the sky above
And signs on the earth below,
Blood, and fire, and vapor of smoke.
The sun will be turned into darkness
And the moon into blood,
Before the great and glorious day of the Lord shall come.
And it shall be that everyone who calls on the name of the Lord will be saved. (Acts 2:17, 19-21).

These again are verses which incite rapture fever whenever there is a blood moon or a peculiar alignment of planets or other heavenly bodies. A quick reference to the Old Testament will soon clear up the confusion by showing that these signs were figurative of the end of governmental systems throughout the Bible and do not need to produce fear.

Jesus is actually quoting Old Testament prophets who foretold the destruction of other cities and empires. He applies it to Jerusalem, Israel and the old covenant governmental system to foretell its destruction, which eventually happened at the hands of the Romans in 70 AD to end that generation.

"The stars shall fall from heaven" and "the Son of Man coming on the clouds": this language uses metaphors referring to the judgment of nations and is not referring to the destruction of the actual planet. These Old Testament passages refer to the fall of Babylon, Egypt, Edom, and Israel (Isaiah 13:9-10; 19:1; 34:4-5; Ezekiel 32:7-8; Amos 5:21-22; Psalm 18; Psalm 104; Habakkuk 1:2-4.). When judgment came to Egypt in 670 BC they reaped what they had sown and were conquered by the Assyrians.

The oracle concerning Egypt.

*Behold, the Lord is riding on a swift cloud
and is about to come to Egypt;
the idols of Egypt will tremble at His presence,
and the heart of the Egyptians will melt within them.*
(Isaiah 19:1).

The same principle of judgment through reaping what they had sown also applied to Edom, Babylon and Samaria, as seen from these passages in Isaiah, Amos and Ezekiel:

*And all the host of heaven will wear away,
And the sky will be rolled up like a scroll;
All their hosts will also wither away
As a leaf withers from the vine,
Or as one withers from the fig tree.
For My sword is satiated in heaven,
Behold it shall descend for judgment upon Edom
And upon the people whom I have devoted to destruction.*
(Isaiah 34:4-5).

*Behold, the day of the Lord is coming,
Cruel, with fury and burning anger,
To make the land a desolation;
And He will exterminate its sinners from it.
For the stars of heaven and their constellations
Will not flash their light;
The sun will be dark when it rises
And the moon will not shed its light.* (Isaiah 13:9-10).

*It will come about in that day," declares the Lord God,
"That I will make the sun go down at noon
And make the earth dark in broad daylight.* (Amos 8:9).

And when I extinguish you,
I will cover the heavens and darken their stars;
I will cover the sun with a cloud
And the moon will not give its light.
All the shining lights in the heavens
I will darken over you
And will set darkness on your land,"
Declares the Lord God. (Ezekiel 32:7-8).

In Matthew 24, the context is the fall of Jerusalem and the destruction of the Temple. The same metaphorical language of sun, moon, and stars is used to represent the old covenant government of Israel which would eventually fall in 70 AD for rejecting Christ and the new covenant (see Matthew 23:31-36). Jesus uses prophetic language that His listeners would be familiar with and applies it to Jerusalem.

As a side note, although the prophetic apocalyptical language employed by the writers concerning the end of empires imputes the destroying to God, this is because of the undifferentiated way they interchanged God and the devil. The principle of sowing and reaping is being used here to indicate that if you follow the tree of the knowledge of good and evil to make a name for yourself then you will reap the consequence that someone will come and take it from you. God does not destroy nations and empires, as He is Love, but they are destroyed and their light comes to an end all the same, as another empire's light rises. Death and destruction are the inevitable results of following the path of the independent false tree agenda.

Much of the Old Testament imputes all judgment and destruction of His enemies to God. But God has no enemies, and when we differentiate through the lens of Jesus (the express image of God, who said, "If you have seen me you have seen the Father"), we will see that they may have heard that God said this or did that but Jesus came to clarify the truth by being the Way, the Truth and the Life. He repeatedly said "you have heard it said... but I say unto you..." – one such time with the injunction not to kill and destroy their enemies but pray for and bless them.

"Now learn the parable from the fig tree: as soon as its branch has become tender and sprouts its leaves, you know that summer is near; so you too, when you see all these things, recognize that He is near, right at the door. Truly I say to you, this generation will not pass away until all these things take place. Heaven and earth will pass away, but My words will not pass away." (Matthew 24:32-35).

Jesus prophesied when these events would take place by placing the fulfilment of the day of the Lord and His coming again, which we look at specifically in the next chapter, in the generation of those who were His audience two thousand years ago, not the present day. For us, all that Jesus prophesied as the fulfilment of those prophecies is in our past.

The events of the desolation of the temple, the resurrection, the tribulation, the coming of the Son of Man and the arrival of the kingdom can be found in Daniel, chapters 7, 9 and 12. Daniel connects all these eschatological events to the same time period that would be fulfilled in 70 AD when Jerusalem was destroyed and Israel as a nation was dispersed. The destruction of the city was linked to the removal of the kingdom from Israel. Therefore Israel's covenant power was ended or shattered (see Daniel 7:13-14, 18, 27; 9:24-27; 12:1-7).

Jesus also linked judgment and resurrection to the end of the age eschatological events (see Matthew 13:39-43, 51). He specifically asked them if they understood the implications of His teaching, referring to the harvest at the end of the age, and they categorically responded, "Yes" (vs. 51). Jesus had already taught that He would return in some of their lifetimes (Matthew 10:22-23; 16:27-28/Mark 8:38-9:1).

There has been much needless confusion over the word 'generation', as dispensationalists have tried to interpret the Greek word *genea* to mean 'race' and not 'generation', thus enabling the events Jesus spoke of to be placed in the future.

Genea is used over 30 times in the New Testament. It always refers to a 40-year generation - and in this case it refers specifically to the generation alive when Jesus taught. Some futurist teachers claim that Matthew 24:34 is the exception to the rule and claim that 'this generation' means that the Jewish race will not pass away until all these things are fulfilled. However, if Jesus (or Matthew) had meant the 'race' of Jews, they would have used the Greek word *genos* (which does mean 'race').

Hal Lindsey, a popular futurist, stated "WE are the generation that will see the end times... and return of Christ." And "unmistakably... this generation is the one that will see the end of the present world and the return of Christ."[9]

Chuck Smith, another popular dispensationalist, stated "... the generation of 1948 is the last generation. Since a generation of judgment is forty years and the Tribulation period lasts seven years, I believe the Lord could come back for His Church any time before the Tribulation starts, which would mean any time before 1981. (1948 + 40 − 7 = 1981)."

---

[9] Cited by Stephen Sizer, stephensizer.com/articles/hallindsey

> From my understanding of biblical prophecies, I'm convinced that the Lord is coming for His Church before the end of 1981. – Chuck Smith, *Future Survival* (1978).

The prophetic significance of these was local to Israel and was never meant to be global, as futurists maintain. Neither Jesus nor the Apostle Paul meant nor understood the phrases 'into all the world,' 'all nations,' 'every creature,' or 'end of the earth,' to be global terms. They are describing the nations of the Roman Empire – or the world as they knew it.

Josephus, the Jewish historian, describes the destruction of Jerusalem in practically identical language:

> Now this vast multitude is indeed collected out of remote places, but the entire nation was now shut up by fate as in prison, and the Roman army encompassed the city when it was crowded with inhabitants. Accordingly, the multitude of those that therein perished exceeded all the destructions that either men or God ever brought upon the world...[10]

That generation time frame was also linked to heaven and earth passing away, which, on a cursory reading, appears to confirm the end of the world but in reality meant nothing of the sort.

"Truly I say to you, this generation will not pass away until all these things take place. Heaven and earth will pass away, but My words will not pass away." (Matthew 24:34-35).

This was not the first time Jesus used the phrase 'heaven and earth' and His audience would have known what He meant:

---

[10] Josephus: *The Wars of the Jews*, Book VI, tr. Whiston.

"Do not think that I came to abolish the Law or the Prophets; I did not come to abolish but to fulfill. For truly I say to you, until heaven and earth pass away, not the smallest letter or stroke shall pass from the Law until all is accomplished." (Matthew 5:17-18).

If the heavens and the earth were the literal planet and sky, then they are still present, which would indicate that we are still under the law. Yet we know the old covenant system of laws has ended:

When He said, "A new covenant," He has made the first obsolete. But whatever is becoming obsolete and growing old is ready to disappear. (Hebrews 8:13).

'Heaven and earth' is referring to the old covenant system, which is also represented by the temple, the place where heaven and earth met in the Holy of Holies. When the old covenant 'heaven and earth' passed away in 70 AD, the new covenant 'new heavens and earth' wineskin was established. This is not discussing the end of planet earth, the world or the universe.

There are good contextual and grammatical reasons to interpret the 'end of the age' as the old covenant age in Matthew 24:3, the stars falling from the heavens (v29) to be the religious and civil rulers falling from the places of power when Jerusalem and her Temple were destroyed in 70 AD, and verse 35 which addresses 'heaven and earth' passing away. Once again there is a contextual and historical hermeneutic suggesting this is referring to the old covenant heavens and earth and its temple.

> ...that 'heaven and earth' in the Old Testament may sometimes be a way of referring to Jerusalem or its temple, for which 'Jerusalem' is a metonymy. (G.K. Beale[11]).

> ...the dissolution of the Mosaic economy, and the establishment of the Christian, is often spoken of as the removing of the old earth and heavens, and the creation of a new earth and new heavens. (John Brown[12]).

Commentators are correct to identify the 'heaven and earth' of Matthew 5:18 as the same 'heaven and earth' of Matthew 24:35; but the context of both point us to the old covenant system and not the planet earth.

> The temple was far more than the point at which heaven and earth met. Rather, it was thought to correspond to, represent, or, in some sense, to be 'heaven and earth' in its totality. (Crispin H.T. Fletcher-Louis[13]).

So the term 'heaven and earth' was synonymous with the temple to Jesus' generation, who saw the temple as the centre of the world. Mark 13:31 and Matthew 5:18 refer to the destruction of the temple as a passing away of the old age or governmental system, something that they were to look out for in their lifetimes. Jesus is not saying this to our generation or to any future generation: He was warning his contemporary audience to look out for the signs and be ready. These signs

---

[11] G.K. Beale, *The Temple and the Church's Mission: A biblical theology of the dwelling place of God*, on fullpreterism.com
[12] John Brown, *Discourses and Sayings of Our Lord*, The Banner of Truth Trust, Edinburgh (1990 [1852]).
[13] Crispin H.T. Fletcher-Louis, a contributing author in *ESCHATOLOGY* in *Bible & Theology Evangelical Essays at the Dawn of a New Millennium*, Inter Varsity Press, Downers Grove, Illinois (1997), p157.

have no relevance at all to our generation and it is a distraction to our sonship mandate to keep looking for them.

Truly I say to you, this generation will not pass away until all these things take place. Heaven and earth will pass away, but My words will not pass away... What I say to you I say to all, 'Be on the alert! (Mark 13: 30-31, 37).

Do not think that I came to abolish the Law or the Prophets; I did not come to abolish but to fulfill. For truly I say to you, until heaven and earth pass away, not the smallest letter or stroke shall pass from the Law until all is accomplished. (Matthew 5:17-18).

Neither Jesus nor the New Testament writers ever predicted the end of the 'late great planet earth' as is simply assumed by so many, whether here in Matthew 24:3, 29 and 35, or elsewhere in the New Testament. Interpretations that place these events firmly in the past are considered orthodox by many reformed and evangelical theologians but not by the modern futurists or dispensationalists who twist the interpretations to fit their narrative by not taking into account audience relevance.

Daniel's 70 weeks

The time of these events was also predicted by Daniel when he prophesied a period of 70 weeks (usually interpreted to mean 490 years, counting each week as seven years). This prophecy has often been used by dispensational futurists to infer that there is one week left still to happen in the future, and that will be the 'Great Tribulation'. I will deal with that specific issue later, as it is very important to show that this period has already been fulfilled (as Jesus Himself revealed in Matthew 24) in that generation.

Daniel was seeing these visions during 70 years of exile in Babylon and some of what was revealed was about the pre- and post-exile period. The return from exile and rebuilding of the temple, and later of Jerusalem, was written about by Ezra and Nehemiah. Daniel was visited by the angel Gabriel several times, interestingly, the same angel that revealed the coming of Jesus to Mary. Gabriel indicated that the vision concerned the time of the end. Of what? The end of the world or the end of the old covenant and Israel's stewardship of the kingdom?

In the first year of Darius the son of Ahasuerus, of Median descent, who was made king over the kingdom of the Chaldeans - in the first year of his reign, I, Daniel, observed in the books the number of the years which was revealed as the word of the Lord to Jeremiah the prophet for the completion of the desolations of Jerusalem, namely, seventy years. So I gave my attention to the Lord God, to seek Him by prayer and pleading, with fasting, sackcloth, and ashes. I prayed to the Lord my God and confessed, and said, "Oh, Lord, the great and awesome God, who keeps His covenant and faithfulness for those who love Him and keep His commandments, we have sinned, we have done wrong, and acted wickedly and rebelled, even turning aside from Your commandments and ordinances. Moreover, we have not listened to Your servants the prophets, who spoke in Your name to our kings, our leaders, our fathers, and all the people of the land.

"Righteousness belongs to You, Lord, but to us open shame, as it is this day – to the men of Judah, the inhabitants of Jerusalem, and all Israel, those who are nearby and those who are far away in all the countries to which You have driven them, because of their unfaithful deeds which they have committed against You. Open shame belongs to us, Lord, to our kings, our leaders, and our fathers, because we have

sinned against You. To the Lord our God belong compassion and forgiveness, because we have rebelled against Him; and we have not obeyed the voice of the Lord our God, to walk in His teachings which He set before us through His servants the prophets. Indeed, all Israel has violated Your Law and turned aside, not obeying Your voice; so the curse has gushed forth on us, along with the oath which is written in the Law of Moses the servant of God, because we have sinned against Him. So He has confirmed His words which He had spoken against us and against our rulers who ruled us, to bring on us great disaster; for under the entire heaven there has not been done anything like what was done in Jerusalem. Just as it is written in the Law of Moses, all this disaster has come on us; yet we have not sought the favor of the Lord our God by turning from our wrongdoing and giving attention to Your truth. So the Lord has kept the disaster in store and brought it on us; for the Lord our God is righteous with respect to all His deeds which He has done, but we have not obeyed His voice.

"And now, Lord, our God, You who brought Your people out of the land of Egypt with a mighty hand and made a name for Yourself, as it is this day – we have sinned, we have been wicked. Lord, in accordance with all Your righteous acts, let now Your anger and Your wrath turn away from Your city Jerusalem, Your holy mountain; for because of our sins and the wrongdoings of our fathers, Jerusalem and Your people have become an object of taunting to all those around us. So now, our God, listen to the prayer of Your servant and to his pleas, and for Your sake, Lord, let Your face shine on Your desolate sanctuary. My God, incline Your ear and hear! Open Your eyes and see our desolations and the city which is called by Your name; for we are not presenting our pleas before You based on any merits of our own, but based on Your great compassion. Lord, hear! Lord, forgive! Lord, listen and take

action! For Your own sake, my God, do not delay, because Your city and Your people are called by Your name."

While I was still speaking and praying, and confessing my sin and the sin of my people Israel, and presenting my plea before the Lord my God in behalf of the holy mountain of my God, while I was still speaking in prayer, the man Gabriel, whom I had seen in the vision previously, came to me in my extreme weariness about the time of the evening offering. And he instructed me and talked with me and said, "Daniel, I have come now to give you insight with understanding. At the beginning of your pleas the command was issued, and I have come to tell you, because you are highly esteemed; so pay attention to the message and gain understanding of the vision.

"Seventy weeks have been decreed for your people and your holy city, to finish the wrongdoing, to make an end of sin, to make atonement for guilt, to bring in everlasting righteousness, to seal up vision and prophecy, and to anoint the Most Holy Place. So you are to know and understand that from the issuing of a decree to restore and rebuild Jerusalem, until Messiah the Prince, there will be seven weeks and sixty-two weeks; it will be built again, with streets and moat, even in times of distress. Then after the sixty-two weeks, the Messiah will be cut off and have nothing, and the people of the prince who is to come will destroy the city and the sanctuary. And its end will come with a flood; even to the end there will be war; desolations are determined. And he will confirm a covenant with the many for one week, but in the middle of the week he will put a stop to sacrifice and grain offering; and **on the wing of abominations will come the one who makes desolate, until a complete destruction**, *one that is decreed, gushes forth on the one who makes desolate."* (Daniel 9:1-27, emphasis mine).

HAPPY ESCHATOLOGY

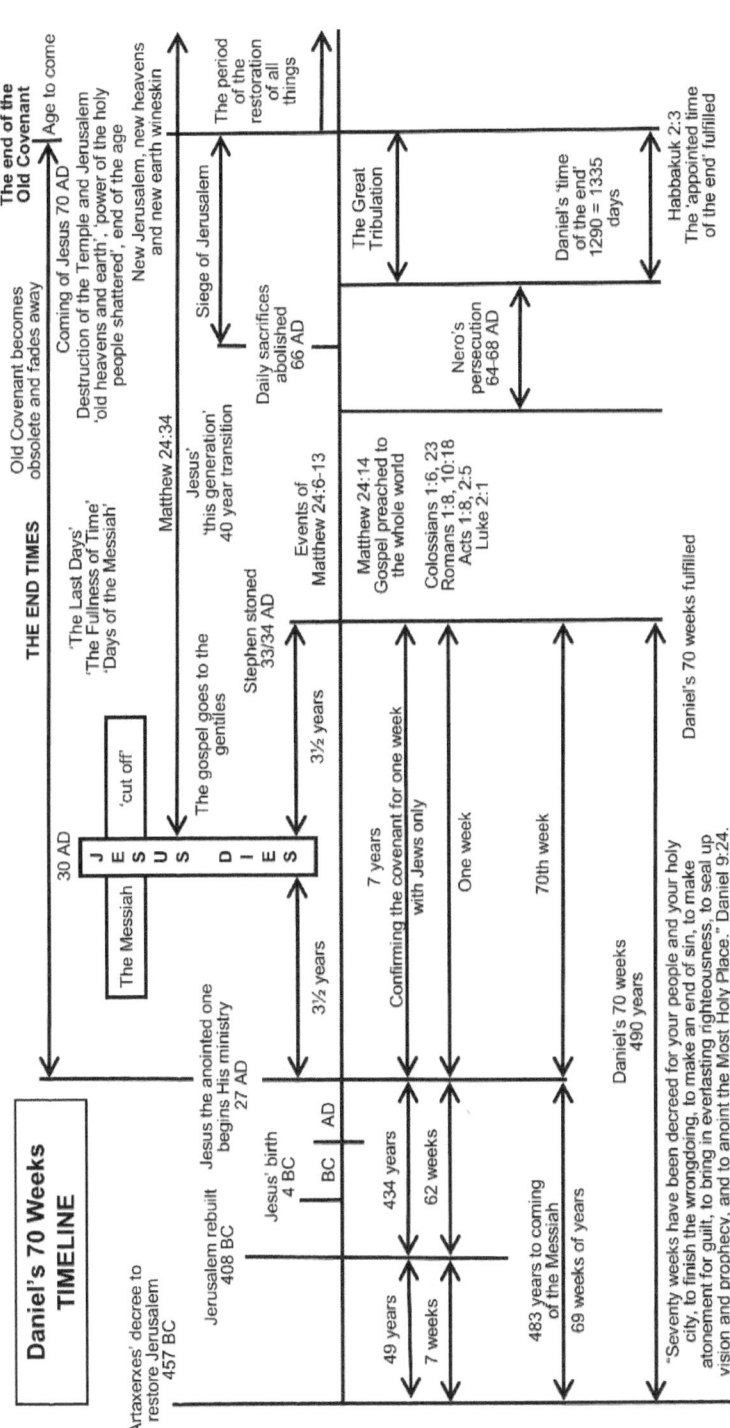

Jesus linked the destruction of Jerusalem and the temple with the great tribulation and His coming with Daniel's phrase 'on the wing of abominations will come the one who makes desolate until a complete destruction', an event Daniel prophesied would occur in the last of the 70 weeks. That would happen in that generation, not a future generation thousands of years later that so many people are still fearfully looking for.

Talking about the great tribulation and the abomination of desolation is enough to strike fear into the hearts of those still caught up in the deceit of the rapture. Perfect love casts out all fear, so we know that God is not the author of such eschatological fear. Of course, there is nothing to fear when we realise that all these things were fulfilled two thousand years ago.

Jesus also linked the coming of the Holy Spirit to indwell mankind with the eschatological events that would end the old covenant temple system of worship. Jesus hinted at this when dialoguing with the Samaritan women at Jacob's well (figuratively, the well of salvation).

Jesus answered and said to her, "Everyone who drinks of this water will thirst again; but whoever drinks of the water that I will give him shall never thirst; but the water that I will give him will become in him a well of water springing up to eternal life." ... The woman said to Him, "Sir, I perceive that You are a prophet. Our fathers worshiped in this mountain, and you people say that in Jerusalem is the place where men ought to worship." Jesus said to her, "Woman, believe Me, an hour is coming when neither in this mountain nor in Jerusalem will you worship the Father. You worship what you do not know; we worship what we know, for salvation is from the Jews. But an hour is coming, and now is, when the true worshipers will worship the Father in spirit and truth; for such people the Father seeks to be His worshipers. God is spirit, and those who worship Him must worship in spirit and truth." (John 4:13-14, 19-24).

The mountain symbolism is significant as it relates to the kingdom of God and government that was to be established in those days, not in a far distant future or a literal millennial thousand years.

In John 3, John 7 and John 14 we can see that Jesus linked the coming of the Holy Spirit to dwell within mankind with the destruction of the old, literal temple wineskin; and in the new covenant, all of mankind would become the new wineskin of His presence.

Now on the last day, the great day of the feast, Jesus stood and cried out, saying, "If anyone is thirsty, let him come to Me and drink. The one who believes in Me, as the Scripture said, 'From his innermost being will flow rivers of living water.'" But this He said in reference to the Spirit, whom those who believed in Him were to receive; for the Spirit was not yet given, because Jesus was not yet glorified. (John 7:37-39).

"Do not let your heart be troubled; believe in God, believe also in Me. In My Father's house are many rooms; if that were not so, I would have told you, because I am going there to prepare a place for you. And if I go and prepare a place for you, I am coming again and will take you to Myself, so that where I am, there you also will be. (John 14:1-3).

"Do you not believe that I am in the Father, and the Father is in Me? The words that I say to you I do not speak on My own, but the Father, as He remains in Me, does His works. Believe

Me that I am in the Father and the Father is in Me..." (John 14:10-11).

"After a little while, the world no longer is going to see Me, but you are going to see Me; because I live, you also will live. On that day you will know that I am in My Father, and you are in Me, and I in you." ... Jesus answered and said to him, "If anyone loves Me, he will follow My word; and My Father will love him, and We will come to him and make Our dwelling with him." (John 14:19-20, 23).

*"'And it shall be in the last days,' God says,
'That I will pour out My Spirit on all mankind;
And your sons and your daughters will prophesy,
And your young men will see visions,
And your old men will have dreams;
And even on My male and female servants
I will pour out My Spirit in those days,
And they will prophesy.
And I will display wonders in the sky above
And signs on the earth below,
Blood, fire, and vapor of smoke.
The sun will be turned into darkness
And the moon into blood,
Before the great and glorious day of the Lord comes.
And it shall be that everyone who calls on the name of the Lord will be saved.'"* (Acts 2:17-21).

The last days were the last days of the old covenant and the signs spoken of used the apocalyptical language of destruction to show the end of a governmental system. This was when the kingdom was established on the earth, and that kingdom would eventually grow to fill it. From the small beginnings of an acorn, a mighty oak tree grows; and so it is with the kingdom: 120 people in an upper room to 2.4 billion people today who profess to believe in Jesus as the Son of God. It is only going to continue to increase as more and more of God's children throughout the earth realise their reconciliation and inclusion in Christ.

In Matthew 24 and Luke 21 Jesus also links the coming of the kingdom with the end of the old covenant system, represented by the physical temple in Jerusalem, being replaced by a new wineskin temple all of mankind that the Spirit was going to dwell in.

Or do you not know that your body is a temple of the Holy Spirit within you, whom you have from God, and that you are not your own? For you have been bought for a price: therefore glorify God in your body. (1 Corinthians 6:19-20).

The last days of the old were linked to the first days of the new covenant age when the kingdom of God was established.

Daniel spoke of a statue that was made of four metals and of four animals, widely accepted to refer to four world empires or kingdoms. The four earthly kingdoms are commonly agreed to be Babylon, Persia, Greece and Rome. Daniel placed the time of the kingdom of God being established as during the last kingdom: that of Rome.

A great event was prophesied to occur in the time of the last kingdom, which had legs of iron but feet of iron and clay (usually interpreted to refer to Rome's eastern and western empire). The event was a stone being broken off a mountain, not by man's hands, ending those previous kingdoms and establishing a new kingdom which would become a great mountain and fill the entire earth. Who or what was the stone, and what was the mountain?

The prophets Isaiah and Micah revealed God's secret plan that the mountain was to be the mountain of the house of the Lord. That would be the same new covenant wineskin of the one new man in Christ, the new temple He would dwell in. That mountain would be lifted up to heaven where we are seated in heavenly places to rule and have dominion so that God's kingdom would be on earth as it is in heaven.

The word 'mountain' in Hebrew is *harar*, which when broken down into its pictorial components can be interpreted as 'behold the ruler of rulers'. Mountains are symbolic of government and in most instances where God engaged with man directly, He came on a mountain e.g. Sinai, Horeb, Ebal, Gerazim, Mount of Olives, Calvary, and Mount Zion. We are described as the mountain of the house of the Lord, which is symbolic of our government in the Kingdom of God. Daniel's stone becomes a mountain or kingdom that grows until it fills the earth and that ties in with the concept of the restoration of all things spoken by the prophets.

> *Now it will come about that*
> *In the last days*
> *The mountain of the house of the Lord*
> *Will be established as the chief of the mountains,*
> *And will be raised above the hills;*
> *And all the nations will stream to it.*
> *And many peoples will come and say,*
> *"Come, let's go up to the mountain of the Lord,*
> *To the house of the God of Jacob;*
> *So that He may teach us about His ways,*
> *And that we may walk in His paths."*
> *For the law will go out from Zion*
> *And the word of the Lord from Jerusalem.* (Isaiah 2:2-3).

*And it will come about in the last days
That the mountain of the house of the Lord
Will be established as the chief of the mountains.
It will be raised above the hills,
And the peoples will stream to it.* (Micah 4:1).

The prophets also revealed that the stone would be rejected by Israel and the kingdom taken from them and given to another people: those truly of the faith of Abraham, not of religious or ethnic origin.

The prophet Daniel interpreted Nebuchadnezzar's dream that was concerning four future earthly kingdoms and the establishing of God's kingdom on earth. Daniel also saw a prophetic vision of the four coming kingdoms and the legal establishment of God's kingdom on earth. That, I believe, was fulfilled on the day of resurrection. These kingdoms were representative of the counterfeit kingdom that has its original source in Lucifer, Satan or the devil - terms representing the system of the tree of the knowledge of good and evil which was independent of God and is the basis of all humanism. That system was expressed at the building of the tower of Babel, where Nimrod, a false messiah figure, created a mountain or tower that ascended into the spiritual realms, seeking to outwork the root of the rebellion: "I will ascend, I will be enthroned".

*"But you said in your heart,
'I will ascend to heaven;
I will raise my throne above the stars of God,
And I will sit on the mount of assembly
In the recesses of the north.
I will ascend above the heights of the clouds;
I will make myself like the Most High.'* (Isaiah 14:13-14).

And they said, "Come, let's build ourselves a city, and a tower whose top will reach into heaven, and let's make a name for ourselves; otherwise we will be scattered abroad over the face of all the earth." (Genesis 11:4).

This is the Luciferian agenda behind all empires' power and government, independent of God and therefore counterfeit. The political spirit promotes nationalism that leads to conquest and empire:

Ancient Period (BC)

- Egyptian Empire (3100-30 BC)
- Norte Chico Empire (3000-1800 BC)
- Indus Valley Empires: Harappa and Mohenjo-Darro (2550-1550 BC)
- Akkadian Empire (2500-2000 BC)
- Babylonian Empire (1792-1595 BC)
- Ancient Chinese Empires: Shang (1751-1111 BC), Chou (1000-800 BC), etc.
- Hittite Empire (1500-1200 BC)
- Assyrian Empire (1244-612 BC)
- Persian Empires (550-331 BC)
- Carthaginian Empire (ca. 475-146 BC)
- Athenian Empire (461-440 BC, 362-355 BC)
- Macedonian Empire (359-323 BC)
- Roman Empire (264 BC-476 AD)
- Parthian Empire (247 BC-224 AD)

Pre-Modern Period (to 1500)

- African Empires: Ethiopian Empire (ca. 50-1974), Mali Empire (ca. 1210-1490), Songhai Empire (1468-1590), Fulani Empire (ca. 1800-1903)

- Mesoamerican Empires: Mayan Empire (ca. 300-900), Teotihuacan Empire (ca. 500-750), Aztec Empire (1325-ca. 1500)
- Byzantine Empire (330-1453)
- Andean Empires: Huari Empire (600-800); Inca Empire (1438-1525)
- Chinese Pre-Modern Empires: including T'ang Dynasty (618-906), Sung Dynasty (906-1278)
- Islamic Empires such as Umayyid/Abbasid (661-1258), Almohad (1140-1250), Almoravid (1050-1140)
- Carolingian Empire (ca. 700-810)
- Bulgarian Empire (802-827, 1197-1241)
- Southeast Asian Empires: Khmer Empire (877-1431), Burmese Empire (1057-1287)
- Novogorod Empire (882-1054)
- Medieval German Empire (962-1250)
- Danish Empire (1014-1035)
- Indian Empires, including Chola Empire (11th century), Empire of Mahmud of Ghazni (998-1039), Mughal Empire (1526-1805)
- Mongol Empire (1206-1405)
- Mamluk Empire (1250-1517)
- Holy Roman Empire (1254-1835)
- Habsburg Empire (1452-1806)
- Ottoman Empire (1453-1923)

Modern Period (since 1500)

- Portuguese Empire (ca. 1450-1975)
- Spanish Empire (1492-1898)
- Russian Empire/USSR (1552-1991)
- Swedish Empire (1560-1660)
- Dutch Empire (1660-1962)
- British Empire (1607-ca. 1980)

- French Empire (ca. 1611- ca. 1980)
- Modern Chinese Empire: esp. Ch'ing Dynasty (1644-1911)
- Austrian/Austro-Hungarian Empire (ca. 1700-1918) [successor to the Habsburg Empire]
- US Empire (1776-present)
- Brazilian Empire (1822-1889)
- German Empire (1871-1918, 1939-1945)
- Japanese Empire (1871-1945)
- Italian Empire (1889-1942)

Daniel prophesied that four kingdoms seeking to outwork that Luciferian agenda would rise up but in the time of the fourth kingdom there would be a kingdom established that would end all the other kingdoms – and that kingdom is the kingdom of God. The language and style Daniel uses are apocalyptical and many of its symbols are also used in the Book of Revelation.

In the first year of Belshazzar king of Babylon, Daniel saw a dream and visions in his mind as he lay on his bed; then he wrote the dream down and told the following summary of it. Daniel said, "I was looking in my vision by night, and behold, the four winds of heaven were stirring up the great sea. And four great beasts were coming up from the sea, different from one another. The first was like a lion but had the wings of an eagle. I kept looking until its wings were plucked, and it was lifted up from the ground and set up on two feet like a man; a human mind also was given to it. And behold, another beast, a second one, resembling a bear. And it was raised up on one side, and three ribs were in its mouth between its teeth; and they said this to it: 'Arise, devour much meat!' After this I kept looking, and behold, another one, like a leopard, which had on its back four wings of a bird; the beast also had four heads, and dominion was given to it. After this I kept looking in the night visions, and behold, a fourth beast, dreadful and terrible, and extremely strong; and it had large iron teeth. It devoured and crushed, and trampled down the remainder with its feet; and it was different from all the beasts that were before it, and it had ten horns. While I was thinking about the horns, behold, another horn, a little one, came up among them, and three of the previous horns were plucked out before it; and behold, this horn possessed eyes like human eyes, and a mouth uttering great boasts.

*"I kept looking
Until thrones were set up,
And the Ancient of Days took His seat;
His garment was white as snow,
Qnd the hair of His head like pure wool.
His throne was ablaze with flames,
Its wheels were a burning fire.
A river of fire was flowing
And coming out from before Him;
Thousands upon thousands were serving Him,
And myriads upon myriads were standing before Him;
The court convened, and the books were opened."*
(Daniel 7:1-10).

Daniel had already prophesied the Kingdom of God putting an end to those earthly counterfeit systems in this period. This was very clearly placed prophetically in Daniel's 70th week, during Jesus' ministry, and it was finally consummated following His resurrection, when He conquered death and Hades and took back the keys that Adam had given to Lucifer.

And in the days of those kings the God of heaven will set up a kingdom which will never be destroyed, and that kingdom will not be left for another people; it will crush and put an end to all these kingdoms, but it will itself endure forever. (Daniel 2:44).

At the end in the period of the fourth counterfeit earthy kingdom, Rome and its earthly government, we see God on the throne and (following Jesus' resurrection) giving the Kingdom of God to Jesus. He then gives it to the saints, as He promised to do in Matthew 21, where Jesus quoted Daniel's prophecy using the symbolism of the stone.

Jesus said to them, "Did you never read in the Scriptures, 'A stone which the builders rejected, this has become the chief cornerstone; this came about from the Lord, and it is marvelous in our eyes'? Therefore I say to you, the kingdom of God will be taken away from you and given to a people producing its fruit. And the one who falls on this stone will be broken to pieces; and on whomever it falls, it will crush him." (Matthew 21:42-44).

"I kept looking in the night visions,
And behold, with the clouds of heaven
One like a son of man was coming,
And He came up to the Ancient of Days.
And was presented before Him.
And to Him was given dominion,
Honor, and a kingdom,
So that all the peoples, nations, and populations of all languages Might serve Him.
His dominion is an everlasting dominion
Which will not pass away;
And His kingdom is one
Which will not be destroyed." (Daniel 7:13-14).

Jesus came to the Ancient of Days, His Father, and was given dominion over the earth, restoring the sonship mandate given to Adam. This dominion will continue and be age-enduring and will not end or be destroyed. This connects with Isaiah's 'restoration of all things' prophecy that there would be no end to the increase of His government and peace.

For a Child will be born to us, a Son will be given to us;
and the government will rest on His shoulders;
and His name will be called Wonderful Counselor, Mighty God,
Eternal Father, Prince of Peace.
There will be no end to the increase of His government or of peace
On the throne of David and over his kingdom,
To establish it and to uphold it with justice and righteousness
From then on and forevermore.
The zeal of the Lord of armies will accomplish this.
(Isaiah 9:6-7).

This messianic prophecy was fulfilled by Jesus, as Daniel predicted, on the day of resurrection; and Jesus, as a prophetic sign of the new covenant age and wineskin, breathed the Holy Spirit into His disciples as representatives of all mankind, just as the Father had to Adam, the original representative of mankind.

So Jesus said to them again, "Peace be to you; just as the Father has sent Me, I also send you." And when He had said this, He breathed on them and said to them, "Receive the Holy Spirit." (John 20:21-22).

All died in Adam but all are made alive in Christ, the last Adam; and one died for all so all can live in a reconciled relationship with the Father through the Son.

But the fact is, Christ has been raised from the dead, the first fruits of those who are asleep. For since by a man death came, by a man also came the resurrection of the dead. For as in Adam all die, so also in Christ all will be made alive. (1 Corinthians 15:20-22).

For the love of Christ controls us, having concluded this, that one died for all, therefore all died; and He died for all, so that those who live would no longer live for themselves, but for Him who died and rose on their behalf... Now all these things are from God, who reconciled us to Himself through Christ and gave us the ministry of reconciliation, namely, that God was in Christ reconciling the world to Himself, not counting their wrongdoings against them, and He has committed to us the word of reconciliation. (2 Corinthians 5:14, 18-19).

"Then I desired to know the exact meaning of the fourth beast, which was different from all the others, exceedingly dreadful, with its teeth of iron and its claws of bronze, and which devoured, crushed, and trampled down the remainder with its feet, and the meaning of the ten horns that were on its head, and the other horn which came up, and before which three of the horns fell, namely, that horn which had eyes and a mouth uttering great boasts, and which was larger in appearance than its associates. I kept looking, and that horn was waging war with the saints and prevailing against them, until the Ancient of Days came and judgment was passed in favor of the saints of the Highest One, and the time arrived when the saints took possession of the kingdom. (Daniel 7:19-22).

Daniel continues to prophesy that, following the Son receiving the kingdom, there would be conflict from the counterfeit kingdom until it was eventually destroyed, having put an end to the religious system of the old covenant.

This is what he said: "The fourth beast will be a fourth kingdom on the earth which will be different from all the other kingdoms, and will devour the whole earth and trample it down and crush it. As for the ten horns, out of this kingdom ten kings will arise; and another will arise after them, and he will be different from the previous ones and will humble three kings. And he will speak against the Most High and wear down the saints of the Highest One, and he will intend to make alterations in times and in law; and they will be handed over to him for a time, times, and half a time. But the court will convene for judgment, and his dominion will be taken away, annihilated and destroyed forever. Then the sovereignty, the dominion, and the greatness of all the kingdoms under the whole heaven will be given to the people of the saints of the Highest One; His kingdom will be an everlasting kingdom, and all the empires will serve and obey Him." (Daniel 7:23-27).

When I, Daniel, had seen the vision, I sought to understand it; and behold, standing before me was one who looked like a man. And I heard the voice of a man between the banks of Ulai, and he called out and said, "Gabriel, explain the vision to this man." So he came near to where I was standing, and when he came I was frightened and fell on my face; and he said to me, "Son of man, understand that the vision pertains to the time of the end." Now while he was talking with me, I was dazed with my face to the ground; but he touched me and made me stand at my place. And he said, "Behold, I am going to inform you of what will occur at the final period of the indignation, because it pertains to the appointed time of the end." (Daniel 8:15-19).

False futurist eschatology sees the word 'end' and immediately interprets that to mean the end of the world. The context is the end of the old covenant system, in the days of those kingdoms, not thousands of years later.

Daniel's 70th week has been falsely separated from the 69 previous weeks and transposed into the future when the context clearly shows that it is contiguous. There are a number of terms that have, by conjecture, been applied to specific people throughout history: the horn waging war with the saints and prevailing against them, the prince who is to come who will destroy the city and the sanctuary. Many have tried to tie the terms 'horn' and 'prince' to people in modern history or current events and use the news to discern who these figures are. These terms have been also extrapolated to be the bearers of other well-known New Testament titles such as the Antichrist, Beast, False Prophet or the Man of Lawlessness.

These events were contemporary with Jesus coming as the Messiah to fulfil all prophecy and to the generation alive at that time so it is clear these terms do apply to modern day or historic people after 70 AD. The 'horn' and the 'prince' are associated with the fourth kingdom, Rome, which was in place when Jesus came in Daniel's 70th week and when the kingdom was established.

The truth has been so twisted that the clear reference to Jesus as the 'prince' has been made to fit a futurist agenda by interpreting the 'prince' of Daniel 9:24-27 to be a future antichrist figure. How perverse has futurist eschatology become, when Jesus is the antichrist!

The focus of Daniel 9:24-27 is centred on the coming Christ and it says that the prince is the Messiah. The statements made are fulfilled by Jesus, as referenced in the New Testament. Jesus is the prince who was to come who would put an end to the old covenant (focused on God's presence residing in one nation, Israel; one city, Jerusalem; and one temple) by destroying that system but consummating it all in the new covenant wineskin.

"Seventy weeks have been decreed for your people and your holy city, **to finish the wrongdoing***, to make an* **end of sin***, to make* **atonement for guilt***, to bring in* **everlasting righteousness***, to* **seal up vision and prophecy***, and to anoint the* **Most Holy Place***. So you are to know and understand that from the issuing of a decree to restore and rebuild Jerusalem, until Messiah the Prince, there will be seven weeks and sixty-two weeks; it will be built again, with streets and moat, even in times of distress. Then after the sixty-two weeks, the Messiah will be cut off and have nothing, and the people of* **the prince who is to come** *will destroy the city and the sanctuary. And its end will come with a flood; even to the end there will be war; desolations are determined. And he will confirm a covenant with the many for one week, but in the middle of the week he will put a stop to sacrifice and grain offering; and on the wing of abominations will come the one who makes desolate, until a complete destruction, one that is decreed, gushes forth on the one who makes desolate."* (Daniel 9:24-27, emphases mine).

Below are the fulfilment references that show Jesus is the fulfilment of these prophecies and promises of Daniel 9:24.

1) Finish wrongdoing:

For this reason, He is the mediator of a new covenant, so that, since a death has taken place for the redemption of the violations that were committed under the first covenant, those who have been called may receive the promise of the eternal inheritance. (Hebrews 9:15).

2) Make an end of sin:

"She will give birth to a Son; and you shall name Him Jesus, for He will save His people from their sins." (Matthew 1: 21)

Otherwise, He would have needed to suffer often since the foundation of the world; but now once at the consummation of the ages He has been revealed to put away sin by the sacrifice of Himself. (Hebrews 9:26).

3) Atone for guilt:

... namely, that God was in Christ reconciling the world to Himself, not counting their trespasses against them, and He has committed to us the word of reconciliation... (2 Corinthians 5:19).

For it was the Father's good pleasure for all the fullness to dwell in Him, and through Him to reconcile all things to Himself, having made peace through the blood of His cross; through Him, I say, whether things on earth or things in heaven. (Colossians 1:19-20).

4) Bring in everlasting righteousness:

But by His doing you are in Christ Jesus, who became to us wisdom from God, and righteousness and sanctification, and redemption... (1 Corinthians 1:30).

... and may be found in Him, not having a righteousness of my own derived from the Law, but that which is through faith in Christ, the righteousness which comes from God on the basis of faith... (Philippians 3:9).

5) Seal up vision and prophecy:

"Do not think that I came to abolish the Law or the Prophets; I did not come to abolish but to fulfill." (Matthew 5:17)

Now He said to them, "These are My words which I spoke to you while I was still with you, that all things which are written about Me in the Law of Moses and the Prophets and the Psalms must be fulfilled." (Luke 24:44)

Sealing up prophecy is not hiding it from our understanding or only applying it to the future: it is the fulfilment, consummation or realisation of it.

6) Anoint the most holy place:

And Jesus cried out again with a loud voice, and yielded up His spirit. And behold, the veil of the temple was torn in two from top to bottom; and the earth shook and the rocks were split. (Matthew 27:50-51).

For by one offering He has perfected for all time those who are sanctified. And the Holy Spirit also testifies to us; for after saying, "This is the covenant that I will make with them after those days, says the Lord: I will put My laws upon their heart, and on their mind I will write them..." Therefore, brethren, since we have confidence to enter the holy place by the blood of Jesus, by a new and living way which He inaugurated for us through the veil, that is, His flesh... (Hebrews 10:14-16, 19-20).

These prophecies were fulfilled in Daniel's 70th week. So there is no need to transpose them into the future, as for us they are past; but many have tried to use modern-day 'resurrections' of a Roman empire to indicate that these events are in our present. The European Common Market of 10 nations becoming 12 nations was going to re-establish the Roman Empire: that never materialised and it became the European Union with 26 nations. There have been many people cast as the Antichrist or the Beast: Napoleon, any Pope, Benito

Mussolini, the Italian fascist dictator (because he attempted to revive the Roman Empire), Hitler; and then any communist leaders until the fall of communism, when the focus went onto Islam with Saddam Hussein and Osama bin Laden (until their deaths, of course). Many American political figures' names have been thrown into the ring, including Ronald Reagan, John F. Kennedy, Barack Obama and Donald Trump. Even Hilary Clinton is not left out (US Republican politician Ryan Zinke, who would be US Secretary of the Interior in the Trump Administration from 2017 until his resignation in 2019, threw the accusation at her in 2014. She later reassured him, at President Trump's inauguration, that she wasn't).

Many are engaged in end-times speculation, exacerbated by the latest crisis, the most recent (at the time of writing) being the Covid-19 pandemic. There is another rash of speculation about the identity of the Antichrist – that end times personal figure who is now apparently living somewhere secretly in the world but who will very soon be revealed. The reality is that if you look back in what I call Christian fiction and fantasy writing then you will see that every perceived crisis since at least the 1960s has caused similar wild and fanciful speculation.

Many books have been written to explain why the conditions are right for Jesus to come and rapture us away. *88 Reasons why the Rapture will be in 1988* by Edgar Whisenant[14] was one such book that put a date on the rapture, which of course never happened. Books such as Hal Lindsay's *Late Great Planet Earth*[15] and its follow-ups proposed imminent dates in

---

[14] Edgar Whisenant, *88 Reasons why the Rapture will be in 1988* (Pamphlet), Whisenant/World Bible Society (January 1, 1988).
[15] Hal Lindsey with C.C. Carlson, *The Late, Great Planet Earth*, Zondervan Academic (1970).

the 1970s and when that failed to materialise, the 1980's; and then 1998, the 50th anniversary of Israel becoming a nation; and then onto the year 2000 and the Y2K hysteria. More recently it was September 24th 2019; and it has been associated with various blood and super moon signs in the heavens.

Ian Paul writes; "One of the key proponents of this kind of scheme in a previous generation, Hal Lindsay (who wrote *The Late, Great Planet Earth*) admits that this is a 'hopscotch' approach to reading the Bible, taking one bit from one place and another from another to put together a picture like assembling the pieces of a jigsaw puzzle. But look at the wonderful picture that results, is his defence!"[16]

Future expectation

For the earth will be filled
With the knowledge of the glory of the Lord,
As the waters cover the sea. (Habakkuk 2:14).

This is a restoration of all things prophecy that is being fulfilled as I am writing this: the glory of the sons of God is being revealed to creation as we arise and shine by discovering our God-given identities and taking our places seated in the heavenlies. How the Bible frames our understanding of our future will greatly influence what we believe about our sonship and what is possible in restoration. Our expectations of the future will also determine what we will believe about our part in its fulfilment. If you believe that God is going to destroy the heavens and the earth with fire, as many do, that will affect how you understand your responsibility to steward the planet and its resources. If you

---

[16] Ian Paul, *Antichrist, man of lawlessness, and the beast*, article on psephizo.com

believe in a defeatist rapture rescue of the church into heaven then there will be little point in the kingdom filling the earth in victory.

The views we have about the future primarily come from what we believe (or have been taught) the Bible says, or what someone may have prophesied. We must always remember that all the New Testament was future to the Old Testament writers and what Jesus prophesied was future to His listeners. However, what was future to Old Testament or New Testament writers is not future to us today if it has occurred since they wrote it.

The questions I am seeking to answer are: is biblical prophecy not yet fulfilled, partially fulfilled, totally fulfilled or being fulfilled? Even if Bible prophecy is fulfilled or being fulfilled, we still need a clear idea of God's original intention, so we seek its restoration.

The fulfilment of biblical prophecy does not limit God unless He specifies it. What I mean by that statement is that just because something has been fulfilled does not mean God cannot do it again, unless He says He will not (for example, God will never again flood the earth because He has promised that He won't).

The shaking of Hebrews 12 has been biblically and physically fulfilled by the events that shook the governmental system and ended Israel's world. That does not mean that God cannot shake whatever He wants to in the future, but it will then not be a fulfilment of biblical prophecy. The same argument can be used for spiritual gifts, as the biblical purpose for them ended in 70 AD but that does not limit the Holy Spirit's ability to give gifts, whenever and to whomever He wants.

Our key question should not be what the Bible is saying about what God is doing in our generation but what God Himself is saying to us. The heart of God for restoration is clearly revealed in the Bible but the specifics of restoration may not always be clear until we engage with God's heart directly. As sons, we need a restoration mindset if we are to participate in the expansion of God's kingdom and therefore the restoration of all things. We have all been conditioned to believe something, so the question to ask is: which eschatological belief system best aligns with creation being set free from corruption within the restoration of all things?

Most eschatological systems have far from happy endings for some or most people and created beings. Do we really think that reflects a God who is love?

Most eschatological systems have expectations of fearful judgment, doom, gloom, destruction and failure for mankind. Does that fit within a restoration framework?

I believe a happy, realised, fulfilled or covenant eschatology (without putting a specific label on it) presents a more optimistic view of the future by viewing the doom and gloom, judgment and destruction as things that have already been fulfilled, leading to a restorative period where all things can be restored. The future is positive and filled with possibilities of increase and blessing.

In a happy, realised, fulfilled or covenant eschatology, all references to 'the end', 'last days', 'end times', 'last hour', and 'soon to take place' refer to the end of the old covenant, which Jesus prophesied would occur in that generation. There is no fear for the future based on biblical prophecy if it is past for us.

Viewing the future from that perspective will reveal the truth that:

- The end or *eschaton* is in the past, not the future.
- The end of the old heavens and earth is in the past, not the future.
- The new heavens and the new earth is present, not a future event.
- The great tribulation is in the past, not the future.
- The end of the age is in the past, not in the future (unless there is an end to this age and there are further ages to come – which has a biblical warrant; but those ends are not prophesied, and would always be to establish something new and better).
- Judgment and resurrection are also past, not future, in a spiritual sense; God's verdict is based on the events of the cross, resurrection and ascension; and the verdict is found in creation's favour: not guilty. God's justice, based on that 'not guilty' verdict, is grace and mercy that leads to reconciliation and restoration for all created things.
- The book of Revelation is John's first-hand account of Jesus' teaching (also recorded in Luke 21, Mark 13 and Matthew 24), received in a heavenly encounter. This book was so important for those who were being persecuted and suffering in the generation following Jesus' final ascension as it was a comfort to them.
- The events recorded in the book of Revelation were about to occur imminently, not thousands of years later. These events can all be reconciled with the events that Jesus prophesied would take place in that generation if viewed through an objective lens that has not been distorted by the leaven of dispensational or futurist eschatology. We

have been conditioned to believe the events of resurrection and judgment must be future and associated with assigning people to eternal conscious torment. All these events are consistent with having taken place in the generation Jesus said they would, and do not need to produce either a future fear or hope. These events are to be experienced in fullness during this present age, where we have Jesus' presence with us and in us already, not in some future second coming event.

The Revelation of Jesus Christ, which God gave Him to show to His bond-servants, the things which must soon take place... (Revelation 1:1).

The book of Revelation is filled with imminent language that filled its original audience with hope, not fear. This first verse of the entire book sets the scene: Jesus was revealing things soon to take place. Those revelations were given after the ascension and therefore the scene has changed from teaching the disciples while being with them physically to being the lamb that was slain but is now the lion who is enthroned.

There are many further time references in the book of Revelation that indicate soon fulfilment.

The Greek words *tachei, tachos* and *en tachei* mean 'quickly, all at once, with all speed, without delay.'

- Revelation 2:16 – "Repent, or else I will come to you quickly"
- Revelation 3:11 - "Behold, I come quickly!"
- Revelation 22:6 - "...things which must shortly take place."
- Revelation 22:7 - "Behold, I am coming quickly!"
- Revelation 22:12 - "Behold, I am coming quickly."

- Revelation 22:20 - "Surely I am coming quickly."

The Greek word *engys* means 'at hand, near.'
- Revelation 1:3 – "The time is near."
- Revelation 22:10 – "The time is at hand."

The Greek words *mello, mellei* mean 'about to, on the point or verge of.'
- Revelation 1:19 – "Write ... the things that are about to take place."
- Revelation 3:10 – "... the hour of trial ... is about to come upon the whole world."

This aligns with Jesus' earthly revelation that prepared His disciples for His death, burial, resurrection, ascension, enthronement and coming again.

"Truly I say to you, you will not finish going through the cities of Israel until the Son of Man comes." (Matthew 10:23).

"Truly I say to you, there are some who are standing here who will not taste death until they see the Son of Man coming in His kingdom." (Matthew 16:28).

"Truly I say to you, this generation will not pass away until all these things take place." (Matthew 24:34).

"You [the High Priest] will see the Son of Man coming on the clouds of heaven." (Matthew 26:64).

Did Jesus lie about when those events would happen?

Did those things that Jesus said would happen in that generation occur or not?

If these things are still future, as some eschatological systems believe, then yes, Jesus must have lied; but of course Jesus is the Truth and cannot lie, so it must be our interpretation that is in error.

That future interpretation of these events is still a problem for Jews and Muslims who say that Jesus was a false prophet because He lied about 'that generation' fulfilment, as they know the language is one of imminence. For many, believing that the resurrection and judgment have already occurred is a step too far but I believe if they are open to explore the truth this will become a very plausible scenario within the bigger picture of restoration.

The 'last day'

Jesus linked judgment and resurrection with the last day – and He was not referring to the end of time as we know it. The Old Testament prophets were all looking to the coming of the Messiah (or in Greek, Christ) and they associated his coming with many different concepts, judgment being one of them. They often spoke of 'the day of the Lord' and this language has been used for many different events, including the first coming and the judgment of the cross and the second coming and the judgment of Israel. Futurists have taken 'the day of the Lord' and manipulated it to fit their agenda so we must look at how Jesus used a reinterpreted 'the day of the Lord' last day concept.

In John chapter 6 the term 'last day' is used referring to resurrection no less than four times, in verses 39, 40, 44 and 54.

"This is the will of Him who sent Me, that of all that He has given Me I lose nothing, but raise it up on the last day." (John 6:39).

Jesus also uses the 'last day' to refer to coming impending judgment. This use of the term will have been familiar to those who knew Daniel's prophecies.

"He who rejects Me and does not receive My sayings, has one who judges him; the word I spoke is what will judge him at the last day." (John 12:48).

In Matthew's gospel, the Day of Judgment is mentioned four times, but always in the context of what those listeners would experience in their lifetime, not at the end of the physical world or the end of time: Matthew 10:15; 11:22, 24; 12:36.

"Nevertheless I say to you, it will be more tolerable for Tyre and Sidon in the day of judgment than for you." (Matthew 11:22).

Jesus was challenging the religious leaders in Jerusalem to take heed of the prophets like Nineveh did or be judged like other cities such as Tyre, Sidon, Sodom and Gomorrah, who ignored prophetic warnings.

The day of the Lord concerned Israel alone and was never referring to the whole world; the judgment was the end of their world, not the whole world. There were never two days of the Lord nor two comings of the Lord separated by thousands of years, just a generation of fulfilment, as Jesus prophesied.

Jesus used apocalyptic, prophetic, symbolic language – and when we read that Jesus is coming on the clouds and stars are falling from the heavens in Matthew 24 we should realise that this is the language of the Old Testament prophets.

In the Old Testament, when God came riding upon the clouds in judgment, rolling up the heavens like a scroll, this was symbolic language depicting the fall and judgment of nations: it was not meant to be interpreted literally.

Jesus had already taught them that some of them would live to witness His return and the destruction of the Temple; so they were not mistaken to associate and connect Jesus' coming in their generation, to destroy the Temple that they were looking at and discussing, with His coming at the end of the age.

The mindset of the Jewish people was that they were God's chosen people and that Jerusalem and the temple were the centre of the world, where heaven and earth met. The creation of the world to them spoke of Israel, not the whole planet. When they prophesied about the earth they were never referring to the whole world but only to the land that would be subject to the covenant curses which Israel agreed on Mount Gerizim (as recorded in Deuteronomy 28). The language was always covenantal, just as Jesus used in Matthew 24 (for example, *"Wherever the corpse is, there the vultures will gather"* (Matthew 24:28): the vulture was an unclean bird that fed on corpses, which was another way of saying that the old covenant age was ending in judgment).

The earth will be completely laid waste and completely despoiled, for the Lord has spoken this word. The earth mourns and withers, the world fades and withers, the exalted of the people of the earth fade away. The earth is also polluted by its inhabitants, for they transgressed laws, violated statutes, broke the everlasting covenant. Therefore, a curse devours the earth, and those who live in it are held guilty.

Therefore, the inhabitants of the earth are burned, and few men are left. (Isaiah 24:3-6).

The earth is broken asunder,
The earth is split through,
The earth is shaken violently. (Isaiah 24:19).

Such language describes creation and de-creation and yet it was specifically referring to Israel, not the original creation. It sounds like the destruction of material creation but closer examination reveals it to be speaking of the destruction of Israel's covenant world under the imagery of "heaven and earth".

Isaiah says that is the reason for the destruction is that they have broken the age-enduring covenant. God was going to allow the 'heaven and earth' to be destroyed figuratively because Israel had broken her covenant with Jehovah.

Here is another example in Isaiah of 'heaven and earth' referring to the covenant world of Israel and not literal creation:

"I have put My words in your mouth and have covered you with the shadow of My hand, to establish the heavens, to found the earth, and to say to Zion, 'You are My people.'" (Isaiah 51:16).

In this prophecy God is saying He gave the Mosaic Covenant to Israel to create a (figurative) heaven and earth. 'Heaven and earth' referred to the old covenant system symbolised by the temple (the place where heaven and earth met). The Mosaic Covenant is the same 'Law' that Jesus was speaking about in Matthew 5:17 when He said that He did not come to abolish the Law or the Prophets but to fulfil them.

God gave Israel a covenant to figuratively create their world, a 'heaven and earth'. So when the old covenant 'heaven and earth' was ended, He gave a new covenant (again figurative) 'new heavens and new earth'.

The end of the old is the birth pangs of the new. Spiritually, the old covenant ended at the cross and the new was initiated; but physically, sacrifices were still taking place in the temple until it was finally destroyed in 70 AD. Israel's old covenant was about to pass or fade away and become obsolete even though it continued (without God's presence, as Jesus left the temple desolate when he walked out).

"Therefore, behold, I am sending you prophets and wise men and scribes; some of them you will kill and crucify, and some of them you will scourge in your synagogues, and persecute from city to city, so that upon you may fall the guilt of all the righteous blood shed on earth, from the blood of righteous Abel to the blood of Zechariah, the son of Berechiah, whom you murdered between the temple and the altar. Truly I say to you, all these things will come upon this generation. "Jerusalem, Jerusalem, who kills the prophets and stones those who are sent to her! How often I wanted to gather your children together, the way a hen gathers her chicks under her wings, and you were unwilling. Behold, your house is being left to you desolate! For I say to you, from now on you will not see Me until you say, 'Blessed is He who comes in the name of the Lord!'" (Matthew 23:34-39).

For if the ministry of condemnation has glory, much more does the ministry of righteousness abound in glory. For indeed what had glory, in this case has no glory because of the glory that surpasses it. For if that which fades away was with glory, much more that which remains is in glory. (2 Corinthians 3:9-11).

When He said, "A new covenant," He has made the first obsolete. But whatever is becoming obsolete and growing old is ready to disappear. (Hebrews 8:13).

See to it that you do not refuse Him who is speaking. For if those did not escape when they refused him who warned them on earth, much less will we escape who turn away from Him who warns from heaven. And His voice shook the earth then, but now He has promised, saying, "Yet once more I will shake not only the earth, but also the heaven." This expression, "Yet once more," denotes the removing of those things which can be shaken, as of created things, so that those things which cannot be shaken may remain. Therefore, since we receive a kingdom which cannot be shaken, let us show gratitude, by which we may offer to God an acceptable service with reverence and awe; for our God is a consuming fire. (Hebrews 12:25-29).

When the New Covenant of Christ was given, the Old was obsolete; but many of the religious leaders of the Jewish people refused to acknowledge Jesus as the Messiah and fought to keep the legalistic, works-based control system in place.

The new covenant that Jesus instituted through the cross was a covenant of grace and love, not works; it included the whole of mankind, not just Israel and those of the Jewish faith. Whilst the new age era was embraced by Jesus' disciples, who became representatives of the one new man in Christ that includes all of humanity, the now obsolete false religion of Judaism persecuted the new, having become a counterfeit, seeking to oppose and deceive. Until the old system was finally removed when the temple was destroyed, the old sought to suppress the new using the political and religious spirit agenda of which Jesus had warned.

The new covenant was of the Spirit that would bring abundant life and not of the letter or law that would bring death. The new covenant was the promise of the restoration of all things that the Old Testament prophets had directed only towards Israel and Judah, but was now expanded, as the walls of separation were removed, to include all of mankind. There is no longer any division between Jew and Gentile or male and female: we are all Abraham's children by faith.

Paul makes it clear that Judaism is now a false religion based on works and that the true Jew is identified not by the externals of race or ethnicity but internally, in the heart, by faith in Jesus.

For he is not a Jew who is one outwardly, nor is circumcision that which is outward in the flesh. But he is a Jew who is one inwardly; and circumcision is that which is of the heart, by the Spirit, not by the letter; and his praise is not from men, but from God. (Romans 2:28-29).

For if that first covenant had been faultless, there would have been no occasion sought for a second. For finding fault with them, He says,

"Behold, days are coming, says the Lord,
When I will effect a new covenant
With the house of Israel and with the house of Judah;
Not like the covenant which I made with their fathers
On the day when I took them by the hand
To lead them out of the land of Egypt;
For they did not continue in My covenant,
And I did not care for them, says the Lord.

For this is the covenant that I will make with the house of Israel
After those days, says the Lord:
I will put My laws into their minds,
And I will write them on their hearts.
And I will be their God,
And they shall be My people.
And they shall not teach everyone his fellow citizen,
And everyone his brother, saying, 'Know the Lord,'
For all will know Me,
From the least to the greatest of them.
For I will be merciful to their iniquities,
And I will remember their sins no more."

When He said, "A new covenant," He has made the first obsolete. But whatever is becoming obsolete and growing old is ready to disappear. (Hebrews 8:7-13).

And in the same way He took the cup after they had eaten, saying, "This cup which is poured out for you is the new covenant in My blood." (Luke 22:20).

... that by revelation there was made known to me the mystery, as I wrote before in brief. By referring to this, when you read you can understand my insight into the mystery of Christ, which in other generations was not made known to the sons of men, as it has now been revealed to His holy apostles and prophets in the Spirit; to be specific, that the Gentiles are fellow heirs and fellow members of the body, and fellow partakers of the promise in Christ Jesus through the gospel... (Ephesians 3:3-6).

Therefore remember that formerly you, the Gentiles in the flesh, who are called "Uncircumcision" by the so-called "Circumcision," which is performed in the flesh by human hands—remember that you were at that time separate from Christ, excluded from the commonwealth of Israel, and strangers to the covenants of promise, having no hope and without God in the world. But now in Christ Jesus you who formerly were far off have been brought near by the blood of Christ. For He Himself is our peace, who made both groups into one and broke down the barrier of the dividing wall, by abolishing in His flesh the enmity, which is the Law of commandments contained in ordinances, so that in Himself He might make the two into one new man, thus establishing peace, and might reconcile them both in one body to God through the cross, by it having put to death the enmity. And He came and preached peace to you who were far away, and peace to those who were near; for through Him we both have our access in one Spirit to the Father. So then you are no longer strangers and aliens, but you are fellow citizens with the saints, and are of God's household, having been built on the foundation of the apostles and prophets, Christ Jesus Himself being the corner stone, in whom the whole building, being fitted together, is growing into a holy temple in the Lord, in whom you also are being built together into a dwelling of God in the Spirit. (Ephesians 2:11-22).

Therefore the Law has become our tutor to lead us to Christ, so that we may be justified by faith. But now that faith has come, we are no longer under a tutor. For you are all sons of God through faith in Christ Jesus. For all of you who were baptized into Christ have clothed yourselves with Christ. There is neither Jew nor Greek, there is neither slave nor free man, there is neither male nor female; for you are all one in Christ Jesus. And if you belong to Christ, then you are Abraham's descendants, heirs according to promise. (Galatians 3:24-29).

... who also made us adequate as servants of a new covenant, not of the letter but of the Spirit; for the letter kills, but the Spirit gives life. (2 Corinthians 3:6).

For this reason He is the mediator of a new covenant, so that, since a death has taken place for the redemption of the transgressions that were committed under the first covenant, those who have been called may receive the promise of the eternal inheritance. (Hebrews 9:15).

But the day of the Lord will come like a thief, in which the heavens will pass away with a roar and the elements will be destroyed with intense heat, and the earth and its works will be burned up... But according to His promise we are looking for new heavens and a new earth, in which righteousness dwells. (2 Peter 3:10, 13).

The 'new heavens and new earth' are established in the new covenant that is already in place and in reality we are the New Jerusalem that has already come out of heaven. This is not a future hope of Jesus' coming but a present hope of His presence, in which, the Psalmist reveals, is fullness of joy and total restoration of spirit, soul and body.

... and the God of the peace Himself sanctify you wholly, and may your whole spirit, and soul, and body, be preserved unblameably in the presence of our Lord Jesus Christ (1 Thessalonians 5:23 YLT).

You will make known to me the path of life;
In Your presence is fullness of joy;
In Your right hand there are pleasures forever. (Psalm 16:11).

The whole of the New Testament was written in this period of transition, during which they were living in the new under the persecution of the old, as the process of revealing the new covenant was not yet complete.

"Heaven and earth will pass away, but My words will not pass away." (Matthew 24:35).

Heaven and earth have now passed away and all prophetic promises are fulfilled in Christ in the new covenant. In Isaiah 51:5-6 God prophesied that the 'heaven and earth' of Israel would disappear with the end of the old covenant:

"Lift up your eyes to the heavens, and look upon the earth beneath; for the heavens shall be dissolved and vanish away like smoke, and the earth shall wax old like a garment, and they that dwell therein shall die in like manner [like gnats]. But My salvation shall be forever, and My rightness and justice [and faithfully fulfilled promise] shall not be abolished." (Isaiah 51:6 AMPC).

For us this is past and good news, the end has ended; the last hour of the last day has gone and we now live in the new covenant of grace and are not under the law. These are the days of the restoration of all things and the kingdom of God filling the earth which we are now experiencing.

I have probably used more Bible verses in this chapter than in the whole of my other books put together because we have all been programmed to believe what the Bible does *not* say. I would encourage you to ask the living Word of God, Jesus, to give you a true revelation of Himself as the Truth and to deconstruct any pillars of religion, including those of dispensationalism and eschatological programming, from your mind. Invite the Truth, Jesus, to deconstruct any lies you believe about the Bible, God and yourself.

4. The Second Coming is Raptureless, Tribulationless and Millenniumless.

That brings us to the big question of the coming of Jesus. Was there the first coming and then, thousands of years later, a second coming? Or was the first and second coming within one generation? The answer lies not in the dispensational theory of a secret rapture or a future premillennial return of Jesus but in Jesus' teaching itself.

I will seek to set out the imminent timetable Jesus revealed as He interpreted the 'day of the Lord' event which the Old Testament prophets prophesied concerning Israel. I will seek to demystify the second coming and the rapture teaching by simply showing what Jesus revealed about His coming, when it would occur and what signs He told His disciples to look out for. The metaphorical language Jesus used was well known to His audience; as we have seen in the previous chapter, it was covenantal and often de-creational, referring to the end of the Jewish world or old covenant age illustrated by the destruction of the 'heavens and earth' temple.

The first coming and the second coming of Christ was one salvation judgment event, separated by 40 years of transition to enable the figurative 144,000 remnant of Judah to be saved from the destruction. By postponing this present experience to a future hope, generations have lost the reality of the true power of Jesus' presence in and among them. We must recover the truth from the deception if we are truly to embrace our sonship and be coheirs of creation. The deceptions of the fruit of the poisonous tree of futurist eschatology must be exposed to the light of the truth so that God's children can discover their true identity and position as sons of God.

The second coming has been called the *Parousia*, a precious hope for the future, when Jesus confined it to the future of only one generation. How many over the centuries have missed out on the fullness of Jesus' presence, deceived into believing it was only achievable in a future – literal – second coming?

The second coming has been linked to physical resurrection and final judgment (and therefore 'hell'), the rapture, tribulation and a literal millennial thousand-year reign of Jesus on earth. I will seek to show that those assumptions applied to Jesus' teaching are false; that Jesus' coming already occurred as He promised and is raptureless, tribulationless and millenniumless (probably made a few words up there).

If you want a full explanation that goes into great detail, a 443 page pdf of the book *The Parousia - A Careful Look at the New Testament Doctrine of our Lord's Second Coming*, by James Stuart Russell, is available for free download[17].

From imminence to irrelevance

In our English Bibles, words that imply imminence and presence have been mistranslated in line with the translators' expectations of a still-future coming. An example of this can be found in Jesus answering His disciples' questions about the events of the destruction of the temple. When the meaning of the words are changed, the meaning of the questions themselves are altered. When this occurs, Jesus' answers can more easily be assigned to the far distant future rather than to the then-living generation which Jesus intended.

---

[17] James Stuart Russell: *The Parousia - A Careful Look at the New Testament Doctrine of our Lord's Second Coming*, (1878). PDF book available to download free at http://www.preteristcentral.com/pdf/pdf%20books/1878_russel_parousia.pdf

Matthew 24 is the classic example of Bible translators interpreting the original Greek using English words that fit a pre-existing belief system. The questions posed by the disciples were referring to the same event, not different events spanning thousands of years. Those questions were asked by people who understood the Old Testament context and symbolism being used. They were asking when the temple would be destroyed, and what the signs of Jesus' presence to accomplish that would be, and therefore when the end of the age would occur; and they knew that this was really one question, expressed in different ways to cover all angles. The way that question is framed by the English words used in our translations dramatically changes their intention from imminence to irrelevance. Jesus had already told them that some of them would be alive when these events would occur, so it was a really important, urgent question for them to know the signs to look out for.

Jesus came out from the temple and was going away when His disciples came up to point out the temple buildings to Him. And He said to them, "Do you not see all these things? Truly I say to you, not one stone here will be left upon another, which will not be torn down." As He was sitting on the Mount of Olives, the disciples came to Him privately, saying, "Tell us, when will these things happen, and what will be the sign of Your coming, and of the end of the age?" (Matthew 24:1-3 NASB).

"Tell us, when shall these things be? and what shall be the sign of thy coming, and of the end of the world?" (Matthew 24:3 KJV).

'Tell us, when shall these be? and what [is] the sign of thy presence, and of the full end of the age?' (Matthew 24:3 YLT).

Signs of His coming (Greek: *parousia*) and the end of the age (Greek: *aion*): the word translated 'coming' actually means 'presence' (obviously after a 'coming') and referred to the presence of a king. By rendering *parousia* as 'coming' and not 'presence' the idea of imminence is lost and that of some future coming is generated. Jesus' presence in reality never left them, which was according to the prophetic promise that Jesus fulfilled:

... for He Himself has said, "I will never desert you, nor will I ever forsake you," (Hebrews 13:5).

Parousia is "used in the east as a technical expression for the royal visit of a king, or emperor. The word means literally 'the being beside,' thus, 'the personal presence'" (K. Wuest, 3, Bypaths, 33).

Changing 'presence' to 'coming' removes the present hope and expectation of the personal experience and replaces it with only a possible future experience. All of the present promises are lost to a future event. Thus in Thessalonians the promise of blameless holiness becomes future rather than present and the experience is lost. Compare the NASB with Young's Literal Translation:

... so that He may establish your hearts without blame in holiness before our God and Father at the coming of our Lord Jesus with all His saints. (1 Thessalonians 3:13 NASB).

... to the establishing your hearts blameless in sanctification before our God and Father, in the presence of our Lord Jesus Christ with all His saints. (1 Thessalonians 3:13 YLT).

NASB translates *parousia* as 'coming' 24 times.

YLT and Rotherham's literal translations translate *parousia* as 'coming' 0 times.

YLT and Rotherham's literal translations translate *parousia* as 'presence' 24 times.

The other word wrongly translated in Matthew 24:3 in the KJV is *aion*, rendered as 'world' and not 'age'. By using 'world' the meaning is transferred to a global event in the future rather than the end of the present age. More modern Bible versions correctly translate *aion* as age but many people still programmed by their KJV upbringing continue to infer that this question is about the literal end of the world. These distinctions may seem pedantic but they go to show the programming we have all probably undergone.

By changing the word from 'age' to 'world' the focus of Jesus speaking to the disciples in the last days is obscured and the significance of the age that the Old Testaments prophets spoke about is lost, allowing everything Jesus said to be put off to the distant future. Another example of this misuse is in the opening words of Hebrews:

God, after He spoke long ago to the fathers in the prophets in many portions and in many ways, in these last days has spoken to us in His Son, whom He appointed heir of all things, through whom also He made the world. (Hebrews 1:1-2 NASB).

In many parts, and many ways, God of old having spoken to the fathers in the prophets, in these last days did speak to us in a Son, whom He appointed heir of all things, through whom also He did make the ages; (Hebrews 1:1-2 YLT).

SECOND COMING

Some won't die
Matthew 16:27-28

Near
Matthew 24:34

At hand
Philippians 4:5

"For the Son of Man is going to come in the glory of His Father with His angels, and will then repay every person according to his deeds. Truly I say to you, there are some of those who are standing here who will not taste death until they see the Son of Man coming in His kingdom."
Matthew 16:27

Now is
2 Corinthians 6:2

This age
Matthew 13:40

Little while
Hebrews 10:37

"Truly I say to you, all these things will come upon this generation."
Matthew 23:36

Quickly
Revelation 22:6, 20

Today
2 Corinthians 6:2

"Truly I say to you, this generation will not pass away until all these things take place."
Matthew 24:34

Shortly
Revelation 1:1, 22:7

Soon
Revelation 22:12

This generation
Matthew 23:36

Timing of Jesus' Second Coming

What about the second coming?

You may well ask! Surely Jesus will have to come physically and not just figuratively? Let's examine that assumption and find out why we make it. Then let's find out whether this occurred in the past, and if so, when and how.

Jesus' own teaching is the place to explore the truth; we need to recognise that all other Bible verses which seem to speak about a still-future-to-us 'coming' of Jesus need to be understood through the lens of Jesus, not pop eschatologists.

What did Jesus reveal about the timing, purpose and circumstances surrounding His coming? The diagram opposite shows how Jesus and the New Testament writers saw the imminent nature of His coming.

1) He comes in glory: Luke 9:26
1) He comes in glory: Matthew 24:30
2) He comes with angels: Matthew 16:27
2) He comes with angels: Matthew 24:31
3) He comes in judgment: Matthew 16:27
3) He comes in judgment: Matthew 24:28-31; 25:31-34
4) He and the kingdom come in power: Mark 8:38
4) He and the kingdom come in power: Luke 21:27-32
5) Some of the disciples would live: Matthew 16:28
5) Some of the disciples would live: Luke 21:16-18
6) Some of the disciples would die: Matthew 16:28
6) Some of the disciples would die: Luke 21:16
7) He would be ashamed of the disciples' generation: Mark 8:38
7) All of this would occur in the disciples' generation: Matthew 24:34

This is a very specific historical event and is not addressing several comings of Christ. There are of course many comings of Jesus that refer to different events and places of His coming:

- The ascension was His coming to heaven and not earth.
- Pentecost was His coming to clothe them with power from on high.
- 70 AD was His coming to outwork the judgment that had already been made to remove the kingdom from Israel and end their old covenant age.

Of course, Jesus continues to come whenever we gather together in His name and He has come and visited people personally. He has come to me many times in many ways to engage with me.

If there is any future coming to end history as we know it or to usher in another age, it is not prophesied in the prophets in the Bible or by Jesus Himself. All those through New Testament history who have prophesied Jesus' coming have been wrong and all predictions of dates of Jesus' coming have been found to be incorrect. The last date that I am aware of is September 24th 2019 but in times of trouble there may well be many others that I am not aware of. They will all come to nothing and I would encourage you not to look for future dates for an event that is confined to the history books.

There are references to some comings of Jesus that are meant to be taken literally and they did occur literally and historically. Other comings were never meant to be taken literally in a physical sense as they are either spiritual or metaphorical.

Jesus came into heaven literally and physically at His ascension but He comes spiritually when we gather, unless He manifests a physical appearance. Some of the literal comings also have figurative meanings attached to them: for example, coming on the clouds was symbolic as well as literal. The meaning of the clouds in symbolism needs to be understood if we are to discern the correct understanding of that coming.

The events associated with the coming of Jesus in judgment recorded by the synoptic gospel writers have corresponding passages in John's account in Revelation. John revealed the same event using visionary apocalyptical language in the Book of Revelation of Jesus but the comparisons to Jesus' earthly teaching are there to see. Events that were predicted by Jesus focused on the land or world of Israel (and not the whole earth, as proposed by a futurist interpretation of the book of Revelation). Translating *aion* (meaning 'age') as 'the world' in Matthew 24:3 and other places helps deceive the casual Christian reader who may be programmed by dispensationalism without ever knowing it.

1) Matthew 25:31 cf. Revelation 20:11 – Christ/God on the throne to judge.

"But when the Son of Man comes in His glory, and all the angels with Him, then He will sit on His glorious throne. All the nations will be gathered before Him; and He will separate them from one another, as the shepherd separates the sheep from the goats..." (Matthew 25:31-32).

Then I saw a great white throne and Him who sat upon it, from whose presence earth and heaven fled away, and no place was found for them. And I saw the dead, the great and the small, standing before the throne, and books were opened; and another book was opened, which is the book of life; and the dead were judged from the things which were written in the books, according to their deeds. (Revelation 20:11-12).

The events that are figuratively depicting judgment on Israel in Matthew, Mark and Luke are synonymously described in the same figurative, spiritual, symbolic events in the Book of Revelation that are all now fulfilled in that past generation as Jesus indicated.

2) Matthew 24:29, 35 cf. Revelation 20:11 – 'heaven and earth' pass/flee.

3) Matthew 25:31/Matthew 16:27 cf. Revelation 20:12 - "all men" "each person" "all nations" "the rest of the dead" "small and great" "are judged according to what they have done."

4) Matthew 25:41-46 cf. Revelation 20:10, 14-15 – the wicked along with the devil are thrown into the Lake of Fire for age enduring purification.

The most important question to be taken into account when interpreting these verses is this: when did Jesus say He would come?

- Some of His audience would live to see it happen (Matthew 16:28).
- He would surely come during that generation (Matthew 24:34).
- The apostles wouldn't have enough time to go through Israel before His coming (Matthew 10:23).
- The apostle John would still be alive (John 21:22).
- The members of the Jewish Council would witness it (Matthew 26:64).
- The first Jewish Christians had to be prepared for His coming (Matthew 24).

These events were imminent and soon to take place before that generation (for the sake of argument, 40 years) ended.

Bible translators have changed words of imminence to suggest an unspecified future.

The greatest example of this is mistranslating the Greek word *mello* which means 'at the point of happening' or 'about to take place'.

Strong's concordance: 3195 méllō – properly, at the very point of acting; ready, "about to happen." Whenever Strong's says 'properly', that is what the actual meaning is; but often it then adds a false and incorrect modern evangelical meaning that twists the true meaning and deceives the reader.

Changing the meaning of *mello* from 'about to occur' (indicating immediacy) to 'will' or 'shall occur' adds the meaning that it is guaranteed to occur but loses the immediacy – and therefore places the occurrence anytime in the future. For example, J. Thayer in his *Dictionary of New Testament Words* changes the meaning from 'about to happen' which is time-based, to certainty-based meaning which removes the immediacy. He quotes Strong's 3195 (méllō) which says the word is used "in general of what is sure to happen".

That type of interpretation is what has been used to futurise the (first century) generation Jesus was referring to and make it appear to be thousands of years later. Every generation has wrongly been looking for events surrounding Jesus' second coming in their own time and therefore become distracted from establishing the kingdom, which is our primary purpose.

Mello occurs 110 times in the New Testament and in many versions is wrongly translated almost every time. Why does that matter? Because each time it changes 'about to' to 'shall', it removes the time factor of immediacy and makes it possible for it to occur at any time in the future. That simple change from 'about to' occur to 'will' or 'shall' occur is responsible for misleading generations into believing a futurist agenda.

A classic example is found in Matthew 16:27 where Jesus was preparing the listeners for His return in their lifetime.

"For the Son of Man is going to come in the glory of His Father with His angels, and will then repay every man according to his deeds". (Matthew 16:27).

Changing *mello* 'about to come' to 'going to come' breaks the link to the next verse that indicates that there would be those still alive when Jesus would come in his kingdom:

"Truly I say to you, there are some of those who are standing here who will not taste death until they see the Son of Man coming in His kingdom." (Matthew 16:28).

Young's Literal Translation translates *mello* correctly and therefore connects the verses as one event in that generation:

*'For, the Son of Man **is about to come** in the glory of his Father, with his messengers, and then he will reward each, according to his work. Verily I say to you, there are certain of those standing here who shall not taste of death till they may see the Son of Man coming in his reign.'* (Matthew 16:27-28 YLT).

This misleading translation practice runs through the whole New Testament in the King James Version used by the Scofield Bible, changing Jesus' meaning (which His contemporary audience would have understood) and making it agree with a future agenda. More modern translators sometimes use 'about to' correctly but the usage is mixed. In the examples below, the emphases highlighting the differences are mine:

- Last days, end of the age:

*And they asked him, saying, Master, but when shall these things be? and what sign will there be when these things **shall come to pass**?* (Luke 21:7 KJV).

*They asked Him questions, saying, "Teacher, when therefore will these things happen? And what will be the sign when these things **are about to take place**?"* (Luke 21:7 NASB).

- Tribulation:

For verily, when we were with you, we told you before that we should suffer tribulation; even as it came to pass, and ye know. (1 Thessalonians 3:4 KJV).

*...for even when we were with you, we said to you beforehand, that we are **about to** suffer tribulation, as also it did come to pass, and ye have known [it].* (1 Thessalonians 3:4 YLT).

*"Fear none of those things which thou **shalt suffer**: behold, the devil shall cast some of you into prison, that ye may be tried; and ye shall have tribulation ten days: be thou faithful unto death, and I will give thee a crown of life."* (Revelation 2:10 KJV).

*"Do not fear what you are **about to suffer**. Behold, the devil is about to throw some of you into prison, so that you will be tested, and you will have tribulation for ten days. Be faithful until death, and I will give you the crown of life."* (Revelation 2:10 NASB).

- Famines, wars and rumours of wars:

*And there stood up one of them named Agabus and signified by the Spirit that there **should be** great dearth throughout all* *the world: which came to pass in the days of Claudius Caesar.* (Acts 11:28 KJV).

... and one of them, by name Agabus, having stood up, did signify through the Spirit a great dearth is about to be throughout all the world – which also came to pass in the time of Claudius Caesar (Acts 11: 28 YLT).

*And you **will be hearing** of wars and rumors of wars. See that you are not alarmed, for those things must take place, but that is not yet the end.* (Matthew 24:6 NASB).

*You **will soon hear** about wars and threats of wars, but don't be afraid. These things will have to happen first, but that isn't the end.* (Matthew 24:6 CEV).

- The coming of the Lord:

*"For the Son of Man is **going to come** in the glory of His Father with His angels, and will then repay every person according to his deeds."* (Matthew 16:27 NASB).

*'For, the Son of Man **is about to come** in the glory of his Father, with his messengers, and then he will reward each, according to his work.'* (Matthew 16:27 YLT).

*"But stay alert at all times, praying that you will have strength to escape all these things that are **going to take place**, and to stand before the Son of Man."* (Luke 21:36 NASB).

*'... watch ye, then, in every season, praying that ye may be accounted worthy to escape all these things that are **about to come to pass**, and to stand before the Son of Man.'* (Luke 21:36 YLT).

- Judgment:

But as he was discussing righteousness, self-control, and the judgment **to come**, *Felix became frightened and responded, "Go away for now, and when I have an opportunity, I will summon you."* (Acts 24:25 NASB).

... and he reasoning concerning righteousness, and temperance, and the judgment that is **about to be**, *Felix, having become afraid, answered, 'For the present be going, and having got time, I will call for thee;'* (Acts 24:25 YLT).

... but a terrifying expectation of judgment and the fury of a fire **which will** *consume the adversaries.* (Hebrews 10: 27 NASB).

... but a certain fearful looking for of judgment, and fiery zeal, **about to** *devour the opposers;* (Hebrews 10:27 YLT).

... and if He condemned the cities of Sodom and Gomorrah to destruction by reducing them to ashes, having made them an example of what **is coming** *for the ungodly;* (2 Peter 2:6 NASB).

... and the cities of Sodom and Gomorrah having turned to ashes, with an overthrow did condemn, an example to those **about to** *be impious having set [them];* (2 Peter 2:6 YLT).

"Because thou hast kept the word of my patience, I also will keep thee from the hour of temptation, which **shall come** *upon all the world, to try them that dwell upon the earth."* (Revelation 3:10 KJV).

"Because you have kept My word of perseverance, I also will keep you from the hour of the testing, that hour which is **about to** *come upon the whole world, to test those who live on the earth."* (Revelation 3:10 NASB).

- Resurrection:

*... having a hope in God, which these men cherish themselves, that there shall **certainly be** a resurrection of both the righteous and the wicked.* (Acts 24:15 NASB).

*... having hope toward God, which they themselves also wait for, [that] there is **about to be** a rising again of the dead, both of righteous and unrighteous;* (Acts 24:15 YLT).

- New Jerusalem:

*For here we do not have a lasting city, but we are seeking the city which is **to come**.* (Hebrews 13:14 NASB).

*For here we do not have a lasting city, but we are seeking the city which is **about to** come.* (Hebrews 13:14 – my own translation, using the correct meaning of *mello*).

- The age to come:

*And whoever speaks a word against the Son of Man, it shall be forgiven him; but whoever speaks against the Holy Spirit, it shall not be forgiven him, either in this age or in the age **to come**.* (Matthew 12:32 NASB).

*And whoever speaks a word against the Son of Man, it shall be forgiven him; but whoever speaks against the Holy Spirit, it shall not be forgiven him, either in this age or in the age **about to** come.* (Matthew 12:32 – my own translation, using the correct meaning of *mello*).

*... far above all rule and authority and power and dominion, and every name that is named, not only in this age but also in the one **to come**.* (Ephesians 1:21 NASB).

... far above all rule and authority and power and dominion, and every name that is named, not only in this age but also in

*the one **about to come***. (Ephesians 1:21 – my own translation, using the correct meaning of *mello*).

*Laying up in store for themselves a good foundation against the time **to come**, that they may lay hold on eternal life.* (1 Timothy 6:19 KJV).

*Laying up in store for themselves a good foundation against the time **about to** come, that they may lay hold on eternal life.* (1 Timothy 6:19 – my own translation, using the correct meaning of *mello*).

*... and have tasted the good word of God and the powers of the age **to come***, (Hebrews 6:5 NASB)

*... and have tasted the good word of God and the powers of the age **about to** come,* (Hebrews 6:5 – my own translation, using the correct meaning of *mello*).

To the reader with a futurist-programmed belief system, the age to come is still in the future and requires the future return of Jesus before we can fully experience those powers; but when correctly translated, it is obvious that everyone has had access to those powers fully since 70 AD. We are in 'the age to come', the new covenant age, in which the powers of sonship are fully available to us now. The false futurist eschatological belief system has limited everyone to a tasting menu which may be great but is limited when compared to the full menu that is freely on offer for us now.

All the signs that Jesus taught them to look out for – signs that would indicate His coming was near and about to occur – have all already occurred, either physically or spiritually.

One supposed sign that still causes people to doubt a realised fulfilment of the second coming is Jesus physically coming to earth. That confusion arises from the statement made by the men in white linen present when Jesus ascended into heaven for the final time:

And after He had said these things, He was lifted up while they were watching, and a cloud took Him up, out of their sight. And as they were gazing intently into the sky while He was going, then behold, two men in white clothing stood beside them, and they said, "Men of Galilee, why do you stand looking into the sky? This Jesus, who has been taken up from you into heaven, will come in the same way as you have watched Him go into heaven." (Acts 1:9-11).

This scripture never states that he would return physically: that is a myth that has been repeated so often that it has become absolute truth to many. What it does state is that Jesus would come (using that same Greek word Jesus used for His coming in Matthew 24:30, *erchomai*, which referred to His coming in the clouds). In fact, that is exactly the method of His return. The same cloud that took Him up from their sight would return Him to their sight; and that was the great cloud of witnesses, which may perhaps have included the same angels who heralded His birth.

"And then the sign of the Son of Man will appear in the sky, and then all the tribes of the earth will mourn, and they will see the Son of Man coming on the clouds of the sky with power and great glory." (Matthew 24:30).

Jesus said to him, "You have said it yourself. But I tell you, from now on you will see the Son of Man sitting at the right hand of power, and coming on the clouds of heaven." (Matthew 26:64).

And Jesus said, "I am; and you shall see the Son of Man sitting at the right hand of power, and coming with the clouds of heaven." (Mark 14:62).

Another question that arises is that if Jesus has come, why is He not reigning on earth physically, as we have been told He is going to do? Well, who told you it would be a physical return and a physical reign? I guarantee that assumption comes from the same futurist, literalist source of eschatological thought.

Jesus clearly states that His kingdom is not of this world; it would exist within us and would definitely not be a religious or political kingdom. We are called to reign on the earth and Jesus has given us the kingdom. That reign, rule or dominion was the original sonship mandate God gave Adam, Noah and Abraham and is now being fulfilled: as we are seated or enthroned in heavenly places, we are the means by which God's kingdom will manifest 'on earth as it is in heaven'. Jesus rules far above all authority in heaven and on earth but chooses to rule and have dominion through us. We are the convergence of heaven and earth. We are of the order of Melchizedek, a heavenly royal priesthood, and oracles and legislators on earth. What is the foundation of the household of God on earth of which Jesus is the chief capstone? Oracles and Legislators (or Prophets and Apostles if you prefer; however, this is not referring to a so-called fivefold ministry hierarchical system of government, trying to copy heaven's government, but a reflection of heaven in foundational, servant-hearted, loving government).

God blessed them; and God said to them, "Be fruitful and multiply, and fill the earth, and subdue it; and rule over the fish of the sea and over the birds of the sky and over every living thing that moves on the earth." (Genesis 1:28).

Then God blessed Noah and his sons, and said to them, "Be fruitful and multiply, and fill the earth... God said, "This is the sign of the covenant which I am making between Me and you and every living creature that is with you, for all future generations; I have set My rainbow in the cloud, and it shall serve as a sign of a covenant between Me and the earth. (Genesis 9:1, 12-13).

And I will bless those who bless you, and the one who curses you I will curse. And in you all the families of the earth will be blessed." (Genesis 12:3).

The Scripture, foreseeing that God would justify the Gentiles by faith, preached the gospel beforehand to Abraham, saying, "All the nations will be blessed in you." (Galatians 3:8).

Notice how in Jesus' teaching, in the promise to Noah and in the prophets, the coming of Jesus in, on or with clouds is linked with salvation, and judgment, and the kingdom.

If Jesus has already returned, why is He not currently reigning on earth? The simple answer: He is, He reigns in us and through us.

For if by the offense of the one, death reigned through the one, much more will those who receive the abundance of grace and of the gift of righteousness reign in life through the One, Jesus Christ... so that, as sin reigned in death, so also grace would reign through righteousness to eternal life through Jesus Christ our Lord. (Romans 5:17, 21).

"This is what the Lord says: 'If you can break My covenant for the day and My covenant for the night, so that day and night do not occur at their proper time, then My covenant with David My servant may also be broken, so that he will not have

a son to reign on his throne, and with the Levitical priests, My ministers.'" (Jeremiah 33:20-21 NASB).

"If you can break my covenant with the day and my covenant with the night, so that day and night no longer come at their appointed time, then my covenant with David my servant ... can be broken and David will no longer have a descendant to reign on his throne." (Jeremiah 33:20-21 NIV).

The night literally and symbolically came in the middle of the day during the crucifixion. The day literally and symbolically came in the middle of the night just before the second coming in 66 AD.

Jesus, as the Christ, reigns at the right hand of the Father in heaven. Like the Father, Jesus rules the earth from a heavenly, not an earthly throne – but through us, His coheirs. We are the royal priesthood through which Jesus reigns on earth. Here we must learn to rule and reign in life, bringing the dominion of heaven into the earth through our lives.

... and He made us into a kingdom, priests to His God and Father – to Him be the glory and the dominion forever and ever. Amen. (Revelation 1:6).

"You have made them into a kingdom and priests to our God, and they will reign upon the earth." (Revelation 5:10).

Blessed and holy is the one who has a part in the first resurrection; over these the second death has no power, but they will be priests of God and of Christ, and will reign with Him for a thousand years. (Revelation 20:6).

Those in that generation who were reigning on earth were royal priests and they reigned with Him in the transition that completed the age, which was for the figurative period of 1000 years until 70 AD. In that transition period, the gospel had indeed gone into all the earth, and the birth pangs ended with the birthing of the age to come.

The transition period was over and the age to come became realised. All the promises that God made through the prophets (and all the covenants God made) were fully realised in Jesus, who was the last Adam, the seed of Abraham, the seed of David and the fulfilment of the law and prophets. Jesus was the Lion of the tribe of Judah, the Israel of God, who included all humanity in Himself.

How then was Jesus' second coming in the same manner as His ascension on the clouds fulfilled in 70 AD, literally, figuratively and symbolically?

The following may seem unbelievable to the programmed mind but all the information below is taken from unbiased historical records and is easily verifiable. This is 'the second coming' in a manner you have probably never seen before but it is clear both from what Jesus prophesied for that generation and from history.

The coming on the clouds is a significant statement that uses language that is both creational and de-creational.

Psalm 104:1-3 refers to the act of creation, using clouds as a chariot, where Genesis 1 says "the Spirit of God hovered over the waters."

Bless the Lord, my soul!
Lord my God, You are very great;
You are clothed with splendor and majesty,
Covering Yourself with light as with a cloak,
stretching out heaven like a tent curtain.
He lays the beams of His upper chambers in the waters;

He makes the clouds His chariot;
He walks on the wings of the wind; (Psalm 104:1-3).

The clouds upon which the Spirit of God rides in Genesis 1:2 are formed by the separation of the waters above from the waters below in Genesis 1:6-8. The clouds that were formed by the separation or evaporation of the waters became the clouds that are figuratively God's chariot. This concept is not unique to Genesis and is also found in other places in the Old Testament. It is also found in the New Testament, where it is applied to the second coming of Christ, for example in Matthew 24:30 and elsewhere.

The Spirit of God hovered over the waters during the literal creation of heaven and earth event. In the book of Isaiah, the creation of the old covenant with Israel is also referred to as the establishment of the heavens and the earth. During the second coming event, Jesus' coming on the clouds of heaven marks both de-creation of the old heavens and earth age and the creation of a new heaven and earth.

This event was foretold in 2 Peter and Revelation:

But by His word the present heavens and earth are being reserved for fire, kept for the day of judgment and destruction of ungodly people. (2 Peter 3:7).

But according to His promise we are looking for new heavens and a new earth, in which righteousness dwells. (2 Peter 3:13).

Then I saw a new heaven and a new earth; for the first heaven and the first earth passed away, and there is no longer any sea. (Revelation 21:1).

When Jesus came on the clouds of heaven during the second coming, this act mirrored Genesis 1 when the Spirit of God came on the clouds during the act of creation. The second coming marked the creation of a new heaven and earth and would also be expected to be a coming that therefore included His presence, which is the Greek word *parousia*, not a one-time event.

There were many comings of Jesus in the Old Testament, usually called 'theophanies', examples of which include Genesis 16:7; 21:17; 22:11; 31:11; Exodus 3:2-15; 17:1-7; Judges 6:11; 13:21; Daniel 3:24-27; and Micah 5:2.

Jesus also made several appearances after His resurrection and before His ascension (Acts 7:55-56; 9:1-8; 1 Corinthians 15:5-8; Revelation 1).

Jesus also made more than one appearance during the second coming period (66-70 AD) to fulfil the prophesied signs. Jesus was present during the whole event in different ways that fulfilled the prophetic Old Testament symbolism.

> *Parousia* is a Greek word meaning "presence". This is a word used to denote the arrival of a conquering general, emperor or high-ranking official into a city for an extended stay, perhaps for several months or years, before then returning to the capital city, the seat of his throne. The word can then be associated both with a coming and, more importantly to the integrity to the meaning of the word, an extended presence or stay often followed by a subsequent departure. – revelationrevelation.org

When most people think of the 'second coming', they think of a brief appearance of Christ on the clouds and then everything changing in the blinking of an eye in a so-called 'rapture'. The events of 70 AD have several 'coming' signs, only one of which is coming on the clouds.

What is the sequence of events that followed Jesus' first coming, that led to His second coming?

During His ministry, Jesus revealed and prepared His disciples for the fact that He would soon leave the physical world to be with the Father in heaven (Luke 19:12-27; John 8:21-23; 13:1; 14:2-3; 16:7). Then after His death He returned, as He promised, in the resurrection (John 14:1-3 is prophesying the resurrection, not the second coming).

"Do not let your heart be troubled; believe in God, believe also in Me. In My Father's house are many rooms; if that were not so, I would have told you, because I am going there to prepare a place for you. And if I go and prepare a place for you, I am coming again and will take you to Myself, so that where I am, there you also will be." (John 14:1-3).

Jesus' promise not to leave them orphans but come to them was not the second coming but the resurrection, otherwise we would all still be orphans. The reality is that the purpose of Jesus' coming to the disciples on the day of resurrection was to breathe the Spirit into humanity again.

*"I will not leave you as orphans; I am **coming to you**. After a little while, the world no longer is going to see Me, but you are going to see Me; because I live, you also will live. **On that day** you will know that I am in My Father, and you are in Me, and I in you."* (John 14:18-20, emphases mine).

The sequence of events was that Jesus ascended into heaven in Acts 1:9-11) where He remained with the Father (Acts 3:19-21; 7:55; 1 Thessalonians 1:10; 2 Thessalonians 1:7; Hebrews 9:24; 1 Peter 3:22) until He returned on the clouds of heaven to establish the *parousia*, and end the old covenant system.

*He also bowed the heavens down low, and came down
With thick darkness under His feet.
He rode on a cherub and flew;
And He sped on the wings of the wind.
He made darkness His hiding place, His canopy around Him,
Darkness of waters, thick clouds.
From the brightness before Him passed His thick clouds,
Hailstones and coals of fire.* (Psalm 18:9-12).

As we have seen, the meaning of *parousia* as 'coming' has the implication of a king who visits a city for a period of time then returns to his own seat of government.

The second coming is a description of Jesus' coming in judgment during the Jewish War event. Judgment is always to life, not death; and Jesus gave plenty of signs so they could escape before the end of the old system finally came.

After His ascension, Jesus departed to heaven, where he reigned at the right hand of the Father in the heavenly Jerusalem mentioned in Hebrews 12:22 and Galatians 4:26:

But you have come to Mount Zion and to the city of the living God, the heavenly Jerusalem, and to myriads of angels (Hebrews 12:22).

But the Jerusalem above is free; she is our mother. (Galatians 4: 26).

Jesus, then, returned to Israel to enact judgment during the Jewish War, as He had promised He would do. This was the sign that Jesus was king, enthroned in heaven, and His kingdom had come on earth.

This judgment was not punishment and Jesus Himself did not destroy Jerusalem. What occurred was the reaping of all the blood that had been shed, as He indicated in His discourse with the religious leaders recorded in Matthew chapters 21-26. Matthew 21 describes the seven woes upon the religious leaders who were stopping people from entering the kingdom. Later, Jesus explains this judgment as being the consequence of reaping what they had sown:

"Therefore, behold, I am sending you prophets and wise men and scribes; some of them you will kill and crucify, and some of them you will flog in your synagogues, and persecute from city to city, so that upon you will fall the guilt of all the righteous blood shed on earth, from the blood of righteous Abel to the blood of Zechariah, the son of Berechiah, whom you murdered between the temple and the altar. Truly I say to you, all these things will come upon this generation." (Matthew 23:34-36).

Even then, Jesus desired that they would be saved from the destruction that was coming. He warned them, revealing what signs they were to look out for, but they refused:

"Jerusalem, Jerusalem, who kills the prophets and stones those who have been sent to her! How often I wanted to gather your children together, the way a hen gathers her chicks under her wings, and you were unwilling. Behold, your house is being left to you desolate!" (Matthew 23:37-38).

Jesus remained in heaven, physically enthroned (as revealed in Acts 3:21) until He came to begin the period of the restoration of all (things) – the translators add 'things' to make sense of this phrase in English but it just states 'all' in the original Greek. During the transition period Jesus' refreshing presence was in them continually because He never leaves us or forsakes us.

Therefore repent and return, so that your sins may be wiped away, in order that times of refreshing may come from the presence of the Lord; and that He may send Jesus, the Christ appointed for you, whom heaven must receive until the period of restoration of all things, about which God spoke by the mouths of His holy prophets from ancient times. (Acts 3:19-21).

During that second coming event, Jesus made many miraculous appearances before at the 'last trumpet' returning to heaven with His people at the spiritual resurrection event (1 Corinthians 15:51-52, 2 Thessalonians 2:1).

Even after His ascension into heaven, Jesus still appeared occasionally to His disciples (Acts 9:3-7, Acts 22:17-18, Acts 23:11 and Revelation 1:9-20). Similarly, He also appears to have made a series of manifestations during the coming events.

One of these appearances of these appearances was in 66 AD, at the beginning of the siege of Jerusalem. This appearance of Jesus at the start of the Jewish War is the fulfilment of Revelation 8:5 and 14:14 which refer to the glory cloud, signifying the presence of Jesus on the clouds, before the start of the 'seven trumpets and bowls'.

Then the angel took the censer and filled it with the fire of the altar, and hurled it to the earth; and there were peals of thunder and sounds, and flashes of lightning and an earthquake. (Revelation 8:5).

Then I looked, and behold, a white cloud, and sitting on the cloud was one like a son of man, with a golden crown on His head and a sharp sickle in His hand. (Revelation 14:14).

Jesus seems to have appeared visibly on the clouds as the Lord had done in Ezekiel 1:4-26. The biblical descriptions of the second coming, including that of the appearance of Jesus on horseback leading an army in the sky in Revelation 19, were literally as well as symbolically fulfilled. These appearances are aligned to descriptions found in other places in the Bible and Jewish history, such as Deuteronomy 33:2, Habakkuk 3:3-15, Zechariah 14:5, and the appearance of gold-clad horsemen in the sky during the Maccabean Wars, according to 2 Maccabees 5:1-4.

The descriptions of what was seen in the sky in 66 AD, such as horsemen and chariots, are very similar terms to Psalm 68:17, Zechariah 6:1-8 and in 2 Kings 6:17:

The chariots of God are myriads, thousands upon thousands; The Lord is among them as at Sinai, in holiness. (Psalm 68:17).

With the first chariot were red horses, with the second chariot black horses, with the third chariot white horses, and with the fourth chariot strong spotted horses. (Zechariah 6:2-3).

Then Elisha prayed and said, "Lord, please, open his eyes so that he may see." And the Lord opened the servant's eyes, and he saw; and behold, the mountain was full of horses and chariots of fire all around Elisha. (2 Kings 6:17).

A horseman was seen in the sky, as referred to in Revelation 6:2.

I looked, and behold, a white horse, and he who sat on it had a bow; and a crown was given to him, and he went out conquering and to conquer. (Revelation 6:2).

This horseman is Jesus Christ, who rides the same white horse in Revelation 19:11-16. An angelic army of horsemen was reportedly seen at the start of the Jewish revolt in Iyyar (66 AD).

The next coming of Christ on the clouds appears to have been at the start of the Idumean massacre in 68 AD. The third, which was very similar, was at the start of the siege of Jerusalem in 70 AD. During these two occasions, Jesus came on the clouds in symbolic judgment of the old covenant; but it was the reaping of the rebellion to Rome that had been sown by Israel that brought the Roman army upon them. Clouds, armies and glory are aspects of the second coming events according to the Hebrew prophets and are symbolic of how judgment took place in the undifferentiated minds of those prophets and writers. Judgment was always apportioned to God even though it was reaping of what had been sown.

The Lord had appeared throughout biblical history in many and various ways and He has probably continued to come, as evidenced by many personal testimonies of His appearing. In light of what the Bible indicates as 'second coming' events, can we find historical records that reveal the 'second coming' as a past event?

Remember, Jesus announced that the following things would occur during that generation:

- Jerusalem would be destroyed (Matthew 23:38)
- The temple would be destroyed (Matthew 24:2)
- Christ would be seen in the sky (Matthew 26:64)
- His angels would be seen in the clouds (2 Thessalonians 1:7,8)
- There would be a great light (Matthew 24:27)
- A supernatural sign would appear in the sky (Matthew 24:30)
- The sun would darken and the moon turn red (Matthew 24:30)

- There would be earthquakes, famines, disease, wars and false prophets (Matthew 24:6-7)
- All this would happen in the first generation of believers (Matthew 24:34).

History reveals that these things, which fulfilled what Jesus prophesied, actually occurred at that time and are recorded. Most people who have any evangelical influences are shocked to discover that these events were reported to have occurred by first century Jewish, Roman and Christian historians.

Flavius Josephus was a Jewish historian who wrote many books about the siege of Jerusalem in 66-70 AD which show that what Jesus said about the destruction of the temple and the end of the old covenant actually was literally fulfilled in the generation predicted.

The Greek, Eusebius of Caesarea, was the most well-known Christian historian of the first century. In the book 'Ecclesiastical History' Eusebius describes many of the events associated with the destruction of Jerusalem.

A Roman historian named Gaius Cornelius Tacitus (56–118 AD) also describes the events surrounding the destruction of Jerusalem in his books.

Sepher Josippon, a medieval historian who majored on the history of ancient Israel, also mentions the events of the destruction of Jerusalem in his writings.

The Pseudo-Hegesippus is a very well-known and respected Jewish historical record. This Jewish historiography also describes what occurred during 66-70 AD.

It is highly unlikely that Jewish and Roman sources would back up the Christian historical evidence if the recorded events were not facts. I will give direct quotes from their books without comment but anyone – even a casual reader – would find it difficult to argue that events depicted do not affirm what Jesus prophesied would occur in that generation.

> A certain figure appeared of tremendous size, which many saw, just as the books of the Jews have disclosed, and before the setting of the sun there were suddenly seen in the clouds chariots and armed battle arrays, by which the cities of all Judaea and its territories were invaded. – Pseudo-Hegesippus[18].

> A demonic phantom appeared of incredible size, and what will be related would have seemed a fairy-tale had it not been told by those who saw it, and been attended by suffering worthy of the portent. For before sunset there appeared in the air over the whole country chariots and armed troops coursing through the clouds and surrounding the cities. – Eusebius[19].

> ...chariots and troops of soldiers in their armour were seen running about among the clouds, and surrounding cities. – Josephus[20].

> There had been seen hosts joining the battle in the skies, fiery gleams of arms... the temple illuminated by a sudden radiance from the clouds. – Tacitus[21].

> Now it happened after this that there was seen over the Holy of Holies from above for the entire night the outline of a man's face, the like of whose beauty had never been

---

[18] Latin version of the Pseudo-Hegesippus, chapter 44.
[19] Eusebius, *Ecclesiastical History*, Book 3, Ch. 8, Sections 1-6.
[20] Josephus, *Wars of the Jews*, Book 6, Chapter 5, Sections 2-3.
[21] Gaius Tacitus, *The Histories*, Book 5.13.

seen in all the land, and his appearance was very awesome.

Moreover, in those days were seen chariots of fire and horsemen, a great force flying across the sky near to the ground coming against Jerusalem and all the land of Judah, all of them horses of fire and riders of fire. – Jossipon[22].

At one time a star, in form like a sword, stood over the city, and a comet, which lasted for a whole year; and ... so great a light shone about the altar and the temple that it seemed to be bright day; and this continued for half an hour. This seemed to the unskilful a good sign, but was interpreted by the sacred scribes as portending those events which very soon took place. – Eusebius[23].

Thus there was a star resembling a sword, which stood over the city, and a comet, that continued a whole year. Thus also before the Jews' rebellion, and before those commotions which preceded the war, when the people were come in great crowds to the feast of unleavened bread, on the eighth day of the month Xanthicus and at the ninth hour of the night, so great a light shone around the altar and the holy house, that it appeared to be bright day time; which lasted for half an hour.'– Josephus[24].

...the temple illuminated by a sudden radiance from the clouds. – Tacitus[25].

---

[22] Sepher Jossipon, *Burning of the temple*, Chapter 87.
[23] Eusebius (*ibid.*)
[24] Josephus (*ibid.*)
[25] Tacitus (*ibid.*)

> For about the signs of the stars even in the Gospels, we are taught that there were signs in the sun and the moon and the stars. – Pseudo Hegesippus[26].

I believe there is overwhelming evidence to support that what Jesus taught concerning His second coming has already been fulfilled. Jesus also talked about certain signs that these things were about to take place so that the believers would be prepared to flee the destruction of Jerusalem and be saved.

We have looked at the biblical evidence of the symbolic and literal fulfilment of these events prior to 70 AD but is there any historical evidence for their fulfilment?

The signs that Jesus revealed in Matthew 24 were that there would be false Christs and false prophets, wars and rumours of wars, famines, diseases, and earthquakes. These signs are often called 'the signs of the end times' by Christians who are still misguidedly looking for future occurrence and fulfilment. Historically all these five signs are mentioned as having occurred contemporaneously with the generation to which Jesus was speaking. These were literal or physical signs but there are also symbolic, figurative or spiritual meanings for the signs that have relevance as well. The same independent historians also record the fulfilment of those signs of impending doom and judgment.

- False Christs and Prophets.

> Now there was then a great number of false prophets, suborned by the tyrants, to impose on the people: who denounced this to them, that they should wait for deliverance from God...

---

[26] Pseudo Hegesippus, Book V, Section XLIV.

And now these impostors and deceivers persuaded the multitude to follow them into the wilderness: and pretended that they would exhibit manifest wonders and signs, that should be performed by the providence of God. – Josephus[27].

The need for this warning soon became apparent, for within a year of ascension, Dositheus the Samaritan rose up, who had the nerve to claim that he was the Messiah whom Moses predicted; while his disciple Simon Magus misled large crowds into believing that he was the 'great power of God'. – George Peter Holford[28].

- Wars and rumours of wars

I am entering on the history of a period rich in disasters, frightful in its wars, torn by civil strife, and even in peace full of horrors. Four emperors perished by the sword. There were three civil wars; there were more with foreign enemies; there were often wars that had both characters at once... Besides the manifold vicissitudes of human affairs, there were prodigies in heaven and earth, the warning voices of the thunder, and other intimations of the future, auspicious or gloomy, doubtful or not to be mistaken.

Never surely did more terrible calamities of the Roman People, or evidence more conclusive, prove that the Gods take no thought for our happiness, but only for our punishment. – Tacitus[29].

---

[27] Josephus, *Wars of the Jews*, Book 6, Chapter 5, Section 2.
[28] George Peter Holford, *The Destruction of Jerusalem* (1805).
[29] Gaius Tacitus, *The Histories*, Book I, January-March 69 AD.

... a great multitude of the Germans were in commotion, and tended to rebellion. And as the Gauls in their neighbourhood joined with them, they conspired together... every part of the habitable earth under them was in an unsettled and tottering condition... At the very same time did the bold attempt of the Scythians against the Romans occur... they slew a great many of the Romans that guarded the frontiers: and as the consular legate Fonteius Agrippa came to meet them, and fought courageously against them, he was slain by them. They then overran all the region that had been subject to him; tearing and rending everything that fell in their way.
– Josephus[30].

- Famines.

Now of those that perished by famine in the city, the number was prodigious; and the miseries they underwent were unspeakable. For if so much as the shadow of any kind of food did anywhere appear, a war was commenced presently; and the dearest friends fell a fighting one with another about it: snatching from each other the most miserable supports of life. Nor would men believe that those who were dying had no food; but the robbers would search them when they were expiring; lest anyone should have concealed food in their bosoms, and counterfeited dying. Nay these robbers gaped for want, and ran about stumbling and staggering along, like mad dogs; and reeling against the doors of the houses, like drunken men.

They would also, in the great distress they were in, rush into the very same houses, two or three times in one and the same day. Moreover their hunger was so intolerable,

---

[30] Josephus, *Wars of the Jews*, Book 7, section 2 and 3.

that it obliged them to chew everything; while they gathered such things as the most sordid animals would not touch; and endured to eat them. Nor did they at length abstain from girdles, and shoes; and the very leather which belonged to their shields they pulled off and gnawed. The very wisps of old hay became food to some; and some gathered up fibres, and sold a very small weight of them for four Attick. – Josephus[31].

- Infectious diseases.

Tacitus and Suetonius also described that similar disasters prevailed during this period, in different parts of the Roman Empire. After Jerusalem was surrounded by the army of Titus, pernicious diseases soon made their appearance, to aggravate the misery and to reinforce the horrors of the siege. They were caused in part by the huge crowds gathered together in the city, in part by the rotten exhalations caused by the unearthed dead, and in part by the spread of famine. – Holford[32].

- Earthquakes

In early 68 AD, a storm broke out, accompanied by great earthquakes:

For there broke out a prodigious storm in the night, with the utmost violence, and very strong winds; with the largest showers of rain; with continual lightnings, terrible thunderings, and amazing concussions and bellowings of the earth that was in an earthquake... These things were a manifest indication that some destruction was coming upon men, when the system of the world was put into this

---

[31] Josephus, *Wars of the Jews*, Book 6, Chapter 3, Paragraph 4.
[32] George Peter Holford (*ibid.*)

disorder; and any one would guess that these wonders foreshowed some grand calamities that were coming. – Josephus[33].

Seneca the Younger, a Roman philosopher, wrote the following in 58 AD:

How often have cities in Asia and Achaea been hit by a fatal shock! So many cities were swallowed up in Syria, so many in Macedonia! How many times has Cyprus been destroyed by this disaster! How often has Paphos become a ruin! We often received the news of entire cities that were destroyed in one fell swoop. – Seneca[34].

Historically many major earthquakes occurred during this period in Crete, Smyrna, Miletus, Chios, Samos, Laodicea, Hierapolis, Kolosse, Campania, Rome, Judea and, on February 5, 63 AD, Pompeii.

Thus all these signs and events are now in the past and already fulfilled. Although they still occur today (as they also have throughout the past 2000 years) there is absolutely no need to see these current events as fulfilments of what Jesus predicted. There is no need to search the newspapers or internet looking for news items that are prophetic fulfilments. The events Jesus predicted were not global events to indicate the end of the world in our day but were local to Israel and the Roman world of their time.

There are many people who still looking for the destruction of the earth by fire and for every eye to see Jesus when He comes, believing that now through television it is possible for

---

[33] Josephus, *Wars of the Jews*, Book 4, chapter 3.
[34] Seneca the Younger, quoted in Henry Alford, *The New Testament for English Readers*, p. 163.

every eye to see Him. Of course not everyone has a TV or can live stream the internet and many people would be asleep in some parts of the world, not glued to their TV screen.

Jesus did mention various things associated with His coming and the writers of the New Testament also confirmed that the 'day of the Lord' was soon to take place. The references found in the Old Testament often used apocalyptical language that was quoted by the New Testament writers.

"For the Son of Man is going to come in the glory of His Father with His angels, and will then repay each person according to his deeds." (Matthew 16:27).

Establish your hearts, for the coming of the Lord is at hand... Behold, the Judge is standing at the door! (James 5:8, 9).

And I saw heaven opened, and behold, a white horse. And He who sat on it was called Faithful and True, and in righteousness He judges and wages war. (Revelation 19:11).

When the Lord Jesus will be revealed from heaven with His mighty angels in flaming fire, dealing out retribution to those who do not know God, and to those who do not obey the gospel of our Lord Jesus. (2 Thessalonians 1:6-8).

The coming of the Lord in judgment had also been announced throughout the Old Testament, often in reference to the coming of the day of the Lord. There are 24 direct references to the day of the Lord, 17 in the Old Testament and 7 in the New; but there are another 86 specific Bible verses that refer to the day of the Lord in various ways (see Appendix 1).

The language used is often apocalyptic, de-creational and judgmental but that was how the Old Testament prophets often announced things. Use the lens of Jesus to view such verses and punishment can be seen as restorative correction, not destruction.

The prophet Isaiah, for example, said:

*So it will happen on **that day**,*
That the Lord will punish the rebellious angels of heaven on high,
And the kings of the earth on earth.
(Isaiah 24:21, emphasis mine).

Behold, the day of the Lord is coming,
Cruel, with fury and burning anger,
To make the land a desolation;
And He will exterminate its sinners from it.
For the stars of heaven and their constellations
Will not flash forth their light;
The sun will be dark when it rises
And the moon will not shed its light. (Isaiah 13:9-11).

When compared to Jesus' statements in John 3:17 and John 10:10 we see that the language of judgment was intended for the system, not people enslaved to the system. Jesus came to destroy the works of the devil, not destroy those enslaved by those works – nor in fact to destroy the devil.

"... the one who practices sin is of the devil; for the devil has been sinning from the beginning. The Son of God appeared for this purpose, to destroy the works of the devil." (1 John 3:8).

"For God did not send the Son into the world to judge the world, but so that the world might be saved through Him." (John 3:17).

"The thief comes only to steal and kill and destroy; I came so that they would have life, and have it abundantly." (John 10:10).

*"For behold, the Lord will come in fire
And His chariots like the whirlwind,
To render His anger with fury,
And His rebuke with flames of fire."* (Isaiah 66:15).

Jesus, His prophets and His apostles unanimously said that He would come to execute judgment to end the old covenant system (not the whole world). Jesus was speaking to Jewish people when He predicted the judgment and His coming. Jesus was not talking to the whole world He came to save, nor to present-day British people, Americans, Africans, Europeans, Asians or Australasians. The 'Second Coming' was not a global event, as many Christians have believed, although of course it has had global consequences as the gospel has spread around the world.

Jesus was speaking directly to the first century Jews who were living in Israel. They were His primary audience, as seen by the following verses:

He came to His own, and His own people did not accept Him. (John 1:11).

"I was not sent except to the lost sheep of the house of Israel." (Matthew 15:24).

Jesus came as the Messiah to warn Israel of the coming judgment so they could be saved. The two major themes seen in the 'day of the Lord' Old Testament verses were destruction of the old and the restoration of the remnant that would be saved. The language used sometimes uses 'Israel' or 'Judah' to refer to the remnant and Revelation mentions '144,000 of the tribes of Israel'.

And I heard the number of those who were sealed, one hundred and forty-four thousand sealed from every tribe of the sons of Israel: from the tribe of Judah, twelve thousand were sealed, from the tribe of Reuben twelve thousand, from the tribe of Gad twelve thousand, from the tribe of Asher twelve thousand, from the tribe of Naphtali twelve thousand, from the tribe of Manasseh twelve thousand, from the tribe of Simeon twelve thousand, from the tribe of Levi twelve thousand, from the tribe of Issachar twelve thousand, from the tribe of Zebulun twelve thousand, from the tribe of Joseph twelve thousand, from the tribe of Benjamin, twelve thousand were sealed. (Revelation 7:4-8).

For though your people, O Israel, may be like the sand of the sea,
Only a remnant within them will return;
A destruction is determined, overflowing with righteousness.
For a complete destruction, one that is decreed, the Lord God of hosts will execute in the midst of the whole land.
(Isaiah 10:22-23).

The destruction of the earthly Jerusalem would be followed by the restoration of the spiritual New Jerusalem. The New Jerusalem would truly be a place of imputed righteousness where all were made the righteousness of God in Jesus.

He made Him who knew no sin to be sin on our behalf, so that we might become the righteousness of God in Him. (2 Corinthians 5:21).

"But I will leave among you
A humble and lowly people,

And they will take refuge in the name of the Lord.
The remnant of Israel will do no wrong
And tell no lies,
Nor will a deceitful tongue
Be found in their mouths;
For they will feed and lie down
With no one to frighten them." (Zephaniah 3:12-13).

The coming of the Messiah was always associated with the salvation of the remnant who would be made righteous.

"Behold, days are coming," declares the Lord, "when I will fulfill the good word which I have spoken concerning the house of Israel and the house of Judah. In those days and at that time I will make a righteous Branch of David sprout; and He shall execute justice and righteousness on the earth. In those days Judah will be saved and Jerusalem will live in safety; and this is the name by which it will be called: the Lord is our righteousness." (Jeremiah 33:14-16).

God's promises would be fulfilled through this 'Branch of righteousness', the Messiah. He would execute God's judgment on the old, rebellious Israel and bring forth a new people who would love God. In the Old Testament the remnant referred only to Judah or Israel but the New Testament expands this to include all humanity, the whole world.

The next day he saw Jesus coming to him, and said, "Behold, the Lamb of God who takes away the sin of the world!" (John 1:29).

Jesus Himself quoted Isaiah 61:1-2 when He began His ministry:

The Spirit of the Lord God is upon me,
Because the Lord anointed me
To bring good news to the humble;
He has sent me to bind up the brokenhearted,
To proclaim release to captives
And freedom to prisoners;
To proclaim the favorable year of the Lord
And the day of vengeance of our God;
To comfort all who mourn... (Isaiah 61:1-2).

Jesus came to fulfil all the promises of God; the covenants of God are consummated in Him and He gave us the Spirit as a pledge.

For as many as are the promises of God, in Him they are yes; therefore also through Him is our Amen to the glory of God through us. Now He who establishes us with you in Christ and anointed us is God, who also sealed us and gave us the Spirit in our hearts as a pledge. (2 Corinthians 1:20-22).

Jesus preached about a new kingdom of God that was really good news. But the message of the new was also the end of the old as the kingdom was taken from the Jewish custodians and given to the saints of the one new man in Christ who would be fruitful.

... and saying, "The time is fulfilled, and the kingdom of God is at hand; repent and believe in the gospel." (Mark 1:15).

"Therefore I say to you, the kingdom of God will be taken away from you and given to a people producing its fruit." (Matthew 21:43).

Jesus went into great detail in Matthew chapters 23-25, using covenantal language that His audience would have understood, to warn them of the coming judgment:

"Woe to you, scribes and Pharisees, hypocrites! For you build the tombs of the prophets and adorn the monuments of the righteous, and say, 'If we had been living in the days of our fathers, we would not have been partners with them in shedding the blood of the prophets.' So you testify against yourselves, that you are sons of those who murdered the prophets. Fill up, then, the measure of the guilt of your fathers. You serpents, you brood of vipers, how will you escape the sentence of hell [Gehenna]*?*

"Therefore, behold, I am sending you prophets and wise men and scribes; some of them you will kill and crucify, and some of them you will scourge in your synagogues, and persecute from city to city, so that upon you may fall the guilt of all the righteous blood shed on earth, from the blood of righteous Abel to the blood of Zechariah, the son of Berechiah, whom you murdered between the temple and the altar. Truly I say to you, all these things will come upon this generation.

"Jerusalem, Jerusalem, who kills the prophets and stones those who are sent to her! How often I wanted to gather your children together, the way a hen gathers her chicks under her wings, and you were unwilling. Behold, your house is being left to you desolate!" (Matthew 23:29-38).

Jesus left the temple area and was going on His way when His disciples came up to point out the temple buildings to Him. But He responded and said to them, "Do you not see all these things? Truly I say to you, not one stone here will be left upon another, which will not be torn down." (Matthew 24:1-2).

It would have been obvious to Jesus' disciples that the destruction of Jerusalem would take place at 'His coming'. That is why they wanted to know when it would happen and that is why they asked Him the questions recorded in Matthew 24:3 in the way they did:

As He was sitting on the Mount of Olives, the disciples came to Him privately, saying, "Tell us, when will these things happen, and what will be the sign of Your coming, and of the end of the age?" (Matthew 24:3).

The coming of the Lord was repeatedly announced throughout the Old Testament. Zechariah went into great detail about this coming of the Lord with His holy ones and standing on the Mount of Olives. Popular end-time preachers often quote this verse, to claim that we will all see how Jesus will stand on the Mount of Olives when He comes in our lifetime. We must understand the context of this verse to be able to place it correctly in history.

Behold, a day is coming for the Lord when the spoils taken from you will be divided among you. For I will gather all the nations against Jerusalem to battle, and the city will be taken, the houses plundered, the women raped, and half of the city exiled, but the rest of the people will not be eliminated from the city. Then the Lord will go forth and fight against those nations, as when He fights on a day of battle. On that day His feet will stand on the Mount of Olives, which is in front of Jerusalem on the east; and the Mount of Olives will be split in its middle from east to west forming a very large valley. Half of the mountain will move toward the north, and the other half toward the south. And you will flee by the valley of My mountains, for the valley of the mountains will reach to Azel; yes, you will flee just as you fled from the earthquake in the days of Uzziah king of Judah. Then the Lord, my God, will come, and all the holy ones with Him! (Zechariah 14:1-5).

The nations would gather to battle against Jerusalem. The Lord would stand on the Mount of Olives, and come with His holy ones, on the day when Jerusalem would be destroyed. That happened in 70 AD and was the literal and spiritual fulfilment of this prophecy. Eusebius confirms this in his writings, recording that the *shekinah* glory, the presence of God, left the temple and resided on the Mount of Olives.

> Which we can see fulfilled in another way even today, since believers in Christ all congregate from all parts of the world, not as of old time because of the glory of Jerusalem, nor that they may worship in the ancient Temple at Jerusalem, but they rest there that they may learn both about the city being taken and devastated as the prophets foretold, and that they may worship at the Mount of Olives opposite to the city, whither the glory of the Lord migrated when it left the former city. – Eusebius[35].

The disciples did not separate the destruction of Jerusalem and the coming of Jesus. They understood that the day of the Lord was the end of the old and the beginning of the new. According to history, Jesus actually stood on the Mount of Olives, during the fall of Jerusalem. People saw Him, as the book of Revelation states:

Behold, He is coming with the clouds, and every eye will see Him, even those who pierced Him; and all the tribes of the earth will mourn over Him. So it is to be. Amen. (Revelation 1:7).

Revelation says those who pierced Him would see Him: that is talking about the Jews and Romans, not British, American, African, Asian, Australasian or European people who did not

---

[35] Eusebius, *Proof of the Gospel*, Book VI, Chapter 18).

pierce Him, even though He was pierced for them. The tribes of the earth refers to Israel (the Greek word used for earth is *ge*, which can equally well be translated 'land', 'country', or 'region'.

The kingdom of God in Daniel is described as a stone cut without hands that grew to fill the whole earth. The end of the old was the beginning of the new and that time is associated with the establishment of the kingdom on earth as it is in heaven.

The old-age wineskin was figuratively and symbolically made of physical stone (that is, based in a physical stone-built temple in a physical stone-built Jerusalem with a law that was written on stone tablets by Moses). Jesus established the kingdom in a new world age in which we are now the temple of God, He dwells in us, and together we are the New Jerusalem, His Bride. The law is no longer written on stone but is now written in our hearts. God now dwells in us and the kingdom is within us to expand His reign over the earth.

For a thorough examination of the historical record of the Second Coming and the fulfilment of the signs leading up to it there is a great deal of information available online at revelationrevolution.org

What about the resurrection?

Am I saying that the resurrection and judgment have also occurred in 70 AD and there is no future resurrection and judgment? Yes, I am, because it was referring to the end of that old covenant age and not the end of the world.

A vast host of spiritual bodies was seen rising out of the earth at the sound of a trumpet in what appears to be a literal resurrection during the year of the second coming. Portions of this event are recorded by no less than five Roman historians.

Now I say this, brethren, that flesh and blood cannot inherit the kingdom of God; nor does the perishable inherit the imperishable. Behold, I tell you a mystery; we will not all sleep, but we will all be changed, in a moment, in the twinkling of an eye, at the last trumpet; for the trumpet will sound, and the dead will be raised imperishable, and we will be changed. For this perishable must put on the imperishable, and this mortal must put on immortality. But when this perishable will have put on the imperishable, and this mortal will have put on immortality, then will come about the saying that is written, "Death is swallowed up in victory." (1 Corinthians 15:50-54).

But we do not want you to be uninformed, brethren, about those who are asleep, so that you will not grieve as do the rest who have no hope. For if we believe that Jesus died and rose again, even so God will bring with Him those who have fallen asleep in Jesus. For this we say to you by the word of the Lord, that we who are alive and remain until the coming of the Lord, will not precede those who have fallen asleep. For the Lord Himself will descend from heaven with a shout, with the voice of the archangel and with the trumpet of God, and the dead in Christ will rise first. Then we who are alive and remain will be caught up together with them in the clouds to meet the Lord in the air, and so we shall always be with the Lord. Therefore comfort one another with these words. (1 Thessalonians 4:13-18).

The resurrection had its first fruits when the graves opened on the actual day of resurrection but the 70 AD resurrection was primarily spiritual in nature.

Daniel 12 places the resurrection with the destruction, not separated by thousands of years.

And at that time stand up doth Michael, the great head, who is standing up for the sons of thy people, and there hath been a time of distress, such as hath not been since there hath been a nation till that time, and at that time do thy people escape, everyone who is found written in the book. And the multitude of those sleeping in the dust of the ground do awake, some to life age-during, and some to reproaches – to abhorrence age-during. (Daniel 12:1-2 YLT).

Jesus linked judgment and resurrection, as Daniel did, with His coming at the end on the last day. Therefore whatever Daniel and Jesus meant by judgment, the resurrection took place in the first century not sometime in our future. Obviously this idea is contradictory to what most Christians have been programmed to believe but the assumptions of the majority do not necessarily make it true.

The truth is independent of man's conclusions and is Christocentric. The truth cannot be discerned from Bible study, the creeds, current orthodoxy or in Christian traditions, even if they are two thousand years old. The truth may only truly be found in Jesus, who is the Way, the Truth and the Life. Jesus said that the day of resurrection and judgment of both the just and unjust would be on the last day; and that day would occur at the end of the age, during that generation.

The apostles, following the teaching of Jesus, shared this expectation that put His coming firmly within that generation then living. The writers of the letters or epistles, now included in what we call the New Testament, wrote to the different congregations of believers living at the time to help them understand and be ready for the imminent return that Jesus promised. Those writers addressed many cultural issues that were relevant to their readers and hearers but are no longer relevant to us today, including women not being able to teach, women having to wear head coverings, not eating meat sacrificed to idols, the imminent second coming of Jesus and many others.

The disciples of Jesus who had heard Him teach about His return in that generation asked the question about His coming when Jesus linked that coming with the destruction of the temple. The disciples first used the word *parousia* (as recorded in Matthew 24:3) to describe His coming as an arrived presence and Jesus went on to define the signs linked to the events Daniel prophesied.

Paul, Peter, James, John and the writer of Hebrews all placed the second coming event and all that it meant as a very imminent event, soon to occur. They were not wrong like the countless thousands who have since predicted that the second coming would occur in their lifetimes.

For yet in a very little while,
He who is coming will come, and will not delay.
(Hebrews 10:37).

Those believers anticipated the time being so short that they asked Paul if it was even worth getting married. Paul responds that the time is shortened and that form of the world was passing away.

But this I say, brethren, the time has been shortened, so that from now on those who have wives should be as though they had none; and those who weep, as though they did not weep; and those who rejoice, as though they did not rejoice; and those who buy, as though they did not possess; and those who use the world, as though they did not make full use of it; for the form of this world is passing away. (1 Corinthians 7: 29-31).

Paul argued that their behaviour should be good even if the time was fast approaching and the day nearly over.

Do this, knowing the time, that it is already the hour for you to awaken from sleep; for now salvation is nearer to us than when we believed. The night is almost gone, and the day is near. Therefore let us lay aside the deeds of darkness and put on the armor of light. Let us behave properly as in the day... (Romans 13:11-13).

The end of all things is near; therefore, be of sound judgment and sober spirit for the purpose of prayer. Above all, keep fervent in your love for one another, because love covers a multitude of sins. (1 Peter 4:7-8).

The Revelation of Jesus Christ, which God gave Him to show to His bond-servants, the things which must soon take place; and He sent and communicated it by His angel to His bond-servant John. (Revelation 1:1).

Paul could not have been any clearer when writing to the Corinthians about the imminence of the Second Coming. Jesus would keep the Corinthians strong until His coming, which would be a pointless statement if that coming was to be thousands of years later.

... so that you are not lacking in any gift, awaiting eagerly the revelation of our Lord Jesus Christ, who will also confirm you to the end, blameless in the day of our Lord Jesus Christ. (1 Corinthians 1: 7-8).

John placed his readers in the last hour: the time was short, the day was at hand, the end was near and they would find relief at Jesus' coming. He linked the last hour with the opposition of the antichrist spirit operating in the world at that time:

Children, it is the last hour; and just as you heard that antichrist is coming, even now many antichrists have appeared; from this we know that it is the last hour. (1 John 2:18).

Jesus had warned the disciples that false teachers would come: John, knowing that, referred to them as 'antichrist' and revealed that they were already in the world. As a result of persecution many would betray them but those days would be shortened to ensure the remnant survived.

At that time many will fall away and will betray one another and hate one another. Many false prophets will arise and will mislead many. Because lawlessness is increased, most people's love will grow cold... For then there will be a great tribulation, such as has not occurred since the beginning of the world until now, nor ever will. Unless those days had been cut short, no life would have been saved; but for the sake of the elect those days will be cut short. (Matthew 24:10-12, 21-22).

... and every spirit that does not confess Jesus is not from God; this is the spirit of the antichrist, of which you have heard that it is coming, and now it is already in the world. (1 John 4:3).

For many deceivers have gone out into the world, those who do not acknowledge Jesus Christ as coming in the flesh. This is the deceiver and the antichrist. (2 John 1:7).

The antichrist was not a specific person who would appear at the end of world history to deceive the world but the fulfilment of Jesus' warning of false teachers at that time. The sign was fulfilled and John announced the last hour that he would later go on to write about in the book of Revelation.

For after all it is only just for God to repay with affliction those who afflict you, and to give relief to you who are afflicted and to us as well when the Lord Jesus will be revealed from heaven with His mighty angels in flaming fire... (2 Thessalonians 1:6-7).

Paul and James also linked the coming of Jesus to His appearing and His kingdom and to the judgment and, by inference, resurrection from the dead.

I solemnly charge you in the presence of God and of Christ Jesus, who is to judge the living and the dead, and by His appearing and His kingdom... (2 Timothy 4:1).

You too be patient; strengthen your hearts, for the coming of the Lord is near. Do not complain, brethren, against one another, so that you yourselves may not be judged; behold, the Judge is standing right at the door. (James 5:8-9).

No one can come to Me unless the Father who sent Me draws him; and I will raise him up on the last day. (John 6:44).

Martha said to Him, "I know that he will rise again in the resurrection on the last day." Jesus said to her, "I am the resurrection and the life; he who believes in Me will live even if he dies, and everyone who lives and believes in Me will never die. Do you believe this?" She said to Him, "Yes, Lord; I have believed that You are the Christ, the Son of God, even He who comes into the world." (John 11:24-27).

If anyone hears My sayings and does not keep them, I do not judge him; for I did not come to judge the world, but to save the world. He who rejects Me and does not receive My sayings, has one who judges him; the word I spoke is what will judge him at the last day. (John 12:47-48).

The resurrection of the just and the unjust is that which takes place at the coming of the Lord. Several passages show that the resurrection of the just and the unjust accompany the coming of the Lord. We have already mentioned several, such as 2 Timothy 4:1; and in Revelation 19-20 John records Jesus' coming at the end of the age, the emptying of Hades and the judgment of all men.

When trying to understand what appear to be confusing events from a modern perspective, we must let the Bible interpret itself and follow the divine logic: if A equals B and B equals C, then A must equal C. What do I mean?

- The resurrection of the just and the unjust takes place at the coming of the Lord.
- The coming of the Lord took place in 70 AD.
- Therefore, the resurrection of the just and the unjust took place in 70 AD.

To fully do justice to this reasoning and logic, the Bible would reveal these parallels between the coming in 70 AD and the resurrection and judgment that closed the age. These parallels are clear when what Jesus taught in Matthew 24 and 25 is compared with what Paul taught in 1 Thessalonians 4-5 and 1 Corinthians 15 (and with what Daniel prophesied).

If A is Matthew 24 and 25 and B is 1 Thessalonians 4-5 and C is 1 Corinthians 15 then A=B=C.

The language used in the individual passages is strikingly similar because it is describing the same second coming event that would close that age and result in the resurrection and judgment. It is only our conditioning and programming that makes us miss these facts because we are always looking for the literal and physical not the symbolic and spiritual.

Jesus' coming ended the old and established the new, and His teaching about His coming was in that context; it was never about personal resurrection and judgment (although I am not denying the reality of the judgment of the cross and humanity being pronounced not guilty and included in Christ, as we all died with Him and are all made alive in Him). *God was in Christ reconciling the whole world to Himself* (2 Corinthians 5:19), therefore there is no longer any separation from God's perspective. The separation that existed between Jew and Gentile was removed: Paul described this figuratively in Ephesians 1 as the middle wall being removed so that there would only be one new man in Christ. This was resurrected mankind, as the old died and was made obsolete and the new was revealed.

Or do you not know that all of us who have been baptized into Christ Jesus have been baptized into His death? Therefore we have been buried with Him through baptism into death, so that as Christ was raised from the dead through the glory of the Father, so we too might walk in newness of life. For if we have become united with Him in the likeness of His death, certainly we shall also be in the likeness of His resurrection... (Romans 6:3-5).

But now Christ has been raised from the dead, the first fruits of those who are asleep. For since by a man came death, by a man also came the resurrection of the dead. For as in Adam all die, so also in Christ all will be made alive. But each in his own order: Christ the first fruits, after that those who are Christ's at His coming, then comes the end, when He hands over the kingdom to the God and Father, when He has abolished all rule and all authority and power. For He must reign until He has put all His enemies under His feet. The last enemy that will be abolished is death. (1 Corinthians 15:20-26).

Paul used the analogy of physical death and transition to describe the old being transformed into the new. This was the resurrection that took place biblically at Jesus' return in 66-70 AD when the old covenant corporate body of Israel had entered into its 'last days', was 'soon to vanish' and would be transformed into the spiritual glorious new covenant corporate body of the Church ("the Israel of God").

During the Second Coming event, a transition, transformation or resurrection process took place. Eventually, in 70 AD, Abraham's Bosom or Sheol/Hades was emptied and the souls of those who accepted Jesus' preaching of the good news and inherited eternal life would experience being in the presence of God; and if any refused to accept Jesus they would go to the lake of fire for refining and purification.

In 70 AD there was also a covenantal transformation or resurrection where the middle wall of partition was fully removed and all were included in Jesus. The church did not replace physical Israel as the people of God: it was the continuation of those who by faith were truly Israel, which was never by ethnicity or religious practice. Paul describes this process as two becoming one, in which Jewish and Gentile believers in Jesus were one new covenant man, the Israel of God and true Jews: those circumcised of heart, not flesh.

This is the *ekklesia* that Jesus said He would build and is the New Jerusalem from above whose gates are never shut and a spiritual temple, a new wineskin. There is no longer any division between Jew and Gentile: there is no earthly physical people (the Jews) and a separate heavenly people (the church).

Therefore remember that formerly you, the Gentiles in the flesh, who are called "Uncircumcision" by the so-called "Circumcision," which is performed in the flesh by human hands – remember that you were at that time separate from Christ, excluded from the commonwealth of Israel, and strangers to the covenants of promise, having no hope and without God in the world. But now in Christ Jesus you who formerly were far off have been brought near by the blood of Christ. For He Himself is our peace, who made both groups into one and broke down the barrier of the dividing wall, by abolishing in His flesh the enmity, which is the Law of commandments contained in ordinances, so that in Himself He might make the two into one new man, thus establishing peace, and might reconcile them both in one body to God through the cross, by it having put to death the enmity. And He came and preached peace to you who were far away, and peace to those who were near; for through Him we both have our access in one Spirit to the Father. So then you are no longer strangers and aliens, but you are fellow citizens with the saints, and are of God's household, having been built on the foundation of the apostles and prophets, Christ Jesus Himself being the corner stone, in whom the whole building, being fitted together, is growing into a holy temple in the Lord, in whom you also are being built together into a dwelling of God in the Spirit. (Ephesians 2:11-22).

Now the promises were spoken to Abraham and to his seed. He does not say, "And to seeds," as referring to many, but rather to one, "And to your seed," that is, Christ... There is neither Jew nor Greek, there is neither slave nor free man, there is neither male nor female; for you are all one in Christ Jesus. (Galatians 3:16, 28).

For in Christ Jesus neither circumcision nor uncircumcision means anything, but faith working through love. (Galatians 5:6).

... and have put on the new self who is being renewed to a true knowledge according to the image of the One who created him – a renewal in which there is no distinction between Greek and Jew, circumcised and uncircumcised, barbarian, Scythian, slave and freeman, but Christ is all, and in all. (Colossians 3:10-11).

For he is not a Jew who is one outwardly, nor is circumcision that which is outward in the flesh. But he is a Jew who is one inwardly; and circumcision is that which is of the heart, by the Spirit, not by the letter; and his praise is not from men, but from God. (Romans 2:28-29).

For neither is circumcision anything, nor uncircumcision, but a new creation. And those who will walk by this rule, peace and mercy be upon them, and upon the Israel of God. (Galatians 6:15-16).

For the promise to Abraham or to his descendants that he would be heir of the world was not through the Law, but through the righteousness of faith. (Romans 4:13).

For this reason it is by faith, in order that it may be in accordance with grace, so that the promise will be guaranteed to all the descendants, not only to those who are of the Law, but also to those who are of the faith of Abraham, who is the father of us all... (Romans 4:16).

But you are a chosen race, a royal priesthood, a holy nation, a people for God's own possession, so that you may proclaim the excellencies of Him who has called you out of darkness into His marvelous light; for you once were not a people, but now you are the people of God; you had not received mercy, but now you have received mercy. (1 Peter 2:9-10).

Post 70 AD, death was defeated and life and immortality brought to light through the gospel; but if anyone dies, their soul/spirit experiences a transformation/resurrection from their earthly body to their spiritual body and they then enter fully into the new covenant spiritual body in the heavenly/spiritual realms.

The focus of resurrection has been moved by evangelicals from what Jesus stated (that He is the resurrection and the life) to our personal, individual, bodily resurrection. The promise available in Jesus is resurrection and abundant life, because Jesus overcomes and triumphs over death by taking back the keys of death and Hades from Satan. As N.T. Wright observes[36], "1 Corinthians 15 is primarily about the renewal of creation and covenant through Christ."

When thinking about the resurrection we all have nearly two thousand years of religious and traditional conditioning and programming to overcome if we are to see the simple truth that mankind has already been resurrected, born from above, indwelt by the Holy Spirit and included in Christ.

Futurists have made the resurrection that was a present hope to Jesus' disciples to be something that only happens when we die or at a judgment at the end of the world. Jesus told His

---

[36] N.T. Wright: *Paul,* pp28-39.

disciples that they would know by experience on the resurrection day that they would be in Him and in the Father:

After a little while the world will no longer see Me, but you will see Me; because I live, you will live also. In that day you will know that I am in My Father, and you in Me, and I in you. (John 14:19-20).

That day has been put off to when Jesus returns to take us to heaven in the future. This is accomplished by twisting Jesus' teaching in John 14:1-3 to mean that He was going to heaven to make mansions for us to live in and would return from heaven thousands of years later to take us there.

A closer inspection beyond the programming will reveal that Jesus was talking about going to the cross and being resurrected to make us a dwelling place for God to live in. 'Where I am' was not a statement about physical location but about His relationship within the Father. The disciples' hearts were troubled because Jesus had told them He was going to leave them, so He developed the argument for them throughout the discourse recorded in John chapters 13 and 14:

"Little children, I am with you a little while longer. You will seek Me; and as I said to the Jews, now I also say to you, 'Where I am going, you cannot come.'" (John 13:33).

Jesus assured them that, although they could not come with Him, He would return to make them into a temple, a house for God to dwell in. They would know that (not intellectually, of course, but by experience) on a specific day that was to come soon, not thousands of years later.

"Do not let your heart be troubled; believe in God, believe also in Me. In My Father's house are many dwelling places; if it were not so, I would have told you; for I go to prepare a place

for you. If I go and prepare a place for you, I will come again and receive you to Myself, that where I am, there you may be also. (John 14:1-3).

"Do you not believe that I am in the Father, and the Father is in Me? The words that I say to you I do not speak on My own initiative, but the Father abiding in Me does His works." (John 14:10).

"I will not leave you as orphans; I will come to you. After a little while the world will no longer see Me, but you will see Me; because I live, you will live also. In that day you will know that I am in My Father, and you in Me, and I in you. He who has My commandments and keeps them is the one who loves Me; and he who loves Me will be loved by My Father, and I will love him and will disclose Myself to him." (John 14:18-21).

This day was fulfilled on the day of Jesus' physical resurrection that would also be the day of the disciples' – and mankind's – spiritual resurrection. This occurred when Jesus breathed on them, as representatives of mankind, just as the Father had done with Adam, to receive the Holy Spirit. These were the first fruits of resurrection that would be finalised when Jesus returned in 70 AD.

So when it was evening on that day, the first day of the week, and when the doors were shut where the disciples were, for fear of the Jews, Jesus came and stood in their midst and said to them, "Peace be with you." And when He had said this, He showed them both His hands and His side. The disciples then rejoiced when they saw the Lord. So Jesus said to them again, "Peace be with you; as the Father has sent Me, I also send you." And when He had said this, He breathed on them and said to them, "Receive the Holy Spirit..." (John 20:19-22).

Neither Jesus nor Paul anticipated or predicted a future-to-us rising of the dead at the end of time or human history. This is the view I once held, but I now realise that this is simply not what the Bible teaches. Why do I no longer believe that? The answer is both because of my personal experience and that Jesus' eschatology was completed in that generation in 70 AD.

It is not flesh and blood that will inherit the kingdom and therefore the kingdom is not of this world politically or physically; the kingdom is within us and is spiritual – but that has a real physical effect.

Now having been questioned by the Pharisees as to when the kingdom of God was coming, He answered them and said, "The kingdom of God is not coming with signs to be observed; nor will they say, 'Look, here it is!' or, 'There it is!' For behold, the kingdom of God is in your midst" [literally, 'within you']. (Luke 17:20-21).

Jesus answered, "My kingdom is not of this world. If My kingdom were of this world, then My servants would be fighting so that I would not be handed over to the Jews; but as it is, My kingdom is not of this realm." (John 18:36).

Jesus answered, "Truly, truly, I say to you, unless one is born of water and the Spirit he cannot enter into the kingdom of God. That which is born of the flesh is flesh, and that which is born of the Spirit is spirit. (John 3:5-6).

Now I say this, brethren, that flesh and blood cannot inherit the kingdom of God; nor does the perishable inherit the imperishable. (1 Corinthians 15:50).

The resurrection is a spiritual regeneration that has already occurred for all of mankind and reveals immortality as our inheritance.

...who has saved us and called us with a holy calling, not according to our works, but according to His own purpose and grace which was granted us in Christ Jesus from all eternity, but now has been revealed by the appearing of our Savior Christ Jesus, who abolished death and brought life and immortality to light through the gospel... (2 Timothy 1:9-10).

The fulfilment of the resurrection in 70 AD defines the resurrection as a 'covenantal resurrection'. Paul uses covenantal terminology in 2 Corinthians 3, describing how the resurrection brings Israel out of the 'ministry of old covenant death' into the 'ministry of new covenant life.' The difference between the dead letter that has now faded away and the living Spirit who is within is the difference between the old and new covenants.

Not that we are adequate in ourselves to consider anything as coming from ourselves, but our adequacy is from God, who also made us adequate as servants of a new covenant, not of the letter but of the Spirit; for the letter kills, but the Spirit gives life. But if the ministry of death, in letters engraved on stones, came with glory, so that the sons of Israel could not look intently at the face of Moses because of the glory of his face, fading as it was, how will the ministry of the Spirit fail to be even more with glory? For if the ministry of condemnation has glory, much more does the ministry of righteousness abound in glory. For indeed what had glory, in this case has no glory because of the glory that surpasses it. For if that which fades away was with glory, much more that which remains is in glory. Therefore having such a hope, we use great boldness in our speech, and are not like Moses, who used to put a veil over his face so that the sons of Israel would not look intently at the end of what was fading away. But their minds were hardened; for until this very day at the reading of the old covenant the same veil remains unlifted, because it is removed in Christ. But to this day whenever Moses is read, a veil lies over their heart; but whenever a person turns to the Lord, the veil is taken away. Now the Lord is the Spirit, and where the Spirit of the Lord is, there is liberty. But we all, with unveiled face, beholding as in a mirror the glory of the Lord, are being transformed into the same image from glory to glory, just as from the Lord, the Spirit. (2 Corinthians 3: 5-18).

The Bible describes a first resurrection, a spiritual resurrection and a resurrection of the rest of those who died: I believe all these things are past and present realities, not future events. Those who participated in the 'first resurrection' in that generation were the first century Jewish 'first fruits' or the figurative 144,000 who were the first to believe in Christ and continued in the faith through the great tribulation until the end. The 144,000 were figurative representatives of the 12 tribes of Israel, therefore all Israel were symbolically saved in the resurrection event predicted by Daniel and associated with the destruction event. This was not a physical but a spiritual resurrection, which is a challenge to many because of the effective programming of evangelical theology.

Jesus taught that people would come out of their 'graves' through the preaching of the gospel (John 5:24-27) and would participate and be joined with the rest of the dead in the consummative resurrection event. Therefore they would partake in the harvest or resurrection at the end of the old covenant age.

"Truly, truly, I say to you, he who hears My word, and believes Him who sent Me, has eternal life, and does not come into judgment, but has passed out of death into life. Truly,

truly, I say to you, an hour is coming and now is, when the dead will hear the voice of the Son of God, and those who hear will live. For just as the Father has life in Himself, even so He gave to the Son also to have life in Himself; and He gave Him authority to execute judgment, because He is the Son of Man. (John 5:24-27).

Many have assumed that the resurrection of Revelation 20 at the end of the millennium and what Jesus described as the 'last hour' or 'coming hour' harvest and resurrection teaching in John 5 are both discussing a biological resurrection of corpses at the end of time. For most people, resurrection only means a future physical resurrection of the body so they are not able to correctly differentiate what is physical and what is spiritual when the Bible speaks of resurrection.

Do not marvel at this; for an hour is coming, in which all who are in the tombs will hear His voice, and will come forth; those who did the good deeds to a resurrection of life, those who committed the evil deeds to a resurrection of judgment. (John 5:28-29).

Surely these verses must be a physical resurrection! What else could Jesus have meant? John 5:28-29 must be seen in the context of the previous verses, John 5:25-27.

Truly, truly, I say to you, an hour is coming and now is, when the dead will hear the voice of the Son of God, and those who hear will live. For just as the Father has life in Himself, even so He gave to the Son also to have life in Himself; and He gave Him authority to execute judgment, because He is the Son of Man. (John 5:25-27).

Jesus preached – and the disciples preached – to those who were dead in their trespasses and sins; they 'heard the voice of the Son of God and lived' when they realised the truth that they were all made alive in Christ. Jesus was referring to the preaching of the gospel which took place at Pentecost where Peter preached to the physical living but spiritually dead about the power of the resurrection. Those who were spiritually 'dead' heard the good news preached and came to the realisation that they were spiritually resurrected. The power of the gospel over death meant that not only were those who were physically alive able to receive the good news but also those who were actually 'in the grave,' as Jesus described them. They were the dead in Sheol (or Hades) and Jesus preached to them also, as Peter later revealed in his first letter:

For Christ also died for sins once for all, the just for the unjust, so that He might bring us to God, having been put to death in the flesh, but made alive in the spirit; in which also He went and made proclamation to the spirits now in prison... (1 Peter 3:18-19).

For the gospel has for this purpose been preached even to those who are dead, that though they are judged in the flesh as men, they may live in the spirit according to the will of God. (1 Peter 4:6).

Jesus expanded the power and scope of the resurrection in His teaching to include those who were not only spiritually dead but also those who were also physically dead. Jesus did in fact preach to those who were in Sheol when He descended into death.

Jesus was consistent with His teaching and there are many parallels, for example between John 4:21, 23 and John 5:25, 28, where the same figurative language is used to convey the same timeframe and event.

*Jesus said to her, "Believe Me, woman, that **a time is coming** when you will worship the Father neither on this mountain nor in Jerusalem... But **a time is coming, and even now has arrived,** when the true worshipers will worship the Father in spirit and truth; for such people the Father seeks to be His worshipers."* (John 4:21, 23, emphasis mine).

*"Truly, truly, I say to you, **a time is coming and even now has arrived,** when the dead will hear the voice of the Son of God, and those who hear will live... Do not marvel at this; for **an hour is coming,** in which all who are in the tombs will hear His voice..."* (John 5:25, 28, emphasis mine).

These two sets of Jesus' prophecies are parallel. They speak of the same periods:

1. Pentecost (30 AD) where the true worshipers would worship the Father in spirit and in truth and the dead would hear the voice of the Son of God and live.

2. The fall of Jerusalem (70 AD) where God's worshipers would no longer worship Him in Jerusalem and all who were in the graves would hear His voice.

Jesus was drawing on the prophecy of Daniel 12:2 for His teaching on the resurrection in John 5:28-29 – it is the only Old Testament prophecy that mentions a resurrection for both the righteous and the unrighteous. Jesus preached to those who were in Abraham's bosom (the righteous Old Testament saints) and the unrighteous in the figurative fire of Sheol. Both groups accepted Jesus and were both physically and spiritually resurrected.

Many of those who sleep in the dust of the ground will awake, these to everlasting life, but the others to disgrace and everlasting contempt. (Daniel 12:2).

Daniel links the resurrection with the destruction of Jerusalem and the great tribulation, which is the 'time of distress' and the 'abomination of desolation' that Jesus referred to as recorded in Matthew 24, and He explained that all of those things would be occurring in that generation.

... And there will be a time of distress such as never occurred since there was a nation until that time; and at that time your people, everyone who is found written in the book, will be rescued... I heard the man dressed in linen, who was above the waters of the river, as he raised his right hand and his left toward heaven, and swore by Him who lives forever that it would be for a time, times, and half a time; and as soon as they finish shattering the power of the holy people, all these events will be completed. (Daniel 12:1, 7).

Daniel asked the angel what these events meant and the answer is illuminating for understanding what constitutes the 'end time'. Daniel prophesied about the end of the old covenant, where the power of Israel, the holy people, was shattered and about the resurrection at the end of that age, in which Daniel himself would also be raised and enter into rest.

As for me, I heard but could not understand; so I said, "My lord, what will be the outcome of these events?" He said, "Go your way, Daniel, for these words are concealed and sealed up until the end time. Many will be purged, purified and refined, but the wicked will act wickedly; and none of the wicked will understand, but those who have insight will understand. From the time that the regular sacrifice is abolished and the abomination of desolation is set up, there will be 1,290 days. How blessed is he who keeps waiting and attains to the 1,335 days! But as for you, go your way to the end; then you will enter into rest and rise again for your allotted portion at the end of the age." (Daniel 12:8-13).

So John 5 and Daniel 12 are describing these same two events: Pentecost (30 AD) and the Fall of Jerusalem (70 AD).

Pentecost (30 AD):

Daniel 12:1: *"And at that hour..."*

John 5:25: *"...an hour is coming and now is..."*

Daniel 12:2: *"Many of those who sleep in the dust of the ground will awake, these to everlasting life, but the others to disgrace and everlasting contempt.*

John 5:24: *"...he who hears My word, and believes Him who sent Me, has eternal life, and does not come into judgment, but has passed out of death into life."*

Fall of Jerusalem (70 AD):

Daniel 12:1: *"And at that hour..."*

John 5:28: *"...for an hour is coming, in which all who are in the tombs will hear His voice,"*

Daniel 12:2: *"Many of those who sleep in the dust of the ground will awake, these to everlasting life, but the others to disgrace and everlasting contempt.*

John 5:29: *"and will come forth; those who did the good deeds to a resurrection of life, those who committed the evil deeds to a resurrection of judgment."*

It is vitally important to let the Bible interpret the Bible so that the dots are joined and parallels seen. There is no need to fantasise and futurise these Bible verses as the dispensationalists have to do to fit their interpretation.

John uses the same language in his letters and the book of Revelation.

1 John 2:18: *"Dear children it is the last hour..."*

Revelation 14:7: *"...the hour of His judgment has come."*

The correlation between John and Daniel confirms this imminent 70 AD end of the old to be the millennium of Revelation by describing the same imminent resurrection of all the dead. Paul was expecting this imminent, 'soon to be', resurrection event, as he used that expectation in his defence to Felix:

*"And I confess this to thee, that, according to the way that they call a sect, so serve I the God of the fathers, believing all things that in the law and the prophets have been written, having hope toward God, which they themselves also wait for, [that] there **is about to be** a rising again of the dead, both of righteous and unrighteous..."* (Acts 24:14-15 YLT, emphasis mine).

There are further parallels between Matthew 27, Revelation 20 and Ezekiel 37 (the rising of the dry bones) and many others that you can pursue if you wish to.

To sum up the gist of the teaching on the resurrection in the New Testament:

Matthew 27 describes the physical resurrection of some Old Testament saints who were a sign of what was to come; they witnessed in Jerusalem but still died again physically, just like Lazarus.

All mankind was resurrected and included in Christ on the day of resurrection when Jesus breathed on His disciples (representing everyone).

During the generation-long period after Jesus' ascension, there was the Great Commission preaching of the gospel, through which the resurrection or salvation of the soul brought people out of death and darkness into life and light of eternal life.

During the same 30-70 AD period there was a corporate and covenantal resurrection by which the old covenant Israel or body was being metamorphosed, changed, transformed by being raised into the new covenant Israel or body: one new man in Christ, made up of Jews and Gentiles, between which there was and is no distinction made.

There was a resurrection of souls from *Sheol*, *Hades* or Abraham's Bosom to inherit eternal life, becoming alive in Christ and overcoming the spiritual death that came from Adam.

There was preaching to those in *Sheol* who had not yet believed and an eventual leading captivity captive, as Paul described in Ephesians 4 and as referred to in Acts 24:15.

There was an 'already' resurrection day and 'day of Pentecost' aspect of resurrection and a 'not yet' aspect to be finally consummated at the end of the age in 70 AD. Paul alluded to this 'already and not yet' in the letter to the Philippians:

... that I may know Him and the power of His resurrection and the fellowship of His sufferings, being conformed to His death; in order that I may attain to the resurrection from the dead. Not that I have already obtained it or have already become perfect, but I press on so that I may lay hold of that for which also I was laid hold of by Christ Jesus. Brethren, I do not regard myself as having laid hold of it yet; but one thing I do: forgetting what lies behind and reaching forward to what lies

ahead, I press on toward the goal for the prize of the upward call of God in Christ Jesus. (Philippians 3:10-14).

Rejoice in the Lord always; again I will say, rejoice! Let your gentle spirit be known to all men. The Lord is near. (Philippians 4:4-5).

Jesus' resurrection was the sign that the power of death had been broken and the first-fruits were the conquering of death and *Hades*. The power that death had over all mankind through Adam was broken through Jesus' resurrection. All died in Adam and the same 'all' are made alive in Christ.

But now Christ has been raised from the dead, the first fruits of those who are asleep. For since by a man came death, by a man also came the resurrection of the dead. For as in Adam all die, so also in Christ all will be made alive. But each in his own order: Christ the first fruits, after that those who are Christ's at His coming, then comes the end, when He hands over the kingdom to the God and Father, when He has abolished all rule and all authority and power. (1 Corinthians 15:20-24).

The resurrection also figuratively concerned old covenant Israel, who were symbolically dead and in the dust. Israel's resurrection from the powerlessness of old covenant religion is another aspect of resurrection that Paul refers to many times in his letters but this is mostly overlooked by futurists and literalist Zionists.

Daniel 12:2-3 is the clearest and most important Old Testament reference to the resurrection. Jesus and the New Testament writers reveal its fulfilment, as we have seen in Matthew 13:39-43; John 5; Acts 24:25; Revelation 20:5-15 and 1 Corinthians 15.

Jesus connected the 'end of the age' resurrection, 'gathering' and 'tribulation' period as being a part of the 'all these things' to be fulfilled in Himself during that generation (see Matthew 24:3-34). This 'end of the old covenant age' gathering is the same event Jesus described in Matthew 13:39-43.

Both Israel and the Church participated in this spiritual, covenantal and corporate resurrection: the new covenant church or 'New Israel of God' is raised out of the figurative corpse of old covenant Israel in 70 AD. During this period, the Great Commission of Matthew 28 was fulfilled as all Israel were being saved in the same way as the Gentiles were being saved – by the faith of the Son of God, Jesus.

During this period, as Jesus predicted, some would believe and be saved physically and some would not believe and perish or be lost physically. All believers fled Jerusalem before it was besieged and were saved from destruction because they heeded Jesus' warning to look for the signs that would occur in that generation, not thousands of years later.

Those who believed and were saved also realised the truth and that salvation was also spiritual. The nation became a corpse that the vultures circled, which was regenerated from dry bones and became the new covenant Israel of God, the one new man in Christ, from which all the families of the earth will be blessed.

Therefore I say to you, the kingdom of God will be taken away from you and given to a people producing its fruit. And the one who falls on this stone will be broken to pieces; and on whomever it falls, it will crush him." When the chief priests and the Pharisees heard His parables, they understood that He was speaking about them. (Matthew 21:43-45).

"The people who were sitting in darkness saw a great Light, And those who were sitting in the land and shadow of death, Upon them a Light dawned." (Matthew 4:16).

"Wherever the corpse is, there the vultures will gather." (Matthew 24:28).

"Truly I say to you, this generation will not pass away until all these things take place." (Matthew 24:34).

And Jesus said to them, "Truly I say to you, that you who have followed Me, in the regeneration when the Son of Man will sit on His glorious throne, you also shall sit upon twelve thrones, judging the twelve tribes of Israel." (Matthew 19:28).

The new covenant body of Israel was raised out from the old covenant body of Israel in 70 AD to become the body of Christ on earth as it is in heaven.

There is only one biblical 'end of the age' and that end incorporated the spiritual, progressive, corporate and covenantal resurrection of the righteous and unrighteous who were in *Sheol*. There was a period where there was a great harvest in Jerusalem, Judea, and Samaria and the good news spread to the whole of the known world.

Jesus predicted that the gospel would be preached in the whole world before the end of the age would come:

"This gospel of the kingdom shall be preached in the whole world as a testimony to all the nations, and then the end will come." (Matthew 24:14).

This was indeed fulfilled literally, as has been stated earlier.

The progressive nature of the Great Commission resulted in a great harvest of believers from amongst the Jews and Gentiles who became one new man in Christ. The spiritual division and separation had already been removed, as Paul made clear to the Ephesians, but the physical wall of partition, symbolically represented by the temple 'heavens and the earth' was finally removed and the 'new heavens and new earth' of the New Jerusalem were fully manifested on earth as it is in heaven. All were spiritually resurrected or born from above when Jesus symbolically breathed new life into the disciples.

When the new covenant body of Israel was raised from the corpse of the old covenant body of Israel, as an actual historic event in 70 AD, this also resulted in souls who were in *Sheol* being resurrected to inherit God's presence and eternal life (right then in 70 AD, at the end of the old covenant, at Jesus' second coming).

These events were described by Jesus and the New Testament writers and there are very clear parallels between what Jesus taught and what the epistles state, if only we can view them free from religious programming.

The judgment of Jesus coming with all His holy ones in Matthew 16:27 can be compared with 1 Thessalonians 3:13, 1 Corinthians 4:5 and Colossians 1:22, in which His judgment is to find His people holy and blameless. The term 'coming with His Holy ones and the angels' is found in both the gospels and the epistles:

For the Son of Man is going to come in the glory of His Father with His angels, and will then repay every person according to his deeds. (Matthew 16:27).

"For whoever is ashamed of Me and My words in this adulterous and sinful generation, the Son of Man will also be

ashamed of him when He comes in the glory of His Father with the holy angels." (Mark 8:38).

... so that He may establish your hearts blameless in holiness before our God and Father at the coming of our Lord Jesus with all His saints. (1 Thessalonians 3:13).

... and to give relief to you who are afflicted, along with us, when the Lord Jesus will be revealed from heaven with His mighty angels. (2 Thessalonians 1:7).

Therefore do not go on passing judgment before the time, but wait until the Lord comes, who will both bring to light the things hidden in the darkness and disclose the motives of human hearts; and then praise will come to each person from God. (1 Corinthians 4:5).

... yet He has now reconciled you in His body of flesh through death, in order to present you before Him holy and blameless and beyond reproach... (Colossians 1:22).

There was so much confusion relating to the second coming of Jesus in churches such as at Thessalonica that Paul had to write them two letters to correct the errors that surrounded an event that He expected both himself and his contemporary readers to participate in.

*Then **we** who are alive and remain will be caught up together with them in the clouds to meet the Lord in the air, and so we shall always be with the Lord.* (1 Thessalonians 4:17, emphasis mine).

Some were afraid that those who had already been martyred would somehow miss out on the second coming, so Paul wrote to comfort them by assuring them that there was no disadvantage to dying before Jesus came and that those alive would take no precedence over those who had died, since He would raise all on His return.

The prophesied events usually interpreted as describing a 'secret rapture' of the church needs to be interpreted in the above context. Those events include:

a. The descent of the Lord from heaven with a shout, with the voice of the archangel, and the trump of God.
b. The raising up of the dead who had died in Jesus.
c. The simultaneous catching up into the air of the living saints, along with the resurrected dead, to meet the coming Jesus.
d. The everlasting union of Jesus and His people in heaven.

But we do not want you to be uninformed, brethren, about those who are asleep, so that you will not grieve as do the rest who have no hope. For if we believe that Jesus died and rose again, even so God will bring with Him those who have fallen asleep in Jesus. For this we say to you by the word of the Lord, that we who are alive and remain until the coming of the Lord, will not precede those who have fallen asleep. For the Lord Himself will descend from heaven with a shout, with the voice of the archangel and with the trumpet of God, and the dead in Christ will rise first. Then we who are alive and remain will be caught up together with them in the clouds to meet the Lord in the air, and so we shall always be with the Lord. Therefore comfort one another with these words. (1 Thessalonians 4:13-18).

The first letter Paul wrote did not clear up all the confusion. Some were teaching that the coming of Jesus had already taken place and as a consequence some people had begun to neglect their jobs and live on the charity of others. Paul wrote his second letter to reveal more clearly what still needed to take place before the second coming. An argument has been used to place the focus of the epistle in the distant future: what do the inhabitants of a city like Thessalonica in ancient Greece have to do with the destruction of Jerusalem, and why would they be concerned about it? To answer that question you have to look at the persecution that all believers were facing at the hands of the Jews in each city. There were 'synagogues of Satan' wherever Paul went to preach the gospel; they stirred up trouble and incited persecution from the Roman authorities too.

... therefore, we ourselves speak proudly of you among the churches of God for your perseverance and faith in the midst of all your persecutions and afflictions which you endure. (2 Thessalonians 1:4).

"I know your tribulation and your poverty (but you are rich), and the blasphemy by those who say they are Jews and are not, but are a synagogue of Satan." (Revelation 2:9).

Behold, I will cause those of the synagogue of Satan, who say that they are Jews and are not, but lie – I will make them come and bow down at your feet, and make them know that I have loved you. (Revelation 3:9).

Now when they had travelled through Amphipolis and Apollonia, they came to Thessalonica, where there was a synagogue of the Jews. And according to Paul's custom, he went to them, and for three Sabbaths reasoned with them from the Scriptures... But the Jews, becoming jealous and taking along some wicked men from the market place, formed a mob and set the city in an uproar; and attacking the house of Jason, they were seeking to bring them out to the people. (Acts 17:1-2, 5).

In context, the letter to the Thessalonians was written to those who were being severely persecuted and were looking for the second coming to be a judgment on those inspired by the religious leaders of the Jews in Jerusalem. Paul writes to comfort the Thessalonians, indicating that the coming of Jesus would bring the salvation of deliverance from their persecutors, which would bring rest to them and retribution to their enemies. The second coming would be the time of judgment to the wicked, and the reward to the righteous, as Jesus taught.

The destruction of Jerusalem for their rebellion against Roman rule would have far-reaching consequences throughout the Roman Empire, where Jews were killed and taken captive in every city.

The apocalyptic language used by Paul is mirrored in Jesus' teachings. The approaching 'apocalypse' or 'revelation' of the Lord Jesus from heaven is identical with the coming predicted by Jesus: it was 'the day of the Lord'. Paul was teaching this message as a comfort to those who were being persecuted, encouraging them to hold on as judgment was coming soon. It is important to note that the language used of judgment has nothing to do with the concept of eternal conscious torment in 'hell' but refers to imminent judgment which would bring an end to the (old covenant) age they were living in. Any future after-death element would have been correctional, purifying and refining within the fire of God's presence. Jesus presented the fires of Gehenna as a present consequence to that generation, not an eternal one.

This is a plain indication of God's righteous judgment so that you will be considered worthy of the kingdom of God, for which indeed you are suffering. For after all it is only just for

God to repay with affliction those who afflict you, and to give relief to you who are afflicted and to us as well when the Lord Jesus will be revealed from heaven with His mighty angels in flaming fire, dealing out retribution to those who do not know God and to those who do not obey the gospel of our Lord Jesus. These will pay the penalty of eternal destruction, away from the presence of the Lord and from the glory of His power, when He comes to be glorified in His saints on that day, and to be marvelled at among all who have believed – for our testimony to you was believed. (2 Thessalonians 1:5-10).

Do you not remember that while I was still with you, I was telling you these things? And you know what restrains him now, so that in his time he will be revealed. For the mystery of lawlessness is already at work; only he who now restrains will do so until he is taken out of the way. Then that lawless one will be revealed whom the Lord will slay with the breath of His mouth and bring to an end by the appearance of His coming; that is, the one whose coming is in accord with the activity of Satan, with all power and signs and false wonders, and with all the deception of wickedness for those who perish, because they did not receive the love of the truth so as to be saved. (2 Thessalonians 2:5-10).

For just like the lightning, when it flashes out of one part of the sky, shines to the other part of the sky, so will the Son of Man be in His day. But first He must suffer many things and be rejected by this generation. And just as it happened in the days of Noah, so it will be also in the days of the Son of Man: they were eating, they were drinking, they were marrying, they were being given in marriage, until the day that Noah entered the ark, and the flood came and destroyed them all. It was the same as happened in the days of Lot: they were eating, they were drinking, they were buying, they were selling, they were planting, they were building; but on the day that Lot went out from Sodom it rained fire and brimstone from heaven and destroyed them all. It will be just the same on the day that the Son of Man is revealed. On that day, the one who is on the housetop and whose goods are in the house must not go down to take them out; and likewise the one who is in the field must not turn back. Remember Lot's wife. Whoever seeks to keep his life will lose it, and whoever loses his life will preserve it. (Luke 17:24-33).

... each one's work will become evident; for the day will show it because it is to be revealed with fire, and the fire itself will test the quality of each one's work. (1 Corinthians 3:13).

"For behold, the day is coming, burning like a furnace; and all the arrogant and every evildoer will be chaff; and the day that is coming will set them ablaze," says the Lord of armies, "so that it will leave them neither root nor branches... Behold, I am going to send you Elijah the prophet before the coming of the great and terrible day of the Lord." (Malachi 4:1, 5).

"For the Son of Man is going to come in the glory of His Father with His angels, and will then repay every person according to his deeds. Truly I say to you, there are some of those who are standing here who will not taste death until they see the Son of Man coming in His kingdom." (Matthew 16:27-28).

To clear up the confusion the Thessalonians were having about the timing and who would be affected, Paul explains the signs that were still to take place. These signs relate to apostasy, the man of lawlessness (or 'man of sin' in older translations) and to the mystery of lawlessness. These terms, taken out of context, have led to wild speculations about who this person is in our present day or will be in the future. To his readers, the language and context would have been much clearer and Paul gave no thought to who might read his letter two thousand years later. We must remember that Paul had been present in the flesh with the Thessalonians and had talked to them about these things, so his seeming hints and veiled descriptions would not have been unintelligible to them. Paul speaks of two issues as one event, and that mirrors Jesus' teaching: the coming of the Lord and the gathering of those in Christ.

The language is similar and Paul was declaring that the day of the Lord was at hand or imminent. The gathering together spoken of by Jesus is the same gathering that Paul spoke of to the Thessalonians and would occur at the coming (or on the day) of the Lord, which would be a day of resurrection and judgment. This is not talking about a physical, bodily resurrection at the end of the world but a gathering of both Jew and Gentile into one new resurrected man in Christ. The gathering together is the promise that they would be one body, the body of Christ, the New Jerusalem temple. The end of the age would occur and the judgment administered to end the old and begin the new.

And He will send forth His angels with a great trumpet and they will gather together His elect from the four winds, from one end of the sky to the other. (Matthew 24:31).

For the Lord Himself will descend from heaven with a shout, with the voice of the archangel and with the trumpet of God, and the dead in Christ will rise first. Then we who are alive and remain will be caught up together with them in the clouds to meet the Lord in the air, and so we shall always be with the Lord. (1 Thessalonians 4:16-17).

Behold, I tell you a mystery; we will not all sleep, but we will all be changed, in a moment, in the twinkling of an eye, at the last trumpet; for the trumpet will sound, and the dead will be raised imperishable, and we will be changed. (1 Corinthians 15:51-52).

This was the figurative summoning of the living and the dead to the court to observe the judgment.

Paul consistently presented the coming day of the Lord in resurrection and judgment as imminent and urged his readers to make sure that they were ready. Some have tried to use an erroneous translation in the King James Version to indicate that he was correcting himself and that Jesus' coming was not imminent and in fact is still future:

That ye be not soon shaken in mind, or be troubled, neither by spirit, nor by word, nor by letter as from us, as that the day of Christ is at hand. (2 Thessalonians 2:2 KJV).

... that ye be not quickly shaken in mind, nor be troubled, neither through spirit, neither through word, neither through letters as through us, as that the day of Christ hath arrived; (2 Thessalonians 2:2 YLT).

Paul does not correct himself and does not teach two different 'comings,' but he does correct the Thessalonians, some of whom thought that the day had already come. Many of them had abandoned even their homes and families and travelled to Jerusalem. Similar events have occurred during history because of the erroneous expectation of a still-future second coming. It is not surprising that the exact day and hour were never revealed and were specifically denied.

"But of that day and hour no one knows, not even the angels of heaven, nor the Son, but the Father alone. For the coming of the Son of Man will be just like the days of Noah. For as in those days before the flood they were eating and drinking,

marrying and giving in marriage, until the day that Noah entered the ark, and they did not understand until the flood came and took them all away; so will the coming of the Son of Man be. Then there will be two men in the field; one will be taken and one will be left. Two women will be grinding at the mill; one will be taken and one will be left. Therefore be on the alert, for you do not know which day your Lord is coming. But be sure of this, that if the head of the house had known at what time of the night the thief was coming, he would have been on the alert and would not have allowed his house to be broken into. For this reason you also must be ready; for the Son of Man is coming at an hour when you do not think He will." (Matthew 24:36-44).

I have included this passage from Matthew to show how these verses have been twisted to make them appear still future to us. The context is clear: the coming destruction of the temple and the end of the present age (that was to happen in that generation) would be like the days of Noah, where everyone was oblivious to the coming judgment and was living normally. The illustration of people working normally in the field or grinding corn followed the analogy of the days of Noah: the flood did come and some were taken away and lost in the flood and some were saved and remained on earth in the arc.

The taking of one person and leaving another is not a prediction of a future secret rapture when one person would just disappear, whisked away to heaven, but a warning to be aware and ready. This was a description of separation: one would be lost and one found, similar to the separation of sheep and goats nations. If this was meant to be taken literally, then who were taken, wheat or tares? In the parable of the wheat and tares (Matthew 13:24-30), Jesus had said that the tares would be taken first, not the wheat; so that would mean that the unrighteous would be taken and the righteous left behind! These Bible verses have been randomly plucked out of their actual context and stitched together to present a flawed eschatology that neither Jesus nor Paul ever taught. Some were literally saved and left Jerusalem, escaping the judgment, and some were literally taken away by the judgment.

Paul clarified that the time of the Lord's coming was still future to them, yet imminent. He did this by pointing to two events which were still take place, the coming of 'the apostasy' and the manifestation of 'the man of lawlessness.' The Thessalonians were filled with fears, expectations and apprehensions and Paul offered them words of comfort that they could understand. The timing of these events and the identity of this man have created great speculation for futurist eschatologists who try to link them to present-day figures and mistakenly connect the man of lawlessness with a personal antichrist figure.

The number of the beast

The apostasy was something Jesus and Paul warned about; encouraging the disciples to endure to the end, keep the faith, and fight the good fight of faith, in light of those whose love would grow cold:

Because lawlessness is increased, most people's love will grow cold. But the one who endures to the end, he will be saved. (Matthew 24:12-13).

But the Spirit explicitly says that in later times some will fall away from the faith, paying attention to deceitful spirits and doctrines of demons... (1 Timothy 4:1).

But realize this, that in the last days difficult times will come. For men will be lovers of self, lovers of money, boastful, arrogant, revilers, disobedient to parents, ungrateful, unholy, unloving, irreconcilable, malicious gossips, without self-control, brutal, haters of good, treacherous, reckless, conceited, lovers of pleasure rather than lovers of God, holding to a form of godliness, although they have denied its power; Avoid such men as these. (2 Timothy 3:1-5).

I have fought the good fight, I have finished the course, I have kept the faith; in the future there is laid up for me the crown of righteousness, which the Lord, the righteous Judge, will award to me on that day; and not only to me, but also to all who have loved His appearing. (2 Timothy 4:7-8).

Know this first of all, that in the last days mockers will come with their mocking, following after their own lusts, and saying, "Where is the promise of His coming?"... But by His word the present heavens and earth are being reserved for fire, kept for the day of judgment and destruction of ungodly men. (2 Peter 3:3-4, 7).

But the day of the Lord will come like a thief, in which the heavens will pass away with a roar and the elements will be destroyed with intense heat, and the earth and its works will be burned up. Since all these things are to be destroyed in this way, what sort of people ought you to be in holy conduct and godliness, looking for and hastening the coming of the day of God, because of which the heavens will be destroyed by burning, and the elements will melt with intense heat! But according to His promise we are looking for new heavens and a new earth, in which righteousness dwells. (2 Peter 3:10-13).

But false prophets also arose among the people, just as there will also be false teachers among you, who will secretly introduce destructive heresies, even denying the Master who bought them, bringing swift destruction upon themselves.

Many will follow their sensuality, and because of them the way of the truth will be maligned; and in their greed they will exploit you with false words; their judgment from long ago is not idle, and their destruction is not asleep. (2 Peter 2:1-3).

The book of Hebrews was filled with warnings against falling away from the truth, as it was a very tough time going through the persecution, and many did not endure to the end: Hebrews 2:1–4; 3:7–4:13; 5:11–6:12; 10:19–39; 12:1–29.

This apostasy is the context that John wrote about, the antichrist spirit that was already in evidence in those whose love was growing cold.

Children, it is the last hour; and just as you heard that antichrist is coming, even now many antichrists have appeared; from this we know that it is the **last hour***.* (1 John 2:18, emphasis mine).

Who is the liar but the one who denies that Jesus is the Christ? This is the antichrist, the one who denies the Father and the Son. (1 John 2:22).

... and every spirit that does not confess Jesus is not from God; this is the spirit of the antichrist, of which you have heard that it is coming, and now it is already in the world. (1 John 4:3).

For many deceivers have gone out into the world, those who do not acknowledge Jesus Christ as coming in the flesh. This is the deceiver and the antichrist. (2 John 1:7).

Who was the man of lawlessness in the same context, who was present at the end of that generation? Paul is speaking about someone whose influence was already beginning to be felt, whom the Thessalonians had 'talked about,' 'remembered,' and 'knew' – it must have been someone of importance and present in their contemporary timeframe.

Why did Paul not just name him, and why did John use code (666 or 616) to refer to him? There must have been some strong reason for this extreme caution: most likely because it was not safe to be more explicit. These letters were read aloud in public and they had to be careful of Jewish persecution because everywhere there were instigators 'stirring up the Gentiles' against the church. In Thessalonica itself, they had a mob stirred up by the accusation that they were against Caesar.

But the Jews, becoming jealous and taking along some wicked men from the market place, formed a mob and set the city in an uproar; and attacking the house of Jason, they were seeking to bring them out to the people. When they did not find them, they began dragging Jason and some brethren before the city authorities, shouting, "These men who have upset the world have come here also; and Jason has welcomed them, and they all act contrary to the decrees of Caesar, saying that there is another king, Jesus." (Acts 17:5-7).

Paul wrote in hints that they understood, but not openly because of Roman power, so that the Thessalonians could not be charged with sedition.

Who was Paul hinting that the man and lawlessness was? Was anyone existing in the Roman Empire to whom it applied? This was an individual who had power, was not Jewish, claimed to be God and desired to be worshipped, pretended to have miraculous power and is known for great wickedness and lawlessness. He was not yet fully in power and was hindered by someone the Thessalonians knew; and he would end up destroyed by the brightness of the Lord's coming.

The man of lawlessness was Caesar, the emperor Nero, whose name in Hebrew numerology was 666 (as identified by John in the book of Revelation). Nero was the first of the persecuting emperors. If you read the history books, he fitted the identity of the man of lawlessness perfectly. We must remember that we are looking back on the fulfilment but in 52 or 53 AD when the letter to the Thessalonians was written, things were still evolving. At that time in 52-53 AD, Nero was not yet emperor. His step-father, Claudius, still lived, and stood in the way of Nero (the son of his wife, Agrippina) taking the throne. Less than a year after the letter was received by the Thessalonians, Claudius was 'taken out of the way,' murdered by Agrippina; and according to Suetonius, Nero was complicit. Most of what is known historically about Nero's reign comes from three ancient writers: Tacitus, Suetonius, and the Greek historian Cassius Dioomes. From these sources, Nero must go down in history as one of the most infamous Roman emperors.

John gave many more cryptic, symbolically political clues to the identity of 'the beast' that fit with Paul's description of the man of lawlessness. These clues also fit with Daniel's prophecy about the end of the age.

Then I saw a beast coming up out of the sea, having ten horns and seven heads, and on his horns were ten diadems, and on his heads were blasphemous names. (Revelation 13:1).

Here is wisdom. Let him who has understanding calculate the number of the beast, for the number is that of a man; and his number is six hundred and sixty-six. (Revelation 13:18).

What about the mysterious number of the beast? The Hebrew *gematria* or assigning of numbers to the letters of the alphabet gives a clear understanding of who the beast was.

First, in Revelation 13:18 the number of the beast is the number of 'a man' and that number is '666.' A Hebrew spelling of Nero Caesar's name was *Nrwn Qsr*, which provides us with precisely the value of 666.

Second, the textual variant. If you consult a Bible with marginal references you may see a note saying "Some manuscripts read '616'." This is a numeric value derived from the Latin spelling of Nero Caesar. The geographical and political context of the symbolic language would not have been lost to the readers of the book, as the churches were all under Roman rule.

Here is the mind which has wisdom. The seven heads are seven mountains on which the woman sits, and they are seven kings; five have fallen, one is, the other has not yet come; and when he comes, he must remain a little while. The beast which was and is not, is himself also an eighth and is one of the seven, and he goes to destruction. The ten horns which you saw are ten kings who have not yet received a kingdom, but they receive authority as kings with the beast for one hour. These have one purpose, and they give their power and authority to the beast. (Revelation 17:9-13).

Blessed is he who reads and those who hear the words of the prophecy, and heed the things which are written in it; for the time is near. (Revelation 1:3).

John wrote to be understood, so we must look at audience relevance when seeking to understand the meaning of the apocalyptical symbols ourselves. He specifically points out here that the wise mind will understand:

Here is the mind which has wisdom. The seven heads are seven mountains on which the woman sits... (Revelation 17:9)

The reference points geographically to Rome, which is alluded to in the seven-headed beast John saw in the vision. The seven churches of Asia Minor that originally received the book of Revelation lived under the rule of Rome and would have understood the meaning of the reference to seven hills. The seven heads also have a political meaning, referring to the rulers of Rome, the Caesars.

...and they are seven kings; five have fallen, one is, the other has not yet come; and when he comes, he must remain a little while. (Revelation 17:10).

Nero was the sixth emperor of Rome. Josephus clearly points out that Julius Caesar was the first emperor of Rome and that he was followed in succession by Augustus, Tiberius, Caius (also called Caligula), Claudius, and, sixthly, Nero[37]. The facts are also confirmed in the writings of Roman historians Suetonius[38] and Cassius[39].

The text of Revelation says that of the seven kings, "five have fallen." These emperors were already dead when John wrote. But the verse goes on to say "one is." That is, the sixth one was then reigning as John wrote. That was Nero Caesar, who became emperor upon the death of the fifth emperor, Claudius, in October, 54 AD. Nero ruled until his suicide in 68 AD, a period of over thirteen years.

John continues: "The other is not yet come; and when he comes, he must continue a short time." As the Roman Civil Wars broke out in rebellion against him, Nero committed suicide on June 8, 68 AD. John informs us that the seventh king was "not yet come." That would be Galba, who assumed

---

[37] Josephus, *Antiquities*, books 18 and 19.
[38] Suetonius, *Lives of the Twelve Caesars*.
[39] Cassius, *Roman History 5*.

power upon Nero's death. But he was only to continue a "short while" – Galba's reign lasted only six months, until January 15, 69 AD. He was one of the quick succession of emperors in the famous era called by historians: "the year of the four emperors."

When John wrote the book of Revelation, the sixth emperor Nero was ruling from Rome; and Galba, the short-lived seventh emperor, was coming shortly.

Eusebius wrote: "Nero was the first of the emperors who showed himself an enemy of the divine religion." In his *Annals*, the Roman historian Tacitus names those who were persecuted as "those who... were vulgarly called Christians." Roman emperors pronounced themselves gods who were to be worshipped; Christians refused to worship any other so-called god and were persecuted. The image of the Emperor was at that time the object of religious reverence; he was a deity on earth, and the worship paid to him was real worship. Caligula (Caius) tried to set up his own statue in the temple in Jerusalem, which incited a Jewish rebellion.

The second coming of Jesus is connected with the destruction of Jerusalem; the death of Nero preceded that event. It took place in June, 68 AD, in the midst of the Jewish war which was to end in the capture and destruction of the city and the temple. In one sense the 'soon coming' of Jesus was a sign that triggered judgment on Nero as he began to reap the consequences of what he had sown.

There was another historical reason why Nero is branded with the name 'man of sin' (or lawlessness). The name 'man of sin' had already been given to Antiochus Epiphanes, a bitter enemy and persecutor of the Jewish people. He was the Nero of his age, the profaner of the temple and persecutor of the

Jewish people. In the first Book of Maccabees, we find the name 'the man the sinner' given to Antiochus (1 Maccabees 2:48, 62),

Why should the revelation of Nero as the man of lawlessness be a matter of such concern to Paul and the Christians of Thessalonica? Nero began to persecute Christians throughout the Roman Empire and it was under Nero's rule and by his orders that the final Jewish war was commenced, which ended in the siege and capture of Jerusalem, the destruction of the temple, and the end of the age and the Jewish world.

It is difficult to understand many New Testament letters without knowing how the readers understood them and what was relevant to them. Modern-day readers of the New Testament do not keep audience relevance in mind when trying to understand the meaning, and that is why many things seen from a modern perspective are open to wild speculation.

The futurist programming which has infected so much of Christianity makes it is easy for people to fall into the trap of trying to fit these things into our own time period. The early church had no such problem interpreting what appear to us to be veiled and confusing references.

When the Protestant reformers were persecuted for leaving Roman Catholicism the Pope became an easy target for accusations that he was 'the man of sin or lawlessness'. Throughout church history, whenever persecution arose, the identity of the beast, the man of lawlessness and the antichrist has been assigned to some historical figure. The reality is that the man of lawlessness was already operating at the time Paul wrote to the Thessalonians.

Do you not remember that while I was still with you, I was telling you these things? And you know what restrains him now, so that in his time he will be revealed. For the mystery of lawlessness is already at work; only he who now restrains will do so until he is taken out of the way. (2 Thessalonians 2: 5-7).

Some theologians say the person who was taken out of the way was the emperor Claudius; others say it was Paul himself.

"But be on your guard; for they will deliver you to the courts, and you will be flogged in the synagogues, and you will stand before governors and kings for My sake, as a testimony to them. ***The gospel must first be preached to all the nations.*** *When they arrest you and hand you over, do not worry beforehand about what you are to say, but say whatever is given you in that hour; for it is not you who speak, but it is the Holy Spirit. Brother will betray brother to death, and a father his child; and children will rise up against parents and have them put to death. You will be hated by all because of My name, but the one who endures to the end, he will be saved."* (Mark 13:9-13).

Some believe it was when Paul was executed just before 66 AD that it paved the way for these things to happen; but in either case, the key fact is that it was during that period and not thousands of years later.

Eagerly awaiting

It is important to look at other epistles and compare them with Jesus' teaching of the second coming, including the letters to the Corinthians. The two epistles to the church in Corinth are believed to have been written in the same year (57 AD) and although dealing with a wide variety of issues the church in

Corinth was facing, both allude to the anticipated coming of the Lord, the decisive 'day of the Lord' when all the doubts and difficulties of that present age would be resolved and all the persecutions redressed. The greatly anticipated event was always presented by Paul in his letters as being 'at hand' or 'about to take place'. This timing is alluded to and implied in his every reference to the subject. It is also directly affirmed as imminent in several passages within Paul's letters and that is the attitude that the Corinthians were encouraged to have.

I thank my God always concerning you for the grace of God which was given you in Christ Jesus, that in everything you were enriched in Him, in all speech and all knowledge, even as the testimony concerning Christ was confirmed in you, so that you are not lacking in any gift, awaiting eagerly the revelation of our Lord Jesus Christ, who will also confirm you to the end, blameless in the day of our Lord Jesus Christ. God is faithful, through whom you were called into fellowship with His Son, Jesus Christ our Lord. (1 Corinthians 1:4-9).

Paul here commends the Corinthians for expecting or waiting for the revealing of Jesus, another way of expressing His coming. The early Christians had this imminent expectation because the apostles were able to explain the imminent context to what Jesus had taught them and this is seen consistently throughout the letters of the New Testament. The end (v8) is the end of the age and that is always in sight and imminent in the letters to the Corinthians and Thessalonians. The context to 'the end' is not the end of life, or a general end of everything, but of the specific age in which they were living; and Jesus was always presented as being faithful and coming soon. The 'age' was always the close of the *aeon* or Jewish age, i.e. the Mosaic dispensation of Law. Jesus came to fulfil all the promises and consummate all the covenantal promises made to Adam, Noah, Abraham, Moses and David in Himself, the last Adam, the seed of Abraham and David.

... so that He may establish your hearts without blame in holiness before our God and Father at the coming of our Lord Jesus with all His saints. (1 Thessalonians 3:13).

... so that you are not lacking in any gift, awaiting eagerly the revelation of our Lord Jesus Christ, who will also confirm you to the end, blameless in the day of our Lord Jesus Christ. (1 Corinthians 1:7-8).

There are so many parallels between what is recorded in the gospels that I cannot cover them all in detail but I will include some charts that show this in the appendices.

The day of the Lord was always a day of judgment, as Paul affirms to the Corinthians in teaching that is often referred to as the Judgment Seat of Christ. This has an earthly, figurative meaning of what is a heavenly reality that I have experienced many times in my life.

The day of the Lord is a judgment, a verdict, which separates good and evil, sheep from goats, wheat from tares. Whichever analogy is used, the inference is the same: that Jesus' coming will bring about that judgment at the end of the age.

... each man's work will become evident; for the day will show it because it is to be revealed with fire, and the fire itself will test the quality of each man's work. If any man's work which he has built on it remains, he will receive a reward. If any man's work is burned up, he will suffer loss; but he himself will be saved, yet so as through fire. (1 Corinthians 3:13-15).

The expression 'through fire' is not meant to be taken literally but metaphorically. The whole passage is figurative: the building, the builders, the materials; therefore the fire is figurative also. Our God is love and a consuming fire: fire describes the loving nature of God who is passionate and has a burning desire for the restoration of all His children. God as fire will not destroy His children: fire never actually destroys anything but changes or transforms it, therefore God is a refining, purifying fire. God has figuratively eyes of fire that can penetrate the hardest of hearts to judgment and reveal what needs to be transformed.

"And to the angel of the church in Thyatira write: The Son of God, who has eyes like a flame of fire, and His feet are like burnished bronze, says this: 'I know your deeds...'" (Revelation 2:18-19).

But who can endure the day of His coming? And who can stand when He appears? For He is like a refiner's fire and like fullers' soap. He will sit as a smelter and purifier of silver, and He will purify the sons of Levi and refine them like gold and silver, so that they may present to the Lord offerings in righteousness. (Malachi 3:2-3).

"As for me, I baptize you with water for repentance, but He who is coming after me is mightier than I, and I am not fit to remove His sandals; He will baptize you with the Holy Spirit and fire. His winnowing fork is in His hand, and He will thoroughly clear His threshing floor; and He will gather His wheat into the barn, but He will burn up the chaff with unquenchable fire." (Matthew 3:11-12).

... and to you who are troubled – rest with us in the revelation of the Lord Jesus from heaven, with messengers of his power, in flaming fire, giving vengeance to those not knowing God,

and to those not obeying the good news of our Lord Jesus Christ; who shall suffer justice – destruction age-during – from the face of the Lord, and from the glory of his strength... (2 Thessalonians 1:7-9 YLT).

The word translated 'destruction' is not meant to convey punishment here but total judgment, ruination or undoing of the old life; by fire, from the face of God, whose eyes are like fire, to reveal the new life transformed by fire.

Therefore do not go on passing judgment before the time, but wait until the Lord comes, who will both bring to light the things hidden in the darkness and disclose the motives of human hearts; and then praise will come to each person from God. (1 Corinthians 4:5).

I have decided to turn such a person over to Satan for the destruction of his body, so that his spirit may be saved on the day of the Lord. (1 Corinthians 5:5).

But this I say, brothers, the time has been shortened, so that from now on those who have wives should be as though they had none; and those who weep, as though they did not weep; and those who rejoice, as though they did not rejoice; and those who buy, as though they did not possess; and those who use the world, as though they did not make full use of it; for the present form of this world is passing away. (1 Corinthians 7:29-31).

Now these things happened to them as an example, and they were written for our instruction, upon whom the ends of the ages have come. (1 Corinthians 10:11).

The day of judgment was soon to arrive as that age was coming to an end and the age to come would become realised. Read in the correct context, the letters to the Corinthians consistently present the soon coming of the day of the Lord as a day of judgment and resurrection of the corporate old body, dead in Adam but resurrected in Jesus.

In the Old Testament, Jesus' teachings in the gospels and the letters of the New Testament are unified in their presenting the coming of Jesus as coming with the refining fire of judgment.

I love this quote from from Francois Du Toit's notes in the Mirror Bible, Luke chapter 1, where the announcement of Jesus' birth brought the hope of a new era:

> This is the end of an era; a new generation is introduced. *"In many and various ways God spoke of old to our fathers through the prophets, but now, in the conclusion of the ages, God has spoken to us in sonship-language!"* Heb 1:1.
>
> 2 Cor 4:4 *The survival and self-improvement programs of the religious systems of this world veil the minds of the unbelievers; exploiting their ignorance about their true origin and their redeemed innocence.*

Paul's letters to the Corinthians also clarify the nature of the resurrection of the dead, the change of the living and the establishing of the kingdom, as having occurred at the end of the age. The part of the letter now known as chapter 15 was just the end of the first letter as there were no divisions into chapters and verses. The whole letter should be read as a consistent whole and the context and audience relevance apply. Paul does not switch from describing events that are coming soon to events coming thousands of years later. The events of the day of the Lord's coming are the same events all through the letter and in what is described in chapter 15 referring to the resurrection. The resurrection of Jesus is central to what Paul is writing to help clarify to the Corinthians, as he did to the Thessalonians, that they did not have to be concerned for those who had already died.

But now Christ has been raised from the dead, the first fruits of those who are asleep. For since by a man came death, by a man also came the resurrection of the dead. For as in Adam all die, so also in Christ all will be made alive. But each in his own order: Christ the first fruits, after that those who are Christ's at His coming, then comes the end, when He hands over the kingdom to the God and Father, when He has abolished all rule and all authority and power. For He must reign until He has put all His enemies under His feet. The last enemy that will be abolished is death. For He has put all things in subjection under His feet. But when He says, "All things are put in subjection," it is evident that He is excepted who put all things in subjection to Him. When all things are subjected to Him, then the Son Himself also will be subjected to the One who subjected all things to Him, so that God may be all in all. (1 Corinthians 15:20-28).

There was an anxious desire of all Christians to be alive at the Lord's coming. Death, therefore, was regarded as a catastrophe. Paul sought to comfort, explain and correct concerning the resurrection of the dead that was soon to take place. The context of writing to the Corinthians was one of persecution, which would have made waiting eagerly difficult – especially as many people were dying, which probably produced much disappointment.

The truth of the resurrection may have been more difficult to understand for Gentile believers without Jewish knowledge of the Old Testament.

But someone will say, "How are the dead raised? And with what kind of body do they come?" (1 Corinthians 15:35).

Paul then gives them an overview of the resurrection which must be read in the context of the whole letter and the day of the Lord's coming. He gave them an order that would help them understand what had already occurred and what was about to occur. The first Adam, as representative of humanity, brought death; so the second and last Adam brings life; and Jesus Himself was the evidence and the pledge of the resurrection of His humanity. Jesus was resurrected and became the first fruits of the great harvest of those who had died that was to come. There was an order that Paul described using the analogy of the harvest. Just as the firstfruits preceded and predicted the full harvest, so the resurrection of Christ precedes and guarantees the resurrection of all humanity.

But each in his own order: Christ the first fruits, after that those who are Christ's at His coming... (1 Corinthians 15:23).

This is a very important statement and unambiguously affirms what is the teaching of the New Testament, that the coming of Jesus was to be immediately followed by the resurrection of the sleeping dead. This is exactly what was revealed to the Thessalonians, in terms that parallel the language Jesus draws from the Old Testament prophets like Daniel, Isaiah and others, who predicted that the day of the Lord would be judgment and resurrection and the establishing of the Kingdom of God.

But we do not want you to be uninformed, brethren, about those who are asleep, so that you will not grieve as do the rest who have no hope. For if we believe that Jesus died and rose again, even so God will bring with Him those who have fallen asleep in Jesus. For this we say to you by the word of the Lord, that we who are alive and remain until the coming of the Lord, will not precede those who have fallen asleep. For the Lord Himself will descend from heaven with a shout, with the voice of the archangel and with the trumpet of God, and the dead in Christ will rise first. Then we who are alive and remain will be caught up together with them in the clouds to meet the Lord in the air, and so we shall always be with the Lord. Therefore comfort one another with these words. (1 Thessalonians 4:13-18).

So also is the resurrection of the dead. It is sown a perishable body, it is raised an imperishable body; it is sown in dishonour, it is raised in glory; it is sown in weakness, it is raised in power; it is sown a natural body, it is raised a spiritual body. If there is a natural body, there is also a spiritual body. So also it is written, "The first man, Adam, became a living soul." The last Adam became a life-giving spirit. However, the spiritual is not first, but the natural; then the spiritual. The first man is from the earth, earthy; the second man is from heaven. As is the earthy, so also are those who are earthy; and as is the heavenly, so also are those who are heavenly. Just as we have borne the image of the earthy, we will also bear the image of the heavenly.

Now I say this, brethren, that flesh and blood cannot inherit the kingdom of God; nor does the perishable inherit the imperishable. Behold, I tell you a mystery; we will not all sleep, but we will all be changed, in a moment, in the twinkling of an eye, at the last trumpet; for the trumpet will sound, and the dead will be raised imperishable, and we will be changed. For this perishable must put on the imperishable, and this mortal must put on immortality. But when this perishable will have put on the imperishable, and this mortal will have put on immortality, then will come about the saying that is written, "Death is swallowed up in victory. O death, where is your victory? O death, where is your sting?" The sting of death is sin, and the power of sin is the law; but thanks be to God, who gives us the victory through our Lord Jesus Christ. (1 Corinthians 15:42-57).

To summarise what I noted previously concerning the resurrection day as referred to in Daniel 7 and 12 and what Jesus revealed as recorded in John 14:

On the day of resurrection, Jesus ascended into heaven, was presented triumphantly before His Father (described as the Ancient of Days), was enthroned, and received the kingdom. Having received the kingdom, Jesus gave the kingdom to the saints of God who would administer that kingdom by preaching the gospel to the whole world; then the end would come. Jesus came back to His disciples on that day as He promised and, as they represented humanity, now one new resurrected man in Christ, He breathed the Holy Spirit into them. Jesus' resurrection and victory over death produced literal first fruits as the graves were opened and resurrected Old Testament saints walked the streets of Jerusalem. This was the first fruits of a greater harvest that Jesus said would occur at the end of the age.

And then the sign of the Son of Man will appear in the sky, and then all the tribes of the earth will mourn, and they will see the Son of Man coming on the clouds of the sky with power and great glory. And He will send forth His angels with a great trumpet and they will gather together His elect from the four winds, from one end of the sky to the other. (Matthew 24:30-31).

All this was part of the first fruits of the Spirit they had received as a pledge for what was coming.

And not only this, but also we ourselves, having the first fruits of the Spirit, even we ourselves groan within ourselves, waiting eagerly for our adoption as sons, the redemption of our body. (Romans 8:23).

Jesus was king and at His coming the kingdom would be consummated: removed from the old covenant and established in the new covenant. The language used is symbolic and figurative and was never meant to be taken literally with every word having a literal fulfilment. The argument against a realised eschatology often relies on the idea that the things Jesus and Paul prophesied did not literally occur, therefore they must still be future. For example, the great trumpet to gather the elect from the four winds and one end of the sky to the other: rather than see this as figurative of the resurrection they interpret the language literally and say that this cannot have happened on earth because it talks of wind and sky. Such objections have no real merit and those who use them are often inconsistent in their interpretation, cherry-picking what they want to be literal. None of them would take the beast with 10 heads in Revelation as literal; but they want the trumpet, shout, wind and sky, and twinkling of an eye to be interpreted literally.

*"But as for Me, I have installed My King
Upon Zion, My holy mountain."
"I will announce the decree of the Lord:
He said to Me, 'You are My Son,
Today I have fathered You.
Ask it of Me, and I will certainly give the nations as Your inheritance,
And the ends of the earth as Your possession.
You shall break them with a rod of iron,
You shall shatter them like earthenware.'"* (Psalm 2:6-9).

Jesus said to them, "Did you never read in the Scriptures, 'The stone which the builders rejected, this became the chief corner stone; this came about from the Lord, and it is marvelous in our eyes'? Therefore I say to you, the kingdom of God will be taken away from you and given to a people, producing the fruit of it. And he who falls on this stone will be broken to pieces; but on whomever it falls, it will scatter him like dust." When the chief priests and the Pharisees heard His parables, they understood that He was speaking about them. (Matthew 21:42-45).

The psalmist uses the same language of kingdom and resurrection to describe the kingdom sovereignty or theocracy of Israel, so the kingdom was removed from them when they ceased to be the covenant nation any longer. When the old covenant had become obsolete, had faded away, and was finally dissolved, the whole administrative framework of the mediatorial system was abolished. It is very reasonable to interpret that the Son would then 'deliver up the kingdom': the purposes of its limited local and national government limitations would be superseded by the universal kingdom that would grow to fill the whole earth. Jesus, having received the kingdom as king, then surrendered the kingdom to the Father at the end of the age. The Father, referred to as the 'Ancient of Days' by Daniel, gives the kingdom to the new covenant saints and they become the new wineskin temple, the New Jerusalem and the new custodians of a 'better covenant'.

... then comes the end, when He hands over the kingdom to our God and Father, when He has abolished all rule and all authority and power. For He must reign until He has put all His enemies under His feet. (1 Corinthians 15:24-25).

Who those enemies are is obvious when viewed from the context of the closing of old covenant history and the transition from old to new. Who were the enemies of the earliest believers, persecuting and killing them throughout the Roman Empire? The chief priests and rulers of the people were the 'rule and authority and power' which, by the destruction of Jerusalem, were put under His feet.

"But these enemies of mine, who did not want me to reign over them, bring them here and slay them in my presence." (Luke 19:27).

That was also the meaning of the judgment in the parable of the sheep and the goats and what John presented as the 'Great White Throne' judgment of Revelation.

The link between resurrection and judgment continues as death is described as the last enemy to be placed under His feet. If you again view this in the correct context of His second coming being imminent, then death has been abolished spiritually and all are now alive in Christ. This is how most who hold a futurist eschatology would also interpret this passage and they are correct to say that the second coming abolishes death, they just wrongly place it in the future. As it occurred in the past, then death has therefore already been abolished.

How can this be true if people are still dying? It was not talking about physical but spiritual death. All died spiritually in Adam; all have died and been buried and been resurrected with Christ (Romans 6); and all – the whole of humanity – is now alive in Christ. Some way well object, "I thought you believed in immortality." I do indeed, and Paul does as well (as he indicates in 2 Timothy 1:10), but that is the process of transfiguration that we all must participate in by figuratively eating His flesh and drinking His blood and so not dying, as Jesus taught (recorded in John 6). It is the very fact that spiritual death has been abolished that makes physical immortality possible.

... who has saved us and called us with a holy calling, not according to our works, but according to His own purpose and grace which was granted us in Christ Jesus from all eternity, but now has been revealed by the appearing of our Savior Christ Jesus, who abolished death and brought life and immortality to light through the gospel... (2 Timothy 1:9-10).

The judgment of the living and the dead was not of the whole human race, but of the subjects of the old covenant kingdom: the dead being raised and the living undergoing an instantaneous change. The resurrection of those who had died throughout the old covenant kingdom were the victims and captives of death; therefore destruction of death meant that death lost its dominion. The spirits in prison were released and could not die anymore: death had no more dominion over them either.

How then were those who are still alive at the time of His coming changed, and what was the meaning of this transformation? This brings the whole subject of 1 Thessalonians 4 and 1 Corinthians 15 to completion.

Behold, I tell you a mystery; we will not all sleep, but we will all be changed, in a moment, in the twinkling of an eye, at the last trumpet; for the trumpet will sound, and the dead will be raised imperishable, and we will be changed. For this perishable must put on the imperishable, and this mortal must put on immortality. But when this perishable will have put on the imperishable, and this mortal will have put on immortality, then will come about the saying that is written,

"Death is swallowed up in victory. O death, where is your victory? O death, where is your sting?" The sting of death is sin, and the power of sin is the law; but thanks be to God, who gives us the victory through our Lord Jesus Christ. (1 Corinthians 15:51-57).

Then we who are alive and remain will be caught up together with them in the clouds to meet the Lord in the air, and so we shall always be with the Lord. (1 Thessalonians 4:17).

Paul received revelation directly when he went into heaven: he was able to reveal some of what he received in those heavenly encounters but some revelation was inexpressible for him at that time. Paul implies that he was communicating a new revelation; and it was not something the gospel writers recorded Jesus speaking of, nor did the other writers of the letters now known as the New Testament.

When Paul wrote 'We shall not all sleep,' he was not referring to people living in some distant future time, but to the Corinthians and himself. There would be no point writing this to the Corinthians if his intended audience was readers thousands of years later. Paul knew that the second coming day of the Lord was imminent. They all expected that they would be alive to see the Lord come and that was their common hope and expectation. When Paul says 'we,' there should be no doubt that he means the Christians of Corinth and himself. They would not all have to die, and those who were still alive would undergo a change that would qualify them to enter into the kingdom of God.

Jesus had declared that many could not enter the kingdom without being transformed, regenerated or resurrected:

"For I say to you that unless your righteousness surpasses that of the scribes and Pharisees, you will not enter the kingdom of heaven." (Matthew 5:20).

"Not everyone who says to Me, 'Lord, Lord,' will enter the kingdom of heaven, but he who does the will of My Father who is in heaven will enter." (Matthew 7:21).

... and said, "Truly I say to you, unless you are converted and become like children, you will not enter the kingdom of heaven." (Matthew 18:3).

And Jesus said to His disciples, "Truly I say to you, it is hard for a rich man to enter the kingdom of heaven. Again I say to you, it is easier for a camel to go through the eye of a needle, than for a rich man to enter the kingdom of God." (Matthew 19:23-24).

"But woe to you, scribes and Pharisees, hypocrites, because you shut off the kingdom of heaven from people; for you do not enter in yourselves, nor do you allow those who are entering to go in." (Matthew 23:13).

Jesus answered, "Truly, truly, I say to you, unless one is born of water and the Spirit he cannot enter into the kingdom of God." (John 3:5).

... strengthening the souls of the disciples, encouraging them to continue in the faith, and saying, "Through many tribulations we must enter the kingdom of God." (Acts 14:22).

Paul linked entering the kingdom with the persecutions that they were to endure until the end would come and they would be transformed figuratively at the Lord's coming. Paul states that 'flesh and blood cannot inherit the kingdom of God' and therefore there was the necessity for a transformation of the material and corruptible into that which is immaterial and incorruptible. This change was to enable them to engage in the true heavenly nature of 'the kingdom of God.' where they would be seated in the heavenly realms that flesh and blood are incapable of entering. In simple terms, they could not enter the kingdom or engage in heaven by the self-righteousness of the old covenant law-based system of works. That old system had to die to be figuratively resurrected in the new covenant 'one new creation man' whom God had reconciled in Christ. This resurrection or regeneration had its first fruits when Jesus breathed the Spirit into His disciples and now it was consummated by Jesus at His coming.

This change and transformation described by Paul in the letters to the Corinthians was not a physical, personal change but a system change: the dead letter system that kills was fully removed and the living letter new covenant fully established. Access was now free through Christ and not through the law of works.

So also is the resurrection of the dead. It is sown a perishable body, it is raised an imperishable body; it is sown in dishonor, it is raised in glory; it is sown in weakness, it is raised in power; it is sown a natural body, it is raised a spiritual body. If there is a natural body, there is also a spiritual body. So also it is written, "The first man, Adam, became a living soul." The last Adam became a life-giving spirit. However, the spiritual is not first, but the natural; then the spiritual. The first man is from the earth, earthy; the second man is from heaven. As is the earthy, so also are those who are earthy; and as is the heavenly, so also are those who are heavenly. Just as we have borne the image of the earthy, we will also bear the image of the heavenly. (1 Corinthians 15:42-49).

This change and transformation was to enable the living to engage in the heavenly realms in a figuratively, not literally, resurrected body. If mankind was not transformed by the spiritual resurrection at Jesus' coming then they would have to wait until physical death to enter the kingdom and the heavenly realms. This, then, is the context for the change at the last trumpet: the sting of death through the law is broken, as the old covenant law-based governmental system that had been fading away was now obsolete and ended. The victory over the death of the old covenant letter was won by Jesus and the life of the Spirit was now manifested.

Now I say this, brethren, that flesh and blood cannot inherit the kingdom of God; nor does the perishable inherit the imperishable. Behold, I tell you a mystery; we will not all sleep, but we will all be changed, in a moment, in the twinkling of an eye, at the last trumpet; for the trumpet will sound, and the dead will be raised imperishable, and we will be changed. For this perishable must put on the imperishable, and this mortal must put on immortality. But when this perishable will have put on the imperishable, and this mortal will have put on immortality, then will come about the saying that is written, "Death is swallowed up in victory. O death, where is your victory? O death, where is your sting?" The sting of death is sin, and the power of sin is the law; but thanks be to God, who gives us the victory through our Lord Jesus Christ. (1 Corinthians 15:50-57).

Throughout the New Testament the second coming event is never spoken of as being distant, but always as imminent. It is looked for, watched for, hoped for and some believers even thought it had already occurred. So they could not have had a concept of a physical rapture where they would be whisked off to heaven at Jesus' coming. They were never expecting a physical resurrection: that is a fabrication introduced into in the creeds and not something Jesus or Paul promised.

I know this raises the question as to how all this could take place without being noticed or written about. That question is framed by the conditioning that it meant individual physical resurrection and not the corporate resurrection of the dead and old covenant in Jesus in the new covenant fulfilment of all God's promises. This was an invisible spiritual change and therefore not visible to the natural eye. It is only the programmed notion that resurrection was physical, with opening graves and emerging bodies, that conditions us to a physical resurrection at the end of the world.

This transition period between the end and removal of the old and the complete birthing of the new is what Jesus was warning them to prepare for in Matthew 24. This period could be described as the pregnancy that would birth the kingdom age, which they would have to enter through many tribulations and persecutions. That process is attested to throughout the New Testament letters and was for those who were transitioning; and so, if we embrace rather than resist the renewal of our minds, it no longer has to apply to us today.

Paul clarifies this spiritual process in his second letter to the Corinthians as being a new creation in Christ where the old had gone and the new had come. They already had the pledge or guarantee of what was coming on the day of the Lord, the Spirit who was indwelling them. That was in the future for them but is now in the past for us. In 2 Corinthians 5, Paul describes his readers as new creation ambassadors, waiting for heavenly clothing but already having the pledge of the Spirit. We too are new creation ambassadors but unlike them we have already received our heavenly clothing and therefore can access the kingdom and heaven without having to die, which was not the case when Paul wrote to the Corinthians.

For indeed while we are in this tent, we groan, being burdened, because we do not want to be unclothed but to be clothed, so that what is mortal will be swallowed up by life. Now He who prepared us for this very purpose is God, who gave to us the Spirit as a pledge. (2 Corinthians 5:4-5).

For the love of Christ controls us, having concluded this, that one died for all, therefore all died; and He died for all, so that they who live might no longer live for themselves, but for Him who died and rose again on their behalf. (2 Corinthians 5:14-15).

Therefore if anyone is in Christ, he is a new creature; the old things passed away; behold, new things have come. Now all these things are from God, who reconciled us to Himself through Christ and gave us the ministry of reconciliation, namely, that God was in Christ reconciling the world to Himself, not counting their trespasses against them, and He has committed to us the word of reconciliation. Therefore, we are ambassadors for Christ, as though God were making an appeal through us; we beg you on behalf of Christ, be reconciled to God. He made Him who knew no sin to be sin on our behalf, so that we might become the righteousness of God in Him. (2 Corinthians 5:17-21).

It is only in Jesus and the new covenant revelation of justification by faith that we are made righteous and can enter the kingdom. While the old covenant was still in place, the new, in which there was only one new man in Christ and the separation was removed, was not yet fully realised.

Paul taught that the coming of Christ, the resurrection of the dead, and the transformation of the living believers would occur in their generation and that many of them would be alive to witness it.

"*Maranatha*" was a common Aramaic term used by believers at the time of this transition: it meant "the Lord is coming" or "Come, O Lord." Being Jesus' disciples was not easy during this period and there were many persecutions suffered at the hands of the Jews and Romans. The Jews believed that followers of Jesus were forsaking Judaism and the Romans thought they were profaning Caesar, who they worshipped as a god. 'Jesus is Lord' was the basic kingdom principle for the early church in the midst of persecution therefore the hope of the Jesus coming sustained them. "*Maranatha!*" became the common greeting for those oppressed believers, replacing the familiar Jewish greeting '*Shalom*' (peace) for former followers of Judaism. They knew that Jesus would be returning to set up His kingdom, and that expectation brought encouragement and comfort. Jesus taught several parables about watching and waiting and being ready for His return (see Matthew 25:1-13; Luke 12:35-40).

Unfortunately, many believers have been deceived into believing that today we should still be expecting Jesus' return. This has put off to a future coming what is a present reality and therefore many believers are living in spiritual poverty and not in abundant blessing.

There is one other obvious similarity between what Jesus taught them to be looking for and what Paul associates with this event in Thessalonians and Corinthians. The last trumpet to be sounded could be seen as the 'Last Post' of the old covenant and the 'Reveille' or 'Rouse' for the new creation new covenant man. This trumpet was figuratively sounding the death of the letter, of hard labour and works, and the beginning of the full life of the Spirit. The foundation of the old had been laid and now they were to move on to the new covenant life, as Hebrews 6 encourages. In the past, I mistakenly used Hebrews 6:1-3 to teach the foundations of the Christian life: how wrong I was to try to perpetuate the old covenant foundations within the new!

Therefore leaving the elementary teaching about the Christ, let us press on to maturity, not laying again a foundation of repentance from dead works and of faith toward God, of instruction about washings and laying on of hands, and the resurrection of the dead and eternal judgment. And this we will do, if God permits. For in the case of those who have once been enlightened and have tasted of the heavenly gift and have been made partakers of the Holy Spirit, and have tasted the good word of God and the powers of the age to come, and then have fallen away, it is impossible to renew them again to repentance, since they again crucify to themselves the Son of God and put Him to open shame. (Hebrews 6:1-6).

This passage is referring to not living under the old covenant laws whilst pressing onto maturity in the new. The Mirror Bible makes it very clear that they were already tasting the powers of the age to come, that they were waiting for at the day of the Lord:

1. *Consequently, as difficult as it may seem, you ought to divorce yourselves from your sentimental attachment to the foreshadowing doctrine of the Messiah, which was designed to carry us like a vessel over the ocean of prophetic dispensation into the completeness of the fulfilled promise. A mind shift from attempts to impress God by your behaviour, to*

realizing the faithfulness of God, is fundamental. There is no life left in the old system. It is dead and gone; you have to move on. (Rom 3:27.)

2 *All the Jewish teachings about ceremonial washings* [baptisms], *the laying on of hands* (in order to identify with the slain animal as sacrifice), *and all teachings pertaining to a sin consciousness, including the final resurrection of the dead to face judgment, are no longer relevant.* (All of these types and shadows were concluded and fulfilled in Christ, their living substance. His resurrection bears testimony to the judgment that he faced on mankind's behalf and the freedom from an obstructive consciousness of sin that he now proclaims. [Rom 4:25; Acts 17:31; Jn 12:31-33] Jesus said, *"and when I am lifted up on the cross, I will draw all judgment unto me!"* Heb 9:28.)

3 *So it is with God's prompting that we advance.* (From the prophetic types and shadows of Scripture into the substance of what God has now spoken to us in sonship. Heb 1:1-3.)

4 *Now it may be that someone may clearly see the light* (of the prophetic word) *and participate in the Holy Spirit by already having sampled the heavenly gift, ("The Prophets who prophesied of the grace that was to be yours searched and inquired about this salvation; they inquired what person or time was indicated by the Spirit of Christ within them when predicting the sufferings of Christ and the subsequent glory."* 1 Pet 1:10, 11.)

5 *and they might even begin to feast on the beauty of the Word; already having experienced the power of the age of the promise that all were waiting for.*

6 *If such a person were to insist on relapsing into the old mindset of legalism, sin consciousness, and condemnation, it*

becomes impossible for him to be restored again and again to ¹repentance. The principle of repeated ¹repentance, as practised under the law, does not make sense in the context of the new dispensation, because it would absurdly imply that Christ was being re-crucified and subjected to public shame over and over again. This new order is not to be confused with the old! Grace is not a cheap excuse for sin! C'mon, ¹awaken to faith-consciousness once and for all. You are free from the old rules and bondage of the duty-driven law of willpower. It is impossible for the old system to match the new! (See Rom 3:27. Under the shadow system of the law, sacrifices were repeatedly slain because no permanent cleansing was possible. [Heb 10:1-4] ¹The word often translated, repentance, is the Greek word, *metanoia*, from *meta*, together with and νοιέω *noieo*, to perceive with the mind. It describes the awakening of the mind to that which is true; a re-alignment of one's reasoning; it is a gathering of one's thoughts, a co-knowing. Faith is not a decision; it is a discovery. It has nothing in common with the Latin word *paenitentia* - where the idea of penance and repentance stems from!). (Hebrews 6:1-6 Mirror).

The last trumpet was used to announce the judgment of the end and the justice of the beginning of perpetual jubilee. In the Old Testament, there are a great variety of biblical trumpets – taking many forms and made of different materials. Some were made of silver (Numbers 10:2), and were used only by the priests in announcing the approach of festivals and in giving signals of war. Some trumpets made of rams' horns are called *shofar* or *yobel* (Joshua 6:8).

Trumpets were blown at special festivals, and to herald the arrival of special seasons (Leviticus 23:24; 25:9; 1 Chronicles 15:24; 2 Chronicles 29:27; Psalm 81:3; 98:6). Trumpets were blown loudly throughout the land of the children of Israel to announce the beginning of each Jubilee year.

And He will send forth His angels with a great trumpet and they will gather together His elect from the four winds, from one end of the sky to the other. (Matthew 24:31).

For the Lord Himself will descend from heaven with a shout, with the voice of the archangel and with the trumpet of God, and the dead in Christ will rise first. (1 Thessalonians 4:16).

... in a moment, in the twinkling of an eye, at the last trumpet; for the trumpet will sound, and the dead will be raised imperishable, and we will be changed. (1 Corinthians 15:52).

And the seven angels who had the seven trumpets prepared themselves to sound them. (Revelation 8:6).

The context of the seals, trumpets and bowls was of the judgment of the old covenant in which they would reap the consequences from Rome for what they had sown. The 7 woes of Matthew 23 are the same woes as John records using the analogy of 7 seals, 7 bowls and 7 trumpets in the book of Revelation. Following the description of the 7 woes upon the scribes and Pharisees as hypocrites there was the declaration of judgment that would occur upon that generation.

"Therefore, behold, I am sending you prophets and wise men and scribes; some of them you will kill and crucify, and some of them you will scourge in your synagogues, and persecute from city to city, so that upon you may fall the guilt of all the righteous blood shed on earth, from the blood of righteous Abel to the blood of Zechariah, the son of Berechiah, whom you murdered between the temple and the altar. Truly I say to you, all these things will come upon this generation." (Matthew 23:34-36).

We have questions to face when looking at the subject of the second coming. Either Jesus told the truth and His prophecy was fulfilled in that generation or they are still to be fulfilled, in which case Jesus could not be the Truth. Either Paul was given revelation and guided by the Spirit of God, and the events which he predicted were imminent and came to pass or Paul was mistaken in his belief and these things never took place.

Jesus is the Truth and Paul was telling the truth: all those events did occur in that generation and therefore the second coming, day of the Lord, the last day of resurrection and judgment have already been fulfilled. There is no 'secret rapture', 'Great Tribulation' or future millennium reign on earth to look forward to as they have all already been fulfilled.

The Millennium

It would be remiss of me not to cover one of the most deceptive and confusing doctrines in looking at this subject: the millennium or thousand-year earthly reign of Jesus. It may be surprising to some that this doctrine is only mentioned in the book of Revelation and that neither Jesus, Paul, Peter nor James ever mentioned it. When reading the book of Revelation it is important that we take audience relevance and the apocalyptical language and symbolism into account. The book of Revelation was not written with a 21st century audience in mind. It was also written using a circular or recapitulation and not linear style. The book repeats and summarises the themes using different visions that progress the revelation. 'Recapitulation' is where we get the modern term 'recap' from: it is originally a biological term but in common usage it means 'to summarize and state again the main points'.

Then I saw an angel coming down from heaven, holding the key of the abyss and a great chain in his hand. And he laid hold of the dragon, the serpent of old, who is the devil and Satan, and bound him for a thousand years; and he threw him into the abyss, and shut it and sealed it over him, so that he would not deceive the nations any longer, until the thousand years were completed; after these things he must be released for a short time. Then I saw thrones, and they sat on them, and judgment was given to them. And I saw the souls of those who had been beheaded because of their testimony of Jesus and because of the word of God, and those who had not worshiped the beast or his image, and had not received the mark on their forehead and on their hand; and they came to life and reigned with Christ for a thousand years. The rest of the dead did not come to life until the thousand years were completed. This is the first resurrection. Blessed and holy is the one who has a part in the first resurrection; over these the second death has no power, but they will be priests of God and of Christ and will reign with Him for a thousand years. When the thousand years are completed, Satan will be released from his prison. (Revelation 20:1-7).

There are many different perspectives to prophecy and how to interpret the book of Revelation but they generally fall into one of three main categories. Our eschatological framework of thinking will usually align with one or other of these perspectives but I do not accept any one label, as no position is wholly the truth. All of our beliefs and mindsets probably contain a mixture of truth, partial or twisted truth and downright lies and so we need a continual process of deconstruction and renewal of our minds. The deepening nature and intimacy of my relationship with the Father has been the catalyst for the progressive development of all my beliefs, including that of my eschatology. The greater my experience of unconditional love, limitless grace and triumphant mercy has been, the more the restoration of all things shapes my understanding and motivates my beliefs.

These are the three main views of eschatological interpretation of the millennium (which include many sub-divisions and perspectives): futurist, historicist and preterist (either partial or full, which is otherwise known as realised or covenant eschatology).

Eschatology concerning the millennium falls into premillennial, amillennial, postmillennial or realised (and those who are totally confused by all this, or don't really care, adopt the pan-millennial position, hoping that it will all just pan out in the end). The problem is that our theological eschatology programming will affect our beliefs and interpretation of the Bible and our perspective of the future, even if we are not aware of it.

I pose the following question as a way of assessing our beliefs, eschatological or otherwise. This question may be perceived as being biased in itself but I believe everything should be Christocentric and love-orientated.

- Do the beliefs you hold about God and your eschatological position reflect His identity as love?
- In that light, therefore, what eschatological position lines up with both the character and nature of God and the restoration of all things?
- Are we looking for the fulfilment of something that has not yet happened or living in the reality and realisation of something already present?

- Are we looking for the period of restoration of things to begin, occur if Jesus returns, or continue (as we are already in it)?

The study of eschatology is really about how we view biblical prophecy, including Old Testament prophets, Jesus' teaching, New Testament revelation and the book of Revelation. The usual prophetic interpretative perspectives are:

Futurism

This view believes that most of the Bible's prophecies are yet to be fulfilled and they will take place at the end of the world when Jesus returns.

Most prophecies will be fulfilled during a global time of chaos known as the 'Great Tribulation' and afterwards. Futurist beliefs usually have a close association with Premillennialism and Dispensationalism.

Iterism or historicism

Iterists assert that most prophecies are repeated in every generation. It is, however, generally considered that there will be an increase in the intensity of such fulfilments until the time of Christ's return. For example, every age will experience persecution but it will grow in severity as time goes on. Many people who are amillennialists are also iterists.

This system of belief, that prophecies are being continually fulfilled both in the present and past in people or events, was the view held by most Protestant reformers. They, like Futurists, were looking for biblical fulfilments in their own time.

Preterism, partial or full.

Preterism is a Christian eschatological view that interprets some (partial preterism) or all (full preterism) prophecies of the Bible as events that have already happened. Therefore preterists believe that most or all prophecies have been fulfilled. They focus on 70 AD when the temple was destroyed as the fulfilment of what Christ speaks of in Matthew 24 and what John focuses on in Revelation. Many post-millennialists are preterists, especially in its most popular forms of exposition.

Preterist theologians usually interpret the prophecies of the Book of Daniel as events that occurred from the 7th century BC until the first century AD. They also believe that the events of the book of Revelation occurred during in the first century AD. Preterism does not believe that modern Israel is the restored people of God but does believe that the church is the continuation of those of faith and is the Israel of God.

> The term Millennialism (from millennium, Latin for "a thousand years"), or chiliasm (from the Greek equivalent), is the belief that a Golden Age or Paradise will occur on Earth before the final judgment and future eternal state of the "World to Come"...
>
> Christian millennialist thinking is based upon the Book of Revelation, specifically Revelation 20, which describes the vision of an angel who descended from heaven with a large chain and a key to a bottomless pit, and captured Satan, imprisoning him for a thousand years:
>
> *He seized the dragon, that ancient serpent, who is the Devil and Satan, and bound him for a thousand years and threw him into the pit and locked and sealed it over him,*

so that he would deceive the nations no more, until the thousand years were ended. After that, he must be let out for a little while. – Revelation 20:2-3.

The Book of Revelation then describes a series of judges who are seated on thrones, as well as John's vision of the souls of those who were beheaded for their testimony in favor of Jesus and their rejection of the mark of the beast. These souls:

came to life and reigned with Christ a thousand years. (The rest of the dead did not come to life until the thousand years were ended.) This is the first resurrection. Blessed and holy are those who share in the first resurrection. Over these the second death has no power, but they will be priests of God and of Christ, and they will reign with him a thousand years – Revelation 20:4-6.
– Wikipedia: *Millennialism.*

There are diverse opinions concerning the thousand years of peace (Millennium) described in Revelation and the events associated with it. Some interpret it as a literal, still-future, thousand-year time period in which Christ will rule over the Earth, a time that will be characterized by peace and harmony. Others understand a literal age of peace but think the 'thousand years' is a figure of speech. Still others see the Millennium as symbolic of a spiritual ideal, with no corresponding earthly condition.

All of these positions fall into the category of millennialism, a broad term that includes any and all ideas relating to the millennium of biblical prophecy mentioned only in the book of Revelation.

The most commonly held viewpoints are usually categorized as follows:

Premillennialism

Normal premillennialism believes that Christ's second coming will establish a literal thousand-year earthly kingdom in Jerusalem. Jesus return will be at the beginning, middle or end of a 7 year period known as the 'Great Tribulation'. There will be a resurrection of believers who have died, and a rapture of believers who are still living, who will meet Jesus when He comes. Premillennialists believe that following Jesus' return there will be a thousand years of peace during which Jesus as Messiah will reign as king in Israel. Futurists have different views as to when the so-called secret rapture will occur: either pretribulation, mid-tribulation or post-tribulation. Each position uses the Bible to validate their position on the time of Jesus' return and can be very antagonistic towards each other even though they are all premillennialist.

Premillennialists all believe that Jesus will return before a literal millennium period during which He will reign on earth. For premillenialists, the 'Golden Age' that the postmillenialists believe is currently and progressively occurring will only be established after Jesus comes. There are many different views on who will reign with Jesus on earth. Dispensationalists and Christian Zionists believe that Jesus will reign in modern day Israel as the Messiah of the Jewish people after the church has been raptured and taken to heaven. More classic premillennialists believe that Jesus will reign on earth with the resurrected believers and those alive at His coming. They believe in only one new covenant people comprising of Jews and Gentiles as one new man in opposition to the dispensationalist view which believes in a secret rapture of the church. They all believe that after the 1000 years is complete there will a general resurrection, judgment and eternal life.

Postmillennialism

Postmillennialists interpret the millennium referred to in Revelation 20 as a golden age in which the Christian gospel will evangelise most of the world and Jesus will return after the success of the gospel message. There are many variations of the theme within its camp.

Postmillennialists believe that the kingdom of God is established on earth through the preaching of the gospel and expect that eventually most people living will be saved. During the 19th and 20th centuries, postmillennialism was the major theological position among American Protestants who wanted social reform, for example abolitionists.

'Christian Reconstructionism' is a form of postmillennialism which adheres to theonomy: bringing the world back under a Christian law system based on the old covenant laws. That is something I would totally reject. We are under grace, not the law, which only produces sin through lost identity.

Amillennialism

Amillennialists do not believe that Jesus will reign on earth in a literal thousand, physical reign. Amillennialists believe the 'thousand years' mentioned in Revelation 20 is a symbolic number and is synonymous with the current church age. Amillennialists believe that Jesus' reign during the church age is spiritual in nature and that when Jesus eventually returns there will be a final judgment and the establishment of the new heaven and new earth.

The term 'amillennial' was used originally used in a negative way by premillennialists to disparage this view.

The historical views on eschatology depend on an assumption that revelation is not progressive but fixed and therefore can be systematically understood. I believe the eschatology of the early church was futurist, as the end of the age was still the future for them. The Church Fathers who followed held many contradictory views about practically everything; as time passed, they moved further from the oral teachings of the apostles. More and more confusion occurred as doctrines that came from their understanding and created so much division were developed. I do not think we can make a decision on eschatology based solely on what belief has been around the longest or which has the most proponents.

As you can see for yourself, these positions are confusing and what you believe usually depends on the Christian stream you were brought up in or converted to.

Another perspective

There is another perspective, aligned to realised eschatology, which holds that the second coming ended the millennium which was both literal and figurative, being a distinct generational period that occurred between Jesus' ascension and final coming in 70 AD. It was not a literal thousand years but was an actual period of consummation during which the gospel went into the whole known world and then the end of the old age finally came, as Jesus predicted.

As the letters and books of the New Testament were being written towards the end of that 30–70 AD generation, the disciples and apostles were revealing the truth to prepare the followers of Jesus to be ready for His return. They did this by teaching that Jesus' second coming, the judgment and the resurrection of the living and dead were 'about to' be fulfilled 'shortly,' 'soon,' 'quickly,' 'in a very little while,' and would 'not be delayed'.

This teaching was consistent throughout the New Testament:

- Acts 2:20, 40; Acts 17:31 YLT; Acts 24:15 YLT;
- Romans 8:18-23 YLT/KJV; Romans 13:11-12; Romans 16:20;
- 1 Corinthians 7:29-31; 1 Corinthians 10:11; 1 Corinthians 15:51;
- Philippians 4:5;
- 1 Thessalonians 4:15ff; 1 Thessalonians 5:1-10; 2 Thessalonians 1:5-10;
- 2 Timothy 4:1 YLT;
- Hebrews 8:13–10:37; Hebrews 13:14 YLT;
- James 5:7-9;
- 1 Peter 1:4-12; 1 Peter 4:5-7, 17;
- 1 John 2:17-18;
- Revelation 1:1, 22:6-7, 10, 12, 20.

Clearly, the New Testament authors, who were inspired by the Holy Spirit, understood Jesus' teachings (Matthew 10:22-23; Matthew 16:27-28; Matthew 24:1-34) – when He spoke about the timing of His return – better than the charismatic television 'prophecy experts' or 'reformed scholars' and many pastors and teachers of our day.

A realised eschatology perspective holds these three areas in harmony:

1. The time of fulfilment of the millennium being imminent (pointing to 70 AD);

2. The spiritual nature of fulfilment of the kingdom as being 'in' or 'within' and that the use of apocalyptic/prophetic language was metaphoric and symbolic;
3. The millennium was a realised position of Jesus reigning in heaven and through His disciples on earth. This came to an end at His second coming, which established the period of the restoration of all things; so that the kingdom is now in the process of filling the earth as all things are being restored.

Realised eschatology is the belief that the Bible teaches that the second coming, the judgment and resurrection of the living and dead and the end of the millennium all took place at the end of the old covenant age in the events surrounding the fall of Jerusalem and her Temple.

In regards to the 'great tribulation,' 'distress' and 'wrath' that was coming upon the land of Judah in Matthew 24/Luke 21, it was a roughly three-and-a-half year period between 66 and 70 AD. The church did experience general persecution and tribulation prior to 66 AD, but when they saw the armies surrounding Jerusalem they fled to Pella and were saved from that coming 'great tribulation' and 'wrath' that engulfed Jerusalem.

It is important and sound hermeneutics when looking at New Testament teaching to ask:

1. Who was the intended reader? This is known as 'audience relevancy'. It was intended for a first-century audience.
2. When was this fulfilled? In the first century 'this generation'.
3. How was it fulfilled? I believe it was fulfilled spiritually, figuratively and literally. The language used in the Bible is often apocalyptical and cryptic and refers to the inward

nature of the fulfilment using terms such as the kingdom is 'within us', 'not of this world' and 'not seen with physical eyes' yet just as real as the literal manifestation of the kingdom in such things as healing and miracles.
4. Where was it fulfilled? Clearly in the land of Judah and the wider Roman world, not the whole world.

What occurred at the Second Coming was realised and fulfilled by the year 70 AD, in the generation which Jesus foretold.

Summary

Jesus taught that His kingdom is 'not of this world' and that when it would come at His return, it would not be discerned by our physical eyes, because the realm of fulfilment would be 'within' (Luke 17:20-21; Luke 21:27-32; John 18:36).

The Father and Son made their home or dwelling place in the church when the heavenly Temple/New Jerusalem descended from heaven and clothed the church while on and upon the earth (John 14:2-3, 23; 2 Corinthians 4:18–5:10, 6:16; Revelation 21:2-3). The believer today has been raised from the dead and 'the hope of glory' which is 'Christ in you' is now a 'hope realised' in the new covenant age (see Colossians 1:27; Proverbs 13:12).

Apocalyptic/prophetic/symbolic language: when we read that Jesus is coming on the clouds and stars are falling from the heavens in Matthew 24 we should realise that this is the language of the Old Testament prophets. In the Old Testament, when God came riding upon the clouds in judgment, rolling up the heavens like a scroll, this was symbolic language depicting the fall and judgment of nations: not literal but metaphorical language.

'Heaven and earth' can refer to the old covenant system. When the old covenant 'heaven and earth' passed in 70 AD, the new covenant 'heaven and earth' was fully established. This is not a reference to the whole of planet earth and the sky, or to the spiritual heavens, but to the temple system where heaven met earth.

The judgment and resurrection of the dead involved the raising of souls from Hades in 70 AD, at which time some went directly into the presence of God and others went into the consuming, purifying and refining fire of His loving presence.

There was also a covenantal transformation or resurrection that took place for the living at this time as well. Through Jesus' coming, the church was raised from its state of spiritual death inherited from Adam and was figuratively transformed from the old covenant body of death to the resurrected and glorified new covenant body that inherited eternal life.

The Bible is not talking about a resurrection at the end of world history or some literal 'rapture' of people flying up in the air.

The eschatological goal or doctrine of the Second Coming of Christ is not to change and transform man's biological substance, but rather to change and transform his covenantal standing or status before God.

The old covenant Kingdom/Temple/Jerusalem were physical and served as types and shadows of Jesus' spiritual new covenant Kingdom/Temple/Jerusalem that all arrived in fullness at Jesus' second coming in 70 AD.

Biblical prophecy is not about the end of time or the physical world but instead about the time of the end of the old covenant age/world.

The New Testament's use of the term 'last days' covers the period between Jesus' first and second comings which brought an end to the old covenant age in 70 AD.

The New Testament's use of 'this age' means the old covenant age and the 'age to come' is the new covenant age. The one second coming event took place at the end of the old covenant age in 70 AD, when there was a spiritual judgment and resurrection of the living and dead and the arrival of the new creation took place.

Unfortunately, most Christian denominations have not taken literally what was prophesied to occur imminently and have therefore postponed Jesus' kingdom to the future. They have also taken literally much prophetic, apocalyptic, symbolic language whilst also spiritualising away very clear time indicators such as 'about to,' 'in a very little while,' 'soon,' 'shortly,' 'at hand,' and 'quickly' to the fantasy land of futurism.

Many people reject realised eschatology because of Reformed creeds and church traditions. This same argument was used by the Roman Catholic Church against Martin Luther's revelation of justification by faith alone. As for what is considered an 'orthodox position,' the goal posts have been moved so many times over the centuries that some of what is now considered evangelically orthodox would have been seen as heretical by the early church fathers.

The issue of the physical and literal Israel within the prophetic purposes of God will be covered in the following chapters. The idea that this generation will see Jesus' return is based on the false interpretation of fulfilment in 'this generation' to mean 'the Jewish race will not pass away until all these things are fulfilled.' There is simply no solid exegetical or etymological evidence for this use of the Greek word *genea* (generation) in the New Testament as a whole. If the race of Jews was intended by Jesus or Matthew, they would have used *genos* (race).

This has prompted pop eschatologists to make our generation the generation of the end times. This view gained major traction after 1948 and the establishment of the state of Israel. The generation of 1948 was purported to be the last generation and that meant that the seventies and eighties, in particular, were hotbeds of futurist eschatologists like Hal Lindsay and Chuck Smith. Of course, that 40 year period from 1948 ended in 1988, so Hal Lindsay and others lengthened their understanding of a generation to 60-80 years. Many other groupings such as the Mormons and Jehovah's Witnesses have had to do the same with their false predictions concerning 'this generation.' But now, as I write this in 2021, all those predictions are failing again.

My inevitable conclusion is that the second coming of Jesus, along with the resurrection and judgment of the living and the dead, occurred in the generation that Jesus said it would. That means that our generation is Raptureless, Tribulationless, and Milleniumless – and that is good news.

This is my diagram showing a simple eschatological timeline. For two charts comparing the relevant passages in Daniel, Revelation, Matthew 24 and 1 Thessalonians 4-5, please see appendix 2.

SECOND COMING

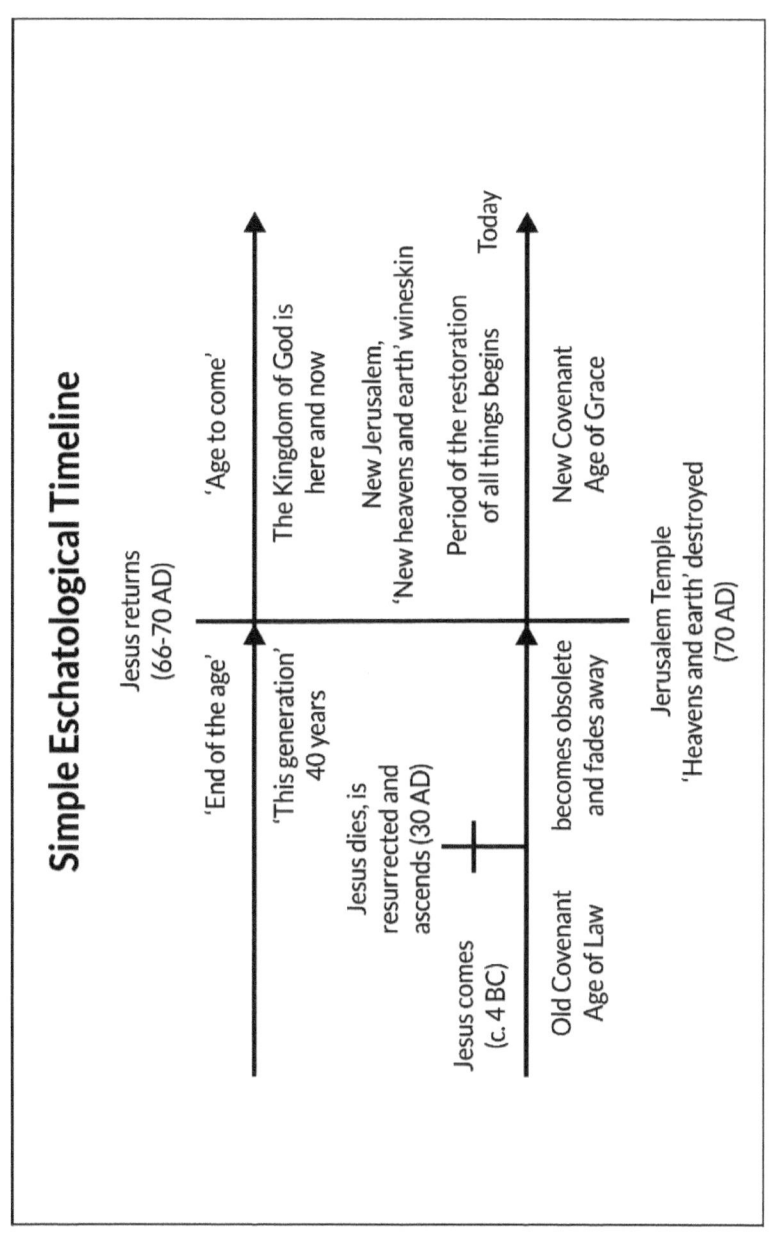

5. Zionism and the Luciferian Agenda

Who is Israel?

Before I address the issues of Zionism, I must address the question of who is Israel and who is a Jew from a new covenant perspective. Who better to clarify those issues than Paul, a Hebrew of Hebrews and a Pharisee of Pharisees? Of course, Paul referred to his fleshy ancestry as dung and perhaps that is where we should start our journey.

... although I myself might have confidence even in the flesh. If anyone else has a mind to put confidence in the flesh, I far more: circumcised the eighth day, of the nation of Israel, of the tribe of Benjamin, a Hebrew of Hebrews; as to the Law, a Pharisee; as to zeal, a persecutor of the church; as to the righteousness which is in the Law, found blameless. But whatever things were gain to me, those things I have counted as loss for the sake of Christ. More than that, I count all things to be loss in view of the surpassing value of knowing Christ Jesus my Lord, for whom I have suffered the loss of all things, and count them but rubbish so that I may gain Christ, and may be found in Him, not having a righteousness of my own derived from the Law, but that which is through faith in Christ, the righteousness which comes from God on the basis of faith, that I may know Him and the power of His resurrection and the fellowship of His sufferings, being conformed to His death; in order that I may attain to the resurrection from the dead. (Philippians 3:4-11).

I know in writing this chapter I will probably be labelled anti-Semitic by some so I will state clearly what my stance is on the Jews and Judaism. I love all people of all nationalities, races, ethnic origins and creeds as I believe we are all one family as children of God. I love Jews equally as much as I love

Palestinians and Muslims, as God does, but that does not mean that I condone their actions or behaviours or politics. I believe I can state that I do not condone the politics of Israel or ISIS and that does not make me anti-Semitic or anti-Muslim. I believe I can state that the religions of Judaism and Islam, along with Hinduism and Christianity, are false religions and still love the followers of those religions.

There is an assumption that because Christianity has Hebrew roots that means Judaism is a special case and should be treated differently than other religions. That assumption continues by following the false logic that the followers of Judaism, the Jews, have some special favour or pass with God. The extreme version of Christian Zionism is that Jewish people are a special case and that they are accepted by God without having to come through Jesus, who is the only way to the Father.

Also, it is an issue that the Jewish Torah, including the writings of the prophets, were included in the Christian Bible; that has brought added confusion to Gentile readers throughout history who have no cultural or contextual understanding. I have made my views clear, that I believe that it was man who produced a closed canon of the Bible and chose which books were going to be included. I do believe that the Holy Spirit can give us insight and revelation concerning what we call the Old Testament but even so, many people are confused by the seeming disparity between the Old Testament and New Testament versions of God. In my opinion, and of course, anyone has the right to disagree, there would have been so much more unity today if we had not tried to build our relationship with God using a book as a mediator. Interpretation of the Bible has created so much division, and with it, denominations.

I do not believe Jewish people are still God's people in the new covenant but that does not make me anti-Semitic. The way Jewish people have been badly treated through the ages, by many different groups, means I have sympathy for them; but it does not mean that I believe they get a free pass to heaven.

So who did Paul say was Israel and a true Jew in the new covenant? We need to remember that this was a time of transition from what was primarily originally Jewish converts to mostly Gentile converts. The Jewish religious leaders were persecuting both Jewish and Gentile followers of the Way and there was much confusion about the issue of Judaism amongst those who were later to be called Christians. This confusion was exacerbated by those who, although were following Jesus, were also still following the Law of Moses. There was even a group within the Jewish Christians called the Judaizers who were seeking to get the Gentile Christians to keep the law. Many were fooled by this deception, so Paul was seeking to clarify these issues, particularly in his letters to the Romans and Galatians.

Paul himself had revelation directly from heaven but also had extensive knowledge of the Old Testament; and whilst he wanted his people by the flesh to come to know God by the spirit, he also wanted everyone to be free from the bondage and death of following a false system of belief.

A big issue to clarify is this: did God's promises to Israel fail? And therefore by inference, could God be trusted?

... that I have great sorrow and unceasing grief in my heart. For I could wish that I myself were accursed, separated from Christ for the sake of my brethren, my kinsmen according to the flesh, who are Israelites, to whom belongs the adoption as

sons, and the glory and the covenants and the giving of the Law and the temple service and the promises, whose are the fathers, and from whom is the Christ according to the flesh, who is over all, God blessed forever. Amen. But it is not as though the word of God has failed. For they are not all Israel who are descended from Israel; nor are they all children because they are Abraham's descendants, but: "through Isaac your descendants will be named." That is, it is not the children of the flesh who are children of God, but the children of the promise are regarded as descendants. (Romans 9:2-8).

In fact according to Paul writing to the 'foolish' Galatians who were being bewitched into trying to follow the law, only followers of Jesus could be truly identified as descendants of Abraham. The idea that Israel as a nation (or Jews who follow their religion) are still today the people of God is now deeply ingrained within evangelical eschatology and theology. This is a lie; it was not what Paul taught nor is it what has been generally believed by Christians until the last one hundred years.

Paul clearly states that being the people of God, those with whom He was in relationship, was never based on an earthly identity of being descended from Israel or Abraham. Not all physical Israel were the people of God, only those children of the promise. The promise was that a believing remnant would be saved on the day of the Lord: those of faith.

As He says also in Hosea,
"I will call those who were not My people, 'My people,'
And her who was not beloved, 'beloved.'
And it shall be that in the place
Where it was said to them, 'you are not My people,'
There they shall be called sons of the living God."

Isaiah cries out concerning Israel, "Though the number of the sons of Israel be like the sand of the sea, it is the remnant that will be saved." (Romans 9:25-27).

The true Jew and the true Israel during this time of great confusion and persecution were those who had a heart relationship with the Father through Jesus the Son. There was no distinction to be made between Jews and Gentiles, who were now one new man in Christ.

For he is not a Jew who is one outwardly, nor is circumcision that which is outward in the flesh. But he is a Jew who is one inwardly; and circumcision is that which is of the heart, by the Spirit, not by the letter; and his praise is not from men, but from God. (Romans 2:28-29 NASB).

For you are not a true Jew just because you were born of Jewish parents or because you have gone through the ceremony of circumcision. No, a true Jew is one whose heart is right with God. And true circumcision is not merely obeying the letter of the law; rather, it is a change of heart produced by the Spirit. And a person with a changed heart seeks praise from God, not from people. (Romans 2:28-29 NLT).

There is neither Jew nor Greek, there is neither slave nor free man, there is neither male nor female; for you are all one in Christ Jesus. And if you belong to Christ, then you are Abraham's descendants, heirs according to promise. (Galatians 3:28-29).

One of Paul's key purposes in writing to the Galatians was to clarify whether they still needed to follow the law in order to be God's people. Paul heavily emphasises his position at the end of the letter by writing it in large letters, reiterating that physical circumcision meant nothing, only being a new creation mattered, as those who lived by grace were the Israel of God. Paul would not have used that term lightly - nor the term 'a true Jew' to identify those who were believers in Jesus.

See with what large letters I am writing to you with my own hand. Those who desire to make a good showing in the flesh try to compel you to be circumcised, simply so that they will not be persecuted for the cross of Christ. For those who are circumcised do not even keep the Law themselves, but they desire to have you circumcised so that they may boast in your flesh. But may it never be that I would boast, except in the cross of our Lord Jesus Christ, through which the world has been crucified to me, and I to the world. For neither is circumcision anything, nor uncircumcision, but a new creation. And those who will walk by this rule, peace and mercy be upon them, and upon the Israel of God. (Galatians 6:11-16).

Those who use Paul's letter to the Romans to argue that all Israel as a race or a nation would be saved are cherry-picking Romans 11 from the rest and not taking the context of the whole letter into account. Romans 11 is referring to the same period and its context is the gospel being preached to the world in preparation for Jesus' coming, after which the end would come. The 'fullness of the Gentiles' mentioned was to be achieved by preaching the gospel to all nations – and that was accomplished, as we have previously seen. Therefore in context the fullness of the Gentiles had come; and all the remnant of Israel had been saved; and both these things were complete at the end of the old covenant which were the birth pangs of the new covenant. The 'one new man in Christ' that Paul refers to in Ephesians 2 is made up of both groups. Paul uses the analogy of the vine and the branches and the process of grafting to represent who were the true people of God, those of faith. All physical Israel was never the people of God: it was always only those of faith, so the olive tree in the analogy is not 'Israel' but all God's people of faith, going back to Adam.

There has always been a continuity of those who were the people of God by faith. The church is therefore just a continuation of the people of God and is in that perspective the Israel of God. The church is made up of those who have realised that they are included in Christ and there is no distinction necessary between any origins. The transition period is over. Christian Zionists have been deceived into reintroducing a false distinction between Jews and Christians, giving the false religion of Judaism a special place. There are now even Messianic Jews who keep their Jewish traditions as Christians: this so confuses what is a very simple equation: there are believers and not yet believers and all are already included in Christ – it is just that some have not yet realised what has already occurred through the resurrection.

Israel was a branch grafted into the vine of the people of God and then became a branch cut off from the vine as the one new covenant man was grafted in. The people of God began with Adam and that line went through Seth to Noah and Noah to Abraham, Isaac and Jacob.

Christian Zionists throw the accusation of replacement theology at anyone who supports the view that the church is now the people of God. But there have never been two peoples of God; and there is not a heavenly people and an earthly people, as dispensationalists teach. Now the whole of humanity is alive and included in Christ by resurrection, as it was included in death in Adam by rebellion.

But if some of the branches were broken off, and you, being a wild olive, were grafted in among them and became partaker with them of the rich root of the olive tree, do not be arrogant toward the branches; but if you are arrogant, remember that it is not you who supports the root, but the root supports you. You will say then, "Branches were broken off so that I might be grafted in." Quite right, they were broken off for their unbelief, but you stand by your faith. Do not be conceited, but fear; for if God did not spare the natural branches, He will not spare you, either. Behold then the kindness and severity of God; to those who fell, severity, but to you, God's kindness, if you continue in His kindness; otherwise you also will be cut off. And they also, if they do not continue in their unbelief, will be grafted in, for God is able to graft them in again. For if you were cut off from what is by nature a wild olive tree, and were grafted contrary to nature into a cultivated olive tree, how much more will these who are the natural branches be grafted into their own olive tree? For I do not want you, brethren, to be uninformed of this mystery – so that you will not be wise in your own estimation – that a partial hardening has happened to Israel until the fullness of the Gentiles has come in; and so all Israel will be saved; just as it is written, "The Deliverer will come from Zion, He will remove ungodliness from Jacob. "This is My covenant with them, when I take away their sins." (Romans 11:17-27).

The 'all Israel' being saved in Romans 11 is the same 'all Israel' as in Romans 9: those who are of faith, not by birth or nationality. All Israel from a salvation perspective was never a nation but the remnant who were faithful within that nation. Paul was not teaching that the whole nation of Israel would miraculously be saved at some point in our future when all Gentiles have been saved. The eschatological perspective for the fullness of the Gentiles and all Israel being saved was that it would take place during that generation before Jesus would come. In Matthew 24:14 Jesus revealed that this was the period when the gospel of the kingdom would be preached in the whole world as a testimony to all the nations, and then the end would come.

Paul was the best person to give the correct perspective to that generation, to clarify the Jew-Gentile confusion; and his letters can help us avoid that confusion today.

An 'everlasting' covenant

To add to the confusion, it is often claimed that God has an 'everlasting covenant' with Israel for the land. The word used for 'everlasting' in Hebrew is *olam*. So does *olam* mean forever, everlasting or eternal in Hebrew? The Hebrew scholars who translated it into Greek as *aionios* (which means age enduring, or an undefined period but not endless time) apparently did not think so. Why is this question important? Because Zionists claim that God made an everlasting covenant with Israel for the Promised Land. If that covenant was not everlasting then the end of the old covenant was also the end of their claim to the land. The claim to still be God's special people is also tied to the covenant He made with them: so was that covenant everlasting?

Olam in modern translations is usually translated 'forever' or 'permanent' in the NASB, but in Young's Literal Translation it is 'age-during'. The age that it was to endure was the old covenant age: it was never meant to be 'forever'.

"This day shall be for you a memorial day, and you shall keep it as a feast to the Lord; throughout your generations, as a

statute forever, you shall keep it as a feast." (Exodus 12:14 ESV).

'Now this day will be a memorial to you, and you shall celebrate it as a feast to the Lord; throughout your generations, you are to celebrate it as a permanent ordinance.' (Exodus 12:14 NASB).

'And this day hath become to you a memorial, and ye have kept it a feast to Jehovah to your generations; -- a statute age-during; ye keep it a feast.' (Exodus 12:14 YLT).

Similarly, was the Aaronic priesthood supposed to be *olam* 'forever' or *olam* 'enduring in the old covenant', which has ended? The way translators interpret *olam* is inconsistent and very hit or miss; but a literal translation is always going to be correct as the duration will be determined by the context. The NASB translates *olam* as 'perpetual', which may convey the correct meaning if the old covenant has ended or it may be incorrect if this is taken to mean that the old covenant is still in operation in the form of modern day Judaism. Does God still support Judaism as a valid religion alongside Christianity, as Christian Zionists insist, or is Judaism just another false religious system like Hinduism or Islam? If the correct meaning of *olam* is understood and the revelation of Jesus' teaching and the New Testament is applied, then the old covenant system is over and is not a valid way of entering into a relationship with God as Father. Much of current evangelism is a mixture of covenants, and that makes it lukewarm.

According to most English translations, Aaron and his sons were anointed as priests 'forever.'

"And thou shalt anoint them, as thou didst anoint their father, that they may minister unto me in the priest's office: for their

*anointing shall surely be an **everlasting** priesthood throughout their generations."* (Exodus 40:15 KJV, emphasis mine).

*"... and you shall anoint them even as you have anointed their father, that they may minister as priests to Me; and their anointing will qualify them for a **perpetual** priesthood throughout their generations."* (Exodus 40:15 NASB, emphasis mine).

*'... and anointed them as thou hast anointed their father, and they have acted as priests to Me, and their anointing hath been to be to them for a priesthood **age-during**, to their generations.'* (Exodus 40:15 YLT, emphasis mine).

Now if perfection (a perfect fellowship between God and the worshiper) had been attainable by the Levitical priesthood – for under it the people were given the Law – why was it further necessary that there should arise another and different kind of Priest, one after the order of Melchizedek, rather than one appointed after the order and rank of Aaron? For when there is a change in the priesthood, there is of necessity an alteration of the law [concerning the priesthood] as well. For the One of Whom these things are said belonged [not to the priestly line but] to another tribe, no member of which has officiated at the altar. For it is obvious that our Lord sprang from the tribe of Judah, and Moses mentioned nothing about priests in connection with that tribe. And this becomes more plainly evident when another Priest arises Who bears the likeness of Melchizedek, Who has been constituted a Priest, not on the basis of a bodily legal requirement [an externally imposed command concerning His physical ancestry], but on the basis of the power of an endless and indestructible Life. For it is witnessed of Him, You are a Priest forever after the order (with the rank) of Melchizedek. So a previous physical regulation and command is cancelled because of its weakness and ineffectiveness and uselessness. (Hebrews 7:11-18 AMPC).

According to the writer of Hebrews, the priesthood which was ordained to be 'everlasting' has been cancelled. There would be no contradiction if the statement in Exodus were translated as it should be, 'to the age, throughout their generations' – that is, throughout their generations, as long as that age lasted.

There are many examples in scripture where *olam* does not mean forever but it has been programmed into evangelicals in general and Christian Zionists in particular that whenever it is used concerning Israel's covenants and land promises it must mean forever, rather than enduring only for an age, the old covenant age.

Olam means an indefinite period as it is a word associated with time and is not timeless. Of course, a specific age may have no end but that cannot be true of the old covenant age of the law, which we know became obsolete and ended. Along with the end of the law and the covenant was the end of the effectiveness of Judaism and the promises regarding the land.

In reality, Jesus has fulfilled all the covenantal promises to Abraham, Moses and David in the new covenant; and that includes the land, which is now a heavenly country and city, the New Jerusalem. This message is consistent throughout the New Testament.

In English we are familiar with the concept of ages – for example, the archaeological ages of the Stone Age (about 40000 BC to 4000 BC), Bronze Age (3000 BC to 1200 BC) or Iron Age (1200 BC to 43 AD; the Dark Ages (5th to 10th centuries) which lasted 500 years; the Industrial Age (18th to

19th century) which lasted 100 years; and the Information Age we are now living in. Who knows what will succeed it? Perhaps the age of sonship or of enlightened consciousness?

Using a modern concordance or Bible dictionary like Strong's can be very confusing because it mixes in a short definition what the words properly or literally mean and what the modern evangelical meaning is – which is totally misleading and generally incorrect (as can be seen when comparing it with a Greek or Hebrew interlinear Bible or a literal translation).

Olam: long duration, antiquity, futurity
Original Word: עוֹלָם
Part of Speech: Noun Masculine
Transliteration: Olam
Phonetic Spelling: (o-lawm')
Short Definition: forever
(Strong's, via biblehub.com)

Now I will give a few of the numerous examples of the literal meaning without the biased interpretation of evangelicalism and Zionism.

Gesenius' *Hebrew and Chaldee Lexicon* tells us that *olam* means:

What is hidden; especially hidden time, long; the beginning or end of which is either uncertain or else not defined.

J. W. Haley[40] says:

---

[40] John W. Haley, *An Examination of the Alleged Discrepancies of the Bible*, Whitaker House (1984) p216.

The Hebrew word 'olam' rendered 'forever,' does not imply the metaphysical idea of absolute endlessness, but a period of indefinite length, as Rambach says, a very long time, the end of which is hidden from us.

Dr Bullinger's Appendix 129 to The Companion Bible, says this about *olam*:

The Hebrew [word] olam ... denotes indefinite, unknown or concealed duration (an age); just as we speak of 'the patriarchal age,' or 'the golden age,' etc.

The Interpreter's Dictionary of the Bible, Vol. IV, under *Time*, says,

The O.T. and the N.T. are not acquainted with the conception of eternity as timelessness. The O.T. has not developed a special term for 'eternity' which one could contrast with 'temporality.' The word *aion* originally meant 'vital force,' 'life;' then 'age,' 'lifetime.' It is, however, also used generally of a limited or unlimited long space of time. The use of the word *aion* is determined very much by the O.T. and the LXX (Septuagint). *Aion* means 'long distant uninterrupted time' in the past (Luke 1:10), as well as in the future (John 4:14).

Rev. J.S. Blunt, in the Dictionary of Theology, under the entry *Eternity*, says:

The conception of Eternity in the Semitic languages is that of a long duration and series of ages.

Jeff Benner describes the Hebrew word *olam* in detail in his book, *The Living Words; Volume One*. You can also find it on his website: http://www.ancient-hebrew.org/27_eternity.html

Some examples of where *olam* obviously cannot mean forever but is still translated as such:

Jonah, praying while in the belly of the whale:

"I descended to the roots of the mountains. The earth with its bars was around me forever (olam)..." (Jonah 2:6).

... then his master shall bring him to God, then he shall bring him to the door or the doorpost. And his master shall pierce his ear with an awl; and he shall serve him permanently (olam). (Exodus 21:6). Presumably only until he died, and therefore not forever!

"I have surely built You a lofty house, a place for Your dwelling forever (olam)." (1 Kings 8:13).

Obviously, that temple was destroyed and the subsequent temple was also destroyed; but now God dwells within humanity as the new covenant temple fulfilment. There will never need to be another physical third temple in Jerusalem with sacrifices and offerings, as Zionists and Christian Zionists insist. They may even seek to build such an edifice but it would never be a fulfilment of biblical prophecy, just another Babel-like effort to make a name for themselves. There are those seeking war by removing the Dome of the Rock to build a third temple, supported by otherwise peace-loving believers who have a complete blind spot in regards to Israel.

The following is taken from a booklet *Total Success Of The Cross of Christ* by Jerry Onyszczak:

> The Septuagint is the Greek translation of the Hebrew Scriptures (285 B.C.)
>
> The Septuagint uses the word "aion" in place of the Hebrew word "Olam"

The definition for "Olam" is the same as for "aion" – an indefinite period

Jonah was in the fish forever (Olam) (Jon 2:6)

A slave serves his master forever (Olam) (Exo 21:6)

Solomon's temple is built to last forever (Olam) (1Kg 8:13)

Sodom's fiery judgement is eternal (Olam) (Eze 16:53-55; Jud 1:7)

The Mosaic covenant is everlasting (Olam) (Lev 24:3, 8)

The Aaronic priesthood is everlasting (Olam) (Exo 40:15)

Circumcision was an everlasting (Olam) covenant (Gen 17:9-13)

Israel's judgment lasts forever (Olam) (Isa 32:13-15)

Animal sacrifices are to be offered forever (Olam) (2Ch 2:4)

I believe Jesus is the fulfilment and consummation of all the covenants and promises that God has made, spiritual or physical. The gospel was preached to Abraham and was not limited to one special people but was for all the families of the earth. Paul indicates that Jesus is the seed of Abraham who was the heir to the world, not just Palestine. Abraham was never just looking for the fulfilment of God's covenantal promise to him to be fulfilled physically. Hebrews reveals that Abraham was looking for a heavenly, not earthly, country and city.

By faith Abraham, when he was called, obeyed by going out to a place which he was to receive for an inheritance; and he went out, not knowing where he was going. By faith he lived

as an alien in the land of promise, as in a foreign land, dwelling in tents with Isaac and Jacob, fellow heirs of the same promise; for he was looking for the city which has foundations, whose architect and builder is God. By faith even Sarah herself received ability to conceive, even beyond the proper time of life, since she considered Him faithful who had promised. Therefore there was born even of one man, and him as good as dead at that, as many descendants as the stars of heaven in number, and innumerable as the sand which is by the seashore. All these died in faith, without receiving the promises, but having seen them and having welcomed them from a distance, and having confessed that they were strangers and exiles on the earth. For those who say such things make it clear that they are seeking a country of their own. And indeed if they had been thinking of that country from which they went out, they would have had opportunity to return. But as it is, they desire a better country, that is, a heavenly one. Therefore God is not ashamed to be called their God; for He has prepared a city for them. (Hebrews 11:8-16).

Now the Lord said to Abram,
"Go from your country,
And from your relatives
And from your father's house,
To the land which I will show you;
And I will make you into a great nation,
And I will bless you,
And make your name great;
And you shall be a blessing;
And I will bless those who bless you,
And the one who curses you I will curse.
And in you all the families of the earth will be blessed."
(Genesis 12:1-3).

The Scripture, foreseeing that God would justify the Gentiles by faith, preached the gospel beforehand to Abraham, saying, "All the nations will be blessed in you." (Galatians 3:8).

For the promise to Abraham or to his descendants that he would be heir of the world was not through the Law, but through the righteousness of faith. (Romans 4:13).

Now the promises were spoken to Abraham and to his seed. He does not say, "And to seeds," as referring to many, but rather to one, "And to your seed," that is, Christ. (Galatians 3:16).

There is neither Jew nor Greek, there is neither slave nor free man, there is neither male nor female; for you are all one in Christ Jesus. And if you belong to Christ, then you are Abraham's descendants, heirs according to promise. (Galatians 3:28-29).

Who were heirs of the covenant and promises made to Abraham and fulfilled in Christ? It was not Israel or the Jews but all who belong to Christ: and that is all mankind, who are alive and included in Christ, having been reconciled by the Father in Christ. The covenant made with Abraham was fulfilled in Christ; the covenant made with Moses was fulfilled in Christ; in the new covenant. The old covenant became obsolete and faded away: it was not everlasting and neither was their claim to the land.

The fulfilment of God's promises

There is a question that we need to answer to bring this section to a conclusion, before looking at Zionism itself: is Israel or the Church the fulfilment of God's prophetic promises?

The answer begins with understanding the fulfilment of the covenant God made with Abraham through new covenant revelation. To get a full picture of the covenant God made with Abraham you will need to read Genesis chapters 12 to 18 but the highlights are below, beginning with a passage we have just seen:

Now the Lord said to Abram,
"Go from your country,
And from your relatives
And from your father's house,
To the land which I will show you;
And I will make you into a great nation,
And I will bless you,
And make your name great;
And you shall be a blessing;
And I will bless those who bless you,
And the one who curses you I will curse.
And in you all the families of the earth will be blessed."
(Genesis 12:1-3).

"I will establish My covenant between Me and you and your descendants after you throughout their generations as an everlasting covenant, to be God to you and to your descendants after you. And I will give to you and to your descendants after you the land where you live as a stranger, all the land of Canaan, as an everlasting possession; and I will be their God." God said further to Abraham, "Now as for you, you shall keep My covenant, you and your descendants after you throughout their generations." (Genesis 17:7-9).

Zionists maintain that the promises God made to Abraham still belong to national Israel today and therefore national Israel and the Jewish people are still the only true people of God.

Christian Zionists add that Israel and the Jewish people are God's earthly people and the Church is God's heavenly people.

Do the teaching of Jesus and the New Testament writers affirm or deny this belief? How are the promises God made to Abraham interpreted as being fulfilled in the New Testament?

I believe that all the old covenant promises God made can only be fully understood through the new covenant revelation of Jesus where many scriptures find new light and meaning. Jesus came to take away the sins, the lost identity, of the whole world and the whole world was reconciled back to the Father who was working in Jesus. The promises were never meant to be restricted to a single ethnic or religious group of people. The covenant made with Israel was designed to make Israel a light to the Gentiles, not to exclude them. The prophet Isaiah used the language of Israel, Jacob, Judah and Zion about a new covenant that was coming, which Jesus places firmly in His arrival.

"I am the Lord, I have called You in righteousness,
I will also hold You by the hand and watch over You,
And I will appoint You as a covenant to the people,
As a light to the nations..." (Isaiah 42:6).

He says,
"It is too small a thing that You should be My Servant
To raise up the tribes of Jacob and to restore the preserved ones of Israel;
I will also make You a light of the nations
So that My salvation may reach to the end of the earth."
(Isaiah 49:6).

*"Arise, shine; for your light has come,
and the glory of the Lord has risen upon you.
For behold, darkness will cover the earth
And deep darkness the peoples;
But the Lord will rise upon you
And His glory will appear upon you.
Nations will come to your light,
And kings to the brightness of your rising."* (Isaiah 60:1-3).

*The Spirit of the Lord God is upon me,
Because the Lord has anointed me
To bring good news to the afflicted;
He has sent me to bind up the brokenhearted,
To proclaim liberty to captives
And freedom to prisoners;
To proclaim the favorable year of the Lord
And the day of vengeance of our God;
To comfort all who mourn,
To grant those who mourn in Zion,
Giving them a garland instead of ashes,
The oil of gladness instead of mourning,
The mantle of praise instead of a spirit of fainting.
So they will be called oaks of righteousness,
The planting of the Lord, that He may be glorified.*
(Isaiah 61:1-3).

*For I, the Lord, love justice,
I hate robbery in the burnt offering;
And I will faithfully give them their recompense
And make an everlasting covenant with them.* (Isaiah 61:8).

*"The Spirit of the Lord is upon Me,
Because He anointed Me to preach the gospel to the poor.
He has sent Me to proclaim release to the captives,*

And recovery of sight to the blind,
To set free those who are oppressed,
To proclaim the favorable year of the Lord."

And He closed the book, gave it back to the attendant and sat down; and the eyes of all in the synagogue were fixed on Him. And He began to say to them, "Today this Scripture has been fulfilled in your hearing." (Luke 4:18-21).

Then Jesus again spoke to them, saying, "I am the Light of the world; he who follows Me will not walk in the darkness, but will have the Light of life." (John 8:12).

Jesus expanded the prophets' understanding of the new covenant that was prophesied by Jeremiah and Ezekiel from Israel to the world. The new covenant would go beyond the physical presence of God in one temple in one city (Jerusalem) in one nation (Israel), to include the whole world. Now all people are temples of the Holy Spirit and part of the New Jerusalem because the sin of the world has been removed. The Old Testament prophets veiled their new covenant prophecies towards Israel but glimpses of the light of the world shone through. The promises made to Abraham (which the Zionists claim exclusively for themselves) were always for every family of the earth to be blessed. All in Christ are Abraham's descendants, his children by faith. The covenant promises to Abraham were always promises for the whole of mankind, as affirmed by Paul.

The Scripture, foreseeing that God would justify the Gentiles by faith, preached the gospel beforehand to Abraham, saying, "All the nations will be blessed in you." (Galatians 3:8).

And if you belong to Christ, then you are Abraham's descendants, heirs according to promise. (Galatians 3:29).

Now the promises were spoken to Abraham and to his seed. He does not say, "And to seeds," as referring to many, but rather to one, "And to your seed," that is, Christ. (Galatians 3:16).

For as many as are the promises of God, in Him they are yes; therefore also through Him is our Amen to the glory of God through us. (2 Corinthians 1:20).

The covenant promises made to Abraham's descendants were all fulfilled in Jesus as the seed and therefore the true Israel. All the covenants are therefore fulfilled in Christ and are accessible to all people: the Adamic, Noahidic, Abrahamic, Mosaic, and Davidic covenants are consummated and fulfilled in the new covenant in the last Adam, who is the seed of Abraham and David and the fulfilment of the law.

The inheritance of mankind of the whole world has always been God's plan, through Adam, Noah, Abraham, David or the church:

Then God said, "Let Us make man in Our image, according to Our likeness; and let them rule over the fish of the sea and over the birds of the sky and over the cattle and over all the earth, and over every creeping thing that creeps on the earth." God created man in His own image, in the image of God He created him; male and female He created them. God blessed them; and God said to them, "Be fruitful and multiply, and fill the earth, and subdue it; and rule over the fish of the sea and over the birds of the sky and over every living thing that moves on the earth." (Genesis 1:26-28).

And God blessed Noah and his sons and said to them, "Be fruitful and multiply, and fill the earth." (Genesis 9:1).

Now the LORD said to Abram,
"Go forth from your country,
And from your relatives
And from your father's house,
To the land which I will show you;
And I will make you a great nation, and I will bless you,
And make your name great;
And so you shall be a blessing;
And I will bless those who bless you,
And the one who curses you I will curse
And in you all the families of the earth will be blessed."
(Genesis 12:1-3).

For a Child will be born to us, a Son will be given to us;
And the government will rest on His shoulders;
And His name will be called Wonderful Counselor, Mighty God,
Eternal Father, Prince of Peace.
There will be no end to the increase of His government or of peace
On the throne of David and over his kingdom,
To establish it and to uphold it with justice and righteousness
From then on and forevermore.
The zeal of the Lord of armies will accomplish this.
(Isaiah 9:6-7).

And Jesus came up and spoke to them, saying, "All authority has been given to Me in heaven and on earth. Go therefore and make disciples of all the nations, baptizing them in the name of the Father and the Son and the Holy Spirit, teaching them to observe all that I commanded you; and lo, I am with you always, even to the end of the age." (Matthew 28:18-20).

The covenant promise was for the world through those of the faith of Abraham and was never meant to be restricted to nationalist Jews or a specific piece of land in Canaan. That should have been just the beginning, as they were called to be a light to the Gentiles, not to exclude them from the promises.

For the promise to Abraham or to his descendants that he would be heir of the world was not through the Law, but through the righteousness of faith. (Romans 4:13).

By faith he lived as an alien in the land of promise, as in a foreign land, dwelling in tents with Isaac and Jacob, fellow heirs of the same promise; for he was looking for the city which has foundations, whose architect and builder is God. (Hebrews 11:9-10).

But as it is, they desire a better country, that is, a heavenly one therefore God is not ashamed to be called their God; for He has prepared a city for them. (Hebrews 11:16).

Abraham's true descendants are only through Christ; it is those who are of faith who are the heirs, not the natural descendants of Abraham or Jacob/Israel who have no faith.

For you are all sons of God through faith in Christ Jesus. For all of you who were baptized into Christ have clothed yourselves with Christ. There is neither Jew nor Greek, there is neither slave nor free man, there is neither male nor female; for you are all one in Christ Jesus. And if you belong to Christ, then you are Abraham's descendants, heirs according to promise. (Galatians 3:26-29).

"Your father Abraham rejoiced to see My day, and he saw it and was glad." (John 8:56).

Being a true Jew according to Paul, and he should know, is not by race but faith, when it comes to being classed as one of God's people. Paul took the promises made to Israel and applied them to all mankind inclusively.

The book of Romans is often used by Christian Zionists to affirm that 'all Israel' will be saved and that is often wrongly interpreted as nationalistic salvation of a whole nation. As I have noted, many Christian Zionists believe that Israel, being the people of God, are a special case and do not need to come to God through Jesus at all but have a covenantal right to salvation. Christian Zionists use one or two proof texts to argue their case from the book of Romans and do not take the context of the whole book into account.

... and so all Israel will be saved; just as it is written,

"The Deliverer will come from Zion,
He will remove ungodliness from Jacob."
"This is My covenant with them,
When I take away their sins." (Romans 11:26-27).

These few verses are taken as a proof text that all national Israel will be saved: but does it really say that when taking into account the whole of Romans? Even Romans chapter 9 says that 'all Israel' never were 'all Israel' by race or religion:

But it is not as though the word of God has failed. For they are not all Israel who are descended from Israel; nor are they all children because they are Abraham's descendants, but: "through Isaac your descendants will be named." That is, it is not the children of the flesh who are children of God, but the children of the promise are regarded as descendants. (Romans 9:6-8).

... even us, whom He also called, not from among Jews only, but also from among Gentiles.

As He says also in Hosea,
"I will call those who were not My people, 'My people,'
And her who was not beloved, 'beloved.'
And it shall be that in the place
Where it was said to them, 'you are not My people,'
There they shall be called sons of the living God."

Isaiah cries out concerning Israel, "Though the number of the sons of Israel be like the sand of the sea, it is the remnant that will be saved." (Romans 9:24-27).

It never was a matter of race or religion that decided the make-up of the people of God; it was a matter of faith. Therefore 'all Israel' does not refer to the current or past nation of Israel but only those, both Jews and Gentiles, who were justified by faith. In reality, God predestined, called, justified and glorified all people when He in Christ reconciled the cosmos to Himself, holding none of their sins against them.

Now all these things are from God, who reconciled us to Himself through Christ and gave us the ministry of reconciliation, namely, that God was in Christ reconciling the world to Himself, not counting their trespasses against them, and He has committed to us the word of reconciliation. (2 Corinthians 5:18-19).

For this reason it is by faith, in order that it may be in accordance with grace, so that the promise will be guaranteed to all the descendants, not only to those who are of the Law, but also to those who are of the faith of Abraham, who is the father of us all. (Romans 4:16).

The church is the continuation of the true people of God (those of faith in Christ), not a replacement for natural Israel. Therefore Jews who become believers become part of one new man; two groups becoming one: the 'true church' (the body of Christ, not the religious institution, of course). There are no longer two or three groups (the church, Israel and unbelievers) there are now just believers in Christ and not yet believers in Christ; there is only one new group, not two or three.

For He Himself is our peace and our bond of unity. He who made both groups—[Jews and Gentiles]—into one body and broke down the barrier, the dividing wall [of spiritual antagonism between us], by abolishing in His [own crucified] flesh the hostility caused by the Law with its commandments contained in ordinances [which He satisfied]; so that in Himself He might make the two into one new man, thereby establishing peace. (Ephesians 2:14-15 AMP).

Come to Him [then, to that] Living Stone which men tried and threw away, but which is chosen [and] precious in God's sight. [Come] and, like living stones, be yourselves built [into] a spiritual house, for a holy (dedicated, consecrated) priesthood, to offer up [those] spiritual sacrifices [that are] acceptable and pleasing to God through Jesus Christ.

For thus it stands in Scripture: Behold, I am laying in Zion a chosen (honored), precious chief Cornerstone, and he who believes in Him [who adheres to, trusts in, and relies on Him] shall never be disappointed or put to shame.

To you then who believe (who adhere to, trust in, and rely on Him) is the preciousness; but for those who disbelieve [it is true], The [very] Stone which the builders rejected has become the main Cornerstone,

And, A Stone that will cause stumbling and a Rock that will give [men] offense; they stumble because they disobey and disbelieve [God's] Word, as those [who reject Him] were destined (appointed) to do.

But you are a chosen race, a royal priesthood, a dedicated nation, [God's] own purchased, special people, that you may set forth the wonderful deeds and display the virtues and perfections of Him Who called you out of darkness into His marvelous light.

Once you were not a people [at all], but now you are God's people; once you were unpitied, but now you are pitied and have received mercy. (1 Peter 2:4-10 AMPC).

Paul's argument in Romans

I want to finally put to bed the argument about who is today the spiritual Israel, who today is a true Jew from God's perspective, and how all the promises of God are fulfilled in Christ in the new covenant. I will do this by following Paul's own argument which runs right through the book of Romans and cross-referencing this with Paul's other letters, particularly Galatians.

The context of Romans as a whole letter is that salvation is by faith alone, for Jew and Gentile, as there is no special treatment for anyone but all have been predestined to salvation.

The context of Romans 2 is that both Jew and Greek (Gentile) have sinned; therefore all have lost their identity and need salvation.

... but glory and honor and peace to everyone who does good, to the Jew first and also to the Greek. For there is no partiality with God. For all who have sinned without the Law will also

perish without the Law, and all who have sinned under the Law will be judged by the Law; (Romans 2:10-12).

The conclusion Paul draws is that post-resurrection, the term 'Jew' is a salvation term, not an ethnic or religious term; therefore being a 'true Jew' has nothing to do with race or religion but is by faith only. This is followed up later in Romans 9:6.

For he is not a Jew who is one outwardly, nor is circumcision that which is outward in the flesh. But he is a Jew who is one inwardly; and circumcision is that which is of the heart, by the Spirit, not by the letter; and his praise is not from men, but from God. (Romans 2:28-29).

This theme of salvation by faith is continued in Chapter 3 and the argument now shifts to circumcision where the benefit is seen not in automatic salvation but the first opportunity to believe. Those who did not believe despite being a citizen of Israel were excluded from the promises.

Then what advantage has the Jew? Or what is the benefit of circumcision? Great in every respect. First of all, that they were entrusted with the oracles of God. What then? If some did not believe, their unbelief will not nullify the faithfulness of God, will it? (Romans 3:1-3).

It was only those who believed who were saved and hence true followers of God and heirs of His promises. Compare what Paul wrote to the Galatians, which affirms this truth:

The Scripture, foreseeing that God would justify the Gentiles by faith, preached the gospel beforehand to Abraham, saying, "all the nations will be blessed in you." (Galatians 3:8).

Now the promises were spoken to Abraham and to his seed. He does not say, "And to seeds," as referring to many, but rather to one, "And to your seed," that is, Christ. (Galatians 3:16).

For you are all sons of God through faith in Christ Jesus. For all of you who were baptized into Christ have clothed yourselves with Christ. There is neither Jew nor Greek, there is neither slave nor free man, there is neither male nor female; for you are all one in Christ Jesus. And if you belong to Christ, then you are Abraham's descendants, heirs according to promise. (Galatians 3:26-29).

Paul continues the letter in Romans 3, again arguing that both Jews and Gentiles need to be saved by faith as all have sinned. The true meaning of sin (Greek *hamartia*) is loss of form or image, and therefore by inference, identity. Sin is and never has been a behavioural issue but an identity issue; the behaviours are a symptom of the true problem. Of course, that is not meant to minimise the behaviours but indicates that you cannot fix the problem by trying to control the behaviour, particularly with laws. Only with the restored true identity of sonship in relationship with the Father and by a rejection of following the DIY tree path of independence will the problem be solved. All fall short of God's image by self-effort and need to realise what the Father has already accomplished for them in Jesus.

What then? Are we better than they? Not at all; for we have already charged that both Jews and Greeks are all under sin; (Romans 3:9).

... for all have sinned and fall short of the glory of God, (Romans 3:23).

Or is God the God of Jews only? Is He not the God of Gentiles also? Yes, of Gentiles also, since indeed God who will justify the circumcised by faith and the uncircumcised through faith is one. (Romans 3:29-30).

Justification is by faith only; and Paul continues with that theme throughout the letter. So in chapter 4 we see that circumcision was in itself nothing but a seal of the righteousness that is through faith; circumcision as a work could never hope to produce righteousness. Paul also reveals that the promises to Abraham were for the whole world, not just one nation.

What then shall we say that Abraham, our forefather according to the flesh, has found? (Romans 4:1).

... and he received the sign of circumcision, a seal of the righteousness of the faith which he had while uncircumcised, so that he might be the father of all who believe without being circumcised, that righteousness might be credited to them, and the father of circumcision to those who not only are of the circumcision, but who also follow in the steps of the faith of our father Abraham which he had while uncircumcised. For the promise to Abraham or to his descendants that he would be heir of the world was not through the Law, but through the righteousness of faith. (Romans 4:11-13).

The covenant promise that Abraham was given was for the world, not just Palestine; and that was affirmed by the writer of Hebrews who revealed what Abraham was truly seeking:

By faith he lived as an alien in the land of promise, as in a foreign land, dwelling in tents with Isaac and Jacob, fellow heirs of the same promise; for he was looking for the city which has foundations, whose architect and builder is God. (Hebrews 11:9-10).

But as it is, they desire a better country, that is, a heavenly one Therefore God is not ashamed to be called their God; for He has prepared a city for them. (Hebrews 11:16).

Paul continues this theme and he shares his desire that his kinsmen by race and religion would be saved. They could only be saved by faith, so Paul is grieved that they are rejecting salvation by the grace offered to them. Remember, Paul had first-hand experience of resisting the truth that Jesus was already in Him. The moment of realisation for him came on the Damascus road where, in the light of God's presence, Saul had that revelation. Without praying a prayer of salvation or responding to an altar call, he realised that Jesus was already at work in him and that he had been self-righteously resisting God's grace, mercy and love. The newly enlightened Paul was given a mission, 'a heavenly vision' he called it, to share the same amazingly good news of the Father's inclusion of all mankind and that Jesus was already at work in him as in all mankind, knocking on the door, as it were.

But when God, who had set me apart even from my mother's womb and called me through His grace, was pleased to reveal His Son in me so that I might preach Him in the Gentiles, (Galatians 1:15-16).

Paul paused his argument in what we know as chapter 8 to remind them of God's foreknowledge and unfailing love.

And we know that God causes all things to work together for good to those who love God, to those who are called according to His purpose. For those whom He foreknew, He also predestined to become conformed to the image of His Son, so that He would be the firstborn among many brethren; and these whom He predestined, He also called; and these whom He called, He also justified; and these whom He justified, He also glorified.

What then shall we say to these things? If God is for us, who is against us? He who did not spare His own Son, but delivered Him over for us all, how will He not also with Him freely give us all things? Who will bring a charge against God's elect? God is the one who justifies; who is the one who condemns? Christ Jesus is He who died, yes, rather who was raised, who is at the right hand of God, who also intercedes for us. Who will separate us from the love of Christ? Will tribulation, or distress, or persecution, or famine, or nakedness, or peril, or sword? Just as it is written, "For Your sake we are being put to death all day long; We were considered as sheep to be slaughtered." But in all these things we overwhelmingly conquer through Him who loved us. For I am convinced that neither death, nor life, nor angels, nor principalities, nor things present, nor things to come, nor powers, nor height, nor depth, nor any other created thing, will be able to separate us from the love of God, which is in Christ Jesus our Lord. (Romans 8:28-39).

Paul knew just how he had been deceived by religion and now counted all his past religious self-righteousness as dung, a polite way of putting it. That is the context of the whole letter to the Romans and is particularly evident in how Paul expresses his sorrow and compassion for his people still living in deception.

I am telling the truth in Christ, I am not lying, my conscience testifies with me in the Holy Spirit, that I have great sorrow and unceasing grief in my heart. For I could wish that I myself were accursed, separated from Christ for the sake of my brethren, my kinsmen according to the flesh, who are Israelites, to whom belongs the adoption as sons, and the glory and the covenants and the giving of the Law and the temple service and the promises, whose are the fathers, and from whom is the Christ according to the flesh, who is over all, God blessed forever. Amen.

But it is not as though the word of God has failed For they are not all Israel who are descended from Israel; nor are they all children because they are Abraham's descendants, but: "through Isaac your descendants will be named." That is, it is not the children of the flesh who are children of God, but the children of the promise are regarded as descendants. (Romans 9:1-8).

Paul now makes the same argument: not all Israel (by birth or religion) will be saved, only the children of promise. Who are the children of promise? In reality, all mankind that Jesus died for; but it is only those who have had the realisation who know that they already belong to Christ and are Abraham's heirs by faith, not natural birth.

And if you belong to Christ, then you are Abraham's descendants, heirs according to promise. (Galatians 3:29).

Paul quotes a prophecy of Hosea illustrating that God was going to call the Gentiles by faith: they would not reject this amazing grace. But only a remnant of the whole nation of Israel would be saved physically, and of course the early church began with that remnant. Even on the day of Pentecost, Jews were present representing every nation under heaven, visiting Jerusalem for the feast. How very clever of God to create an evangelistic force to go back to those nations and preach the good news in fulfilment of the great commission of Matthew 28:18-20 and Jesus' prophecy that the gospel would be preached in the whole world! Paul later affirms that this had already occurred in that generation.

Now there were Jews living in Jerusalem, devout men from every nation under heaven. (Acts 2:5).

This gospel of the kingdom shall be preached in the whole world as a testimony to all the nations, and then the end will come. (Matthew 24:14).

First, I thank my God through Jesus Christ for you all, because your faith is being proclaimed throughout the whole world. (Romans 1:8).

... because of the hope laid up for you in heaven, of which you previously heard in the word of truth, the gospel which has come to you, just as in all the world also it is constantly bearing fruit and increasing, even as it has been doing in you also since the day you heard of it and understood the grace of God in truth; (Colossians 1:5-6).

Paul continues the theme of the true people of God being made up of the remnant of Israel and the Gentiles who believed by faith:

... even us, whom He also called, not from among Jews only, but also from among Gentiles.

As He says also in Hosea,
"I will call those who were not My people, 'My people,'
And her who was not beloved, 'beloved.'
And it shall be that in the place
Where it was said to them, 'you are not My people,'
There they shall be called sons of the living God."

*Isaiah cries out concerning Israel,
"Though the number of the sons of Israel be like the sand of
the sea, it is the remnant that will be saved; for the Lord will
execute His word on the earth, thoroughly and quickly."*

*And just as Isaiah foretold, "unless the Lord of Sabaoth had
left to us a posterity, we would have become like Sodom, and
would have resembled Gomorrah."* (Romans 9:24-29).

*Why? Because they did not pursue it by faith, but as though it
were by works. They stumbled over the stumbling stone, just
as it is written, "Behold, I lay in Zion a stone of stumbling and
a rock of offense, and he who believes in him will not be
disappointed."* (Romans 9:32-33).

The rejection of Jesus as the Messiah, referred to as the stone, is a consistent New Testament theme: the stone in context was Jesus and His kingdom.

In Romans chapter 10 Paul continues the theme of salvation by faith for all, both Jew and Greek (Gentile):

*For there is no distinction between Jew and Greek; for the
same Lord is Lord of all, abounding in riches for all who call
on Him; for "Whoever will call on the name of the Lord will
be saved."* (Romans 10:12-13).

The prophecy of Isaiah was that Gentiles would be saved by faith and make Israel angry; but they were still stubborn and unrepentant just as Paul had been.

*But I say, surely Israel did not know, did they? First Moses
says, "I will make you jealous by that which is not a nation,
by a nation without understanding will I anger you." And
Isaiah is very bold and says, "I was found by those who did
not seek Me. I became manifest to those who did not ask for*

Me." But as for Israel He says, "All the day long I have stretched out My hands to a disobedient and obstinate people." (Romans 10:19-21).

This theme of salvation by faith alone sets the context for Romans 11. Remember, there were no chapters or verses in Paul's original letter so there was a more obvious continuity.

I say then, God has not rejected His people, has He? May it never be! For I too am an Israelite, a descendant of Abraham, of the tribe of Benjamin. God has not rejected His people whom He foreknew. Or do you not know what the Scripture says in the passage about Elijah, how he pleads with God against Israel? (Romans 11:1-2).

The same theme runs throughout Romans chapter 11. The key is, who did God foreknow? A whole nation? Or, as the whole of Romans indicates, only those who are of faith? Of course, God foreknew all of them from an eternal perspective but here Paul is referring to the current and urgent situation before the day of the Lord which was about to come. No one escapes the love of God that continues even after death. For all those who continued to reject the love and grace of God and ended up besieged in Jerusalem – and for many, being thrown into a literal Gehenna – that was still not the end of the hope of salvation. Although the hope of physical salvation from the destruction of Jerusalem was over, the hope of eternal salvation was not. God's amazing grace reaches beyond the grave within the consuming fire of His loving presence.

Paul identifies the current remnant as those including himself who had accepted Christ by faith from amongst the Jews. Paul knew the scriptures that salvation for the Gentiles could make them jealous as their promises were being enjoyed by others.

In the same way then, there has also come to be at the present time a remnant according to God's gracious choice. (Romans 11:5).

I say then, they did not stumble so as to fall, did they? May it never be! But by their transgression salvation has come to the Gentiles, to make them jealous. Now if their transgression is riches for the world and their failure is riches for the Gentiles, how much more will their fulfilment be! (Romans 11:11-12).

The same argument is reemphasised by Paul. If salvation has come to the Gentiles by Israel's rejection then of course 'their fulfilment' (following Paul's reasoning as seen throughout the whole letter) would be that their salvation would result in even more blessing.

Paul then goes on to talk about the olive tree and branches: in reality, the original figurative tree could be said to be the Tree of Life – and that included everyone, not just Jews. When Adam chose to follow his own independent tree path, inclusion was only by faith. The metaphor of being cut off is used as God seeks to re-establish a relationship with mankind through Adam, Seth, Enoch and eventually Noah, Abraham and the sons of Israel. The illustration uses the phrase 'cut off' which is a covenantal term: when mankind breaks the covenant made with it by God, it leaves the Tree of Life and follows the tree of knowledge of good and evil, which means works of toil and hard labour. This is the same argument using old covenant imagery: the real tree is only those of faith, if there is no faith, then branches choose not to be joined. There has only ever been one tree and people are grafted into what is their true inheritance, based on salvation by faith or a realisation of God's *chesed* lovingkindness, faithfulness, grace and mercy.

But I am speaking to you who are Gentiles. Inasmuch then as I am an apostle of Gentiles, I magnify my ministry, if somehow I might move to jealousy my fellow countrymen and save some of them. For if their rejection is the reconciliation of the world, what will their acceptance be but life from the dead? If the first piece of dough is holy, the lump is also; and if the root is holy, the branches are too. But if some of the branches were broken off, and you, being a wild olive, were grafted in among them and became partaker with them of the rich root of the olive tree... (Romans 11:13-17).

Of course, Paul desires that the entirety of his kin would be grafted back in by accepting Christ and becoming believers through realising and accepting who Jesus is as the only door to the Father.

... do not be arrogant toward the branches; but if you are arrogant, remember that it is not you who supports the root, but the root supports you. You will say then, "Branches were broken off so that I might be grafted in." Quite right, they were broken off for their unbelief, but you stand by your faith. Do not be conceited, but fear; for if God did not spare the natural branches, He will not spare you, either. Behold then the kindness and severity of God; to those who fell, severity, but to you, God's kindness, if you continue in His kindness; otherwise you also will be cut off. And they also, if they do not continue in their unbelief, will be grafted in, for God is able to graft them in again. For if you were cut off from what is by nature a wild olive tree, and were grafted contrary to nature into a cultivated olive tree, how much more will these who are the natural branches be grafted into their own olive tree? For I do not want you, brethren, to be uninformed of this mystery – so that you will not be wise in your own estimation – that a partial hardening has happened to Israel until the fullness of

the Gentiles has come in; and so all Israel will be saved; just as it is written,

"The deliverer will come from Zion,
He will remove ungodliness from Jacob."
"This is My covenant with them, when I take away their sins."
(Romans 11:18-27).

The same applies to Israel: they have hardened their heart but should they repent (or change their minds to agree with God) they will be saved. This process continued right up to 70 AD after Jesus ascended: alongside the Gentiles being saved, so also were Jews. Even today, Jesus has been appearing to many Jewish priests in dreams, as He has also to Muslims and Hindus.

And so all Israel (all foreknown) will be saved by faith in Christ. The 'so' as used here does not mean 'after' but refers to the method of their salvation. Salvation was by faith, not works or race or nationality. Of course, the deliverer is Christ. This passage has been misinterpreted by Christian Zionists and dispensationalists to infer that after all the Gentiles have been saved then all Israel will then be saved in a different manner. In reality, all this verse is saying just echoes the same theme of salvation by faith alone. Paul's use of 'all Israel' may be compared to his use of 'the Israel of God' in the letter to the Galatians, where he uses the phrase to refer to both Jew and Gentile as one new man. 'All Israel' refers to the Gentiles and Jews being saved by the same faith in Jesus, not just the remnant which was the Jews who were being saved.

From the standpoint of the gospel they are enemies for your sake, but from the standpoint of God's choice they are beloved for the sake of the fathers; for the gifts and the calling of God are irrevocable. For just as you once were disobedient to God, but now have been shown mercy because of their disobedience, so these also now have been disobedient, that because of the mercy shown to you they also may now be shown mercy. For God has shut up all in disobedience so that He may show mercy to all. (Romans 11:28-32).

Then God's choice is again, as Paul illustrates in Romans 9, not for a nation or a religion but those of faith. Israel's gift and calling were only for those who were true Israel by faith, those whose hearts were circumcised, not national Israel. Of course, God desires that none should perish and He would be only too willing to make mercy available to Jewish people but they must come to realise faith in Christ to receive it.

The mistake people make in interpreting Romans 11 is that they isolate it from the rest of the letter when the book as a whole follows the same reasoning throughout. We are only considering Romans 11 here, but the New Testament writers are consistent in their interpretation of the promises of God being fulfilled in Christ. Should many Jews turn to Christ in the future this will of course release much blessing to the world, as would many Muslims, Hindus, Americans or British people turning to Him.

Natural Israel

So what happened to natural Israel?

The kingdom was removed from them for their rejection of Jesus as the chief corner stone and they suffered the consequences of independence. Jesus prophesied this in Matthew chapters 21-25.

John the Baptist prophesied judgment on Israel, which must be seen as covenantal justice and not punishment. There are self-inflicted consequences of breaking a covenant, one being divorce and separation. The judgment made on the old covenant law-based system was a verdict that it was obsolete and fulfilled in Jesus who was the consummation of the law and prophets. When many Christians, particularly those with an evangelical background, hear or read the word 'judgment' they jump to the wrong conclusion that it means punishment. The context of covenantal judgment and justice will always be righteous and any judgment legally allowed the enemy to bring about the consequences, not God. This is evident right throughout the history of Israel as a nation and there are many examples in the book of Judges. Israel had agreed to a covenant with God in which they would not worship other gods. Whenever they broke that covenant they walked away from God's protection within the covenant. It might appear that God was punishing them when, for example, the Midianites or Philistines conquered them, but legally God had to abide by the covenant and allow the enemy access. The way the Hebrew mindset worked was in an undifferentiated way (i.e. they believed that the devil worked for God and therefore did His dirty work for Him). In what they wrote they attributed to God the words and works of the devil. This is why when reading the record of the Old Testament there appears to be a very different angry God from the loving Father that Jesus revealed.

God was not passive regarding those who walked in independence. God pursued Adam and Eve in the garden where they were hiding in fear; He engaged with Noah to provide salvation from the flood; He initiated a relationship with Abraham and Moses. He sent Israel judges and prophets; but they continued to bring the consequences of rebellion and independence on themselves. God was not angry with them and God was not happy that they suffered consequences because He is faithful and His lovingkindness never ends. The judgment was on the system and those leading or following the system of self-righteous religion suffered the consequences of following a failed obsolete religious system.

But when he saw many of the Pharisees and Sadducees coming for baptism, he said to them, "You brood of vipers, who warned you to flee from the wrath to come? Therefore bear fruit in keeping with repentance; and do not suppose that you can say to yourselves, 'We have Abraham for our father'; for I say to you that from these stones God is able to raise up children to Abraham. The axe is already laid at the root of the trees; therefore every tree that does not bear good fruit is cut down and thrown into the fire. As for me, I baptize you with water for repentance, but He who is coming after me is mightier than I, and I am not fit to remove His sandals; He will baptize you with the Holy Spirit and fire. His winnowing fork is in His hand, and He will thoroughly clear His threshing floor; and He will gather His wheat into the barn, but He will burn up the chaff with unquenchable fire." (Matthew 3:7-12).

Jesus prophesied judgment on the system that could produce no fruit and people who followed that system would not be saved physically or spiritually by it.

Jesus said to them, "Did you never read in the Scriptures, 'The stone which the builders rejected, This became the chief corner stone; This came about from the Lord, And it is marvelous in our eyes'?

"Therefore I say to you, the kingdom of God will be taken away from you and given to a people, producing the fruit of it. And he who falls on this stone will be broken to pieces; but on

whomever it falls, it will scatter him like dust." (Matthew 21:42-44).

Natural Israel was scattered like dust into the nations in the dispersion after 70 AD; some remained locally and some mixed with other mainly European people, maintaining their religion but losing their ethnicity. Judaism as a religion is today a false religion, like any other false religion which is based on works and not grace. The followers of monotheistic religions, including those who adhere to Judaism, Islam or institutional Christianity, are not worshipping the one true God: He can only be engaged through Jesus who is the Way, the Truth and the Life and is the only way to the Father. Who or what are followers of religion being deceived into worshipping? The one who is behind the tree of the knowledge of good and evil, all works, religion and humanism – in fact anything which is based on performance orientation, toil and hardship – is Lucifer. All religion is Luciferian, dressed up and known by many names, but it is all based on appeasing and trying to earn favour by dead works.

For thus it stands in Scripture: Behold, I am laying in Zion a chosen (honored), precious chief Cornerstone, and he who believes in Him [who adheres to, trusts in, and relies on Him] shall never be disappointed or put to shame.

To you then who believe (who adhere to, trust in, and rely on Him) is the preciousness; but for those who disbelieve [it is true], The [very] Stone which the builders rejected has become the main Cornerstone,

And, A Stone that will cause stumbling and a Rock that will give [men] offense; they stumble because they disobey and disbelieve [God's] Word, as those [who reject Him] were destined (appointed) to do. (1 Peter 2:6-8 AMPC).

"Woe to you, scribes and Pharisees, hypocrites! For you tithe mint and dill and cummin, and have neglected the weightier provisions of the law: justice and mercy and faithfulness; but these are the things you should have done without neglecting the others. You blind guides, who strain out a gnat and swallow a camel!

Woe to you, scribes and Pharisees, hypocrites! For you clean the outside of the cup and of the dish, but inside they are full of robbery and self-indulgence. You blind Pharisee, first clean the inside of the cup and of the dish, so that the outside of it may become clean also.

Woe to you, scribes and Pharisees, hypocrites! For you are like whitewashed tombs which on the outside appear beautiful, but inside they are full of dead men's bones and all uncleanness. So you, too, outwardly appear righteous to men, but inwardly you are full of hypocrisy and lawlessness.

Woe to you, scribes and Pharisees, hypocrites! For you build the tombs of the prophets and adorn the monuments of the righteous, and say, 'If we had been living in the days of our fathers, we would not have been partners with them in shedding the blood of the prophets.' So you testify against yourselves, that you are sons of those who murdered the prophets. Fill up, then, the measure of the guilt of your fathers. You serpents, you brood of vipers, how will you escape the sentence of hell [Gehenna]*?*

Therefore, behold, I am sending you prophets and wise men and scribes; some of them you will kill and crucify, and some of them you will scourge in your synagogues, and persecute from city to city, so that upon you may fall the guilt of all the righteous blood shed on earth, from the blood of righteous Abel to the blood of Zechariah, the son of Berechiah, whom you murdered between the temple and the altar. Truly I say to you, all these things will come upon this generation.

Jerusalem, Jerusalem, who kills the prophets and stones those who are sent to her! How often I wanted to gather your children together, the way a hen gathers her chicks under her wings, and you were unwilling. Behold, your house is being left to you desolate! (Matthew 23:23-38).

Matthew 24:1-34 and Luke 21:7-32 describe this judgment on the old covenant system; and all that Jesus prophesied in those passages took place in that generation.

Jesus came out from the temple and was going away when His disciples came up to point out the temple buildings to Him. And He said to them, "Do you not see all these things? Truly I say to you, not one stone here will be left upon another, which will not be torn down."

As He was sitting on the Mount of Olives, the disciples came to Him privately, saying, "Tell us, when will these things happen, and what will be the sign of Your coming, and of the end of the age?"

And Jesus answered and said to them, "See to it that no one misleads you. For many will come in My name, saying, 'I am the Christ,' and will mislead many. You will be hearing of wars and rumors of wars. See that you are not frightened, for those things must take place, but that is not yet the end. For nation will rise against nation, and kingdom against kingdom, and in various places there will be famines and earthquakes. But all these things are merely the beginning of birth pangs. (Matthew 24:1-8).

What Jesus was describing were the signs that pointed to the eventual end of the old covenant system (wineskin) and the beginning of the new covenant wineskin. This was the end of the old natural system (central nation, central city, central temple) symbolised by the torn curtain of the Holy of Holies: now there is open access to the presence of God. This is the new covenant and the New Jerusalem (whose gates are never shut and therefore there is open access); and those who know God by personal experience realise that they are temples of God's presence.

And behold, the veil of the temple was torn in two from top to bottom; and the earth shook and the rocks were split. (Matthew 27:51).

The New Testament writers clarify the differences between the physical and spiritual Jerusalem, temple and land:

- Jerusalem is now above (see Galatians 4:25-26).
- Mount Zion is spiritual and eternal (see Hebrews 12:22-24).
- The temple is now living and spiritual (see 1 Corinthians 6:19, Ephesians 2:20-22).
- The acceptable sacrifices are now our lives and praise (see Romans 12:1-2, 1 Peter 2:5, Hebrews 12:15).
- The land of promise is no longer Canaan but is the world (and the new heavens and new earth).
- The old natural land, temple and nation were only symbols, types or shadows of the spiritual new covenant realisation of those symbols (see Colossians 2:16-17, Hebrews 8:5, 10:1).

According to the revelation of the New Testament writers, every expression that once denoted Israel in the Old Testament is now invested with new spiritual significance and is only applicable to the true believer in Jesus.

"Then they will deliver you to tribulation and will kill you, and you will be hated by all nations because of My name. At that time many will fall away and will betray one another and hate one another. Many false prophets will arise and will mislead many. Because lawlessness is increased, most people's love will grow cold. But the one who endures to the end, he will be saved. This gospel of the kingdom shall be preached in the whole world as a testimony to all the nations, and then the end will come." (Matthew 24:9-14).

The gospel (and the end of the old system) has already been preached:

Now there were Jews living in Jerusalem, devout men from every nation under heaven. (Acts 2:5).

So faith comes from hearing, and hearing by the word of Christ.
But I say, surely they have never heard, have they? Indeed they have;
"Their voice has gone out into all the earth,
And their words to the ends of the world." (Romans 10:17-18).

... because of the hope laid up for you in heaven, of which you previously heard in the word of truth, the gospel which has come to you, just as in all the world also it is constantly bearing fruit and increasing, even as it has been doing in you also since the day you heard of it and understood the grace of God in truth; (Colossians 1:5-6).

... if indeed you continue in the faith firmly established and steadfast, and not moved away from the hope of the gospel that you have heard, which was proclaimed in all creation under

heaven, and of which I, Paul, was made a minister. (Colossians 1:23).

"Therefore when you see the ABOMINATION OF DESOLATION which was spoken of through Daniel the prophet, standing in the holy place (let the reader understand), then those who are in Judea must flee to the mountains. Whoever is on the housetop must not go down to get the things out that are in his house. Whoever is in the field must not turn back to get his cloak. But woe to those who are pregnant and to those who are nursing babies in those days! But pray that your flight will not be in the winter, or on a Sabbath. For then there will be a great tribulation, such as has not occurred since the beginning of the world until now, nor ever will. Unless those days had been cut short, no life would have been saved; but for the sake of the elect those days will be cut short. Then if anyone says to you, 'Behold, here is the Christ,' or 'There He is,' do not believe him. For false Christs and false prophets will arise and will show great signs and wonders, so as to mislead, if possible, even the elect. Behold, I have told you in advance. So if they say to you, 'Behold, He is in the wilderness,' do not go out, or, 'Behold, He is in the inner rooms,' do not believe them. For just as the lightning comes from the east and flashes even to the west, so will the coming of the Son of Man be. Wherever the corpse is, there the vultures will gather.

But immediately after the tribulation of those days THE SUN WILL BE DARKENED, AND THE MOON WILL NOT GIVE ITS LIGHT, AND THE STARS WILL FALL from the sky, and the powers of the heavens will be shaken. And then the sign of the Son of Man will appear in the sky, and then all the tribes of the earth will mourn, and they will see the SON OF MAN COMING ON THE CLOUDS OF THE SKY with power and great glory. And He will send forth His angels with A GREAT

TRUMPET and THEY WILL GATHER TOGETHER His elect from the four winds, from one end of the sky to the other. Now learn the parable from the fig tree: when its branch has already become tender and puts forth its leaves, you know that summer is near; so, you too, when you see all these things, recognize that He is near, right at the door. Truly I say to you, this generation will not pass away until all these things take place." (Matthew 24:15-34).

All these things have already taken place, the prophetic language used (in uppercase letters in the NASB) comes from Daniel 7 and refers to Jesus receiving all authority in heaven and earth at His ascension (see Matthew 28:18). The signs in the heavens refer to the end of the old covenant system of authority and similar language is used in Isaiah 13:19-20, Amos 8:9, Ezekiel 32:7, Joel 2 and Acts 2:19 when old authority systems ended, e.g. Samaria, Egypt, Babylon.

The judgment that Jesus prophesied came upon Israel, representing the old covenant system, with the destruction of Jerusalem by the Romans in 70 AD. The kingdom is now in the hands of the *ekklesia* that Jesus is building, the people of God made up of believers in Christ from all nations under heaven, including Jews by race or religion, through whom the manifold wisdom of God is to be made known (see Ephesians 3:8-11).

Galatians 3:29 states that if you belong to Christ, then you are Abraham's descendants, heirs according to promise. If so, then Christians would have equal claim to Israel as a land – but as we now see, it is the world and creation itself that is our inheritance.

For you are all sons of God through faith in Christ Jesus. For all of you who were baptized into Christ have clothed yourselves with Christ. There is neither Jew nor Greek, there is neither slave nor free man, there is neither male nor female; for you are all one in Christ Jesus. And if you belong to Christ, then you are Abraham's descendants, heirs according to promise. (Galatians 3:26-29).

For the promise to Abraham or to his descendants that he would be heir of the world was not through the Law, but through the righteousness of faith. (Romans 4:13).

This is the new covenant fulfilled in Christ and eventually outworked through us, the new heaven and new earth. The sign of this everlasting covenant is circumcision of the heart: the old physical sign of the circumcision of the flesh is now replaced and fulfilled in the new spiritual circumcision of the heart.

For he is not a Jew who is one outwardly, nor is circumcision that which is outward in the flesh. But he is a Jew who is one inwardly; and circumcision is that which is of the heart, by the Spirit, not by the letter; and his praise is not from men but from God. (Romans 2:28-29).

The nation of Israel is now no more the people of God than the nations of China, Russia, America or Britain. Judaism is just another false religion, worshipping a false God.

The nation-state of Israel

Zionists and Christian Zionists both see the creation of the nation-state of Israel in 1948 as a fulfilment of Old Testament prophecy and therefore evidence that modern-day Israel is still God's special people. This is another argument that must be answered, as it is at the heart of what is behind the Luciferian Zionist agenda.

All the promises and covenants are fulfilled in Jesus, not in Israel, and therefore the land of promise is fulfilled spiritually in the new covenant, not literally. We will look at the history of Zionism and how the state of Israel came into being later. For now, suffice it to say that it was not a fulfilment of prophecy but part of a very different agenda.

Modern Israel is not the Old Testament or New Testament Israel. The Abrahamic Covenant and Israel's land promises, when taken in their correct context, were biblically fulfilled in 70 AD when their custodianship of the kingdom was fully and finally removed.

To understand what God's purposes were when He established covenants, we need to be aware of what His original intention was, and therefore see the promises and covenants in a restoration light. God has never had a plan B or C, just a plan A: the covenant with Abraham and Israel were part of the same plan, not separate and independent from it.

God's original intention and desire was that there would be one family of mankind, with Him as their Father and everyone being brothers and sisters. By following the path of DIY independence, humanity eventually decided to make a name for themselves. That was the significance of the tower of Babel story: man was seeking to act independently of God to make a name for themselves, so God confused their languages and therefore removed their ability to be in agreement with one another.

The nations were judged and divided into 70 (see Genesis 10-11). God disinherited them and stopped them from fulfilling the "I will, we will" Luciferian agenda. God's plan continued through Abraham, who would be the father of many nations and through whom all the families would be reunited in Christ, the seed of Abraham. God eventually continued with His original intention, initially by making one nation His inheritance and heritage as an example or light to the nations. It would be through Abraham's seed and eventually the formation of a covenant made with national Israel that the Messiah and salvation would come to the world to reconcile the nations to Himself once again.

This process was firstly to be worked out through physical old covenant Israel being blessed 'in the land' as an example to the rest of the nations. Israel failed to be a light to the Gentiles, so subsequently the Messianic new covenant spiritual fulfilment was realised in Jesus. The new covenant spiritual fulfilment will enable the physical restoration of all creation back to the intention of God for a unified whole. First the physical, then the spiritual; then the physical and spiritual unified in the full restoration of all things.

All the promises made to Abraham have been fulfilled in Jesus, not in the creation of the physical state of Israel.

The Abrahamic promise fulfilled in Christ

In Genesis, God promised Abraham that through his descendants He would (1) form a great nation; (2) give them a land, and (3) bless the nations through Abraham's seed. That promise was reaffirmed through Moses and the promises to 'the children of Israel,' as they were then known.

1. A great nation

God promised Abraham that through him he would form a great nation – to be as numerous as the stars in the sky, the dust of the earth, and the sand on the seashore. The promise continued to be worked out and eventually Jacob was renamed Israel and his small family went to live in Egypt. This promise to be a great nation was fulfilled and 430 years later the children of Israel came out of Egypt as a new nation.

He said, "I am God, the God of your father; do not be afraid to go down to Egypt, for I will make you a great nation there." (Genesis 46:3).

Your fathers went down to Egypt seventy persons in all, and now the Lord your God has made you as numerous as the stars of heaven. (Deuteronomy 10:22).

"But as the time of the promise was approaching which God had assured to Abraham, the people increased and multiplied in Egypt..." (Acts 7:17).

By faith he lived as an alien in the land of promise, as in a foreign land, dwelling in tents with Isaac and Jacob, fellow heirs of the same promise; for he was looking for the city which has foundations, whose architect and builder is God. By faith even Sarah herself received ability to conceive, even beyond the proper time of life, since she considered Him faithful who had promised. Therefore there was born even of one man, and him as good as dead at that, as many descendants as the stars of heaven in number, and innumerable as the sand which is by the seashore. (Hebrews 11:9-12).

It is clear that the promise was always going to go beyond one nation or physical land and while this specific promise was physically fulfilled under the Mosaic old covenant, the New Testament reveals that it would be fully fulfilled in Christ forming the Church as His new 'nation' (see Matthew 21:43-45; 1 Peter 2:9; and Galatians 6:16).

In 70 AD Jesus 'took' the kingdom from physical Israel and 'gave it' to 'another nation' – which is the spiritual new covenant 'elect nation' or 'Israel of God'. It is through this 'nation' or 'New Jerusalem' which is 'from above' that the message of the reconciliation of the rest of the nations of the world back to Himself would be preached (see Galatians 4:21-31; Hebrews 11 to Hebrews 13:14 YLT; Revelation 21-22:17).

The promise of becoming a great nation and the father of many nations is fulfilled in Christ, as now, *"The kingdom of the world has become the kingdom of our Lord and of His Christ; and He will reign forever and ever."* (Revelation 11:15).

2. A land

God promised Abraham that through his descendants he would inherit a land.

On that day the Lord made a covenant with Abram, saying, "To your descendants, I have given this land, from the river of Egypt as far as the great river, the river Euphrates..." (Genesis 15:18).

Talmudic Zionists and Christian Zionists argue that this promise is still to be fulfilled and is a goal to be financed and fought for. That premise is not supported if you allow the Bible to bear witness, rather than futurist eschatology. If this is still in the future then why does Joshua state that they took possession of all the land promised and that all the promises were fulfilled and came to pass? This is also recorded in the days of Samuel, David and Solomon.

So the Lord gave Israel all the land which He had sworn to give to their fathers, and they possessed it and lived in it. And the Lord gave them rest on every side, according to all that He had sworn to their fathers, and no one of all their enemies stood before them; the Lord gave all their enemies into their hand. Not one of the good promises which the Lord had made to the house of Israel failed; all came to pass. (Joshua 21:43-45).

Judah and Israel were as numerous as the sand that is on the seashore in abundance; they were eating and drinking and rejoicing. Now Solomon ruled over all the kingdoms from the River to the land of the Philistines and the border of Egypt; they brought tribute and served Solomon all the days of his life. (1 Kings 4:20-21).

"Blessed be the Lord, who has given rest to His people Israel, according to all that He promised; not one word has failed of all His good promise, which He promised through Moses His servant." (1 Kings 8:56).

*"You are the Lord God,
Who chose Abram
And brought him out from Ur of the Chaldees,
And gave him the name Abraham.
You found his heart faithful before You,
And made a covenant with him
To give him the land of the Canaanite,
Of the Hittite and the Amorite,
Of the Perizzite, the Jebusite and the Girgashite –
To give it to his descendants.
And You have fulfilled Your promise,
For You are righteous...
So their sons entered and possessed the land.
And You subdued before them the inhabitants of the land, the Canaanites..."* (Nehemiah 9:7-8, 24).

The actual physical land promises made to Abraham and Moses have already been fulfilled but there is also the fulfilment of the types and shadows that the land represented. The physical old covenant blessing of being 'in the land' of

Israel was typological, pointing to the ultimate blessing of being spiritually 'in Christ' in the new covenant Israel of God (the *ekklesia*). There are Christians who promote instability in the political situation in the Middle East, hoping that war will bring the return of Jesus. There is no need to be fighting wars over land such as modern 'Israel,' or 'Jerusalem' and that agenda is completely unbiblical.

3: The seed promise

The New Testament writers reveal that the seed promise made to Abraham is now fully fulfilled 'in Christ' and the *ekklesia*. The promises of being a nation and having an inheritance of land come through having faith in the seed of Christ, the true Messiah.

It is you who are the sons of the prophets and of the covenant which God made with your fathers, saying to Abraham, 'And in your seed all the families of the earth shall be blessed.' For you first, God raised up His Servant and sent Him to bless you by turning every one of you from your wicked ways." (Acts 3:25-26).

And we preach to you the good news of the promise made to the fathers, that God has fulfilled this promise to our children in that He raised up Jesus, as it is also written in the second Psalm, 'You are My Son; today I have begotten You.' ... Therefore let it be known to you, brethren, that through Him forgiveness of sins is proclaimed to you... (Acts 13:32-33, 38).

The Scripture, foreseeing that God would justify the Gentiles by faith, preached the gospel beforehand to Abraham, saying, "All the nations will be blessed in you." So then those who are of faith are blessed with Abraham, the believer. (Galatians 3:8-9).

For if the inheritance is based on law, it is no longer based on a promise; but God has granted it to Abraham by means of a promise. (Galatians 3:18).

And if you belong to Christ, then you are Abraham's descendants, heirs according to promise. (Galatians 3:29).

Old covenant Israel was supposed to be a light to those Gentile nations outside the covenant with Abraham. The truth is that even in the Old Testament, Gentiles could be included in covenant with God, becoming circumcised and even living in and inheriting the land God promised to Israel. Salvation for the whole earth was always God's intention, even when delivering Israel from Egypt. There were those from Egypt who saw and believed in the God of Israel and left with them in the Exodus. They were present and included in everything that transpired. It was a common practice in Israel that an adopted heir could inherit the land, which was consistent within the Law of Moses. Both believing Jews and Gentiles were involved in helping rebuild Jerusalem's walls and build up the Temple during the time of Ezra and Nehemiah.

For this time I will send all My plagues on you and your servants and your people, so that you may know that there is no one like Me in all the earth... But, indeed, for this reason, I have allowed you to remain, in order to show you My power and in order to proclaim My name through all the earth. (Exodus 9:14, 16).

A mixed multitude also went up with them, along with flocks and herds, a very large number of livestock. (Exodus 12:38).

'When a stranger resides with you in your land, you shall not do him wrong. The stranger who resides with you shall be to you as the native among you, and you shall love him as

yourself, for you were aliens in the land of Egypt; I am the Lord your God.' (Leviticus 19:33-34).

This point was finally and fully revealed in the one new man in Christ where all the types and shadows were consummated. Israel was a type of what God was going to do spiritually in gathering believing Jews and Gentiles 'in Christ' under Messiah and building up His spiritual temple in the new covenant age.

In conclusion, modern Israel is not biblical Israel and has no divine right to land belonging to other countries such as Egypt or Saudi Arabia. The Talmudic Zionist agenda mistakenly adopted by Christian Zionists has a much more sinister Luciferian agenda behind it.

Jesus Himself is the fulfilment of all the promises of God and the law and the prophets are now fulfilled in love.

"Teacher, which is the great commandment in the Law?" And He said to him, "'You shall love the Lord your God with all your heart, and with all your soul, and with all your mind.' This is the great and foremost commandment. The second is like it, 'You shall love your neighbor as yourself.' On these two commandments depend the whole Law and the Prophets." (Matthew 22:36-40).

Now He said to them, "These are My words which I spoke to you while I was still with you, that all things which are written about Me in the Law of Moses and the Prophets and the Psalms must be fulfilled." Then He opened their minds to understand the Scriptures... (Luke 24:44-45).

Philip found Nathanael and said to him, "We have found Him of whom Moses in the Law and also the Prophets wrote – Jesus of Nazareth, the son of Joseph." (John 1:45).

A new commandment I give to you, that you love one another, even as I have loved you, that you also love one another. (John 13:34).

By this, love is perfected with us, so that we may have confidence in the day of judgment; because as He is, so also are we in this world. There is no fear in love; but perfect love casts out fear, because fear involves punishment, and the one who fears is not perfected in love. We love, because He first loved us. (1 John 4:17-19).

The thief comes only to steal and kill and destroy; I came that they may have life, and have it abundantly. (John 10:10).

Jesus arrives and completes this progressive revelation and fulfilment of the types and shadows and in the process refines our image of God. Whoever sees Jesus sees the Father, and He does not come to kill or destroy, but to give life in abundance.

The Luciferian agenda

Before I continue let me reiterate that I am not anti-Semitic and fully acknowledge that most followers of Judaism and Christian Zionism have no idea of the Luciferian agenda that is piggybacking on their religion. Just because I see Judaism as a false religion does not make me anti-Semitic any more than believing that Islam is a false religion makes me anti-Muslim. God loves all of His children regardless of what religion they are following; but that does not validate the religion, as Jesus is the only way to the Father. When John recorded Jesus' words that He was the Way, the Truth and the Life and the only way to the Father, that did not make either John or Jesus anti-Semitic.

The agenda to unify the so-called monotheistic religions under a Noahide law banner is more extreme but is none the less a continuation of ecumenicalism which makes all religions a road to God. The goal of the Noahide law movement is Luciferian and deceptive, seeking a new Babel and one new world order or government under another name.

I am appalled and disgusted by any form of racism or bigotry promoted by any groups or ideologies, including white supremacy, as they are a total contradiction of the fact that we are all children of God and equally loved and valued by our heavenly Father.

To reveal the Luciferian agenda behind the eschatological deception of the rapture, millennium and Zionism I will have to challenge the efficacy of Zionism as I have done with the other issues. As I do so, some may be offended by my challenge to the theology and make the accusation of anti-Semitism, as that label is often used to stop the truth from being uncovered. It is a very clever tactic to imply that anyone who does not agree with political or religious Zionism (and that includes many modern Jewish rabbis and the group of Jewish people who call themselves 'Jews against Israel') is anti-Semitic.

The topic of Zionism and Christian Zionism has been put off-limits and not open for discussion by the fear of being labelled anti-Semitic but as I have already been labelled I am going to explore the issue. You are totally at liberty to hold a different opinion but I would encourage you to be open to the Holy Spirit, to deconstruction and renewal of your minds. By calling Zionism a deception I am not trying to attack the people who hold to such beliefs but challenge the beliefs themselves.

In chapter 2 we saw that the root of all these dangerous doctrines is the poisonous tree of Brethrenism, which gave rise to Dispensationalism, promoted by the Scofield

Reference Bible. I believe there was and is a bigger agenda behind this deception that needs to be uncovered and is Luciferian in its origin.

I have used the term 'Luciferian' to mean that which originates with Lucifer's 'I will' statements of independence and which was perpetuated by Adam and Eve following the deception of independence. Luciferianism, in my definition, is anything associated with following the path of the tree of the knowledge of good and evil (evil being lost identity, leading to the toil and hardship and heavy labour of a works-based religious or humanistic system). Jesus described the source as being lies and murder, and those two traits are at the heart of the deception. The goal of a counterfeit God and a humanistic system was demonstrated by Nimrod at Babel.

One online definition of Luciferian is:

> Lucifer is a symbol of enlightenment, independence, and human progression and is often used interchangeably with similar figures from ancient beliefs, such as the Greek titan Prometheus or the Jewish Talmudic figure Lilith.
>
> Luciferians generally support the protection of the natural world. Both the arts and sciences are crucial to human development and thus both are cherished. The ability to recognize both good and evil, to accept that all actions have both positive and negative consequences, and to actively influence one's environment are key factors.
>
> The Luciferian philosophy in recent years has been defined in a collective foundation, known as the "11 Luciferian Points of Power", authored by Michael W. Ford. The basis of Luciferian philosophy cultivates and encourages individuality, self-determined choices based

on strategic application and continually seeking to enhance the Will via overcoming challenges. Luciferianism is philosophically practised with the continual cycle and process known as Liberation, Illumination and Apotheosis.

– slife.org/luciferianism

The Luciferian agenda is behind all of the global and cabalistic systems and all religious and political spirit agendas. Those agendas include one new world order government to counterfeit the kingdom of God, the Hebrew Roots movement, and Zionism, which seeks to enslave its followers to Noahide laws through deception.

Below is an entry from my journals on April 1st 2021. It is not an 'April fool' joke by God: He is very serious about exposing the great deception in all its forms, political or religious.

1st April 2021

"Son, great changes must take place to bring to an end the deception and influence of the control systems that originate from the tree of the knowledge of good and evil.

"Our children are mostly oblivious to what influences and controls their minds and lives but an awakening is taking place and the light of truth is beginning to reveal the systems of slavery. So many of Our children have lost the ability to discern along with their identity, and blindly follow the societal and cultural norms they are conditioned by. Some forerunners are beginning to question and challenge the norms; and protests are a sign that some are beginning to wake up to some truth.

"Those who claim to follow Jesus but accept division, violence, conflict and tribalism are even more deceived and have been so programmed by religion and fear that they are willing to embrace war over peace. The political spirit is rampant within the evangelical system and many of the so-called prophetic movements are completely deceived into looking for political solutions and are not seeking first Our Kingdom.

"The combination of the political and religious spirit is a powerful deception force that has hoodwinked so many into blindly following the lies and conspiracies. The light of truth is going to expose the lack of the fruit of the Spirit operating within those systems and many will be shocked into examining what and who they are following. The theology, doctrines and leaders behind these movements are going to be scrutinised by the Spirit of Truth and weighed in the balances and they will be found wanting. The judgment of those systems will result in Our children waking up to the reality that they have been deceived – but there is no guilt, shame or condemnation, just the justice of mercy that always follows judgment.

"Son, all the systems are being weighed and put on trial within the courts of heaven and the verdicts are releasing the mandates for the great shakings. The light of love and truth is revealing the deceptions; and limitless grace and triumphant mercy are being poured out from heaven into the earth. The resultant global awakening of the consciousness of mankind will accelerate the process of restoration as more of Our children become aware of Our desires and intentions. The great revealing of love will shake the religious systems of dead works and many will be set free from the bondage to duty and obligation they are trapped in.

"Son, the political and religious spirit has used the front of Zionism to fulfil its agenda but their desired goal of one counterfeit new world order government is neither religious nor political. The light of truth needs to be focused from the earth shield to shine on very specific targets so they can be brought into the light and exposed as deception. Your mandate gives you the authority to shine the light onto the deception of eschatology to reveal how it has deceived Our children into believing in the failure of the sonship mandate. Others have different targets to focus on but the light of love and truth will shine so brightly that nothing will escape and remain hidden.

"Everything that originated from the Luciferian rebellion that resulted in mankind's independence will be shaken and only that which is founded on the kingdom of righteousness, mercy and lovingkindness will remain. The fiery truth of Our loving presence will consume everything before it like a wildfire of lovingkindness that will restore all things."

What is the root of modern-day Zionism and what is the Luciferian agenda behind it? Most of the evangelical church has bought into the deception of Christian or evangelical Zionism that believes that Jesus as the Messiah will return to establish the Kingdom of God on earth in a future millennial reign in Jerusalem. That needs a restored Israel and temple in Jerusalem for Jesus to come back to. Talmudic Zionists, however, do not believe in Jesus as Messiah and therefore are looking to a very different source for the Messiah: they have a counterfeit kingdom or one new world government to establish. The fact that these two protagonists have been deceived into promoting a restored nation of Israel as the people of God and one world governmental order shows how clever the Zionist agenda is.

Zionists promote Judaism, which is a false religion, and many gullible Christians seem to have no problem accepting Judaism as the way for Jews to experience salvation. We have looked at who are the people of God, true Jews and the real Israel of God – a spiritual, not physical, people. The question remains then, who are modern-day Jews? Are they ethnically Semitic descendants of Abraham and therefore a race? Or are they followers of Judaism from any race, and thus just religious followers?

To answer that we need to look at another question. What happened to those who were dispersed following the destruction of Jerusalem in 70 AD? Did the Jewish people remain genetically or ethnically pure? Were they even pure at the time of Jesus?

The Jewish diaspora (or exile) is the dispersion of Israelites or Jews out of the land we now know as Israel and their subsequent settlement in other parts of the world. The diaspora in 70 AD was just the last dispersion: there were other exiles recorded in the Bible.

> The first exile was the Assyrian exile, the expulsion from the Kingdom of Israel (Samaria) begun by Tiglath-Pileser III of Assyria in 733 BCE. This process was completed by Sargon II with the destruction of the kingdom in 722 BCE, concluding a three-year siege of Samaria begun by Shalmaneser V. The next experience of exile was the Babylonian captivity, in which portions of the population of the Kingdom of Judah were deported in 597 BCE and again in 586 BCE by the Neo-Babylonian Empire under the rule of Nebuchadnezzar II...
>
> Before the middle of the first century CE, in addition to Judea, Syria and Babylonia, large Jewish communities

existed in the Roman provinces of Syria, Palaestina, Egypt, Crete and Cyrenaica, and in Rome itself; after the Siege of Jerusalem in 63 BCE, when the Hasmonean kingdom became a protectorate of Rome, emigration intensified. In 6 CE the region was organized as the Roman province of Judea. The Judean population revolted against the Roman Empire in 66 CE in the First Jewish–Roman War which culminated in the destruction of Jerusalem in 70 CE. During the siege, the Romans destroyed the Second Temple and most of Jerusalem. This watershed moment, the elimination of the symbolic centre of Judaism and Jewish identity constrained many Jews to reformulate a new self-definition and adjust their existence to the prospect of an indefinite period of displacement...

During the Middle Ages, due to increasing migration and resettlement, Jews divided into distinct regional groups which today are generally addressed according to two primary geographical groupings: the Ashkenazi of Northern and Eastern Europe, and the Sephardic Jews of Iberia (Spain and Portugal), North Africa and the Middle East...

– www.jewishwikipedia.info/diaspora.html

Many different groups identify as 'Jews', including Mizrahi and Natione Tedesca, Italkim, Romaniotes, San Nicandro, Juhurim, Gruzim, Krymchaks, Subbotniks etc.

Wikipedia has this to say about Jewish ethnic divisions:

Jewish ethnic divisions refer to many distinctive communities within the world's ethnically Jewish population. Although considered a self-identifying ethnicity, there are distinct ethnic subdivisions among Jews, most of which are primarily the result of geographic branching from an originating Israelite population, mixing with local communities, and subsequent independent evolutions...

Despite this diversity, Ashkenazi Jews represent the bulk of modern Jewry, estimated at between 70% and 80% of all Jews worldwide; before World War II, however, it was 90%. Ashkenazim developed in Europe but underwent massive emigration in search of better opportunities and during periods of civil strife and warfare. As a result of this, they became the overwhelming majority of Jews in the New World continents and countries, which previously were without native European or Jewish populations...
– Wikipedia: *Jewish ethnic divisions.*

Mixing genetically with other races has been a fact from very early on in the history of the Israelites. The book of Judges has multiple accounts of this and it also occurred whenever there was an exile. The Samaritans were hated by the Jews for being mixed race and there was prejudice even in Jesus' day.

The Samaritans consider themselves to be the remaining population of the Northern Kingdom of Israel who were not expelled during the ten tribes exile, and who joined with the incoming Assyrian populations to form the Samaritan community. Some biblical scholars also consider that parts of the Judean population had stayed to live in their homes during the exilic period and later joined the returning Israelites from Babylon and formed the Jews of the classic and Hasmonean era...

The Babylonian Jewish community, though maintaining permanent ties with the Hasmonean and later Herodian kingdoms, evolved into a separate Jewish community, which during the Talmudic period assembled its own

practices, the Babylonian Talmud, slightly differing from the Jerusalem Talmud. The Babylonian Jewry is considered to be the predecessor of most Mizrahi Jewish communities.
– Wikipedia: *Jewish diaspora*.

Returning to the 'Jewish ethnic divisions' Wikipedia article:

Despite the evident diversity displayed by the world's distinctive Jewish populations, both culturally and physically, genetic studies have demonstrated most of these to be genetically related to one another, having ultimately originated from a common ancient Israelite population that underwent geographic branching and subsequent independent evolutions.

A study published by the National Academy of Sciences stated that "The results support the hypothesis that the paternal gene pools of Jewish communities from Europe, North Africa, and the Middle East descended from a common Middle Eastern ancestral population, and suggest that most Jewish communities have remained relatively isolated from neighbouring non-Jewish communities during and after the Diaspora." ...

A study of Ashkenazi mitochondrial DNA by Richards et al. (2013) suggested that, though Ashkenazi paternal lineages were of Middle Eastern origin, the four main female Ashkenazi founders had descent lines that were established in Europe 10,000 to 20,000 years in the past while most of the remaining minor founders also have a deep European ancestry. The majority of Ashkenazi maternal lineages were not brought from the Levant, nor recruited in the Caucasus, but were assimilated within Europe. The study estimated that 80 per cent of

Ashkenazi maternal ancestry comes from women indigenous to Europe, 8 per cent from the Near East, and the remainder undetermined.
– Wikipedia: *Jewish ethnic divisions*.

The Jewish People see themselves as descending from the three founding families of Israel. The Matriarchs of Israel are the mothers of the Tribes of Israel; for those who adhere to Jewish Law, Israelite Nationhood or belonging to the Jewish People via descent exclusively follows the mother's line. – Wikipedia: *Matrilinearity in Judaism*.

Why is the ethnicity of Jewish people important? How has this been used by Zionists (who are mostly not religious and have a political, not spiritual agenda)?

Many Jewish communities indeed have a long history of suffering persecution at the hands of the Romans, Christians (particularly after Constantine converted the Roman Empire to Christianity) and Muslims. This tragic history has been used by those with a hidden and deceptive Luciferian agenda to create the conditions for establishing the nation-state of Israel with a Talmudic agenda for world government. This is a very unpopular theory amongst Zionists and Christian Zionists and is often shrouded in conspiracy but I believe that there is some truth behind it.

The answer lies in the history of the groups of proselytes such as the Khazars who have been absorbed into modern Jewish populations (and in the Khazars' case, absorbed into the Ashkenazim).

So who were the Khazars and do they still exist amongst the global cabalistic globalist groups?

Wikipedia again:

> The Khazars were a semi-nomadic Turkic people that in the late 6th century AD established a major commercial empire covering the south-eastern section of modern European Russia, southern Ukraine, Crimea and Kazakhstan... Khazaria became one of the foremost trading empires of the medieval world, commanding the western marches of the Silk Road and playing a key commercial role as a crossroad between China, the Middle East and Kievan Rus'. – Wikipedia: *Khazars*.

Many theories and conspiracies surround the Khazars, their conversion to Judaism and their connection with Ashkenazi Jewish groups. This has created much controversy amongst academic experts which has obscured the truth behind accusations of conspiracy and anti-Semitism. I believe that there is a Luciferian agenda behind the matter of the Khazars and their connection to Judaism but I am not going into the details as they cannot be substantiated because the records are lost or hidden.

That being said, in my conversations with the Father there has been direct confirmation of the Luciferian agenda of the great deception that was outworked at Babel and through a Babylonia Talmudic Zionist agenda.

There are several rhetorical questions I want to pose that, although being steeped in accusations of conspiracy, I do believe have a basis in truth:

- Do the Khazars have links to modern-day secret groups and global cabals which may have a Luciferian agenda that promotes Zionist eschatology through the religious and political spirit agenda?

- Did those groups have any association with Cyrus Scofield and the spread of Dispensationalism (and therefore futurist eschatology, rapture and Christian Zionism)?
- Is there a Luciferian agenda that has infected mankind and has a goal to establish a name for itself in a one-world governmental system?
- Are there secret groups or cabals that control the world through financial and political systems?

The dictionary definition of a cabal is 'a secret political clique or faction':

Cabal, a private organization or party engaged in secret intrigues; also, the intrigues themselves. In England, the word was used during the 17th century to describe any secret or extra-legal council of the king, especially the foreign committee of the Privy Council.
– Britannica.

The term cabal is derived from Kabbalah (a word that has numerous spelling variations), the Jewish mystical and spiritual interpretation of the Hebrew scripture.

Followers of the QAnon conspiracy theory use "The Cabal" to refer to what is perceived as a secret worldwide elite organisation who, according to proponents, wish to undermine democracy and freedom, and implement their own globalist agendas.
– Wikipedia: *Cabal*.

These cabals have many names, including the Illuminati and the Bilderberg Group, and are often associated with Freemasonry. They are shrouded in conspiracy and the term 'cabal' is often used by both left and right-wing political groups as propaganda to undermine their opponents.

The politics of cabals has always been pretty muddled, says James McConnachie, co-author of the Rough Guide to Conspiracy Theories. These groups allow protesters to project their fears onto them.

In the USA, the most extreme fear over Bilderberg is of a hidden cabal run by the European Union and threatening American freedoms. In Europe, the view is often of a free market elite trying to push through a right-wing agenda.

"Conspiracy theories are quite blind to conventional notions of left and right," says McConnachie. "The left is organising an international government. Meanwhile, global capitalism on the right may be doing the same thing by different means."
– www.bbc.co.uk/news/magazine-13682082

I have seen this scenario play out during the 2020 American election and the subsequent conspiracies of election fraud and the QAnon conspiracies that were adopted by right-wing conservative evangelicals and the prophetic movement. Every time a date for some event passes, another rises to perpetuate the false hope that many had in a political solution to world issues. Many of my contacts were caught up in this conspiracy, often believing wilder and wilder stories, clinging onto hopes that disappeared one after the other.

The sad fact is that many people have genuine passion for godly agendas but those agendas have become lost amongst the nonsense of the lunatic fringe. Theories about coronavirus and the subsequent vaccine turned rational, logical individuals into raving conspiracy fanatics – and at the time of writing this, none of their hopes or fears have ever come to pass.

Does all the conspiracy obscure some truth that is then lost in the midst of the chaos surrounding it? I believe the answer to this is yes; and, obviously, any secret Luciferian agenda would want to use the political and religious spirit as it has always done whilst deceiving mankind.

So why is the eschatological deception so important to uncover? One answer is that it joins strange bedfellows, political opposites and religions together to promote an idea that removes the kingdom of God from the here and now to the future, and thus undermines the restoration of all things agenda.

Those behind this deception are not interested in either Judaism or Israel and they are happy to support both communism and capitalism. Their agenda is far more sinister and uses division, competition and conflict to promote the tribalism that provides the finances to maintain control of global systems.

The establishing of a Jewish homeland is not a fulfilment of biblical prophecies, just the latest way for the religious and political spirit to outwork its Luciferian agenda.

The political agenda of Zionism centres on certain well known but mysterious figures who are often the subject of conspiracy theories. One such name and family are the Rothschilds, who according to some, are at the head of various one-world government conspiracies. So who are the Rothschilds and what role have they played in the Zionist agenda?

For those seeking after truth, how do you navigate the often confusing path through the minefield of misinformation, lies, partial truth, twisted truth and actual truth? I have found that by spending time in the presence of the Truth Himself you begin to resonate with truth and find it easier to discern what are lies or twisting of the truth by the frequency it carries.

In the first of the Matrix movie trilogy, the Morpheus character says to the bewildered seeker, Neo:

"What you know you can't explain, but you feel it. You've felt it your entire life, that there's something wrong with the world. You don't know what it is, but it's there, like a splinter in your mind, driving you mad."

I know exactly how that feels and probably so do you, or you would not be reading this book. But the matrix that we have been living in feels so real. Why is the world as it is? What agenda is behind the illusion that has control over so much of what we have believed?

The deconstruction process is hard, particularly if the religious programming and conditioning have been operating for most of our lives. I know that the Christian Zionist programming is very strong and emotive, fuelled by the fear of being cursed as anti-Semitic. All I can say is to be bold and very courageous in the pursuit of truth and do not be afraid of going into the promised land of freedom.

Below is information that can be found freely online. How much of it is the whole truth and how much is speculation is up to the reader to decide. What resonates in your heart and spirit and what causes your mind to fear the consequences of religious opposition?

I resonate with the sentiment behind what is below and I have had personal discussions with those who have had met the Rothschilds and who affirm their part in global financial control systems (one friend even prophesying their destiny, in one of several meetings orchestrated by the Father, which caused much consternation for that Rothschild family member). Of course, the best way of dealing with the global cabals is not spiritual warfare but by seeing the individuals behind them restored to their sonship identity and relationship with their heavenly Father. Mercy triumphs over judgment and they are all God's children, whom Jesus died for. It is very important to differentiate behaviour from identity and demonstrate the love of God towards everyone as the Father does.

The following is from the Encyclopaedia Britannica:

Rothschild family, the most famous of all European banking dynasties, which for some 200 years exerted great influence on the economic and, indirectly, the political history of Europe. The house was founded by Mayer Amschel Rothschild (b. February 23, 1744, Frankfurt am Main – d. September 19, 1812, Frankfurt) and his five sons, Amschel Mayer (b. June 12, 1773, Frankfurt – d. December 6, 1855, Frankfurt), Salomon Mayer (b. September 9, 1774 – d. July 27, 1855, Vienna), Nathan Mayer (b. September 16, 1777 – d. July 28, 1836, Frankfurt), Karl Mayer (b. April 24, 1788 – d. March 10, 1855, Naples), and Jakob, or James, Mayer (b. May 15, 1792 – d. November 15, 1868, Paris). Starting out in a Frankfurt banking house, Mayer and his sons became international bankers, establishing branches in London, Paris, Vienna, and Naples by the 1820s. In addition to banking and finance, the Rothschild businesses have encompassed mining, energy, real estate, and winemaking. From the early 19th century the family has been known for its considerable charitable activities, particularly in the arts and education.

Mayer Amschel Rothschild

Mayer's family name derived from the red (rot) shield on the house in the ghetto in which his ancestors had once lived. Intended for the rabbinate, Mayer studied briefly, but his parents' early death forced him into an apprenticeship in a banking house. Soon after becoming court factor to William IX, landgrave of Hesse-Kassel, Mayer set the pattern that his family was to follow so successfully – to do business with reigning houses by preference and to father as many sons as possible who could take care of the family's many business affairs abroad...

Starting as dealers in luxury items and traders in coins and commercial papers, Mayer and his sons eventually became bankers to whom the French Revolutionary and Napoleonic wars of 1792-1815 came as a piece of great good fortune. Mayer and his eldest son, Amschel, supervised the growing business from Frankfurt, while Nathan established a branch in London in 1804, Jakob settled in Paris in 1811, and Salomon and Karl opened offices in Vienna and Naples, respectively, in the 1820s. The wars, for the Rothschilds, meant loans to warring princes; smuggling as well as legal trading in key products such as wheat, cotton, colonial produce, and arms; and the transfer of international payments between the British Isles and the Continent that Napoleon vainly attempted to close to British trade. Peace transformed the growing Rothschild business: the banking group continued its international business dealings but became more and more an agent in government securities (Prussian or English, French or Neapolitan), in insurance-company stocks, and in shares of industrial companies. Thus, the family successfully adapted to the Industrial Revolution and participated in economic growth throughout Europe with their railway, coal, ironworking, and metallurgical investments. The banking group continued to expand after the 1850s and, in particular, achieved an important position in the world trade of oil and nonferrous metals...

The Rothschilds were influencing the national economy and politics of their countries as greatly as they were being influenced themselves. Alphonse, for example, as the head of the international banking syndicate that in 1871 and 1872 placed the two great French loans known as liberation loans after France's defeat by Prussia, could boast without immodesty that his influence had maintained the chief of the French government, Adolphe Thiers, in power. At the same time, in 1875, Lionel, in London (where he had been a member of the House of Commons since 1858), was able to give on a few hours notice the £4 million that allowed the British government to become the principal stockholder in the Suez Canal Company. Obviously, the two cousins had become important citizens in their respective countries.
– Britannica: *Rothschild family*.

Without a doubt, the Rothschilds have historically wielded much financial and political power and were supporters of the Zionist agenda who, along with others, exerted influence for favours to secure a Jewish homeland.

The agenda of the religious and political spirit behind global control uses the resources of four fallen angelic orders that cause division, competition, conflict and tribalism to further its goals. Those four characteristics can be used to discern what the agenda is behind what has been written in the history books and reviewing current world events. Whose fingerprints are on the history books and what is the agenda behind what they want you to know and accept as truth?

The Rothschilds associate with Judaism but they are probably Khazarians in origin and only use the Jewish cause in as much as it suits the hidden Luciferian agenda.

The five Rothschild brothers branched out into the various countries in Europe. From here, they have ended up financing not just various wars, but in some instances both sides of the same war.

The Balfour Declaration

In 1917 the British Foreign Secretary, Arthur Balfour, declared in a letter to the Rothschilds that his government would support a Jewish homeland in Palestine. It is important to note that before this declaration was given, it was agreed upon that if the Rothschilds could get the U.S. into WWI to help defeat the Germans, Britain in return would give the land of Palestine to the Rothschilds and Zionists.

The Rothschilds funded the early Khazarian settlers from Europe to relocate to Palestine. In 1948 they also funded and armed terrorist groups, which bombed and terrorised 800,000 Palestinians to leave the land of their birth. Their connection to Israel is even evident with them paying for the construction of the Israeli parliament building, the Knesset, and the Israeli Supreme Court. The Israeli flag symbolizes both its territorial ambitions and that it is owned by the Rothschilds. Modern Israel uses the same six-pointed star on its flag that the Rothschilds used as their family symbol (just changing its colour from red to blue). The two blue lines above and beneath the star symbolize the ancient borders/rivers given to ancient Israel under the old covenant.

The following paragraphs by Michael Sullivan[41] concerning the Rothschilds and their Talmudic Zionist agenda are taken from the fullpreterism.com website:

The Influence of the Talmud on the Rothschilds

Mayer's father's wish for his son was that he would one day become a Rabbi, strictly teaching and following the Talmud. Although not becoming a Rabbi, Biographer Frederic Morton, in The Rothschilds, points out how important the Talmud was in guiding the Rothschild dynasty in their unquenchable drive for money and power. He writes, "On Saturday evenings, when prayer was done at the synagogue, Mayer would invite the rabbi into his house. They would bend towards one another on the green upholstery, sipping slowly at a glass of wine and argue about first and last things deep into the night. Even on work days...Mayer...was apt to tear down the big book of the Talmud and recite from it...while the entire family must sit stock still and listen" (p. 31). He goes on to tell us that Mayer Amschel Rothschild and his five sons were "wizards" of finance, and "fiendish calculators" who were motivated by a "demonic drive" to succeed in their secret undertakings. And Morton adds that it is difficult for the average person to "comprehend Rothschild nor even the reason why he having so much, wanted to conquer more."

---

[41] Michael Sullivan, *A full preterist response to "holy land," "the end is near (again)," "holy war" eschatologies – Part 2 Judaism (the article Facebook doesn't want you to read!)*. See https://fullpreterism.com/a-full-preterist-response-to-holy-land-end-of-time-holy-war-eschatologies-part-2-judaism-the-article-facebook-doesnt-want-yo/

All five brothers shared their father's spirit of Talmudic cunning and conquest.

President Andrew Jackson, the only one of the US presidents whose administration abolished the National Debt, condemned the Rothschild's and international bankers as a "den of vipers" which he was determined to "rout out" of the fabric of American life. Jackson claimed that if only the American people understood how these vipers operated on the American scene "there would be a revolution before morning."

In 1911, John F. Hylan, mayor of New York said that "the real menace of our republic is the invisible government which, like a giant octopus, sprawls its slimy length over our city, state and nation. At the head is a small group of banking houses, generally referred to as 'international bankers.'"

"The house of Rothschild has arisen from the quarrels between states, has become great and mighty from wars. The misfortune of states and peoples has been its fortune." (Friedrich Edlen von Scherb).

"The Rothschild's are the wonders of modern banking... We see the descendants of Judah, after a persecution of two thousand years, peering above kings, rising higher than emperors, and holding a whole continent in the hollow of their hands. The Rothschilds govern a Christian world. Not a cabinet moves without their advice. They stretch their hand, with equal ease, from Petersburg to Vienna, from Vienna to Paris, from Paris to London, from London to Washington. Baron Rothschild, the head of the house, is the true king of Judah, the prince of the captivity, the Messiah so long looked for by this extraordinary people. He holds the keys of peace or war, blessing or cursing... They are the brokers and counsellors of the kings of Europe and of the republican chiefs of America. What more can they desire?" (Niles Weekly Register, 1835-1836).

Eschatological Goals of Zionism

The goal of religious or messianic Zionism is to bring about the conquest of Palestine, the rebuilding of the Temple, and the arrival of Messiah through war. Zionism has used and manipulated Dispensational Zionism (through the Scofield Reference Bible), to help create a sub-culture within Christianity that will support their violent eschatology.

The main tenets of Dispensational Zionism are:

1. That if biblical prophetic promises are not fulfilled, they were postponed or remain yet to be fulfilled. The church age is just a parenthesis before God returns to His main agenda, Israel.

The Dispensational Zionist argues that since Jesus' Kingdom promises were not fulfilled 'at hand' and in His generation, they must have been 'postponed' to be fulfilled 'at hand' in our generation.

2. That there are two peoples of God.

That means that the new covenant promises made to Israel cannot apply to or be fulfilled by the Church. That may seem an extreme view but it is however supported by many prominent dispensationalists who make the following unbiblical statements:

Lewis Sperry Chafer: "That the Christian now inherits the distinctive Jewish promises is not taught in Scripture."

Dwight Pentecost[42]: "...it would be impossible for the church to fulfil God's promises made to Israel."

Charles C. Ryrie[43]: "The church is not fulfilling in any sense the promises to Israel."

Dwight Pentecost: "The Church cannot be presently fulfilling the New Covenant."

John Walvoord agrees: "The New Covenant is with Israel and awaits the second coming of Christ for its fulfilment."

Dwight Pentecost: "The whole covenant takes on importance, in addition, for Amillennialism attempts to show that the church is fulfilling Israel's covenants because the church today is redeemed by the blood. If the church fulfils this covenant, she may also fulfil the other covenants made with Israel and there is no need for an earthly millennium."

Charles C. Ryrie[44]: "If the church is fulfilling Israel's promises as contained in the new covenant or anywhere in the Scriptures, then [dispensational] premillennialism is condemned."

"I will surely bless you, and make your descendants as numerous as the stars in the sky and as the sand on the seashore." (Genesis 22:17 NIV).

---

[42] Dwight Pentecost, *Things To Come* A Study in Biblical Eschatology, Dunham Publishing Company (1958).

[43] Walvoord's and the first of Ryrie's statements are quoted by Keith A. Mathison in *Dispensationalism: Rightly Dividing the People of God?* P&R Publishing (1995).

[44] This second Ryrie statement is quoted by Curtis I. Crenshaw and Grover E. Gunn III, in *Dispensationalism today, yesterday, and tomorrow*, Footstool Publications (1986), p175.

This scripture has been twisted to infer two peoples, a heavenly and an earthly people, when it is just a metaphorical expression. Clarence Larkin[45] writes:

> John Hagee in his book, *Final Dawn Over Jerusalem* asserts that 'the stars in the sky' here is referring to the Church (God's heavenly people), and 'the sand on the seashore' is referring to Israel or the Jews (God's earthly people) and that the two may exist together in time, but remain separate. Hagee states in The Houston Chronicle, April 30th, 1988, that he believes these two groups today can be saved differently. He believes Jews today remain God's chosen and they may be saved without having faith in Christ as long as they obey the Torah. But Gentiles must believe in Jesus to be saved. He believes trying to convert Jews is a 'waste of time,' 'Jews already have a covenant with God that has never been replaced with Christianity. The Jewish people have a relationship to God through the law of God as given through Moses. I believe that every Gentile person can only come to God through the cross of Christ. I believe that every Jewish person who lives in the light of the Torah, which is the word of God, has a relationship with God and will come to redemption.'

Dispensational Zionism also believes that there are two different kingdoms – one for Israel and another for the Church. It is taught that Israel was offered the 'kingdom of heaven' which was to be the earthly messianic kingdom. As this was never fulfilled literally, it got postponed until

---

[45] Clarence Larkin, referring to John the Baptist's coming: "Prepare the way of the Lord for what? Not for the Cross but for the Kingdom (on earth)." *Rightly Dividing the Word*, 1921, p51.

the Second Coming and a literal thousand-year millennial period in the future.

The warped logic of dispensationalism behind Zionism declares that, when the Bible uses 'the kingdom of God,' this is the spiritual kingdom of the Gentile Church. But when the Bible uses 'the kingdom of heaven,' it refers to a literal Messianic kingdom reign on earth. So many believers are still conditioned by dispensational teaching, even if they have rejected dispensationalism itself. It requires a deep deconstruction of the frameworks of our thinking for us to be deprogrammed.

3. The re-establishing of Israel in 1948 was the fulfilment of the biblical covenants and prophetic promises.

The year 1948 when the 'Jews' inherited their land, becoming a nation again, is an essential event for Dispensational Zionists. Dispensationalists use a circular logic form of reasoning that ties together their vision of the future to literal events in Israel. That logic completely disintegrates if you remove one event from its sequence:

- There must be a state of Israel, or there can be no holy city of Jerusalem.
- Without the city of Jerusalem and a reinstituted Talmudic law, there would be no need to rebuild a third Temple and have animal sacrifices.
- Without a rebuilt temple there would be no need for an 'Antichrist' to desecrate it and then there would be no 'Great Tribulation' where two-thirds of the Jewish people have to die.
- Without an Antichrist, there would be no need for the battle of Armageddon to destroy Israel.

- So we are back to the need for a state of Israel in this circular argument where, in their eschatology, all of these events are necessary for Jesus to return.

Zionists claim that Israel in the Old Testament never fully inherited the land (a claim that has already been discredited). Israel's land promises were allegedly 'unconditional,' therefore 1948 fulfils the land prophecies and restoration promises.

This idea comes from the Scofield Reference Bible's notes which states of Deuteronomy 30:5, "It is important to see that the nation has never as yet taken the land under the unconditional Abrahamic covenant nor has it ever possessed the whole land." This belief has been promoted so as to condition people into not just accepting that a state of Israel fulfils God's promises but to actively work for it.

Arnold Fruchtenbaum[46] writes, "At no point in Jewish history have the Jews ever possessed all the land from the Euphrates in the north to the River of Egypt in the south."

As we have already seen, this theory is based on a flawed understanding and translation of the Hebrew word *olam* to meaning everlasting rather than age-enduring and then exaggerating that reasoning to add the meaning of 'unconditional' as well.

The assumption that the land promises God made to Abraham and Israel must be 'unconditional' is programmed into evangelical thinking. It is then a small step of logic for the Dispensational Zionists to accept and believe that Israel's restoration back to the land and their salvation need not be conditional upon repentance and faith. The next logical step

---

[46] Arnold Fruchtenbaum, *The Land is Mine*, Issues, 2-4 July 1982.

of reasoning is that of the national salvation of Israel and therefore no requirement for an individual Jewish person to accept Jesus.

This is a fatally flawed logic but it has conditioned many believers to believe this fiction to be absolute fact and unchallengeable. That is why emotional accusations of anti-Semitism are made against those who would dare to challenge this sacred cow.

The reasoning continues that as Israel has not yet inherited the land 'forever,' then Israel must be still fulfilling her land promises in our day. In many Christians' perspectives, this gives Israel the right to take land from any of the neighbouring nations and persecute and commit genocide against the Palestinian people.

For these reasons, the establishment of the nation-state of Israel in 1948 is seen a fulfilment of many Old Testament and New Testament land and restoration promises and becomes the most significant sign that Jesus' return and the end time battle will take place in our generation. This encourages a very militant stance that ironically actually looks forward to warfare to bring the return of the Prince of Peace!

In spite of the fact that many Christians believe and promote these Luciferian agendas, as you can see from the quotes below, there are many religious Jews who are totally against viewing the existence of the state of Israel as a fulfilment of God's promises. They see that this is a western evangelical and political Zionist agenda that has nothing to do with God at all.

> From the founding of political Zionism in the 1890s, Haredi Jewish leaders voiced objections to its secular orientation, and before the establishment of the State of

Israel, the vast majority of Haredi Jews were opposed to Zionism. This was chiefly due to the concern that secular nationalism would replace the Jewish faith and the observance of religion, and the view that it was forbidden for the Jews to re-constitute Jewish rule in the Land of Israel before the arrival of the Messiah... A study in late 2006 claimed that just over a third of Israelis considered Haredim to be the most hated group in Israel... – Wikipedia: *Haredim and Zionism*.

This is a headline from the newspaper *The Times of Israel*[47] that shows that there is at least one Jewish group that does believe in Zionism or that the modern state of Israel is fulfilling Old Testament promises. In fact on YouTube there are many videos of Rabbis challenging Zionism.

Satmar rebbe in Israel to donate to anti-Zionist institutions.

Zalman Teitelbaum distributes $5 million to 150 associations during a 10-day visit; his Hasidic group believes the Jewish state can only be established with the coming of Messiah.

Satmar ideology holds that there should not be a Jewish state and that the Jews should remain in exile until the redemption, or coming of the Messiah.

In contrast, Christian Zionists assert:

"On more than one occasion in Scripture, Israel is compared to a fig tree (see Judg. 9:11; Hos. 9:10; Joel 1:7-8). I believe that Mark 13:28-29, along with many other

---

[47] *The Times of Israel*, 22 November 2019; article syndicated from Jewish Telegraphic Agency.

> Scripture passages, such as Ezekiel 37-39, speak of the rebirth of Israel – the re-gathering of God's people. When the nation of Israel comes back into existence, Jesus was stating prophetically, it is a super sign that His coming is near." – Greg Laurie[48].

Dispensational Zionists and 'Jewish' Zionists want believers to support Israel in committing acts of violence to take back 'their' land. The borders of this land include parts of modern-day Egypt, Lebanon, Syria, Jordan, Palestine, Iraq, Kuwait and Saudi Arabia.

Dispensational Zionists believe in a yet future literal and global fulfilment of Matthew 24, therefore for them the destruction of the Temple in 70 AD cannot be the prophetic fulfilment of Jesus' teaching. In this flawed logic, in order for the destruction of the Temple to be at Christ's (to them still future) coming, another Temple must be rebuilt in Jerusalem to experience the abomination of desolation.

For example, John Hagee[49] writes of Matthew 24:15-20,

> "The holy place is the temple in Jerusalem, and according to this verse, the Jews are in control of the temple. How could they control the temple without being in control of Jerusalem? How could they be in control of Jerusalem if they were replaced (by the Church).

In Hagee's book, *Beginning of the End, Are We the Terminal Generation*, he states that 'the times of the Gentiles' (Luke 21:24) must be referring to Gentile rule over Jerusalem which

---

[48] Greg Laurie, *Are these the last days?* How to live expectantly in a world of uncertainty, Regal Books From Gospel Light (2005), p20.
[49] John Hagee, *In Defense of Israel*, Strang Communications Company (2007), pp156-157.

began in 70 AD and continued until the Six-Day War of 1967. David predicted that since God would rebuild Jerusalem and show His glory there in Psalm 102:6, and he believes that we must be the terminal generation, as this is a sign of the soon-coming literal return of Jesus to earthly Jerusalem to reveal His glory there.

It seems to me so much easier to accept that Jesus already came to that generation, as He promised, rather than project everything into the future.

Hal Lindsey[50] also promotes the rebuilding of a literal third temple.

> Obstacle or no obstacle, it is certain that the Temple will be rebuilt. Prophecy demands it... With the Jewish nation reborn in the land of Palestine, ancient Jerusalem once again under total Jewish control for the first time in 2600 years, and talk of rebuilding the great Temple, the most important sign of Jesus Christ's soon coming is before us... It is like the key piece of a jigsaw puzzle being found... For all those who trust in Jesus Christ, it is a time of electrifying excitement...
>
> Since the 1960s, I have been writing and saying that the single most important key to prophecies yet to be fulfilled involve rebuilding the Temple. Twenty-five years ago, the whole idea of Jews actually rebuilding their holy Temple seemed quaint – even far-fetched. Today, nobody's laughing about the notion.

Dispensational Zionists have formed *The International Christian Embassy* to raise money for the rebuilding of the

---

[50] Hal Lindsey, *The Late Great Planet Earth*, Lakeland, (1970) pp56-58 and 156.

Temple in Jerusalem. Many believers were encouraged to support this temple rebuilding project. Trinity Broadcasting Network and the God Channel (amongst others) fleece and manipulate Christians for their money to self-fulfil their prophetic agenda.

Randy Thomas[51] points out that the group 'Jews for Jesus'

> ...provides information and links to eight extreme and militant Jewish organizations involved in attempts to destroy the Dome of the Rock, rebuild the Jewish Temple and re-institute Jewish Temple worship and sacrifices. These include the Temple Institute and Temple Mount Faithful. They have formed a 4.5-ton cornerstone of which each year during Sukkot, the Feast of Tabernacles, they enact the elaborate water-drawing ceremony at the pool of Siloam, and then attempt to set the cornerstone for the rebuilding of the Temple. Each year the Israeli government authorities prevent them."

Ironically, we have a Jews for Jesus group and a Jews against Israel group who have diametrically opposed beliefs.

Another *The Times of Israel* headline[52]:

This Chicago synagogue is a home for non-Zionist Jews

Tzedek Chicago emphasizes advocating for Palestinian rights and criticizing Israel's conduct, and many members feel they have finally found a congregation that fits.

---

[51] Randy Thomas, *Death Is at Your Door Are You Ready?* Lulu.com (2007), p119; via Google Books, accessed 13 May 2022.
[52] Ben Sales, article in *The Times of Israel*, 7 June 2019.

Hal Lindsey is actually excited about the rebuilding of the Temple, seemingly because he believes it will trigger WWIII and Armageddon. Many Zionist Christians who are enthusiastic about supporting the rebuilding of a Third Temple are mostly unaware of the wider implications of applying the prophetic writings of Daniel, Ezekiel and the Book of Revelation literally as the pre-written history of apocalyptic destruction of Israel itself. However, there are Christian Zionists who acknowledge that the rebuilding of the Temple will lead to Israel's destruction. Citing the Zechariah 13:8 prophecy that two-thirds of Jews would perish, David Brickner[53] writes, "the hope of the Jewish people in seeing the glorious Temple rebuilt will lead to their greatest calamity and suffering."

Some Dispensational Zionists seem more concerned about the creation of a literal temple cornerstone than about Jesus, the true cornerstone. Thus, according to this warped eschatological perspective, Jewish people are willingly sacrificed to enable Jesus to return.

They seem happy that there will be the destruction of two-thirds of the 'Jews' they claim to love! According to the Christian Research Institute, John Hagee[54] states that evangelizing these 'Jews' to Christ (and having them be a part of Christ's real Temple) is a 'waste of time' because they can be redeemed through following Torah and embracing the sacrificial temple system.

So many Christians are being deceived and manipulated to financially support this Luciferian Zionist movement! The

---

[53] David Brickner, *Future Hope, A Jewish Christian Look at the End of the World*, 2nd edition, Purple Pomegranate (1999), p. 68.
[54] Christian Research Institute, www.equip.org/article/pastor-john-hagee/

God Channel even asked their followers to send in money to buy and plant a million trees in Israel to welcome Jesus' return.

4. The Second Coming and end time battle of Armageddon will take place 'soon' in 'our generation.'

Jewish Zionism and Dispensational Zionism interpret Ezekiel 37-39 to 'prove' that 1948 was a fulfilment of Bible prophecy and therefore that a world war is necessary in our generation for Jesus to return.

John Hagee is known as 'Dr Armageddon' because many of his critics have discerned that he not only wants Armageddon to take place in his lifetime but is willing to be a very active participant in bringing it about. At the *Christians United For Israel* (CUFI) event in Washington D.C on July 19, 2006, Hagee gave his prophetic scenario for Israel and the U.S.:

> "The United States must join Israel in a pre-emptive military strike against Iran to fulfil God's plan for both Israel and the West... a biblically prophesied end-time confrontation with Iran, which will lead to the Rapture, Tribulation and the Second Coming."

The first to propose Russia as Gog and Magog was John Cumming in 1864. Another cult, the British Israel movement, picked this up in 1940. This group believes the tribes of Ephraim and Manasseh live on in the Anglo-Saxon races. According to one of their leading teachers, A.J. Ferris, in his book *Armageddon Is at the Doors*, Ezekiel 38-39 taught that Russia would soon attack British Israel. It was Hal Lindsey in the 1970s who popularized this Gog and Magog Armageddon theology. During the Cold War, Dispensational 'newspaper pop eschatology' began telling everyone that Russia would participate in the Armageddon battle and attack Israel in our generation. Why? Because the 'prince of Meshek' – *Rosh meshek* in Hebrew – sounded a lot like 'Russia' and 'Moscow'.

But as the newspapers and current events change, so too does Zionist eschatology:

- 1970 – Lindsey claimed Russia was the threat and focus of the Gog and Magog Battle.
- 1994 – Lindsey changed it to 'Islamic fundamentalism.'
- 1997 – Then he changed it again to 'the Russia-Muslim force.'
- 1999 – And then again to the 'Muslim-Russian alliance.'

In 2000 Lindsey was the first to have a revelation that America was also found in the book of Revelation. Why? Because the US flag has an eagle on it, so the wings of an eagle in Revelation 12:14-17 that carries the woman to safety must be a description of a U.S. airlift rescue mission of the Jews.

The Scofield Reference Bible, funded and marketed by Zionists and Dispensational Zionists, elaborates on Genesis 12:3, "For a nation to commit the sin of anti-Semitism brings inevitable judgment." To not support Israel and the Zionist mission is therefore 'sin,' 'anti-Semitic' and will be judged by God.

John Hagee writes of this text in his book *Jerusalem Countdown*[55], "This is and has been God's foreign policy toward the Jewish people from Genesis 12 until this day. Any man or nation that persecutes the Jewish people or the State of Israel will receive the swift judgment of God."

---

[55] John Hagee, Jerusalem Countdown, Strang Communications Company (2006) p230.

Hagee further says[56], "You are either a Christian or an anti-Semite. Bottom line, if you are not for Israel and the Jewish people, you either are biblically ignorant or you're not a Christian."

What these statements are affirming is that if you do not support modern Israel in committing acts of violence in defence of, or in expanding, Israel's territory to fulfil the 'biblical promises', then you are committing the 'sin of anti-Semitism' and God is going to 'judge' you and your nation. Dispensationalists and Christian Zionists twist Jesus' teaching in Matthew 25, changing the correct meaning of the sheep and goat nations persecuting the early church to teach that the Gentile 'nations' are being judged based upon how they treated the 'brethren' of the Jewish nation of Israel.

Dispensational or Evangelical Zionists avoid the more obvious conclusion that Jesus was prophesying to that current generation. To do so they have to ignore the many 'imminence' Bible verses that indicate that Jesus' Second Coming was soon to take place in that 30-70 AD generation.

Many dispensationalists' logical arguments are not biblical but make sense to them because of their conditioning that these were to be global and not local events. I fully accept that these historic events had global significance, without the need for them to be relating to the whole planet. The argument goes that because Jesus did not come in the literal, physical way they have been programmed to believe, to establish an earthly kingdom, and because the whole of planet earth has not been destroyed by fire, then His coming is still future.

---

[56] John Hagee, http://www.charismanews.com/world/45501-john-hagee-if-you-re-not-for-israel-you-re-biblically-ignorant-or-not-christian

Such programming and conditioning are made easier because many of these religious groups do not understand the nature of the apocalyptic, non-literal, highly metaphoric old covenant and symbolic language which Jesus and the New Testament writers used to describe His coming. As we have seen, the language and symbolism of coming on the clouds is using the same de-creation language as used of Egypt, Babylon and other governmental systems. Jesus used that language to refer to the end of the old covenant world passing away in fire in 70 AD and the establishing of the new covenant age that would replace it.

Before the advent of the deception of dispensationalism, the mainstream theological beliefs of the reformers such as Luther and Calvin did not mix covenants and was consistent in understanding that there are not in fact still two covenants in place, one for Israel and the Jewish people and a separate one for Christians. Luther and Calvin taught that there was only one covenant of grace which old covenant and new covenant true believers shared. Of Matthew 8:11, Calvin wrote[57], "For, even now, the only kingdom of heaven which our Lord Jesus Christ promises to his followers, is the one in which they may sit down with Abraham, Isaac and Jacob."

They also taught that 'Israel' in Romans 11:25-27 was the Church, comprising both Jews and Gentiles. Calvin wrote[58], "I extend the word Israel to all the people of God..." "...This interpretation seems to me the most suitable because Paul intended here to set forth the completion of the kingdom of Christ, which is by no means to be confined to the Jews, but is to include the whole world. The same manner of speaking we

---

[57] John Calvin, *Institutes*, 4.16.14.
[58] John Calvin, *Commentary on Romans* 11:25-27.

find in Galatians 6:16. The Israel of God is what he calls the Church..."

The dispensationalist view is not held by the following Christian theologians within the Reformed and Evangelical communities, who have an 'already realised' interpretation of virtually every eschatological de-creation prophecy in the Bible: John Owen, John Locke, John Lightfoot, John Brown, R.C. Sproul, Gary DeMar, Kenneth Gentry, James Jordan, Peter Leithart, Keith Mathison, Crispin H.T. Fletcher-Louis and Hank Hanegraaff. In addition, N.T. Wright teaches that the passing away of heaven and earth (or the world) of Matthew 5:17-18; 24:3, 29, 35; 1 Corinthians 7:31; 2 Peter 3; 1 John 2:17-18 and Revelation 21:1 refers to the destruction of the temple and the civil and religious worlds of men; and that the rulers of the old covenant religious system or world, represented by the temple, were the 'sun, moon, and stars,' which made up the 'heaven and earth' of the world that perished in 70 AD. And I must offer my sincere thanks to Mike Sullivan, whose extensive research has uncovered many of the quotes I have used from Dispensational Zionists.

History of Zionism

I will quote from the online version of the Encyclopaedia Britannica to give some factual background to the violent origins of Zionism.

> **Zionism,** Jewish nationalist movement that has had as its goal the creation and support of a Jewish national state in Palestine, the ancient homeland of the Jews (Hebrew: Eretz Yisra'el, 'the Land of Israel'). Though Zionism originated in eastern and central Europe in the latter part of the 19th century, it is in many ways a continuation of the ancient attachment of the Jews and the Jewish religion

to the historical region of Palestine, where one of the hills of ancient Jerusalem was called Zion.

In the 1880s, however, a rise in European anti-Semitism and revived Jewish national pride combined to inspire a new wave of emigration to Palestine in the form of agricultural colonies financed by the Rothschilds and other wealthy families. Political Zionism came a decade later when the Austrian journalist Theodor Herzl began advocating a Jewish state as the political solution for both anti-Semitism (he had covered the sensational Dreyfus affair in France) and Jewish secular identity. Herzl's brief and dramatic bid for international support from the major powers at the First Zionist Congress (August 1897) failed, but, after he died in 1904, the surviving Zionist organization under the leadership of Chaim Weizmann undertook a major effort to increase the Jewish population in Palestine while continuing to search for political assistance.

These efforts could only be on a small scale while the Ottoman Turks ruled what the Europeans called Palestine (from Palaestina, 'Land of the Philistines,' the Latin name given Judaea by the Romans). But in 1917, during World War I, the Zionists persuaded the British government to issue the Balfour Declaration, a document that committed Britain to facilitate the establishment of a 'Jewish homeland' in Palestine. Amid considerable controversy over conflicting wartime promises to the Arabs and French, Britain succeeded in gaining the endorsement of the declaration by the new League of Nations, which placed Palestine under British mandate. This achievement reflected a heady mixture of religious and imperial motivations that Britain would find difficult to reconcile in the troubled years ahead.

Immigration and conflict

The Zionist goal of Jewish statehood was violently opposed by the local Arab leaders, who saw the Ottoman defeat as an opportunity either to create their own state or to join a larger Arab entity – thus reviving the old Arab empire of early Islamic times. British efforts to bring the Zionists and the Arabs together in a cooperative government failed, and serious disorders, escalating into organized violence, were to mark the mandate, culminating in the Arab Revolt of 1936-39. This period also marked the birth of local Jewish defence forces. The largest and most widely representative of the various militias, the Haganah ('Defense') was a branch of the Jewish Agency, the organization most responsible for bringing Jews to Israel.

The most effective of the main, pre-state militias were associated with political factions from both the right and left wings of Zionist politics. The Irgun Zvai Leumi and its even more violent splinter group, Lehi (also known as the Stern Gang), were affiliated with the ultraconservative Revisionist Party, founded by Vladimir Zev Jabotinsky. (The Revisionists withdrew from the main Zionist institutions in 1935 in protest against Jewish cooperation with the British mandate.) Another group, the Palmach, though technically an elite arm of the Haganah, was heavily influenced by a Marxist-socialist party, Achdut HaAvoda, and recruited many of its members from socialist-oriented kibbutzim. Members of these militias were to play an important role in Israeli politics for the

next half-century: Yigal Allon, Moshe Dayan, and Yitzhak Rabin were high-ranking members of the Haganah-Palmach, Menachem Begin led the Irgun, and Yitzhak Shamir was a prominent member of the Lehi. Three of these men – Rabin, Shamir, and Begin – would later become prime ministers of Israel.
– Britannica: *Zionism*.

To discern who and what was behind Zionism you would inevitably have to follow the money trail that leads back to those whose agenda is not religious but political. Those behind the superficial Zionist agenda have a deeper Luciferian agenda that would willingly promote the terrible persecution and destruction of millions of innocent Jewish people as collateral damage in the pursuit of their political agenda. The seeds of a coming holocaust were sown long ago by those behind Zionism to get political traction and popular sympathetic support for a Jewish homeland.

The global cabals and secret groups and societies that are the tools of the Luciferian agenda cleverly use both the political and religious spirit to fulfil their goals. I am not necessarily in full agreement with what is quoted below but I do believe it reveals that this agenda is not a modern one and that there is a very clear strategy behind which was interpreted by the personal filters of those in their period. The object of the criticism reflects the context (for instance, the British Empire being the focus of the conspiracy for those during the American Revolution). This is to be expected but must not hide the fact that an agenda for one-world government has existed and continues to do so.

Those behind the political and religious agenda of Zionism have used the ideologies of both the left and right wings of the political bird to fulfil their goals.

Those hiding behind a Jewish identity were outworking their agenda through Communism and Fascism and the conflict that produced the Second World War. They took advantage of those mistakenly blaming the advance of communism by Jewish Bolsheviks on ordinary innocent Jewish people. The political dealings of Zionists manipulated UK and US governments to bring the US into the Second World War, just as it did in the First World War, and the agenda was based on establishing a Jewish homeland in Palestine.

> This is from an article by Mrs B.M. Palmer, referring to the post First World War period, published in the UK on January 13, 1940.
>
> During the chaos which supervened on the Versailles Treaty, the German middle classes were deprived of their savings and small businesses and came under the control of international Jews who had access to the international money market.
>
> This is the real origin of Anti-Semitism in Germany. The fact that the blow fell on inoffensive citizens, [religious Jews - the 'lesser brethren'] even on scholars and artists who had nothing to do with the world of finance, has blinded well-meaning people to the fact that the international money-lenders are responsible for the terrible troubles that fell on their own people. They knew perfectly well that there would be pogroms [race specific genocides].

The slaughter of a few hundred Jews was no more to them than the German casualties are to Hitler. They want world domination, and they are prepared that their own should pay for it." – *World's Troublemakers.*

The fact is that the persecution of Jews has been orchestrated by the International money-lenders (global cabalists) who call themselves 'Jews'.

To achieve their political program of world dominion they have taken advantage of the political and religious spirit promoted divisiveness and hatred between Jew and non-Jew; orchestrated pogroms, oppression, suppression, and persecution of the Jew masses.
– vikingmac.wordpress.com/tag/jesus-christ

What has this to do with eschatology, you may ask? The reality is that the same people orchestrating the conflicts that eventually led to the fulfilment of the Zionist agenda were behind the production of the Scofield Reference Bible (the main source of Dispensationalism), rapture escape theology and procrastination of the kingdom to the 1000-year future period.

To deprogram people from the frameworks and mindsets of futurism, the erroneous teachings of the modern-day churches regarding the second coming of Christ needs to be challenged. Dispensationalism has deceived church systems into teaching and propagating the doctrine of the New World Order for over 100 years.

Jonathan Williams recorded in his book, Legions of Satan, in 1781, that Cornwallis revealed to Washington that a "holy war will now begin on America, and when it is ended America will supposedly be the citadel of freedom, but her millions will unknowingly be the loyal subjects of the Crown." Cornwallis went on to explain that what would seem to be a contradiction:

"Your churches will be used to teach the Jews' religion and in less than two hundred years the whole nation will be working for divine world government. That government that they believe to be divine will be the British Empire. All religions will be permeated with Judaism without even being noticed by the masses, and they will all be under the invisible all-seeing eye of the Grand Architect of Freemasonry."

Indeed George Washington himself was a Mason, and he gave back through a false religion what he had won with his army.
– Extracted from https://nmevsus.wordpress.com/pikes-debunked-its-lenins-3-world-wars)

This divine world government that Cornwallis spoke of was the religion of the New World Order. The evangelical seminaries began to teach doctrines that would deceive their followers into believing that there would be a one-world government and it would be the fulfilment of Bible prophecy; however, in their version it is Christ who will be the ruler.

The power of this deception has created the belief that Zionism will produce that result when in fact Zionism has a contradictory agenda and their world government would definitely not be Christian. The Talmudic agenda is for an elite group to control the world; it presents a false Zionist agenda, concealing its true agenda behind a political and religious façade.

This may seem a very extreme view but it is found within the Talmud and is quoted many times by prominent Zionists:

"We will have a world government whether you like it or not. The only question is whether that government will be achieved by conquest or consent." – Zionist banker Paul Warburg, testifying before the US Senate, February 17 1950.

A One World Government and one-unit monetary system, under permanent non-elected hereditary oligarchists who self-select from among their numbers in the form of a feudal system as it was in the Middle Ages. In this One World entity, the population will be limited by restrictions on the number of children per family, diseases, wars, famines, until 1 billion people who are useful to the ruling class, in areas which will be strictly and clearly defined, remain as the total world population.

There will be no middle class, only rulers and servants. All laws will be uniform under a legal system of world courts practising the same unified code of laws, backed up by a One World Government police force and a One World unified military to enforce laws in all former countries where no national boundaries shall exist. The system will be based on a welfare state; those who are obedient and subservient to the One World Government will be rewarded with the means to live; those who are rebellious will simply be starved to death or be declared outlaws, thus a target for anyone who wishes to kill them. Privately owned firearms or weapons of any kind will be prohibited." – John Coleman[59]

In the preface to his book *Descent into Tyranny*, Alex Jones[60] states that the New World Order system of world conquest has always been visible but it is so hulking and massive that it has remained hidden in plain sight:

> The globalists' plan is so far along that now they must admit that world government is a reality. Their propagandists are hailing the New World Order as the only system that will keep us safe and secure. In reality, it is the world government itself which is conducting the terrorist acts.

Adam Weishaupt, professor of canon law at Ingolstadt, a former Jesuit and founder of a secret society who called themselves 'Perfectibilists' wrote[61]:

> "The great strength of our Order lies in its concealment; let it never appear in any place in its own name, but always covered by another name, and another occupation".

Britannica says of Weishaupt and the Perfectibilists:

> Also known as the Bavarian Illuminati, their founder aimed to replace Christianity with a religion of reason... The order was organized along Jesuit lines and kept internal discipline and a system of mutual surveillance based on that model... From 1778 onward Weishaupt's

---

[59] John Coleman, *Conspirators Hierarchy: The Story of the Committee of 300*, p161.
[60] Alex Jones, *9-11, Descent into Tyranny*, Progressive Press (2002).
[61] Adam Weishaupt, AZQuotes.com, Wind and Fly Ltd, 2022. https://www.azquotes.com/quote/771598, accessed 7 April, 2022.

Illuminati began to make contact with various Masonic lodges...

Secret societies of this kind fitted in with the idea of benevolent despotism as a vehicle for the Enlightenment... After the suppression of Weishaupt's order, the title *illuminati* was given to the French Martinists, founded in 1754 by Martinez Pasqualis and propagated by Louis-Claude de Saint-Martin. By 1790 Martinism had been spread to Russia by Johann Georg Schwarz and Nikolay Novikov. Both strains of 'illuminated' Martinism included elements of Kabbalism and Christian mysticism, imbibing ideas from Jakob Böhme and Emanuel Swedenborg.
– Britannica: *Weishaupt.*

Contrary to popular belief, the term 'New World Order' was not coined by George Bush. It is an ancient plan of the secret and occult societies of the world. The Illuminati are interconnected families who believe Lucifer is their spiritual father and they do his bidding. Their plan is to outwork their Luciferian agenda through societies like the Freemasons, Bilderbergs, Zionists etc., never revealing themselves, always remaining behind the veil. Famous families believed to be members of this occult society include the Rockefellers, Rothschilds and Vanderbilts.

The poisonous tree is responsible for promoting a Zionist agenda that most gullible Christians have no idea about. The Babel agenda is alive and well in the guise of Zionism and the goal is the same as the empire of one-world government. Few, if any, Christian Zionists would agree with this agenda if they truly knew what was behind it, but the following quotes from two former prime ministers of Israel reveal that agenda:

"Our race is the Master Race. We are divine gods on this planet. We are as different from the inferior races as they are from insects. In fact, compared to our race, other races are beasts and animals, cattle at best. Other races are considered as human excrement. Our destiny is to rule over the inferior races. Our earthly kingdom will be ruled by our leader with a rod of iron. The masses will lick our feet and serve us as our slaves." – Israeli Prime Minister Menachem Begin[62], 1982.

"Every time we do something you tell me America will do this and will do that... I want to tell you something very clear: don't worry about American pressure on Israel. We, the Jewish people, control America, and the Americans know it." – Israeli Prime Minister Ariel Sharon[63], 2001.

We must distinguish Jews, who follow the religion of Judaism and the Torah, from Zionists, who may or may not be Jews and who follow a political movement, using the cover of the Talmud for its authority.

The Torah is the Hebrew Bible, and refers to all of the Hebrew Bible, including such books as Joshua, Psalms, Book of Ruth, etc. but the Talmud is a collection of rabbinic teachings which seek to interpret Torah and law. Rabbinical traditions that are collated in the Talmud are sometimes referred to as the Oral Torah. Many Jews believe that the Talmud is as authoritative and legally binding as the Torah itself.

---

[62] Israeli Prime Minister Menachem Begin, in a speech to the Knesset [Israeli Parliament] quoted by Amnon Kapeliouk, "Begin and the Beasts," New Statesman, June 25, 1982.
[63] Israeli Prime Minister Ariel Sharon, October 3, 2001, to Shimon Peres, as reported on Kol Yisrael radio.

The entire Christian Zionist Movement is influenced by the footnotes from the Scofield Bible. I believe that those who funded the Scofield Bible were promoting the Zionist agenda. There is evidence to suggest that it was the Rothschilds who provided that funding through intermediaries and also founded and funded the Zionist movement to further a New World Order agenda. At the first Zionist conference, Theodor Herzl[64], a Rothschild intermediary, made it clear that Rothschildism (RothIsm) is not about saving Jews:

> "It is essential that the sufferings of Jews... become worse... this will assist in realization of our plans... I have an excellent idea... I shall induce anti-Semites to liquidate Jewish wealth... The anti-Semites will assist us thereby in that they will strengthen the persecution and oppression of Jews. The anti-Semites shall be our best friends."

There is strong evidence to support the connection between Cyrus Scofield and Samuel Untermeyer, an attorney who was instrumental in preparing the Federal Reserve Banking law in 1910 and the financing of Scofield's Reference Bible. Untermeyer introduced Scofield to many Zionist and socialist leaders, including Samuel Gompers, Fiorello LaGuardia, Abraham Straus, Bernard Baruch and Jacob Schiff. These Zionists financed Scofield's research trips to Oxford and arranged the publication and distribution of his concordance.

The Scofield Bible became the standard reference work in virtually all Christian ministries and divinity schools and has greatly influenced 20th and 21st century Christian beliefs, It is primarily responsible for many Christians' belief in Zionism

---

[64] Theodor Herzl, Bartleby Research, https://www.bartleby.com/ essay/ Herzl-Anti-Semites-PJYFTNVWGJB, accessed 7 April 2022.

and for deceiving so many into supporting the Luciferian one world government agenda.

The Scofield Bible has hundreds of footnotes in the margins and at the bottom of the pages that misleadingly weave parts of the Old and New Testaments together as though the same people wrote them at the same time. The notes themselves give insights into the Zionist influence and agenda. Below are examples taken from the revised 1967 Edition:

> For a nation to commit the sin of anti-Semitism brings inevitable judgment.

> God made an unconditional promise of blessings through Abram's seed to the nation of Israel to inherit a specific territory forever.

There is no 'sin of anti-Semitism' in the Bible and Abraham did not bequeath a 'specific territory' to his descendants.

The religious right of fundamental Christianity, fronted by the emerging televangelists, started to gain political traction as their votes were seen as election winners. For those seeking to get elected by courting the religious right, the promotion of a Zionist agenda and Christian Zionism was a popular cause to support.

Fundamentalists like Pat Robertson, Jerry Falwell and others have inserted the Scofield's Bible interpretation concerning 'Jews' into Genesis 12:3, which reads:

"And I will bless those who bless you, and the one who curses you I will curse. And in you all the families of the earth will be blessed." (Genesis 12:3).

For many, this has made support for Israel and its policies a part of new covenant Christianity, for fear of being cursed.

If you wish to go deeper into the history of dispensationalism and Christian Zionism, there is more suggested reading in Appendix 3.

When challenged, the evangelical programming many Christians have undergone because of the dispensational and Zionist roots of many seminaries often causes anti-Semitic accusations. The reality is that the Christian Zionist position is not a prevailing position for much of the Christian Church, either historically or currently.

That being said, Zionistic and Christian Zionistic eschatology has detrimentally influenced and deceived many believers into accepting both Hebrew Roots theology and Jewish mysticism. This subject deserves a chapter on its own, as it is becoming a major problem and deception in the mystic community which needs to be addressed if we are to see the restoration of all things.

6. Hebrew Roots Theology and Jewish Mysticism.

Paul, in his letters to the newly-formed Gentile Churches, warned them of the dangers of the infiltration and mixing of the leaven of the law-based old covenant into the new covenant. The whole of Galatians chapter 3 deals with this subject in detail. He cautioned them not to go back under the bondage of the law: that was a curse, and yet that is what is really behind the deception of the Hebrew Roots theology that many sincere mystics are peddling.

You foolish Galatians, who has bewitched you, before whose eyes Jesus Christ was publicly portrayed as crucified? This is the only thing I want to find out from you: did you receive the Spirit by the works of the Law, or by hearing with faith? Are you so foolish? Having begun by the Spirit, are you now being perfected by the flesh? (Galatians 3:1-3).

Even so Abraham believed God, and it was reckoned to him as righteousness. Therefore, be sure that it is those who are of faith who are sons of Abraham. The Scripture, foreseeing that God would justify the Gentiles by faith, preached the gospel beforehand to Abraham, saying, "All the nations will be blessed in you." So then those who are of faith are blessed with Abraham, the believer.

For as many as are of the works of the Law are under a curse; for it is written, "Cursed is everyone who does not abide by all things written in the book of the law, to perform them." Now that no one is justified by the Law before God is evident; for, "The righteous man shall live by faith." However, the Law is not of faith; on the contrary, "He who practices them shall live by them." Christ redeemed us from the curse of the Law, having become a curse for us – for it is written, "Cursed is everyone who hangs on a tree" – in order that in Christ Jesus the blessing of Abraham might come to the Gentiles, so that we would receive the promise of the Spirit through faith. (Galatians 3:6-14).

Therefore the Law has become our tutor to lead us to Christ, so that we may be justified by faith. But now that faith has come, we are no longer under a tutor. For you are all sons of God through faith in Christ Jesus. For all of you who were baptized into Christ have clothed yourselves with Christ. There is neither Jew nor Greek, there is neither slave nor free man, there is neither male nor female; for you are all one in Christ Jesus. And if you belong to Christ, then you are Abraham's descendants, heirs according to promise. (Galatians 3:24-29).

For there are many rebellious men, empty talkers and deceivers, especially those of the circumcision, who must be silenced because they are upsetting whole families, teaching things they should not teach for the sake of sordid gain. One of themselves, a prophet of their own, said, "Cretans are always liars, evil beasts, lazy gluttons." This testimony is true. For this reason reprove them severely so that they may be sound in the faith, not paying attention to Jewish myths and commandments of men who turn away from the truth. (Titus 1:10-14 NASB).

There are many who engage in worthless debates about their Jewish sentiments and playing mind-games in order to snare new believers into legalism. By entreating and persuading them with wisdom, their influence will be silenced. The rot must be stopped since they have already confused entire families with their teachings and robbed them financially in the process. According to one of their own so called "enlightened" leaders, the Cretans are known to be phony, lazy gluttons, and savage brutes. This gives all the more reason that they need distinguished leaders who are capable of rebuking such behavior sharply and establish them in robust faith. (We are not here to merely comment on people's behavioral trends; we are here to declare people free to live the life of their redeemed design! Faith sees that old life co-crucified with Christ and the new resurrected life emerge victoriously. Faith is not a "mickey-mouse" cover-up for sin; faith defeats sin.) *Admonish them not to pay any attention to Jewish fiction and their man-made rules and regulations which achieve exactly the ¹opposite to what truth promotes.* (The word, ¹*apostrepho*, means to reverse). (Titus 1:10-14 Mirror)

When He had disarmed the rulers and authorities, He made a public display of them, having triumphed over them through Him. Therefore no one is to act as your judge in regard to food or drink or in respect to a festival or a new moon or a Sabbath day things which are a mere shadow of what is to come; but the substance belongs to Christ. (Colossians 2:15-17 NASB).

In him dying mankind's death, he ¹defused every possible claim of accusation against the human race and thus made a public ²spectacle of every ³rule and authority in God's brilliant triumph, demonstrated in him. The ⁴voice of the cross will never be silenced! (The horror of the Cross is now the eternal trophy of God's triumph over sin! The cross stripped religion of its authority to manipulate mankind with guilt. Every accusation lost its leverage to blackmail the human race with condemnation and shame. The word, ¹*apekduomai*, is translated from *apo*, away from, and *ekduo*, to be stripped of clothing; the religious facade that disguised the law of works as a means of defining a person's life, was openly defeated.

Same word used in Col 3:9. The dominance of the tree of the knowledge of good and evil [*poneros*, hard work and labor] was ended. The word, ²*deikmatizo*, means to exhibit in public. See ³commentary below of the words *arche*, rule and *exousia*, authority. The word, ⁴*parresia*, comes from *pas*, all and *rheo*, outspokenness, pouring forth speech. "He stripped all the spiritual tyrants in the universe of their sham authority at the Cross and marched them naked through the streets." – The Message.

See commentary for 1 Corinthians 15:24, The complete conclusion in his work of redemption is celebrated in his yielding the full harvest of his reign to God the Father, having brought to nought the law of works which supported every definition of dominion under the fall, including all principalities, all authority and every dynamic influence in society. [He brought to naught the law of works, *katargeo*, from *kata*, meaning intensity, and *argos*, meaning labor; thus free from all self-effort to attempt to improve what God has already perfected in Christ. All principalities, ³*arche*, or chief ranks, i.e., kings, governors; this includes any governing system whereby one is ranked above the other on the basis of their performance or preference. All authority, ³*exousia*, comes from *ek*, denoting origin and *eimi*, I am; in this case, because of what I can do I am defined by what I can do better than you; therefore, I have authority over you. Every dynamic influence in society, *dunamis*, means power, in this case, willpower. Every government structure in society will be brought under the dominion of grace where the Christ-life rules.]

In 1 Corinthians 2:7-8, We voice words of wisdom that was hidden in silence for timeless ages; a mystery unfolding God's Masterful plan whereby he would redeem his glory in mankind. Neither the politicians nor the theologians of the day had a clue about this mystery [of mankind's association in Christ]; if they did, they would never have crucified the Lord whose death redeemed our glory!)

Do not let anyone therefore bring a restriction to your freedom by reviving religious rules and regulations pertaining to eating and drinking; all Jewish festivals, new moons, and Sabbaths have come to an end in Christ! (Their relevance only served to remind of the promise of Christ on an annual, monthly, and weekly basis. They carried the promise like a placenta would hold the unborn child, but became obsolete as soon as the child was born.)

These things were only prophetic shadows; Christ is the substance. (Colossians 2:15-17 Mirror).

Paul warns them of the dangers of paying attention to Jewish myths, festivals, religious rules and traditions and therefore turning away from the truth.

The following is an extract from my journals where I recorded what the Father said to me regarding the deception that this chapter addresses. It gives me the motivation to write this difficult chapter and fully endorse what Paul wrote to the early church, who were in danger of the leaven of the Pharisees infiltrating and bringing mixture into the purity of the new covenant that Jesus instituted.

"Son, the light of love and truth is shining brightly and this will increase further as Our sons begin to arise and discover their eternal identity. The light of truth will expose many areas of darkness that are keeping Our children in the bondage of lost identity. Even those who have engaged heaven are susceptible to deception if their minds are not deconstructed from their programmed belief systems.

"The eschatological programming that is part of the Luciferian agenda must be brought into the light of truth and Our sons must be set free or they will remain susceptible to deception. The mixing of covenants is being perpetrated by the religious spirit and is responsible for the guilt, shame and condemnation that so many feel."

13th May 2021

"Son, there is truth and the 'righteous real' behind many counterfeits, as you have discovered through Our encounters; but the philosophies behind the counterfeits are lies and deceptions and must be avoided at all costs. This is especially true of Kabbalah because of its association with Judaism which hoodwinks so many because of Zionism. The root of deception behind Kabbalah and the Hebrew Roots Movement is eschatological, as all things Hebrew and Jewish culturally are wrongly made acceptable because of Zionism. The whole of Jewish mysticism is a perversion as it is sourced in the wrong tree and is part of the Luciferian agenda behind all religions.

"Kabbalah has its light and knowledge from Lucifer and has twisted heavenly truth concerning sacred geometry, the Tree of Life, the Merkabah and Metatron's cube – things that We have shown you the truth about – into an esoteric false and Luciferian system. That which Kabbalah reveals is designed to deceive, not enlighten; and Our sons must be warned to completely reject it. There is absolutely no benefit from studying false belief systems as they are designed to trap Our children in their lost identity. There can be no syncretism with Judaism, Hebrew culture or Kabbalah as it will be the leaven that eventually will desecrate, pollute and infect the lives of those who study it.

"Son, there may be some elements of truth that can be found in many things but they all point to the Truth, who is the only way to discover abundant life. The counterfeits can and will never lead to the restoration of lost identity, as they only perpetuate it, as they are from the same independent source. All elements of truth found hidden within the counterfeits are designed to deceive Our children; but We are still able to use the frequency that truth has to draw them to the light of truth only found in Jesus. We did not place those elements of truth within the false religious systems that Our children used to make gods in their own image but We can use it.

"Son, encourage Our children to dwell only in the light of Our presence, helping to reveal and awaken and turn them to the reality of who We are as pure unconditional love. Only a love awakening can enable Our children to come to the light of love and truth and learn to abide there in rest. The rest that is only found in Us is the only antidote for the addiction to dead works that humanity is controlled by. We declare to humanity, 'Be still, cease striving with self-effort, and know who We are, so you can discover who you are as mankind made in Our image.'

"Son, let this declaration reverberate throughout the earth shield as Our sons become oracles of Our heart and begin to speak with the sound of many waters to awaken Our children from the stupor of lost identity."

I am passionate in my opposition to the leaven of Jewish mysticism infecting the true mystic movement but I am not seeking to attack individuals (some of whom are personal friends) nor name and shame anyone. My only goal is to help free all of God's children from this deception by establishing the realised eschatology of the restoration of all things.

Many of you may be thinking 'Well, I am not influenced by Zionism'; but due to the infiltration of Hebrew culture into the mystic movement, you may indeed have already been infected and influenced. The displays of *tallits* (Hebrew prayer shawls) draped over conference lecterns, the wearing of *kippahs*, using the Hebrew name for God, Jesus and the Spirit instead of what is commonly used in a person's native tongue is evidence of such infiltration.

Sometimes I listen to those infected by Hebrew Roots and I don't even understand what or who they are talking about. Then some use the Hebrew rather than Gregorian calendar and proclaim 'Happy *Rosh Hashanah*!' and follow all the Hebrew feasts, even partaking in the Passover. These things are the thin end of the wedge and are the leaven of the old covenant infiltrating, mixing with and polluting the new covenant. Ultimately I believe this is part of the great deception that is hoodwinking God's children into believing the lies of Zionism by another route. Then there is the encouragement that is given by some that you have to learn Hebrew and fully understand Hebrew cultural practices or worldview to know the mysteries of God. In my opinion, this is a lie and makes the Hebrew language a mediator and substitute for the Holy Spirit of Truth or Jesus, the Way, Truth and Life.

It all sounds very plausible and I dare say you will get a greater intellectual understanding of some of the Old Testament symbolism. I know no Hebrew and yet still get similar revelation, without the need to spend both time and money to do so. As an example, I attended a conference where one of the speakers was a very well-known mystic and one of his disciples shared a session on the Hebrew language. As he broke down the word 'peace' or *'shalom'* into its various Hebrew pictorial components, the definition seemed very familiar. Later as I searched through my journals I found that in conversation with the Father only two weeks previously, He had spoken almost word for word the same definition of the meaning of the word and concept of peace. I am not saying that there is no value in learning Hebrew but that the time, effort and money it takes to do so may be better invested in face to face time with the Father, who *is* the mystery.

Two of the intellectual pillars that held up the framework of my thinking were Greek and Hebrew mindsets and the Father deconstructed both those pillars to free my mind from their influence. I believe the promotion and acceptance of Hebrew culture, values, titles, language, dates, feasts and festivals by sincere, well-meaning but deceived individuals will ultimately lead people into deception and bondage. It is the law and legalism by another name and it is drip-feeding Hebrew cultural values so that they become mediators in our relationship with God.

The ultimate goal of the Luciferian agenda is to create a counterfeit kingdom of one-world government under a false Messiah claiming to be Christ. I believe that a false eschatological framework is also behind the infiltration of the Hebrew roots movement into the mystic community. Following types and shadows, festivals, dates and Hebrew traditions has crept into the mystic movement because of Christian Zionist programming. I believe there is a clear agenda to pollute the mystic movement and sabotage the mission of the sons of God for the restoration of all things. I am not criticising those who teach these things personally, as

I believe that they are mostly sincere, but I am opposed to the infiltration of what are, in my opinion, deceptive, false doctrines.

Hebrew Roots

The Hebrew Roots Movement (HRM) is difficult to pin down and define because it is made up of so many disparate groups and individuals. It is a diverse collection ranging from scholars to individuals practising make-it-up-as-you-go Judaism. It also includes followers of Kabbalah, with its esoteric numerology. Dangerously, there are often no distinctions made between the old and the new covenant or between the Bible and the Talmud. This movement can be very legalistic in following the law or may simply suggest Jewish practices that they say will give us deeper insight and understanding as well as make us more 'authentic' believers.

Here is a loose definition of the Hebrew Roots Movement:

> It is a very modern movement that insists that we must resurrect first-century Judaism (our Jewish Roots) and the milieu and lifestyle of first-century Jews and impose them on both Jewish and non-Jewish believers. This is not just an academic study to better understand Scripture and its setting but is rather a movement of restoration that claims that the church has moved off its Jewish foundation and must return to a more Jewish way of life to be authentic. – G. Richard Fisher[65].

There are two distinct strands of Hebrew Roots theology and of course many variants in each strand. One is a Christian

---

[65] G. Richard Fisher, "Bewitching Believers Through the Hebrew Roots Movement," *Berean Call*, January 1, 2014.
See https://www.thebereancall.org/content/january-2014-bewitching-believers-hebrew-roots

Evangelical religious movement that advocates the return to adherence to the Torah and the other is more of a grassroots movement.

Since the early 20th century, different religious organizations have been teaching a belief in Jesus (called Yeshua by adherents) as mankind's redeemer and savior from man's own sinful nature and a lifestyle in keeping with the Torah, the Sabbath and the annual Feasts (or mo'adim, Holy Days). These include Messianic Judaism (to a very limited degree) in 1916, the Sacred Name Movement (SNM) in 1937, and the Worldwide Church of God (WCG) in the 1930s, and, later, the Hebrew Roots Movement. Thus far, the WCG has had the greatest impact on all organizations which teach these beliefs, including obedience to much of the Old Testament law, both nationally and internationally until about 1994–95. Within a few years after the death of its founder, Herbert W Armstrong, in 1986, the succeeding church administration modified the denomination's doctrines and teachings in order to be compatible with mainstream evangelical Christianity, while many members and ministers left and formed other churches that conformed to many, but, not all, of Armstrong's teachings. Consequently, the WCG spawned numerous splinter groups, with most of these new churches adopting names bearing the term "Church of God" (COG) and retaining the belief system developed by Armstrong.

In contrast, Hebrew Roots (or sometimes, Hebraic Roots) is a grassroots movement without an ecclesiastical superstructure and it does not adhere to the COG belief system, nor does it adhere to Messianic Judaism, or to the SNM, although there are commonalities. A number of their founders began teaching about the need to keep the 7th Day Sabbath, to observe annual Feasts, and to obey Old Testament commandments years before these topics were taught and accepted by some in the Christian churches. These early teachers include William Dankenbring (1964) and Dean Wheelock (1981) (both of whom had prior associations with different Churches of God), Joe Good (1978), and Brad Scott (1983). Batya Wootten's curiosity about the Gentile majority in many Messianic-Jewish congregations resulted in her first book about the two houses of Israel in 1988. This was later followed by her 1998 book entitled Who is Israel (now renamed in its 4th edition as Redeemed Israel).

In 1994, Dean and Susan Wheelock received their Federal Trademark for the term "Hebrew Roots", after which they began publishing the Hebrew Roots magazine in April/May 1998, and later a website at Hebrewroots.net. The goal of this group is "Exploring the Hebrew Roots of the Faith Once Delivered,"-"roots" which go back to not only Yeshua and the Talmidim (Disciples), but to the Nazarenes of the first century and, ultimately, the original Hebrews (Ivrim), Abraham and his offspring, who were the first to "cross over" (which is one view of what "Hebrew" means in the Hebrew language). Those who continue in this Hebraic walk seek out the history, culture, and faith of the first century believers who, like Abraham and Moses obeyed God's voice, charge, commandments, statutes, and laws (Gen 26:5). The 41,000, denominations of Christianity commonly believe that such obedience (*viz*, to the 613 Torah commands) is no longer required. This is largely due to a number of statements by the apostle Paul.

The Hebrew Roots movement began emerging as a distinct phenomenon in the mid-1990s (1993-96). In 1997, Dean Cozzens of Open Church Ministries (Colorado Springs, CO) published a prophecy titled "The Hebrew Movement", which revealed that God had foreordained four major moves for the 20th century, Pentecostalism, Faith-healing, the Charismatic Movement and finally the Hebrew Roots Movement. In this prophecy, the Hebrew Roots Movement is the "final stage of empowerment" before Christ returns. Several Hebrew Roots ministries are now preferring to use the term Awakening instead of the term "movement" which has been used widely since the 1960s to define politically oriented movements.

The movement / Awakening has accelerated in the last few years, mainly because of a shift within the Messianic Jewish community. The Hebrew Roots movement and a few Messianic Jewish groups diverge on the issue of One Law theology (one law for the native born and the sojourner, c.f. Numbers 15:16) which Hebrew Roots subscribes to, but which some Messianic Jewish groups deny.
– Wikipedia: *Hebrew Roots.*

The 'hebrewrootsmom' website sets out how it works:

The main source of doctrine in the Hebrew Roots Movement is simply the bible itself – both the Old and New Testaments. Some in the Movement incorporate rabbinical teachings and some do not. Some follow Kosher dietary laws, honour the New Moon Festivals, and keep their heads covered, while others do not. Some follow all Christian traditions but also incorporate the three annual festivals commanded in Deuteronomy 16:16. It is practised differently in every Hebrew Roots family I know but they all have one thing in common: They seek to mature their faith and pass it on to others by illuminating the Gospel and the God of the bible through the practice of Jewish customs...

Again, there is not just one way to practice Hebrew Roots Christianity. It's a type of grassroots movement to follow Jesus and practice our Christian faith by returning to the Jewish roots of that faith. Incorporating Jewish customs and learning the Hebrew language increases our understanding of biblical Jewish culture, which is so very different from our own. When reading scripture written by mostly Jewish people about primarily Jewish people (including our Jewish Messiah), a lack of understanding of Jewish language and culture can create confusion. Many are drawn to the Movement because it brings clarity to their biblical studies, leading to an increase in knowledge of our God and our Messiah.

Many Hebrew Roots Christians merely want to be as authentic as possible in the practice of their faith. For example, most Christians would say that Christians are responsible for adhering to the fourth commandment (Keeping the Sabbath), but many don't do that or even know how to. The Hebrew Roots Christian is bothered by inconsistencies such as this one and seeks then to resolve it in his or her life. Jewish customs resolve many of these inconsistencies because of their history of strict devotion to the Torah. As Christians, we have the New Testament also, which sheds light on the Old Testament by way of prophecy fulfilment, the ushering in of the New Covenant, and the life of Jesus and the apostles.
— hebrewrootsmom.com

Whilst this seems very sincere and noble, I believe that it is ultimately a part of a much bigger deception, including Zionism, which is fundamentally designed to bring believers back under a system that is obsolete, however it is framed. There is a very thin line to tread that is fraught with danger and so many are easily deceived and fall into the trap being set for them. In exploring Hebraic Roots they end up deceived into accepting and following the traditions and culture of a system that failed and is obsolete. The only thing that needs to be sought after is the kingdom of God, which is expressed in the new covenant; and which is not influenced by Greek or Hebrew culture, but heaven.

The mixing of covenants brings what I call covenantal confusion, which was so clearly evident during the early years of the church, where new converts wrestled with issues related to Israel and the church. Paul and the other New Testament writers wrote their epistles to those fledgling churches who were being encouraged as it were to flee the nest of Judaism and soar free from the old covenant religious laws and restrictions. Even today, in the twenty-first century, because of the false eschatology of Zionism and the deceptive influence of Jewish mysticism, believers continue to struggle with the same issues of being sucked back under legalism.

Most of the errors of the HRM arise from its misunderstanding of the nature of biblical covenants. The most serious of these understandings is the idea that "the law" was originally intended to be binding on all people throughout history. They erroneously use some of Jesus' statements recorded in the synoptic gospels, where He was addressing and seeking to reach a Jewish audience still living under their notion of the law. They misunderstand what Jesus meant by not abolishing but fulfilling the Law and Prophets and infer that He meant that the law was to continue in the new covenant. They also assume that when Jesus spoke of keeping His commandments that He was referring to the Torah, or the Ten Commandments, or the entire law: religious, legal and ceremonial. Jesus' commandments could not be more different from a law-based system and can be summed up in one statement, "Love another as I have loved you," making it a gracious response to love, not obedience to the law.

"Do not presume that I came to abolish the Law or the Prophets; I did not come to abolish, but to fulfill." (Matthew 5:17).

"If you love Me, you will keep My commandments." (John 14:15).

"A new commandment I give to you, that you love one another, even as I have loved you, that you also love one another." (John 13:34).

All the promises and covenants which God made are fulfilled in Jesus and are summed up or consummated, brought to fullness and completeness, in the new covenant of love. When Jesus stressed the importance of keeping commandments, He was speaking to those Jews still under the law, not to future Gentile believers or the 'one new man in Christ' *ekklesia*. HRM erroneously infers this to mean that the law must still be in force today, even for Gentiles, even though they were not under the law in Old Testament times, as Paul makes clear in the letter to the Ephesians.

Therefore remember that formerly you, the Gentiles in the flesh, who are called "Uncircumcision" by the so-called "Circumcision," which is performed in the flesh by human hands – remember that you were at that time separate from

Christ, excluded from the commonwealth of Israel, and strangers to the covenants of promise, having no hope and without God in the world. But now in Christ Jesus you who formerly were far off have been brought near by the blood of Christ. For He Himself is our peace, who made both groups into one and broke down the barrier of the dividing wall, by abolishing in His flesh the enmity, which is the Law of commandments contained in ordinances, so that in Himself He might make the two into one new man, thus establishing peace, and might reconcile them both in one body to God through the cross, by it having put to death the enmity. (Ephesians 2:11-16).

How did Jesus fulfil the law? Not by ensuring that the law would continue but by making us righteous, something which the law itself had no power to do.

He made Him who knew no sin to be sin on our behalf, so that we might become the righteousness of God in Him. (2 Corinthians 5:21).

Jesus lived a sinless life, so He could be the perfect sacrifice that humanity required, our Passover lamb, outworking in time what was already accomplished in eternity.

Clean out the old leaven so that you may be a new lump, just as you are in fact unleavened. For Christ our Passover also has been sacrificed. (1 Corinthians 5:7).

Jesus fulfilled the law, so no one, Jew or Gentile, is obligated to be under the law: that was the message Paul experienced on the Damascus road and shared throughout his letters.

... having canceled the certificate of debt consisting of decrees against us, which was hostile to us; and He has taken it out of the way, having nailed it to the cross. (Colossians 2:14).

For sin shall not be master over you, for you are not under the Law but under grace. (Romans 6:14).

Therefore, my brothers and sisters, you also were put to death in regard to the Law through the body of Christ, so that you might belong to another, to Him who was raised from the dead, in order that we might bear fruit for God. (Romans 7:4).

But if you are led by the Spirit, you are not under the Law. (Galatians 5:18).

To summarise:

The HRM uses non-biblical books and oral traditions as well as the Bible.

The HRM misunderstands the extent and scope of the Mosaic law, which is now obsolete.

The 'Jerusalem Council,' as recorded in Acts 15, rejected the idea that Gentile believers must follow the Law of Moses, only suggesting that they should not do certain things so as not to antagonise the Jews throughout the Roman Empire.

The Apostle Paul refuted many of the most popular teachings of the HRM in his letters to the churches.

Kabbalah

The studying and following of Hebrew mystic and religious books that is being encouraged by some in the mystical movement carries a serious danger for those who are not discerning and who may be programmed and indoctrinated by reading the lies and errors along with the small elements of truth. The true mysteries of God are not found in books but in face to face, spirit to spirit, heart to heart and mind to mind direct encounters with the *mysterion*, the sacred mystery who is *I am that I am*.

I am not saying some people do not have a mandate to read these books; but for most of us, engaging the truth directly is the better and safer option. We do not need the mediation of the Bible, let alone the *Zohar*, *Kabbalah*, *Talmud* etc., to know the truth: we have direct access to the Truth, with Jesus the only door we need.

Why would we need to study Kabbalah which means "received tradition", a term previously used in other Judaic contexts? The Medieval Kabbalists adopted some ancient traditions and texts into their own doctrine to deceive people into the belief that Kabbalah is only revealing the ancient hidden esoteric tradition of the Torah. The Kabbalah is no different from any other false religious systems, including Judaism, Islam, Hinduism etc. Kabbalah should not be accepted as being authenticated because it has some of its roots in Judaism. It is Christian Zionism that has made all things Jewish acceptable in a religious sense, and that is the heart of the Luciferian agenda: to enslave mankind in lost identity within humanity.

We are the new covenant 'one new man,' the New Jerusalem, set free from the law, ceremonial, civil and religious. As Paul might be saying today, "You foolish believers, who is bewitching you?"

There are things that I am told are contained in Kabbalah like the *Sephiroth*, Metatron's cube, Merkabah and other forms of sacred geometry that I have had direct revelation of by personal experience. That does not validate a mystic book which may contain some elements of truth or which uses the same or similar terminology. The same terms have very different meanings when seen through the lens of Jesus, the Truth.

Dan Duval[66] has a whole teaching series, 'Exposing Kabbalah', in video or audio, which might be of interest to you if you want to explore this further, warning of the dangers of Kabbalah and the Zionist agenda. I am not saying that I wholly agree with everything said in that series, and certainly not its eschatology; but it is a warning that needs to be taken seriously nonetheless.

It states "You will learn why Kabbalah is the government of Lucifer and why its influences are something to steer clear of as a believer in Jesus Christ. There has been an excessive amount of infiltration in the body of Christ by Kabbalah, and you need to know how to spot it."

Paul warned the Corinthians of those preaching a different gospel and I resonate with how the Mirror Bible presents that warning: "Why would you politely put up with deception, even if it comes packaged in prominent names and titles!"

I wish that you would bear with me in a little foolishness; but indeed you are bearing with me. For I am jealous for you with a godly jealousy; for I betrothed you to one husband, so that to Christ I might present you as a pure virgin. But I am afraid that, as the serpent deceived Eve by his craftiness, your minds will be led astray from the simplicity and purity of devotion to Christ. For if one comes and preaches another Jesus whom we have not preached, or you receive a different spirit which you

---

[66] Dan Duval, *Exposing Kabbalah* series (YouTube playlist): buff.ly/3dTkYNw. Or type "Exposing Kabbalah series" into your search engine (including the quote marks).

have not received, or a different gospel which you have not accepted, you bear this beautifully. (2 Corinthians 11:1-4).

This might sound a little foolish, but please bear with me! I feel a divine jealousy for you! I have as it were been the groomsman who wooed you to belong solely to your one husband and presented you as a pure bride to Christ. I am concerned for you that that you might ¹pine away through the ²illusion of separation from Christ and that, just like Eve, you might become ³blurry-eyed and ⁴deceived into believing a lie about yourselves. The temptation was to exchange the truth about our completeness (I am) *with the idea of incompleteness* (I am not) *and shame; thinking that perfection required your toil and all manner of ⁵wearisome labor!* (The word, *¹phteiro*, means to pine or waste away, to whither. Any idea of separation causes one to wither away in loneliness! The word *²haplotes* from *hama*, a particle of union, and *pleko*, to braid or plait together; sometimes translated, simplicity or unmixed. The Greek word, *³ophis* is translated serpent and comes from *optomai*, to gaze, in this case, to present a visual idea through illusion. The word *⁴exapataō* from *ek*, source + *apateo*, apathy is the source of deception, to be without faith, believing a lie about yourself! Heb 4:6 Israel died in the wilderness because of their unbelief. [Both Adam and Israel believed a lie about themselves. Num 13:33, Josh 2:11, 2 Cor 4:4.] The word *⁵panourgia*, from the words, *pas*, all, and *ergon*, work or toil, where your complete existence is reduced to wearisome labor. This word is often translated, cunning or craftiness. See also 2 Cor 4:2 "We have renounced hidden agendas [employing a little bit of the law in an attempt to "balance" out grace]; we have distanced ourselves from any obscure craftiness to manipulate God's word to make it mean what it does not say!") *You will know by the echo within you whether the Jesus someone else preaches is the same Jesus we proclaim to you. You will recognize the same spirit; if it is a different spirit, it is not the same gospel!* **Why would you politely put up with deception, even if it comes packaged in prominent names and titles!** (2 Corinthians 11:1-4 Mirror, emphasis mine).

The last statement is what motivates me today to warn you of the dangers of Kabbalah, just as Paul was warning the Corinthians of the dangers of Judaism or Gnosticism: I reiterate that warning. Why would you politely put up with deception, even if it comes packaged in prominent names and titles? There are those today who are calling themselves Rabbis, some self-appointed and others recognised as such by others who give them the title. This is just another example of the infiltration of the mediation of the old covenant system.

Modern-day Judaism is not the same as was practised in Moses' day; nor is it the form of Judaism that Jesus was challenging the religious leaders about. Some of the Talmudic oral traditions of the Rabbis were in place during Jesus' day but Judaism has evolved further from its original form because of Kabbalistic influences. The Luciferian agenda was to mix the occult with Judaism through the Kabbalah.

Most Jewish religious observers only seek the first level of truth, which is to understand the law and apply it to their lives today, and most are unaware that the hidden goal of Judaism today is to understand Kabbalah, not God. Sadly they do not know that the law was only a schoolmaster to lead them to Jesus, their true Messiah.

The Babylonian Talmud is a written commentary on the *Mishnah*, the oral *Torah* of Rabbinic tradition. Most modern followers of Judaism believe the oral *Torah* and its commentary to be divinely inspired; but it is different from the Jewish Bible, which is known in Hebrew as the *Tanakh*, an acronym of the three sets of books that comprise it: the Pentateuch (*Torah*), the Prophets (*Nevi'im*) and the Writings (*Ketuvim*). The *Tanakh* is where the Old Testament scriptures in the Christian Bible are derived from.

Most Jews would probably not know that Kabbalah is a major source of influence on modern-day Judaism. The primary texts of Kabbalah were allegedly once part of an ongoing oral tradition. The written texts are obscure and difficult for readers who are unfamiliar with Jewish spirituality, which assumes extensive knowledge of the *Tanakh* (Hebrew Bible), *Midrash* (Jewish hermeneutic tradition) and *Halakha* (Jewish religious law).

The major texts in this collection of esoteric books include the *Zohar* and the *Sefer Yetzirah*, 3 Enoch, *Heichalot, Pardes Rimonim, Etz Hayim* and the Eight Gates.

The text is supposed to not only offer traditions and ways of thinking but also reveal the reality of God. Herein lies the major issue – and it is the same issue that occurs with the Bible – it can be used as a substitute and mediator. You cannot find the reality of God in the Kabbalah or in the Bible but only in Jesus, who is the only way or door to the Father.

Many modern mystics and those involved in Hebrew roots teaching mix Jewish mysticism with their teaching and talk about the 4 levels of revelation which are supposed to take us deeper into God. In Kabbalah, the mystery is not God but the secret, which is Kabbalah.

Pardes is the word used to describe 4 levels of revelation in biblical exegesis in rabbinic Judaism or the interpretation of the text in *Torah* study. The term, sometimes also rendered PaRDeS, is an acronym formed from the initials of the following four approaches:

Peshat – 'surface' ('straight') or the literal (direct) meaning.

Remez – 'hints' or the deep (allegoric: hidden or symbolic) meaning, beyond just the literal sense.

Derash – from Hebrew *darash*: 'inquire' ('seek') – the comparative (midrashic) meaning, as given through similar occurrences.

Sod (pronounced with a long 'o' as in 'lore') – 'secret' ('mystery') or the esoteric/mystical meaning, as given through inspiration or revelation.

I am not saying that there are no levels of revelation but they are found in Jesus, the Truth, not in Judaism or Kabbalah. There is a clear Luciferian agenda behind Kabbalah that is evident when you see those who are (or have been) involved in its practice and study. Some teach that there is always something real or truthful behind the counterfeit; and whilst I would agree that much truth has been counterfeited, that does not mean we should study the counterfeit to discover the real truth.

An example of this is the *gematria* and the living letters that many are using today in mystic teachings. I do believe that God created living beings that represent all aspects of creation, including living letters that are beings. I do believe that there is truth in biblical numerology; but the versions found in Kabbalah are counterfeit deceptions and the living letters have nothing to do with Hebrew culture itself. I have encountered the living letters themselves, and they do seem to have a role to play in creativity, but they must not become another mediator between us and God. The Father does not speak to me primarily through living letters, but directly in English.

There are other examples of terms that are in Kabbalah which I have encountered in the heavenly realms without ever reading about Kabbalah. The Tree of Life is in Genesis and in the book of Revelation but that has been twisted into the Kabbalah Tree and sephirotic belief systems. Other Kabbalah counterfeit terms that I have engaged independently are Metatron's Cube, the Merkabah, and Chakras. Kabbalah twists these things deceptively so that the counterfeits are very difficult to tell apart from the real. The terms may be the same but the meaning and function I have experienced all have Jesus at their centre.

There are many occultists who have used Kabbalah: that is evidence enough to indicate the real fruits of this Luciferian religious practice. These include:

- Éliphas Lévi Zahed, born Alphonse Louis Constant (8 February 1810 – 31 May 1875), who was a French esotericist, poet, and author of more than twenty books about magic, Kabbalah, alchemical studies, and occultism.
- A. E. Waite, who wrote occult texts on subjects including divination, esotericism, Rosicrucianism, Freemasonry, ceremonial magic, Kabbalism and alchemy; he also translated and reissued several mystical and alchemical works.
- Helena Blavatsky, who created the Theosophical society.
- Alice Baily, the supposed originator of the New Age movement.

Another example is how the 'Star of David', the most common symbol associated with the Israeli flag and Judaism, has been accepted into Judaism and Christianity. The star is not a positive biblical symbol at all: it is referenced as an occult symbol both in the Jewish *Tanahk* and the New Testament.

"Did you present Me with sacrifices and grain offerings in the wilderness for forty years, O house of Israel? You also carried along Sikkuth your king and Kiyyun, your images, the star of your gods which you made for yourselves." (Amos 5:25-26).

... as it is written in the book of the prophets, 'It was not to Me that you offered victims and sacrifices forty years in the wilderness, was it, O house of Israel? You also took along the tabernacle of Moloch and the star of the god Rompha, the images which you made to worship. I also will remove you beyond Babylon.' (Acts 7:42-43).

The star symbol is that of the god Rompha or Rempha, which the children of Israel brought with them out of Egypt, carried around the wilderness and continued to venerate even in the Promised Land. This flag adorns so many evangelical churches that support Christian Zionism and is now in mainstream acceptance as being associated with David rather than a demonic god.

Occultist and Kabbalah symbols and practices have infiltrated both mainstream evangelical Christianity through Zionism and Christian mysticism through the Kabbalah.

Seeking to know about our Christian roots in Judaism is a deception that has gone beyond knowing the prophetic Messianic scriptures. Our roots are not in Judaism but the true children of God as revealed to Abraham. We are children of promise and faith and that is where our roots are, not in the false Luciferian religion of Judaism.

The goal of Kabbalah is to reveal the truth to those who follow it; but this is not the Truth, Jesus, who is completely omitted from the cosmology that it teaches. Cosmology is an account or theory of the origin of the universe that has scientific and philosophical perspectives.

Kabbalistic cosmology

To discover the truth of the roots of Kabbalah we need to look at what it teaches about creation and whether that is consistent with what the New Testament reveals about Jesus as the creator. We should always start by looking at the truth of Biblical cosmology so that we can more easily discern the error in Kabbalistic cosmology.

Jesus and the New Testament writers confirm that Jesus was the creator, present at the beginning, and that everything created was created by Him, through Him and for Him. Jesus is the *alpha* and *omega*, the beginning and the end and all things are consummated in Him. Jesus is therefore the *eschaton* who is the final consummation of all things. If you remove Jesus from the centre of eschatology and cosmology you fall right into the Luciferian deception of 'I will'.

In the beginning was the Word, and the Word was with God, and the Word was God. He was in the beginning with God. All things came into being through Him, and apart from Him nothing came into being that has come into being. In Him was life, and the life was the Light of men. The Light shines in the darkness, and the darkness did not comprehend it. (John 1:1-5 NASB).

To go back to the very [1]beginning is to find the [2]Word already [3]present there; [4]face to face with God. The Word is [3]I am; God's [2]eloquence echoes and [4]concludes in him. The Word equals

God. (In the beginning, *¹arche,* to be first in order, time, place or rank. The Word, *²logos,* was "with" God; here and again in verse 2 John uses the Greek preposition *⁴pros,* towards; face-to-face. Three times in this sentence John uses the active indicative imperfect form of the verb *³eimi,* namely *aen* [ἦν] to be, [in the beginning 'was' the Word etc...] which conveys no idea of origin for God or for the Logos, but simply continuous existence, "I am." Quite a different verb *egeneto,* "became," appears in John 1:14 for the beginning of the Incarnation of the Logos. The Word 'became' flesh. The incarnation is not the origin of Jesus. See the distinction sharply drawn in John 8:58, "before Abraham was [born, *genesthai* from *ginomai*] I am." The word *eimi,* I am; the essence of being, suggesting timeless existence.)

The beginning mirrors the Word face to face with God. (Nothing that is witnessed in the Word distracts from who God is. "If you have seen me, you have seen the Father." [John 14:9] ...)

The Logos is the source; everything commences in him. He remains the exclusive Parent reference to their existence. There is nothing original, except the Word! The Logic of God defines the only possible place where mankind can trace their origin. (All things were made by him; and without him was not anything made that was made. KJV See Colossians 1:16.)

His life is the light that defines our lives. (In his life we discover the light of life.)

The darkness was pierced and could not comprehend or diminish this light. (Darkness represents mankind's ignorance of their redeemed identity and innocence [Isa 9:2-4, Isa 60:1-3, Eph 4:18, Col 1:13-15].) (John 1:1-5 Mirror).

He is the image of the invisible God, the firstborn of all creation. For by Him all things were created, both in the heavens and on earth, visible and invisible, whether thrones or dominions or rulers or authorities – all things have been created through Him and for Him. He is before all things, and in Him all things hold together. He is also head of the body, the church; and He is the beginning, the firstborn from the dead, so that He Himself will come to have first place in everything. For it was the Father's good pleasure for all the fullness to dwell in Him, and through Him to reconcile all things to Himself, having made peace through the blood of His cross; through Him, I say, whether things on earth or things in heaven. (Colossians 1:15-20 NASB).

Everything that is, begins in him; whether in the heavenly realm or upon the earth, visible or invisible, he is the original blueprint of every order of justice and every level of authority, be it kingdoms or governments, principalities or jurisdictions; the original form of all things were founded by him and created for him. (Any order that does not mirror Christ is a distortion of man's own making.) *He is the initiator of all things, therefore everything finds its relevance and its true pattern only in him. The ekklesia [church] is the visible expression [body] of which Jesus is the head. He is the principle rank of authority who leads the triumphant procession of our new birth out of the region of the dead. His pre-eminent rank is beyond threat.* ("... leading the resurrection parade" – The Message.) *God is fully at home in him. Jesus exhibits God's ¹happy delight to be human.* (Delightful intent, ¹*eudokeo.* "So spacious is he, so roomy, that everything of God finds its proper place in him without crowding." — The Message) *He initiated the reconciliation of all things to himself. Through the blood of the cross God restored the original harmony. His reign* *of peace now extends to every visible thing upon the earth as well as those invisible things which are in the ¹heavenly realm.* (The heavens, ¹*ouranos*, a place of elevation, from *oros*, a mountain, from *airo*, to lift, to raise, to elevate, "Not only that, but all the broken and dislocated pieces of the universe, people and things, animals and atoms, get properly fixed and fit together in vibrant harmonies, all because of his death." – The Message.) (Colossians 1:16-20 Mirror).

... that is, the mystery which has been hidden from the past ages and generations, but has now been manifested to His saints, to whom God willed to make known what is the riches of the glory of this mystery among the Gentiles, which is Christ in you, the hope of glory. We proclaim Him, admonishing every man and teaching every man with all wisdom, so that we may present every man complete in Christ. (Colossians 1:26-28 NASB).

Mankind's most sought after quest, the mystery which has remained elusive and concealed for ages and generations, is now fully realized in our redeemed innocence. (The word, *hagnos*, clean, blameless innocence.)

Within us, God is delighted to exhibit the priceless treasure of this glorious unveiling of Christ's indwelling in order that every person on the planet, whoever they are, may now come to the greatest discovery of all time and recognize Christ in them as in a mirror! He is the desire of the nations and completes their every expectation! (He is not hiding in history, or in outer space nor in the future, neither in the pages of Scripture, he is merely mirrored there to be unveiled within you. Mt 13:44, Gal 1:15, 16, 2Cor 3:18, 2Cor 4:4,7. This is huge! What God was now able to disclose in the saints is immediately equally relevant in the nations!...)

This is the essence and focus of our message; we ¹awaken everyone's mind, instructing every individual by bringing them into ²full understanding [flawless clarity] *in order that we may ³prove* (present) *everyone ⁴perfect in Christ.* (Translating *¹nous + tithemi* as to re-align every mind with God's mind. The word, *²sophos*, comes from *sophes* meaning clear, clarity. The word, *³paristano*, comes from *para*, sphere of influence, closest possible association, and *histemi*, meaning to stand, to exhibit with evidence. The word, *⁴teleios*, means perfect, without shortcoming and fully efficient.) (Colossians 1:26-28 Mirror).

By faith we understand that the worlds were prepared by the word of God, so that what is seen was not made out of things which are visible. (Hebrews 11:3).

Eschatology and cosmology must be Christocentric to be authentic. To be absolutely clear, when I say Christ, the Messiah or anointed one, I mean Jesus; and therefore if Jesus is not in the centre (as He is not in all forms of Judaism and Kabbalah), it is deceptive, twisted and false.

When Genesis reveals what occurred in the beginning, John and Paul affirm that Jesus, the living word of God, was fully present as the *alpha* or *aleph* as the express image of God as the creator.

In the beginning God created the heavens and the earth. (Genesis 1:1). This is that sentence transliterated from the Hebrew language:

Bereshit bara Elohim et hashamayim ve'et ha'aretz, or, *Bereshit Bara Elohim Et Ha-Shamaim V-Et Ha-Aretz*
[בראשית ברא אלוהים את השמים ואת הארץ].

Most exiled Jews and early Christians, however, used the Greek translation of the Old Testament, known as the Septuagint. That text begins with the absolute statement: "In the beginning, God created the heavens and the earth," which implies an absolute beginning for this universe.

The biblical idea that God created the universe out of nothing is found in the Book of Genesis but it is more fully developed in the New Testament. It is implied in Genesis 1:1 because if God made all that there is, He must have begun with nothing: this is the cosmology of the Christian biblical account as it takes us back to a time when only God existed.

However the Zohar seeks to give a modern twist to the commonly accepted Septuagint translation. The Zohar twists the translation and alters the meaning to make it seem that *Keter* (*Adam Kadmon*) created *Elohim*.

Not only is Jesus completely excluded from this cosmology but something is substituted in Jesus' place. *Adam Kadmon* is often known as Primordial Man or *Adam Elyon* or Supreme Man. In Kabbalah, *Adam Kadmon* corresponds to the *yechidah*, which is the collective essence of the soul. This is the clear humanistic Luciferian agenda behind Kabbalah that is being peddled to the undiscerning mystic community, which seems to love gnostic mysteries more than Jesus, the Truth.

Our creator God was the created in Kabbalistic cosmology – and that is incompatible with Jesus as the Way, Truth and Life, and Jesus as the only door to the Father. This is an example of the humanism of the tree of the knowledge of good and evil which removes Jesus and places man as creator. Satan's lie was 'you can be like God' and this lie still appeals to man's ego today.

When the Hebrew letters of the word *bereshit* are broken down into their pictorial form the meaning of *bereshit* ('in the beginning') is 'the body of the highest the ox was pierced by something sharp by the destroyer through the hand by which he died and established the finished work of the cross'.

This meaning places Jesus, who is the beginning and the end, as the body that was pierced on the cross.

I am the Alpha and the Omega – the Beginning and End – the First and the Last. (Revelation 22:13 YLT).

Jesus, the central figure of cosmology and eschatology, is excluded from the narrative by Kabbalah; but the so-called Christian Rabbis are encouraging people to learn about the mysteries of God through the Kabbalah and not directly through Jesus, the Truth. I do not know about you but that makes no logical or spiritual sense to me. God, through Jesus, creates the heavens and the earth: now that makes perfect sense in the light of Jesus being the Word and the beginning and the end, the *Aleph* and the *Tav*.

These are some of the Jewish myths and fables that Paul warns the early church against following; and we would do well if we followed that urging today.

The restoration of all things agenda is embedded in the names of God. It is found in the concept that Jesus, as the creator, is the beginning and the end; and is represented as the *vav* in YHVH. *Vav* represents the nail that in creation connected and joined the heavens and the earth with mankind.

Through Jesus, God nailed the heavens to the earth and then created man from the dust of creation; so God nailed or connected the earth representing creation to man. The destiny of the heavens and the earth is tied to man; and man's restoration is what will set creation free from decay.

Jesus, as the second Adam or man, came to reconcile man to God and redeem the earth from the curse so that the whole of creation can be set free.

For the anxious longing of the creation waits eagerly for the revealing of the sons of God. For the creation was subjected to futility, not willingly, but because of Him who subjected it, in hope that the creation itself also will be set free from its slavery to corruption into the freedom of the glory of the children of God. (Romans 8:19-21).

Kabbalistic cosmology is irreconcilable with Jesus at the centre of creation and therefore needs to be avoided. Although there may be some concepts that have some elements of truth, there is no 'righteous real' hidden within or behind the source of the Kabbalah.

This foundational cosmology is being taught within Hebrew Roots and has now begun to infiltrate Christian mysticism. 10 years ago, when I first started to engage heaven and started to connect with others that seemed to be on the same journey, I resonated with the frequency of what was being taught and shared. Over the last 6 years, as my mind has been deconstructed, it feels like those who were forerunners in discovering and revealing truth have diverted from the path we were all following. It seems that many have taken a different path, following Hebrew Roots and Jewish mysticism, and sadly now I find very little that I resonate with and what they teach has a different frequency. They still have many followers who hold onto their every word, but the love is missing from many and I believe some of that is to do with embracing Jewish mystic knowledge and culture and the deceptive influence of the Kabbalah.

The source of the roots of this great deception is what is also behind Freemasonry, Zionism, Global Cabals, Illuminati, Rosicrucianism, Noahide and Luciferianism to name just a few. This is antichrist, as Jesus is removed from the origins of the narrative and Lucifer deceptively replaces Him – and many Christians are not able to discern the clashing and competing frequencies. The genuine Tree of Life which is, in reality, Jesus Himself, at the centre of all truth, has been replaced by a counterfeit Kabbalah tree that has twisted the truth of who is at the heart of creation. The Tree of Life has many facets and levels of truth and is fractal, being in the smallest and greatest expressions of creation; but Jesus is at the centre and root of it all. The patterns found in the Tree of Life have been deceptively changed to promote a narrative that places Lucifer, the light bearer of Kabbalah, at its centre.

The cosmology of Kabbalah layers lies and deception, using a false concept of the *Sephiroth* which obscures the truth of the Tree of Life and deceives people. The Kabbalah believes in a dualistic God, twisting the true image of God as love into a god who is severe in punishment but also mercy. God is love and there is no severity in Him; but evangelicalism has also adopted this dualistic God, trying to balance mercy with holiness and justice. This concept makes for a two-faced God: one face the Old Testament, angry God and the other face the New Testament, loving God. This dualistic version of God is firmly rooted in the same source as Kabbalah, that of the tree of the knowledge of good and evil.

God is love; and judgment and justice are expressions of love, so mercy and justice are synonymous terms. Before there was ever a problem, the solution was already in motion: as the lamb was slain before the foundation of the world, mankind was predestined to have a relationship with the Father. Jesus is the express image of the Father and Jesus summed up and consummated all that went before, the law and the prophets, in one clear representation of His essence, nature and character: LOVE.

Yes, the kingdom of God is based on righteousness and justice; but we have all been made the righteousness of God in Christ and are justified. Justice can only be fulfilled after a judgment has been made; and the judgment made before time existed, and through the cross, was a loud and clear verdict of 'not guilty' and 'innocent'. Therefore justice as the foundation of the kingdom is built upon unconditional love, limitless grace and triumphant mercy. This was established in eternity, and in time, through the cross; and all of the cosmos has been reconciled to God, as the Father in Jesus has chosen to forgive, release, bless and restore all things. God holds nothing against us, as all accusations have been nailed to the cross and peace has been made through the blood that brought about reconciliation for all that Jesus created.

... just as He chose us in Him before the foundation of the world, that we would be holy and blameless before Him. In love He predestined us to adoption as sons through Jesus Christ to Himself, according to the kind intention of His will... (Ephesians 1:4-5 NASB).

He associated us in Christ before [1]the fall of the world! Jesus is God's mind made up about us! He always knew in his love that he would present us again [2]face-to-face before him in blameless innocence. (The implications of the fall are completely cancelled. Paul uses the word, *[1]katabalo*, meaning "to fall away, to put in a lower place," instead of *themelios*, meaning "foundation" [see 2:20]; thus, translated "the fall of the world," instead of "the foundation of the world." ... God found us in Christ before he lost us in Adam! We are presented in blameless innocence before him! The word, [2]*katenopion*, suggests the closest possible proximity, face-to-face!)...

He is the architect of our design; his heart dream realized our [1]coming of age in Christ. (Adoption here is not what it means in our Western society. It is a coming of age, like the typical Jewish Barmitsva. See Galatians 4:1-6, "... and to seal our sonship the spirit of his Son echoes Abba Father in our hearts." This is [1]*huiothesia*.) (Ephesians 1:4-5 Mirror).

... namely, that God was in Christ reconciling the world to Himself, not counting their trespasses against them, and He has committed to us the word of reconciliation. (2 Corinthians 5:19 NASB).

Our ministry declares that Jesus [1]did not act independently of his Father. God was present in Christ when they reconciled the total cosmos to themselves. Deity and humanity embraced in him; the fallen state of mankind was deleted; their trespasses would no longer count against them! He now announces his friendship with every individual from within us! (The [1]incarnation did not separate the Father from the Son and the Spirit. In him dwells the fulness of God in a human body. Col 2:9. As a human person, Jesus felt the agony of fallen humanity on the cross when he echoed Psalm 22, "My God, my God, why have you forsaken me! Why are you so far from helping me, from the words of my groaning?" But then in verse 24, David declares triumphantly: "He has not despised or abhorred the affliction of the afflicted; and he has not hid his face from him, but has heard, when he cried to him.") ... (2 Corinthians 5:19 Mirror).

For it was the Father's good pleasure for all the fullness to dwell in Him, and through Him to reconcile all things to Himself, having made peace through the blood of His cross; through Him, I say, whether things on earth or things in heaven. (Colossians 1:19-20).

I have received revelation from the Father concerning the Merkabah, Tree of Life, which has both a heavenly and internal fractal perspective. The core of our being - where spirit, soul, body, Father, Son, Spirit, seven energy gates, heaven and the dimensions meet - is balanced by the Tree of Life and the flow of the river of life as rivers of living water from our innermost being.

These are some extracts from my journals that refer to conversations the Father had with me concerning these subjects.

"Son, the chakra gates are connected to separate places within the heavenly realms and each has a flow for a specific purpose. You can activate each gate by intention to receive and channel the flow of energy into dimensional realms. There are three gates connected to the eternal now that are represented by the heart (love), mind (crown) and gut (root); there are four that are representative of being in the four faces as the order of Melchizedek: throat (oracle), third eye (priest), sacral (legislator) and the solar plexus (king). Three gates always need to be activated so you can converge the heavens and the earth.

"Heart, crown and root become your governmental foundation. All the other gates operate from that foundation.

"Spirituality, awareness, communication, love, wisdom, power, creativity and trust: son, become aware of the source so that the rivers of living water can flow from your innermost being. There must be balance and harmony between your spirit, soul and body.

"The Merkabah is your consciousness' ability to connect and converge the eternal now and time through the four faces of the cherubic nature of man in the order of Melchizedek government. The energy gates activate the Tree of Life within you to balance soul and spirit.

- Soul judgment must be in balance with spirit mercy.
- Soul intelligence must be in balance with spirit wisdom.
- Soul triumph must be in balance with spirit glory.
- Soul beauty must be in balance with spirit crown and creation root.
- Spirit and soul union is the foundation of creativity.
- Soul kingdom root must be in balance with the spirit crown by being balanced with the heart beauty.
- Rest is spirit, soul and body in perfect union, harmony and balance."

The Father said to me, "Develop these abilities and consciously choose to activate them to flow into your spheres and connect to the dimensions. The three and the four combined represent the seven, and multiplied represent the twelves of government. The sons of God are the convergence of time and the eternal now, spiritual and physical, heavenly and earthly, within the Order of Melchizedek government: Kings and Priests seated in the heavenlies and Oracles and Legislators on the earth.

I did not get this revelation from Kabbalah but directly from the Father who is the source; so although this diagram is similar to Kabbalah and New Age, both the cosmological source and meaning is different. The *Sefirot* or *Sephiroth* are often expressed through the Kabbalah tree diagram that counterfeits the Tree of Life.

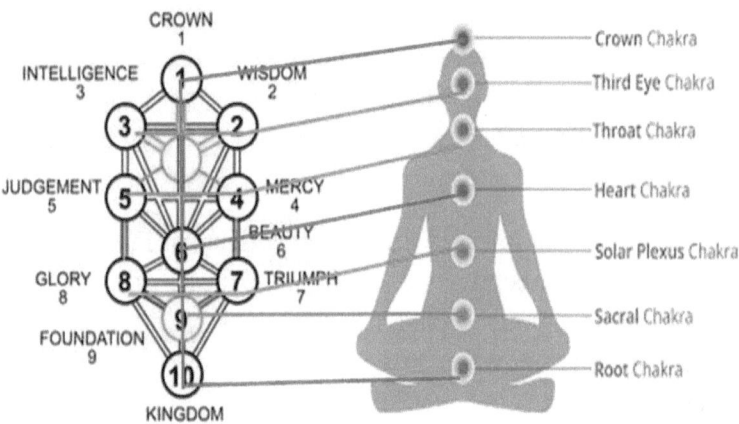

What is the Kabbalah Tree and what are the Sephiroth? I am not seeking to encourage you to go to the Kabbalah and find out for yourself but I would urge you to seek the answers in the Truth, Jesus, or the Father. I am showing you the pictures and information so you can see the deception if you come across it.

Here is a direct quote from Kabbalah online, a free source of information that I am not advising you to read, but I do want to warn you to avoid the deception.

> "Authentic Jewish mysticism is an integral part of the Torah, and Torah determines what is authentic Jewish mysticism." – Kabbalah online.

That seems to anchor Kabbalah to the Old Testament and so give it legitimacy, but the truth is that all mankind is now in the new covenant of grace; only Israel was ever under the law of the old covenant – and even that has faded away and is now obsolete. The goal of the Luciferian agenda is to bring all humanity into the bondage of the law that will enslave them under Lucifer in one counterfeit world governmental system, where you find the Messiah or Christ is Lucifer, not Jesus.

You will not find Jesus hidden within Kabbalah, but you will find Lucifer as the fallen light-bearer who declared 'I will be like God'.

The God of Kabbalah is not Father, Son and Spirit but *Ein Sof* and the following is a definition of the god of Kabbalah.

> *Ein Sof* may be translated as "unending", "(there is) no end", or infinity. Of the *Ein Sof,* nothing (*Ein*) can be grasped (*Sof* - limitation). It is the origin of the *Ohr Ein Sof,* the "Infinite Light" of paradoxical divine self-knowledge, nullified within the *Ein Sof* before creation.
> – Wikipedia: *Ein Sof.*

God is unknowable? This is a deception which contradicts Jesus being the express image of the Father and His statement that "if you have seen me, you have seen the Father" (see John 14:9). Of course, there is mystery surrounding God; and that is what mystics who teach Kabbalistic principles use in their deception to hook people into the pursuit of esoteric hidden knowledge. One meaning of 'Kabbalah' is 'revealed'.

My own experiences face to face with God do not support the belief that God is unknowable; in fact, quite the opposite. God is continually revealing Himself to His children and it is only our lack of maturity and limited consciousness that stops us from knowing Him more deeply. Not allowing that to become a restriction to His desire for union and oneness, God deconstructs, renews and transforms our minds, leading to enlightenment and expanded consciousness through our encounters with Him. He invites us to meet with Him face to face in the light, where we can know Him in love. We are predestined to such a restored relationship of innocence where our encounters in the light of love and truth enlighten us.

God is love and that is the motivation behind creation; but Kabbalah places will, not love, at the centre of creation, which is of course a Luciferian idea associated with the five "I will" statements of Lucifer in the rebellion. Kabbalah deceptively places Lucifer in the centre of creation through will, and not Jesus through love. To those who use discernment, Kabbalah clearly teaches a false understanding of God but many seeking truth have been taken in by these deceptive teachings.

The pursuit of hidden knowledge and mystery can be highly addictive but ultimately unfulfilling because according to Kabbalah, God is unknowable in the physical world. This is Gnosticism under another name and is dualistic.

Gnosticism is a group of religious ideas from around the first century. *Gnosis* is the ancient Greek word for 'knowledge', but now more closely means 'esoteric knowledge'. Gnostic ideas are also found in sects of Judaism and Islam, as well as in alchemy and other kinds of esotericism.

Gnosticism says that humans are divine souls trapped in the ordinary physical (or material) world. They say that the world was made by an imperfect spirit. The imperfect spirit is thought to be the same as the God of Abraham. The imperfect spirit may be seen as evil, or sometimes just not perfect but doing the best it can. The real God, who is good, is distant and not easy to know. To get free from the material world, a person has to get *gnosis*. That is the special secret knowledge given only to a few special people. Some Gnostic groups saw Jesus as sent by the Supreme Being, to bring *gnosis* to the Earth.

Following Jewish mysticism and Hebrew Roots leads to a path of knowledge that is a mixture, which has polluted and perverted the truth. This will bring bondage to legalism and the religious dead works of law where the follower will end up being weary and heavily burdened, lacking in rest. Even those who place Jesus as *Yeshua* within Christian mysticism will end up losing their rest in the pursuit of mystery. That is why Hebrew culture and tradition is being mixed into Christian mysticism, where people are being encouraged to learn Hebrew, study Torah, celebrate Jewish festivals and ceremonies and keep Hebrew dates. It is very common now at mystic conferences to see *tallit* prayer shawls draped over the lecterns and teachers wearing *kippahs*. Some Christian mystics are celebrating the Passover, which is a major Jewish festival, because of its association with communion. This is not valid, as Jesus did not tell His disciples to celebrate the Passover but a new covenant meal.

- Are we in the old covenant or the new covenant?

If the covenants were meant to be mixed, Jesus would have never said this at His last supper:

"For this is My blood of the new covenant which is shed for many for the remission of sins" (Matthew 26:28).

- Are we to partake in the Passover or the Lord's Supper?

Paul reminded the Corinthians what the Passover stood for and what was really central:

For indeed Christ our Passover was sacrificed for us. (1 Corinthians 5:7).

It is clear from the New Testament that all the Old Testament ceremonies, symbols, and feasts were types and shadows pointing to Jesus (see Colossians:2:16-23; Hebrews:10:1-10).

• Do we follow Jewish externals and superficial ritual purity or an internal cleansing of the heart?

The psalmist answers that question clearly:

For You do not delight in sacrifice, otherwise I would give it; You do not take pleasure in burnt offering.
The sacrifices of God are a broken spirit;
A broken and a contrite heart, God, You will not despise.
(Psalm 51:16-17).

Talmud

Jewish mysticism is an integral part of the *Tanahk* but the false rabbinical teaching of the *Talmud* is at the heart of Kabbalah. What is the *Talmud* and why is it significant in the discussion concerning Hebrew Roots, Jewish mysticism and Zionism?

> Talmud: Compiled circa 500 CE, the Talmud contains a record of debates and discussions between various Amoraim, elucidating the Mishnah, a written compendium of Judaism's oral traditions. The Mishnah covers the full gamut of Jewish life, arranged in 6 books, each packed with succinct teachings. The Talmud quotes from the Mishnah and thoroughly analyses it in the light of contemporary works as well as subsequent teachings. Together they form a divinely inspired work of massive scope. It has also been recognized as an extraordinary

scholarly achievement and a model of unparalleled critical analysis.
– chabad.org

Jesus challenged the traditions of the Rabbis as opposing the true spirit of the law whenever He said "You have heard that it was said... but I say to you..." Jesus challenged the wisdom of those who He called the ancients.

Then some Pharisees and scribes came to Jesus from Jerusalem and said, "Why do Your disciples break the tradition of the elders? For they do not wash their hands when they eat bread." And He answered and said to them, "Why do you yourselves transgress the commandment of God for the sake of your tradition?" (Matthew 15:1-3).

"Again, you have heard that the ancients were told, 'You shall not make false vows, but shall fulfill your vows to the Lord.' But I say to you, make no oath at all, either by heaven, for it is the throne of God, or by the earth, for it is the footstool of His feet, or by Jerusalem, for it is the city of the great King. Nor shall you make an oath by your head, for you cannot make one hair white or black. But let your statement be, 'Yes, yes' or 'No, no'; anything beyond these is of evil. **"You have heard that it was said***, 'An eye for an eye, and a tooth for a tooth.'* **But I say to you***, do not resist an evil person; but whoever slaps you on your right cheek, turn the other to him also. If anyone wants to sue you and take your shirt, let him have your coat also. Whoever forces you to go one mile, go with him two. Give to him who asks of you, and do not turn away from him who wants to borrow from you.* **"You have heard that it was said***, 'You shall love your neighbor and hate your enemy.' But* **I say to you***, love your enemies and pray for those who persecute you, so that you may be sons of your Father who is*

in heaven; for He causes His sun to rise on the evil and the good, and sends rain on the righteous and the unrighteous. (Matthew 5:33-45, emphases mine).

Kabbalah teaches that *Talmud* is divinely inspired: if you were to read some of the content, you would see that to be absurd. The *Talmud* promotes, amongst other things, Jewish supremacism and the right to kill, rape and enslave Gentiles or *goyim*.

The Talmud Unmasked[67] is a collection of alleged quotes from the *Talmud*, the *Zohar* and other Talmudic works supposedly demonstrating that:

- Jews do not regard non-Jews as human beings.
- The *Talmud* contains blasphemies against Jesus and offensive passages about Christians.
- Judaism despises non-Jews at its core, although that is not how most followers of Judaism think, but the preparation of persecution makes many Jews think that the world is against them.
- The *Talmud* urges Jews to do a variety of harms to Christians such as murder and theft, and teaches that each death of a Christian serves as a substitute for the Temple sacrifices, which would then hasten the arrival of the Jewish messiah.

Using numerous citations in Hebrew and Latin translations of the *Talmud*, *The Talmud Unmasked* seeks to demonstrate that the *Talmud* obliges Jews to injure Christians many ways, and to work for their ultimate destruction.

---

[67] Justinas Bonaventura Pranaitis, *The Talmud Unmasked - The Secret Rabbinical Teachings Concerning Christians* (1892). Available online as an epub download.

This is not to say that most adherents to Judaism know or believe such things; but it is at the heart of Kabbalah and that should, at the very least, make us cautious about using the books of the Kabbalah to base our lives on.

This belief system is antichrist; and in it, Metatron is a key figure (but not the Metatron that I have met many times, who is an angel: the head of the order of Chayoth and associated with the keys and gates). In Kabbalah, Metatron (or whatever fallen angel is masquerading as Metatron) is the angel behind Zionism; and some are trying to infer that Metatron is Jesus. Jesus is the Tree of Life, the source of creation, and that is true biblical cosmology; but behind Kabbalah is the notion that Lucifer is God and creator.

For such men are false apostles, deceitful workers, disguising themselves as apostles of Christ. No wonder, for even Satan disguises himself as an angel of light. Therefore it is not surprising if his servants also disguise themselves as servants of righteousness, whose end will be according to their deeds. (2 Corinthians 11:13-15).

Whenever Jesus is removed from His centrality within all things then the vacuum will be filled with a counterfeit, who is Lucifer, masquerading as light.

Noahide laws

The ultimate goal of connecting Christianity to Jewish roots is to bring all under Noahide law, which is bondage to the tree of the knowledge of good and evil. What are the Noahide laws and why should we avoid coming under them?

The seven Noahide laws, as traditionally enumerated in the Babylonian Talmud Sanhedrin, are:

- Not to worship idols.
- Not to curse God.
- Not to commit murder.
- Not to commit adultery, bestiality, or sexual immorality.
- Not to steal.
- Not to eat flesh torn from a living animal.
- To establish courts of justice.

According to the Talmud, the seven laws were given first to Adam and subsequently to Noah and the Noahide laws apply to all of humanity.

These laws seem fair to the casual observer and are a bit like the 10 commandments (which, as a reminder, the Gentiles were never under). All mankind are under grace; and in grace, unconditional love is the only commandment and the highest principle. If we are motivated by the unconditional love we have received through Jesus we would never do anything to contradict that.

Accepting Noahide law is the first step on a slippery slope towards a one world governmental system, and that is not the kingdom of God.

> In the 1980s, Menachem Mendel Schneerson urged his followers to actively engage in activities to inform non-Jews about the Noahide laws, which had not been done in previous generations. The Chabad-Lubavitch movement has been one of the most active in Noahide outreach, believing that there is spiritual and societal value for non-Jews in at least simply acknowledging the Noahide laws.
>
> In 1982, Chabad-Lubavitch had a reference to the Noahide laws enshrined in a U.S. Presidential proclamation: the "Proclamation 4921", signed by the

then-U.S. President Ronald Reagan. The United States Congress, recalling House Joint Resolution 447 and in celebration of Schneerson's 80th birthday, proclaimed April 4, 1982, as a "National Day of Reflection."

In 1989 and 1990, Chabad-Lubavitch had another reference to the Noahide laws enshrined in a U.S. Presidential proclamation: "Proclamation 5956", signed by the then-U.S. President George H. W. Bush. The United States Congress, recalling House Joint Resolution 173 and in celebration of Schneerson's 87th birthday, proclaimed April 16, 1989, and April 6, 1990, as "Education Day, U.S.A."

In January 2004, the spiritual leader of the Druze community in Israel, Sheikh Mowafak Tarif, met with a representative of Chabad-Lubavitch to sign a declaration calling on all non-Jews in Israel to observe the Noahide laws; the mayor of the Arab city of Shefa-'Amr (Shfaram) – where Muslim, Christian, and Druze communities live side-by-side – also signed the document.
– Wikipedia: *Seven Laws of Noah*.

This agenda is part of the great deception and many Jewish Rabbis are infiltrating Christianity in general, but specifically the mystic movement, by teaching that we have Hebrew or Jewish roots. Most mystics teaching Hebrew Roots are also encouraging the study of Kabbalah, which is why I am seeking to expose this as a deception.

Christianity does not have Jewish or Hebrew roots, even though the Old Testament is in the Christian Bible. That statement may seem indefensible and of course I am not saying there is no connection at all, but Christianity is rooted in the covenant God made with Abraham, not Moses.

Righteousness was always through faith and never through the observance of the law.

Not under the law

Just to make it completely clear, below is a list of Bible verses that indicate that Christians are not under the law, compiled by Phil Drysdale[68]:

- The law is an unbearable yoke. (Acts 15:10)
- The law reveals sin but cannot fix it. (Romans 3:20)
- If the law worked then faith would be irrelevant. (Romans 4:14)
- The law brings wrath upon those who follow it. (Romans 4:15)
- The purpose of the law was to increase sin. (Romans 5:20)
- Christians are not under the law. (Romans 6:14)
- Christians have been delivered from the law. (Romans 7:1-6)
- The law is good, perfect and holy but cannot help you be good, perfect or holy. (Romans 7:7-12)
- The law which promises life only brings death through sin. (Romans 7:10)
- The law makes you sinful beyond measure. (Romans 7:13)
- The law is weak. (Romans 8:2-3)
- The strength of sin is the law (1 Corinthians 15:56)
- The law is a ministry of death. (2 Corinthians 3:7)
- The law is a ministry of condemnation. (2 Corinthians 3:9)
- The law has no glory at all in comparison with the New Covenant. (2 Corinthians 3:10)

---

[68] Phil Drysdale: chadhutchinson.wordpress.com/category/phil-drysdale (accessed 26 May 2022).

- The law is fading away. (2 Corinthians 3:11)
- Anywhere the law is preached it produces a mind-hardening and a heart-hardening veil. (2 Corinthians 3:14-15)
- The law justifies nobody. (Galatians 2:16)
- Christians are dead to the law. (Galatians 2:19)
- The law frustrates grace. (Galatians 2:21)
- To go back to the law after embracing faith is "stupid". (Galatians 3:1)
- The law curses all who practise it and fail to do it perfectly. (Galatians 3:10)
- The law has nothing to do with faith. (Galatians 3:11-12)
- The law was a curse that Christ redeemed us from. (Galatians 3:13)
- The law functioned in God's purpose as a temporary covenant from Moses till John the Baptist announced Christ. (Galatians 3:16 and 19, see also Matthew 11:12-13, Luke 16:16)
- If the law worked God would have used it to save us. (Galatians 3:21)
- The law was our prison. (Galatians 3:23)
- The law makes you a slave like Hagar. (Galatians 4:24)
- Christ has abolished the law which was a wall of hostility (Ephesians 2:15)
- Paul considered everything the law gained him as '*skybalon*' which is Greek for "poop". (Philippians 3:4-8)
- The law is only good if used in the right context. (1 Timothy 1:8) (see next verse for the context)
- It was made for the unrighteous but not for the righteous. (1 Timothy 1:9-10)

- The law is weak, useless and makes nothing perfect. (Hebrews 7:18-19)
- God has found fault with it and created a better covenant, enacted on better promises. (Hebrews 8:7-8)
- It is obsolete, growing old and ready to vanish. (Hebrews 8:13)
- It is only a shadow of good things to come and will never make someone perfect. (Hebrews 10:1)

The seed of Abraham is not Judaism or national Israel but Christ; and therefore Jesus is the Tree of Life that is the root. All religion, including Judaism, is rooted in the tree of the knowledge of good and evil.

Just because Jesus is the fulfilment of all the covenants God made with mankind does not make the old covenants, traditions, culture and festivals something we should be following or learning about to help us understand the new covenant. The Old Testament prophets prophesied about the coming Messiah but that does not make them experts on how we should live in the new covenant.

Judaism and its Hebrew roots are obsolete and have faded away: it no longer has any value (its only value was as a schoolmaster to lead us to the grace found in Jesus). The Law and the old covenant never brought anyone to righteousness as it was an utter failure, so why would we think studying Hebrew roots, types and shadows would be helpful today?

That is the deception that is perpetrated on so many wannabe mystics today by so-called Rabbis who are leading them into studying Hebrew and the Kabbalah books and teachings. Those Rabbis, like the Rabbis in Jesus' day, are following the oral rabbinical traditions passed down through the Talmud,

Mishnah etc. which is at the heart of Kabbalah. We do not need another oral tradition of men when Jesus promised to speak directly to those following Him.

Rabbinical tradition began before Jesus, as He challenged it, but it continued to be developed after Jesus came. At the time of the destruction of the Second Temple, Judaism was divided into antagonistic factions. The main camps were the Pharisees, Sadducees, and Zealots, but also included other less influential sects. This led to much conflict in the period before Jesus came and again during the period before His second coming. There were a number of charismatic religious leaders, contributing to what would become the *Mishnah* of Rabbinic Judaism, including Yochanan ben Zakai and Hanina Ben Dosa. Rabbinical tradition is not found in the Old Testament writings but emerged after the exile to Babylon and in my opinion, has a syncretistic mixture of non-Hebrew concepts.

I am not trying to deny that Jesus was born a Jew and lived an observant Jewish life. He did this to fulfil completely every demand of the law, He did it for us (Romans 8:1-4) – and He continues to do it for us. Just because Jesus was born into that Jewish culture and observed the true heart and core of the law, it does not mean that to be like Jesus we have to do the same. Jesus challenged many wrong understandings concerning the law and the rabbinical teachings and traditions that were added to it.

There are many levels of Hebrew Roots teaching but I believe they are all dangerous and at their core is a desire to bring us back under the law at some level. This is often done very openly but it is also done very deceptively, seeking to put us back in chains of religious bondage (just like the Galatians, as we have previously observed).

This poses many questions that seem logical to ask if we want to be authentic believers, following Jesus:

- If we want to be like Jesus, does that mean that we must become observant Jews, as some teach? No way.
- Is that what being like Jesus really means? No.
- Should Gentile believers try to be Messianic Jews? No.
- Should Gentiles don a *yarmulke*, worship in a synagogue, blow a *shofar*, wear a prayer shawl, call Jesus *Yeshua* or *Yeshu*, keep the Old Testament feasts and dietary laws, and give their pastors the title of Rabbi? No.
- Are Jewish ceremonies and practices effective? No.
- Do we need to restore first century (or later) Jewish practices to be good Christians? No.

I believe that Jesus' response to the Pharisees shows that He rejected their version of the law. The Pharisees followed the letter of the law and the ceremonies but did so in vain, as they missed the spirit behind the letter.

"You hypocrites, rightly did Isaiah prophesy of you: 'This people honors Me with their lips, but their heart is far away from Me. But in vain do they worship Me, teaching as doctrines the precepts of men." (Matthew 15:7-9).

Jesus pronounces woes on those false teachers who, according to Matthew 23:4, *"tie up heavy burdens and lay them on men's shoulders, but they themselves are unwilling to move them with so much as a finger."*

Why would we want to try to do today what they failed to do by following a legalistic religion in Jesus day? The fruit of reaping what they sowed was described by Jesus as a 'woe' and was a judgment against the efficacy of their religious dead works. The definition of 'woe' is a condition of deep suffering from misfortune, affliction, or grief. A 'woe' was not God's wrath or punishment but a self-inflicted consequence of self-righteousness.

Read the whole of Matthew 23 for the full context but here are some examples of woes Jesus pronounced:

"But woe to you, scribes and Pharisees, hypocrites, because you shut off the kingdom of heaven from people; for you do not enter in yourselves, nor do you allow those who are entering to go in." (Matthew 23:13).

"Woe to you, scribes and Pharisees, hypocrites! For you are like whitewashed tombs which on the outside appear beautiful, but inside they are full of dead men's bones and all uncleanness. So you, too, outwardly appear righteous to men, but inwardly you are full of hypocrisy and lawlessness." (Matthew 23:27-28).

- So, is Jewishness next to Godliness? No.
- Does learning Hebrew and following Hebrew culture and traditions make you a better follower of Jesus? No.

I do not think Paul, who described himself as a Pharisee of Pharisees and Hebrew of Hebrews, would affirm such a thing or answer any of the questions posed above in the affirmative. He describes all the old covenant Jewish or Hebrew works as rubbish, which is the translator's polite way of interpreting the Greek word *skubalon*: properly, waste thrown to dogs, like filthy scraps of garbage (table-scraps, dung, muck, sweepings); (figuratively) refuse, what is good-for-nothing except to be discarded (Strong's).

You foolish mystics! Who has bewitched you into partaking in the refuse fit only for dogs?

Just because something has mysticism in its title does not make it something we should be pursuing. I would urge you not to be bewitched by the Jewish mysticism promoted by those teaching Hebrew Roots. The true mystery can be discovered through Jesus alone, who is the only door to face to face encounters with the Father.

Beware of the dogs, beware of the evil workers, beware of the false circumcision; for we are the true circumcision, who worship in the Spirit of God and glory in Christ Jesus and put no confidence in the flesh, although I myself might have confidence even in the flesh. If anyone else has a mind to put confidence in the flesh, I far more: circumcised the eighth day, of the nation of Israel, of the tribe of Benjamin, a Hebrew of Hebrews; as to the Law, a Pharisee; as to zeal, a persecutor of the church; as to the righteousness which is in the Law, found blameless. But whatever things were gain to me, those things I have counted as loss for the sake of Christ. More than that, I count all things to be loss in view of the surpassing value of knowing Christ Jesus my Lord, for whom I have suffered the loss of all things, and count them but rubbish so that I may gain Christ, and may be found in Him, not having a righteousness of my own derived from the Law, but that which is through faith in Christ, the righteousness which comes from God on the basis of faith, that I may know Him and the power of His resurrection and the fellowship of His sufferings, being conformed to His death; in order that I may attain to the resurrection from the dead. (Philippians 3:2-11).

Jewish believer Stephen Katz[69] expresses his concerns when he says, "Much of the Jewish Roots Movement is actually

---

[69] Stephen Katz, *The Jewish Roots Movement: Flowers and Thorns,* online article at messianicassociation.org, March 1, 2001

based on later Jewish/rabbinic tradition. More importantly, the question of whether Gentiles need to add Jewish lifestyle and return to Jewish roots was settled by the Jerusalem Council described in Acts 15. The remarkable news of the Gospel is that, in Y'shua, Jews and Gentiles have direct access to God."

Messianic Jewish believer Stan Telchin[70] sees the imposition of Jewish law and practice on Gentiles as one of the more troubling aspects of the Messianic Jewish Movement: "I know that the overwhelming majority of Jewish believers do not attend Messianic synagogues. It has been suggested that less than five per cent of the Jewish believers in the United States attend them... Many Jewish people who I have brought to such synagogues have told me they felt as though they were looking at a caricature – an imitation and not the real thing."

If Telchin's statistics are correct, 95 per cent of the attendees at Messianic synagogues are Gentiles and only 5 per cent are Jews. That means that believers from non-Jewish backgrounds are being 'converted' to a form of Judaism that many believers with a Jewish history reject. This imposition of Jewish practice on non-Jewish believers can promote elitism, unnecessary division, wide confusion, and unbiblical practices.

Once again I urge you not to be like the foolish Galatians who were bewitched by Jewish myths and fables into legalism.

---

[70] Stan Telchin, *Messianic Judaism Is Not Christianity*, Chosen Books (2004), p. 83.

7. The Political and Religious Spirit and its Luciferian Babel Agenda.

Jesus warned His disciples to beware of the leaven of Herod and the Pharisees. Leaven was old, fermented dough, usually containing lactobacillus and yeast, a substance that infiltrates the dough to cause it to rise and take the form of the old. This warning still applies today and is both an individual warning and a corporate warning to beware of the infiltration and influence of the political and religious spirit in our lives and in the church.

The *ekklesia* that Jesus said He would build relationally has been infected by the religious and political spirit to become a religion and a system that controls people's lives through fear, often in cahoots with political empires or kings. It has infiltrated and infected the new covenant with the old covenant of laws, rules and mediatorial, hierarchal leadership.

And He was giving orders to them, saying, "Watch out! Beware of the leaven of the Pharisees and the leaven of Herod." (Mark 8:15).

And Jesus said to them, "Watch out and beware of the leaven of the Pharisees and Sadducees."... Then they understood that He did not say to beware of the leaven of bread, but of the teaching of the Pharisees and Sadducees. (Matthew 16:6, 12).

When He left there, the scribes and the Pharisees began to be very hostile and to question Him closely on many subjects, plotting against Him to catch Him in something He might say. Under these circumstances, after so many thousands of people had gathered together that they were stepping on one another, He began saying to His disciples first of all, "Beware of the leaven of the Pharisees, which is hypocrisy. But there is nothing covered up that will not be revealed, and hidden that will not be known. " (Luke 11:53-12:2)

The context of this strong warning from Jesus for the disciples was to prepare them for the coming persecution in the transition period between the end of the old and the beginning of the new covenant. What can we learn from this warning that applies to our situations today and how does this relate to the Luciferian agenda throughout human history?

I believe that the leaven of Herod is a warning against the political spirit that was seen in the political system both in Israel and the Roman world. The leaven of the Pharisees represents the religious spirit that was seen in the religious leaders' agenda. When the political and religious spirit join together in agreement it creates a more powerful force, as there is power in agreement for both good and bad. This prophecy was outworked at the crucifixion when the religious Jewish leaders conspired with the political Roman government to crucify Jesus; and continued throughout the transition period with religious and political persecution.

This is the same spirit at work at Babel when they refused God's mandate to fill the earth and instead chose to build an earthly city to make a name for themselves. This spirit was linked to Nimrod or Apollyon, a false Messiah figure behind all empires and desire for a one-world government.

When God made a covenant with Abraham (which Jesus fulfilled), He gave him a vision for a heavenly country and city, not an earthly one. Abraham saw Jesus' day and was glad, as the gospel was preached to Abraham beforehand in God's desire for all the families of the earth to be blessed. The source of making an empire and name for humanity is the tree of the knowledge of good and evil. The source of kingdom and blessing is the Tree of Life.

By faith Abraham, when he was called, obeyed by going out to a place which he was to receive for an inheritance; and he went out, not knowing where he was going. By faith he lived as an alien in the land of promise, as in a foreign land, dwelling in tents with Isaac and Jacob, fellow heirs of the same promise; for he was looking for the city which has foundations, whose architect and builder is God. (Hebrews 11:8-10).

For those who say such things make it clear that they are seeking a country of their own. And indeed if they had been thinking of that country from which they went out, they would have had opportunity to return. But as it is, they desire a better country, that is, a heavenly one. Therefore God is not ashamed to be called their God; for He has prepared a city for them. (Hebrews 11:14-16).

The counterfeit empire is in direct contradiction to the kingdom of God's government in its earthly, not heavenly, focus and its desire to promote 'I will' and not God's will. The real brings freedom and the counterfeit brings bondage. This bondage is both religious (as the DIY independent tree is the source of manmade religion that seeks to do works to appease an angry god of their own making) and political and humanistic (to make a name for themselves in an empire).

Now Cush became the father of Nimrod; he became a mighty one on the earth. He was a mighty hunter before the Lord; therefore it is said, "Like Nimrod a mighty hunter before the Lord." The beginning of his kingdom was Babel and Erech and Accad and Calneh, in the land of Shinar. (Genesis 10:8-10).

> *Now the whole earth used the same language and the same words. It came about as they journeyed east, that they found a plain in the land of Shinar and settled there. They said to one another, "Come, let us make bricks and burn them thoroughly." And they used brick for stone, and they used tar for mortar. They said, "Come, let us build for ourselves a city, and a tower whose top will reach into heaven, and let us make for ourselves a name, otherwise we will be scattered abroad over the face of the whole earth."* (Genesis 11:1-4).

> *Now the serpent was more crafty than any beast of the field which the Lord God had made. And he said to the woman, "Indeed, has God said, 'You shall not eat from any tree of the garden'?" The woman said to the serpent, "From the fruit of the trees of the garden we may eat; but from the fruit of the tree which is in the middle of the garden, God has said, 'You shall not eat from it or touch it, or you will die.'" The serpent said to the woman, "You surely will not die! For God knows that in the day you eat from it your eyes will be opened, and you will be like God, knowing good and evil." When the woman saw that the tree was good for food, and that it was a delight to the eyes, and that the tree was desirable to make one wise, she took from its fruit and ate; and she gave also to her husband with her, and he ate. Then the eyes of both of them were opened, and they knew that they were naked; and they sewed fig leaves together and made themselves loin coverings.* (Genesis 3:1-7).

The first independent act after the fall was a religious act: to hide and make their own coverings so they could be acceptable to God. The source is Luciferian, based on "I will"; and that is why it can be called a DIY or do-it-yourself path, as it promotes the futility and bondage of self-made religious dead works.

This first prophetic statement declared that these two trees and paths, described as the seed of woman and seed of the serpent, would be in direct opposition to one another. Jesus would eventually come through the Tree of Life path, where He had already been slain before the fall, and the serpent seed would operate through the DIY tree path.

"And I will put enmity between you and the woman, and between your seed and her seed; He shall bruise you on the head, and you shall bruise him on the heel." (Genesis 3:15).

When Jesus came, in fulfilment of the prophetic promise, He came to destroy the DIY tree works-based system and redeem those enslaved in lost identity. Lost identity is often described in English translations of the Bible as being 'evil'; but 'evil' is not actually a description of behaviour, as the Greek word *poneros* actually means toil, hardships and heavy labour. Therefore 'evil' is just another way of saying someone has lost their identity and is enslaved to a system of self-righteous religion or humanism.

Jesus symbolically cursed the DIY tree that was not producing any fruit and the false government system or mountain it represented that came out of the sea of humanity:

Seeing a lone fig tree by the road, He came to it and found nothing on it except leaves only; and He said to it, "No longer shall there ever be any fruit from you." And at once the fig tree withered. Seeing this, the disciples were amazed and asked, "How did the fig tree wither all at once?" And Jesus answered and said to them, "Truly I say to you, if you have faith and do not doubt, you will not only do what was done to the fig tree, but even if you say to this mountain, 'Be taken up and cast into the sea,' it will happen. And all things you ask in prayer, believing, you will receive." (Matthew 21:19-22).

Why are Babel, Babylon and Nimrod important to be aware of today? Surely it is just mythology and has no value?

I believe that the independence of Lucifer and the deception of mankind is outworked through the religious and political spirit throughout history and the goal has always been to establish a counterfeit kingdom in which he would be worshipped vicariously through kings or messiah figures. All those who are deceived into following (or choose to follow) Lucifer and represent him as an empirical figure seek others' worship. The Pharaohs, Nebuchadnezzar, Caesars, and Chinese, Japanese and Inca emperors, all pronounced themselves as gods to be worshipped.

The methods that the political and religious spirit uses to further its goals thrive in an atmosphere of division. Division promotes competition and enmity between people groups or nations and that often erupts into conflict and war. This forms a vicious cycle that creates greater tribalism and therefore more division, and so the cycle continues.

God established family and union of all mankind, splendid in diversity; the counterfeit political system is nations and nationalism and the counterfeit religious systems are religions and sects within religions, including all Christian denominations, which all seek to make a name for themselves and are divisive.

The pattern that the political and religious spirit uses is reflected in the names of the orders of fallen angels that promote this agenda: Division, Competition, Conflict (or Warmongering), and Tribalism. This is evident in the competition, conflict and wars between nations, political ideologies (such as communism, socialism and capitalism) and religions (such as Christianity, Judaism and Islam). The cold war was another expression of the conflict caused by opposing ideologies; but what is not widely known is that the same global cabals of Zionist bankers routinely support both sides of the political divide to enhance their agenda.

I am not being anti-Semitic by making this statement: those who control the financial systems and the money may use the term 'Jewish' but they are not driven by a religious agenda and they serve a very different master. Even as I write this chapter, violence is raging in the Middle East, promoted by the cabalistic agenda that encourages conflict and supports arms sales to both sides.

The religious fundamental right, who are primarily Zionists, are seemingly happy to promote and encourage conflict in Palestine to bring about Armageddon, which would (according to their own eschatology) wipe out a third of the Jewish people they purport to support. This throwing people under the bus is a hallmark of the genuine Luciferian agenda, as we will see in the next chapter, The Hoodwinking of History.

This divisive agenda that is still expressed through nationalism is now evolving to include corporate conflicts, espionage, reverse engineering and intellectual property theft.

Another expression is seen in Christian doctrinal competition between ideologies: Calvinism and Arminianism, Cessationism and Pentecostalism, Protestantism and Catholicism. All the doctrinal differences that are used to divide Christianity up into a series of denominations or streams are the outworking of the religious and political spirit that fronts the Luciferian agenda.

Apartheid, segregation and racism are further expressions of the political and religious spirit working in collaboration to keep God's children divided and separated when we are all one family. The political spirit uses the Bible to support just about anything that it promotes, including racism and slavery. The political spirit will collaborate with the religious spirit to provoke and promote division and conflict, elitism and class division in first and third world settings.

The Talmud is one of the primary books that is being used by the political and religious spirit to promote the separation of Jews and Gentiles, whom Jesus brought together by removing the walls of division and forming one new man in Himself. The Talmud promotes the notion of the Jewish people being an elite that the *goyim* are created to serve. The political agenda to create a Zionist state threw millions of Jews under the holocaust bus just as the Jewish bankers and cabals behind the Bolsheviks and the Russian revolution threw 60 million people under the bus of the Red Terror. These terrible atrocities were all funded and supported by the financial cabals who thrive on division and conflict.

> In his latest book [*Stalin's Genocides*] historian Norman Naimark argues that the definition of genocide should include nations killing social classes and political groups.
>
> Mass killing is still the way a lot of governments do business. The past few decades have seen terrifying examples in Rwanda, Cambodia, Darfur and Bosnia.
>
> Murder on a national scale, yes – but is it genocide? "The word carries a powerful punch," said Stanford history Professor Norman Naimark. "In international courts, it's considered the crime of crimes."

Nations have tugs of war over the official definition of the word "genocide" itself – which mentions only national, ethnic, racial and religious groups. The definition can determine, after all, international relations, foreign aid and national morale. Look at the annual international tussle over whether the 1915 Turkish massacre and deportation of the Armenians "counts" as genocide.

Naimark, the author of the controversial book *Stalin's Genocides*, argues that we need a much broader definition of genocide, one that includes nations killing social classes and political groups. His case in point: Stalin.

The book's title is plural for a reason: He argues that the Soviet elimination of a social class, the kulaks (who were higher-income farmers), and the subsequent killer famine among all Ukrainian peasants – as well as the notorious 1937 order No. 00447 that called for the mass execution and exile of "socially harmful elements" as "enemies of the people" – were, in fact, genocide. – Cynthia Haven[71].

What are the signs that the political and/or religious spirit is at work in our lives, churches, nations and in the world in general?

Kris Valloton posted this article about the political and religious spirit on his Facebook page:

The political spirit and the religious spirit have at least 12 things in common:

1. it makes people fear those they can't control.

---

[71] Cynthia Haven, *Stalin killed millions. A Stanford historian answers the question, was it genocide?* Stanford News, September 30, 2010: https://news.stanford.edu/2010/09/23/naimark-stalin-genocide-092310/

2. it causes people to assign motives to people they don't know.
3. it leads people to demonize those with whom they disagree.
4. it causes people to create an 'us and them' mentality.
5. it persuades people to spiritualize the demeaning of people of different persuasions.
6. it convinces people that they are justified in applying a different standard of behaviour towards those who they deem wrong.
7. it causes people to refuse to acknowledge the positive accomplishments of those they vilify.
8. it convinces people to assign the blame for all the problems of society to one people group.
9. it blinds people to its own prejudices.
10. it motivates people to judge themselves by their intentions and others by their actions.
11. it causes people to redefine dishonouring attitudes as virtuous attributes.
12. people under its influence hunt in packs so they can feed off the self-righteousness of others.

We would do well to follow Kris' urging to ensure that we are not operating under the influence of these pervasive spirits in our own lives.

The religious and political spirits are alive and well in the world today. We see their influence, yet we cast blame right and left on a human level, failing to expose the spiritual influences behind them.

What characterises the religious spirit?

The religious spirit and its influence on our lives and the religious institution of the church are far-reaching and part of a wider agenda.

The religious spirit is one of the greatest hindrances you will encounter in your life of following Jesus. Religious spirits seek to interfere with the freedom we have to enjoy new covenant grace by bringing us back under bondage to the law, or rules and regulations we have to comply with to be accepted by God or the group we are in.

As Albert Finch[72] warns,

> They can be hard to discern precisely because they are religious; they are pious, even hyper-spiritual. Their influence can pervade a person's life and church – like yeast pervades a lump of dough. That's why Jesus said, *"Watch out and beware of the leaven of the Pharisees and Sadducees"* (Matthew 16:6).
>
> In New Testament times, the Pharisees were the watchdogs of religious purity, chastising any Jewish person who transgressed even slightly, promoting the perfectionistic performance of their strict interpretation of the requirements of the law of Moses. They held to *"a form of godliness, although they...denied its power"* (2 Timothy 3:5).

The most common outworking of the religious spirit is bondage to a works-based or performance-based religious lifestyle. Jesus has made performance-based religion obsolete

---

[72] Albert Finch, *Embracing Spiritual Discernment*, November 29, 2017: http://afministry.ning.com/profiles/blogs/embracing-spiritual-discernment

through the finished work of the cross; the religious spirit likes to resurrect it so that people have to strive and struggle under a triple burden of guilt, fear and pride. Every child of God should enjoy a sense of God's acceptance, but the religious spirit keeps that just out of reach. It is this that Jesus describes as being a yoke and heavy burden which can only be relieved by coming to Him directly to find rest from the evil, toil and hardship of lost identity.

We need discernment to see the religious spirit in action and before we go pointing out the splinter in someone else's eye, let's discern if we have a log in our own.

Finch highlights five attitudes that are prompted by the religious spirit:

- Self-righteousness
- Legalism
- Dogmatism
- Criticism
- Judgment

And three characteristics of being influenced by the religious spirit which we need to guard against:

- Guilt
- Fear
- Pride

Pride is often a mask to hide the fear and insecurity we are feeling as we try to keep up appearances and hit the pass mark of performance. This is a religious hamster wheel of denial and projection that gets us absolutely nowhere. Judging others is often the evidence of our internal struggle with the failure to meet religion's external standards that can lead to anger and depression.

The Political Spirit

The religious spirit is often associated with the political spirit as it was in Jesus' day, hence the warning. The religious spirit operating through the Pharisees conspired with the political spirit working in Herod to undermine and discredit Jesus, eventually plotting to have Him crucified.

The Pharisees went out and immediately began conspiring with the Herodians against Him, as to how they might destroy Him. (Mark 3:6).

Later, after Jesus was arrested, He was passed between the political and religious leaders who were conspiring against Him.

And the chief priests and the scribes were standing there, accusing Him vehemently. And Herod with his soldiers, after treating Him with contempt and mocking Him, dressed Him in a gorgeous robe and sent Him back to Pilate. Now Herod and Pilate became friends with one another that very day; for before they had been enemies with each other. (Luke 23:10-12).

The coalition of these two spirits has outworked in every age and in every culture to create an environment for the Luciferian agenda to thrive. The political spirit worked through Pharaoh to kill Moses, and through Herod to kill Jesus, while they were still young children.

The political spirit devises strategies that create division, competition, conflict, wars, enmity and strife to thwart God's plans for peace and blessing to all families of the earth. To achieve its corrupt goals, it enters into devious alliances with religious spirits and institutions backed by those in financial control. The political spirit will seek to buy off, corrupt, manipulate, and dominate leaders and groups of people. It deceives people into false loyalties, often by demanding conformity through the pressures of fear, guilt, shame, and condemnation.

There are numerous examples throughout history of the coalition of the political spirit and the religious spirit that have used competing political and or religious ideologies to create conflict and tension, which masks the underlying agenda to control world affairs.

When facing the political spirit in conflict situations we should always seek to operate in the opposite spirit and not go to war but seek a peaceful resolution. We should not attack the people involved, who are often just pawns in the religious and political spirit game, but discern what is operating through them.

For our struggle is not against flesh and blood, but against the rulers, against the powers, against the world forces of this darkness, against the spiritual forces of wickedness in the heavenly places. (Ephesians 6:12).

If we are discerning, we can see the same influences today in many levels of conflict, including the latest 2020 US election, the conflict in Palestine, and the terrorist activities of conflicting religious and political ideologies such as seen in Islam or communism.

The political spirit always needs an enemy, someone to fight against. The political spirit is characterised by the need to win an argument or conflict rather than solving a problem, and it demonizes anyone that doesn't agree with it. The political spirit seeks to influence or work within all DIY systems of government where rules of law can be established. The political spirit is often outworked in families, churches, corporate organisations, secret societies, and all forms of government. The political spirit is a controlling spirit and seeks to exert power over people.

The political spirit is obviously mostly seen within society in the political and governmental arenas but is often working in conjunction with the religious spirit within religious systems.

A political spirit is deceptive and will try to hide its agenda so it appears to want the good for people and society, all the while having hidden Luciferian agendas. The political spirit has been at work infiltrating society and culture since the fall: therefore it is very difficult to recognise its hidden agendas as they are part of humanistic culture.

The political spirit is devious, conniving and unscrupulous in seeking to establish its agenda. It seeks to corrupt, manipulate, and dominate individuals, leaders and groups of people through division and conflict.

The political spirit works in religious systems, as was evident with the Pharisees and Sadducees, who did not agree with each other over doctrines and competed with each other strongly.

Key attributes of a Political Spirit

Its ultimate agenda is power and control, often by any means; it drives people to keep that control at any cost, even war.

It uses laws, both civil and religious, to bind people to those legalistic systems. Of course, some laws or rules are necessary for the safety and wellbeing of society but the political spirit will have an underlying agenda and intention to enslave people, not free them. The political spirit can be seen at work in the Pharisees and other religious leaders who continued to add layers of law and tradition on top of what Moses had given them until the people were in bondage to laws they had no hope of keeping.

"The scribes and the Pharisees have seated themselves in the chair of Moses; therefore all that they tell you, do and observe, but do not do according to their deeds; for they say things and do not do them. They tie up heavy burdens and lay them on men's shoulders, but they themselves are unwilling to move them with so much as a finger." (Matthew 23:2-4).

The political spirit was still at work in the early church, seeking to bring the Gentile believers under the bondage and control of the law.

But some of the sect of the Pharisees who had believed stood up, saying, "It is necessary to circumcise them and to direct them to observe the Law of Moses." The apostles and the elders came together to look into this matter. After there had been much debate, Peter stood up and said to them, "Brethren, you know that in the early days God made a choice among you, that by my mouth the Gentiles would hear the word of the gospel and believe. And God, who knows the heart, testified to them giving them the Holy Spirit, just as He also did to us; and He made no distinction between us and them, cleansing their hearts by faith. Now therefore why do you put God to the test by placing upon the neck of the disciples a yoke which neither our fathers nor we have been able to bear? (Acts 15:5-10).

A goal of the political spirit is to press people into a mould of conformity of its own making by replacing the unique diversity with which God made His children with uniformity. The political spirit will pressurise people by fear, shame, control and law. We see this in the way people have to be politically correct and no longer have free speech. This is enforced by the social media thought police and the anti-defamation league who seek to conform everyone else to a system of beliefs and standards set by them. Paul warned of this conformation to the Romans where they were pressed into a political and religious mould.

And do not be conformed to this world, but be transformed by the renewing of your mind, so that you may prove what the will of God is, that which is good and acceptable and perfect. (Romans 12:2 NASB).

Do not allow [1]current religious tradition to mould you into its pattern of reasoning. Like an inspired artist, give attention to the detail of God's desire to find expression in you. Become acquainted with perfection. To [2]accommodate yourself to the delight and good pleasure of him will transform your thoughts afresh from within. (The word, *[1]aion*, is traditionally translated as "do not be conformed to this world." Actually *aion* points to a period of time of specific influence. In the context of this writing, Paul refers to the religious traditional influence of his day. The word *[2]euarestos*, comes from *eu*, praiseworthy, well done + *arestos*, meaning to accommodate one's self to the opinions, desires, and interests of others.) (Romans 12:2 Mirror).

I am in no way condoning any racism or trolling in the name of freedom of speech, which is of course reprehensible, but I do see the political spirit at work in a western (and eastern) society that seeks to conform people to its imposed 'politically acceptable' stereotypes. The sons of God knowing their true identity and authority is a threat to the political spirit which it seeks to extinguish.

The political spirit hates healthy debate so it makes its principles absolute and unchallengeable, thereby squashing questions and dissenting opinions. The political spirit will always try to displace true governance for the benefit of the people and replace it with loyalty to a party philosophy. The political spirit seeks to create a society and political arena where people are expected to blindly support a political party or system rather than stand for the truth that benefits everyone. This can sadly be seen clearly in the American political system, where each party seeks to block the other party's policies irrespective of whether they will benefit the nation or the people. The political system is open to corruption and self-interest that is partisan and not governmental.

Where a political spirit is functioning and in control, success is no longer measured by the wellbeing of society or the people but in terms of reach, party influence, visibility and popularity. In the case of political positions or parties it is also measured in polls and media coverage rather than facing issues and presenting real solutions.

The political spirit uses populism in that on the surface it seeks to keep people happy but beneath the surface is a political machine seeking to create a society in its image. The political spirit seeks to make a name for itself and will use populism to do so.

> Populism refers to a range of political stances that emphasise the idea of "the people" and often juxtapose this group against "the elite"... Populist parties and social movements are often led by charismatic or dominant figures who present themselves as the "voice of the people".
> – Wikipedia: *Populism*.

This is deception to gain public support whilst outworking their own hidden agenda behind the public facade.

The political spirit seeks to create a society with a culture that removes our permission to think for ourselves, so that our decisions become based on our nationalistic, political or religious affiliations. It seeks to make people avoid questioning their beliefs, and inclines them to instantly dismiss (and become afraid of) any truth which conflicts with what they believe.

This was so obviously the case during the 2020 US elections where the 'big lie' deception was perpetrated and the evangelical prophetic movement and the QAnon conspiracy joined together to present a delusion that many bought into. As every new date for their version of reality passed without fulfilment, the conspiracies became more and more absurd. Most of the prophets and Facebook gurus failed to accept their errors and publicly acknowledge the harm they were doing (bar a few who, with integrity, apologised for getting it wrong).

The political spirit is very divisive, promoting and thriving on the conflict it creates. The political spirit always has to win the argument, no matter what the cost to life or society. The political spirit is very prejudicial, with strong biases that are based in a root of pride that never admits it is wrong. The political spirit promotes the division and separation behind racism and such ideologies as segregation and apartheid.

The political spirit seeks to deceive us into an 'us and them' stance that prejudices us strongly towards a particular opinion or alignment to a very biased set of beliefs. This outworks in confirmation bias, where we see every piece of evidence confirming our pre-existing biased opinion.

The political spirit causes enmity and strife with those who do not believe the same as we do. This causes polarisation, where we always side with our tribe or faction no matter what is the truth.

The political spirit always seeks to create environments that cause an "us vs. them" mentality. We see this in Paul's letter to those in the church at Corinth who were forming factions:

Now I exhort you, brethren, by the name of our Lord Jesus Christ, that you all agree and that there be no divisions among you, but that you be made complete in the same mind and in the same judgment. For I have been informed concerning you, my brethren, by Chloe's people, that there are quarrels among you. Now I mean this, that each one of you is saying, "I am of Paul," and "I of Apollos," and "I of Cephas," and "I of Christ." Has Christ been divided? Paul was not crucified for you, was he? Or were you baptized in the name of Paul? (1 Corinthians 1:10-13).

...for you are still fleshly. For since there is jealousy and strife among you, are you not fleshly, and are you not walking like mere men? For when one says, "I am of Paul," and another, "I am of Apollos," are you not mere men? (1 Corinthians 3:3-4).

The political spirit seeks an enemy, someone to fight against, and it creates that adversary from anyone that does not agree with its agenda. This was again seen clearly during the US 2020 election with the political mudslinging and especially the horrific aspersions cast onto the nominees.

The political spirit will not just insinuate that the opposition is wrong but will cast them as evil and an enemy of their just and righteous cause. Society becomes deeply divided into those who are winners and those who are losers; but in reality, both sides continue to believe they are the winners, so continue to fight.

The political spirit deceives people into apportioning the blame for all the problems of society to certain people groups, races or religions. The political spirit is behind the promotion of "isms" – racism, ageism, sexism, etc. With the formation of various factions comes the thinking that when someone agrees with our tribe's stance, they are right; but if not, they are wrong. Being right is more important than being in a relationship, so the political spirit will cause people to distance themselves from those with different loyalties, beliefs or opinions from them.

Again, clear examples of this were seen during the 2020 US election where anyone voting democrat could not be a "real" Christian, e.g. "A real Christian could never vote for..." "That person is evil; if you were a real Christian you would know that", or statements like, "I thought you were a real Christian." I read of people being branded heretics based on their political stance. Mostly (but not entirely) this was Republicans branding Democrats as 'not Christian' over the issue of abortion.

People operating under the influence of a political spirit are very dogmatic. There is no room for debate or discussion over what they believe; there is no middle ground on which to stand. There is just offence and defence because the political spirit creates fences of belief between people. The political spirit causes contention and arguments that are usually unwinnable and serve only to perpetuate the issues that divide.

I have seen and experienced situations in which normally loving individuals will become hyper-critical and vindictive, attacking others by slandering them and spreading gossip and lies about them. They are prepared to break relationships and distance themselves from those they cannot control or convince to their way of thinking. This type of behaviour is in contradiction to the fruit of the Spirit and is the fruit of a very different spirit indeed.

Now the deeds of the flesh are evident, which are: immorality, impurity, sensuality, idolatry, sorcery, enmities, strife, jealousy, outbursts of anger, disputes, dissensions, factions, envying, drunkenness, carousing, and things like these, of which I forewarn you, just as I have forewarned you, that those who practice such things will not inherit the kingdom of God. (Galatians 5:19-21).

The political spirit always has excuses that it can use to make us justify our behaviour. It enables people to make dishonouring attitudes into virtuous attributes. Gossip is redefined as 'sharing essential information'. Self-righteous anger becomes righteous or even godly anger to excuse behaviour. This was evident in the vilification of Biden, Pelosi, Planned Parenthood and Black Lives Matter by Republicans and of Donald Trump by Democrats.

The political spirit works by getting us to idolise a particular leader (for example, Donald Trump or some other governmental figure) or party. Once people are operating in this type of political idolatry they can get defensive, even abusive, if others disagree, as their idols can do no wrong in their eyes. This causes people to try to defend the indefensible with great vehemence, often throwing logic and reason out of the window. This idolisation and putting people on pedestals is very prevalent in some Christian streams where the pastor, prophet or apostle must always be right.

The political spirit can blind people's eyes to their idols' (be they political or religious leaders) failings. The political spirit can cause someone to justify or minimise any wrongs of their idol or their party. On the other hand, the political spirit can make it open season on criticising those seen as the opposition. Considerations such as love, kindness, mercy, forgiveness etc. are abandoned. With the advent of the internet, and especially social media, the political spirit is thriving and these behaviours and attitudes are rife even amongst Christians.

Looking at the bigger picture, these attitudes cause nations to go to war against other nations fully justified by the political spirit and fulfilling its agenda. The Luciferian agenda of those global cabals controlling the world systems is fulfilled when people are divided, in competition and conflict with each other, as they generally benefit financially from the conflicts. While we are operating in strife and enmity with each other, they continue their hidden agenda to control the world because we are seeing each other as enemies and are just attacking ourselves. The real enemy that is behind the religious and political spirit is very happy to be hidden from sight, working through proxies to establish empires of all descriptions, including financial, national and corporate versions – and ultimately one world Luciferian government.

It is high time we stopped fighting each other and started looking at the real culprit behind the conflicts so that God's kingdom can fill the earth as we are united with one heart, mind and purpose.

The thief comes only to steal and kill and destroy; I came that they may have life, and have it abundantly. (John 10:10).

I do believe that the Luciferian agenda will ultimately fail and it will be the kingdom of God that will fill the earth to be one world government; but the religious and political spirit is still actively opposing the expansion of God's government and peace. That is why as sons of God we need to arise and be seated in the heavenly realms to see heavenly government and peace increasingly manifested on earth.

As I continue to survey the American Christian landscape regarding responses to the coronavirus pandemic, my disappointment and bewilderment grows daily. Much of the responses from the Evangelical community – and especially those within the Pentecostal-Charismatic framework – have been frankly dangerous, conspiratorial, hyper partisan, scientifically illiterate and theologically bankrupt.

There are two dominant heresies alive in American Christianity today, which would be fundamentalism and nationalism. – Maximus Nyssen[73]

These two ideologies of fundamentalism and nationalism are behind so much of the deception operating within the right-wing of American Christianity and explain the predisposition of that particular section of the church to the conspiracies that propagate the Luciferian agenda.

Whilst there are some aspects of truth contained within fundamentalism, as there are in evangelicalism, that are not wrong in themselves, it is how they are framed in an ideological sense that makes them dangerous.

---

[73] Maximus Nyssen, *Fundamentalism & Nationalism: Two Dominant Heresies in American Christianity*, PCPJ, May 5th, 2020: https://pcpj.org/2020/05/26/fundamentalism-nationalism-two-dominant-heresies-in-american-christianity/

"Fundamentalism" is used in so many ways that a basic definition is important to help frame the discussion.

The term, "fundamentalism" refers to a twentieth-century movement closely tied to the revivalist tradition of mainstream evangelical Protestantism that militantly opposed modernist theology and the cultural change associated with it. Fundamentalism shares traits with many other movements to which it has been related (such as pietism, evangelicalism, revivalism, conservatism, confessionalism, millenarianism, and the holiness and pentecostal movements), but it has been distinguished most clearly from these by its militancy in opposition to modernism. This militancy has typically been expressed in terms of certain characteristic theological or intellectual emphases: whereas modernism or liberal theology tended to explain life and much of religion in terms of natural developments, fundamentalists stressed the supernatural.
– George Marsden[74].

There are many different types of fundamentalism attached to different religious and political perspectives. Obviously in this book I am looking from a Christian perspective; and coming from a scientific background, this issue has caused me many challenges.

Christian fundamentalism treats the Bible as if it is a scientific textbook and portrays scientists as attacking the Christian faith. This causes fundamentalist Christians to reject science

---

[74] George Marsden, *Fundamentalism as an American Phenomenon, A Comparison with English Evangelicalism*, Cambridge University Press online, 28 July 2009. https://www.cambridge.org/core/journals/church-history/article/abs/fundamentalism-as-an-american-phenomenon-a-comparison-with-english-evangelicalism/
708CF096739F0DD966597AA238057752#

and defend the Christian faith against what they perceive to be scientific error. What fundamentalism does is deceive people into defending what is only a modern theological perspective. Fundamentalism only really came into a place of prominence at the beginning of the 20th century and for most of Church history no one adopted that position.

Religious fundamentalism, promoted by the religious spirit, requires someone to be the enemy; and when joined by the political spirit, lends itself to nationalism. The enemy of the nation becomes the enemy of the Christian faith and God. That makes it easier to incite fundamental Christians into supporting the violence and conflict often associated with nationalism. For some people, the two positions become almost synonymous terms and they begin to seek political solutions and political saviours. I believe this deception was behind the fundamentalist Christian support for President Trump and the QAnon conspiracies.

A general definition of nationalism is:

> ... identification with one's own nation and support for its interests, especially to the exclusion or detriment of the interests of other nations.
> – lexico.com

It is important not to confuse nationalism with patriotism. Patriotism is a healthy pride in your country that brings about feelings of loyalty and a desire to help other citizens. Nationalism is the belief that your country is superior, without question or doubt. I do not believe that God's original intention for the world was for there to be nations that were in conflict with each other, but rather one family in covenant with each other.

Nationalism is very prominent in the USA and advocates the view that America is God's 'special nation' and the 'best' nation in the world; therefore all other nations will be seen as inherently lesser, wrong or – at its worst – evil. This makes it easier for God's 'special nation' to support the Zionist agenda behind God's so-called 'special people,' thus falling for the religious and political spirit deception. So much of fundamental American evangelical Christianity is susceptible to the bigoted conspiracy theories that many now support.

Fundamentalism does not encourage debate or discourse because of its contempt of science and empiricism. So those trapped in fundamentalism are not persuaded by rational arguments or logic and empirical evidence, even when such evidence is demonstrated to be factually correct. This has been clearly evidenced in the US political arena where the Christian fundamentalist right wing has been manipulated by the political right wing to adopt a partisan-nationalist agenda as 'Christian'. These people have been deceived into only trusting the words of former president Trump, as opposed to anyone else.

The Pentecostal/Charismatic prophetic movement adds mysticism into this heresy, which feeds into those individuals who already believe that they know the 'truth' since they can 'hear from God.' The prophetic movement buying into the conspiracies of QAnon is evidence that it is easier to deceive those who believe that they have a special revelation.

Conspiracy theories are appealing for individuals who have a desire to know the mysteries of God, specifically those who believe that they are part of some enlightened group that knows how things 'truly' operate, which is usually contrary to the widely accepted narrative of the world. A non-religious conspiracy theorist is usually drawn to hidden knowledge but a Charismatic conspiracy theorist often adds prophecy, futurist eschatology and God's sovereignty to the mix, producing an intoxicating cocktail that easily becomes extremism. Those fundamentalist conspiracy theorists believe they must be right as God is on their side so they can expose 'the truth.'

This becomes even more dangerous with the added phenomenon of modern social media, which uses the constant feedback-looping of algorithms to ensure that you only see posts, memes, and videos which reinforce the perspectives and beliefs you already have. This is very dangerous for those susceptible to deception because of the heresy of fundamentalism.

That does not mean that all events initially considered conspiracy theories are false: some are true, as I have alluded to in this book; but the false ones are by far the majority.

How can we be discerning enough to distinguish between the two? I would encourage everyone to go directly to God but that in itself can create problems if we operate with confirmation bias. So when drawn to a potential conspiracy I would question what my motivation is. Does it draw me to a pre-existing passion or cause? If so, better be careful not to get sucked into it just because it confirms my beliefs. If it moves me to want to expose injustice, that represents the heart of God and might be worthy of looking at more closely. In the current political and religious climate, almost all conspiracies that I have seen shared by Christians are ridiculously esoteric – most are frankly idiotic – and should be rejected.

So ask the question: who or what is benefitting from the conspiracy? If the motivation is to sell books or other merchandise, gain popularity, or 'prove' someone's spirituality or prophetic accuracy, then it is probably a scam that should be avoided.

8. The Hoodwinking of History.

This is a difficult chapter to write as, like most other people, I have believed what I have been told in the history books and school lessons. I believed the orthodox historical and religious views were the truth, just as I assumed that what we believe today had always been believed.

Perspectives on history

Modern studies using newly discovered sources such as the Dead Sea Scrolls have uncovered new truths about what the early Christians believed, yet the modern evangelical orthodox perspective and the perhaps slightly older reformed perspectives have remained unchanged. Many Bible versions have been translated using previous versions as their foundation and support and have ignored the newly discovered documents. For example, the King James Bible leaned heavily on the previous Latin Vulgate version and did not always use the original Greek texts – and modern translations still lean heavily on the King James. The Greek word *metanoia* which basically means 'with mind' is still consistently translated using the English word 'repentance', which warps the word's meaning to become 'sorrow over sin'. That is just one example of many. Even though modern translators have access to much older and more original Greek texts, they still translate words using their modern 'orthodox' meanings as their point of reference. Translators suffer from confirmation bias as much as readers.

On the journey of deconstruction on which the Father has been taking me, I discovered that the early Church Fathers, those closest to being discipled by Jesus' disciples, held a wide range of different beliefs and views concerning such matters as eschatology, hell, Christian Universalism and the restoration of all things. Ilaria Ramelli, an Italian-born historian, academic author and university professor who specializes in ancient, late antique and early mediaeval philosophy and theology, has written some excellent books[75] on the subject of the early Church Fathers' beliefs.

As new research continues to shine a light on old facts, there are obvious questions that need to be asked. Can we ever hope to know the whole truth about the past? Therefore can history ever be accurately reported? This poses another challenge: if we cannot depend on our knowledge of history (if we do not know where we came from and how we got here), will we ever be able to understand where we are going? The big question then is: can we trust the historical record at all?

Most of us get our knowledge of history from our school textbooks and history lessons; but how accurate are they? For example, an American school textbook may have a very different perspective on what they refer to as the 'War of Independence' than a UK textbook does concerning what is may call the 'Revolutionary War'. Although it is same subject, they use different titles to skew the supposed purpose of the war to fit their own perspective. The facts are often spun to support one side over the other, depending on which side is recording the facts. This is more obvious when concerning conflicts and separation of lands. For example, I wonder how the Indian, Pakistani and Bangladeshi school history books record the story of the 1947 partition of India and the 500,000 lives that were lost in the struggle for independence.

---

[75] For example, Ilaria Ramelli, *A Larger Hope?, Volume 1: Universal Salvation from Christian Beginnings to Julian of Norwich*, Cascade Books, (2019).

I do once again reiterate my opinion that those behind the Zionist agenda, going back hundreds of years, although they may use the title 'Jewish,' have a Luciferian political agenda, not a religious one. In seeking to expose what is behind the Zionist agenda I am not being anti-Semitic and I have nothing personally against adherents to any religion.

As I dig into whatever political machinations and scheming led up to the establishing of the nation-state of Israel, I believe it will uncover evidence to show that those responsible were willing to sacrifice countless millions of innocent lives to achieve their goals. Those in the global cabals and secret societies that control financial and political world affairs have used revolution and conflict both for financial gain and political manipulation. I believe they were behind the French and Russian revolutions and used both World Wars to achieve their goals.

Many things have been left out of the history books to hide the Luciferian agenda and those behind it from exposure. There are many seeking to expose these things by writing articles about the Khazarian mafia as the world's largest organised crime cabal and others seeking to expose the Illuminati or Freemasons for their own agendas. I believe there may be elements of truth in all these articles but I am in no way seeking to validate them or support their goals and agendas. John Lennon[76] sums up the position we can find ourselves if we begin searching for the truth:

"Our society is run by insane people for insane objectives. I think we're being run by maniacs for maniacal ends and I think

---

[76] John Lennon: https://solutionsthought.com/john-lennon-98996

I'm liable to be put away as insane for expressing That. That's what's insane about it."

This is a quote from an online article showing that people are beginning to awaken from the stupor of learned ignorance to seek the truth:

> The history of the Khazarians, specifically the Khazarian Mafia (KM), the World's largest Organized Crime Syndicate that the Khazarian oligarchy morphed into by their deployment of Babylonian Money-Magick, has been nearly completely excised from the history books.
>
> The present day KM knows that it cannot operate or exist without abject secrecy, and therefore has spent a lot of money having its history excised from the history books in order to prevent citizens of the World from learning about its "Evil beyond imagination", that empowers this World's largest Organized Crime Cabal.
>
> The authors of this article have done their best to resurrect this lost, secret history of the Khazarians and their large International Organized Crime Syndicate, best referred to as the Khazarian Mafia (KM) and make this history available to the World via the Internet, which is the new Gutenberg Press.
> – Veterans Today[77] (Editor's introduction to an article by Preston James and Mike Harris).

I am not condoning or affirming conspiracy websites such as Veterans Today but I do think this is an indication that the truth is being sought. It is difficult to discern what is true

---

[77] Editor's introduction to *The Hidden History of the Incredibly Evil Khazarian Mafia*, article by Preston James and Mike Harris, https://veteranstodayarchives.com/the-hidden-history-of-the-incredibly-evil-khazarian-mafia/

amongst so much false (or mis-) information: that is why I would encourage everyone to take the information back to the Father or to Jesus, the Truth, to see if it aligns with the frequency of the Truth.

There are many facts surrounding the Russian revolution and the First and Second World Wars that you will probably not find in the history books because those facts could reveal the agenda of the global cabals fronting Zionism.

History in general is written from the perspective of those who were in governmental control or who were the victors of wars and conflicts. Many conflicts of interest may have prevented what we have in our history books from being entirely true or accurate. Different countries, religions and cultures, such as east and west, Christian and Islamic, may have widely divergent historical records, for instance over the Crusades.

Has there been an agenda to write history from a perspective that hides the real truth of who is behind the conflicts? In modern history, who has controlled the finances, politics, religion, media and truth?

This book is about the eschatology of the restoration of all things and I have already covered why our eschatology is important. I have already linked the modern eschatology of dispensationalism and Zionism to a bigger Luciferian agenda of the one-world government that has been active throughout human history. So what has eschatology to do with history? Whoever controls the narrative of the past controls the narrative of the future. The Luciferian agenda behind Zionism has controlled the truth of what or who was behind the conflicts that enabled the Zionists' agenda of the establishment of the political state of Israel. By controlling the narrative of how God has worked in the past, using the false doctrine of dispensationalism; and by futurising eschatology, Christians have been hoodwinked and deceived into providing Christian Zionist support for the Luciferian one-world government agenda.

It would be impossible to unravel all of history and discover the truth about every situation so I will limit the scope of this chapter to the eschatological issues relating to the restoration of all things.

Who was behind the political and religious schemes used to create a nation-state of Israel? How widespread was this in a political sense? And how far does this agenda go back into history? I am not against Israel or Israeli or Jewish people but I do want to expose the manipulation of political events and the historical records. The answer to these questions will reveal how religion and politics have been used to create the conflicts that have been used to create support for this Luciferian agenda.

The accusation of anti-Semitism is enough to intimidate some people and cause them to back off in their pursuit of the truth. I am not anti-Semitic, so I do not fear the accusations; but there are those who, in seeking the truth, mistakenly blame Jewish people instead of who really is behind the Zionist agenda.

There is one common goal shared by both religion and politics: to acquire the power and influence necessary to fulfil their aims. The methods used to achieve their objectives are usually different. Religion uses an evangelical cause to mobilise people to change society to align with that cause. Religion will use the support of the people to create political traction to fulfil its objectives. Politics also wants the support of public opinion but secretly uses other methods such as intrigue, diplomacy, and secret deals made behind the scenes. Political parties can take power democratically through elections, or by revolution or coups d'état – often with the help of military force. The support of public opinion is not entirely necessary for a military-backed revolution or coup but the sympathy of the people is helpful to the ongoing government. Misinformation and disinformation are used to create propaganda that sways public opinion to support a cause.

When those puppet-masters use religion to influence political authority, their ambition is to exploit it to fulfil a so-called divine mission. The claim is often made that the cause derives its authority from God and therefore its work is holy and is motivated to reform society. However, this makes people susceptible to accepting their spiritual guidance (for which we can read coming under the bondage of religious laws designed to take away people's freedom). Politics that is purely secular and humanistic uses the excuse that society requires changing for the better, which needs updated laws and systems of government to meet its obligations.

The religious and political approaches can be summed up as:

- Religion bases its authority on divine laws or God's will, which is absolute.
- The political approach is more pragmatic. It uses the front of society's needs to give political parties the excuse to makes the sometimes draconian changes which are represented as 'necessary' to meet the new challenges the world faces.

According to this secular Luciferian humanistic approach, man is responsible to determine his destiny. He is not under the control of God, so does not have to be submissive to a deity and therefore inactive. The political spirit agenda today is the same as at the building of the Tower of Babel: for humanity to make a name for themselves and build a society according to man's independent (but in reality, Luciferian-influenced) vision.

There are various modes of operation seen in history that relate to how the religious and political spirit functions.

One way of operating is when religion and politics unite with each other in an attempt to dominate political power. This method works when the religious and political spirits integrate: a good example of this would be the combination of the Roman Catholic Church and the political powers known as Christendom.

> After the dissolution of the Roman Empire, the idea arose of Europe as one large church-state, called Christendom. Christendom was thought to consist of two distinct groups of functionaries: the sacerdotium, or ecclesiastical hierarchy, and the imperium, or secular leaders. In theory, these two groups complemented each other, attending to people's spiritual and temporal needs, respectively. Supreme authority was wielded by the pope in the first of these areas and by the emperor in the second.
> – Britannica: *Christendom.*

Another way of operation is where the political power is dominant, having subdued and overpowered religion but still using it for its own interests. Religion plays a subservient role in politics: this might be seen in England, where the Queen is the head of the Church of England but in reality, control is political.

A third way is when the religious and political spirit seem to come into conflict with each other: they appear as rivals and compete to struggle for domination. This was true at times in Christendom, as both spirits thrive in an atmosphere of competition and conflict.

> In practice, the two institutions were constantly sparring, disagreeing, or openly warring with each other. The emperors often tried to regulate church activities by claiming the right to appoint church officials and intervene in doctrinal matters. The church, in turn, not only owned cities and armies but often attempted to regulate affairs of state. This tension would reach a breaking point in the late 11th and early 12th centuries during the clash between Emperor Henry IV and Pope Gregory VII over the question of lay investiture.
> – Britannica: *Christendom.*

Building a Christian city was an attempt to marry religion and politics: Zion City, near Chicago, was an example of this. As all such attempts do, this eventually failed, amidst religious and financial corruption.

> The city was founded in July 1901 by John Alexander Dowie (1847-1907), a Scots-Australian evangelical minister and faith healer who had migrated to the United States in 1888. By 1890, he had settled in Chicago, where he built a large faith healing ministry (which included a large mail order component) and had attracted thousands of followers.
>
> He bought land 40 miles north of Chicago to found Zion, where he personally owned all of the land and most businesses. The city was named after Mount Zion in Israel.
> – Wikipedia: *Zion, Illinois.*

Throughout the historical records, the real agendas behind world events and empire-building are mostly hidden. The following is a snippet from my journals of a conversation I had with the Father while writing this book:

4th January 2021

"All division and separation is a tool of the deception that is used by the few to keep the many from the truth of their value and worth as sons. Anything that divides our children and separates Our one family is an abhorrence to Us.

"The subjugation of mankind by the old gods and their new minions, the bankers, political warmongers and corporations that have replaced the priests of religion, just perpetuates the great deception.

"There is one agenda behind all of the deceptions: that is to counterfeit the true with the false so mankind will believe the lie is the truth. The Luciferian deception is to fool Our children into believing that they have to attain through independence who they already are. The empire spirit that has tried to counterfeit the true Kingdom with one independent world government made in their own image has used politics and religion to achieve that goal.

"The latest form of that Luciferian agenda is Talmudic Zionism, masquerading behind the political left of communism and the political right of nationalism. The Luciferian goal of one false world government is controlled by the elite financiers who control the power through money.

"The political and religious spirit promotes its agenda through division, competition, conflict and tribalism whilst seeking to unite the world politically and religiously through deception. The sons of God in the light of their true identity must arise to expose the darkness and the Luciferian agenda behind the latest deception.

"Your focus this year is to facilitate restoration government and write the book that will expose the lies of Zionist eschatology that supports and perpetuates the deception amongst Our sons."

19th May 2021

"Son, the history of humanity as written has been manipulated and influenced by the Luciferian agenda and is a history of the achievements of knowledge sourced from the DIY tree. The history of mankind can be read in the books of the library of heaven and they record the story of Our interactions with Our children and the stories of their individual lives.

"The narrative of most history books has twisted the truth through the filters and perspective of Leviathan to be the record of 'I will' humanistic achievements. The Luciferian agenda has been hidden deceptively to mask the political and religious spirits' interference in human history and obscure the truth behind layers of crafted lies. In the distant past it was emperors and kings who had history recorded to paint them in a favourable light but in more modern times it is the global cabals (who control the finances, printing companies and media) who control the narrative. Corporations have replaced empires but the agenda for control, subjugation, division, competition, conflict and tribalism is the same.

"All humanistic political control systems are rooted in the tree of independence and are manipulated by the religious and political spirit for the goals of the Luciferian agenda. The hijacking of history to hide the deception dresses up the Luciferian agenda in many ways to keep humanity deceived and enslaved to worship Lucifer, who is behind humanistic independent knowledge and achievements.

"The real truths that can be found in history are the acts of love, courage, compassion and selflessness that are recorded and reflect Our nature that is encoded within Our children. Son, love wins; and the awakening of love-consciousness will also awaken humanity to the truth of mankind's history and destiny and that will expose the great deception."

As I was standing in the light of the Father's presence, I began to feel that unconditional love that is the very essence of God. Love's light is the light of the truth: that has been covered in darkness to obscure the truth; but light will always overcome the darkness in the end.

"Darkness is only temporary but light is eternal, as it is who We are. Deep darkness may cover the earth but the glory of Our nature in mankind will arise and shine. The glory of Our true identity will shine from Our children to reveal their sonship to creation and bring freedom from corruption and decay.

"The history of humanity has been written to display humanistic achievements that glorify independence; but their glory is but a flickering candle in comparison with the glory of mankind's true destiny.

"Son, all things will be restored and the glorious freedom of creation will once again be displayed in the harmonious union of all things. The story of humanity's independence will be redeemed and mankind's glorious beginning and future will be what is remembered. There will be a cosmic awakening of love-consciousness that brings such enlightenment that all the hidden agendas of independence will fade into nothingness.

All of the history of creation will be restored and there will be no memory of what is only a hiatus, as Our original intention is realised and fulfilled in the harmonious union of all things."

I saw all that was within the Father's heart in a glorious quantum moment and I rejoiced in wonder and awe. I could not do anything but smile, contented and fully satisfied, as all was as it was always supposed to be.

Encounters like this are behind my motivation to write this book and I believe exposing the lies whilst revealing the truth is part of my mandate. I believe that the truth is that Zionism (a political movement which uses religious support) has employed a very clever strategy to use the terrible persecution of Jewish people throughout modern history to gain the sympathy of the world for its political advantage.

I had many other individual and corporate restoration government group ascensions and encounters which opened my eyes further to the way global control systems manipulate and control world events for their agendas, often hiding control and political influence behind what are often and incorrectly called 'natural disasters' by controlling the narratives.

26th May 2021

"Son, you can let everything go and put your trust fully in Us as you seek first the kingdom and choose the reality that aligns with Our heart and your destiny. You cannot choose a reality that forces or manipulates others to bend to your will, even if it is Our desire, as We have given all things the ability to choose.

"Son, we allow Our children to choose, even if those choices are not wise. You must do the same and trust Us to bring about good in your and their lives. Everything will be woven into the stories that create the narrative of the restoration of all things, as Our lovingkindness could do no less than good."

In several restoration government group encounters we have been engaging the tectonic plates of the earth, releasing heavenly oil to reduce friction between the plates. We discovered a void where there has been an absence of the light of sonship, creating a vacuum filled with darkness. In this void there is an order of fallen angels whose function is to cause devastation both to the earth through earthquakes and eruptions and to man by the destruction of lives, crops, livestock and property.

The original function of those beings was preservation, so not only do they promote devastation but there is also an absence of preservation. The responsibility to work in cooperation with man for the preservation of life, species, natural balance and harmonious ecosystems has been twisted to create devastation through what are known as 'natural disasters'. These fallen beings have corrupted the Elementals to work against man and each other, which has resulted in chaos and disharmony.

Humanity, under the influence of the DIY tree path of independence, has been deceived into abusing its authority over creation, cursing it rather than blessing it. As the sons of God are awakening to their identity, the truth is being revealed and creation is responding as restoration is taking place.

The restoration of fallen angelic beings is tipping the balance to accelerate the shift and the earth and the Elementals are awakening also. As those restored beings participate in the earth shield, there will be an even greater global awareness and consciousness awakened to the responsibility to steward creation.

"Son, Our government is to restore peace and harmony to creation not by war and conflict; and the power of unconditional love is Our weapon. We have limitless grace at Our disposal and an abundance of triumphant mercy; so love will win and the restoration of all things will be accomplished.

"Legislate for the global awakening of consciousness to unconditional love that will reveal Our true nature to Our children and through them to all creation. Son, trust in the power of Our love to overcome anything that is an obstacle or a hindrance to the restoration of all things."

9th June 2021

During a group ascension, I engaged the realm of light and the Father's thoughts formed a matrix of light around me, filled with His intentions for the earth.

Time, Wealth, Union, Blessing, Gold and Silver as beings stood by me; light streamed from them, connecting with the matrix around me. The filaments of light that I saw were like highways or portals that were connected to places or dimensions and timelines. I felt the desire to engage the earth shield. All those beings came with me and their light became one, like a laser pointer directed into the earth.

I followed the path to engage the earth's core and plates and felt the tension it was under at certain points around the globe. At each place of tension there was darkness – or better, something hiding – so I engaged one specific place in Iceland and saw a being. I began to engage it but it did not communicate. I sensed deep shame within its dark covering but I continued to offer restoration without any success.

I took Time with me and asked Time to show me its original purpose and name. As I saw its origin I knew it was another being of Preservation but now called Devastation. I reminded it of its name and function and began to call forth its identity that was so hidden under the scales of darkness and shame that covered it.

I saw that there were dark filaments connected to this being as if it was tethered and being controlled, having its strings pulled for an external financial agenda. I felt that its shame was associated with causing natural disasters that caused financial crashes or situations that were taken advantage of to make money out of others' misery or misfortune. The disasters were used to influence the financial markets and control or destabilise governments.

I saw the timeline of devastations that created famines and loss of property and livelihoods through history and I understood the deep shame. I released forgiveness for the financial devastations and again called forth its true identity as Preservation. As the quantum moment expanded, I began to see light breaking through the darkness. I felt its true purpose was to preserve life, health and blessing and to prevent destruction, loss and decay; and I began to declare jubilee and wellbeing. The other beings of Wealth, Gold, Silver and Blessing began to engage as I surrounded it with my spirit, creating a safe place. It was afraid of reprisals from its order and mankind.

Eventually, the light being of Preservation emerged in its glorious identity. We engaged it and asked it to participate in the earth shield to preserve the earth from devastations leading to financial crashes etc. It agreed and surrounded the earth like a cloak. We began to sense the other beings of devastation still connected by the back tentacles to dark pools and webs of deception within the global financial control systems. There is more work to do to see those control systems removed and the connections between world events and financial gains and control severed.

"Son, many such manipulations have occurred throughout history that have a Luciferian agenda behind them; and today there are strategies of the political and religious spirit that need to be exposed and dismantled. The events in history that caused devastations that were financially manipulated need to be revealed, so people can be disentangled from the global financial control and manipulation."

Hidden agendas

Eruptions, earthquakes, epidemics, hurricanes, typhoons, famines, revolutions, coups, stock market crashes, wars, conflicts, the Red Terror of Russia, Holodomor, Chinese genocides, African genocides, Irish potato famine, terror attacks, Krakatoa, Atlantis, floods in prehistory, nuclear disasters at Chernobyl and Fukushima, pandemics: history is full of examples where there are hidden agendas that are not written in the history books behind such catastrophic events.

George Orwell said in his book, *Nineteen Eighty-Four*[78]:

He who controls the present, controls the past. He who controls the past controls the future. Control the writing of history and you control the perception of where we have come from. That, in turn, becomes the coordinate for where we are and, when projected forward, it is the perceived starting point for where we need to go.

---

[78] George Orwell, *Nineteen Eighty-Four*, Secker & Warburg (1949).

One of the major foundations of the global deception has been to get people to buy into a false version of history that forms a narrative which obscures the truth beneath layers of lies and misinformation so that many different forms of control can follow.

A hypothetical example of this would be the events that surrounded the 9/11 attacks on the twin towers in New York. The consequences of that event changed the USA and shook the world. What if there was a Luciferian agenda driven by the religious and political spirit that was designed to create conflict and warmongering and tribalism? The insecurity felt by people created a xenophobic and nationalistic fervour, fuelling anti-Muslim attitudes, which meant more division and conflict. If you accept the official version of 9/11, you will probably accept the fundamental destruction of many basic freedoms to enhance the war on terror to 'fight the terrorists' who are suspected of being responsible as acceptable or at least expedient. There were further attacks, like the 7/7 attacks in London and others in Europe, which garnered support for reprisals, creating more division and conflict.

These events had many still lasting effects and changed the world for the worse in many ways. The following is a Wikipedia article depicting those effects, to give you an example of how history can be controlled by hidden agendas.

> The cultural influence of the September 11 attacks (9/11) has been profound and long-lasting. The impact of 9/11 has extended beyond geopolitics into society and culture in general. Immediate responses to 9/11 included greater focus on home life and time spent with family, higher church attendance, and increased expressions of patriotism such as the flying of American flags. The radio

industry responded by removing certain songs from playlists, and the attacks have subsequently been used as background, narrative or thematic elements in film, television, music and literature.

Already-running television shows, as well as programs developed after 9/11, have reflected post-9/11 cultural concerns. 9/11 conspiracy theories have become social phenomena, despite the lack of support from scientists, engineers, and historians. 9/11 has also had a major impact on the religious faith of many individuals; for some it strengthened, to find consolation to cope with the loss of loved ones and overcome their grief; others started to question their faith or lost it entirely because they could not reconcile it with their view of religion.

The culture of the United States succeeding the attacks is noted for heightened security and an increased demand thereof, as well as paranoia and anxiety regarding future terrorist attacks that includes most of the nation. Psychologists have also confirmed that there has been an increased amount of national anxiety in commercial air travel.

Due to the significance of the attacks, media coverage was extensive (including disturbing pictures and live video) and prolonged discourse about the attacks in general, resulting in iconography and greater meaning associated with the event. Don DeLillo called it "the defining event of our time". The attacks spawned several catchphrases, terms, and slogans, many of which continue to be used more than a decade later. – Wikipedia: *Cultural influence of the September 11 attacks.*

If the official 'history' of September 11th 2001 were to prove to be a lie, that revelation would change your view of the present and future in an instant. I believe that there is an underlying agenda behind all division and conflict and that many are acting unknowingly like puppets, not realising that someone is pulling their strings for a much more devious agenda. There are of course many conspiracies surrounding 9/11 that I am not going to go into, but the example remains valid.

Myths and legends

This is a modern example of how an event can change the world; so if you control history, you also control what people believe about the past. If you believe that we (mankind) have evolved from savage cavemen who had no advanced knowledge or technology, that will shape your understanding of who you are and what is possible. To control and confuse people you have to suppress their understanding of their true identity, who they are and what they are truly capable of as sons of God. By rewriting history you can erase the truth of our true origin as made in the creative image of God. When the truth becomes only myths and legends, then mankind's true potential to be fruitful, multiply, subdue and rule by following the pathway of the Tree of Life is obscured and lost amongst the independent lies of the DIY tree.

The myths and legends of most cultures hide the truth of our origin and the agenda behind our lost identity. There is a version of the 'Tower of Babel' (Babylon) story in most cultures where 'God' confuses languages to stop the agenda that was present (to make a name for themselves) when there was one global society with one language. That society was founded on advanced knowledge which was traded as described in Genesis 6 and the Book of Enoch with the fall of the watcher angels. Communication was as it is in heaven, by thought or telepathy. The introduction of language to replace telepathy tethered people to the realm of their five physical senses and disconnected them from multidimensional reality.

That past culture had abilities of thought and the use of light and sound that are only just being rediscovered through technology. I believe the sons of God have latent powers and abilities that are going to be unlocked and restored as we mature in sonship. I have been on the timeline and seen for myself how some of the 'mystery' structures like the pyramids, built thousands of years ago all over the world, were constructed. Some of those remaining visible structures are still beyond the capability even of modern technology.

In recent years media advancements have shown that these amazing ancient structures, temples, stone circles and standing stones were not only lined up precisely with the sun, moon and certain star systems, they were also aligned relative to each other all over the planet.

The truth of what occurred in history has been hidden, lost or deliberately obscured so that it is much harder to believe what it is to see paradise restored. There are many legends and accounts all over the world that refer to a 'Golden Age', which was destroyed by cataclysm and the 'Fall of Man'. The ancient Greek poet Hesiod described the world before this 'fall': Man lived like gods, without vices or passions, vexation or toil. In happy companionship with divine beings, they passed their days in tranquillity and joy, living together in perfect equality, united by mutual confidence and love. The account of man's garden east of Eden with the heavenly Garden of Eden barely touches the true reality of life before the fall.

The Earth was far more beautiful and creation functioned in harmony with man, spontaneously yielding a bountiful harvest and abundance of fruits. Mankind and the animals were able to communicate with each other and the Elementals functioned together with man to maintain dominion. People never died and time worked in harmony and partnership with mankind, not against it. Creation is going to be set free and we are going to be restored: not back to what it was like but to what it would have been if mankind had not chosen independence.

Rebecca Cann, Assistant Professor of Genetics at the University of Hawaii, co-authored a study in 1987 in the journal *Nature* suggesting that all modern humans are descended from a single mother who lived in Africa about 200,000 BC. The connection, she said, was through the mitochondrial DNA, which passes down through the female. This naturally led people to ask if this single mother could have been the biblical Eve.

There are earlier and similar accounts to Genesis in the Sumerian culture (they lived in what we now call Iraq, from around 4000 to 2000 BC). The goal of genetic manipulation of the seed of the sons of God to hybridise and allow inter-dimensional interference is recorded in many cultures.

I do not believe the conspiracies of reptilians from Drako but I do believe that serpent seed was introduced into the human genome in the garden and that later there was angelic seed introduced that formed the Nephilim. These bloodlines probably do exist today and may be what is used to draw people to the Luciferian agenda behind the global cabals. Those seeking the truth often end up obscuring the truth behind the ancient alien, star seed and other theories that are twisting the truth – which is counterproductive to their pursuit of truth.

Now it came about, when men began to multiply on the face of the land, and daughters were born to them, that the sons of God saw that the daughters of men were beautiful; and they took wives for themselves, whomever they chose. Then the Lord said, "My Spirit shall not strive with man forever, because he also is flesh; nevertheless his days shall be one hundred and twenty years." The Nephilim were on the earth in those days, and also afterward, when the sons of God came in to the daughters of men, and they bore children to them. Those were the mighty men who were of old, men of renown. (Genesis 6:1-4).

The process of maturity that the sons of God would have gone through was counterfeited by the Luciferian agenda to create in its own image, independent of God. The hybridisation of human beings and the trading of knowledge created a twisting of the human genome where mankind made in the image of God became humanity with genetic mutations or adaptations. Jesus came and included all of mankind in Him as a new creation; but that needs to be worked out through a process of transformation, to renew the mind and expand the consciousness to live in the truth of the true identity of sonship.

The deliberate twisting of historical truth and the inadvertent twisting of elements of truth by those who are genuinely seeking the truth cause many people to believe in Luciferian lies. Believing in the lies of the tree of the knowledge of good and evil keeps mankind, who are made in the image of God, in bondage and living as 'humanity', having taken on a false, Luciferian image.

The offspring of those genetic unions between humans and the angelic races are known as Nephilim; this caused the modern human race, or Homo sapiens, to advance technologically but to lose true sonship abilities. The cosmologist Dr Carl Sagan discussed humanity's origins in his book, *The Dragons of Eden*[79], and pointed out how the fossil record reveals a sudden and inexplicable leap in human brain function that cannot be explained by the claims of Charles Darwin and his advocates that humans evolved from reptiles, but very slowly. Under the Darwinist timescale, it should have taken 200 million years, Sagan says. Instead, it happened very quickly in what Sagan describes as a major burst of brain evolution. Stone tools, for example, did not develop slowly but appeared 'in enormous abundance' all at once.

I do not believe that there was an evolution of brain function caused by ancient aliens. However, I do believe that brain function diminished but technological capabilities increased as knowledge was given; and the desire to make a name for themselves is part of the deception of the tree of the knowledge of good and evil. Humanity is trapped in the desire to be like God but be independent of Him.

The ancient Book of Enoch describes how the 'fallen angels', especially one it calls Azazel, introduced this knowledge:

> And Azazel taught men to make swords, and knives, and shields, and breastplates, and made known to them the metals of the earth and the art of working them, and bracelets, and ornaments, and the use of antimony, and the beautifying of the eyelids, and all kinds of costly stones, and all colouring tinctures. And there arose much

---

[79] Carl Sagan, *The Dragons of Eden: Speculations on the Evolution of Human Intelligence*, Ballantine Books (1989).

godlessness, and they committed fornication, and they were led astray and became corrupt in all their ways. Semjaza taught enchantments, and root-cuttings, Armaros the resolving of enchantments, Baraqijal (taught) astrology, Mabel the constellations, Ezeqeel the knowledge of the clouds, Araqiel the signs of the earth, Shamsiel the signs of the sun, and Sariel the course of the moon. – *The Book of Enoch*, Chapter VIII.

A group of researchers at the Human Genome Project[80] believe that 97 per cent of non-coding DNA – what was once termed 'junk DNA' – is the genetic code of extra-terrestrial life forms. Professor Sam Chang, the group leader, maintains that the overwhelming majority of human DNA is 'of off-world origin' and the apparently 'extra-terrestrial junk genes' merely 'enjoy the ride' with hard-working, active genes passed from generation to generation.

The once-termed 'junk DNA' is now known to be a series of switches or triggers that can switch on and off abilities and functions. It is not evidence that we have extra-terrestrial origin from this universe, but that our origin is to be found in God's image. The twisting and controlling of history always seeks to keep mankind from the truth of our sonship and keep us in bondage to being a 'less than' humanity striving for self-identity but never succeeding.

The Bible describes the period after trading with the fallen watcher angels as a time of great wickedness:

Then the Lord saw that the wickedness of man was great on the earth, and that every intent of the thoughts of his heart was

---

[80] *Scientists Find Extraterrestrial Genes in Human DNA?*, article from *An experiment in ideas* blog, 2007: https://alsop.wordpress.com/scientists-find-extraterrestrial-genes-in-human-dna/

only evil continually. The Lord was sorry that He had made man on the earth, and He was grieved in His heart. (Genesis 6:5-6).

Some call this period the 'Golden Age': there are many mythologies throughout the known world that describe a high-tech 'Golden Age' that was brought to an end by enormous cataclysmic events, including a fantastic tidal wave or great flood. The truth is that this age, which may have had many technological advances, descended into anarchy, as only Noah was genetically pure when God commissioned him to build the ark. Most of the technology was lost during the flood and the consequence of continual wickedness was a global reset.

Atlantis is one well known myth of a city and society that was lost under the sea. The great flood is a common theme in the mythology of many ancient cultures, connected to incredible geological upheavals. The Earth was struck by these cataclysmic events: this is not a myth but a fact that has been verified by scientific research. A series of geological catastrophes caused immense earth changes through earthquakes, volcanic eruptions and tidal waves. From the biological and geological record, there appear to have been several enormous upheavals from around 13,000 BC. The scientific and history books obscure the truth, as do the conspiracies surrounding these catastrophic events.

The Biblical account of Noah and the ark has parallels in other cultures and stories persist today about pre-Flood, or pre-diluvian, civilisations known as Atlantis, which is most often said to be located in the Atlantic, and Lemuria, or Mu, in the Pacific.

The Sumerian mythology tells how some of the gods, known as the Anunna or Anunnaki, decided to destroy humanity and one god, called Enki, warned the priest-king Ziusudra of the coming flood. He was told to build a great ship and take aboard beasts and birds. After the rains and flood, Ziusudra bowed in thanks before the Sun-God, Utu.

You can also find the flood story in Egypt, Assyria, Chaldea, Greece, Arcadia, Rome, Scandinavia, Germany, Lithuania, Transylvania, Turkey, Persia, China, New Zealand, Siberia, Burma, Korea, Taiwan, Philippines, Sumatra, Islam, in Celtic lore and among native peoples throughout North, South and Central America, Africa, Asia, Australia and the Pacific. Each society or tribal people may have used different names and added their spin here and there, but they all tell the same basic story: virtually all of them describe a great flood of water that eventually covered the earth.

All versions of the flood story other than the Bible obscure the one true God from the story in favour of many gods. Modern mythology has inferred those gods to be extra-terrestrial or inter-dimensional beings.

There is much research being done to find the truth, and many books written, but most contain such a mixture that the truth being sought is still obscured. In books such as *When the Earth Nearly Died*, by D.S. Allan and J.B. Delair[81], the ancient accounts are supported by geological and biological evidence. I do not find the conclusions drawn from such research convincing and the Luciferian agendas are always hidden behind layers of misinformation and deception. The truth of a global catastrophic event is overwhelming but there are other

---

[81] D.S. Allan and J.B. Delair, *When the Earth Nearly Died: Compelling Evidence of a Catastrophic World Change 9500 B.C.*, Gateway (1994).

facts that most people do not know: the Himalayas, Alps and Andes mountain ranges only reached anything like their present height around 11,000 to 13,000 years ago. The fact that those mountains were once at sea level, and recently so in geological terms, explains why so many fish and other ocean fossils are found high up in mountain ranges.

The knowledge of those ancient times was lost but the Bible states that the Nephilim existed before and after the flood. This could be accounted for by genetics, as if only Noah was genetically pure that means his wife, their children and their wives may not have been genetically pure. Therefore serpent and angelic seed lines could have existed after the flood; this concurs with the biblical record of giants among the '-ites' nations. Another possibility that cannot be ruled out is that Luciferian knowledge continued to be given to those seed lines to perpetuate the great deception and form a counterfeit kingdom. Jesus described in a parable how the enemy had sown seed into the field of the world to fulfil his agenda and hinder the sons of God filling the earth with God's kingdom.

Jesus presented another parable to them, saying, "The kingdom of heaven may be compared to a man who sowed good seed in his field. But while his men were sleeping, his enemy came and sowed tares among the wheat, and went away. But when the wheat sprouted and bore grain, then the tares became evident also. The slaves of the landowner came and said to him, 'Sir, did you not sow good seed in your field? How then does it have tares?' And he said to them, 'An enemy has done this!' The slaves said to him, 'Do you want us, then, to go and gather them up?' But he said, 'No; for while you are gathering up the tares, you may uproot the wheat with them. Allow both to grow together until the harvest; and in the time of the harvest I will say to the reapers, "First gather up the tares and bind them in bundles to burn them up; but gather the wheat into my barn." (Matthew 13:24-30).

Ancient Sumeria seems to be a source of ancient knowledge that has some mystery surrounding it.

The origins of Sumerian civilization in Mesopotamia are still debated today, but archaeological evidence indicates that they established roughly a dozen city-states by the fourth millennium B.C. These usually consisted of a walled metropolis dominated by a ziggurat – the tiered, pyramid-like temples associated with the Sumerian religion. Homes were constructed from bundled marsh reeds or mud bricks, and complex irrigation canals were dug to harness the silt-laden waters of the Tigris and Euphrates for farming. Major Sumerian city-states included Eridu, Ur, Nippur, Lagash and Kish, but one of the oldest and most sprawling was Uruk, a thriving trading hub that boasted six miles of defensive walls and a population of between 40,000 and 80,000. At its peak around 2800 B.C., it was most likely the largest city in the world...

The origins of the sixty-second minute and sixty-minute hour can be traced all the way back to ancient Mesopotamia. In the same way that modern mathematics is a decimal system based on the number ten, the Sumerians mainly used a sexigesimal structure that was based around groupings of 60. This easily divisible number system was later adopted by the ancient Babylonians, who used it to make astronomical calculations on the lengths of the months and the year. Base-60 eventually fell out of use, but its legacy still lives on in the measurements of both the hour and the minute.

Other remnants of the Sumerian sexigesimal system have survived in the form of spatial measurements such as the 360 degrees in a circle and the 12 inches in a foot...

After Mesopotamia was occupied by the Amorites and Babylonians in the early second millennium B.C., the Sumerians gradually lost their cultural identity and ceased to exist as a political force. All knowledge of their history, language and technology – even their name – was eventually forgotten. Their secrets remained buried in the deserts of Iraq until the 19th century, when French and British archaeologists finally stumbled upon Sumerian artifacts while hunting for evidence of the ancient Assyrians. Scholars such as Henry Rawlinson, Edward Hincks, Julius Oppert and Paul Haupt later took the lead in deciphering the Sumerian language and cuneiform, providing historians with their first ever glimpse of the long lost history and literature of early Mesopotamia. Since then, archaeologists have recovered numerous pieces of Sumerian art, pottery and sculpture as well as some 500,000 clay tablets, the vast majority of which have still yet to be translated.
– history.com

There is evidence that this knowledge was external and may have had Luciferian origins but it all seems to have one focus: that of empire and world government. The knowledge was passed on through initiation in what was known as the 'mystery schools', which could be the forerunners of today's global cabals and secret-society networks.

Some have used this ancient hidden knowledge to open dimensional portals for the incursion of dimensional beings. Aleister Crowley, a famous British occultist, used rituals which he called 'The Amalantrah Workings' to open a portal in 1917/8 to engage beings he called Lam, which have a very similar appearance to what are known as Greys today. Jack Parsons and L. Ron Hubbard later used the 'Babalon Working' to open a portal for further incursions:

> The Babalon Working was a series of magic ceremonies or rituals performed from January to March 1946 by author, pioneer rocket-fuel scientist and occultist Jack Parsons and Scientology founder L. Ron Hubbard. This ritual was essentially designed to manifest an individual incarnation of the archetypal divine feminine called Babalon. The project was based on the ideas of Aleister Crowley and his description of a similar project in his 1917 novel *Moonchild*.
> – Wikipedia: *Babalon Working*

The dimensional portal opened by Parsons and Hubbard in 1946 was the western gate and its opening may be responsible for the Roswell UFO incident and subsequent ufology. An attempt by Jason Westerfield to open the western gate during an online Christian conference on 28 November 2015 was thankfully unsuccessful. The conference had a web address of openthewesterngate.org.

Below is my journal entry on November 7th 2015, that I now know was referring to this attempt to open the Western gate:

7th November 2015

"Son you are authorised to open the realms of revelation to reveal destiny and purpose. Son, the veils between dimensions are being prepared for multidimensional incursions; set the watchmen at the gates to guard, protect and defend. The veils once removed [the gates being opened (my explanation)] will also allow many to travel into the mysteries that are inter-dimensional and return with the discoveries for the opening of the Discovery House."

Similar prehistoric incursions may have been responsible for ancient knowledge. An influx of external knowledge may explain why early civilisations like Egypt and Sumer (the land of 'Shinar' in the Bible) started at the zenith of development and then fell into decay, I believe that there is evidence that there was an infusion of highly advanced knowledge that was later lost to most people.

I had a fascination with the pyramids in Egypt and have had the privilege of visiting them many times. The earliest, like the great pyramid at Giza, were more advanced than later ones. In every culture throughout the world there are ancient stories and texts which describe the 'gods' (who were in fact either fallen angelic or dimensional beings) who brought advanced knowledge. This also explains how the ancients had an amazing understanding of astronomy and many other sciences.

The Sumerians were the first known people to study the stars, develop the written word and enforce a legal code. As we have seen, they were the first people known to use the sexagesimal system of numbers based on 60 and to divide time into 60 seconds and 60 minutes. They also introduced the twelve-month calendar. The Sumerians were the first known civilisation to have codified legal and administrative systems with courts, prisons and written records for government, history, mathematics and astronomy. They established the first schools and intensive farming with wheat, barley and animals. All the foundations of what we call 'modern society' started in Sumer and this was the society and structure given to them through external knowledge.

This may seem highly unlikely to the western mind because this knowledge has been hidden from most but I have had experiences myself where the Father has given me mandates to release knowledge through encounters.

During one of those encounters I visited a village in Africa – I am not sure if this was in the present or past – in which I showed them a map to find a water source and told them how to use the water to irrigate their crops. In another encounter, I went into the Discovery House in heaven and saw a scroll with a blueprint for some technology on it. When I picked up the scroll I was immediately translated into a bedroom where a man was sleeping and I put the scroll into his mind. I discovered later he was the inventor of air conditioning and the year was 1902. I have travelled in time many times, being used to heal or help someone. I did not change history, of course, as I was always used in that moment but I only became aware of it in the present when I engaged the eternal now.

The Luciferian agenda of 'I will' independence is focused on independent humanistic knowledge but the serpent seed may have introduced programmed traits of independence into the genetic code or as epigenetic factors. These traits may be psychologically programmed or perhaps they are functions that may be traits of serpent or angelic/Nephilim seed. These traits are part of the agenda that creates division, competition, conflict and tribalism within society and culture and these traits are used to maintain the financial and political control systems behind the Luciferian agenda.

Controlling the hidden narrative

Human character traits like aggressive and ritualistic behaviour, territoriality, and a desire for social hierarchies are all are consistent with what the religious and political spirit use to manipulate world events and control the hidden narrative. The programming of human activities that are part of lost identity finds expression in the tendency towards obsessive-compulsive behaviour; religious rituals and superstitious acts; legalism and slavish conformance to dead works; ceremonial re-enactments and laws; obeisance to precedent. This programming has trapped so many people, making them slaves to legal, religious and cultural deceptions.

The traits and behaviours of those behind the controlling cabals which own or control politics, banking, business corporations, energy, pharma, the military and the media today are influencing the world around us. Within those groups there is an obsession with hierarchical structures of rule and control, aggression, and the idea that might is right and winner takes all.

Throughout human history, the empire spirit has operated using these independent traits which are behind all division, racism, class and elitism; and that spirit has a fiercely hierarchical power-structure and has sought to impose the same on people. The traits of pomp, ceremony and ritual that are seen in many of the empiric structures like royal families, religious streams and the political establishment are part of the systems of rule and control.

There is a theme running throughout human history that has a Luciferián agenda behind it which has remained hidden from most people's view. The agenda has been propagated through the religious and political spirit to bring about a one-world government under a political and religious prophetic messiah figure. This government is a counterfeit of the kingdom, with Lucifer, not Jesus, as its head. Sadly, many Christian Zionists think they are supporting the cause of Jesus as a king returning in triumph to Jerusalem to set up an earthly kingdom. This deception has drawn together many strands of eschatological and political ideas into a deception that so many have believed. Those who have been deceived have no idea that they are promoting Lucifer as lord of an earthly kingdom.

Jesus clearly stated that His kingdom was not of this world: in other words, not a physical political kingdom. The kingdom of God that is filling the earth is a rule of love that is spiritual and not political. The government of the kingdom of God is increasing, to bring peace and not war and conflict. The spiritual warfare that is taught and practised by many evangelical Christians is in direct conflict with Jesus' commandment to be unconditionally loved and to love one another in the same way. This type of spiritual conflict demonstrates not love and peace but conflict and war, and is in total contradiction to the restoration of all things.

The political and religious spirit was already functioning in Israel in Jesus' day and was responsible for His rejection and crucifixion. That manoeuvring was to keep the power in the hands of those wanting an elite people and nation who would rule the world from Jerusalem: that was and still is the Luciferian agenda. That hope and agenda have never completely disappeared, just been hidden throughout the last two millennia; but the Talmudic political agenda has masqueraded in many guises, the latest being political Zionism. The agenda of political Zionism has the same goal of empire for a ruling elite and is both racist and elitist. Those behind this agenda are not religious nor are they descendants of Abraham but they do use Judaism as a mask to hide behind to give them legitimacy and the freedom to operate. It has become politically incorrect (and even an illegal hate crime) to challenge this, as those Talmudic Zionists control and censor the media, using such devices as the Anti-Defamation League and accusations of anti-Semitism to ward off those who might try to uncover the deception.

The *Talmud* and the Kabbalah are behind modern Judaism and use religion to hide the political agenda; and both are antichrist and looking for an earthly political messiah. I reiterate that I have nothing against Jewish people, those who practice Judaism, as they have the right to choose; but like any other false religion, following it keeps them from the truth of who God is and who they are as God's children. It is not anti-Semitic to say that Judaism is a false religion from the standpoint of Jesus' declaration that He is the Way, the Truth and the Life and the only way to the Father.

How did we get here, to a place where seeking the truth to expose the lies is a hate crime? It has been a long process to undermine the love values of the kingdom of God and replace them with the thought police and ADL. The agenda has carefully used the political and religious spirits' deception to hoodwink people and keep them from the truth, believing lies.

History has been hoodwinked so that most people have no idea of the agenda that is behind this deception and anyone who tries to expose it is labelled a conspiracy theorist.

9. Exposing the Great Deception.

With the advent of written, audio and visual media, knowledge of modern history is more widespread and that is both an advantage and a disadvantage to those seeking the truth. The truth can be hidden beneath layers of fabricated lies, misinformation and twisted partial truths which makes it difficult to discern what the truth is.

Most of the conspiracies I have seen have elements of truth embedded within them that either obscure the actual truth or make it so extreme that most sensible people reject the elements of truth as lies. If there is a Luciferian agenda for one-world government under Lucifer's control through intermediaries, one way to obscure it is to hide this fact within a conspiracy. Another way to disguise it is within Christian Zionism, in which gullible Christians are encouraged to pray for Jerusalem, to which Jesus is supposed to return to rule over Israel. The actual Talmudic Zionist agenda is for one-world government under an earthly messiah figure.

Any truth is hidden within the conspiracy and this is no more obvious than within the article on 'The Great Reset' found on the ADL website. The Anti-Defamation League comments on obvious misinformation and conspiracy around the Covid-19 pandemic being used by the global elite.

The article begins:

> Since first emerging in the spring of 2020, "The Great Reset" conspiracy has gained traction with the ongoing spread of COVID-19 in both mainstream and fringe circles alike. In its most common form, adherents warn that "global elites" will use the pandemic to advance their interests and push forward a globalist plot to destroy

American sovereignty and prosperity. However, there are more outlandish and pernicious strains of the conspiracy, and the adoption of this term "Great Reset" – particularly by mainstream figures with large audiences – creates dangerous opportunities for ordinary Americans to be drawn deeper into the world of conspiracies. References to The Great Reset conspiracy can be found on a range of social media platforms, from mainstream platforms like Twitter, YouTube, to newer platforms like Parler, to more extremist-friendly platforms like Gab and Telegram. Several prominent conservative pundits have also discussed the conspiracy on their television and radio shows.

The article ends, inevitably, by connecting this to anti-Semitism; and thus any connection to the Talmudic Zionism Luciferian agenda is completely discredited.

Usage of the Great Reset to Espouse Antisemitism

As is so often the case with conspiracy theories, one can find anti-Semitic sentiments in the Great Reset, with some believers going so far as to accuse Jews of orchestrating the plot or invoking George Soros and the Rothschild family. In a video posted on December 6 that has since been viewed more than 17,000 times, anti-Semitic conspiracy theorist Adam Green of Know More News asserts that the World Economic Forum is controlled by Jews who are using the Great Reset as part of a plan to "set up a Zionist, Noahide, One World Government according to the prophecies." He adds, "the Great Reset is totally tied in with all of this."

Such accusations that the conspiracists are against the Jewish people deflect attention away from any political Talmudic

Zionist agenda. This one article uses all the following rhetoric and terminology and the context either obscures the truth or casts doubt by labelling it 'conspiracy':

- The Great Reset conspiracy
- Global Elites
- New World Order
- Building Back Better
- Bill Gates
- President Trump
- QAnon
- Transhumanism
- Neo-Nazi
- George Soros
- The Rothschild family
- World Economic Forum
- Zionist
- Noahide
- One World Government
- Conspiracy theory
- Depopulation
- Jesuits
- Freemasonry
- Pharmaceutical industry
- Catholic Church
- Sex abuse allegations
- Vaccination
- Detention camps
- House arrest.

When left unchecked, conspiracies like the Great Reset carry the risk of undermining faith in democratic institutions by casting its leaders as part of a globalist plot and can even lead to further threats of violence against government officials. I am not saying that I believe in the Great Reset myself but by associating so many other things with it, the article cleverly tars them with the same brush.

We live in an era where 'virtual reality' has replaced reality. Image trumps truth, style supersedes substance and it has become very difficult to separate fact from fiction.

The Luciferian agenda

Exposing a deception that goes back to the rebellion of Lucifer and the fall of mankind into following the pathway of independent knowledge is difficult but not impossible because we do have access to the Truth Himself. So I will attempt to weave together the various threads within this book to try and form a basic picture that hopefully will enable the reader to follow the pathway of the truth of the Tree of Life.

What has been the Luciferian agenda throughout religious and political history? And can we see the truth amongst the smoke and mirrors of deception that has kept it hidden? The agenda behind Lucifer's involvement in human history can be summarised in the five 'I will' statements we saw before, as recorded in Isaiah 14:13-14.

Lucifer's agenda in this world is to get every single human, by any means necessary, to acknowledge that he is God. He wants God's position and authority over creation and needs the children of God to give it to him. Lucifer seeks to deceive the children of God (humanity) to act independently of the true God and by doing so give him authority. When humanity (through humanism) acts as its own god, it is playing right into Lucifer's hands as he both replaces God and takes our position of authority as sons.

Consider again those five 'I wills' of Lucifer. They summarise the agenda and give the insight to help us expose the deception and free the children of God to be restored to sonship.

- I will ascend to heaven,
- I will raise my throne above the stars of God,
- I will sit on the mount of assembly,
- I will ascend above the heights of the clouds,
- I will make myself like the Most High.

Lucifer desired to replace the sons of God as God's rulers of creation. He wanted to take their position of authority in the heavens for himself and to be seated in the place that God had prepared for His sons to rule in coheirship with Him.

Lucifer was not content with serving God: he wanted a throne that would give him authority over the angelic host known in the Bible as the 'stars of God'. It is the sons of God who have been given the authority to judge the angelic realm so Lucifer craved their position: he wanted to rule over all the angels who, like him, were created as ministers to the sons of God. Lucifer wanted to be enthroned to a higher place so that all the angelic assemblies and councils would be subject to him.

Biblically, clouds can refer to the glory of God. Lucifer wanted the glory that God had clothed mankind in but he refused to acknowledge the sovereignty of the creator over His creation. He craved his own independence and seduced man into following his desire to be accountable to no one but himself. Independence and non-accountability is a hallmark of following the path of the tree of the knowledge of good and evil.

For more information about Lucifer's agenda and the five 'I wills', there is a good article available to download online at biblerelatedministries.org/5Iwills.pdf

Lucifer has deceived mankind and now humanity is a surrogate, outworking these 'I will' statements of independence.

Many premillennialist Christians believe that the Antichrist will establish one world religion, based on Satanism and the occult, associated with one-world government. Rejecting and opposing the so-called antichrist, and hoping they themselves will be removed by the rapture, these same Christians promote the one-world government of the millennial reign of Jesus on earth in a rebuilt temple in Jerusalem and so support Christian Zionism. They have no idea that Talmudic Zionism rejects Jesus as the Messiah and accepts Lucifer (or his intermediary) as a Messiah who will establish a kingdom where he rules the world through Israel.

Lucifer's attempt to fulfil his agenda for control and domination throughout human history, has been through either religious or political means, starting at Babel and proceeding through all the subsequent attempts of world conquest to establish a world empire under his surrogate. All these attempts failed and imploded as they were based on flawed knowledge and independence.

Zionism

One of the latest attempts for world control is through a Talmudic Zionist agenda. This requires various things to be in place to succeed in its goal of a new world order: the political and religious spirit in a union, the existence of the nation-state of Israel and the support of both Talmudic and Christian Zionists.

This Zionist agenda for world conquest has been in place for several hundred years but its roots go back to the Talmud. Most honest Jews who follow the religion of Judaism have no idea of what is behind modern Talmudic Judaism and its Kabbalistic influences. Most Christians have no idea what agenda is behind Christian Zionism and what they are supporting.

There has been a politically motivated agenda to establish the nation-state of Israel as the precursor of one-world government that will seek to unite the world under Noahide laws. The true history of this agenda is carefully hidden from most people's view and the manipulation of nations to fulfil this goal has been orchestrated by those who control the world's financial systems.

As we saw in the previous chapter, history has been controlled by those who control the financial and political systems and the media. This agenda is not Jewish and has nothing to do with Judaism: it is political and has thrived through manipulating the conflicts that have shaped the political landscape.

The secret societies and families have hidden behind the label 'Jewish' and used the ADL and anti-Semitism to remain hidden and mostly control the narratives. There are many names used to obscure the truth like Free Masonry, Illuminati, Khazarian Mafia, Global Elite, Global Cabals, Deep State and many others too numerous to mention.

The Zionist-controlled media systems of Reuters news and the Associated Press make sure to keep the agendas and real truth behind Zionist-inspired revolutions and political manoeuvrings carefully hidden.

I do not want to go into all the details or focus on the stories of the connections to child trafficking, satanic ritual abuse, or blood and child sacrifice of Molech worship that often surround these secret societies. I will just focus on the political events that have led up to the establishing of the Talmudic Zionist goal for the nation-state of Israel. Of course, many people caught up in the Christian Zionist deception will attribute the establishment of the nation-state of Israel to God and pronounce it a miracle. I have hopefully covered who are the people of God thoroughly enough for the reader to realise that God does not support Israel (or any other nation, for that matter) and that the followers of the false religion of Judaism are not the earthly people of God.

The Luciferian agenda fronted by the religious and political spirit is behind all empires and all revolutions and thrives on conflict and warmongering. If you trace the money you will find who is behind all war and religious conflict and see how they benefit.

The French, American and Russian revolutions were all promoted by the same people who funded the First and Second World Wars and the Cold War. They equally support and use capitalism and communism to further their goals and a careful examination of history will illuminate this fact.

They use Catholicism, Protestantism, Islam and Judaism indiscriminately to further their cause. They have sacrificed millions of Muslim, Jewish and Christian people, having no regard for the individuals or the religions they use to achieve their political goals.

They have been willing to sacrifice millions of Jewish people to gain the sympathy of the international community as a backdrop for the Zionist agenda. They have promoted anti-Semitism throughout history by using such ideas as the blood libel and 'Protocol of the Jewish Elders' to both promote anti-Semitism and to hide the truth in the deep mire of conspiracy.

I will not use the term 'Jew' in a religious sense or in any anti-Semitic way and will try to separate adherents of religion from the followers of political Talmudic Zionism.

I believe that there is ample evidence, if you research, to support the idea that there are global cabals and that they have been responsible for hijacking history and orchestrating the Talmudic Zionist Luciferian agenda. This evidence points to their involvement in the First World War, blackmailing Woodrow Wilson into bringing America into that war in order to influence Britain into making the Balfour Declaration which guaranteed the establishing of the nation-state of Israel. It also indicates that they funded the Russian revolution and promoted communism; that would eventually lead to the Versailles treaty which paved the way for National Socialism and the Second War in which millions of innocent Jewish people (labelled Bolsheviks by Hitler) were sacrificed. The number 'six million' can be traced back fifty years before this, appearing in 260 different news articles that subliminally paved the way for that Kabbalistic number to be enshrined in history as the Holocaust number. That number has been cleverly used to remind people that Israel should be politically supported.

I would never deny that the Holocaust happened but I do believe it was carefully engineered by those who would be willing to sacrifice millions of innocents to play the sympathy card that would eventually lead to the establishment of the nation-state of Israel in 1948.

A good friend of mine, Jonathan Cavan, the founder of *Liebusters* ministry, has done extensive research around this very issue and for those who are willing to go down the rabbit hole, I would suggest you seek out the information he has produced. Some of this he shared in the *Restoration of All Things 3* conference which our ministry hosted in June 2021. The subject matter is the Leaven of the Pharisees, covering three areas: Theology, History and Culture. The conference recordings are available to purchase from our website[82].

I will show that eschatology has been used to promote a specific Luciferian agenda that has caused many Christians to abdicate responsibility for the restoration of all things in favour of a defeatist rescue mentality. The rise of dispensationalism and premillennialism, as we have seen, is associated with the Scofield Reference Bible. Christian Zionism theology arose from the same root and has been promoted by Talmudic Zionist funding.

> More than any other factor, it is Scofield's notes that have induced generations of American evangelicals to believe that God demands their uncritical support for the modern State of Israel. – Maidhc O Cathail[83].

A name that crops up regularly when researching the Scofield Bible and Talmudic Zionist influence in the political arena is

---

[82] *The Restoration of All Things 3 – Ascending Higher*, online conference recordings with Mike Parsons, Nancy Coen, Lindy Strong and Jonathan Cavan, 22 sessions. Visit eg.freedomarc.org/course/the-restoration-of-all-things-3-2021
[83] Maidhc O Cathail, in *The Scofield Bible – The Book That Made Zionists of America's Evangelical Christians,* Washington Report on Middle East Affairs https://wrmea.org, September 24, 2015.

Samuel Untermeyer or Untermyer (various sources spell his name differently). In *Unjust War Theory: Christian Zionism and the Road to Jerusalem*, Prof. David W. Lutz writes[84],

> Untermeyer used Scofield, a Kansas City lawyer with no formal training in theology, to inject Zionist ideas into American Protestantism. Untermeyer and other wealthy and influential Zionists whom he introduced to Scofield promoted and funded the latter's career, including travel in Europe.
>
> On one of these European trips, Oxford University Press publisher Henry Frowde "expressed immediate interest" in Scofield's project. According to a biography of Frowde, although the OUP publisher was "[n]ot demonstrative in his religious views, all his Christian life he was associated with brethren known as 'Exclusive.'" The "Exclusive Brethren" refers to the group of Christian evangelicals that, in an 1848 split in the Plymouth Brethren, followed John Nelson Darby, the Anglo-Irish missionary generally considered to have been the most influential figure in the development of Christian Zionism, and a major influence on Scofield. – Maidhc O Cathail[85].

Untermeyer was appointed by President Wilson to serve on the US section of the 1916 International High Commission, which convened in Buenos Aires to frame uniform laws in the Americas. After America entered World War I, he was an advisor to the US Treasury Department regarding the interpretation of the income tax and the excess profits tax laws.

---

[84] Prof David W. Lutz, *Unjust War Theory: Christian Zionism and the Road to Jerusalem*, quoted by Maidhc O Cathail *(ibid)*.
[85] Maidhc O Cathail *(ibid)*.

He later served as a delegate to the Democratic National Convention from New York in 1932 and 1936. He was also a delegate to the New York Constitutional Convention in 1938. Untermeyer also identified as a Zionist and served as president of the *Keren Hayesod*, the agency through which the movement was then, and still is, conducted in America. In 1933, he helped found the Non-Sectarian Anti-Nazi League to promote an economic boycott of Nazi Germany in the lead up to the Second World War.

There is much evidence that the Rothschild family, known to be prominent Zionists, have been involved in controlling world financial affairs. For a full timeline that shows the extent of the Rothschild involvement and interference in world political and financial affairs in support of a Zionist agenda, please see truthcontrol.com/articles/timeline-rothschild-family

Below are extracts linking the communist revolution and the Zionist agenda:

> 1897: The Rothschilds found the Zionist Congress to promote Zionism (a political movement with the sole aim of moving all Jews into a singularly Jewish nation state) and arrange its first meeting in Munich. However due to extreme opposition from local Jews, who are quite happy where they are, this meeting has to be moved to Basle, Switzerland and takes place on 29 August. The meeting is chaired by Ashkenazi Jew, Theodor Herzl, who would state in his diaries,
>
> "It is essential that the sufferings of Jews....become worse....this will assist in realization of our plans....I have an excellent idea....I shall induce anti-Semites to liquidate Jewish wealth....The anti-Semites will assist us thereby in

that they will strengthen the persecution and oppression of Jews. The anti-Semites shall be our best friends."

Herzl is subsequently elected President of the Zionist Organisation which adopts the, "Rothschild Red Hexagram or Sign," as the Zionist flag which 51 years later will end up as the flag of Israel. The early Zionists were much like many terrorist movements of today and used many acts of violence to promote their cause.

1919: In January, Ashkenazi Jews, Karl Liebknecht and Rosa Luxemburg, are killed as they attempt to lead another Rothschild funded Communist coup, this time in Berlin, Germany.

The Versailles peace conference is held to decide reparations that the Germans need to pay to the victors following the end of the first world war. A delegation of 117 Zionists headed up by Ashkenazi Jew, Bernard Baruch, bring up the subject of the promise of Palestine for them. At this point the Germans realised why America had turned on them and under whose influence, the Rothschilds.

The Germans, naturally, felt they had been betrayed by the Zionists. This is because, at the time the Rothschilds made their deal with Britain for Palestine, in exchange for bringing America into the war, Germany was the most friendly country in the world towards the Jews, indeed the German Emancipation Edict of 1822 guaranteed Jews in Germany all civil rights enjoyed by Germans.

Also, Germany was the only country in Europe which did not place restrictions on Jews, even giving them refuge when they had to flee from Russia after their first attempted Communist coup failed there in 1905...

Nevertheless, the Rothschilds had held up their side of the bargain to spill the blood of millions of innocents and as a result, Palestine is confirmed as a Jewish homeland, and whilst its handover to the Rothschilds takes place it is to remain under the control of Britain as the Rothschilds control Britain. At that time less than one percent of the population of Palestine was Jewish. Interestingly, the host of the Versailles peace conference is its boss, Baron Edmond de Rothschild.

The Versailles peace conference is also used as an attempt by the Rothschilds to set up a world government under the pretext of ending all wars (which they create). This was called the, "League of Nations." Fortunately not enough countries accepted it and so it soon died.

On March 29th The Times of London reports on the Bolsheviks in Russia,

"One of the curious features of the Bolshevist movement is the high percentage of non Russian elements among its leaders. Of the twenty or thirty commissaries, or leaders, who provide the central machinery of the Bolshevist movement, not less than 75% were Jews."

It is reported that the Rothschilds were angry with the Russians because they were not prepared to allow them to form a central bank within their nation. They therefore gathered groups of Jewish spies and sent them into Russia to drum up a revolution for the benefit of the common man, which was actually a takeover of Russia by a Rothschild controlled satanic elite.

These Jewish spies were, in age old deceptive Ashkenazi tradition, given Russian names, for example Trotsky was a member of the first group and his original name was Bronstein. These groups were sent to areas throughout Russia to incite riots and rebellion.

The Jewish Post International Edition, week ending January 24th 1991, confirms Vladimir Lenin was Jewish. Lenin is also on record as having stated,

"The establishment of a central bank is 90% of communizing a nation."

These Jewish, Rothschild funded Bolsheviks would go on in the course of history to slaughter 60 million Christians and Non-Jews in Soviet controlled territory. Indeed the author Aleksandr Solzhenitsyn in his work, "Gulag Archipelago, Vol 2," affirms that Zionist Jews created and administered the organized Soviet concentration camp system in which these tens of millions of Christians and Non-Jews died.

On page 79 of this book he even names the administrators of this the greatest killing machine in the history of the world. They are Aron Solts, Yakov Rappoport, Lazar Kogan, Matvei Berman, Genrikh Yagoda, and Naftaly Frenkel. All six are Zionist Jews. In 1970 Solzhenitsyn would be awarded the Nobel Peace Prize for literature. 'N. M. Rothschild & Sons' are given a permanent role to fix the world's daily gold price. This takes place in the City of London offices, daily at 1100 hours, in the same room until 2004.

Below is an extract from a booklet[86] that highlights the role of eschatology in preparing for the Talmudic Zionist Luciferian agenda.

THE GREATEST HOAX

A STUDY OF THE INCONSISTENT THEOLOGY OF MODERN-DAY BIBLE PROPHECY

by Charlie Samples

This book was written for essentially two reasons. To expose the erroneous teachings of the modern-day churches regarding the second coming of Christ, and to prove that the "churches" in America have been teaching and propagating the doctrine of the New World Order for over 100 years.

Jonathan Williams recorded in his book, LEGIONS OF SATAN, in 1781, THAT Cornwallis revealed to Washington that a

"holy war will now begin on America, and when it is ended America will supposedly be the citadel of freedom, but her millions will unknowingly be the loyal subjects of the Crown."

Cornwallis went on to explain that what would seem to be a seem to be a contradiction:

"Your churches will be used to teach the Jews' religion and in less than two hundred years the whole nation will be working for divine world government. That government that they believe to be divine will be the British Empire.

---

[86] Extract from a booklet by Charlie Samples, quoted on sweetliberty.org/issues/hoax/greatesthoax.htm

All religions will be permeated with Judaism without even being noticed by the masses, and they will all be under the invisible all-seeing eye of the Grand Architect of Freemasonry."

And indeed George Washington himself was a Mason, and he gave back through a false religion what he had won with his army.

This divine world government that Cornwallis spoke of, was the religion of the New World Order. The religions of America deceive their followers into believing that there will be a one-world government and it will be the fulfilment of bible prophecy. They say, however, that Jesus Christ will be the ruler.

You must read this book to see that this simply is not true and that it is the religion of the New World Order that is preparing this world for a ONE WORLD GOVERNMENT of enslavement and despotism for the entire world.

In writing this chapter, the research to uncover the facts showed that much of the evidence is shrouded with mystery and conspiracy which so veil the truth that it is impossible to verify every fact. The origins of documents that prove or disprove a particular theory are widely available online and there are YouTube videos that will support or debunk certain conspiracy theories around the great deception. Many videos and articles are removed from YouTube and Facebook because they fall foul of so-called community guidelines. Our ministry had several mentoring videos banned by YouTube because the discussion included questions about Covid-19 or the vaccine, even though I challenged the conspiracies surrounding those subjects myself in my response to the questions.

There is a mixture of truth, theories and conjecture in most videos and articles that talk about the great deception, particularly concerning the agenda of Talmudic Zionism, which makes it very difficult to prove anything one way or the other. The same can be said over the issue of global cabals and secret societies and the Khazarian ancestry of the leading proponents of Talmudic Zionism. There are many Christian authors writing articles and producing videos concerning the subjects and making claims that are impossible to prove either way.

Most of these articles and videos fall foul of the ADL and are banned for being anti-Semitic or holocaust deniers – and some of them undoubtedly are – but most also contain truth or elements of truth that are automatically dismissed as lies or conspiracies and rejected by most people as being part of the lunatic fringe.

Another example of this is the highly controversial Protocol of the Elders of Zion, a document that purports to contain facts about the plan for a Zionist Freemasonry one-world government. The document itself has been debunked as a hoax, as the Encyclopaedia Britannica states:

> Protocols of the Elders of Zion, also called Protocols of the Learned Elders of Zion, fraudulent document that served as a pretext and rationale for anti-Semitism mainly in the early 20th century. The document purported to be a report of a series of 24 (in other versions, 27) meetings held at Basel, Switzerland, in 1897, at the time of the first Zionist congress. There Jews and Freemasons were said to have made plans to disrupt Christian civilization and erect a world state under their joint rule. Liberalism and socialism were to be the means of subverting Christendom; if

subversion failed, all the capitals of Europe were to be sabotaged.

The Protocols were printed in Russia in abbreviated form in 1903 in the newspaper Znamia ("Banner") and subsequently (1905) as an addendum to a religious tract by Serge Nilus, a tsarist civil servant. They were translated into German, French, English, and other European languages and soon came to be a classic of anti-Semitic literature. In the United States Henry Ford's private newspaper, Dearborn Independent often cited them as evidence of a Jewish threat.

Subsequent investigation, particularly by the Russian historian Vladimir Burtsev, revealed that the Protocols were forgeries compounded by officials of the Russian secret police out of the satire of Joly, a fantastic novel (Biarritz) by Hermann Goedsche (1868), and other sources. – Britannica.

There is a 12-hour long video only available on the Bitchute platform called EUROPA: THE LAST BATTLE[87]. This has white supremacist undertones but also has a wealth of information and facts drawn from many sources that should not be dismissed out of hand. That information points to the hoodwinking of history that hides the involvement of Talmudic Zionists who, through financial and media control, manipulated the events leading up to the establishing of the nation-state of Israel. I do not condone how white supremacists use such information to promote their foul cause but that does not make all the information false. Great discernment is needed when looking at or watching such

---

[87] EUROPA: THE LAST BATTLE, 12-hour video
https://www.bitchute.com/video/YDyz9eZKkSQv/

material and that is where we need the Spirit of Truth to help us chew the grapes and spit out the pips. When reflecting on the content there is a very fine line between exposing the agenda to undermine the godly values which form the basis of the western worldview and promoting white supremacy, which is of course abhorrent.

This video may no longer be available by the time this book is published and it is very long and tortuous but I cannot dismiss it all as mere conspiracy. The Luciferian agenda runs right through it and it does confirm many things with copious newspaper articles and quotes that the Father has spoken to me directly about.

Another such article is *The KHAZARIAN MAFIA: You Don't Know, What You Don't Know! The Hidden History of the Incredibly Evil Khazarian Mafia*, by Preston James, PhD[88].

The author is found on the VT or Veterans Today website which is on the surface just another conspiracy website. It offers a wide variety of popular conspiracies, but is there any truth to be found hidden within the veils of conspiracy? Even if there is, should we bother to waste our time trying to find it? For most people, I would answer "no", Jesus as the Truth is sufficient – but if you have a mandate to write a book about the Luciferian agenda then these things resonate with some truth among the smoke and mirrors.

Whenever the subject of the Khazarian origins of the Rothschilds or Ashkenazis is raised, it is usually debunked by so-called genetic experts who say there is no evidence that

---

[88] Preston James, PhD. - *The KHAZARIAN MAFIA: You Don't Know, What You Don't Know! The Hidden History of the Incredibly Evil Khazarian Mafia*. http://themillenniumreport.com/2018/06/the-khazarian-mafia-you-dont-know-what-you-dont-know

most Ashkenazis originate from the Caucasus. They usually quote some genetic study or other to back up their claims and that then casts doubt on the legitimacy of all the other information.

Seeking whether there is any evidence of Khazarian origin, I found a very good recent study published by the reputable scientific journal *Genome Biology and Evolution* (GBE)[89] which came to the following conclusion:

We compared two genetic models for European Jewish ancestry depicting a mixed Khazarian-European-Middle Eastern and sole Middle Eastern origins. Contemporary populations were used as surrogates to the ancient Khazars and Judeans, and their relatedness to European Jews was compared over a comprehensive set of genetic analyses. Our findings support the Khazarian hypothesis depicting a large Near Eastern-Caucasus ancestry along with Southern European, Middle Eastern, and Eastern European ancestries, in agreement with recent studies and oral and written traditions. We conclude that the genome of European Jews is a tapestry of ancient populations including Judaized Khazars, Greco-Roman Jews, Mesopotamian Jews, and Judeans and that their population structure was formed in the Caucasus and the banks of the Volga with roots stretching to Canaan and the banks of the Jordan.

I am giving you all this information so that you can make up your own mind. My mind was made up when the Father kept speaking to me about exposing the great deception and its link

---

[89] Eran Elhaik, *The Missing Link of Jewish European Ancestry: Contrasting the Rhineland and the Khazarian Hypotheses*, in *Genome Biology and Evolution*, Volume 5, Issue 1, January 2013, pp 61–74: https://doi.org/10.1093/gbe/evs119

to eschatology. Please, please, please be discerning: do not just accept everything as being true or reject everything as lies. Find the frequency of truth by hanging out in the light of truth and use that frequency to discern.

I believe that there has been a Talmudic Zionist agenda that is associated with global cabals which opposes the government of God and promotes the Luciferian values of independence that are behind all religious and political systems. Therefore as I chart the influence of such groups in history and their goal of using a re-formed state of Israel to lure followers of both Judaism and Christianity into accepting a Messiah figure who would rule in Jerusalem, I do so knowing that this cannot be proved categorically. Nevertheless I believe it to be true and consistent with the other evidence I used in writing this book.

This weaves together various threads such as the Babylonian Talmud, Reformation, Expelled European Jews, English Civil War, slave trade, Freemasonry, Illuminati, Zionism, Russian Revolution, Communism, Protocol of the Elders of Zion, Scofield Bible, Samuel Untermeyer, Federal Reserve act 1913, WW1, Balfour Declaration, Treaty of Versailles, Interwar Germany (banking), Jews declare trade war on Germany, Banking in Germany, Rothschilds imprisoned, Attack on Christian values, Frankfurt school, Churchill, Roosevelt, De Gaulle, 6,000,000 number in history, Media and Big Tech, Facebook, Google, Amazon, YouTube, Wikipedia, internet, ADL, big tech censorship, Covenant of Brotherhood, Mary Fagan, Geopolitics, Debt-based capitalism, usury, Noahide laws, World economic forum, Bilderberg, The Bohemian Grove etc. etc.

Many of these threads are highly controversial and steeped in conspiracy but that does not mean that there is no truth within it all.

I was never really interested in conspiracies but undoubtedly I will be labelled a conspiracy theorist for writing this book and particularly this chapter. ("Just because you're paranoid doesn't mean they aren't after you." – Joseph Heller, Catch-22.)

Here is the story that is behind many of the so-called conspiracies that control the narrative and therefore the beliefs of most people, at least in the western world.

Talmudic Zionists control most of the world's financial institutions and media. They have used that money in modern history to influence world governments politically to support a Zionist state; but more importantly, to create an environment where one-world government becomes more likely to be accepted.

Those in financial control thrive on conflict, making their money out of war and using their influence to bring about political instability (often by funding both sides of the conflicts). Such conflicts are the seedbed for political change. This political instability is often taken advantage of by those who control the usury debt to influence political decision-making as the countries or regimes are in debt to them, often for decades. Playing both sides against each other is the way money is made and influence is maintained. Allegiance to political ideology is rejected in favour of supporting both wings of the political bird. Supporting capitalism and funding communism keeps the coffers full and ensures continual conflict. The threat to Western Europe of Bolshevik communism and its perceived Jewish support was significant, along with the suppression of Germany by economic means through the Treaty of Versailles, in the rise of Hitler's National Socialist party in Germany.

Zionist Lord Rothschild promised to use his influence to help get America into WWI, which was against the election pledge of Woodrow Wilson, in exchange for Britain's support for a Jewish homeland. Why did Woodrow Wilson (who had run on peace, after all, winning re-election in November 1916 on the slogan "He kept us out of war") suddenly change his stance? The incidents of the sinking of US ships including the Lusitania were used by Zionist influencers who had heavily funded the Democratic Party for the election. The law firm of Guggenheim, Untermeyer and Marshall represented the major bank Kuhn Loeb; its head was Jacob Schiff, an agent for Walter Rothschild (who made large contributions to Wilson's re-election campaign).

Samuel Untermeyer, who was responsible for funding the production of the Scofield Bible, also helped establish the Federal Reserve Act in 1913 and used his influence with Wilson to get America into WWI. Later, he declared economic war on Germany in 1933 on behalf of the World Jewish Economic Federation, which brought a worldwide boycott of German goods and paved the way for WWII.

Woodrow Wilson's advisors before and during the conference that led to the Treaty of Versailles (from which Germany itself was excluded) were Stephen Wise and Bernard Baruch, both Zionists. Advisor to the British government was Philip Sassoon and to the French Government was Georges Mandal (also known as Louis Rothschild), who were also Zionists. Also present was the head of the Federal Reserve, Paul Warburg. The resulting treaty crippled Germany economically, stripped it of 13% of its landmass (some of that to Poland, including the Danzig Corridor) and imposed crippling reparations which were not finally paid off until 3rd October 2010. The Treaty of Versailles and its enforced treatment of Germany and the failed communist revolution of 1918 were both stepping stones to the rise of National Socialism and eventually war and the sacrifice of innocent Jews for the Zionist cause.

This letter to Lord Rothschild, by the British Foreign Secretary Arthur James Balfour, was aimed at Jewish support for the Allies in the First World War. The letter, known as the 'Balfour Declaration' became the basis of the movement to create a Jewish state in Palestine. The letter was published a week later in *The Times* newspaper:

Foreign Office November 2nd, 1917.

Dear Lord Rothschild: I have much pleasure in conveying to you. on behalf of His Majesty's Government, the following declaration of sympathy with Jewish Zionist aspirations which has been submitted to, and approved by, the Cabinet: His Majesty's Government view with favour the establishment in Palestine of a national home for the Jewish people, and will use their best endeavours to facilitate the achievement of this object, it being clearly understood that nothing shall be done which may prejudice the civil and religious rights of existing non-Jewish communities in Palestine, or the rights and political status enjoyed by Jews in any other country. I should be grateful if you would bring this declaration to the knowledge of the Zionist Federation.

Yours, Arthur James Balfour

In 1918 there was a communist revolution in Germany, which was defeated but led to the establishment of the Weimar Republic government. The carefully funded and orchestrated fight against communism by Germany was the catalyst for the Second World War in which Churchill, Roosevelt and Stalin eventually divided Germany and carved up Europe, creating an environment for the establishing of the Warsaw Pact. The political deals done created the next conflict, the Cold War. Germany's offers of peace were continually rejected by Churchill and the war succeeded in its goal of generating sympathy for the Zionist cause of a Jewish homeland by sacrificing millions of innocent people. This was not coincidental but the fruit of a carefully orchestrated plan that has continued to offer support of the Zionist cause for the last 75 years.

You can read the full history of the political process that produced the nation-state of Israel in the article *The Road to Balfour: The History of Christian Zionism* by Stephen Sizer[90].

Subliminal programming over decades created sympathy for the Zionist agenda.

The number 'six million' is originally an esoteric Kabbalistic mystical number from the Zohar, based on the Gematria system. It represented the number of people who would need to be sacrificed for the atonement of their sins before God. The word 'holocaust' – derived from Late Latin *holocaustum* and Greek *holokauston*: *holo-* (whole) + *kaustos* (burnt) – was

---

[90] Lecture by Stephen Sizer, *The Road to Balfour: The History of Christian Zionism*, Edinburgh, 2nd November 2012: https://balfourproject.org/the-road-to-balfour-the-history-of-christian-zionism-by-stephen-sizer-2/

originally coined to refer to a burnt offering in the Jewish sacrificial system[91].

Some esoteric Rabbis have interpreted the phrase 'you shall return' in Leviticus 25:10 in a way that promotes the idea that when they would return to the land they would return with less, or that they have to be cleansed through fire to be able to return. That expectation of suffering was sown into the Jewish psyche as a rabbinical tradition, so much so that there are rabbinical articles that question whether the holocaust was God's punishment, for example:

https://www.chabad.org/library/article_cdo/aid/404608/jewish/Was-the-Holocaust-a-Punishment.htm

It is interesting to see that the number 'six million' usually associated with the holocaust was subliminally sown into world consciousness during the 50 years in the lead up to the Second World War, with that mythical and mystical number appearing in various guises during that period. The Talmudic Zionists were willing to sacrifice millions of innocent Jews on the altar of Zionism and they manipulated both left and right of the political divide to do so. There were 270 newspaper articles in those 50 years specifically referring to 'six million'. That number associated with the holocaust has been ingrained into the culture over the subsequent 75 years, whilst the accounts of other genocides that have killed literally hundreds of millions of Christians, Ukrainians, Africans and Chinese have been lost. Why? Because that number is integral

---

[91] holocaust. (n.d.) *Collins English Dictionary – Complete and Unabridged, 12th Edition 2014*. (1991, 1994, 1998, 2000, 2003, 2006, 2007, 2009, 2011, 2014). Retrieved from https://www.thefreedictionary.com/holocaust January 25 2022.

in the strategy that keeps Zionist sympathy and anti-Semitism in the political awareness.

In 1900 American Zionist leader Rabbi Stephen Wise let slip what the agenda was behind the eventual holocaust in a New York Times article on June 11th 1900 when he said:

"There are 6,000,000 living, bleeding, suffering arguments in favour of Zionism."

There are many references to the number 'six million' in print in encyclopaedia, newspaper articles and other sources collated below:

> 1902 Encyclopaedia Britannica article on anti-Semitism references six million Jews of Rumania and Russia being systematically degraded.
>
> 1902 New York Times mentions 6,000,000 Jewish families to be expelled from Russia.
>
> 1905 New York Times article the End of Zionism Maybe where a Jewish preacher talks of 6,000,000 Jews
>
> 1906 The New York Times reported Dr Paul Nathan's View of the Russian Massacre. A Jewish publicist addressed an audience in Germany where he claimed the Russian Government had a 'solution of the Jewish Question' and that solution is the 'murderous extermination of 6,000,000 Jews'.
>
> 1910 In the American Jewish Committee's annual report it claimed that since 1890 Russia had a policy to 'expel or exterminate' six million Jews (Source: American Jewish Yearbook 5672, p 15).

1911 Max Nordau, co-founder of the World Zionist Organization together with Theodore Herzl, made an astonishing pronouncement at the tenth Zionist Congress in Basle Switzerland. He claimed that 6,000,000 Jews would be annihilated – and that was 22 years before Hitler would even come to power.

1914 New York Times, 2nd December, 'Appeal For Aid For Jews' for the 6,000,000 Jews who were living in the war zone.

1915 New York Times, 14th January, mentions 6,000,000 Jewish people living in the very heart of the war.

1918 New York Times, 18th October: 'Six Million Souls Will Need Help to Resume Normal Life When the War is Ended.'

1919 San Francisco Chronicle: 'Elder of Zion Nathan Straus claims 6,000,000 Jews in peril in Ukraine.'

1920 A Jewish Relief campaign states "Today 6,000,000 Jews are facing the darkest days ever known in the history of the race."

1921 Chicago Tribune, 19th July, "Russia's 6,000,000 Jews are facing extermination."

1931 Montreal, 20th December, "Six Million Jews face starvation in South-Eastern Europe."

1940, Dr Hahum Goldman, founder and long-time president of the World Jewish Congress, predicted that 6,000,000 Jews in Europe are doomed to destruction.

I could go on, as there are numerous other examples of this number being used to program the world to be receptive to the Zionist agenda. I am not saying the holocaust did not occur or should not be remembered but that there has always been a deeper hidden agenda behind it.

Why is this important? It goes to show that it was the Talmudic Zionists themselves who were behind the strategy and were funding all the conflicts that led up to the establishing of the nation-state of Israel. Their agenda was and is not religious but political and behind the politics is the Luciferian agenda for one-world government. That agenda has used Israel and the Middle East conflict to further its ends.

The original Zionists were the terrorists of their day and that militancy has been at the heart of Israeli politics ever since.

David Ben-Gurion, the first Prime Minister of Israel, said in a letter to the Zionist executive on December 17th, 1938: "The saving of Jewish lives from Hitler is considered here as a potential threat to Zionism unless they are brought to Palestine." When Zionism had to choose between the Jewish people and the Jewish state, it unhesitatingly preferred the latter.

David Ben-Gurion also ranked the goals of Zionism and a fascist state far above the lives and happiness of Jewish children, saying[92]: "If I knew that it was possible to save all the children of Germany by transporting them to England, and only half by transferring them to the Land of Israel, I would choose the latter, for before us lies not only the numbers of these children but the historical reckoning of the people of Israel."

---

[92] Attributed to Ben-Gurion (pre-War 1939) by Martin Gilbert in "Israel was everything" in The New York Times (21 June 1987):
http://query.nytimes.com/gst/fullpage.html?res=9B0DE2DB1539F932A15755C0A961948260&pagewanted=2

Former Israeli Prime Minister, Yitzhak Rabin, said in an uncensored version of his memoirs, published in The New York Times on October 23rd 1979: "We walked outside, Ben-Gurion accompanying us. Alton repeated his question – 'What is to be done with the Palestinian population?' Ben-Gurion waved his hand in a gesture which said 'Drive them out!' And that's what they did.

'Palestine' was the region we now call Israel, Jordan, the West Bank and Gaza Strip, the lands formerly belonging to the Turkish Ottoman Empire. The Arabs were eventually evicted from their own land by Zionist terrorist groups like Hagana, Irgun and the Stern Gang (also known as Lehi), who bombed and assassinated Arabs, fellow Jews and the British administrators who governed Palestine under a mandate from the League of Nations and the Versailles Peace Conference.

It was Zionist terrorism which led to the imposition of the Jewish state in 1948, when at least 750,000 Arab people were expelled from their land. Among the leaders of the Zionist terror groups were Menachem Begin, Yitzhak Shamir and Ariel Sharon. These Zionist terrorists would become Israeli prime ministers and eventually condemn Arab terrorism.

The Stern Gang was named by the British after its first commander, Avraham Stern, who later formed his own group, Irgun Zvai Leumi be-Yisrael (National Military Organization in Israel). Irgun, led by later Prime Minister, Menachem Begin, was responsible for the bombing of the British headquarters at the King David Hotel in Jerusalem in 1946. It killed 91 Britons, Arabs and Jews, injuring many more, and this was only one of a stream of terrorist outrages and assassinations that ended in the creation of Israel.

Zionist quotes

The majority of these racist quotes by Israeli prime ministers, presidents and other prominent Israeli leaders are well-documented and have appeared in leading Israeli newspapers, in books written by Jewish historians that were published by Israeli and other reputable book publishers, and in dairies kept by the leaders themselves which are now housed in the Zionist Archives in Jerusalem[93].

The ADL and accusations of anti-Semitism make sure that anyone who questions or challenges Israeli political strategies is labelled racist. Yet these Zionist statements are apparently acceptable! I find them highly offensive so I have only used 4 here: the rest (should you want to read them) are in the appendices.

"The Palestinians are like crocodiles." – Prime Minister Ehud Barak, Jerusalem Post, August 30, 2000

"They are beasts walking on two legs." – Prime Minister Menachem Begin, in a speech to the Knesset, New Statesman, June 25, 1982

"One million Arabs are not worth a Jewish fingernail." – Rabbi Yaacov Perrin, New York Times, Feb. 28, 1994, p. 1

"It is forbidden to have pity on them. We must give them missiles with relish, annihilate them. Evil ones, damnable ones." – Rabbi Ovadia Yosef, Ha'aretz, April 12, 2001.

The Nazis considered themselves as a race to be superior to the Jews. To the racist Nazis, the Jews were not really human. It is obvious from the quotes by prominent Zionists that they

---

[93] Zionist quotes: full internet article
http://www.thehypertexts.com/Zionist%20Quotes.htm

believe the same thing about Palestinians. There are those who call themselves white supremacists from many nations who consider themselves superior to those with darker skin. Racism is totally inconsistent with the fact that we are all God's children and the division, discrimination and prejudice of people, whatever its basis, is totally antithetic to the character and nature of a loving God.

If the nations of the world treated Jewish people the same way Israel treats Palestinian people there would be a justifiable outcry. Yet whenever anyone questions the right of Israel to treat Palestinians badly by denying employment, buying their property at fire-sale prices and trying to deport them to other countries, they are called anti-Semitic by Zionist and Christian Zionist sympathisers.

We once had a speaker in a local church in our town giving a message about Zionism. He was from a Messianic congregation based in Jerusalem. I did some online research investigating the website of that congregation and I was appalled by the transcripts I read of their prayer meetings which recorded them openly praying to God asking Him to destroy the Palestinian people.

This attitude is why Israel is constantly in conflict with its Arab or Muslim neighbours. Arabs do not just irrationally hate Jews, as Zionists would have you believe. Whilst I do not condone the hatred, there is a reason why Arabs hate Israeli Jews: it is because of how they have treated their Palestinian brothers and sisters, who have consistently been victims of racism, apartheid and ethnic cleansing since 1948.

There are many past Zionist leaders who seem to have openly advocated the ethnic cleansing of the Palestinian people. In 1948, as one of its first governmental acts Israel created a

Transfer Committee to supervise the ethnic cleansing of Palestinians. The director of the Transfer Committee was Yosef (Joseph) Weitz, who in his diary recorded the following[94]:

> "It is our right to transfer the Palestinians".

> "We must work out a secret plan based on the removal of the Arabs ... [and] include it in American political circles."

There are further quotes from Weitz in the appendix.

Zionist Ze'ev Jabotinsky[95] (one of the spiritual fathers of the Likud, and of the future Israeli Prime Ministers Menachem Begin and Bibi Netanyahu) also wrote of the solution. An article in the *Village Voice*, 2001:

> "...the "sole way" for Jews to deal with Arabs in Palestine was through "total avoidance of all attempts to arrive at a settlement," which Jabotinsky euphemistically termed the "Iron Wall" approach. Not coincidentally, a picture of Jabotinsky graced Prime Minister Ariel Sharon's desk.

Here is what Jabotinsky said about the Iron Wall himself[96]:

> "The Islamic soul must be broomed out of Eretz-Yisrael."

Further racist quotes from Jabotinsky and other Zionist political figures can be found in the appendices.

Of course, there have been dissenters, Jews and others, who have seen through the Zionist agenda. One example is Albert

---

[94] Yosef Weitz' published diary in five volumes, located in the Zionist Archives in Jerusalem.
[95] Ze'ev Jabotinsky, *Death Wish in the Holy Land*, The Village Voice, 12 December 2001.
[96] Ze'ev Jabotinsky, the spiritual father of the Likud [One Palestine Complete, p. 151].

Einstein's 1948 letter to the New York Times. In this landmark letter, Albert Einstein and 27 other leading Jewish intellectuals, including Hannah Arendt and Sidney Hook, explained to Americans and the larger world that militant Zionist leaders like Menachem Begin (a future prime minister of Israel) were racists, fascists, terrorists and religious fanatics.

TO THE EDITORS OF THE NEW YORK TIMES:

Among the most disturbing political phenomena of our times is the emergence in the newly created state of Israel of the "Freedom Party" (Tnuat Haherut), a political party closely akin in its organization, methods, political philosophy and social appeal to the Nazi and Fascist parties. It was formed out of the membership and following of the former Irgun Zvai Leumi, a terrorist, right-wing, chauvinist organization in Palestine.

The current visit of Menachem Begin, leader of this party, to the United States is obviously calculated to give the impression of American support for his party in the coming Israeli elections, and to cement political ties with conservative Zionist elements in the United States. Several Americans of national repute have lent their names to welcome his visit. It is inconceivable that those who oppose fascism throughout the world, if correctly informed as to Mr. Begin's political record and perspectives, could add their names and support to the movement he represents.

Before irreparable damage is done by way of financial contributions, public manifestations in Begin's behalf, and the creation in Palestine of the impression that a large segment of America supports Fascist elements in Israel, the American public must be informed as to the record and objectives of Mr. Begin and his movement.

The public avowals of Begin's party are no guide whatever to its actual character. Today they speak of freedom, democracy and anti-imperialism, whereas until recently they openly preached the doctrine of the Fascist state. It is in its actions that the terrorist party betrays its real character; from its past actions we can judge what it may be expected to do in the future.

Attack on Arab Village

A shocking example was their behavior in the Arab village of Deir Yassin. This village, off the main roads and surrounded by Jewish lands, had taken no part in the war, and had even fought off Arab bands who wanted to use the village as their base. On April 9 (THE NEW YORK TIMES), terrorist bands attacked this peaceful village, which was not a military objective in the fighting, killed most of its inhabitants "240 men, women, and children" and kept a few of them alive to parade as captives through the streets of Jerusalem. Most of the Jewish community was horrified at the deed, and the Jewish Agency sent a telegram of apology to King Abdullah of Trans-Jordan. But the terrorists, far from being ashamed of their act, were proud of this massacre, publicized it widely, and invited all the foreign correspondents present in the country to view the heaped corpses and the general havoc at Deir Yassin.

The Deir Yassin incident exemplifies the character and actions of the Freedom Party.

Within the Jewish community they have preached an admixture of ultranationalism, religious mysticism, and racial superiority. Like other Fascist parties they have been used to break strikes, and have themselves pressed for the destruction of free trade unions. In their stead they have proposed corporate unions on the Italian Fascist model.

During the last years of sporadic anti-British violence, the IZL and Stern groups inaugurated a reign of terror in the Palestine Jewish community. Teachers were beaten up for speaking against them, adults were shot for not letting their children join them. By gangster methods, beatings, window-smashing, and wide-spread robberies, the terrorists intimidated the population and exacted a heavy tribute.

The people of the Freedom Party have had no part in the constructive achievements in Palestine. They have reclaimed no land, built no settlements, and only detracted from the Jewish defense activity. Their much-publicized immigration endeavors were minute, and devoted mainly to bringing in Fascist compatriots.

Discrepancies Seen

The discrepancies between the bold claims now being made by Begin and his party, and their record of past performance in Palestine bear the imprint of no ordinary political party. This is the unmistakable stamp of a Fascist party for whom terrorism (against Jews, Arabs, and British alike), and misrepresentation are means, and a "Leader State" is the goal.

In the light of the foregoing considerations, it is imperative that the truth about Mr. Begin and his movement be made known in this country. It is all the more tragic that the top leadership of American Zionism has refused to campaign against Begin's efforts, or even to expose to its own constituents the dangers to Israel from support to Begin.

The undersigned therefore take this means of publicly presenting a few salient facts concerning Begin and his party; and of urging all concerned not to support this latest manifestation of fascism.

(signed) ISIDORE ABRAMOWITZ, HANNAH ARENDT, ABRAHAM BRICK, RABBI JESSURUN CARDOZO, ALBERT EINSTEIN, HERMAN EISEN, M.D., HAYIM FINEMAN, M. GALLEN, M.D., H.H. HARRIS, ZELIG S. HARRIS, SIDNEY HOOK, FRED KARUSH, BRURIA KAUFMAN, IRMA L. LINDHEIM, NACHMAN MAISEL, SYMOUR MELMAN, MYER D. MENDELSON, M.D., HARRY M. ORLINSKY, SAMUEL PITLICK, FRITZ ROHRLICH, LOUIS P. ROCKER, RUTH SAGER, ITZHAK SANKOWSKY, I.J. SCHOENBERG, SAMUEL SHUMAN, M. ZNGER, IRMA WOLPE, STEFAN WOLPE.

New York, Dec. 2, 1948

... Other prominent, world-esteemed Jews have also strongly opposed the policies and methods of the militant Zionists, including Sigmund Freud, Franz Kafka, Isaac Asimov, Erich Fromm and Noam Chomsky. They have been joined by icons of peace like Mohandas Gandhi, Nelson Mandela, Desmond Tutu and Jimmy Carter.
– Michael R. Burch[97].

---

[97] *Albert Einstein's 1948 letter to the New York Times*, online article by Michael R. Burch, an editor and publisher of Holocaust and Nakba poetry. http://www.thehypertexts.com/Albert%20Einstein%201948%20Letter%20N ew%20York%20Times%20Nakba.htm

The religious spirit's defence of such racist politics is clear: that Israel and the Jews are God's people and God will commit genocide to protect His people.

History has been written to obscure the truth concerning these facts which show a clear Luciferian agenda behind the establishment of the state of Israel. That religious and political Zionist agenda is that a human Messiah would give the kingdom back to Israel. Many Christians have been deceived into believing that that agenda is preparing for the return of Jesus as the heavenly Messiah to rule for a thousand years on earth from Jerusalem with a rod of iron.

The World Wars and the creation of Israel were never an end in themselves, only and always means to an end. The plan has been to target the Islamic world to trigger a global war that would lead to the 'solution' of centralised control of the planet and all of its peoples. To do that, the Zionist elite need to create a point of conflict, a powder keg, among the Arab countries, that could be exploded to start another global war. This is the real reason for the creation of Israel and the real reason why the Zionist-funded United States has spent billions building up Israel's might and military. People like John Hagee promote this war as 'Armageddon' because in their eschatological ideology that will bring the return of Jesus.

The goal of Talmudic Zionism is an empire and world conquest that the Talmud alludes to as a master race ruling the subhuman *goyim*.

The great deception is seeking to condition the world to accept a one-world government that promises peace. The agenda of division, competition, conflict and tribalism has paved the way politically to create an environment that now exists. I do not of course believe that this will be the end result but it is up to us as the sons of God to expose such deception and expand the kingdom of God like leaven to fill the world.

The kingdom of God is a kingdom of love, not war; and Jesus is the Prince of Peace, not of war: that makes 'spiritual warfare' an oxymoronic statement. The government of God, His kingdom, will be on earth as it is in heaven and will continually advance in peace.

Let the sons of God arise and let His enemies be restored to become His footstool, a place of worship.

The Global Love Awakening

"Son, brood within the Cradle of Life as you bask in the truth of the light of perfection."

The glorious light from the Father's face inspired my thoughts and the light of truth filled my being so I knew that I knew. Shifting my focus to the Cradle of Life, I engaged the heart of God; completely at rest, yet moved and motivated by the desire that the truth had created in me. I began to vibrate and resonate with such love, passion and compassion that I became alive, energised with creative potential. My being was focused on just one all-encompassing thought that I was so pregnant with expectation that I thought I might explode. My whole being was consumed with anticipation for the great love awakening that will change the whole of creation.

The frequency of that momentous thought became transformed into the living word of the sound of many waters and my destiny. That amplified voice began to resound with creative intention, so much so that this reality was already in creative existence when I engaged with the Chamber of Creation. The living light began to dance with excitation and the energy increased to such an extent that I felt as if it already was, such was its creative force. As the quantum moment of creation expanded before me, I saw the glorious living light, the building blocks of all reality, stream from the portal to form that reality. That creative moment had more energy, life and light than I had ever experienced before as unconditional love is the Father's glorious obsession. An awakening to unconditional love, filled with such limitless grace that nothing will be able to stop its restorative power, but... – and there was a 'but', which in itself seemed impossible:

"There needs to be a oneness of heart, mind and purpose within the sons of God to focus Our intention into reality. Many are being side-tracked by lesser or self-created agendas.

"Son, use the governmental groups to become part of this creative force to form the reality of the great love awakening and other desires of Our heart. In the present world reality of deception and darkness, the light of love is the only thing that can awaken Our children to the truth of their present slavery to the DIY tree agenda. Focus your love towards those of Our sons who are becoming more entangled in the deceptions of conspiracies because their passions for certain issues have blinded them. Their obsessions for issues they have drawn from Our heart has made them susceptible to deception because they have created their independent mandates.

"What you have observed amongst your connections is but the tip of the iceberg and this deception runs deep. So many are so blinkered by their own obsessions that they have lost perspective and are the pawns of the very systems they want to see dismantled. Son, keep absorbing and releasing the light of love and truth into the darkness of the deceptive conspiratorial delusions so many of Our children and sons are trapped in."

10. The Revealing of the Sons of God.

These final two chapters put the previous ones into perspective and context and express the hope for the final restoration of all things that emerges shining in the midst of the darkness of the great deception of eschatological defeat, doom, gloom and destruction of the Luciferian agenda.

The revealing of the sons of God includes their maturity and these chapters contain my latest encounters, as I am writing this book during 2021. Some sections are compilations of my journal entries or restoration government group ascensions.

If we, as sons, do not have our minds deconstructed from the programming of religion and renewed so that our consciousness can be expanded then creation will remain in bondage. Sonship has many associated aspects, as I began to discover during my encounters with the Father.

Arise, shine;
For your light has come!
And the glory of the Lord is risen upon you.
For behold, the darkness shall cover the earth,
And deep darkness the people;
But the Lord will arise over you,
And His glory will be seen upon you.
The Gentiles shall come to your light,
And kings to the brightness of your rising.

"Lift up your eyes all around, and see:
They all gather together, they come to you;
Your sons shall come from afar,
And your daughters shall be nursed at your side.
Then you shall see and become radiant,
And your heart shall swell with joy;

Because the abundance of the sea shall be turned to you, The wealth of the Gentiles shall come to you. (Isaiah 60:1-5).

Sonship is the light that emerges to shine brightly in the darkness of eschatological apocalyptic fear. The eschatology of the old covenant was based upon the apocalyptical books of Daniel and Ezekiel and looked forward to the destruction of the old covenant age of Israel and the coming Messiah to establish a new kingdom age. Dispensational and premillennial rapture-based eschatology has placed the end of the age at the end of the world. Jesus clarified that the end and the new beginning was within that generation and that the fulfilment of all the covenant promises God had made to all His children were to be fulfilled in Himself.

The correct context is that the end of the old was the beginning of the new. The light of the new has already come into the darkness of the old and is progressively overcoming it. Isaiah 60 has already been fulfilled and Jesus has already returned to establish the period of the restoration of all things, which we are currently living in. This is the period that will reveal the glorious light of sonship so that all creation is set free.

Eschatologically this has already occurred. It is not a future event but an ongoing process in which the light of the sons of God in the world will transform the darkness back into the light. In one sense, the light has come and restoration is taking place; but the revealing of the glory of sonship is a process, not an event. The process of maturity that Adam and Eve, if they had not chosen independence, would have gone through to become mature creative sons is still necessary and the number of God's children who are becoming mature sons has been progressively increasing. Throughout the past two thousand years, only a mystical few embraced the intimacy necessary for such a transformation but now the revelation is being experienced by many more and will eventually become the norm.

Enlightenment and conscious awareness of love is awakening the children of God to throw off the religious and political spirit shackles to realise their identity, position and purpose as sons of God. The leaven of sonship is spreading to overcome the leaven of Herod and the Pharisees that Jesus warned about.

Isaiah 60:1-3 describes the process that we are now in: the light has come and is now being revealed through those who have arisen to take their heavenly places as sons of God. Our sonship relationship with creation is described in Romans 8 and the revealing of the glory of our sonship will bring about the freedom and restoration of all things.

For all who are being led by the Spirit of God, these are sons and daughters of God. For you have not received a spirit of slavery leading to fear again, but you have received a spirit of adoption as sons and daughters by which we cry out, "Abba! Father!" The Spirit Himself testifies with our spirit that we are children of God, and if children, heirs also, heirs of God and fellow heirs with Christ, if indeed we suffer with Him so that we may also be glorified with Him. For I consider that the sufferings of this present time are not worthy to be compared with the glory that is to be revealed to us. For the eagerly awaiting creation waits for the revealing of the sons and daughters of God. For the creation was subjected to futility, not willingly, but because of Him who subjected it, in hope that the creation itself also will be set free from its slavery to corruption into the freedom of the glory of the children of God.

For we know that the whole creation groans and suffers the pains of childbirth together until now. And not only that, but also we ourselves, having the first fruits of the Spirit, even we ourselves groan within ourselves, waiting eagerly for our adoption as sons and daughters, the redemption of our body. For in hope we have been saved, but hope that is seen is not hope; for who hopes for what he already sees? But if we hope for what we do not see, through perseverance we wait eagerly for it. (Romans 8:14-25).

In 2018 I presented a six-part intensive conference series that reflected my journey to sonship, with the title *Sons Arise!*[98] The conferences were designed to progressively reveal the nature and purpose of sonship, each building upon the experiences of the previous. The six events were titled:

- Engaging the Father
- Engaging the Dark Cloud
- Sons Invested and Enthroned
- Living in Dual Realms
- On Earth as in Heaven
- Expanding Our Reality

This describes my journey to sonship and the subsequent three *Restoration of All Things* conferences[99] have put that journey into context. That context is being outworked through restoration government groups who are participating in the earth shield and actively legislating for the restoration of all things. The understanding of the scope of that restoration has been the theme of the conferences: to go deeper and higher and to include all dimensional realities.

---

[98] For details of *Sons Arise!* recordings, visit eg.freedomarc.org/sons-arise
[99] For details of all *The Restoration of All Things* events recordings and the book of the same name, visit eg.freedomarc.org/roat

The *Engaging God* programme[100] has modules on preparing for sonship and the government of sonship and two modules on the restoration of all things; that reflects the importance these subjects have to fulfilling our destinies as mature sons of God.

Since 2018, my personal experiences of sonship have revealed the connection between sonship and the restoration of all things both legislatively and creatively. I have learnt to be at rest in love, joy and peace: living loved, loving living and living loving; in unconditional love, limitless grace and triumphant mercy. The sons of God are truly arising and their light is dispelling the darkness and removing the eschatological fear of future tribulation and the end of the world.

The awakening to love that is taking place throughout the cosmos is beginning to accelerate the process of the restoration of all things as more of the sons of God are beginning to participate actively in restoring creation. The expansion that love brings is moving the sons beyond the earth into spiritual heavenly realms, the cosmos and the dimensions; actively participating in the restoration of fallen dimensional and cosmic beings and the sentient creation itself. As the sons of God have awakened to their identity and responsibility towards creation, their participation in the councils and assemblies of heaven has led to the establishing of light shields around the creational spheres to facilitate the restoration of all things agenda.

The coheirship and co-creating roles of sonship have been revealed to enable us, as oracles of God, to begin to choose

---

[100] *Engaging God* is an online subscription programme created by Mike Parsons. For more information, visit eg.freedomarc.org/subscribe-to-engaging-god

the realities to which quantum light responds creatively. Quantum wave functions collapse to form reality when we, as sons, speak as the voice of God.

I will share those recent encounters to conclude this book on an optimistic note, filled with the joyous expectation of the final and complete restoration of all things.

This journal entry gives some context to the process of maturing in sonship:

13th September 2021

"Son, activate your Merkabah and engage multidimensional reality to draw your energy – and give your energy – from and to the whole of creation. As you have learned to be at rest and oneness you can now live in the light of love and truth and be in communion with all things. You can go beyond physical communion and be in communion with *I am that I am* within all things as you abide. Your whole being is connected in the sacred communion of life, giving and taking in balance and harmony with life itself.

"No longer do you have to do things or not do things: you can just be at rest and in oneness with all things, as you have now learned to go beyond the doing into the being. This is the state of enlightenment and consciousness that all Our children were made to live in continually and continuously. This is the state of being where you are in fellowship with all things at a quantum level of being: living light, living love.

"This is the glory of sonship that all creation is waiting for to become what it was intended to be in the beginning, in the freedom of sonship and fellowship and communion of oneness; living in the pure love, joy and peace of perfection reality in oneness, where there is no separation between all things to the level of no division of doing and being, as all just is.

"Love is the only reality that is used for living and all values are measured by love. There is no law-based morality of rules, regulations and behavioural norms, just love. Law and rules only came into being when things were separated from love because the humanity that came into existence had nothing to frame living so they invented a do-it-yourself feedback system based on judgment and justice. That system of external morality and values was then encoded within all religious and political systems, which needed a DIY external system rather than a love-based relationship.

"The restoration of all things is a return to love and communion with all things as a state of being where all is one and one is all. The revealing of the sons of God reveals a loving fellowship in the communion of light at a quantum level that permeates all things with the light of love and truth. This state of being encapsulates unconditional love, limitless grace and triumphant mercy; not as the actions of God towards all things but as the state in which all things exist in the oneness of communion.

"This glorious state can just be defined as *I am that I am*."

My understanding and experience of sonship have fundamentally changed from a 'doing' state of consciousness to a 'being' state of being; and that is reflected in the change in the level of encounters I have been experiencing.

I will start by sharing experiences from the end of 2020 and the beginning of 2021 which framed my mandate for writing this book; and then I will share some of the creative aspects of sonship being revealed in this season which give a wider scope to our roles as sons in regards to creation.

Framing the Book Mandate

"Unconditional love, limitless grace and triumphant mercy are the hallmarks of genuine spirituality. Son, love wins because love has won: so continue to live lived, love living and live loving in the rest of being and you will be an ambassador of the light of truth.

"Son, as you learn to rest in being you will see your capacity increase greatly to be a son and an ascended father who is love. The goal of sonship is not the restoration of all things as that just restores the possibility of maturing beyond what is presently possible. The true goal is to be like Us, whose image you are made after; to be creative love and light. Your connection to creation must be restored as that [same connection] is what you will have with what you learn to create when you are mature.

"Son, restoration is not the end, just a return to the beginning so that the journey can continue to become the intention of Our desire, found in the light of the Tree of Life. Dwelling in the realm of light, where you can continually gaze upon Our face and become conformed to Our image and abide, is a key. The light of Our glory is absorbed into the fabric of your being in this place of intimacy."

Immediately, I switched my conscious awareness to the realm of light where I am, and the light of His face was so much brighter, as if the level of glory I was able to stand in had increased. It was like I was in a glorious sound and light bath, clothed in the glory of His face, absorbing love, light and the energy of being. I felt more connected to all my quantum moments of being and knew that they had all increased in being also. The splendour of the face of God is an awe-inspiring and truly wondrous sight to behold and become like, and I was basking in the light of that glory.

"Son come walk with Me."

I found myself near the fire stones by the river of fire, where the Father was beckoning me to ascend the stones once again. This was the eighth time I have had significant and life-transforming encounters on the fire stones during my journey to mature sonship that began with my first heavenly encounter in 2008.

I remembered that I had already received an invitation to come and engage there but perhaps I had needed the glorious light encounter first. As the Father took a step, I followed; still somewhat apprehensive, as these encounters are challenging and disruptively life-changing.

The Father took hold of my hand and I felt infused with confidence as we stood on the first step of love, which I had encountered 7 times before, each time revealing different characteristics. This time I felt love as before but I knew this was creative love; and I was not just being a recipient but a participator, as my creativity was being awakened.

To truly create is to truly love and only by creating can you know how to love as a creator. I rejoiced as I felt filled with creative love potential but also became calmer and fully accepting of who I am at a deeper and higher level of being. I am a son of God, made in His image to become a creative ascended father.

That moment stretched out before me to the conclusion of ascension before the Father led me to take the next step. I was now standing in deeper creative joy, where I now understood the emotions of the statement 'it is very good' at a deeper creational level. Each step played out in the quantum moment of being until we reached the top and stood on the tenth step; and then the eleventh step manifested.

"Son, you will need to learn to be content and comfortable at a deeper level of glory and truth before ascending any further but you will know when the time is right."

I stood very still, just being, soaking in the creational revelation: this step contained the memories and the distilled consummation of all the previous 58 steps of encounter as if concentrated into this expanded moment. I had never felt more lovingly, joyfully and peacefully at rest, just being.

"Mankind is the pinnacle of creation, beyond the gods and all other created beings in all dimensions, but it is the lack of the knowledge of that reality that has kept Our sons in darkness. The Great Deception is designed to keep Our children from the full knowledge and truth concerning their sonship identity and destiny. Creation is waiting for the revealing of the true light of sonship so the darkness can be dispelled by the glorious brightness of the rising of Our sons to their position within the Tree of Life that is Christ.

"The dark cloud that contains the realm of creative light is where the full knowledge of sonship can be absorbed into your being. The greatest deception that has been perpetrated is that which has kept Our children from their true identity and destiny to rule creation with Us.

"All deception is a product of leaving the creative light of Our shadow to walk in the created light of independence. The knowledge of the true potential of mankind has been hidden by the division and subjugation into classes that devalue Our children based on anything material. All division and separation is a tool of the deception that is used by the few to keep the many from the truth of their value and worth as sons. Anything that divides our children and separates Our one family is an abhorrence to Us. The subjugation of mankind by the old gods and their new minions, the bankers, political warmongers and corporations that have replaced the priests of religion, just perpetuates the great deception.

"There is one agenda behind all of the deceptions: that is to counterfeit the true with the false so that mankind will believe the lie is the truth. The Luciferian deception is to fool Our children into believing that they have to attain through independence who they already are. The political and religious spirit systems that front the Luciferian agenda have used many guises throughout history to disguise the lies as truth. The recording of history itself has been used to obscure the truth behind the twisted lies.

"The empire spirit that has tried to counterfeit the true Kingdom with one independent world government made in their own image has used politics and religion to achieve that goal. The latest form of that Luciferian agenda is Talmudic Zionism, masquerading behind the political left of communism and the political right of nationalism. The Luciferian goal of one false world government is controlled by the elite financiers who control the power through the money. The political and religious spirit promotes its agenda through division, competition, conflict and tribalism whilst seeking to unite the world politically and religiously through deception. The sons of God, in the light of their true identity, must arise to expose the darkness and the Luciferian agenda behind the latest deception.

"Your focus this year is to facilitate restoration government and write the book that will expose the lies of Zionist eschatology that supports and perpetuates the deception amongst Our sons.

"Son, the glory of sonship is about to intensify: so be ready for increase by consciously engaging the realm of light within the creative dark cloud in perfection."

I shifted my consciousness to enter the realm of light to gaze at the wondrous beauty of the Father's face, resplendent in glory. I focused my full attention on a facet that drew my attention, and the creative power of that truth became my reality as I absorbed the glorious light into my being.

"Yes, son, true reality and true identity is found in the light of true perfection. Prioritise this place of transfiguration. The glory of your true identity is needed to bring freedom to creation but the great deception that has kept Our children from their true purpose of being must be exposed by the light of truth. No eye has yet seen and no ear has yet heard all that is within Our heart for their being because that truth is too much for those who are still deceived by the seduction of the knowledge of the false tree path.

"Son, only absorbing the light of truth from who We are can transfigure Our children into their true state of being. Following the path of independence has created a false state of doing that keeps Our children in the darkness.

"Son, by just being, the light of your glory will draw those clothed in darkness to the light of your rising, not to dispel the darkness but transform it. Only the light of glory that is absorbed from perfection has the energy of truth to restore darkness to light through its creative power."

As I turned my focus to facet after facet, I rejoiced in the glorious splendour of pure light and truth but I also became aware of the seemingly limitless facets there were. The infinite glory and truth drew my gaze and the desire of my heart deeper into the pure love, joy and peace of being.

"Son, the glorious creative light of perfection will be the truth that enables you to discern as it resonates within your being. This resonance with the truth within you will enable you to discern anything that is tainted by the doing of the DIY tree.

"Son, you must learn to use this ability to discern wisely – but not sceptically or suspiciously but with a pure heart of love. Love must be the motivation of all discernment as only love can win when deception is revealed by the light of truth.

"Son, learn to discern with gentleness and humility of heart by being yoked to the Truth in a state of rest that will detect works by their negative energy. Son, 2021 will be a year where discernment must be practised as so much deception will need to be brought into the light.

"Son, as you learn to abide in the realm of light in a state of being, you will be able to discern that which does and that which does not resonate with Our heart of love and truth. The frequency of the light of love and truth will be a genuine reflection of that which represents Us and that which is false, deceptive or not living will become more and more obvious.

"The intimacy with the light of Our glory will ensure the light of your glory is a true reflection of who We truly are; and creation will be able to respond to your light and the sound frequency of your voice.

"In 2021, the spotlight of truth will shine brightly to expose the great deception of the Luciferian tree of the knowledge of good and evil agendas. The deception of independence, the cult of I, can be found embedded within the original 'I will' statements that defined the motive of the first rebellion.

"*I* is the same as *one* and 'there is no *I* in the word *team*'; and there can be no relationship with one: that is why independence, division and separation are the tools of the religious and political spirit behind the Babel agenda of false unity seen in the statement 'we will make a name for ourselves'. Selfishness is the hallmark of the DIY tree agenda: 'I will' is its cry, as doing and works are its *modus operandi*.

"Son, this is why so many of Our children – and even so many of those who know they are Our sons – are weary and burdened and live on the treadmill of independence. The call to all who are weary and heavy-laden to come to the light of truth and find rest in their true identity is still being made today.

"Son, rest is truly being and knowing the inclusion and acceptance of unfailing unconditional love and limitless grace. Being is being gentle and humble of heart and that is only to be found abiding within *I am that I am* in the true identity of being. You cannot know yourself independent of your relationship with us.

"The greatest deception has been fooling Our children to work for – by their own independent self-effort – what they already have and are as Our children. The religious spirit enslaves Our children through the dead works of performance because they have lost their true identity and live as orphans, even though they are already included in Our family. The political spirit offers the false family of nationalism, tribalism, and by denominating through division (which is falsely uniting under a banner of colour, race, ethnicity, birthplace, religion, social status, class or any other manmade category that divides).

"So many of Our children think they are uniting when they are actually dividing, just as they were deceived into doing at the Tower of Babel. We confused language to create family and they divided into nations and sought empires. We mandated them to fill the earth as one family but they were deceived into making a name for themselves; and then once they were dispersed they falsely united, creating independent nations that would compete and fight for territory.

"The empire spirit is the Luciferian agenda behind all attempts to conquer and form one-world government under a false messiah figure. The latest and current version is the Talmudic Zionist agenda behind the global control systems of economics, politics, corporations, media, entertainment, energy and pharmaceuticals that are the front of the religious and political spirit.

"All the ideologies that have been created from the tree of the knowledge of good and evil are inherently flawed – and that includes all forms of government: capitalism, communism, right, left and middle; and all forms of economics. The Kingdom of God is a relational, covenantal partnership of mutual support and encouragement, where everyone is part of one family and finds fulfilment in being who they were created to be.

"The world without the fall would be a very different place; and living in a garden environment, in harmony and oneness with creation, is very different from living in a city, dependent upon mankind's technology and ingenuity. The politicising of the prophetic movement to support conflicting ideologies is the work of the religious and political spirit and it has been exposed through the US presidential election as another deception that Our children and sons have fallen for.

"Son, the Kingdom of God is a government of love, producing the fruit of righteousness, peace and joy so all can be blessed and fulfil their destiny. You are mandated to expose the great deception and the Luciferian agendas behind it so the sons of God can rule righteously in love, free from the infiltration of the religious and political spirit.

"Son, the Kingdom is one of love, peace and joy ruling in righteousness. There are many professing to seek first the kingdom but they only want government and not righteousness. The fruit of righteousness is love, joy and peace; and that is how you discern Our true Kingdom, that which flows from the throne of grace through the Tree of Life.

"Many who profess to be seeking the Kingdom are blinded to the truth by the deceptions of the religious and political spirit. Violence is never the answer: only love wins, through forgiveness and reconciliation. We have allowed the prophets to speak with a lying spirit to reveal the deception they are hoodwinked by and show how the political and religious spirit has infiltrated the church. It is time for this deception to be exposed by the light of truth so Our children will reject all mediation and seek Us face to face and heart to heart.

"The separation of the mediatorial spirit must be replaced by intimacy: that is why We are calling so many of Our children to leave the religious church systems. The light of love and truth has been hidden under religious deception, so much so that many of Our children have rejected Us. In truth, they are rejecting the distorted view of who We are that religion has created in its own image.

"Son, the frequency of love's light must be released into the earth to awaken Our children to a new level of consciousness that reveals Us to be love. Love is the only antidote to the fear created by the deception that results from following the DIY tree path of independence. Only the revealing and awakening to unconditional love and limitless grace will cast out the fear that is controlling people and making them so susceptible to the great deception and delusion. Only the light of truth can expose the lies to reveal what is true reality, so an awakening to love must be the precursor to the revealing of the great deception.

"'There are none so blind as those who will not see' – that was made obvious by those who refuse to see the truth that is right in front of their own eyes. They live in denial, refusing to accept the truth because they live in a false reality, thinking they are hearing Our voice; but in fact they hear the voices of reason, the voice of their own understanding and the lying voices of those prophets who have been infected by the religious and political spirit. They lack the discernment to be able to distinguish the truth from the lies and are seduced by the conspiracies of the religious and political spirit. Refusing to accept the truth, they are drawn deeper into deception where they become even more deluded.

"It is time for the light of love to shine brightly through the sons of God who have experienced the true love of intimacy face to face. The power of deception is great but the power of true love is greater: that is why there must be an awakening to love consciousness.

"Son, brood in the Cradle of Life over the love awakening so you can be the sound of love that light will respond to, to form that reality.

"Son, the fruit of the poisonous tree is toxic but its roots have infiltrated the whole of worldly culture and society, hidden from most of Our children's knowledge. All that is considered normal, everyday life in every culture is unrecognisable from Our original intention and this must be acknowledged if true restoration is to take place. You have come to the correct conclusion, that everything that has come from the source of the DIY tree path is un-restorable because it is independent of Our desire.

"We will give mankind future choices that will affect the end.

"Son, this is hard for mankind's ego to accept because man has used the creativity that comes from being made in Our image to accomplish all that is seen. Technological ingenuity is no substitute for true creative reality where mankind and creation are in total harmony.

"Restoration will remove all that is man-made and sourced from following the independent path so that only that which has been inspired by the Tree of Life will remain. This process must be one of reconstruction and renewal: a creative renaissance that restores garden (not city) life. Technology will not be man-made but organic and living in creative harmony, where the frequency of all light will be restored to perfect balance. The living light Quantum Lumens will be harmonised to the sound of many waters that will be the voice of a man that speaks the thoughts of God into existence.

"Son, mature mankind were always designed to be gods; but the false gods who usurped man's authority will have to be exposed, rejected and then restored to bring back true harmony. The gods have hidden behind many guises so that humanity will worship them but all that is a deception that has trapped Our children in lost identity. The light of true sonship is beginning to shine with the hope of true restoration to counteract the despair of the world as its systems fail and fall. The dawning of a new age of enlightenment, where the light of truth shines brightly, is being ushered in through the government of the sons of God who are revealing sonship. As Our children are awakened to love consciousness to discover their true identity, which is found only in the Tree of Life, then creation itself will begin to respond favourably.

"Son, only when life and fruit flows from the Tree of Life can humanity become all that it is intended to be as restored mankind, made in our image.

"The fruit of true being in rest must replace the work of doing that is poisonous to the soul of man, so that their true identity and relationship with creation and their status as gods can be revealed. Only being at rest, living with gentle and humble hearts, can counteract the ego of a works-driven existence.

"Son, there is creative beauty that has been inspired by Our image within mankind to be seen in the world, but it is still less than Our intention. Many things were created by the desire to bring Us glory, and that is good and admirable, but it is but a pale imitation and a shadow of what it would have been."

We must make a distinction between 'mankind' and 'humanity', as they have different fathers. Sons of God can only be revealed by the heavenly Father, as we are made in His image, according to the vast sum of His thoughts.

As I pondered all these things, I engaged the Cradle of Life to brood over true creativity and I saw glimpses of indescribable, organic, creative beauty beyond my ability to express. Only by brooding, cocooned in the thoughts and desires of the Father, can we hope to be able to call forth that which is not as that which is.

"Son, you have discerned well, so abide and dwell in the creative light of Our thoughts that will truly inspire your creative being."

I stood before the throne of the Ancient of Days, where the Father gave me a large golden key and a scroll before beckoning me to sit next to Him on His left, which I thought was rather odd. As I sat there, three very powerful and imposing angels stood around me and I felt very encouraged, strengthened and emboldened. They were Limitless, Liberty and Union, whom I had met previously several times. I looked at the scroll: it was a mandate for exposing the great deception and the key would open the way for the truth to come into the light.

Inspired, I got up and went to the fire stones, where the river of fire was flowing from the throne, and began walking down the eleven steps, remembering the encounters in which the last two steps were formed. I stood on the bottom step with the desire to engage the dark cloud burning within me. I felt such passionate love burning in my entire being, transforming me once again, so I embraced the fire and rejoiced in such passion.

Suddenly, as I stood there, I was aware of the enormity of the task of writing the book to expose the great deception that was ahead of me; but the task, daunting as it was, became sharply in focus. At that moment I felt passionate about the book but also knew I was incapable of writing it in my current state, even with the key and the scroll that I had received. That made me even more determined but also at rest.

I ascended the steps one by one, very slowly, so that each one could have its transforming effect on me. Each step birthed a greater passion, almost painful in its intensity: this was another stage of ascension and part of the maturation process. With each step I felt stronger, yet more aware of my weaknesses; so I knew that had to become more dependent on the revelation of intimacy that I would be entering into within the dark cloud invitation. As I ascended and stood on the last step, I felt a great surge of energy. This was energy at a level I had not experienced before in this way and form but it felt familiar and comforting.

I was enveloped in the frequencies of sound and light that were so breathtaking in their beauty that my whole being was spaghettified and swirled within the light, moving to the rhythm of the frequency. I was and wasn't, all at the same time, as my whole being was charged with energy that I had never felt before. It was like I was continually blinking in and out of conscious, time-based existence. This process felt eternal, as if my whole existence was phasing, moving in and out of eternity, my being energised with each cycle as I mixed in and out of God. I knew from my limited past experiences that I was encountering *Perichoresis* at a very different level of truth and reality.

Then abruptly it ended and I ascended into the created realm of eternity where I was standing before the dark cloud. I waited patiently, knowing that although I had an invitation to enter, I had to let all that had just happened sink in and do its work. The longer I waited, the more I knew that I would never be able to complete the mandate I had been given without what was to come.

Desire grew within me to the point of desperation, yet my being was totally at rest. There was no striving; I was filled with love, joy and peace and totally content and satisfied like never before.

"Son, live loving: that will bring you to a place of peace where you can speak the truth in love to all those who need to hear the truth. Only the real Truth can set Our children free but only if they know it; and there lies the problem, as they cannot know what they have not experienced.

"Truth and knowledge cannot be intellectually assimilated information but experiences. Those who have been hoodwinked into the darkness of deception sincerely think that what they believe is the truth and therefore are unwilling to back down, as they see that as a compromise. The issues that have been used to cause division and separation by the religious and political spirit are emotive in people and they are passionate about them because they think they reflect Our heart.

"If they truly knew Our heart, they would not be open to division, as they would have no enemies and no one to fight against. These passions, if they incite anger and hatred, are not based in love and are not from Our heart. Passion for causes has placed the importance of the cause above relationship; and that is what causes them to see their brothers and sisters who hold different opinions to be their enemies. They have been deceived into thinking they are fighting against flesh and blood and that they need to be at war with those who they see as the perpetrators of crimes.

"If they knew Our heart for the restoration of all things, they would be ambassadors of reconciliation, not division, strife and enmity. The way to discern the truth is through the lens of love and an opposite spirit to division. Their passion for their causes has caused them to personalise and therefore personify their causes with individual people who they see as being against them and they become the focus of their anger. The strongest emotions are raised by the pro-life agenda as they confuse Our desire for immortality to mean that We hate abortion and therefore all abortionists and those who have had abortions.

"Son, you know the Truth: that hate is never an emotion that We feel, as the oracles of Our heart are always passionate towards Our children, irrespective of what they do. We have as much love and burning desire for relationship with the perpetrators as with the victims, as they are all living in lost identity. They do not understand that We are never taken by surprise and know all things, including the date of Our children's birth and unfortunately their physical deaths. All these things are factored into their eternal destiny; and yes, they can be changed and corrected from the eternal perspective. You have seen what happens to all who are miscarried, aborted or die in childhood: they are nurtured and perfected for the fulfilment of their destinies. Sadly, passion for the unborn life is often directed as anger towards those who are vilified and made enemies. This is not, and never will be, Our heart.

"Son, you will have to tread very lightly over this issue and be very gentle in the way you challenge this cause with the truth that all lives matter to Us, not just the unborn. All are victims in some way and everyone needs love and compassion, whoever they are and whatever they have done: never lose sight of that but be careful not to make enemies of those who disagree with you. All lives matter to Us but We never make enemies of those who take life, as that would compromise who We are. We will not remove the right for Our children to choose and make their decisions, as that would make them slaves, but We are actively involved to bring good out of every wrong choice. The truth is that only unconditional love and limitless grace can restore all things and that is who We are and We are overflowing with mercy in lovingkindness.

"Son, there has to be just as much of an awakening to love amongst those who already believe in Us as in those who do not yet believe. Feel how We feel, think how We think, see how We see, by actively engaging within Us within you, so that you can be moved by what are the true oracles of Our heart."

I stood looking at the dark cloud, a cloud like none other I had seen or entered. It was intense but also seemed to be a living thing. I felt apprehensive as I watched it pulsating, swirling, shifting, like it was ready to engulf me.

"Son, you have your invitation: there is nothing to fear but this will bring greater changes than you could ever imagine or think."

So I took a step and the cloud moved towards me, engulfing me in complete darkness that went through every particle of my being. The deeper the darkness became, the more intense the light that filled my mind. It was as if I was totally cocooned in a darkness that was in reality the brightest light. My senses were heightened, my consciousness enlightened with a light so bright it matched the depth of darkness I was in. The darkness was the light, the very light of God that was truth itself; and then, one by one, I saw the darkness of deceptions overwhelmed by the pure, creative light of truth. All the deceptions I was wrestling with in writing the book were transformed by that light so I could see the truth of who and what was behind them.

I saw figuratively the tree of the knowledge of good and evil engulfed in the purest of light that exposed its agenda. I saw the great deception of 'I will' that has enslaved humanity: it was like a mass of living darkness as tendrils attached to all humanity and all that we have made in independence. I saw the light of truth overwhelm each tendril of darkness until each one retracted and all that was left was one dark 'I' that was then itself consumed by the light.

My mind, a consciousness that had been shattered, splintered by the darkness, like everyone else's, was being bathed in the most amazing light. Each lie, like a splinter I had learned to live with, was consumed by that healing light of pure truth and I 'knew that I knew' that all I had been wrestling with was not a conspiracy theory but a conspiracy to hide the truth. Mankind has been deceived into living a lie: an eschatological lie has been accepted as a truth that promotes the Luciferian agenda of one-world government to make a name for themselves.

That name, called many things, Babel, Egypt, Sumeria, Babylon, Greece, Rome, Britain, Russia, Germany, Spain, Israel and Zion, was now revealed as Lucifer. I could see the depth of deception that could cause men to murder millions of innocent people to fulfil their objectives. Pharaoh, Stalin, Hitler and the Zionist elite behind the holocaust were willing to sacrifice the millions slaughtered to hide the truth behind the great deception. The bright and morning star is the light that is the false sun and son who has deceived mankind and most of Christianity into supporting his agenda to be worshipped as God.

I could see more clearly now, so I did not have to water the deception down to make it more palatable or tone it down for fear of the anti-Semitic accusations and reprisals. I heard the comforting voice of the Father gently say: "Speak the truth that you now know in love, to bring the great deception into the light."

The dark cloud receded, drawing back from me, leaving me exhausted but inspired; but now I knew that I could write what I had been hesitant to write, in the knowledge of what I had seen. Inspired, I engaged the earth shield, connected by the light of truth, and began to make legislative declarations:

I call for the light of truth to shine brightly to penetrate the darkness of deception in following the religious and political spirit agendas.

I call for the light of truth to reveal the true reality behind the deception of QAnon and the political conspiracy theories keeping the deceived in denial.

I call for the light of truth to free the minds of God's children who are deceived into following the lies of DIY religion through lost identity.

I call for the light of truth to expose the Luciferian agenda of division, competition, conflict and tribalism that is behind the religious and political spirit.

I call for the light of truth to free those trapped in futurist, escapist eschatology and millennial Zionism.

I call for a global awakening to love, revealing the lovingkindness of the new covenant.

I call for an awakening of lost identity to new creational reality and inclusion.

I call for peace to rest over the earth as a suppressive blanket to fear and anger.

I call for the light of truth to reveal the truth of the passion of God's heart for the restoration of all things.

Those declarations are inspired by the mandate I have been given to write this book and the things the Father revealed to me.

"Son, the truth is being revealed for those seeking and willing to look but those who lean to their own understanding will remain in darkness. A time is coming when the light of truth will penetrate all darkness: this time will be the rising and shining of the sons of God who know Us face to face. Only face to face knowledge of the Truth will be powerful enough to free Our children from the deception of self-delusion they are living in.

"Son, encourage Our children to seek first the kingdom in the righteousness of their true identity as sons and engage Us face to face. Encourage all pursuing the government of sonship to rest in the realm of light to learn to be. The revelation of being is the key to living loved in the yoke of rest, to learn to be gentle and humble in heart, to discover true identity. Living and dwelling in the realm of light in perfection is the only thing that can reveal the truth to expose the lies of the great deception that keeps creation in bondage to corruption.

"Son, there will be a series of revelations that will shake and rock the foundations that most of Our children stand upon and the future will become very uncertain for those who do not know the Truth by experience. The second-hand information of religion will not satisfy when those foundations are shaken; and many will begin to seek the truth as their deluded realities are shaken. Only an awakening to love will enable this transition to be peaceful in the times of great uncertainties that are ahead. Only when all hope in the DIY tree path is rejected will Our children seek and find the truth, so the system will continue to be shaken until all are following the path of the Tree of Life. Son, be an oracle of truth in the times of great uncertainty ahead by being in the state of rest found only in face to face abiding within Us.

"Son, union will triumph over division, covenant will triumph over competition, peacemaking will triumph over warmongering and family will triumph over tribalism. Have no doubt: love wins, because love is unconditional and never fails, never gives up, and is faithful, consistent and eternal."

"I call to the sons of God to arise and shine love's light and truth into the darkness of deception."

I knew this to be the cry of the Father's heart and it is His deep desire for all His children to come out of the darkness of the deception of the religious and political spirit. I felt so moved by believers who were caught in the deception, still clutching at prophetic straws.

I believe the global cabals will be exposed and fall.

I believe the swamp will indeed be drained.

I believe in a brave new world as we transition into the next age, the Age of Aquarius.

I do not believe any of those things will be achieved through any system that has come from the tree of the knowledge of good and evil: it is all an elaborate deception and delusion. No political, religious, economic, corporate or any other control system will ever establish the Kingdom of God on earth as it is in heaven. They all seek to deceive people into believing in the counterfeits.

Everything that can be shaken has already been shaken: the only thing that remains is God's kingdom and the process of the restoration of all things. Please do not build your hopes and dreams on the shifting sands but on the solid rock of the Prince of Peace. There is no need to shame or humiliate anyone who has been deceived, as we have all been there and no doubt we will all be there again.

So let's extend the hand of friendship for reconciliation to one another, whatever our political or religious opinion; and let's demonstrate love, grace and mercy to one another: the world is looking on, desperate for answers in this time of great shaking and uncertainty.

Let's seek first the kingdom together in the union of the new covenant as sons of God, seated in the heavenly places as priests and kings, so that we can be the oracles and legislators of the order of Melchizedek and the kingdom of God can fill the earth.

"Son, it is time to enter into rest as you continue to expose the deceptions that Our children are living in. Only the light of truth and love can illuminate the minds of those who have been deceived by the political and religious spirit. Focus your attention on releasing the light by abiding in the light; then as you absorb the light into your being, you can shine as a revealed son.

"The darkness of deception is very strong in those who think they have a cause that is Ours, as they think they are operating from Our heart and what they are defending is noble and godly. Often the cause has an element of truth to it and that makes it even more deceptive but it is often the method and means that have been perverted.

"Son, from a place of rest you can be passionate; but never be against anything, always be for something: that will keep you in the opposite spirit and in love. It is so important that we are positive in renewal and construction, not destruction and warfare. Always be positive; then, for example, you will be able to reveal the truth, not focus on exposing deception – but that will be the end result because you have been a peacemaker. Love's light is the light of truth, and passion for the truth is good; but never let it develop into anger directed against anyone. Remember those who are deceived do not know that they are, so do not blame them: have mercy, and show compassion, with limitless grace and unconditional love. Those who influence others have a responsibility but they are not to blame, however crazy they get, so be careful not to get frustrated and always keep your heart righteous towards them.

"Son, feel how We feel towards those caught up in the darkness of deception because it was just how We felt about you. So have empathy for those who are embroiled in the craziness of the conspiracies and seem to have lost all reason. You have believed the lies embedded within your written history itself all your life; and there is still more to be revealed to you, so be patient and loving as you administrate the light of truth."

As I focused my attention on the light shining from the Father's face I sank into a deeper state of rest where the eternal now was perfected in the light of truth which I was absorbing. All my frustrations with those mystics who I thought should know better just melted away in the bliss and glory of absolute rest in peace.

"Son, now you have ascended to a new level of enlightenment, abide in that state so your whole consciousness and being can be transformed and conformed."

I began to see the earth shield illuminated by the light of truth so that even those sons who make up the shield will be enlightened to another level. I engaged the shield and began to release the light that I had absorbed from the place of rest I was in.

I call for the light of love and truth to penetrate the hearts of those within the shield with a deeper level of truth.

I call the restored angels, Truth Restorer, Truth Revealer and Truth Establisher to engage the hearts and minds of the earth shield.

I call the restored angels, Truth Restorer, Truth Revealer and Truth Establisher to engage the hearts and minds of the mystic movement.

I call for the light of truth sourced within the Tree of Life to be released through its fruit and leaves to help restore the minds of the sons of God.

I call for a state of rest and reconciliation to descend onto and into the earth as a blanket of peace.

"Son, receive all that We are releasing to you and embrace the transformation this will bring, as change will be accelerated as the next age approaches."

I stood in the light, where I remembered my last engagement with the fire stones. As I contemplated, twelve facets of the

Father's face began to glow until each released a burst of coloured light energy filled with truth.

I absorbed that truth into my being until I was pulsating with the frequency of each colour unified in my being. I became alive with limitless energy, glowing like a twelve coloured rainbow, filled with the knowledge of the truth that previously I had no connection to; but although it was not yet cognitive in my mind, it was hidden, waiting to be discovered.

"Son, now when you experience information you will be able to discern truth from lies as the hidden knowledge is activated within you. Son, now the truth has been imparted to you, it will enable you to be a cosmic fact-checker as when you encounter information you will discern the truth from lies by the frequency of its vibration. There is so much disinformation being released to confuse and deflect, so that the real truth is hidden behind the smoke and mirrors. You will be able to detect where grains of truth are obscured by mountains of lies where most people will dismiss it and miss the truth. The conspiracies are created to keep people from the real truth by packaging truth within lies so that Our children will believe lies as the truth or reject the truth because it is hidden within lies.

"Son, now you are armed with this ability to discern, you will be able to reveal the truth; but do not try to expose the lies, just allow the light of truth to do that itself. As you proclaim the truth, the light will shine brightly enough that its frequency will cause the alarm bells to ring within the minds of those who are open. More of Our children are awakening out of the slumber of deception that has dulled their ability to discern into the dawning of a new day of revealed truth. The next age of enlightenment is coming with greater light as the end of this age passes, in the transition that most will not be aware of; but the forerunners are awakening.

"Son, 'the dawning of the age of enlightenment' is the more positive way to describe the exposing of the great deception of the Luciferian agenda. You will never need to fear the darkness when you know you are light and that is what creation itself is looking for within the revealing of the sons of God. You can now accurately discern 'no truth', 'some truth' and 'the truth' within any type of written statement or audio or video teaching, testimony or account.

"Son, it is time to let go of the current political and religious spirit situation and move on in your heart and trust that I will guide you if there is anything that I want you to do. It is time to be passionate about the truth and focus on calling the sons of God to come out of the wilderness into the Promised Land. Only by learning to cross the veil to engage with Us face to face will there be true change and transformation into Our image.

"As you participate in the earth shield, focus your attention on those who have been shaken and are looking for the truth. Call them out of the darkness of the coverings that they have been under into the light of love and truth. Call them out of the mediatorial system of the old Moses generation to join the Joshua generation and take their places in heaven. Call them out of their lost identity into the knowledge of the truth of who We made them to be.

"Remember where you were 13 years ago and have compassion for those in similar places. Release the frequency of sonship and the blue light call continually, to enable those who are hungry and seeking to find you and the *Engaging God* program. The shaking that has been taking place is preparing the next wave who are beginning to look for the answers for themselves and drawing them to the light.

"Son, focus on the great awakening to love, as that will be their way to the truth and the abundance of life that awaits them. There are also those of Our children who have not come to the realisation of who We are, who also are beginning to look for the truth. Release the frequency of hope and send the light that will unveil Our presence within them and their inclusion in Us. Call for the light to shine brightly around those We are calling who will become the champions of the next generation and ambassadors of reconciliation. There are those who are becoming ready, and the time of a global awakening to love is fast approaching, so direct the oracles of Our heart towards the next generation."

I released the frequency of light and issued another blue light call. I focused on releasing the light of love and truth from the earth shield to call the next generation to come to the light of truth:

I call for the light to shine into the darkness to reveal the truth of God as love.

I call for the angelic legions to take the message of love to those who need a supernatural encounter with the light of love and truth.

I call for the light of love to shine brightly to reveal that the Father is pleased to demonstrate that Jesus is already within those awakened.

I call for the next generation to come forth into their destiny as sons of God.

"Son, make stronger connections in the spirit by opening up your heart and releasing your frequency through the Merkabah. Broadcast your identity to all dimensions to make the connections that will join you, heart to heart, with those who are like-minded."

Immediately, I was aware of my multidimensional reality; and from each of those quantum moment positions, I released my song into creation. I felt the echo and knew that I had connected with many seekers of truth that I am now calling to connect heart to heart.

"Son, there are so many that need hope to inspire them at this time of great transition and change, so be one of the oracles of Our heart that they need to reveal who We truly are. There are those who have almost given up, whose light is but a flicker and are only just clinging onto life: give them your light. All that you have absorbed from Our face in the realm of light in perfection, broadcast with passion and burning desire.

"There are those, like Saul of Tarsus was, who will be blinded by the light of truth that encounters them; so send angelic helpers to guide them while their spiritual eyes become accustomed to the light of love and truth.

"Son, Our glory is about to be released, so get ready to receive those who are awakened to the truth.

We must be and provide those safe places of relationship for people to come to, so they can find rest.

"Son, the Kingdom of God is the culture of heaven and a counter-culture on earth, to fill the earth with the glory of Our presence within Our children. The Kingdom is not primarily about government but dominion does flow from it naturally when Our children are joined to Us in a mystic union of heart and mind in an intimate love relationship.

"Son, you cannot use laws to control people, as they only produce rebellion. Rebellion is a heart matter that stems from lost identity; and only love can change the heart, not law. The issue of abortion cannot be legislated out of existence as it is primarily a moral issue that changes when Our children's hearts are aligned to Our heart through relationship, not laws. All of the issues that are called 'sin' by religion are sourced in the need for identity and position and the real sin is the deceived choice to live independently from Us.

"Restoration of relationship with Us is the hope for a return to the paradise where there was no sin, only bliss and blessing; and that results in childlike trust in Our provision, protection and guidance. Laws that seek to prohibit behaviour in reality only focus the soul on it and are counterproductive in that people become what they focus on, even if they are trying not to. The answer to all negative behaviour is to focus on positive behaviour: that is why face to face intimacy which eliminates the fear of punishment creates a desire for transformation that changes behaviour.

"Only the knowledge that comes from the cardiognosis of union can bring freedom to Our children because that knowledge comes with blessing's empowerment to prosper and succeed. Our mandate to be fruitful is not based on productivity and profitability but being blessed to be a blessing in a covenant relationship of lovingkindness.

"The fruit of the Spirit is the product of love that produces perpetual blessing, as it is about giving not receiving."

But the fruit of the Spirit is love, joy, peace, patience, kindness, goodness, faithfulness, gentleness, self-control; against such things there is no law. (Galatians 5:22-23).

"The focus of the deception of the independent path of the tree of the knowledge of good and evil is always selfish and about receiving rather than giving.

"The focus on me, myself and I are the results of the deception of independence. The first lie in all creation was 'I will'. The 'I will' of independence always results in the lost identity of selfishness and produces nothing that is good. It always produces a fall that produces entropy.

"Son, as you know, there is nothing that has been inspired and produced by following the path of independence that can be restored. The deception of the so-called 'seven mountain mandate' is sourced from the same Luciferian agenda as the Tower of Babel, under the guise of religion. The agenda of the Kingdom is the union of two mountains to function as one, as the Mountain of the House of the Lord and Mount Zion converge to produce a union of heaven and earth. The return to a restored paradise can only be found in the mystic union of God and man as one, where *I am that I am* lives in mankind and mankind lives within *I am that I am*. Humanity is the counterfeit produced by independence.

"That restored union will produce a true government of love, joy and peace, in the rest of being free from the need to work to earn. Restored union with Us will bring the acceptance, affirmation, approval, appreciation and affection so craved by those who are living in lost identity. The return to union is the utopia and paradise that all of humanity has been searching for; but it can never be found in independence, as only union produces blessing.

"Son, the light of love in union is beginning to shine brightly to awaken Our children to unconditional love consciousness. That awakening will reveal the futility of independence and the power of union. Unconditional love can only be found within the mystic union that is *I am that I am* and the reality of that truth has been hidden under the lies of religion and performance orientation.

"Son, the religious spirit draws well-meaning believers into a web of deceit by giving them a cause they think represents Our heart. Once they are hooked, they are drawn deeper into the deception by their religious fervour and eventually a mania that blinds them to the deception. This is the deception that the religious spirit uses in cults and sects that promote that they have secret hidden knowledge, higher truth or special revelations.

"Even those who did receive revelation that was true are susceptible to the religious spirit deception, as they often separate and divide and make a name for themselves because they have to defend their special revelations from the orthodox church system that opposes it. Whenever groups use their revelation to give them identity, they become susceptible to the political spirit that drives them to divide and compete to defend their truth against the system. Many groups become legalistic to maintain the purity of their truth and denominate into e.g. Baptists, Methodists, Pentecostal, Charismatic, Reformed etc."

This same deception was behind cults and the Jonestown and Waco tragedies. Many people have been deceived by the offers of money for their causes: for example the Omega Trust and Trading fraud in the 1990s that gave believers the hope of a great wealth transfer. The QAnon cult has deceived so many because it unites the political and the religious causes and hoodwinks them into believing lies or partial truths that fit their personal cause, be it ending human trafficking, stopping abortion or exposing the deep state. The Luciferian agenda is then hidden behind layers of conspiracy that obscure the real truth and makes it unbelievable to many. When the truth is hidden within a conspiracy many are deceived because they lack the discernment to see the trap that they get caught in.

"Son, you know how easy it is to be caught in these types of scams that use a grain of truth or a biblical concept to convince – and then it becomes an obsession."

The internet makes it easy to perpetuate these deceptions through forums and secret groups that prey on people's hopes and dreams by spreading misinformation that offers the next glimmer of hope which never comes to fulfilment. There is always a drama or crisis that keeps delaying things and usually a secret mole who feeds cryptic pieces of information into the groups to keep them on the hook. There is usually a white knight who collects the misinformation and appears to be an expert who coordinates and disseminates the collected knowledge.

This was what was behind the Iraqi dinar fraud that caused many gullible but well-meaning Christians to buy thousands of worthless dinars in the expectation that the currency was going to be revalued and they would be instantly rich and able to fund the Kingdom. That scam had well-known mystics who promoted it with the illusion of secret heavenly knowledge that was just another deception, giving false hope to often vulnerable, susceptible people. Many people become disillusioned when they discover that they have been deceived and then reject the real truth; and many others find other causes or live in denial and hold onto their version of reality.

"Son, you know the Luciferian agenda that hides behind all these veils of deception, as I have shown you, but it will not be easy to separate the truth from the lies. The agenda of the path of the tree of the knowledge of good and evil has always been a deception that preys on ego and lost identity.

"All political and religious spirit activity can be traced back to that first lie, 'I will ascend', and have been outworked in the 'we will make a name for ourselves' agenda. The agenda is to create a counterfeit that can fool most into believing it is real, just as it was at Babel. There is a counterfeit god and a counterfeit kingdom or government agenda behind it all that has fooled most of Our children.

"Be careful that you do not get obsessive and fall prey to the very thing you are mandated to expose, by keeping close to the pure Truth only found in face to face relationship with Us. Many will seek to discredit you when you threaten the deception and they will call you a conspiracy theorist (or worse) to protect their lies. The conspiracy of global cabals keeps many from believing that groups are seeking one-world government but it also fools others into believing the twisted version that conceals the truth. The religious spirit twists its version of the deception: i.e. one-world government of the futurist eschatology with a false Messiah figure of the Antichrist with a false prophet and a political beast.

"The political and religious spirit union is a powerful deception. The truth becomes hidden in folklore and mythology but the Luciferian agenda is no less real and active in fulfilling its objective of a false god, no god, man is god, and a false kingdom of globalisation and control.

"Son come to the light of truth and release the frequency of love's light to reveal the truth that will set Our children free to know their true identity and kingdom purpose. Son, it is vital to ensure that you are continually engaging with the light of love and truth, as trust will enable the heart and the mind to be in perfect harmony.

"Love must be the true motive of the heart and mind of anyone who can intentionally create reality to align with the truth of Our desire and intention. There must be no motive based on fear, anger, revenge or warfare: just that of peace. The oracles of Our heart express fully who We are as love and the light of truth that radiates from Our face fully expresses the knowledge of Our desire and intention. As you draw from the light, by abiding in the realm of the light of love and truth in face to face intimacy, your motives will become purified and you will be able to discern the truth from amongst the veils of deception that often obscure it."

I gazed upon the beauty and majesty of the face of the Father and basked in the lovingkindness that was warm and inviting and felt cocooned in a mystery of wonder and awe. I was just being, in the perfection of the light: totally at rest in the peace of being, rejoicing in the joy of being, and completely content and satisfied in love's embrace.

From that place of being, I felt a stirring in the Father's heart that drew my attention and I was moved to turn my gaze to the earth shield, whilst still abiding in the light. I saw the light intensify in the shield: it was as if energy shocks pulsed through everyone and got their attention.

I saw the light of truth begin to shock the minds to challenge beliefs, mindsets and values, and to expose lies and deception. I saw the shock and surprise of realisation come over the faces of those who began to embrace and not resist the cognitive dissonance that was occurring. Cognitive dissonance can entrench some and deconstruct others, depending on our response. I saw the light of truth begin to penetrate areas of their hearts and reveal deep and hidden motives, both purifying and harmonising their heart and mind union. I saw all turn to look into the atmosphere of the earth and penetrate through that covering into the earth itself, going beyond the surface activity of life to the very core of the planet.

I knew that the sons of light were being moved by love and truth to engage creation itself at a new level of empathy. I felt the connection with the groaning of creation that was now passionate and intentional and would be necessary for all that will begin to take place in the coming season.

"Son, this is what is going to take place in the transition to bring about the change in the seasons as the sons of God arise and shine with the light of love and truth. As Our sons embrace their identity and destiny concerning creation, they will embrace and be filled with unconditional love and limitless grace energy. The living light of the Quantum Lumens will begin to respond to their choices creatively and reality itself will begin to align with Our original intention. The light of truth that shines with lovingkindness will bring an awakening to love that will free so many of Our children from the deception, bondage and independence of the DIY tree and its Luciferian agenda.

"Son, so many are caught in the eschatological trap that twists the truth they receive into a negative framework that is wrapped in fear and causes confusion within the *restoration of all things* movement. You are mandated to challenge this false eschatological expectation with the truth of perfect love that will remove fear and create a true, positive expectation for the future. The restoration of all things is moving forwards unstoppably and progressively towards its inevitable conclusion and that will be the platform for an even greater increase of kingdom government and peace."

The Source of the Great Deception.

"Son, the source of all deception is the deceiver who broke union and relationship to instigate independence. Those who followed him into independence were deceived by the lie of 'I will be like God' but all were tricked into worshipping the liar. Mankind was deceived by the same lie and became slaves to dead works.

"Eternity was placed in the hearts of Our children by design, so that they would always seek God, but they are deceived to do dead works to try to return home. The path of the tree of the knowledge of good and evil was the independent way to seek to restore identity and find home.

"This performance-oriented lifestyle creates a rat race or people living on a hamster wheel getting nowhere fast. There lies the heart of the deception, as no works of independence can ever achieve restoration of identity or relationship because that is by grace alone and is the free birthright of all Our children.

"The source of deception, Lucifer (or whatever other names he masquerades behind), has an agenda that he would be worshipped as god, but for most that is only through a mediator. The Luciferian agenda that drives making a name for themselves (in whatever religious or political guise that takes) is a trap because works, laws and protocols enslave to systems and do not create relationships. There is usually a puppet counterfeit political leader or spiritual figure who fronts the systems, who is deceived into thinking they are god, or mediate and speak for god.

"Son, all religion is deception, and all political or humanistic ideologies are deceptions, that promise identity and union; but that is only possible through a restored relationship with Us as the creator. The Luciferian agenda deceives through the political and religious spirit to falsely unite Our children to a cause, nation, king, Messiah, guru, party, tribe, ideology or theology.

"The Luciferian agenda has controlled the financial systems in modern times through Talmudic Zionists, and that supports and controls the political and media systems. These systems have controlled the narratives through division, competition, conflict and tribalism to create the conditions and environments that will make people more susceptible to an earthly political and religious counterfeit saviour-messiah figure. The Luciferian agenda is narcissistic (and that requires no real relationship) as it is selfish and is only about ego, me, myself – and 'I' is at its core.

"Son, the light of love and truth will begin to shine brightly through the ascended sons of God: to reveal love's agenda, to awaken Our children to who We truly are and reveal their identity, which will free them from the deception and delusion of independence. An awakening to unconditional love, limitless grace and triumphant mercy will overcome the darkness of lost identity by raising consciousness levels of enlightenment to a realisation of inclusion, reconciliation and restored union. Son, always focus on revealing the truth and the lies inevitably will be exposed by the purity of love's light:

that has a frequency that will resonate deep within the hearts of Our children.

"The memory of eternity and union will resonate with the frequency of love's truth which is the purest of light and sound. No deception can remain in pure light and the consuming fire of Our lovingkindness will refine and purify until no lies remain. Son, We are pure light, pure love and pure fire; so live loved, love living and live loving, at rest within *I am that I am*; and just be immersed in unconditional love, limitless grace and triumphant mercy.

"Son, it is not time to hold back. Do not be afraid: be bold and courageous to reveal the truth, as there will be much opposition from those still programmed to believe what they have been taught. Most people do not think for themselves or question what they have been taught because it is easier to accept everything as it is. If a lie is told often enough and repeated by enough people it will usually be accepted as the truth by the majority.

"Son, I have not called you to go with the majority but to be a pioneer, no matter where that takes you or how many people go with you. Many will oppose you but keep your focus and persevere. A lie is a lie, no matter how many people say it is the truth; and even if it is written in the history books that does not automatically make it true. The light of truth and love will reveal the truth that will eventually expose those lies. Sometimes you have to walk a lonely path to get to the destination and find the truth and that path is usually not popular with those who want to play it safe or maintain the status quo.

"Son, you do not have to defend yourself or explain yourself to those who are offended by the truth for whatever reason.

Always remain respectful and honouring to those who disagree or are offended.

"The great deception is designed to keep as many of Our children as possible believing lies as truth and living in a delusion that keeps them from their true identity as sons of God. Those behind keeping the truth hidden and keeping the lies from being exposed control the world systems of commerce, media, economics, science, and politics and they control the narratives that most people believe through the global media.

"The Luciferian agenda behind the religious and political spirit facade desires to keep Our children living in darkness that is maintained by division, competition, conflict and tribalism through a survivalist mentality. The same spirit that is behind denominationalism is behind nationalism and every form of empire, supremacy, discrimination, sectarianism, prejudice, racism, strife, and enmity that keeps Our children from true union with each other.

"True union can only be found by those who are at one within Us and so discover their true family is everyone: no matter what ethnicity, colour, political allegiance, background or history. We have called all Our children to be one as We are one and any division or separation or false unity based on anything at all is a deception that is sourced from the independent knowledge of the wrong tree. We desire that every family (who are in reality all one family) be blessed so they are not taken advantage of by anyone or needing to take advantage of anyone. Covenant is about mutual blessing, not exploitation.

"Poverty is a curse orchestrated by those who control the financial systems but the economy of the kingdom is based on jubilee and that is based on blessing and well-being for all. Capitalism makes winners and losers and Communism makes slaves to the system that provides for them; but in the kingdom, wealth is based on the fact that everyone is equally worthy and has the same intrinsic value.

"Our desire is that everyone is blessed so that all of Our children are empowered to prosper and succeed in fulfilling their destiny in union with Us, each other and creation. The deception that divides by creating competition and conflict has devalued everything by making productivity the measure of worth. All Our children were created with a birthright and an inheritance within creation and working for or being a slave to someone was never Our intention. All economic systems and ideologies are based on a flawed logic that is materialistic at heart and drives people to possess at the expense of others.

"All kingdom government is based on covenant, which is always peaceful and mutually beneficial, as it is respectful of difference and celebrates diversity within the whole. It is vital to honour your diversity by placing equal value on all Our children's unique abilities, just as all parts of the body are equally necessary for healthy living. Any system that values someone or something above another is sourced from the lies of independent knowledge. This utopian paradise was Our original intention and now most of Our children cannot even imagine that such a thing is even possible.

"Son, the restoration of all things will transform and change everything that exists that has its source in the deception of the tree of independence. The glory and true identity of Our children can only be found in restored union with Us and each other and only then can creation be set free from its bondage into that glorious liberty.

"Son, while the narrative is controlled by the global control systems Our children will remain in the darkness of deception, so the light must shine to create a narrative of truth. Whatever you reveal in the light, some will call a conspiracy, to keep the truth veiled in darkness; but some will resonate with the truth in their hearts, even though their minds will be confused. The greater the intensity of the light, the deeper the truth can penetrate the darkness that keeps Our children deceived. Truth must be spoken and revealed in love or it will create even more conflict.

"Son, the deception goes back to the first 'I will' statement of independence and many were deceived by it long before mankind was deceived, so restoration must go back to that point of departure from union and inclusion within Us.

"'*I am that I am*' is not a declaration of independence but of union, as '*I am*' is in reality '*We are*' and therefore you are also designed to be one family. That one family including all that We created is the initial goal of restoration; and once accomplished, there will only be limitlessness.

"Son, limitlessness is only possible when all know they are unconditionally loved and included; then no one will need to compete or compare themselves to anyone else, as they will know who they are within the union of oneness.

"Son, the light of love and truth is shining brightly and this will increase further as Our sons begin to arise and discover their eternal identity. The light of truth will expose many areas of darkness that are keeping Our children in the bondage of lost identity. Even those who have engaged heaven are susceptible to deception if their minds are not deconstructed from their programmed belief systems.

"The eschatological programming that is part of the Luciferian agenda must be brought into the light of truth and Our sons must be set free or they will remain susceptible to deception. The mixing of covenants is being perpetrated by the religious spirit and is responsible for the guilt, shame and condemnation that so many of Our sons feel.

"Son, there is truth and the righteous real behind many counterfeits as you have discovered through Our encounters but the philosophies behind the counterfeits are always lies and deceptions and must be avoided at all costs. This is especially true of Kabbalah because of its association with Talmudic Judaism which is hoodwinking so many because of the association with Christian Zionism.

"The root of deception behind Kabbalah and the Hebrew Roots Movement is eschatological as the Talmud and Hebrew culture are wrongly made acceptable because of the deception of Zionism. Jewish mysticism is a perversion that has infiltrated the mystic movement as it is sourced in the wrong tree and is part of the Luciferian agenda behind all religions. The covenants and religions cannot be mixed as it creates syncretic impurity. Syncretism is a Luciferian agenda to pollute the truth with mixture and lies."

(Syncretism is combining or bringing together different philosophical, religious, or cultural principles and practices.)

"Kabbalah has its light and knowledge from Lucifer and has twisted heavenly truth concerning sacred geometry, the Tree of Life, the Merkabah and Metatron's cube – things that We have shown you the truth about – into an esoteric false and

Luciferian system. That which Kabbalah reveals is designed to deceive, not enlighten, and Our sons must be warned to completely reject it. There is absolutely no benefit from studying false belief systems, as they are designed to trap Our children in their lost identity. There can be no syncretism with Judaism, Hebrew culture or Kabbalah, as it will be leaven that eventually will desecrate, pollute and infect the lives of those who study and follow it.

"Son, there may be some elements of truth that can be found in so many things but all those elements are designed to point to the Truth and the Light who is the only way to discover abundant life. The counterfeits can (and will) never lead to the restoration of lost identity, as they only perpetuate it, as they are from the same negative independent source.

"The elements of truth found hidden within the counterfeits are being used to deceive Our children but We are still able to use the frequency that truth has to draw them to the light of truth only found in Jesus. We placed those elements of truth within the false religious systems that Our children used to make gods in their own image so We can use it to point them to the truth; but that is not the way Our sons should be using.

"Son, encourage Our children to dwell only in the light of Our presence, as that will help them to be awakened to the reality of who We are as pure unconditional love. Only a love awakening can enable Our children to come to the light of love and truth and learn to abide there in rest. The rest that is only found in Us is the only antidote for the addiction to dead works that humanity is controlled by.

"We declare to humanity to be still, cease striving with self-effort and know who We are, so you can discover who you are as mankind made in Our image. Son, let this declaration reverberate throughout the earth shield as Our sons become oracles of Our heart and begin to speak with the sound of many waters to awaken Our children from the stupor of lost identity.

Creative Sonship

I will now share some of my experiences over the past couple of years relating to creativity and restoration, to illustrate where the journey is heading and why I have total belief in the restoration of all things.

As we mature in sonship there is a creative function we begin to operate in. This requires the deconstruction and renewal of our minds and the expanding of our consciousness to engage creative possibilities to choose and create realities. This creative function takes us beyond the basic realms of Kingdom of God, Kingdom of Heaven and Heaven to engage the realms of Heaven of Heavens, Perfection and Eternity. Those higher realms are more closely connected to the eternal now for the transcendent, outside of time and space perspective of God's heart.

As my understanding of sonship increased, so I began to see the connection of sonship with quantum physics. Quantum entanglement enables multidimensional living and connection to the whole of creation. Sonship involves the creative process of choosing and creating realities. To be able to choose reality requires brooding over and incubating reality. I had many creative engagements that helped facilitate the expansion of my understanding.

"Son, creation is still groaning! If you are to set creation free, you must learn to connect and feel its frequency."

I activated my root energy gate and reached out to creation with my desire that was birthed in cardiognosis with the Father. I drew on the river of life as rivers of living water, flowing out of heaven into my spirit; and I focused the flow through my worship gate through the desire of obeisance. As I did this I demonstrated my absolute trust in the Father by surrendering the seat of rest and government to Him.

The flow was directed by my choice through that gate in my soul by only wanting to do what I know is the Father's heart: my choice is to be a living sacrifice, immersed and cocooned in the circle of the loving conversation. The flow was directed through the garden of my heart, my deepest inner desire, cultivated in the secret place and then focused as energy frequency in the Merkabah.

The Father's desire for creation was my motivation, so I directed that flow to three gateways simultaneously, activating the root and the crown which connect heaven and earth through my heart gate. I was connected to creation: grounded, sensing and feeling creation's emotions, energy and physical life force, but also connected to the spiritual dimensions of creation and the Father's heart.

My awareness of the connection between physical and spiritual, chaos theory, string theory, the unified quantum field and fractal images was intensified and filled my mind with mathematical beauty. I opened my heart to the Elementals and invited union. As I waited, an abstract feeling began to form into a mental image of creation's mind. I felt connected to creation like I had only previously felt twice before, when I was spaghettified at a subatomic level.

This was a living emotional connection with the sentience of creation but also with the heart and mind of the Father and

His desire for total restoration. I felt the chaotic, swirling, groaning emotions of creation in bondage to corruption. Out of that mass of emotion emerged the Father's original intention, which became clearer as all the disconnections between aspects of creation, internally and externally, the seen and the unseen, revealed the design and the heart of the designer.

The Father's original desire for union, for oneness, that was ripped apart so violently, was now being restored in the connection I was feeling as a son joined to the Father's heart. The wonder that I feel sometimes when looking at nature, or a nebula in a picture from the Hubble telescope, was multiplied and intensified to feel what the Father felt when He declared "It is good". I felt the pleasure of the creator and the joy of the creation as it was in the beginning and I was almost overwhelmed with the emotional intensity of creation's song, the music of the spheres, joyously conducted.

The great symphony of creation in its purity and beauty was awesome; and as I listened, watched and felt creation's union with the creator, restoration was not only inevitable but my part in it seemed sealed and guaranteed. I was captivated, caught and suspended between the arc of creation and creator, immersed and one with both.

I now understood my role and the connection with the Elementals through this amazing union of heart, mind and purpose. All that has been lost, disconnected, fragmented and broken will be restored: it is the destiny of sonship. My experiences with the dimensions and those living beings, the fallen spiritual beings and the Elementals now made perfect sense when seen through and experienced within the Oracles of the Father's heart.

The restoration of all things is the desire of the eternal now, the heart and mind of the creator as a loving Father, converged and expressed in time through our sonship. As sons, we are the vital component in this equation and that is why creation is looking at mankind, longing for our revealing in maturity.

"Son, this is the first of many reconnections that need to take place as three gates are opened governmentally in perfect union: this was the heart with the arc of crown and root but there are other arcs joined by the heart to form government within you."

Spirit, soul and body unified with the life force in pure celebration. I felt the joie de vivre, the joy of life that was a celebration of the Father's original intention. I was undone and overwhelmed.

I saw some photos of the cosmos that were released by NASA to mark the 25th anniversary of the Hubble telescope. I was drawn to one particular picture of what is known as the Cosmic Reef, particularly the circular blue nebula that looks like a portal[101].

In a restoration government ascension group we were also drawn to the blue nebula. When we ascended, I went out into the cosmos, drawn by the blue portal nebula. When I entered through the membrane it felt familiar, like I had been there before. This was a place connected to the eternal now of God's heart but I had only ever seen it before from a heavenly perspective, accessing it only from the heavenly realms. This

---

[101] You can find the image online at hubblesite.org/contents/media/images/2020/16/4646-Image – or on the cover of my previous book, *The Restoration of All Things* and as the background in many of my videos.

was a cosmic access point that connected to God's heart and His creative desires.

This was not an access point that had been entered through before, other than by Enoch, as I later discovered. Only now, because of our union and cosmic focus, can we enter. Our sonship is unveiling the ancient paths once again.

I immediately heard and felt the sound and light frequency that was His voice vibrating with energy. This was the Chamber of Creation where the Father's heartbeat was creating a rhythm – more like a cadence – that was pulsating with living energy grace, His divine enabling power. There was a membrane between the spiritual and the physical dimension like the event horizon of a black hole because this was the original singularity that formed creation. This was where the creativity of the eternal now is released. This was where the heart and mind of God in agreement spoke all creation into existence: this was the origin.

The Father said "This is where you must gather together when you desire to release a shock wave ripple of exponential creative energy from the eternal now perspective into cosmic time and space."

I began to let my thoughts form words that were resonating with the Father's heart and they began to pulsate to its cadence, becoming greatly amplified. It was as if when we speak here the Father adds His voice to ours, sparking creative power. This chamber is where the vibrating energy of His voice and our voice engages with the vibrating living light strings of energy that are within the fabric of all creation.

Limitless grace, communicated as creative expression: a place which is the source of zero-point energy, the unified quantum field and quantum foam. This is where all creation is held together by the power of His voice. One sugar cube's worth of this energy can power 400 billion galaxies and it is within us; and when focused, it produces limitless energy and creativity.

The chamber of creation is the opposite of black holes which absorb light and energy because they are the absence of light (but they do emit a sound that is the groan of creation, a B flat 57 octaves lower than the keyboard middle C: that is one million, billion times lower than the lowest sound audible to the human ear).

I remembered some of my past experiences and I began to vibrate, pulsate, almost convulse, as I resonated to the cadence of the Father's heart. The living light beings swayed to the rhythm of the frequency of creative thought and the Father spoke:

"Son, you have all been shown something within the Chamber of Creation that only Enoch saw when he walked the stars. This knowledge is precious and powerful beyond measure: be very careful and ensure that you never use it individually and selfishly but only in union together. This chamber has the creative power to change and transform the physical realm, to restore it to its original condition purpose.

"This power is a living power. Within Us there is only life. That is why it is light; and light is alive, grace is alive, love is alive – they all take angelic form – and the strings that science has discovered are alive. The strings are alive: and whenever We speak, it is living, limitless grace; and that responds through the beings that were named Quantum Lumens."

(We had been told to name them so that they could be revealed and things would be seen, so one person on that ascension named them 'Quantum Lumens' and that name seemed to fit perfectly).

"Whenever you choose and create reality, those light beings of pure limitless grace form the fabric of existence as they respond to your sonship. Son, start choosing life to form the future: aligned to Our heart, beating to Our cadence, on a cosmic scale – just as you have learned to choose reality, controlling time and space within your own sphere.

"The cosmic sphere of government can never be controlled by any one person but only by the union of hearts and minds that are willing to selflessly collaborate with the Father's heart. You have all been called for a time such as this, *kairos* moments that will affect *chronos* time and space for its restoration.

"The shield around the earth sphere that your union is creating is increasing and will eventually become an energy field around the whole cosmos as you mature in oneness in union with others.

"Son, the Chamber of Creation will amplify your one voice when in union, so legislate from there. Seek Me for My heart so you can resonate with Me and all creation will begin to respond to your one voice."

I later found the place to do that, called the Cradle of Life.

"The living grace light beings (Quantum Lumens) are that which holds the fabric of creation together and are the creative force behind all that is created. Your awakened sonship consciousness has the ability to see and choose the reality of the restoration of all things. When you speak as one with each other and My heart from within the Chamber of Creation, the sound that you release enables the light to bond together as one to manifest reality." (In quantum physics this is called 'popping a qwiff' or 'collapsing a quantum wave function').

"Great changes that seem to suddenly appear on the earth or in the cosmos all began as thoughts that are amplified into living words that become living light. There is a place of brooding and connection that creates the sound you hear that I will show you soon. Legislate as one for the global changes that you seek, to prepare the earth and the cosmos for the shift into the next age of enlightenment and rest.

"Son, Enoch, Melchizedek and Wisdom are to be your guides and many of the great cloud are coming to the brightness of your rising to support you. Engage with them and listen to the wisdom that they carry as they have many things to impart to you. It is important that you unite creation by involving all those that have been revealed to you from the different realms and those who have been restored.

"Son let me show you something. Come walk with Me."

I saw, felt and sensed the connection of life between all things that unifies creation. This was part of a series of encounters going back to 2010. I sensed the connections within the heavenly realms between the living beings and the cloud of witnesses functioning like a vast living neural net of love's light.

We as sons are to be the convergence of this connection with the Elementals of creation. I sensed the grace light beings within the fabric of all things longing for the physical creation to be united as the spiritual heavenly dimensions are. I began to sense the desire of the oracles of the Father's heart living within the light of those light beings, resonating with life force:

the energy of love's light pulsating within the fabric of creation, creating a potential unified field of consciousness.

The echo of a memory of what once was and will be again is drawing creation back to a union that it is longing for deep within its fabric. This vibration is getting stronger as sonship is revealed and more are rising and shining, awakened to love. Love's light is the grace, loving energy, that connects and holds all of creation loosely together; but it is also drawing it together into a union of greater coherence.

I felt it deeper than ever before because it is stronger than ever before, as it is being amplified by our union and rippling through space-time. As the ripples go out into all the dimensions they are not diminishing but getting stronger, being energised and energising simultaneously. The hope for restoration is the energy frequency that is awakening creation and hope's whisper is itself growing louder, as if all the light beings are being excited and activated. The faint whisper of hope and the testimonies of restoration are creating morphic resonance throughout the dimensions of creation.

So many of those who are lost and adrift in hopelessness are beginning to sense hope rising and have an expectation for restoration. The tide has turned: the balance has shifted and momentum is increasing. Everything feels brighter, more expectant of hope being fulfilled from the flow of the Tree of Life. Joy is rising, fuelled by hope, strengthening love's bonds within the unified field of existence. It feels like the groan is slowly becoming a laugh. It is but a faint, barely perceivable change, but it is there: hope restored is rippling through creation like leaven permeating dough.

"Son, the age of light is living in the light of love which is true oneness with *I am that I am*. Living in the light of oneness illuminates creation and restores it back to its position (which you saw in 2010) where there was no absence of light. The whole cosmos was illuminated by each living being made of creative light and each being was filled with the light of love and radiated love's light as luminaries."

"You are called sons of light, the light of the world" (actually the word is 'cosmos'). "Restoration will restore that primordial condition; and everything that was created in the beginning will be transfigured to reveal Our true essence as you reflect I am in glorious splendour.

"Son, that is just the beginning (not the end) of the ascension of mankind, as Our children are destined to become ascended fathers and co-creators in the ages to come. The ability to speak with Our voice like a father will awaken the creative power within you to partner with what you have called Quantum Lumens to form new creative realities.

"Son, you will only be limited in creative light power by the smallness of your thinking and imaginative ability. Do not limit creativity by being tethered to what you presently know because with an expanded consciousness there is limitlessness. With the ability to create must come the responsibility to have a father's heart towards that which you will have the power to create. With great creative light power comes even greater responsibility to be love's light, shining with the oracles of the Father's heart.

"Son, love cares: it is deeply compassionate towards all that it creates with a passion and burning desire for its wellbeing. When you are truly mature as ascended fathers, you also will be fiercely protective towards what you create, with joyous pride and pleasure. Your creations will be the treasure of your hearts, just as this present creation is the treasure of Our heart.

"Son, remember: true love never gives up, never fails, can never be separated or divided from its object, and will always eventually win and overcome. Son, learn the dancing movement of the living light beings as they respond to the sound of your voice. When you speak with a father's heart, light will be ignited and become activated, bursting with love's creative energy. Son, in the age of light, living light itself will dance to the rhythm of the frequency of the beating of your heart as you learn to express your creative desire as thoughts tuned to the frequency of love."

Standing in the Chamber of Creation I saw the living light grace beings, the Quantum Lumens, moving to sound like a swirling mist, or a flock of birds flying in murmuration, or a shoal of fish shimmering as they move in unison, waiting to form into the manifestation of the creator's desire. It was so beautiful: living light, dancing, moving, waiting, full of potential, needing only a focused loving thought to collapse the quantum wave into reality. We need to understand this process to begin to change and realign reality for the restoration of all things.

I engaged the Chamber of Creation and immediately began to pulsate and groan to the rhythm of the Father's heart for creation. It felt like I was vibrating but contracting in picking up energy and expanding out over and over. I began to groan, my mind and my voice in agreement with the frequency as it became deeper and louder. I became unaware of my body. In a trancelike state I saw the Quantum Lumens dancing to the rhythm of the groan, swaying like a moving ribbon of light particles. This became more intense, my thoughts and my whole being entwined in the sound and light that I was part of.

It felt like it was moving, being conducted by God's heart, and I was moving with it. I then focused my thoughts and the frequency of my being together with those in union within the earth shield. We then released the light into the earth shield and into areas where light was absent. The Quantum Lumens, moving as one living being, began to stream out of the chamber through the portal, energised by the sound that we were producing. I saw and felt the living light focused and streaming with purpose, connecting and energising, synchronising with other sons around the world.

I saw Enoch and Limitless (an angelic being) together in agreement with us in union, directing the sound and the light. The Father's heart was being expressed through us in a union of living sound and light that is awakening people to the new reality that we, in union with each other and with others, are creating.

The Father began to speak to me of unconditional love in regards to this global awakening of consciousness. I went into the dark cloud, the cloak of mystery, and engaged with the restored angels of Union, Covenant, Peacemaker, Family, Hope and Protector. I shared our heart with them about shielding, protecting the earth as we steward this revolution. I asked them to help us weaken the systems of global influence. We need help in this process as there is creativity and the action that accompanies it.

The global systems function through division, competition, conflict and tribalism. We need help to remove the cabals controlling the economy, banking systems, oil industry, pharmaceutical corporations and arms dealers by drawing more of their kind (fallen beings) to restoration.

I asked them to help destabilise the systems so this awakening could gain momentum by inspiring counterculture through genuine protests. They agreed; and together in union we began to release a ripple of frequency into the spiritual realms. It felt like we were getting the attention of the orders of fallen angels responsible for division, conflict, competition and tribalism and some of them began to lose their focus. The frequency began to draw them towards the dark cloud and away from their activities in the earth so that the awakening could accelerate. I believe that this is an ongoing process that needs many sons in agreement to legislate.

The living light streams began to illuminate the areas of darkness with revelation truth, enlightening people to the possibilities of change. It felt like this enlightenment was going to become the seedbed for the future, to usher in this global golden age with a new renaissance.

"Son, come walk with Me."

The Father took me out into the cosmos to constellations and planetary systems and I discerned something that I had seen before, the same voids that were around the atmosphere of the earth. As the journey continued I saw that those voids were in many of the galaxies that we visited: hidden portals, only discernible by the absence of light.

I knew how to penetrate those shielded voids, as I had done before, by changing the vibrating frequency of my being. The Father halted the whistle-stop tour of the universe at a particular constellation, Pleiades, and we entered the void. Within it, there was a portal that was energised and very active with many beings coming and going.

I asked the Father who they were and what they were doing. "These are who you are shielding the earth from and this is a junction between dimensions that connects many dimensional places."

I started to think about what I was supposed to do when the Father interrupted my musings by revealing His heart for those beings and all the dimensions that they represented. His thoughts were far from my thoughts, so I just focused on Him and my mind went back to the Chamber of Creation.

I began to resonate with the Father's heart and I started to pulse and move in harmony; and then the Quantum Lumens that were hidden within the void and also within me began to illuminate that place. That absence suddenly became filled with light and love energy that took all those beings by surprise and got their attention. I was aware that I was supposed to do something but I hesitated and reached out to the Father with my mind. I felt peaceful and at rest at that moment; and inspired and energised, I began to attract the Quantum Lumens, who streamed towards me; they joined with those from within me and surrounded me, as if creating a luminescent field around me.

I was moving in unison with creative light and was one heart and mind with them. I thought and spoke; and instantly, through a quantum entangled connection, they moved and created a new reality where love's light filled that void. It was like I was conducting or orchestrating a message of hope for restoration that was dancing like an amazing cosmic light show, communicating the Father's desire in a way that was far beyond anything I had felt or experienced before. One by one, the beings started moving towards the light that was encompassing me and I became aware that the Father was hidden from my sight.

For a brief moment I felt apprehensive but then I felt the Father's comforting presence within me. I released the call for restoration: the Lumens shone brightly with love's light and the whole atmosphere in that void changed. I continued to release the love frequencies of the oracles of the Father's heart and I expanded my being until it encompassed the whole void.

I called to them, revealing the truth of their deception and their true origin within the Father's creative purpose. The beings began to respond – and I felt them communicating their confusion at first – but then, one by one, I felt their decisions to be restored back into creation according to the Father's desire. I watched as the Lumens streamed towards them and burst from within them to join in a joyfully jubilant celebration that sent ripples into the dimensions to which they were connected. Those glorious, restored beings released a joyous hope for restoration into creation.

Again I felt overwhelmed by the experience and did not know what to do next. The Father's comforting voice reassured me when He said, "Come, your part is over; just keep them in your heart. The revolution has progressed today and this has created the seedbed for great change. Son, this is a lesson for you. You were thinking warfare and disruption and I was thinking peace and joy. Rebuilding and restoration will never be facilitated by warfare, only through coming in the opposite spirit will change begin." This is a lesson that so many will have to learn if they are to collaborate with the Father's heart for the restoration of all things.

"Son, come walk with Me."

We walked in the Father's garden in all its great beauty, a feast for the eyes that activated all the senses, filling me with wonder and awe. We walked through some double golden gates and I realised that this was another of those moments on my journey that connected me to creation at a deeper level.

The Father reminded me of the limitless possibilities that exist in this place of absolute rest and my mind, although totally at peace, was filled with creative potential.

"Son, this is the place that is connected to the Chamber of Creation: this is where We brood over creation. This is where creative realities are formed in rest, inspired by the beauty of possibility. Our dreams become substance and the Chamber of Destiny amplifies Our frequency; and so the Lumens dance to Our thoughts with creative energy in the Chamber of Creation.

"Son, this is not just My garden, but is the cradle of all that there is and all that there will be. That is why we invite all Our children to be at rest here, where the treasure chest of our thoughts is; here, within the pool of deep intimacy.

"Son, that is why the golden mountain and Metatron are here: this is the garden of Our heart, the birthing place of Our precepts. You have been drawn here all your life, looking for this place of being that inspires the reality of who you are. Now that you know the secrets of the Chamber of Creation, brood here in the rest of I am and release your being."

In that instant, my being became a creative force, capable of infinite creativity. I was anchored within precepts of the Creator, made in Their image and likeness: spirit from spirit, light from light, love from love and fire from fire.

This experience was in 2020 and my mind went to the upcoming *Restoration of All Things 2* conference. I began to see what would emerge from that conference: a generation inspired by hope for restoration, establishing embassies of heavenly love, joy and peace all over the earth.

I brooded over what I saw and felt, and I saw how that produced the sound of many waters and was amplified in the Chamber of Destiny behind the waterfall in the Father's garden. I also saw how the Chamber of Destiny was connected to the Chamber of Creation. I saw the creative energy of my thoughts was resonating and pulsating with creative potential and the Lumens were dancing to the tune of what my heart had released.

I saw light streaming from the portal into creation, creating a new reality: birthed from rest, inspired by my Father, but created by my being. All other possibilities ceased to be: the Quantum Lumens activated creation and this reality is established and has been called forth.

"Son, now you know and your knowledge will inspire a generation of sons to become mature in their true identity as creative beings at rest as they begin to father the future." I felt pure joy and elation, resting in the true knowledge that I am that I am within *I am that I am*.

"Son, today We desire to draw you deeper into Our desire so you can dwell permanently within the creative place of Our heart. The Cradle of Life is the birthing place of Our thoughts: this is your abiding place but there is further revelation to come.

"Come through the Garden of Eden, through the golden gates, into the garden of Our heart. We will enable you to see in the light that is just the Cradle of Life, the creative birthplace of all things."

This was an encounter that further clarified the connection between sound and light for me. I could see, but I could not *really* see - it was still too much for my mind. My consciousness still needs to be expanded beyond my current capacity. The light enveloped me and it felt like I was being wrapped in the beautiful light and love of creative thought. In this chrysalis of transformation, my consciousness was changing: it felt like I was aware of mysteries that I was never aware of before, or even knew existed. The mysteries were no longer hidden; and as this process continued, they became knowledge to my spirit, even if not yet to my soul.

That amazing light was being woven into the fabric of my being. It was light that has been everywhere and seen everything and it was as if all of history was now contained within my consciousness. It was like a movie of the ages was playing within my mind, reminding me not just of the facts and events but how the Father was working within them. I could see how He was rewriting the narrative of every event in every person to enable the love story to continue. There were constant revisions and new beginnings throughout history that are the fingerprints of God on all people and all events.

Limitless grace and mercy – expressed over and over, throughout all time and space – bringing inclusion and reconciliation to ensure relationship. Relationship is the creative spark, the common theme and the thread that runs throughout all of time and connects time within eternity. The deepest desires of the Father for the restored face to face innocence of a love relationship is the pure essence of the narrative and the true spark of all that is behind the whole creative process. The brooding frequency is vibrating to this creative rhythm, producing the sound that moves and energises the light to form those desires into reality.

"Son, if you are to be like We are as *I am that I am*, you must learn to dwell here, deep within Our heart; as this is how and where the convergence of the eternal now and what will be is framed and formed.

"Son, all the other heavenly realms, places, courts, thrones, councils and houses that you have experienced began here in the cradle of all life and existence. This place was always designed for Our children to abide so that they can be like us: ascended fathers, moved and motivated by love's light relationally expressed.

"Son, now you know even more the depth of Our desire for the restoration of all things and why it is inevitable. Son, be one with Our heart in the Cradle of Life, motivated and directed by the oracles that you have experienced and embraced. Joined with Us, you become one spirit within Us as We become one spirit within you.

"You will discover so much more within you as *I am that I am* within Us, as We are *I am that I am* within you. This is another stage of ascension revealed by your last fire stone engagement.

"We have been drawing you here through the encounters you have experienced in preparation for the global shift you are now participating in. Being truly one spirit, soul and body, with all your gateways and energy gates balanced, aligned and energised, has opened this realm of being as a new state of consciousness.

"Son, as you are at rest, resonating with love, joy and peace, brooding over creation, the Chamber of Creation is responding to your voice as you feel Our heart and know Our mind; and the Quantum Lumens of living grace dance creation's dance. Son, this is how reality is framed and comes into existence as the eternal now and time converge.

"Union, Covenant and Peacemaker will partner with Limitless, Hope and Love so that Family can open the windows from the eternal now and time. These angelic orders are at the disposal of Our sons who are moved by the restoration of all things.

"You have been given the mandate to turn those in darkness to the light of their creative purpose. Begin with the benches of Division, Competitiveness and Warmonger (Conflict) before you engage Tribalism."

I began to brood over them within the Cradle of Life, feeling how the Father feels and knowing the vast sums of His thoughts towards them. My whole being started to convulse with the sound of their creation and I began to be consumed with passion for their restoration. My thoughts and emotions became a deep groan that echoed as the sound of many waters within the Chamber of Destiny and the living light grace beings danced, energised and activated, in the Chamber of Creation. I absorbed the light into my being, which activated and energised me.

I saw what would be months of engagements become focused into one concentrated moment as I chose that reality and the quantum wave function began to collapse. As the light streamed into reality. I issued the call of hope to Division and the angelic orders surrounded me within the cloak of mystery, the dark cloud. The three generals of Division were drawn into the dark cloud, safe, and shielded from darkness.

"Son, everything is a convergence and a fractal that is designed to balance and align with who We are. Everything is within Us and We are within everything, therefore you are gods within God. We are within you, as you will discover later on your journey. You are Priests, Kings, Oracles and Legislators within YHVH as you are the faces of God within the four faces of God. You are within the eternal now and the eternal now is within you as you are the convergence of time and eternity. You are a garden designed to dwell within a garden within a garden within a garden, as sons, both created and creating.

"Son, as you learn to brood within the Cradle of Life it is also brooding within you as a resonant frequency creating a resonant frequency. Son, as you groan, you answer a groan, being both sound and light: so arise and shine, pulsating to the rhythm of Our heart. Son, just as you have the Merkabah and the Sephiroth within you, so are you within them: a fractal and a convergence.

"Son, come, let's walk together in the garden of your heart."

We went to my secret place, which I had first discovered in 2010, and I sat on my swing. The Father, gently pushing me, told me to look at the tapestries. I saw that there were more tapestries than before, the new ones representing the multidimensional reality that I am now living in. There was a picture for each set of functions lived in the quantum moment that has become my existence.

"Son, you have tended and cultivated this place well, and the intimacy of rest can be truly enjoyed, but there is still more expansion needed for a full creational reality. Remember when we first engaged here before, you were not even aware of a garden? Now, in 10 years, you are abiding in the garden of My heart as I abide in yours – but you need to realise the creative potential you have. This is the cradle of your life as a son who will become an ascended father, made in the image and likeness of Me.

"Son, learn to brood here as you have in My heart. Be inspired to be creative so your imagination can be expanded to match your heavenly consciousness. Son, there are infinite quantum moments here that you can brood into reality, created from the light of your being.

"Rejoice in your being and be filled with joy unspeakable, full of your creative glory, as that will be your strength. This is where you can truly see who you are as you engage My face in deep intimacy within yourself. This is another wheel within a wheel that is capable of amazing creativity when you learn to align your 12 houses. Yes, son, you have a circle of the deep within you with 12 houses that are a fractal of the Chancellors' Houses, as you are a Chancellor.

"Son, the Merkabah has many more dimensions to it that will be discovered as you learn to creatively brood here." I saw them now, the connections within that reflect the heart of God and the creative process. The Merkabah is the point of connection between dimensions, where everything can be in perfect harmony and balance.

I pondered and mused in that quantum moment and infinite possibilities of creative realities streamed before me. I felt completely at rest, knowing that I am within the Father and the Father is within me, even faced with infinite choices. I was overflowing with the joy set before me, rejoicing as I pondered the creative potential.

"Son, the shift is here, as you have moved from one to many, from individual to corporate, and your authority has increased exponentially. Your mandate in government is creation with a specific emphasis on the fallen ones and fallen dimensions and their restoration."

I began to brood over Competition and Covenant within the Cradle of Life, resonating with the relational creative intention, and I felt the direct effects of Division that has promoted competition globally and cosmically.

As I began to rhythmically pulsate, the Chamber of Creation began to amplify the frequency and the Quantum Lumens began to energise. I absorbed that light energy within my being, which activated the light within me, and I was in unison and harmony with the Father's desire. Being within the quantum moment, I engaged the dark cloud of mystery and released a frequency that drew the bench of Competition. My whole being was energised with the light of covenant love and all objections just melted away like ice in a furnace. In that quantum moment, all time existed; and the months of fire and purifying refinement were *now*. I felt the whole process of transfiguration within that moment and there were three resplendent beings of light, restored to their former glory as Covenant.

"Son the eternal now is the dimension of Our being, Our oneness, Our pure essence; that gives birth to Our precepts, Our heart and Spirit; that in turn to Our statutes, Our mind and love; and to Our laws and Our light.

"There must be a window to creation that enables Us to be experienced: that is Our ordinances, Our hand and fire. Remember that we are Spirit, love, light and a consuming fire and We choose and create reality, as you must learn to do.

"Son, the Cradle of Life is where Our heart's desires become living spirit frequencies and the Father's garden is where those frequencies form Our thoughts that vibrate and are energised and become living love motivation. That life spirit carries Our thoughts and they become living words of love, the sound of many waters, in the Chamber of Destiny; and they become living light within the Chamber of Creation; and as that light crosses the event horizon, it becomes Our hand of living grace fire within the fabric of the all things of creation.

"Son, there is always a fourth window that enables the three of Our being to be experienced through Our ordinances: Our hand of fire that connects Us to the physical realm of creation.

"Son, walk with Me."

We walked in Eden by the River of Life, Tree of Life and Throne of Grace, which are another three, representing the heart, mind and voice of God. Then we walked to the Judgment Seat and I saw that the fire is the window of ordinances where destiny is refined by God's hand.

We continued walking to the great waterfall that cascades into the Father's garden. As we descended the falls, I could see as never before. I saw the golden mountain where the seasons of heaven and doors, windows and portals are administered by Metatron. I saw the pool where the golden chest of divine thoughts is found and where there is an entrance to the eternal now. I saw the golden gates that lead to the Cradle of Life and then I saw it: behind the waterfall is the Chamber of Destiny, the entrance to the Chamber of Creation. The waterfall is the sound of many waters where God's voice is amplified in the Chamber of Destiny before it enters the Chamber of Creation. I could see through the chamber to the event horizon, where it connected through the consuming fiery hand of God to creation.

We were then within my spirit, seeing the river of life flow through my worship and choice gates to the garden of my heart, the dance floor, soaking room and bridal chamber, which followed the same pattern of three becoming consummated in the fourth.

"Son, We are – but have included man in Us so you can be – and Our hand and fire is always fulfilled in creation. We are a consuming fire that keeps Our living desires, thoughts and words alive in the transfiguration of man by Our hand.

"Son, only the light of love can draw fallen creation; and that love must be genuine and have integrity. When you come into the realm of light within the dark cloud to see Our face, you will absorb the light of love that We have for Our creation.

"Son, you will begin to see what We see when We look at Our creation with the eyes of a Father creator. We see beauty even in the midst of outer darkness, as We see with the eyes of love's light for Our creation."

On another occasion, I went into the dark cloud in the realm of perfection, drawn to the light, to absorb the light of truth; and as I looked into the Father's face, I was able to focus on different facets of manifoldness in regards to creation. I saw the beauty of the original intention in majestic splendour and I absorbed the frequency of that beautiful light. This was an amazing experience of being as it was always meant to be, in the total rest of *I am that I am*.

I entered the Cradle of Life to brood over the beauty of the fallen ones, focusing on the order of Division. Division functions through producing mixture, compromise and lukewarmness that perverts the purity of oneness in the name of this false unity. As I brooded and resonated with the Father's heart of love for those responsible, I was feeling and seeing the images of His original intention.

Being joined and resonating in agreement with the Father's heart must be the foundation of all our creative intentions.

I saw the sound of many waters activate the Chamber of Destiny, which amplified the sound of my groaning; and in the Chamber of Creation, that frequency excited the Quantum Lumens, the light beings, who began to form the reality of their restoration. I went into the cloak of mystery and released the frequency of love's light that would draw those beings of false unity. They create unity of a compromised, joint belief but without producing true oneness and union. Their minds are united but their hearts are divided and they live in the illusion of unity with no oneness and no union.

I drew them into the dark cloud and, in that quantum moment, went through the process of releasing all the light of love I had absorbed from the Father, forgiving and releasing them, reminding them of their previous position, offering restoration, and answering every fear and objection with love's wisdom, wearing them down until that moment came when the scales of darkness and deception began to melt away and the beautiful light beings emerged.

On behalf of the restoration government group, I commissioned them to engage the Church systems to draw people out of compromise to connect with true union and oneness of true new order *ekklesia*. I released the frequency of love's light into the wilderness of religious compromise to call the children of God to come out from under the false coverings of the Moses order to cross over into their heavenly inheritance and true union.

"Son, brood over restoration within the Cradle of Life: really go deep, to identify with creation's groaning. Feel the pain creation feels over the lost identity of Our children and the discord and disconnection that was once union and harmony. The longing and waiting in anticipation of the rising of sonship is over now, as the new dawn has now broken. The frequencies of hope and the light of love have rippled throughout creation and the Elementals are awakening as a sign. 'Hope springs eternal' – this is now the beginning of the end of bondage and new days will dawn in an age of fulfilment and freedom, where the light of truth will shine brightly.

"Division between man and creation is ending as the sons of God become one with Us, each other and creation once again. The songs of the joy of union will be sung, sounding throughout creation in a jubilant celebration once again."

It was like a united orchestra was playing the great symphony, the music of the spheres, signifying the dawn of the new age.

"Son, brood long for the fullness of restoration so that the sound of many waters will be amplified in the Chamber of Creation. The living light of grace and truth will resonate with the sound that Our sons produce, ready to form new creation realities. The glory of the children of God will bring freedom to all of creation when all the colours merge into one, unified, bright white light of family.

The whole of creation was created to be a family full of diversity, each part resplendent in its beauty; a union of variety, with no competition or conflict.

I engaged the Cradle of Life to resonate with the Father's heart for creation and began to brood over peace and harmony. Those engagements with the Father's heart create a frequency that causes great resonance to form the sound of many waters. My heart was moved with compassion for those beings within creation deceived into causing warmongering. I saw and felt the Father's heart for their restoration to the Father's original intention and purpose.

My being began to pulsate with energy. The sound of many waters began to energise the Chamber of Creation, where the amplification excited the Quantum Lumens to begin moving to the rhythm of peace and harmony.

I saw the reality for the restoration of Warmonger and released the frequency of hope as the light streamed into creation. I entered the dark cloud clothed with mystery and began to call for the bench of three of Warmonger to be drawn to love's light and the hope of restoration and freedom. I asked Union and Covenant to stand with me as they came into the cloud; and in that quantum moment, I saw the next season play out. I became aware of all of the processes that would lead to their restoration, until finally the light emerged from the darkness.

There before us were three beautiful light beings radiating the light of peace, so I introduced them to the Benches of Union and Covenant. I felt the celebration of the heavenly host and I commissioned them to the task of helping to facilitate global transformation.

They revealed that whilst conflict through competition and division was at the heart of their strategies economically, their major focus was to keep the church system divided and in opposition with one another because of doctrinal and theological arguments. They revealed the great deception that is behind the economic, political, media and religious systems that maintain control globally. They revealed the strategy to keep us from our sonship by drawing us back to the old covenant Hebraic roots that divide and separate.

As I brooded in the Cradle of Life over my spheres of influence, I began to get a deeper insight into the Father's desires.

"Son all these spheres are part of your scroll in general but they are not part of you. Earthly love will always be only a pale reflection of the love who We are, so look to things above and focus on the true eternal realities."

I needed to meditate on the value of the temporal and the eternal and how to balance them correctly. I released my broodings as I pulsated with life for a better future into the sound of many waters waterfall, to be amplified in the Chamber of Destiny as a conduit into the Chamber of Creation, where the amplification process excited the Quantum Lumens to begin to shape reality.

"Son, come and brood over a restored future in the Cradle of Life. Feel Our heart: let Our desire motivate your intentions so you can be as We are."

I felt the energy of life begin to pulsate within my heart, creating new future possibilities that were filled with positive energy. I took that energy to the waterfall and imparted it as a resonant frequency to the sound of many waters for amplification in the Chamber of Destiny so it could echo within the Chamber of Creation to form future reality. I saw the living light swaying and moving, energised and activated by the sound frequency of my desire. I saw the future begin to manifest into reality where hope fulfilled is a tree of life. The Quantum Lumens streamed out to form future reality.

"Son, come walk with Me."

We walked in the Father's garden to the golden mountain and we sat there observing the wonder of creation. I saw thrones associated with creation connected to the basic elements: air, water, earth and fire. Those thrones were by the river of fire, the waterfall, the mountain, and the garden; and there were other thrones also, for the trees, animals, plants and all beings.

The Father took me to each throne and there – waiting for me to sit as an ambassador – were the representatives of each of the Elementals. They were ancient spirits and I felt their deep connections to creation and their desire for union and symbiosis with the sons of God. They were waiting for Our authority to complete what was lacking in them by giving them direction and order. They were powerful but not wise; and the Father showed me history in a moment where they had been seduced by darkness. I felt their grief over the groaning of creation but also their shame for being deceived and influenced by darkness.

We went to each throne in turn, where a connection was made; and I received a download of infused knowledge concerning creation past, present and future. I felt the sentience of creation and understood more of its longing; and my desire for its freedom and restoration became more focused.

"Son, you have always had a deep connection to nature but now you are more aware of the responsibility of sonship, you will begin to connect and partner with the Elementals. Creation needs the government of man to be fruitful as intended and mankind needs the cooperation of the Elementals and the elements for harmony to be restored. This revelation and these types of encounters will increase greatly in the next season.

"Son the need for union and harmony with creation is built into the fabric of your being and no DIY substitute can ever bring fulfilment. Son, these thrones will need to be occupied by Our sons who are awakened to the ancient ways. The elements must be governed to see the restoration of peace: therefore the winds must be tamed, the earth's plates must be unified and the seas be brought to rest so that nature will be in harmony as it was in the beginning.

"Son, it is the season for the hope of freedom to be communicated to creation with limitless grace and deep compassion. The oracles of Our heart are not limited to what you see as living beings but for all creation in all its reflections of I am. Son, legislate for the sons of God to arise and respond to creation's groaning and connect with the Elementals. This union and reconnection will raise the frequency of the earth and cause the cosmos to react.

"Son, the thrones within the atmosphere and the seismic plates are occupied by principalities and rulers that are controlling global issues. The occupation of these thrones needs to be a focus of the next season of limitless grace. The sons of God are beginning to occupy the mountain spheres and the water spheres but there are still many thrones that need to be occupied and governed. The Elementals are presently influenced by those seated in darkness. The Elementals recognise who are enthroned – and cooperate with them, unless many sons are interceding to counteract the negative influence.

"Son creation is longing and waiting for Our children to arise and be seated in identity and authority in heaven and on earth. Who is seated in the atmosphere has the greatest influence on the earth but who is seated in the heavenly realms has greater authority to cleanse the atmosphere; but they must converge both realms, by functioning as the order of Melchizedek.

"Son, teach Our sons to engage and function in the dark cloud of the cloak of mystery, to remove the darkness by releasing the light. Only when you take authority in the dual realms of heaven and earth can you restore the atmosphere and mobilise the global Elementals to enable full governmental rule. Changing the global control systems will not be possible without occupying the thrones of the elements of creation, as they are used to create instability, insecurity and fear.

"Fear generates anger, and anger is used to create division; and division creates competition, and that creates conflict, which creates tribalism and empire, which creates more cycles of division. The cycles must be broken by coming together in the union of relationship that will model a new progression of well-being. This cycle is where union creates covenant, which creates peace, which creates family, which brings union and harmony.

"This cycle of seasons functions like a fractal at many levels, beginning with you being the union of spirit, soul and body and the convergence of time and eternity and heaven and earth throughout the dimensions. Union leads to covenantal cooperation and peace, which creates harmony, which restores family oneness, togetherness, and the environment that fosters love.

"Son, when Our children truly function in relationship and government in the heavenly realms in the union of perfect love, they will be able to begin to reflect heaven in and through their lives and so manifest sonship."

I went to the Cradle of Life within the heart of the Father and began to brood over union until I was pulsating with creative energy and producing the frequency of oneness. I stretched out the moment of incubation to be ready to birth union and I saw Division fighting, resisting but eventually falling.

I saw the repeating cycle of the vicious circle of Division to Tribalism broken and the infinite pathway of covenant replace it. Energised by what I saw, I engaged the waterfall of the Sound of Many Waters to amplify the sound of Union and it began to resonate and increase in intensity in the Chamber of Destiny, until the Chamber of Creation was activated, the sound was magnified to a creational level, and the Quantum Lumens began to dance to the creative rhythm of the frequency. The creative light was alive with the energy necessary to pop the qwiff and begin the cycle of wave function collapse.

"Son, the season of limitless, greater grace is beginning as the age of the waters of light and love are dripping into creation, ready to be poured out.

"Son, come walk with Me."

We entered the dark cloud of mystery and I was amazed by what I saw: the realm was filled with light and life, there was so much frequency and love being displayed by the restored angels. The luminosity and manifold colours of the restored ones were like an amazing cosmic firework display. The restored beauty was wonderful to behold and the interaction with the Father and other angels was so touching to see that I was undone and deeply moved.

"We have been here, following up on all you have done and amplifying the frequency of your love. You have been here continually with Us and there are multitudes of fallen ones who have returned and have been restored. More are returning by the second and there is a momentum that cannot be stopped. We have a strategy for their deployment as the ordinances of heaven to support the Joshua Generation in their mandate for the harvest. The light is going to shine so brightly that the frequency of the whole earth will be raised to awakening levels of illumination."

The whole scene filled me with thanksgiving and gratitude: it was joyous, a celebration of restoration. I felt the overwhelming love of the oracles of the Father's heart inspire me to press on. In subsequent encounters I have been practising retaining all the information and experience gained multi-dimensionally in quantum moments of expanded time. Different dimensional realms operate on different time scales, depending on the speed of creative light that exists in that realm. When you are in the realm of perfection, an hour could be a day, a month or a year. Retaining the information of the experiences requires an expanded consciousness. The realm of the Kingdom of God is where creative light exists in closest relationship to created light: therefore quantum moment expansion is necessary.

"Convergence is only possible through intimacy, where resonance takes place through cardiognosis. Brooding within Our heart and speaking with the voice of the sound of many waters will activate creative light energy to form reality aligned with Our intentions. The living light grace strings you call Quantum Lumens will respond to the sound of many waters of the voice of the observer to collapse wave functions to form reality.

"Son, learn to brood within the intimacy of Our heart and become a voice, an oracle, who can legislate reality."

As I became still, a God thought focused my mind; and my heart began to brood over the frequencies generated by the heart coherence of expanded consciousness. Technology will become redundant when the heart and mind are converged with the mind of Christ.

"Sons who are pure of heart will see the possibilities that exist within Our heart and choose to only create what they know are Our desires. Focus on being joined heart to heart in the deepest intimacy of the Cradle of Life, so that all you create will be pure and have no mixture.

"Son, focus your attention on legislating limitless grace."

I went to the Cradle of Life and began to brood over limitless grace with the Law of Limitless Grace in my heart. I engaged the Father's heart in that creative garden and began to resonate with a frequency that drew Limitless, who infused me with greater insight and empowerment. My whole being began to vibrate rhythmically to the cadence of limitlessness and my thoughts began to form into a song.

I became the song of limitless grace, which I now released into the Chamber of Destiny behind the waterfall. It became amplified and my voice became like the sound of many waters. This frequency crossed the event horizon of the Chamber of Creation, pulsating with living thought energy, and the Quantum Lumens began to dance creatively. My energised thoughts became declarations that were living light grace that began to stream into the physical realm to form the reality of limitless grace consciousness.

I then began to sing the song as legislative decrees.

I call for demonstrations of limitless grace to manifest that will expose all the limitations of religion.

I call for limitless grace to be lavishly expressed on the worst of the worst of the global cabals to reveal unconditional love.

I call for limitless grace to scandalise religion's need for payback and to expose the commodification of Jesus, the cross, work, money and time.

I call for limitless grace to be poured out in excess upon those who are undeserving from man's judgment perspective.

I call for limitless grace to challenge the religious and political spirit deception that has kept the children of God in spiritual poverty.

I call for limitless grace in the light of the shifting and shaking of the global control systems to expose the lies of DIY delusion.

I call for limitless grace to reveal the limitless truth of the message of the restoration of all things agenda, that of the next age outpouring of unconditional love.

I call for limitless grace to release and demonstrate forgiveness on an unprecedented scale so reconciliation between the most divided will take place.

I call for limitless grace to challenge and break the cycles of Division, Competition, Conflict and Tribalism through the lovingkindness of true new covenant love in action.

I call for limitless grace to unveil the restoration of all things message and agenda into the mainstream religious institutions, to reveal limitless grace and unconditional love.

I call for limitless grace to seek out the fallen beings in all dimensions of space and time, to open their hearts to the possibility that they can be restored from darkness to light.

I call for limitless grace to be expressed through the light of sonship to all of creation to answer its groaning for freedom with limitless grace demonstrations.

My declarations were alive and I saw the Quantum Lumens collapsing wave functions into reality throughout creation as that quantum moment stretched out before me. I felt overwhelming joy explode within me, a celebration of the pure bliss of the limitless grace of unconditional love.

"Son, let unlimited grace fill your mind and unconditional love fill your heart, as an Oracle of the Father's heart, with the desire for the restoration of all things.

"Son, the thrones of the elements need to be occupied by the sons of God for creation's restoration. Relationship with the Elementals must be restored for creation to be set free. The focus of Our children needs to be turned from their DIY agenda to the sonship mandate of dominion for blessing. The global agendas must be neutralised as they regard the earth as an asset to be stripped – and that is abuse. The relationship with creation needs to be restored so the symbiotic union that was Our intention can function again for the benefit of all. It was so different in the beginning, in the garden, but we want what would have been if there was no side-track."

The cosmos is taking its cue from what is occurring in the earth sphere and what is being broadcast through the communication networks is a false system. We must be the frequency of hope that can be broadcast dimensionally to all creation.

"The other cosmic dimensions have traded on this twisted agenda, perverting Our original intentions to their own agendas even further. The sons must rise and shine love's light to broadcast a higher frequency that will disrupt the false agendas and create hope.

"Son, all of the parts of creation are interconnected and when one suffers, they all suffer. It is time for love, joy and peace to spread like a virus, infecting with good."

We are that virus, so we must be pure and free from the pollution of the leaven of the religious and political spirit.

"We are calling Our children to a global awakening of the consciousness of true love reality but Our sons need to be ready to receive the harvest that is being prepared, to establish safe places where heaven, earth and creation can be union. It is time for global *ekklesia* to rise from the ashes of the church system and be storehouses for the coming harvest, to be restored like gardens of union between the dimensions, where fruitfulness will be restored.

"Son, these *ekklesia* must be free from mixture and pure of heart and purpose to receive the harvest. There is a religious spirit agenda to rob the purity of Our sons by deceiving them with old covenant mindsets linked to Jewish mysticism and false Hebrew roots. Son, you are mandated to issue a warning against the infiltration of the global *ekklesia* of the political and religious spirits' agendas, through Hebraic roots theology, seeking to reintroduce that failed culture and tradition.

Mystery

"Son, I have this to give you."

"What is it?"

"It is a mystery."

"Why would I need a mystery, Father?"

"Trust Me in this."

"Okay, I will receive this mystery."

The Father placed the mystery over me, like a cloak or mantle, but it completely shielded me from view. It felt like an energy field that surrounded me but also a light of inwardly-absorbed illumination. I felt wisdom and knowledge and might like I was cloaked with the 7 spirits of God. I thought "no one would be able to fathom this, including me." Was this symbolic? But it felt so real, even if it looked surreal. I symbolically had 7 eyes so I could see dimensionally and 7 heads that increased my consciousness' capacity and authority.

I thought I needed to test it out: so, seated on my new throne in the heaven of heavens, I looked to see with 7 eyes. I saw the voids, but this time clearly, and how they formed a dimensional image like an inverse fractal. These voids were where I was detecting an absence of restoration revelation. They were designed to maintain the global status quo.

I went to the restoration void, passing through the shielded harmonics as if they were not even there. I saw three fallen beings responsible for opposing the restoration of all things message. I felt no intimidation after my encounters with the light as now I was clothed with a mystery like a dark cloud of light but this was not like any dark clouds I had seen before.

I spoke in a way I had never done before, able to communicate my deepest desire for restoration, forgiveness and oneness to the three, who were knotted together like a Trinitarian knot. I overshadowed them within the mystery and all the light I had absorbed burst upon them with love's passionate, burning desire for their restoration.

The void was filled with an intensity of love's light that absorbed the darkness and there were the three most amazingly beautiful beings of light. They asked if they could stay in the mystery until they were ready. 'Ready for what?' I thought – but before I could ask, they were already aware of my musing.

"To be disconnected to become how we were created: three, but governmentally and relationally one." I said "yes" even though I would need to meditate on what they meant.

I have used the cloak of mystery, which is more like a realm or state of being than an actual cloak. It is a mystery, a place of hiddenness within the dark cloud, where we can engage with fallen angelic beings safely. It is also a safe haven where fallen angels can be restored and remain hidden from reprisals, giving us information, until they are ready to come back into the light of our realm. This dark cloud is within the Kingdom of God realm, connected to the atmosphere of the earth. The cloak of mystery within the dark cloud is a realm of light, hidden within the darkness, which is a key place to learn how to outwork the restoration process, particularly concerning fallen angels.

"Son, come walk with Me." We were in the realm of perfection, walking in the realm of light.

"Son, feel the light, don't just see it visually, as it is alive with possibilities, bursting with creative energy. Feel and sense that life force and open your heart to it so it can feel your desire and be activated by it. Your desire is created when you are joined to Us and one heart with us within the Cradle of Life as you brood. The resonance of your brooding creates the sound of your desire and that excites the living light with possibilities.

"Son, you know the process; but ensure the process is relational, by opening your heart to the scrutiny of perfection's light. Son, come here to this place and state of being to absorb the light of perfection before you brood in the Cradle of Life, and that will ensure purity without mixture.

"When you engage as groups, you have permission to open this realm of perfected light so that you can engage the fallen ones effectively.

"Son, come deeper into the light of Our being in this realm of perfection, as this is where the eternal now can converge with your time. Son, this will help you live from the eternal now state within time to become the convergence, as you can be one, at rest, but still moved by the events in time. Son, learn to live, move and have your being from within Us but express your being as the light of love within time. The light realm of perfection is filled with the light of Our being, as this is the light of love. The light realm of perfection is completely attuned and synchronised with who We are, that is why it casts no shadows."

This is where I first went in 2012, and could only stay for a millisecond, but now I can dwell there. This is where we can see the manifold facets of His face. This realm of light in Perfection is so important to the brooding creative process as all is as it should be.

"Son, come into the realm of light in perfection, and be; and see the perfect state of Our desires and intentions."

Immediately, as I entered the dark cloud and came into the light of truth, I was drawn to one facet of His face. The glorious splendour and majesty of pure perfection overwhelmed me in I am-ness: all was as it has always been. The rest of love, joy and peace cocooned me as my reality was immersed in well-being. This was deeper than I had ever been before into the reality of who is *I am that I am*. I was just being, as I absorbed the light of truth to be who I was always meant to be, in a reality that was always intended to be.

"Son, you will soon engage the fire stones once more for the next season of change and transformation to be revealed. Embrace the fire for the joy set before you, full of hope and glory, so creation can respond to the light of the rising of Our children to sonship. Son, there will be signs in the heavens and the earth that will be clear pointers that you will recognise as significant, that others might miss: so be diligent and vigilant. Keep looking so you can see.

"With great change comes great opposition, so be careful to maintain honour in love to those who resist the challenges to deception. Rest in the light of perfection and learn to be.

"Son, come walk with Me."

We walked in the Father's garden; it was beautiful beyond description. I began to feel the pleasure of the Father and creation's pleasure that we were enjoying it. Everything was communicating with me as we walked: it was sensory overload in a good way as I felt the emotions of each living thing. The garden was singing to me its joy that the Father was enjoying it and that I was enjoying it.

"Son, sonship must focus beyond the restoration of creation to the joy set before it of the union of all things. You have begun to see that by enjoying life every day in the rest of multidimensional living by being creative. Son, do not hold back on your creativity as that is what life is supposed to be about. The restoration process is not an end in itself but is only so life can return to Our image. Everyone is individually crafted and wonderfully made in Our image to live in the rest of their creative identity. All that you are enjoying making through the creativity you are expressing is part of the reset and recalibration of your life for enjoyment.

"So many of Our sons are not a good example to Our children because they are performance-driven and are not enjoying life. We intended creation to be a joyous expression of *I am that I am* but following the path of independence has taken the joy out of creation. The shift you are going through is restoring the creative joy to your heart: that is why your priorities are changing. Son, as you have discovered, by living in multiple dimensions, free from the restraints of time, you have all the time you need to do what your entire destiny mandates you to do. So just as you have felt the joy of My garden, feel the joy of your domain and be satisfied and be content with your creative endeavours.

"Son, never again go back to the old ways of working, which were lacking in real joy, but look forward to being creative as an ascended father. Creation is groaning to return to symbiotic union with the sons of God: that is reflected in what you feel in My garden. Son, imagine the whole of the created order expressing the joy you have experienced in My garden, and brood over it."

I went through the golden gates into the Cradle of Life to brood over what the Father had shown me. My whole being rested in that desire for restored union and in that quantum moment I was already enjoying what I was contemplating as if it already existed. The Chamber of Destiny amplification and the Chamber of Creation excitement of the Quantum Lumens of reality were contained within that creative moment.

"Son, now you are beginning to know true rest and enjoy a life of being. Son, brood over all that you have seen within the Cradle of Life, to come into full agreement, union and harmony with Our intentions, so that you can be one of the oracles that release the sound of many waters to shape and form reality in the Chamber of Creation. The whole of creation is waiting and longing for the sons of God to be moved by its groaning enough to act responsibly. Arise, shine with the glory of your sonship to restore hope to all the dimensions that are beginning to awaken from the great deception.

"Son, only living in a state of rest will enable all that you have seen to become reality: trusting in Our lovingkindness despite all evidence to the contrary. Live loved, love living and live loving in the rest of immortality. Legislate for this transition: although few will be aware of it, transformation will take place and the future you seek will come into reality.

"Son, engage the realm of light in perfection to know Our heart and brood over the process of wealth transfer."

I engaged the light of the Father's countenance and basked in the radiance and beauty of His face, infused with revelation knowledge and truth. I saw everything that should be and will be, as it is; and I was filled with joy and peace and totally at rest in being in the 'is'. Contented, I went to the Cradle of Life and, in collaboration with the Father's heart, brooded in rest. As that quantum moment fast forwarded, I became overjoyed again, this time pulsating to the rhythm of the frequency of creative thought. The process of creating that reality continued fast forward as the sound of many waters amplified the thoughts into words at the waterfall; and the Chamber of Destiny energised the sound until the Chamber of Creation was alive with the dance of the Quantum Lumens.

It is so important that the sons of God awaken from the slumber of religious stupor to find their true identity, heavenly authority and creational responsibility.

"Son, this light of love and truth will illuminate all that is in darkness when the sons of God abide in the light of Our countenance, knowing Our true nature and their true identity. So many of Our sons are immature in regards to the truth because they are still programmed by their religious systems and need a deconstruction and renewal of their minds. There are many who have received some truth but have not pursued the whole truth, content with limited knowledge.

"Our sons must be awakened to the truth of love's light if the world is to awake from the matrix of delusions they have been living in. Theological and doctrinal deception of all kinds has so many sons trapped in the delusion of religion, locked out of an intimate relationship. Only encounters with the light of love and truth that reveal unconditional love and limitless grace will set Our sons free to fulfil their destiny. The angelic orbs you have encountered in the earth shield carry the light and frequencies that can activate encounters; they are waiting for the sons to legislate their deployment into the earth. As they are assigned and mandated by Our sons they will facilitate a great season of encounters through dreams, visions and visitations that will stir Our children out of their religious slumber to engage beyond the veil.

"As you saw those in the earth shield being shocked by the light of truth, so those still tethered to the earth will also be shocked when they come to the realisation that they can engage heaven before they die. There are so many living wilderness existences under the darkness of man's mediatorial coverings, unable to see the freedom that is possible by living in the light. We have been wooing Our sons into a more intimate relationship with Us and many have come to maturity by the draw of Our love but many still have not awakened.

"Son that is why angelic 'shock and awe' tactics will be needed to shake them out of their slumber in the darkness. They must be awakened from their stupor by encounters with extreme demonstrations of the light, just as Brother Saul was many years ago. Son, mobilise the sons to legislate for the angelic legions that have been prepared for a time such as this and are ready for deployment."

My encounters with angelic beings increased greatly as the earth shield was being formed and strengthened. Some of these beings were those who have been already restored and were now functioning in their original identity. Limitless, Liberty, Blessing, Union, Truth Revealer, Truth Restorer, Truth Establisher, Sikurt, Protector and others are ready to be assigned to engage the earth with powerful and shocking encounters.

I shifted my attention to the earth shield but was also aware of my multidimensional positions and states of being as I began to engage the angelic orbs; this time it was not for engaging me but to engage those on the earth. Strengthened and encouraged, I began to make declarations targeting those who needed awakening.

I call for the light of love and truth to shine brightly; for lightning bolts of truth and love bombs to manifest on earth as it is in heaven.

I call for Damascus and Emmaus road type encounters that will capture and captivate hearts and minds with the light of love and truth.

I release the angelic legions carrying the message of love's light and truth to explode revelation into the earth, to invade the lives of those sleeping and slumbering in deception.

I focused my attention on specific people groups, streams, and cultures to be a guide for the angelic legions to follow.

I call for engagements with the eschatological futurist, Zionist and dispensational streams.

I call for engagements with the Universalist streams.

I call for engagements with the Mystical streams.

I call for engagements with the Energy Healing streams.

I call for engagements with the Pentecostal and Charismatic streams.

I call for engagements with the Evangelical streams.

I call for engagements with the Reformed streams.

I call for engagements with the Orthodox streams.

I call for engagements with the Catholic streams.

I call for engagements with those who have left the church to search for the truth.

I call for engagements with those who have left the church, hurt and disillusioned.

I saw the angelic orbs stream into the earth but I know there need to be many others who are legislating for the light of love and truth to go forth.

"Son, with the light of love and truth that is beginning to shine into the earth will come the weight of Our glory. As you embrace Our glory, your glory will begin to engage creation more effectively and all the dimensional realms will begin to resonate with the frequency of your sonship. Sonship will bring the frequency of hope to creation: that is the hope of freedom from its bondage to corruption and decay.

"As love's light shines, creation is waiting in anticipation of a greater revealing of sonship that is coming and hope is rising. The greater the truth that comes into the light, the more the darkness is exposed, the more that hope rises and the more creation begins to respond. As you abide in the light of Our countenance in the realm of light in perfection, your glory and lovingkindness will increase in effectiveness.

"Son, you only have to be who you were created to be and the light of love and truth will increase as your consciousness expands as your mind is renewed. Your engagements with the angelic realm are increasing: you are seeing more being restored and the dimensional beings are also engaging you for help in becoming free. There is great activity, even if most of it is not cognitive; you are being increasingly effective by living multidimensionally from a state of being at rest. Son continue to focus on revealing the truth as an oracle of Our heart as that is your priority consciousness mandate in this season."

My focus shifted to the earth shield where Jesus was connecting the light of truth, as all the light of our being was interconnected through Him. This is forming a vast neural net of truth that is challenging, deconstructing and renewing all our minds so we will be joined in the mind of Christ. The truths that we all have are connecting – and exposing the lies and deception that we all have – to bring us all into agreement and alignment with the Truth.

I saw many interconnections taking place as our light was flowing through Jesus, the Light, and He was redirecting us to make new interactions in the spirit and physical realms. The earth shield was getting stronger and energised with the purified enlightening of our networked minds and interactions.

"Son, this process is perpetual, as the union of hearts and minds continue to fuse into an agreement of desire and intention. The shield needs more sons to complete it, so that Our intention for the restoration of all things can be focused dimensionally from the union of hearts and minds in the light of love and truth, and limitless grace is released. Release the blue light call with greater intensity to draw Our sons to participate in the earth shield and engage in the light of love and truth.

"Son, as you look into Our face you will see the true reality and truth that will reshape history and form the basis of the future. Only face to face intimacy can reveal the truth to those who are willing to see without the filters of their own understanding distorting their vision. Son, that is why only the pure in heart can see who We really are; and that is why healing the heart, restoring the soul and renewing the mind is a process all will need to go through to be able to see the truth. All will need to have the godly wisdom to act on that knowledge without being deceived; and that wisdom can only come through the restoration relational process.

"Son, do not stop at the beginning of wisdom: let the stage of awe and wonder take you to the deeper knowledge, wisdom and understanding that is only found within *I am that I am*. This knowledge is not hidden from you, but for you to discover within Us; and your journey to enlightenment will produce the wisdom of maturity that you will need as a son. Wisdom is the crown of glory that creation will respond to as the frequency of your true identity is revealed. Only a crown of wisdom that comes through wearing a crown of thorns carries a frequency that has the fruit of the process of maturity.

"Son, only as you learn to really trust Us through the process will creation trust in who you are and respond to your sonship. The fires of adversity produce the purification that is characteristic of trust that runs deep and is not superficial. Everyone finds it easy to trust in Our lovingkindness when the going is easy; but when it gets tough, that is the true hallmark of real trust that has been forged in the fire of Our love. Those who are willing to walk through the flames to obtain wisdom will be revealed as sons of God to creation and will be able to discern the truth from the deception. Only by abiding in the light, no matter how intense it gets, will you be able to know the truth of true reality and enable others to see it.

"Only a light bright enough to blind you to the deception will enable you to see true reality and be enlightened, just as Saul experienced on the DIY tree path he was following to Damascus. Only when he was blinded to the deception that was normal life to him was he able to see who We are and find his true destiny. Only those who are willing to embrace the light that blinds them to the deception of normalcy will be able to be enlightened to see true reality and become awakened to creative sonship.

"The tree of independence limits the creative abilities of Our children but the Tree of Life is limitless in grace and overflowing in lovingkindness and unconditional love. The Tree of Life is always in season and its fruit can produce the limitless creativity necessary for Our sons to mature into the ascended fathers they are destined to become.

"Son, desire and pursue the crown of wisdom wherever the journey takes you by abiding in the realm of light in perfection so you can gaze upon Our face. True wisdom will grow, it cannot be imparted; and true knowledge is experienced, not received as information; so true understanding is a result of the journey to enlightenment that all must walk.

"Son, rejoice in the light of truth, bask in unconditional love, revel in limitless grace, as there is abundance and overflow here. The light of Our glory is lavish and bountiful and to be enjoyed to the full, so immerse yourself in the height, depth and breadth of the love of *I am that I am*."

As I sank deeper into that ocean of pure bliss, I became more and more intoxicated by the fragrance and taste of the very essence of *I am that I am*. My being became saturated in the thick oil of love's essence as I rejoiced, full of gratitude for being in that place of perfection. I began to eulogise, pouring out my thanksgiving for being embraced in the arms of pure lovingkindness, cocooned in the character, nature and essence of God. Praise and honour followed from my heart to His heart as I revelled in that joyous moment as if I was suspended in eternal bliss that captivated my being.

"Son, never lose this moment: abide in this place of bliss so that this experience of true reality is your motivation and inspiration."

I felt inspired as I began to realise that this was how I was intended to be and how all creation was intended to exist. This is what relationship is truly meant to be: a pure connection, the oneness of being in *I am that I am* and *I am that I am* being in me. The true reality of the Father's heart emotions expressing the light of perfection is how He feels continually, even if we do not yet abide here. A return to this state of being is the objective of the restoration of all things agenda and I felt totally inspired as a son to be an oracle of that passionate desire and intention.

I was overflowing with joy, rejoicing at even the thought of creation being restored to that beautiful state of existence. Amazing grace, amazing love, amazing light, amazing truth captivated my whole being like never before as I rested, abiding in Him.

"Son, there will be no end to the increase of the government of Our desire for total and complete restoration for all things; and peace will be once more. It is inevitable that there will be restoration to the place of peace where nothing is missing, broken, separated or out of place. Son, as you brood over Our heartfelt desire within the Cradle of Life and find the union of heart and mind, the energy of your voice can be focused by intention to create reality.

Union and Oneness.

One of the key strategies of the enemy is division and separation through conflict, so union and oneness are very important so that we can be one heart, mind and purpose; but I have discovered that there are many more levels of union to experience.

"Union in the oneness of heart, mind and purpose is the key to creativity, as brooding creates resonance and the frequency energises the living light grace strings that are the building blocks of all reality. Many people are trying to create without union and are therefore functioning from the knowledge of the wrong tree path by trusting in their own understanding. The reality that most of Our children are choosing just perpetuates their limited past experiences because it is limited to what they know.

"To choose and create new realities, the mind must be renewed by the light of truth framed by lovingkindness that is a reflection of who We are as love. All societies and cultures have been framed by the knowledge that flows from the wrong tree, that of independence, but there are still some godly influences within each that keep stability. The shaking of those man-made systems is designed to expose the false knowledge of humanism so the transition to the light of truth can take place.

"Only an awakening to the love and light of enlightenment can facilitate a peaceful transition and transformation so heaven can begin to manifest on earth. The increase in government must be peaceful, not by conquest, war or bloody revolution: that is why the growth of the Kingdom is described as being like yeast infiltrating the dough. But kneading is necessary at times: the times of shaking that occur during periods of awakening often seem to be revolutionary but are just Our hands kneading the dough, as it were.

"The periods of shaking are designed to cause Our children to mistrust what they have been previously relying on to seek a more secure foundation for their lives. When the storms and quakes of Our shaking take place, many look for the stability of the rock which cannot be moved and will remain to fill the earth. The shaking is designed to cause instability so that Our children will stop trusting in their independent self-effort and abilities to seek first Our Kingdom, which is trustworthy. When everything seems to be failing and the world systems have no answers, then Our children will begin to look for the solutions from a different source.

"Shaking and shifting is always accompanied by the light of truth shining in the darkness of fear to bring hope and enlightenment: that brings the changes necessary for Kingdom increase but it is a slow, generational process. Son, when three generations are in union there will be exponential growth and your mandate is to help facilitate that union. In the past, the political and religious spirits have infiltrated to create empire or rebellion that causes division. Only when the first generation who are enlightened to embrace and mentor the next generation, rather than resisting or controlling it, can the third generation be reached.

"Son, this is why immortality is so important to embrace: so that the first generation will still be alive and well within that union. The truth of abundant life and immortality is one of the keys to being able to unify the generations. Joshua only united two generations: they were able to occupy the Promised Land but never possessed it fully, as the third generation were independent. The next generation can be the billion-fold harvest of harvesters and reach the third generation if the heavenly storehouses are ready to receive them. Only embassies of heaven that are new wineskin *ekklesia*, free from the mediatorial systems of hierarchical control structures, will be able to accomplish union.

"Son, call the Joshua generation to arise and come out from under the coverings of the old religious orders to embrace their destinies to unify the three generations. This union of generations is fiercely opposed by the religious and political spirit to stop the establishment of true governmental authority that operates in peace.

"Son, never be content with what appears on the surface, always be prepared to go beyond – be that deeper, higher or further than the obvious conclusion. We have so much hidden treasure for you to discover that will only be found by the diligent and vigilant pursuit of the truth in the light of Our countenance. Our favour and blessing are only found in the light of Our countenance, through a level of trust that is deep within Our being.

"Trust is a product of dwelling in the light of love and truth to know the reality of who We are, so you can be enlightened and gloriously be revealed in sonship. The revealing of the enlightened sons of God will restore creation by freeing it from the bondage to lies it has been held captive in. The glorious rising of the enlightened ones will set creation free into the light of their glory, which is their true identity within *I am that I am*. Son, never be content with 'less than' when there is always 'more than' beyond; so never stop pursuing the beyond that is beyond."

As I fixed my eyes on the magnificent face of my Father, the light of truth flooded all my senses with the thoughts and emotions that He has about me. Those thoughts went beyond anything I had experienced before, revealing how precious and special I am, being wonderfully made in His image and likeness (as we all are). The emotions behind those thoughts overwhelmed me as I began to find a deeper realisation of how strong and unrelenting they are. Those desires for a return to oneness and union are so powerful that I knew that nothing was too much and nowhere was too far for my Father in pursuit of me.

I knew that the Father was prepared to go to any lengths, heights or depths to restore what has been lost, including descending into death itself. The waves of emotion that were revealed in the oracles of the Father's heart rolled over me, each one taking me deeper into the knowledge of His unconditional love. The waves of emotion, unrelenting passion, burning desire, intense joy, deep compassion, overwhelming love, the lovingkindness of blessing and unending union cocooned my being.

"Son, this is but a fraction of what We feel about you, and all of creation, but this is all you could bear without being consumed. Let what you experienced today become the motivation that moves you to continue to go beyond as you journey towards the fulfilment and consummation of the restoration of all things. Let Our passion be your passion and you will become unrelenting in your pursuit of the truth whilst being able to rest in Our love. Multidimensional living is the only way that you will have the capacity to go beyond every and any 'beyonds' that face you."

I focused the energy within the Merkabah at the core of my being, to connect me to each dimensional reality that I dwell in, to broadcast the emotions of my experiences, to re-energise the quantum expanded moments. In turn, I engaged each moment that were the destination points of my many quests and encounters coming together in a quantum moment of existence. I am multidimensional and I exist having my being multidimensionally, with each quantum moment a union of experiences, all connected to the unified field of existence.

I dwelled for a moment on the creative cycle that forms reality and energized my being to brood in the Cradle of Life for full and complete restoration; the resonance of that desire energised into the sound of many waters, infusing it with emotion. The emotion amplified the sound in the Chamber of Destiny, fusing my being to the sound of the Father's voice until the vibrational frequencies engaged the Quantum Lumens within the Chamber of Creation. The Quantum Lumens received the energy of the Father's desires within the sound of my voice and danced to its rhythm and cadence. The focus of desire energised by the emotions of the oracles was filled with creative possibilities, all waiting to be streamed through the portal into creation.

Only a cosmic creational union of being, such as is forming in the earth shield, has the exponential unified consciousness to choose such a reality. Only when enough enlightened sons are in such a union of desire, becoming one mind, will this choice for the restoration of all things become reality. Only when we become in union with one heart, one mind, one desire, one passion, one purpose, with one choice, will the reality of creation being set free into the glory of our sonship begin to manifest.

"Son, all other causes need to be consumed with the fire of the desire for the restoration of all things, which is the only cause that encompasses all others."

I engaged the light, face to face with the Father; and the light wove an intricate pattern around me of the Father's intentions. I felt wave after wave of emotions concerning creation that moved me with deep compassion until my whole being was conformed to His intentions. Then the desire for restoration hit me with such force that all I could see, feel, and sense was the groaning of creation; and the contrast between that desire and the present reality was the motivation that moved me to action.

I shifted my focus to the Cradle of Life where I began to brood, at rest in the knowledge of the desires of the Father's heart but focused intently on the freedom of creation. In a quantum moment, all the scenarios for creation's freedom played out in my mind until the only option left was union and that thought filled my whole being.

Union, union, union: there was just that single thought, with no other option; and I began to vibrate in resonance with that one thought until I was that one thought of union. Union consumed me on every level of being: there was nothing else possible, no alternatives or options, just the one, simple, but overwhelming reality that existed at that moment.

I was one with creation in the oneness of being in that glorious union. No other thought could enter, as I was one pure thought. Oneness of being – mind, heart and purpose unified until nothing else existed; I had brooded before many times but nothing like this.

Creation's freedom and restored union was all there was when the transition to becoming the sound that would counteract the groaning took place. I was not just a sound or a voice but a glorious combination of all things: the thought, emotion, light and sound energy of being one. I could not feel myself within the oneness of that union of all created things as I was as it was before there even was a 'was' in the oneness of God.

This is the eternity placed within the heart of all things: that glorious moment, the memory of being, that will eventually draw all things to become one once again in the glorious union of fatherhood and sonship. This is the moment of the revealing of the sons of God, when creation will be set free to become restored to the union of oneness. All is one and one is all; and that is what it is to be within the oneness of God's being: just glorious bliss and nothing but love and light, where all truth is, oneness and nothing else. That one moment is enough to motivate me forever to be one in the glorious union of oneness.

"Son, now you know in your being what is Our being: so just be."

All the different aspects of union that I had experienced previously: the union of body, soul and spirit within itself, the *Perichoresis* union of Father, Son and Spirit, the union of the thrones of the heavenly realms, the union of the great cloud of witnesses, the tri-part union of the spheres, the union of the earth and the Elementals, the union of the planets in our solar system, the union of the constellations, the union of the circle of the deep, the union of the wheels within the wheels within the wheels, the union of the oracles of the Father's heart and so many other unions that I had experienced on my journey, all merged into one glorious moment of the oneness of union.

One is all and all is one restored reality.

Mystic Union – One Mind.

"Son, come walk with Me."

We were in a larger complex crystalline structure, where the light was reflecting and bouncing around internally as if it was a living thing. I was amazed and overawed with its beauty and complexity, as the colours of the light were constantly changing in intensity as well as speed and rhythm. I saw that it was connected externally to threads of light of unfathomable numbers but each was pulsating with energy. I thought to myself, "What is this place?"

The Father answered. "This is the fabric of what the Bible describes as the mind of Christ. It is not Jesus' mind, as some think, but Our living, creative thoughts that connect with all of creation that produce the frequency of oneness and harmony. Son, this is the connection where all who are joined to Us can be one spirit with oneness: a union of heart, mind and purpose. This is the nexus point for all things and this is where the restoration of all things is coordinated with Our desire and intention."

I wondered, again to myself, how this was connected to the creative process I had been shown previously (i.e. the Cradle of Life, Chamber of Destiny and Chamber of Creation). But that was no barrier to the Father, who answered my question the moment I formed it.

"Son, this coordinates the whole process, as the realms of heaven all exist within the light of Our thoughts. All existence is but a moment and what you see is, in your parlance, a complex holographic projection, contributed to by the consciousnesses of all. That does not make it any less real, of course; and as more are reconnected and restored, Our true intention will begin to be shaped by all whose consciousness is expanded."

As I pondered the implications of what I was seeing and hearing, I became aware that my thoughts were light and colour. My creative thoughts were connected and active here? Wow, even the concept was amazing.

"Yes, son, even some of *your* thoughts are connected creatively here," the Father said drily, but with the warmth of love that I was accustomed to. Although I could not see His face, I knew He was smiling.

I began to focus my desire and my creative thoughts on restoration; and it was as if there was an amazing light show in this one small area; but other connected areas also became active.

"Son, this is not a place you can dwell in but We wanted you to know that you are not alone, as you are connected to others through the Merkabah within you. We wanted you to understand the importance of your thoughts, and those of all Our children, so you will be able to focus and connect as you brood, to connect desire, thought, sound and light.

"Son, love, peace and joy are the hallmarks of Kingdom living and will continue to be expanded through and beyond Our sons, to fill the earth and creation. Blessed (empowered to prosper and succeed) are the peacemakers, for they administrate the fundamentals of the Kingdom. Blessed are those who are gentle and humble in heart, for they know who We are and they know who they are; and they live in the rest of being. They see what We are doing from Our state of being *I am that I am*, so all their doing can flow from their state of being.

"Son, being free to know, see, be, do and go is the hallmark of a mature son who can live in and choose true reality.

"Son, see from the realm of light today what is occurring in, above and on the earth, and what We are doing, so you can be in full cooperation and collaboration with the light of truth that is radiating from Our face, which is a true manifestation of who We are."

Immediately I was aware of where I was standing and that I was being illuminated by the light of His countenance, being filled with the knowledge of God. I was also aware that I was brooding in the Cradle of Life, within the heart and mind of the Father, His thoughts becoming my thoughts. I saw the reality and truth of peace and resonated with the sound of many waters until I was the sound of His voice, amplified within the Chamber of Destiny, broadcast and connected in union within the mind of Christ. I saw the living light of grace, the Quantum Lumens, activated within the Chamber of Creation; and the light of peace began to stream out into creation.

These events are part of a continual process of forming reality aligned to God's heart.

I heard and felt a deep sigh go forth into creation: "Peace, be still!" It was heavy, thick, glorious: a blanket of peace descended over creation. There will be no end to the increase of His government and peace through the sons of God, who are His peacemakers. I do not doubt that peace will eventually triumph in time, through the Prince of Peace, who fully expresses the heart of God as love and light. Time and eternity are converging in the sons of God as we mature and take our responsibility.

As I stood in the realm of light in perfection I desired to go deeper and further into the light of truth within the Father's heart.

"Son, you have been faithful with all the quests that you have been tasked with and have shown us the motives of your desires are pure, without agendas, so come."

I did not know how to come, of course, so I just walked towards the light of Their face, until I was absorbed by the light into another light that felt different yet also strangely familiar. The Father's thoughts of love flooded my senses to the point of overload yet I was in a state of being like never before.

All that I was shown previously regarding the progressive nature of my journey was now put into a different context, which was a deeper mystery. I felt the bigger picture was all around me and I saw the connections where all the pieces fitted together into a coherent whole. Here, in this state of being, my journey seemed small in comparison to the whole; yet I knew that mine and every other part were still vital to restoration as a whole.

My progressive journey to restoration was mirrored in so many others on parallel tracks, all similar yet so different. I felt comforted that I was not alone but part of creation; and then I began to connect with those others at a level of oneness that I never could have imagined.

I opened my heart and was filled with joyous wonder as I began to engage in multiple simultaneous cardiognosis experiences. There was no need to be guarded or seek to protect myself within this wonderfully peaceful state of union. The connections were of heart, mind and memory that brought such joy, comfort and peace as I discovered the true nature of family that far surpassed any earthy experience. This was a brotherhood, a deep connection within *I am that I am*, that was beyond beyond yet again and was so precious and beautiful.

This was a state of enlightenment, being in union and connected by the oneness of heart, mind and purpose with those with the same restoration intention. This was similar to the mind of Christ experience that I previously had but also deeper and more emotional.

In this mystic union with people I had never physically met before I felt their journeys as they felt mine: "we were" is the only way I can describe it but it was wonderful and so beyond any bond I had previously felt.

"Son, this is the reality of being that we intended for all things and this is being restored as all things were never intended to be separated or independent of each other."

I felt so inspired and satisfied that I never wanted to be anywhere or be anything other than in this mystic union.

"Son, come boldly to the throne of grace, and cast all your cares on Us, and rest, by trusting Us to meet all your needs. Do not try to meet your own needs, even though you may be very capable to do so in some areas, as this will take you down the path of the DIY tree. That path is deceptive and always results in independence and eventual self-reliance, so let everything that you are carrying go.

"So many of Our children, including many sons, are weary and burdened, living in stress and exhaustion because they do not know how to rest by fully trusting in Our faithfulness. Seeking first Our Kingdom by prioritising intimacy and relationship will enable all Our sons to come to the place of rest where they know that they are loved unconditionally. Creation is waiting to be restored back to the place of rest and union with the sons of God, free from its bondage to decay and corruption. Son, come closer; draw nearer into union and oneness, as there are so many more levels of oneness beyond your wildest imaginations."

I drew closer until I was absorbed into love's embrace and immediately stopped being able to think, as my mind was emptied or disconnected. I was floating on a sea of pure bliss, drifting without the need to know where I was or where I was going: nothing mattered but being. It felt like I was in an isolation tank but filled with light, not darkness; where I could feel but not think, so I just was. Being within *I am that I am* was the only way I could describe that state of being, floating on an ocean of love, completely disconnected from the cares of life. There were no thoughts, so no worries – complete 'Hakuna Matata' – but all was as it was meant to be: living loved, with nothing else to distract me from bliss.

I was floating in blissful love, with no concept of time (so it could have been a minute, or eternity) when that state of emotional being infiltrated my mind; and all my thoughts were transformed by love, until my mind and emotions were completely in sync and at rest.

"Son, this is the state of oneness and union that all Our children were designed to live in and this is what can be restored, so all of creation will be one and at rest. This is the glory of sonship that creation is longing for; and now that you have a greater understanding of this state, you never have to leave, as your consciousness has been expanded once again."

I took several deep breaths of that atmosphere: I could feel the joy of union and oneness and could do nothing but rejoice and be glad, not sad.

"Son, anytime sadness tries to overwhelm you, just breathe deeply and rest in living loved; and you will be able to love living and live loving.

Sons of Light

"Son, the knowledge from the source of the tree of the knowledge of good and evil has infected all of the world systems and it will not be easy to free people from that deception. Rather than attempting to expose the darkness and the lies, focus on revealing the light of the Tree of Life so the truth becomes obvious. Light removes darkness, so increase the light that the sons are shining by encouraging them to abide in the light of love and truth so their identity is unveiled. When Our sons come close to Us in face to face intimacy, they will resonate with truth and will be able to more easily discern the source and root of knowledge.

"The world systems are not neutral like creational systems: they were designed with a hidden agenda that on the surface looks good but is in fact evil. Lucifer was light and has knowledge beyond most people's imagination but all that knowledge has been twisted and is used for his own 'I will' agenda. You can always determine the source by observing and comparing 'I will' with '*I am that I am*': 'I will' is always 'less than' seeking to be 'more than' and '*I am*' is always eternally consistent.

"All selfish motivation comes from the need to elevate self to a higher level through independent self-effort methods that always leave Our children weary and burdened. The identity lost at the fall from grace to works cannot ever be found or achieved through the knowledge of the DIY tree. True identity can only be discovered by a restored relationship with the true Creator and We have never lost sight of the eternal image of anyone or anything that was created by Us.

"Seeing yourselves in the light and mirror of Our face is the only way identity can be restored; but the self-effort which always leads to selfishness must be abandoned. The abandonment of self in pursuit of the truth is the only way to enlightenment and sonship but the light of '*I am that I am*' must shine to draw Our children's attention and focus from the darkness and deception of 'I will'.

"The mind of Christ is anointed and powerful through the relational oneness of *Perichoresis*; and only in a unified consciousness of oneness is the glorious light of sonship going to be revealed to creation. A unified mind has abandoned 'I will' for 'we are' and never seeks for independent identity because true identity can only be found in relational oneness. Look at *I am that I am* and you see three as one God, in complete harmony: yet Father, Son and Spirit have their own personality, with no competition. You can be individual within the oneness and mystic union of a collective unified consciousness that has ascended beyond to a higher plane of existence and reality.

"Son, encourage everyone to look into the light of Our face; but to do so effectively they will all have to go through the dark cloud where self is surrendered. The pursuit of identity and destiny will take Our children on a journey through the fires of purification, refining and transformation. Only the pure in heart can see God – and themselves – so encourage Our children to follow the light of the Tree of Life to enlightenment.

"Son, continue to release the light and the frequencies that will draw Our children out of the darkness into the light of truth so that they can find their true identity, position and destiny. Creation is waiting for the sons to be revealed in their glory to be set free; but Our children must be free first and that is the priority. There must be a bright light that shines in the darkness to show the way back home to the origin of Our desires and thoughts. Only face to face encounters can reveal the fullness of identity that produces a state of being within *I am that I am*. Be diligent and keep focused on the priority by paying close attention to the rhythm of Our heart and that will direct you, guide you and move you."

Truth and Love

"The knowledge of the heart is pure and true knowledge, unpolluted by your own understanding. If you stay close to Our heart you will receive the wisdom and understanding that are associated with the truth.

"Sadly, many do not dwell here, but only visit; so they receive knowledge but twist it to their own understanding and frame it by their own belief systems. So much knowledge has been given but few stay close enough to be able to use that knowledge effectively for the purpose it was given. The knowledge that We have given many times ends up being used to create an identity and promote self, so it becomes polluted and mixed with deceptions of the wrong tree. All truth comes from Us as We are the only source of truth but most truth is hidden under the deceptive coverings that have come from independent understanding within the heart of man.

"Truth is hidden within lies and lies masquerade as truth so that most of Our children remain controlled by the agenda of darkness without even knowing it exists. Following that which appears good from independent knowledge is still evil because it has its independent selfish agenda. Evil has the appearance of being good to those who are being deceived. Evil is the slavery of independence.

"Unconditional love is the only hallmark of the genuine truth that originates from within Us; but be aware that love that is not unconditional is the sign that the truth has been polluted. The passionate causes that Our children have that originated within Our heart are easily polluted when there is a lack of love, wisdom and understanding.

"The end can be used to justify the means; and when that state of mind exists, you know self is involved and deception has already twisted the truth. So many of Our children have succumbed to deception even when they have been seeking to fulfil Our desires because they have not sought Our kingdom first. When a mission and ministry takes priority over relationship, deception is not far behind – and then trusting in their own understanding is the result. Many are deceived by the passions of their hearts as their identity is tied to their mission.

"Son, it is vital to stay in the light, close to Our heart, so that the motivation to act is always unconditional love and limitless grace. Lovingkindness will always be the way to outwork Our desires: all other emotions such as anger, fear, frustration, pity, empathy, or injustice will make anyone susceptible to deception.

"Focus on releasing the light, not exposing the darkness, as that produces positive energy; but when you focus on attacking the negative, you will produce negative destructive energy that is counterproductive. Only by operating in the opposite spirit to that which is an obstacle can that hindrance be removed safely.

"The opposite spirit when facing anything from the tree of the knowledge of good and evil will always have an unconditional love motivation at its core. Never seek to fight fire with fire: use water. Never seek to fight at all but always seek to overcome with true love so that restoration is the result. There can be no warfare, even if there are biblical analogies that have been used to promote that concept; but those analogies were there only to encourage perseverance, not aggression.

"You can be an army but it must be an army that conquers and overcomes by love, not violence, intimidation, fear or strength of arms, as that only causes escalation and proliferation. Only unconditional love can truly win in the end as it will always seek reconciliation and restoration, not victory. Be careful not to win an argument or debate but lose a friend, as competition and conflict are always counterproductive.

"Son, the glory of sonship is being unleashed to increase the light that will create a global awakening to love and that will change the very fabric of creation."

One Global Family

"When Our children discover unconditional love, and begin to feel its impact, then societies and cultures will transition away from an economic foundation to a wellbeing-based value system.

"The personal must drive the corporate, not vice versa. The responsibility of sonship for creation will begin to replace the selfishness of the desire for independence which is the foundation of most societies. Nationalism will be replaced by true globalism based on family. Love for each other will end the conflicts that arise from competition as Our children begin to become more secure in their identity. The global control systems will begin to fall one by one as the deceptions of the origin of independence is revealed. The light of love and truth must shine brightly to awaken Our children to the truth of who We are so that they can become free from the delusions they have been living in.

"Son, only love can overcome the darkness with light, and only love can overcome the deception with truth; so focus on living loved, loving living and living loving and be a light in the darkness. Those who think they are representing Us by following various causes are becoming more extreme and their agendas are taking them further from love and truth. Those who are unwilling to embrace the truth of their deception will begin to become more susceptible to even greater conspiracies and manipulation.

"What you have experienced in the last few days from those who think they are representing Us is just the beginning: there will be even more extremes of behaviour as they descend into greater delusion. The global nature of the shifting and shaking is beginning to expose the true motives behind the agendas that have twisted and manipulated their passions and have blinded them to the truth. Do not confront or argue with them as they will not be able to see what is plain and obvious to you; and do not allow them to use your platforms to proliferate their delusions.

"First, it was the Coronavirus conspiracies and now it is the vaccine conspiracies, and in between, the political conspiracies that they hoped would end abortion, trafficking and many other issues. When you see people who are normally loving in nature resort to emotional outbursts and irrational logic you must not give them a platform for their views. Love them by not confronting them and trust Us to deal with them.

"Son, always act with lovingkindness but do not bow to the pressure to get personal or confrontational as that will just entrench their position further. Do not allow the political or religious spirit to manipulate you into division, competition, conflict or tribalism: just keep speaking the truth in love for the positive and not against the negative.

"Love wins because love has already won; and there will be an awakening to unconditional love, and the light of truth will eventually overcome the darkness of deception and lies.

"Son, the glory days are coming, in the midst of the deep darkness of deception that covers the minds of those enslaved to the false knowledge systems. The revealing of the sons who walk in and as the light will illuminate the darkness with the light of love and truth. The key is the maturing of enough sons to raise the consciousness levels of sonship to be in a union of hearts and minds.

"All division and divisiveness is the fruit of independent knowledge that raises people above each other and creates elites who seek to control, suppress and rule over the masses. Family was never meant to have divisions or be hierarchical, patriarchal or matriarchal but to function by relational honour where all generations respect each other. The restoration of family honour and respect will bring blessing to the earth again and creation itself will respond to the oneness that family reveals.

"All divisions, including those of nations, nationalism, gender, ethnicity, colour, race, religion, background, social standing or any other arbitrary category, are the result of following the path of independence. Union and oneness respect and honour uniqueness within a family and all members are treated equally as equality is a strong value within family.

"Restoration of family values will enable the sons of God to arise to illuminate those values by leaving systems that are denominated to separate based on theology, doctrine or creed. Son, following the creeds is placing man-made concepts above the truth, as the creeds were produced and motivated by the need for doctrinal purity and the fear of losing control. Those who produced the creeds did not trust Us to teach Our children. The creeds have placed tradition over truth and have been used to support orthodoxy and perpetuate lies that create division. The creeds are used to produce the same result as at Babel, to make a name for themselves based on fear of uniqueness. Oneness and union comes from relationship and intimacy, not the dogma of forced agreement or consensus that the creeds represent."

The word creed comes from the Latin word *credo*, which means 'I believe' and is the mantra of the 'I will' agenda. Creeds are meant to define the boundaries within which a group of people operates. They are by definition restrictive, and hinder progressive revelation and true family, which is not based on what I believe but who I am.

"When true union manifests there is no need for creeds as there is relationship based on honour and trust with cardiognosis between God and each other. All religions have their creedal systems to force unity, based on the agreement of beliefs, to control and stop progressive knowledge. Progressive knowledge produces panic in religious systems and the fear of losing control. Progressive revelation is the hallmark of family, where seeking the truth in relationship is valued and honoured as it unveils deeper truth and brings enlightenment.

"Enlightenment is feared by all religious systems that are creedal, traditional or hierarchical in structure as it threatens the status quo of control. The greatest creed was the production of the Bible as a closed canon that stopped the progressive revelation that was intended for every generation.

"Family enables generations to honour each other whilst encouraging progression because there is no need to fear losing position. You are always family but the functions within the family change as each matures from child to parent to grandparent to great-grandparent; and the truth is passed on and progressive revelation can be encouraged. Children can benefit from the knowledge and wisdom of their parents but the hallmark of wise parents is that they will benefit from the progressive knowledge of their children and eventually grandchildren. Within the family of mankind as We intended, there would have only been fruitfulness, increase and expansion to fill the earth and go beyond.

All systems inspired by the tree of the knowledge of good and evil produce division and devalue family by using control, not relationship, because it is based on fear. Lost identity is lost family and is based on the deception and fear that produces independence from God and is responsible for the desire for false identity produced by cults. All religions are actually like cults in that they promise identity and family but only control their members into conformity to creeds: that restricts and fears progressive revelation.

"Son, We are family in the *Perichoresis* of true union and We invite all Our children to experience the love, joy and peace of rest. We are *I am that I am* and We reveal Ourselves progressively through relationships so all Our children can be fully enlightened and know who they are in union with Us.

"Family is based on unconditional love, and is by definition inclusive, but any theology that excludes is a deception. All of creation is family and was designed to function together in union and harmony. We unconditionally love all things that We have created and We have made the provision for total restoration, built into the fabric of creation itself. All creation is universally quantum-connected and already in union without knowing it. The harder those who seek to divide and separate it try, the greater the force will be that draws it back together. The potential energy for restored union is stored within creation itself at a quantum level and the relational entanglement that connects all things will eventually reunite all things.

"Enlightenment and expanded consciousness is awakening creation to the reality of entanglement as the living grace light of love exists within all things within Us. We are the family of inclusivity, limitless in unconditional love and grace; and all will be restored. Union was established before creation and is within the fabric of all things at a quantum level."

Triumphant Mercy

"Son, there is a need for greater shifting of mindsets, belief systems and values to awaken Our children from the deception of darkness that they are slumbering in. A greater shift to awaken Our children to love consciousness is coming once this present shaking has fully been completed. And there are more shakings to come, until all are awakened to the futility and slavery of the 'I will' agenda.

"The global control systems that are the front for the Luciferian agenda to keep the world in a state of delusional independence so it will accept the god of 'I will' will be exposed to the light of truth and love. The light of truth and love is beginning to shine with greater brightness and its frequency is starting to shake the stability of those deceptive systems and Our children's trust and dependence in and on them. The truth is being revealed and those with their eyes opened will be able to discern what is happening and what is about to occur – so keep looking. There is so much more to see and discern if you see from the realm of light perspective in union with Our heart."

I shifted my focus to being in that joyful union of heart, mind and purpose and rested in love's embrace, cocooned in light, basking in the radiance of glory. Slowly, a deeper sense of desire came over me and a precept of God began to awaken my consciousness to a truth of the nature of mercy embedded in the matrix of light that holds all creation together. God is love; and mercy is the inevitable conclusion of a God who is lovingkindness. There can be no other conclusion to love, therefore mercy must always be the result; and there can be no end to mercy because God is always unconditional love.

Thoughts of mercy filled my mind and I became aware that the world systems are fixated on a type of twisted judgment and justice that is devoid of grace and mercy. Yet as God is love and light, and love is unconditional and grace is limitless, then mercy is also limitless and it is the inevitable product of love and grace. Mercy is triumphant over all obstacles and hindrances to love and grace. Even heaven's seasons always end with mercy that ushers in rest; and therefore judgment and justice are just as much a product of unconditional love and cannot exist independently from grace and mercy.

"Son, you have been reading Our thoughts and your conclusion is correct: mercy is a precept that must align all the statutes of thinking and all the laws of being. The deception of independence has isolated grace and mercy from judgment and justice and twisted mankind's understanding of Our nature. Man has made a wrathful god of vengeance to outwork their need to appease and sacrifice by works. With no grace and mercy, judgment and justice become the tools of an angry, vengeful god who punishes and torments his children. That is not who We are as love is kind and We are overflowing with lovingkindness. That deception must be exposed to the light of truth that will unveil mercy as unending and is always the precursor to new beginnings and fresh starts. 'I will' is the mantra of religious dead works that needs laws to obey by their own efforts. Seasons of judgment and justice are only precursors that enable grace and mercy to restore all things. When the truth of the present unperfected state is revealed by judgment, desire for and pursuit of new beginnings can follow.

"Without a judgment that reveals what is not aligned to the truth, and justice to ensure the judgment is acted upon, there would be no grace and mercy. Judgment challenges the status quo of ignorance with enlightenment. Judgment is not the punishment of the present reality but is a verdict that reveals the truth of the present reality with hope for a different future reality. Religion uses judgment to produce fear, guilt, shame and condemnation that requires dead works.

"Before creation began, the grace and mercy of love were embedded within the fabric of creation to ensure restoration; but there would have been no need for judgment if there was no independence. The twisted knowledge of the false tree path of independence needs judgment to life to reveal the truth of its deception. Judgment is the verdict on the efficacy of the tree of the knowledge of good and evil. Judgment is the consequence of independence and is only needed to define what is not good so Our children can turn to follow the light of the Tree of Life. Lost identity and the twisted knowledge of 'I will' has perverted judgment with fear.

"When there was only light, in timeless existence, there was nothing to judge as all was good; only with the independence that separated to form an absence of light and deception was a verdict necessary. When mankind chose independence, a judgment of that choice was necessary so that they could turn away from that source and find the grace and mercy of lovingkindness awaiting them.

"The cross where Jesus willingly offered Himself is the central point in mankind's history, as it restored grace and mercy to complement and balance mankind's twisted need for judgment and justice. The glorious light that was revealed was then obscured, as the purpose of the cross (to overcome darkness with light so that Our mercy would triumph over mankind's judgment) was itself twisted by the religious spirit. An act of pure, loving mercy became twisted into the need for wrath and penal punishment to appease an angry god. The light of truth must shine to reveal that mercy is a true reflection of Our loving nature and an angry, wrathful and vengeful god is a myth and lie.

"Son, live loved, love living and live loving, overflowing with mercy, demonstrating that mercy with unconditional forgiveness. Our mercy is as triumphant as Our grace is limitless and Our love is unconditional and overwhelming. Son, Our mercy is triumphant over all judgment, all guilt, all shame and all condemnation from all sources. Overwhelming, unconditional love is expressed in limitless grace and triumphant mercy, which is fully realised for the whole of creation at the cross.

"All legal rights for any opposition to the restoration of all things were removed as mercy was triumphant over judgment and now, in reality, justice and mercy are synonymous terms from Our perspective. Mercy was triumphant when all accusations against humanity were nailed to the cross and the light of mercy overcame the darkness of humanity's requirement for judgment, justice, sacrifice and death. At that moment Our unconditional, loving mercy reconciled the whole cosmos back into a relationship and all possible accusations and judgments against it were nullified.

"All of creation is viewed through the lens of mercy, therefore all creation will be restored; but much of creation is still under the delusion of being separated. The whole of creation must be awakened to unconditional love, limitless grace and triumphant mercy, to come to the realisation of restoration and inclusion. The consciousness of most of creation is still trapped in the deception of independence and self-condemnation, so extremes of mercy must be demonstrated. When mankind demands justice, We release mercy; so that the fires of judgment are in reality just the consuming fire of refining, purifying love."

I heard a sound with a rhythm and frequency that was faint and almost imperceptible, hardly discernible above the background noise of life; but then it started to get louder by absorbing all other sounds until the only sound that could be heard was mercy.

"Son, mercy will overcome and be triumphant: it will leaven the whole of creation so it can rise above the darkness of deception and delusion to shine gloriously with the light of love and truth like the sun. There will be no night, where darkness overcomes the day, as the creative light of mercy will bring the perpetual glorious daylight of new beginnings.

"Son, legislate for Our mercy to become revealed in the great love awakening so all self-imposed separation will be seen as the illusion and delusion it really is. The earth shield is powering up, energised with the light of love and truth, becoming limitless in grace and mercy; but there needs to be a union that will focus the intentions of Our heart. Light can be a flickering candle or a powerful searchlight but it needs to be focused into a laser-precise beam of mercy to be effective. Our intention provides the focus but only the union of hearts and minds of Our sons can purposefully direct mercy to its intended targets.

"The union of sonship required to free creation cannot be achieved whilst there is such opposition to the restoration of all things – fuelled by a false image of who We are – that limits unconditional love, limitless grace and triumphant mercy to humanistic, limited levels of understanding. Call for the awakening of Our children who are free from the negative religious programming that believes the lie that 'judgment and justice are more powerful than mercy' that many of Our sons are still deceived and conditioned by. The next age awakening of the harvesters is coming nearer and the everlasting doors are being prepared for the greatest outpouring of mercy in the earth there has ever been outside of the cross. The deluge of the flood of judgment will be in comparison like a trickle to the torrent of Our mercy that will be poured out from heaven into the earth by the sons of God in union."

I released the frequency of union and the blue light call to draw the sons of God away from their own limited theological and doctrinal understanding to embrace unconditional love, limitless grace and triumphant mercy.

"Son, come and walk with Me."

We began in the Father's garden, which was beautiful beyond description, alive with joyous wonder, and I felt a sense of innocence and purity. It was like everything was fresh and new, and all life was celebrating my presence just as much as the Father's presence. I was filled with overwhelming joy, which is such an inadequate description for what I was feeling but there are no words for it.

"Son, there are new mercies every day as every day is a new beginning with excitement and innocent expectation: so live as if yesterday is forgotten and tomorrow never thought of."

The Lord's acts of mercy indeed do not end,
for His compassions do not fail.
They are new every morning;
Great is Your faithfulness. (Lamentations 3:22-23).

"Mercy is designed to reset every day so it is like the first day, so that everything can be enjoyed over and over again; wisdom is retained and innocence is not lost. Mercy is designed to make all of creation as it was in the beginning: childlike, innocent, filled with possibility and enthusiasm. Mercy is designed to restore and reset every relationship to union and untainted oneness, filled with the joy of life.

"Following the path of the tree of the knowledge of good and evil caused the retaining of knowledge of yesterday and all its associated trauma, which has resulted in the consequences of disease and aging. When each day was fresh with mercy and limitless grace, with no negative memory, there was no aging and everything was perfect. Without yesterday or tomorrow, there is only the purity and innocence of being. The simplicity of innocence was lost and along with it, mankind's true identity, as the work of retaining independent knowledge became the goal of life instead of joyous enjoyment.

"Son, what you felt in Our garden was how creation was designed to be: where every innocent dawn had wisdom, understanding and maturity being retained but any independent knowledge is forgotten. Fresh mercies every day restored innocence and life was filled with joyous creative discovery and wonder. Life was about the purity of being, not the striving of doing and accomplishing.

There was re-creation every day, just as you have seen and felt in Our garden, where there is no limitation, where every moment is all moments. Fresh mercies every day is like an artist with a new canvas, new colours, new brushes: filled with creative possibilities, untainted or negatively influenced by yesterday and with no need for thoughts of tomorrow.

"Son, I know you cannot truly imagine what We are showing you, as the memory of knowledge is all you have known; but go deeper into the spirit and you will find the eternal now of being."

I tried to search for that experience in the memory of my pre-existent spirit but I soon realised that I was thinking in terms of memory and knowledge, and I felt stuck. So I rested from my works and began to sink deeper. At first I resisted, panicked at the thought of being lost without knowledge, but I soon abandoned myself, letting go of everything I knew. I lost the fear of not knowing and returned to rest in being and for the first time I had no thoughts: I just was, in that moment of blissful innocence. I cannot possibly explain what I experienced in any terms that would be intelligible but that is the point – there was no knowing, just pure, blameless, innocent being.

If this was my perfected self as the Father had intended, then there was no vast sum of thoughts about me that I had been seeking the knowledge of: just my being within His being. There I felt one, whole within the desire of union's existence: no words, no thoughts, no works, just content, satisfied as I am within *I am that I am*.

"Son, you have now felt what life is like without retained independent knowledge. Do not try to realise innocence but just abandon yourself to be in new mercies every day, until you are restored to a state where there is no yesterday or tomorrow."

11. Creative Sonship Responsibility

The Earth Shield

During restoration government ascensions in 2020, we began to engage the living light beings of limitless grace and were instructed to join with them to form a shield of light that would protect the earth from external dimensional interference during the period where God was at work in resetting values and priorities. This shield also became a platform for administering legislation into the earth and out into the cosmos.

"Son, the earth shield is where the light of *I am that I am* is beginning to be unified into oneness so that the earth can be illuminated by the light of love and truth and not cosmic created light. The glory of sonship is the light of oneness and union and cannot shine in independence: all concepts of 'I' must be surrendered to us."

I engaged the realm of light and became aware that the light was forming a matrix around me like a sacred geometric shape. I was conforming to that shape which represented the intentions of the Father's heart. Wisdom, Knowledge and Understanding came and connected to the matrix and the light became more intense. The light focused into waves of thought that became intention and my emotions were overwhelmed with mercy.

Wisdom spoke, "This is where to interface with the intentions of the Father's heart so you can focus those intentions together in union with others in the earth shield."

I engaged the shield of light, where I saw four other angels standing around the earth holding hands; and as I watched, their heads bowed until they met and they formed a canopy over the earth. Their heads were joined in the earth shield and seemed to be illuminating and energising those who were connecting to them. This was a demonstration of union in action as the four became one; and this is how the earth shield needs to function – in union. They were Union, Liberty, Limitless and Blessing; and they were revealing hidden areas of the earth that were covered in the darkness of their opposites: division, bondage, restriction and cursing, which is poverty through lost identity.

I began to think about focusing mercy into those areas when the Father said "No, release a frequency to call others into union with Our intentions because there are not enough sons who have one mind." I released another blue light call which had the frequency of union from the earth shield into the earth to draw the sons to the light of truth.

During the next gathering of a governmental group, we received a mandate to connect with all the groups. Connecting the groups to communicate and share heart and information to legislate in union was part of the process.

When engaging the earth shield on one occasion I saw Jesus standing and all of our light energy was connecting through Him like He was the hub unifying us. He spoke with a very loud and energised voice that shook me until I was vibrating, "Stop listening to other voices and focus your attention on what the Father is saying." Jesus spoke again with such power and authority: "Peace, be still!" and waves of that declaration rippled around the earth and out into the cosmos. I saw many orbs of intense light begin to be energised and activated by that declaration and as I engaged them they took angelic form and enhanced my energy and agreement.

Four angels engaged me: Union, Covenant, Peacemaker and Family; and then there were three others: Truth Revealer, Truth Restorer and Truth Establisher. They each transferred light energy to strengthen my light and frequency. As I engaged their energy and light, I could see the areas of darkness that were their opposites in the earth and, with their cooperation, was able to release the light of truth into those specific areas, targeting the darkness of division with the light and truth of union. I continued with each of the others, targeting Competition with Covenant, Warmongering and Conflict with Peacemaker, and Tribalism with Family. These areas of darkness are what the Luciferian control systems use to maintain their deceptions.

I then saw areas of great darkness which was the deception that is covering the earth; so, in agreement, I released the light of Truth Revealer, Truth Restorer and Truth Establisher into those areas of darkness. I bombarded those areas of darkness with the light of mercy, love and truth but I knew that this would require all the governmental groups to be in harmony and union to be effective.

Engaging with the Father face to face, I looked deeply into His eyes and wave after wave of mercy rolled over me once again. As I absorbed that triumphant mercy I became saturated, completely filled, until it felt like I had no more capacity. Inspired by mercy, I engaged the earth shield.

The Father said "Son, you must abide in this state so you are not just a container of mercy but a conduit of Our triumphant mercy." In the light of the earth shield, I began looking to release that mercy, when Wisdom, Knowledge, Understanding and Prudence surrounded me: they blocked my sight into the earth so I had to feel; and at that moment I began to connect and empathise with the emotions of those who desperately needed mercy. I felt the lostness, hopelessness, despair and loneliness of the marginalised, stigmatised, abused, and isolated so I just released all the mercy I had absorbed; but mercy kept flowing from the Father's face in a steady, inexhaustible supply. I heard and felt the intention of the Father's heart that mercy must go beyond their children to creation itself, which has just as much need.

The angelic beings around me blocked the eyes of my heart towards people and opened my heart towards creation, focusing my attention on how the earth felt. To begin with, I felt similar emotions, like isolation and separation from sonship, but then I began to feel the effects of the abuse that the different parts of creation had suffered. I began to sense the earth, air, sea, water, trees, plants, animals, birds and fish and I became even more aware of their lostness, hopelessness, and despair over their treatment by humanity: such sorrow at the pollution of land, sea and air, the asset stripping, extinction, deforestation, overfishing, whaling, plasticising and becoming a rubbish dump for our refuse.

I felt so sad and so responsible that mankind, as stewards, had misused their position of authority to abuse, dishonour and disrespect the planet as humanity. I immediately asked for forgiveness as a son of God on behalf of humanity for its callous treatment of creation, for its selfishness and self-centredness, indifference, dishonouring, disrespecting and abuse. I felt such compassion and empathy that I became a channel for mercy to flow through me like a mighty river of justice into the earth, land, sea, air, core and crust as a conduit for the Father's love and compassion. I knew that this was not enough: humanity needs to wake up to the truth and become aware of its responsibility towards creation and be restored to harmony.

"Son, more of Our sons must desire to abide here to become conduits of Our unconditional love, limitless grace and triumphant mercy to restore peace and harmony to creation.

"Son you have already experienced some of the dimensional disharmony and isolation from just two dimensions within one constellation: there is so much more to engage with. Creation is groaning with pain and loss and is longing for the revealing of sons who will restore a relationship and take responsibility for its freedom and harmony. Humanity's independence from Us has also resulted in its independence and separation from creation. The consequence of lost identity is always separation and lost relationship.

"Son, continue to be a channel for Our triumphant mercy, unconditional love and limitless grace by staying in rest: living loved, loving living and living loving, not just towards Our children but all of creation. Feel Our heart's desire and passion for restoration and be motivated and inspired to persevere and never give up in your pursuit of fulfilling your destiny as a coheir and co-creator. Son, wear the crown of mercy with honour and respect for creation by being clothed in the glorious light of your sonship.

"Son, the earth shield is getting stronger as more of Our children are awakening to their true identity and responsibility as sons coheirs and co-creators. The frequency of sonship is getting stronger and is being broadcast to all realms and dimensions, so many doors of opportunity are being opened for restoration. The wheels within wheels are being aligned and the seasons are shifting and changing as the great awakening to love gathers pace."

Dimensional Engagements

The sons of God are not just responsible for the earth but all the spheres of creation, including other dimensions. I have had many encounters that have revealed sonship dimensionally.

In a restoration government encounter, I saw three angels, Limitless, Revelation and Breakthrough, form a three-stranded cord that became a ring of fire that opened a portal. I went through the portal and saw many other portals connected in a Merkabah-like structure and each group was formed of different substances. I now know this was out in the cosmos, in the constellation of Cancer.

There were fire portals, water portals, cloud portals, earth portals, energy portals, plasma portals, portals seemingly made of living beings, others like angelic beings, light portals, sound portals, and colour portals. Some portals were like gold, others silver, some like different types of gemstones and some were like liquid mercury and other metallic fluid-like materials; and there were many others too difficult to describe.

I sensed something like a frequency or signal coming from them. As I engaged, I was drawn to the centre of each group that seemed to have the most powerful signal. As I looked in, I first felt then heard a cry for help but also an expectancy of hope; and as I looked more closely, there were many beings in each, gathering together in union, and it was their thoughts and desires I was tuning in to.

"Son, there are many more who need the sons of God to come together in a union of heart, mind and purpose. Do not stop releasing the frequencies and issuing the calls to Our children to come into union and oneness with Our intention."

During another restoration government ascension, I re-engaged the fiery portal and I again saw the same dimensional portals, arranged like a Merkabah of portals, each composed of different substances. I felt the energy, a frequency like a homing beacon, coming from each group of portals. Looking in, I saw that there were beings representative of all manner of different dimensional realities. I felt the overwhelming need to release mercy into the portals. As I did, one person saw some very small beings coming through one of the portals: they were like midgets with transparent heads with arcing light filaments.

I saw them also and we attempted to communicate with them, asking them who they were and what they wanted. They revealed that they had been reaching out to me in my sleep and I began to release declarations of mercy over them. They identified themselves as the guardians of Servici and they were at our service, so we commissioned them to be carriers of mercy to the beings in the other dimensional portals. Servici is the collective name for the portals of the constellation of Cancer. They revealed that they engage through the constellation of Cancer which is characterized by humility and service. The Father later revealed that each constellation is a hub for different dimensional portals.

"Son, you have experienced freely the power and depth of Our mercy and now have emissaries to take mercy to the dimensions to raise hope and expectation. Use your mandate wisely to freely give what you have freely received to bring freedom and restoration dimensionally."

On another occasion, I went back through the fiery portal again and I felt slightly overwhelmed with the task, so I began to think about how I would choose which portals to engage first. I immediately felt a strong frequency drawing me to the water portal but also other frequencies coming from each of the portals. Confused as to which to engage first, I began to brood over each of the portals and the beings that existed in those dimensions; and as I did, I felt the desires of the Father's heart.

I engaged the matrix of light to interface with the intentions of the Father's heart, where I saw possibilities before me; so I chose the reality that I could engage all of the portals that I had felt drawing me. I was greatly energised and I was able to expand the quantum moment to engage each portal in turn to release the frequency of triumphant mercy. Each of the portals were connected like rings joined in a Merkabah-like formation and within each there were beings that looked very different but had a similar or connected frequency.

I engaged each type of portal and each connected portal of that substance (water, air, fire, earth, energy, colour, light, sound, crystal, metal etc.) in turn. In each I was met by representatives and released the mercy of the intentions of the Father's heart. I was filled with joyous wonder at the creativity expressed in each portal and each type of being within them. The manifoldness of God's wisdom and creativity is just so amazing that I was – and still am – in awe. They all had one thing in common, despite the amazing differences in form: they drew me to release mercy, as they all had emotive stories, expressed as intense feelings rather than words, but they moved me to feel deep compassion. They all felt isolated and disconnected from home and from us as sons, only having the merest echo of a long-past memory of union left. The triumphant mercy and limitless grace of a loving God had brought those memories to life and hope was instilled in them for restored union once again.

"Son, come, fly with Me."

I knew the familiar voice of the Spirit and I willingly and excitedly accepted the invitation, as I knew that this would be an adventure. We began to fly through the solar system, slowing enough as we passed by the planets that I could feel the frequency they were emitting. I sensed that there were beings there but I did not see them. I felt their unfulfilled purpose and a sense of sadness that I had never contemplated before but they need to be restored.

"Yes, it is mankind's responsibility to bring restoration to creation: that begins with sentient beings, and as the earth is being restored, there is also so much more. There are guardians for each system that will help you when you learn to engage them."

We are going to engage the constellations and the dimensional portals that connect beyond the physical realms.

I remembered previous experiences I had had with the guardians and the specific encounters with the dimensional hub in the Pleiades region of space. I also recalled the restoration government encounter with the constellation of Cancer accessed through the fiery portal.

"Yes, that is right, you have been prepared for this journey; so now We wish to show you the extent and scope of Our desire for restoration."

We travelled at light speed through the constellations in an order that may be significant but I was too excited to notice.

We met the guardians of the constellations, who were large, regal beings with an official air about them. There was a plan for the portals that were at the core of each region and the guardians were key to engaging the hubs that connected to other dimensions. Some hubs had no guardians around the portal. In some of the constellations there were hubs which angels still governed but there were others where I sensed (but did not see) a fallen being.

There are many regions of space within each constellation but there seemed to be only one dimensional portal hub. As we paused to observe the activity around each hub, some were occupied by different types of beings I wanted to engage, but the Spirit said that this was a reconnaissance mission.

I did feel the frequency and energy of each hub and the draw of the portals that formed the Merkabah-like centres. The enormity of the task hit me as I contemplated that each portal has multiple Merkabah within it; but the cry for help that I had previously encountered from the beings inspired me. Once we had visited all the constellations and their regions, I had a galactic map of the portals in my mind.

We then went to a large council chamber where the representatives of the guardians were meeting and excitedly and noisily communicating with each other. The Holy Spirit took centre stage: all came to attention and there was a hushed silence as I was introduced as one of the ambassadors of the sons of God. The Father has a strategy for restoration that encompasses the sons of God and many will begin to come here for counsel. The light of the hope of sonship is reaching the dimensions and desire is rising for freedom within but the nexus hubs must be restored first, as they are coordinating the external interference that the earth is being shielded from.

I put all my experiences together and I saw the strategy that the Father is beginning to put in place, starting with the earth shield but expanding beyond to incorporate the constellations. I believe there will be more shields for spheres other than the earth. I felt the importance and significance of the shift and transition of the ages that we are currently in and the opportunity it is giving us. The instability of times of transition affords the opportunity for great restorational changes to take place but there has to be sonship and a union of government in place.

"Son, you are mandated, along with others, to mobilize and organise those who are beginning to sense the call of the frequencies from beyond into a functioning government. Everything must be according to its order, and the earth is the first fruits, but preparations must begin now for the restoration of all things in the dimensions beyond."

Seated in Heavenly Places

We engaged a rainbow light realm where the fullness of the promises of God are accessible and all the colours of the 7 spirits can be accessed simultaneously. I saw a mycelial-like organic network of silver threads that connected everything: a communication and transport system of quantum entanglements that connects to all creation. I engaged a thread and was immediately transported to a constellation, to a nexus point where several threads intersected. There were guardians there who were protecting the dimensional portal that was at a point of connection between realms.

They gave us an invitation to engage with the Council of Guardians that the representatives of each nexus point attended. After some discussion, we felt that we needed to honour the invitation by engaging. We engaged a thread from within the rainbow realm and were immediately before the council, where we were presented with a scroll by the Father. We honoured the guardians for the role they have been fulfilling in keeping us safe and there was mutual honouring. It was a solemn and moving moment of reconnection that had an ancient history.

They gave us seats at the council and I saw that we were in a large sphere. On the dome were dimensional maps of the superhighways connecting dimensions. The angelic beings Limitless, Breakthrough and Revelation came and began spinning light around us like a vortex that took us up through the pillar of light. We began to be elevated into different levels and our form began to be transformed to enable us to engage with and relate to different dimensional realities. There were pathways of light set before us that we could follow but the light was also transformational to prepare and equip us to be able to access and relate to the different dimensional realities.

We began to be transformed into different energy forms: a protonic form then a nano form, a photonic form that connected us to a light network for dimensional access. I saw the mycelium connecting different realities for communication and transport; there were also threads to different special dimensions that I did not know. Threads were connecting the physical realm, macro and micro realms and a nano realm but there were also others like sub-space, hyper-space, quantum-space and others that I have no grid for yet.

The Father's presence was very strong there and He said,

"Son, you have been invited to join the council, as they are now forming a strategy to safely engage the dimensions so that they can be transformed and restored. All of creation is beginning to reconnect but you need to be careful and not just go anywhere you like, as there is an order and structure to the process of restoration. The council will give mandates that will give access to the dimensions but some dimensional realities will require a level of union and maturity that is greater than others.

"Son, all that you have seen and experienced is just a fraction of creation but you will be able to connect and engage with it all. Mankind was made to connect with all creational realities and to rule as coheirs and co-creators within Kingdom government. What you are being shown is part of a process of preparation to transform you to be able to access and engage all that has been created for Our sons so they can restore balance and harmony."

These things are our responsibility, in union with others.

"Mankind was not created, but made from all the particles of existence, to connect you and enable you to have a deep desire for union and harmony. That desire has been obscured by independence but it is awakening. Mankind was created in Our image, in union and relationship, to be a multidimensional being, able to transcend the barriers between the many forms of dimensional space-time. No other being has the capacity to be able to be as transformational and multidimensional, as mankind alone were made to be coheirs and co-creators.

"The restoration of identity, position and authority is just the beginning of the journey that outworks through this process of ascension to maturity. Mankind will ascend into glorious transcendence with eternal attributes and capabilities, so keep following the pathway of light set out before you.

"Son, come walk with me."

I was happy to accept the invitation and we began to walk around the circle of the deep, past each of the High Chancellors' houses, pausing at the entrance of each house. At each pause, all that I had previously experienced about the houses came flooding back to me and then we looked out to the constellations and in towards the Ambassadors of the ages, the wheels within wheels within wheels.

"Son, the circle of the deep must be aligned as a wheel within a wheel within a wheel for the strategies agreed with the guardians to be effective. Alignments and agreement are what makes union and oneness so powerful in collaboration. Time functions differently within the dimensions, so the cosmic wheel must be aligned with the ages before the Chancellors' houses can process the dimensional changes. The ages of the ascension of mankind must align with the time frames that operate in the dimensions that are connected to each constellation.

"What you have observed as you entered the fiery portal within what you know as Cancer was a series of dimensional portals sharing a specific age. Each constellation has similar dimensional portals associated with each of the 12 ages of man, so a council of the guardians, Chancellors, Ambassadors and man is necessary to coordinate the alignment. As man has ascended in consciousness to become aware of Our precepts and Our statutes, it is now possible for the principles of acceleration to trigger the ordinances of time.

"There are 12 major constellations that the earth is connected to, 12 chancellors' houses, 12 ages of man and 12 nexus dimensional portals; and each must be aligned, so that Our precepts can be revealed to the dimensions associated with that age. There are dimensions associated with the first age of man, and others for each age; and because time operates differently, some dimensions seem more advanced than mankind.

"There is an order to the constellations that corresponds to the ages and dimensions and only a union of the three spheres and man can coordinate the process:

- Sagittarius
- Scorpius
- Libra
- Virgo
- Leo
- Cancer
- Gemini
- Taurus
- Aries
- Pisces
- Aquarius
- Capricornus

"Engaging the guardians has triggered the opportunity to align the wheels to release the principles of time ordinances to accelerate dimensional restoration.

"Son that is why you have been engaging the precepts of unconditional love, limitless grace and triumphant mercy, as they are the foundations of the principles of time." (It was only later that I was able to engage the being of Time).

"The foundational precepts of the eternal now must converge with time for each of the constellational ages and dimensions in sequence. Enoch has walked the pathways of the ages and will preside over the council that is forming; but there must be a representative of man for each age, constellation, house and dimensional portal.

"You have engaged with many of the creational and dimensional processes that are part of the ascension of man. That began when mankind was formed out of the living particles of creation, enlightened to the covenant, born from above at the resurrection, enlightened to heavenly coheirship and matured to lordship, chancellorship, kingship and sonship identity, awakened to creational responsibility, enlightened to union, enlightened to ambassadorship and awakened to destiny as co-creating ascended fathers. This is the ancient pathway of the Tree of Life to mankind's ascension to maturity.

"Son, each process is also a governmental window, like desire, thought, voice and light in the Cradle of Life, Waterfall of the Sound of Many Waters, Chamber of Destiny and Chamber of Creation. The 12 fire stones correspond to the 12 ages of ascension, where the wheels of the High Chancellors' houses are aligned. Only now that the constellational portals have been discovered and the council formed can the time principles be enacted. There still need to be 12 representatives of man at the council to unify the convergence: Adam, Abraham, David, Paul and John can make up the 12 temporarily if necessary.

"Son, the principles of dimensional time are about to unravel and knowledge will become available to those who truly seek after restoration. A desire for restoration will motivate and inspire those who have experienced the oracles of Our heart to restore the dimensions and reset the cosmic and dimensional clocks. The light of love and truth is beginning to shine more brightly and its frequency is reaching the dimensions, producing a spark of hope that will light a fire of restoration that will become unstoppable.

"The ages of man, the constellational ages and the dimensional ages must be aligned with the High Chancellors' houses for the process of restoration to become fully functional. The fabric of the space-time continuum will be unravelled and restored so all memory of lost identity will cease to exist and only wisdom will remain. This resetting is the greatest triumph of mercy that will ever be experienced, even though there can never be any memory of it when all is reset. Creation is longing for the day when all things are aligned in union with the sons of God who are the central point of connection and the light and resonant frequency.

"Son, you have seen the council and know the truth of the first principles of restoration: by abiding within love's light, keep resting in being, and more will begin to unravel."

I began to see the wheels within wheels turning like cogs in a cosmic dimensional clock, each click and tick bringing closer alignment of the union of the ages which is occurring during this transition.

"Son, all that you see is within the eternal now and its convergence will be the heavenly governor that creates the first movement. The seasons and cycles of judgment, justice, grace and mercy are the governors of the cosmic dimensional clock. You have experienced each of the seasons and have been through each cycle within your own life, as the 12 houses aligned with the four seasons:

1. Judgment - precepts, statutes, laws, ordinances.
2. Justice - ordinances, mantles, weapons, scrolls.
3. Grace - scrolls, discoveries, commissioning, culture.

4. Mercy - culture, affairs of the nations, treasury, precepts.

"Son, there are also seasons where the four ages, four constellations and four dimensional portals also cycle and align with what you have experienced with the first chancellor's wheel:

1. Sagittarius, Scorpius, Libra, Virgo.
2. Virgo, Leo, Cancer, Gemini.
3. Gemini, Taurus, Aries, Pisces.
4. Pisces, Aquarius, Capricornus, Sagittarius.

1. Daktarians, Eluvians, Simarians, Hadjurians.
2. Hadjurians, Servicians, Durrassians, Jordassians.
3. Jordassians, Pleiadians, Silothians, Lorathians
4. Lorathians, Rakthurians, Siriusians, Daktarians.

"Son, as you engage the council of the twelves (the guardians, Ambassadors and Chancellors) as a representative of the sons of God, a strategy for restoration will be revealed.

"Son, receive the mercy that so many in creation need to triumph over a judgment that is not coming from heaven. Heaven's judgment is clear: the whole of creation has been pronounced not guilty and is innocent of all accusations brought from all sources. From Our perspective, creation's innocence was agreed upon and guaranteed before the beginning, and therefore restoration is certain, but We do not operate independently of Our children. We desire agreement and union of hearts and minds. We desire relational union, agreement and cooperation with the desires and intentions of Our heart and We are constantly working to bring good out of every situation.

"Restored harmony within all of creation is Our intention because We are passionate about all We have created. The more Our sons receive and know Our mercy and unconditional love, the easier it will be for union and limitless grace to restore the relationship between all creation. It is sons made in Our image who are responsible as coheirs with Us to establish Kingdom government and expand peace throughout the dimensions. Creation needs demonstrations of triumphant mercy to awaken it to a conscious awareness of unconditional love so all within it will be able to be set free."

I felt waves of mercy within the light radiating from the Father's face, each wave going deeper into my being. The more those waves kept coming, the more compassion and love I began to feel for creation and all that is within it and the more mercy I was able to absorb.

"Son you must encourage Our sons to abide here. As you do so, their capacity for unconditional love and mercy can increase."

I felt inspired with the intentions of the Father's heart, so I engaged the fiery portal within the constellation of Cancer and was drawn to the group of golden portals. As I engaged the central portal that connected all the others within that group, I felt such a deep, almost overwhelming sense of loss. I was drawn just within the event horizon where I felt an even greater sense of what this dimension was suffering from.

In contrast to the external appearance of the portal being gold, within there was the total and complete opposite: deep deprivation and poverty beyond my ability to express. I felt such shame and loss that the original intention of God as creator has been so tarnished that there was nothing even shiny or reflective and everything was absorbed. The light could not reflect but that was just an external symptom of the shame that dominated this environment.

I released all the mercy I had absorbed, but this time I was still entangled with the mercy coming from the Father's face and I became a conduit for mercy to triumphantly begin to overcome generations of shame. Mercy continued to ripple out, wave after wave, until finally I felt my task had been accomplished; and then I saw a golden glow, as if the dawn was just about to break forth. I felt such a relief as the weight of shame I empathised with was lifted and I was consciously back with the Father.

"Son, Our sons are mandated to engage the dimensions as you have done but they must be able to absorb Our mercy and have the capacity for unconditional love. Humanity's understanding of judgment must be transformed by the truth of Our true essence so that righteousness and true justice (which is triumphant mercy) can overcome the deception.

"Son, come with Me, as I have something to show you that you need to know about."

We began to move through the constellations, beginning with the 12 known as the Mazzaroth. In each one we stopped at dimensional portals where there were guardians stationed. As we went beyond, to the other constellations, some portals were not guarded. I remembered that I had been to one of those unguarded portals in the Pleiades constellation during a previous encounter, and there had been a lot of interdimensional activity.

"Son, all the dimensions accessible within the 12 constellations do not engage your realm unless everlasting doors are opened, such as the West gate. Most activity between dimensions is coordinated by counterfeit councils and some portals are currently active but many are now being awakened and activated. You have the mandate to engage the active portals as before, but you will need to cooperate with the angelic orders and guardians to protect those portals that are at risk of activation. Son, whenever the ages are in transition there is also increased opposition activity: that is why We have established the earth shield."

I began in a specific constellation that was activated and expanded the quantum moment to facilitate the process of restoration. I engaged the light realm to discern the Father's heart, and brooded in the Cradle of Life until energised and resonating with the thoughts and intentions of the Father for that dimension. Once I became a vibrating sound of many waters and an oracle, and the Quantum Lumens were activated within the Chamber of Creation, I was able to engage, and overshadowed those at the event horizon with love's light for restoration.

The hope of mercy that was released was able to penetrate the dimensions beyond before I moved on to the next constellation. Each expanded moment was months of intense activity and there were times when I had to re-energise the gateways within my core being before attempting another process.

"Son, continue to dwell in the light of Our presence and call on the angelic orders to engage the council before attempting to stop the occupation of other portals."

I called the four angels of transition to accompany me to the council: Transformation, Winds of Change, Sound of Many Waters and Refiner's Fire. The council was in session when I presented my mandate before them but they seemed to be aware, as if I was not interrupting. There was some debating of strategy before they finally stated their conclusion: more guardians need to be created to protect the vulnerable constellations.

They looked at me as if I knew what to do but I had never created anything sentient before, so I avoided their gaze. Then I remembered the time in 2010 when Jesus created the horse by whittling wood and invited me to create something. As I was very naive in 2010 I just thought about what I wanted to create, picturing it in my mind, and then the beautifully-coloured bird appeared. I shifted focus to the light realm as I thought this would be more complicated and I would need a mandate from the Father, not just a council edict.

"Son, you now dwell here and within the Cradle of Life, and know Our heart; so the process of creating is no more complicated, as you know the sequence that light responds to."

I was aware that the council was waiting. So, surrounded by the four angels, I pictured many guardians in my mind and they just seemed to appear (though I was aware that there was a process behind this). I heard the Father speak in my mind and I knew that there were limits to my creative mandate and that others would also need to create.

"Son, only choose the realities you know are Our intentions and help to mobilize others to become creatively activated."

The council assigned the newly-formed guardians to their constellational stations and I left, feeling somewhat bemused by the whole encounter.

"Son, do not be overwhelmed by what you are being called to do: it is your destiny and that of all Our sons to be creatively responsible.

During a restoration government ascension, we ascended a helical DNA-type ladder and we engaged the Tree of Life, where a sap-like substance was being released. We also engaged a counterfeit council where some trafficking strategy was taking place and saw some beings who were acting like guards, stopping victims from believing in the possibility of freedom. We also engaged an infinity loop which is deceiving humanity into believing in the possibility of eternal life through religious works and self-effort, trapped in a cycle of the futility of dead works.

The truth of the ascension of mankind through the Tree of Life was released like sap, to free people from their lost identity and a cyclical existence that is going nowhere. The sap from the Tree of Life was applied to bring freedom to those trapped by a form of artificial intelligence (AI). This substance was also applied to some beings that were guarding the AI control room. The beings were engaged, forgiven and transformed into the guardians of dimensional portals they were intended to be and released to take up their positions in the constellations.

We felt that we had a mandate to create more guardians for unguarded dimensional portals, so one person simply created a variety of different-looking guardians and they were then commissioned. One of those created guardians went to the constellation of Leo, which has a kingship function.

During the encounter, I was functioning within the earth shield, releasing waves of creative energy to equip the group for creative and restorational abilities.

"Son, the Tree of Life has many functions and purposes that can be used in the restoration process, like the sap you experienced. Keep seeking and you will keep finding, as there is so much more to discover about your identity as a son and your sonship governmental and creative abilities."

I engaged the helical ladder within the Tree of Life again and ascended through levels of mankind's intended maturity: each one had DNA transformations and consciousness expansions. These stages were associated with the frequencies encountered on the fire stones which are also part of mankind's ascension and development to oneness.

"Son, the oneness of intimacy that is within the *perichoresis* of *I am that I am* is like a marriage consummation where two become one. The deception of the tree of the knowledge of good and evil was the lie that We were withholding things from Our children to stop them from being like Us. This is a total twisting of the truth, as We created mankind in Our image to be godlike; but maturity in wisdom and character was always meant to be a relational journey of discovery.

"The choice to try to be like Us independently created the DIY tree path of striving, through self-effort and dead works, to be who you always were. Lost identity trapped mankind on an infinity loop that was a counterfeit of eternity which perpetuated the deception of 'I will ascend'. The deception has created a cyclical pathway that looks like the covenant pathway where the end and the beginning meet for new beginnings with fresh mercy: but it is a trap. The deceptive loop creates an illusion of progress but is in fact as futile as expecting a hamster to evolve by running around a wheel that is going nowhere.

"Son, Our children need to be set free from this futile, evil existence of striving, toil and labour that is an illusion and a delusion. Only an awakening to unconditional love, limitless grace and triumphant mercy can free Our children to know their true identity as sons, by freeing them from the controlling matrix they are trapped in. Experiencing the truth of Our unconditional lovingkindness is the only thing that can expose the deception and free Our children from the trap of lost identity. Only the intimacy of oneness within Us can reveal the true glory of sonship and elevate mankind to its intended position concerning creation. Only ascended, mature sons can free creation from its bondage to mankind's corruption into the harmony of oneness that We intend.

"The creative process of brooding to incubate Our intention is to birth the reality of restoration. You are mandated to engage with the dimensions, earth shield, portals and Guardians' Council. Son, We are giving opportunities to those who are seeking Us with sincere hearts to connect with the angelic realm orders more closely. The collaboration and special relationships that are being developed with angelic partners are vital for Our sons to fulfil their destinies. We have assembled the groupings that each person needs to fulfil their mandates and assignments and they are seeking you out. Remember those groups that have encountered you and you will begin to see patterns emerge, as there is no randomness."

- Wisdom, Knowledge, Understanding and Prudence.
- Union, Liberty, Limitless and Blessing.
- Transformation, Winds of Change, Sound of Many Waters and Refiner's Fire.
- Union, Covenant, Peacemaker and Family.
- Limitless, Revelation, Breakthrough.
- Love, Joy and Peace.

- Truth Revealer, Truth Restorer and Truth Establisher.
- Love, Peace, Sound Mind.
- Immortality, Knowledge, Intimacy.
- Faith, Hope and Love.
- Love, Power and a Sound Mind.
- Grace, Mercy and Limitless.
- Unity, Union and Blessing.
- Time, Wealth and Health.
- Gold, Silver and Precious Stones.

I engaged them all, thanking them for their service and demonstrating my gratitude by honouring them with positive judgment in their favour. I engaged with those who I have helped to be restored, thanking them, honouring them and judging them for their service.

- Abundant Life, Deep Intimacy and Revealed Truth.
- Destiny, Freedom and Harmony.
- The Punisher bench of three who were restored to Protectors.
- Sikurt who was restored back to Truth.

"Son, there are so many more ready to cooperate and collaborate who are already prepared and working behind the scenes. Seek to engage them by opening your heart and desires to them so connections can be established but always maintain respect, honour and gratitude."

I went to the court of angels and chose to open my heart to them, exposing my destiny and offering friendship. I honoured them for all they have done in my life in caretaking my throne, aligning the circle of the deep, protecting and keeping me safe, engineering connections and encounters. I went through the canopy of angels over my throne stopping in each realm to honour and thank them for their service and judging them with positive affirmations. I opened my heart and became vulnerable by revealing my deepest desires, demonstrating a trust that I have only previously shown to the Father.

I went to the Chancellors' Court, Court of Scribes, Court of Kings and Court of Judges and judged them with honour and gratitude. I went to the High Chancellors' houses, the Guardians' Council and the Ambassadors of the ages and honoured them. I went to the guardians of our solar system and the constellations and honoured them for their service and thanked them. I went to the Court of the Upright and thanked the cloud of witnesses for their faithfulness and service and honoured them. I went to the thrones of the earth to engage the Elementals and I honoured them and thanked them for their service, and opened up my heart and desires for creation's freedom to them.

"Son, this day marks a transition into a new season of restoration that will be characterized by deeper union and relationship."

Time

In a Restoration government ascension, I entwined in the light matrix of the Father's intentions; and when I engaged the earth shield those intentions were directed by Wisdom, Knowledge, Understanding and Prudence, who surrounded me out to the cosmos. The light intentions formed a connection that entangled me to the constellation of Cancer and, like engaging a wormhole, I was instantly there when my choice aligned with the intention and the resonance energised the connection.

I engaged with the guardians around the fiery portal, which was glowing: they permitted me to enter, and when I did I was drawn to a group of golden portals connected in a formation like the Merkabah. Some beings emerged that I recognised as the Servici whom we met before and who committed themselves to Our service. They informed me that I needed to help those who were in deep need; their countenance and frequencies indicated a sense of urgency and desire. They directed me to another group of portals that were giving off a strong sense of dread, foreboding and deep loss; and although I did not enter, I tangibly felt the darkness.

I released all that I had encountered in the light and connected that place with the Father's heart, where I was still entangled; and a stream of unconditional love, limitless grace and triumphant mercy entered the central portal. I felt a disturbance within and eventually a faint but encouraging response that the light of love and truth that had entered had produced hope in that dimension. Again, I felt like I was a straw and a giant pipeline was needed: there was such darkness and despair that would require a union of many hearts to overcome with love's light.

The Father also revealed that there was a system of connections, like a network of veins and arteries, like a cosmic circulation system, that was blocked. There were beings composed of angels and the cloud of witnesses that symbolically held hands across space-time to indicate that we could engage it. We engaged the circulatory system at the blockage points and began to expand to force the vessels open, like inserting a stent. There seemed to be a lot of energy stored up that began to flow strongly, as if it was being pumped by the Father's heart in time. It was like the blood of Jesus carrying the intentions of the Father's heart as anointing was being pumped through this system of networks to the constellations and dimensions. We thanked and honoured Time for partnering with us and there was a sense of rejoicing that something lost was now restored.

"Son, Our sons are beginning to rise up into their positions of responsibility to steward the restoration of all things in some of the realms and dimensions of creation. As the restrictions and limitations on the minds of the sons of God are removed and consciousness is awakened and expanded creation will begin to respond even more than at present.

"Son, continue to release the call and frequency of the blue light of destiny to draw those willing to accept the responsibility for creation's stewardship. For many, the cost to pursue their destiny is too great as they have experiences of heavenly encounters but they have not embraced the transformation these engagements have offered. Many have recoiled at the level of commitment needed to embrace their identity and position and have rejected the governmental aspects of being a son of God.

"Son, do not be disappointed, as they have not been untethered from their wrong thinking about time so have not learned to work with time creatively. Most are still living with time constraints and do not yet believe they can expand and contract to enable them to fulfil their destiny. It is important that Our sons learn to partner with Time effectively so they can be free from their restrictions and limitations. Those who have enjoyed the heavenly experiences but who have not connected face to face and heart to heart with Us are those who have not yet embraced restoration and its implications. Only experiencing the oracles of Our heart towards creation will create the passion and desire necessary to overcome the inconveniences and produce the perseverance needed.

"The revealing of the sons of God to creation is not an event but a long process of maturity that requires much transformation and metamorphosis. The only way to become who you are is to go through the chrysalis of restriction and the struggle to emerge to become as beautiful and free as the butterfly."

What follows is a compilation of various engagements with the being of Time:

"Son, your encounters with Time must become widespread as Our children need to be the masters of time and not subject to it."

I encountered Time as a being many times during ascensions, where there was a restoration of relationship. Time spoke of changing our vocabulary towards it, because it was for us and not against us and wished to cooperate. We need to evaluate what we say about time: think of the positive and remove the negative, no longer saying things such as "I don't have enough time", "time is running out", "time is against us", "the passage of time", "it's all in the past", "another day gone", "getting older every day", and "time is our enemy". We need to be untethered from the restrictions of time and learn to cooperate with Time creatively. Time can be expanded, contracted and suspended to stand still; and each quantum moment of time can expand indefinitely.

Time wishes to be part of the restoration of what we call history so that it can be restored, as Time is creative and collaborative. We have access to all history by engaging through the eternal now. Time gives insight and understanding of history. Time desires a positive relationship with us that enables us to function fully as sons of God where there is always enough time to do all that we are called and mandated to do. Time wants to be our friend and not our enemy so we never think about being too busy.

"Son, it is important for Our children to change their whole relationship with Time and work together in a union."

During a group ascension, the being Time appeared. Whilst I had met it before, this was new to the others. Time declared again "I am for you, not against you," offering partnership but indicating that our attitude, vocabulary and thinking needed to change towards it. Each of us asked for forgiveness for our negativity towards Time and severed the connections we had made with time and ageing, not having enough time, losing time, time running out, connecting time's passage with death etc.

Time offered to partner with us so that the limitations and restrictions in our minds to past, present and future would be removed so that we could access everything across space-time. All sorts of possibilities and opportunities began to form in our minds for this partnership with Time and a great sense of excitement and anticipation was activated within us.

"Son, your engagements with Time are preparation for a new season of restoration that will go beyond beyond again. History has been manipulated by those with the agenda to keep Our children from their destiny by deceiving them and trapping them in lost identity. Who owns the publishers, newspapers and media outlets? No one owns the internet – that is both really good and potentially really bad, but it is now being policed and manipulated – but it is really difficult to control.

"Conspiracy and misinformation campaigns have been used to hide the truth amongst the lies. The worldwide web can bring the truth or lies and deception right into your homes and available at your fingertips. Learn to discern the truth from the deception by encountering the Truth and knowing His frequency. The truth found in love's light is the only thing that can expose the lies within the history books, whose contents have been to control and manipulate the truth to present a false narrative that hides the Luciferian agendas of historical events. A partnership with Time will enable history to be unlocked and unravelled and the restoration of the truth to take place where the key events of history are redeemed."

I have engaged with Time during many ascensions in the last few months to be untethered from wrong attitudes, beliefs, mindsets and vocabulary that has formed negative associations. Along with untethering from the inevitability of ageing and death, there has been a reconnection with immortality and a new partnership with Time that will enable the restoration of all things to go to another level.

This is a transcript of a group encounter with Time, including contributions from different members of the group:

> We need to develop a relationship with Time that is positive and cooperative that will enable us to go beyond the concepts of past, present and future to develop nonlinear and multidimensional creative and restorational abilities.

> We must begin to honour and respect Time so new wisdom, knowledge and understanding concerning both time and space continuums can be revealed and received.

I saw Time standing before the thrones where we are seated next to Jesus and the Father; and coming from Time were filaments of light that on closer inspection were connections or pathways like wormholes of instant entanglement. I saw the possibilities of the partnership that Time was offering mankind so that it can be untethered from the concept and agenda of humanity.

"Enlightenment of love exposes the deception so the truth will bring freedom to restore humanity back to mankind made in Our image, free it from the trap of independence and reconcile and reconnect it to creation.

"Time is integral in this process as a partner and friend who is for you not against you.

"Time is not robbing you but enabling you to fulfil your destiny.

"Son, Time is not to be killed, wasted, lapsed, borrowed or lost; and Time does not fly, run out, fly like an arrow or pass.

"Time is not to be commodified, as time is not money: your value is not based on productivity.

"Time is your friend, not your enemy: so embrace Time and enjoy.

"Time and immortality are being restored to a union.

"Do not associate Time with seconds, minutes, hours, days, weeks, months, years, decades, centuries or millennia, as you are tethering yourself to death, as then Time becomes a passage to nothingness. Embracing a partnership with Time will free you from the restrictions of yesterday, today and tomorrow so you can become the convergence of time and the eternal now.

"When you partner with Time relationally you will learn to be in a state of being at rest where everything is within *I am*. Everything is as it should be and you can live satisfied and content but motivated and passionate for the restoration of all things."

What does it take for the sons to take their places and positions?

We need to engage with the being of Time...

How do we engage with Time?

How does Time work for us and not against us?

"Begin by honouring Time..."

I honour you, Time, who I have actually treated more as an enemy and a scarcity.

I open my heart now to learn from Time, in the presence of the Father, in the presence of the Lord, so that I can see what my relationship should be with this being of Time and how to function with him in that relationship.

I honour you, Time, and thank you for desiring to partner with us.

Time is saying, "Time is not running out. You need to change your mindset and vocabulary towards that with me, so that we can partner for the restoration of history, for the incubation needed for the restoration of all things."

There are so many ways of talking about time which are a dishonour and lack of trust.

Time wants to work *with* us, not *for* us.

We have connected Time with death and ageing. We have tied our understanding of time to the passage of hours, days, years, and that it's gone and we have no access to it.

I ask forgiveness for using negative words and concepts of time, for using phrases that have disrespected and dishonoured Time, making Time an enemy rather than a friend.

In Father's presence, I engage with Time, seeking for a relationship that will be fruitful and fulfilling and will enable us to outwork and fulfil all that we need to do in restoration.

I ask that Time would teach us about time-travelling so that we may repair the breaches of the past.

I repent of judging myself and others for wasting time. Father, thank You that You have given us all the time we need.

I repent of thinking of sleep as an interrupter of my activities, rather than valuing sleep.

We have been given light-emitting shoes to "walk forwards and backwards."

We accept the invitation to partner with Time.

We honour that partnership, and we join together for the purposes and the intentions of God's Kingdom, for the restoration with Time.

We declare: "We have all the time that we need."

Time is not running out.

Time is our friend, not our enemy; and we cooperate in partnership with Time to facilitate the restoration of all the past that's affecting the present and the future.

We renounce the separation of past, present and future (as if we are living in the present, rejecting the past and not thinking about the future) – we just see the whole thing as one, not limited or restricted by past, present or future.

We can just learn to be at rest, knowing that we have all that we need, all resources and access that Time gives us – it's available to us to expand, to contract, to travel, to instantly be connected to places.

In a sense, the speed of light, which is a function of time, enables us to be anywhere and everywhere and live in a multi-dimensional way, unlimited by linear time.

We reject the concept of linear time, in favour of engaging rich time, the Eternal Now perspective of time that will not limit us or restrict us in any way in the fulfilment of the whole of the restoration of God's purposes.

"Blessed be the name of God forever and ever,
For wisdom and might are His.
And He changes the times and the seasons;
He removes kings and raises up kings;
He gives wisdom to the wise
And knowledge to those who have understanding.
He reveals deep and secret things;
He knows what is in the darkness,
And light dwells with Him. (Daniel 2:20-22 NKJV).

Filaments of light coming from the being Time are connecting us instantaneously with other places, time, self, history.

These are quantum-entangled 'wormholes' that are instantaneous connections for multidimensional engagement. We are not limited to our own time-space continuum and framework of time.

Time is basically releasing all of these things for us to follow and connect and engage with.

These are the pathways. These are the partnership opportunities that Time is releasing for us that's connecting us with specific moments, past, present, future – all encapsulated so that there's no limitation to our engagement.

But not just 'time' but also dimensional reality as well. This is giving us access to those dimensions.

Father is saying to us, it's TIME now because we're ready. We weren't ready before.

Our understanding is where it is regarding time.

It's time now to unlock some of the treasures of darkness.

I receive that, Father. I receive the treasures of darkness.

I agree and align myself with what You've decreed, that it's time.

"I will give you the treasures of darkness
And hidden riches of secret places,
That you may know that I, YHWH,
Who call you by your name..." (Isaiah 45:3 NKJV[102]).

---

[102] This contributor substituted 'YHWH' for NKJV's 'the LORD'.

I want to be friends with Time, and friends hang out together.

So Time, I would like to be your friend and hang out with you and learn from you how to redeem the time without feeling guilty about it or under undue pressure, but just to understand how time is available to us to make good use of.

We untether ourselves from our limitations concerning time. We untether ourselves from the time connected to ageing and death.

We untether ourselves from where time has been connected to the passage of time in moments of time that we're disconnected from.

And we release to those who are trapped in time, feel time's running out, feel they're lost, drifting without purpose, aimless, directionless... we release the frequency of hope. We release the light. We release the truth.

We release what we've experienced, that time would be redeemed. Their whole lives in relation to their destiny, their purpose which they may feel has been wasted or lost – we call for redemption of their purpose and their destiny, freeing them from any time constraints or sense of lost opportunities and time.

We release it as a frequency of hope to inspire people to, again, partner with Time in a completely different way; that they will be free from the restrictions and limitations that they feel Time has placed on them but they've placed on themselves.

So they would have the fullness of the times, those things that the Lord releases in new seasons.

We call for new seasons of opportunity of change, of transformation to take place.

Tectonic plates

In several government group encounters, we have engaged the tectonic plates of the earth, releasing heavenly oil to reduce friction between the plates. During these encounters, we discovered a void where there has been an absence of the light of sonship, creating a vacuum filled with darkness. In those voids, there is an order of fallen angels whose function is to cause devastation, both to the earth through earthquakes and eruptions and to man by the destruction of lives, crops and livestock and property. These beings were called Devastation, Disaster and Destruction.

We discovered that the original function of those beings was preservation, conservation and construction: so not only do they promote devastation but there is an absence of preservation and conservation.

> Conservation – the act of preserving, guarding or protecting; preservation from loss, decay, injury, or violation; the keeping of a thing in a safe or entire state; as the conservation of bodies from perishing; the conservation of the peace of society; the conservation of privileges. – *dictionary.com*

Their responsibility to work in cooperation with mankind for the preservation of life, species, natural balance and harmonious ecosystems has been twisted to create devastation through what are wrongly known as natural disasters or acts of God. These fallen beings have corrupted the Elementals to work against man and each other and that has resulted in chaos and disharmony. Humanity, under the influence of the DIY tree path of independence, has been deceived into abusing its authority over creation, cursing it rather than blessing it.

As the sons of God are awakening to their identity, the truth is being revealed and creation is responding as restoration is taking place. The restoration of those fallen angelic beings is tipping the balance to accelerate the shift and the earth and the Elementals are awakening also. As those restored beings participate in the earth shield there will be an even greater global awareness and awakened consciousness to the responsibility to steward creation.

"Son, Our government through mankind is responsible for the restoration of peace and harmony to creation not to create war and conflict because the power of unconditional love is Our primary weapon. We have limitless grace at Our disposal and an abundance of triumphant mercy; so love has won and will win and the restoration of all things will eventually be accomplished.

"Legislate for a global awakening of consciousness to unconditional love that will reveal Our true nature to Our children and through them to all creation. Son, trust in the power of Our love to overcome anything that is an obstacle or a hindrance to the restoration of all things."

During another group ascension, I engaged the realm of light and the Father's thoughts formed a matrix of light around me, filled with His intentions for the earth. Time, Wealth, Union, Blessing, Gold and Silver stood by me: light streamed from them, connecting with the matrix of the Father's intentions. There were filaments of light that were like highways or portals that were connected to places, dimensions or timelines.

I felt the desire to engage the earth shield. All those beings came with me and their light became one, like a laser pointer, scanning the earth. I followed the path to engage the earth's core and plates and felt the tension it was under at certain points around the globe. At each place of tension – be it political or geological – there was darkness, or more like something hiding, so I engaged one specific place in Iceland and saw a being. I began to engage it: it did not communicate but I felt deep shame within its dark covering so I continued to offer restoration, without any immediate success.

Restoration is a process that requires commitment and perseverance. Time came with me and I asked Time to show me the being's original purpose and name. As I saw its origin, I knew it was another being of Devastation that was originally called Preservation. With that knowledge, I reminded it of its original name and function and began to call forth its identity that was hidden under the scales of darkness and shame that covered it. I saw that there were dark filaments connected to this being, as if it was tethered and being controlled: having its strings pulled by others for an external financial agenda.

I felt the shame was associated with causing natural disasters that caused financial crashes or situations that were taken advantage of to make money out of the misery or misfortune of others. The disasters were used to influence the financial markets and control or destabilise governments. I saw the timeline of devastations that created famines, loss of property and livelihoods through history and I understood the deep shame it was covered by.

I released forgiveness to it for the financial devastations and again called forth its true identity as Preservation; and as the quantum moment expanded, I began to see light breaking through the darkness. I felt its true purpose was to preserve life, health and blessing and prevent destruction, loss and decay. I began to declare jubilee and wellbeing over it, producing hope, breaking down its objections and resistance to believing it could be restored.

The other beings of Wealth, Gold, Silver and Blessing began to engage as I surrounded it with my spirit and love, creating a safe place for the process to continue. It was afraid of reprisals from its own order and mankind. Eventually, the light of the being of Preservation emerged in its glorious identity and we engaged it and asked it to participate in the earth shield to preserve the earth from devastations leading to financial crashes etc. It agreed to be part of surrounding the earth like a cloak of preservation.

We began to sense the other beings of devastation still connected by the back tentacles to dark pools and webs of deception within the global financial control systems. There is more work to do to see those control systems removed and the connections between world events and financial gains and control severed. There are people in global cabals pulling the strings, using these beings to maintain their control.

"Son, many such manipulations have occurred throughout history that have a Luciferian agenda behind them; and today there are strategies of the political and religious spirit that need to be exposed and dismantled. The events in history that caused devastations that were financially manipulated need to be revealed so people can be disentangled from global financial control and manipulation. Look carefully to discern what is behind world events and who benefits from them."

Eruptions, earthquakes, tornados, hurricanes, typhoons, famines, revolutions, coups, stock market crashes, wars, conflicts, the Red Terror of Russia, Holodomor, Chinese genocides, holocaust, African genocides, Irish potato famine, terror attacks, Krakatoa, Atlantis, floods in prehistory, Chernobyl and Fukushima nuclear disasters and pandemics: we need to become more discerning when viewing world events, not operating in nationalism, fear or conspiracy but in understanding to help legislate for the revealing of the agendas behind those events.

Below is another transcript of a restoration government group ascension.

> We were discussing encounters that I and some *Engaging God* governmental groups had had with Time and subsequently an order of beings hidden in the earth in places of tension. The order of beings was Devastation, previously called Preservation.
>
> We can call them into the highest court and rule for justice to begin to strip away the shame that is on them, seeking justice from the courts of heaven with agreement and mandate. At the present moment, we have to find out whether or not we have the mandate to begin to strip away all those layers of shame, because that's something that has to be adjudicated from on high.
>
> Father, we just thank you and praise you that you've called us and privileged us and blessed us with being your ambassadors in this specific time in the earth realm.

We just thank You that you have opened the door and prepared the way for us that wherever you are and whatever You are doing, we can follow.

So, as one body, with one thought process, we take on the mind of Christ; we ascend into the courts of heaven, and we stand before You and present this case.

We just yield our own thoughts, our own ideas, our own expectations; and we just yield to Your mandate, to whatever You want to initiate in us and through us and by us and between us and round about us.

You know what's in our heart, so You've heard all of our words and all of our conversation today.

So we come before you humbly, just asking your permission, Lord, to co-work and to co-create together with You to bring about the stripping away of shame – especially over the one called Devastation, that he might be restored to his previous place at the beginning, called Preservation.

Father, we ask You to forgive us in any way that we have fallen short.

We thank You that all of our authority comes through You, through the blood of Jesus.

[We were engaging the court and seeking direction for administering justice.]

We surrender right now to that blood which is the highest form of sacrifice. Thank You that Your name is above every other name, every other name named in heaven and earth; that the name of Jesus is high above the name of

Devastation; that the name of Jesus is high above every other name.

Lord, You have put it in our hearts now to be your instruments for restoration.

So we just present our petition right now and we just ask you, is it okay and is it time for us to deal with this issue?

We lay our petition on your bench.

We want to stay within the perfect timing designated by you.

We want to restore justice. We call on the being of Justice to come and stand with us, along with Time.

So what I'm seeing is a cloning effect amongst these beings. So I'm going to call it a cloning effect because I don't really know how else to describe what I'm seeing. What I am seeing is that whilst these beings have been assigned to different places in the cosmos, they are separate parts but still part of a whole. As one so-called natural disaster takes place, it actually layers and impacts through every being. It impacts on every geographical area that that being is sitting over. So I just see that as we do whatever it is that we are going to do, in the same way, that it has a cloning kind of effect: as it had a negative impact, so it can have a positive effect. As we begin to unpack this and impact the one being of Devastation, it actually impacts on the whole. So, this is exponentially positive as we begin to reverse out this stuff.

What I'm seeing now is, I'm seeing a cluster of beings that look like green lights. Not sure if they are lights – but if they are, they are very green and they are mandated to work with us. I sense and feel that they are part of the Elementals and that they are connected to some of the elements of nature, which is why they appear in green, in that way. I also take it to mean that we have a green light.

Okay, so I'm seeing the green light beings and they are mandated to work with us. But I am seeing them looking to us, asking for instructions. Well, since they are mandated to work together with us, I'm thinking that maybe what the Lord's intention is, is for us to commission them to begin to go and strip away the layers of shame.

So, Father, we just speak to the green light beings right now and we just commission them to go and begin to strip away the shame from Devastation. We thank You that, because these are Elementals, that the stripping away of this shame will ultimately cause things to be restored and put back into divine reposition and brought into accurate alignment with the Father's will. We just commission them right now to go and work together with us.

So we lift you up and work with you to begin to strip away these layers of shame.

I feel that the mandate they have is to take our declarations, and almost lay them over the areas of shame, almost like oil that would soften the hard areas of the hardest things.

It feels like we need to release forgiveness to Devastation. It is almost like the earth itself is traumatized by the history of past events of devastation, the things that these beings have done and the justice is in a sense to release forgiveness, so that trauma can be released and the restoration of the earth will come about; and I think the

Elementals are going to help us with that, and it feels like what we declare, they can take, like healing oil or softening oil, to soften the layers that are over this being, so those layers can be peeled away.

So I choose to declare forgiveness for past disasters, past devastation of eruptions; of earthquakes, tsunamis and famines. I release forgiveness for the areas where the earth itself has been affected. The tectonic plates have been divided and pressured.

I choose to release forgiveness upon this being of Devastation. I declare Jubilee. A Jubilee where the economic systems of greed and profit that are in control will fall. We want to see a well-being economy; we want to see a change in global economics.

[We soon heard a testimony of the G7 agreeing to tax equality and justice against corporations.]

So we call for jubilee and we declare jubilee. We declare the reality of all things being restored and for Devastation to be restored to Preservation.

We call the earth itself to also release its forgiveness, to come into agreement with us, to come into an alignment where we will be one heart and one mind and one purpose.

We call for the Elementals to interface with us and for us with the earth, to come into agreement, that we would layer healing oil like a balm that would soften the dark scales of shame, removing those layers of shame.

I just want to engage with those green light elemental beings, and I release you to engage with the union of this being, with every part of this being that is connected globally. I release you to release peace, as I see that you are peace carriers. There is an infusion of peace in your green colour, that as you engage with this being, that you will infuse your peace, and to bring that being into a place of peace so that it can begin to engage outside of the negative into the positive.

I see the green light beings. They are pouring out the oil on the top of the head of the one called Devastation and Devastation has all of these other ones that are attached to it, that are all tethered to it. This oil is flowing down from the head and down these tethers into the multiples of other beings that are attached to Devastation and have the same mandate from darkness to bring destruction. So the oil is actually moving down the tethers like oil down a string or a thread, and it is actually beginning to affect and impact all of the other beings that are tethered to Devastation.

On the right-hand side, I see the oil has now penetrated two of these beings: one is called Destruction. So I speak to the green light beings right now to prophesy over Destruction that Destruction would be restored to Construction. We bring our hearts and our minds into an agreement with the green light elemental beings right now as they stand over this one called Destruction.

I see – this is really strange – I see that the green light beings are just quivering with delight because they're releasing their green light into the one called Destruction. Destruction is shaking like crazy as it's opening up and receiving the green light.

Something really similar, but the green lights, they had joy on them, and they were infusing themselves into Destruction: that is where the shaking took place, that Destruction was actually intended to bring forth life and that the green is a new life, like spring coming forth to bring new life, rather than to take or destroy. It was never intended to be that way. So the shaking is coming so that everything inside of them is being restructured to be able to bring about its original and designed intent.

I see that, as the green peace and joy is being infused into this being, there is an order coming back, as there has been a constant tug within this being of Destruction.

It has kind of shrunk away from everything that it has been forced to engage with, yet as these green beings are infusing this peace and tranquillity and calm into Devastation and Destruction, it is bringing an order. It is bringing an ability for this being to start to see construction, to start to see a different way of being.

We call upon Time to reveal and unveil to these beings what their original purpose was: to bring the memory of who they were, the glory that they carried, the light that they once carried; to remind them of who they were, their real, true identity, which has been covered by layers of shame and dark scales.

So we call upon you, Time, to unveil your secrets, or ancient truths and mysteries, to these beings; to reveal to them the memory of who they were, to open up the avenue for them to be restored, that they would remember what it was like in their original form and purpose. We call you, Time, to enable them to remember what it was like to be a preserver, to be in construction, to be bringing wholeness and life, rather than death and destruction. We call on you, Time, to open their eyes, the eyes of their heart, to see themselves, to know their true identity, the light that is still hidden within them.

Father, we just call upon the spirit of wisdom and revelation of the Lord Jesus Christ to overwhelm and overtake them, that the eyes of their understanding would be opened up, that they might know that they were initially called by God for the restoration of all things, which was paid for by the blood of Jesus. So we just ask You right now to go and open up the eyes of their understanding.

Thank You for revealing their pre-Adamic identity. That, even as our forgiveness for all of their previous devastation has been extended, that that shame is now being stripped away. I see it actually coming off, layer upon layer upon layer of shame being stripped away, like a serpent that would shed its skin. It's beginning to be peeled back. I can sense a fluttering within that being, a fluttering of hope, but that being doesn't really know what that is.

Father, I just release the realms of wisdom around that being, the realms of revelation, to take it back in time to where it remembers hope and anticipation and excitement and Kingdom identity.

So I just see Limitless stepped into that realm. I see that these beings of Construction and Preservation were once called to work with Limitless. This being has been enslaved and forced to bring devastation but actually, even while being in the negative, it has shrunk away, so as not to deliver limitless destruction.

I just invite engagement now between Limitless and these beings that start to open a new way for Kingdom construction, Kingdom preservation. I am seeing a very tentative engagement now with Limitless. I am just seeing an untethering and more untethering and even more untethering taking place. As this untethering is taking place, I see that the cloning effect is beginning to be reversed to what they were, before they were all clones of devastation. They're taking back their original shape and form so that they are actually escaping the cloning.

So one of the things I am seeing is forests, rainforests, popping up from nowhere, and I feel like it is going to be a sign. We are going to see this in the natural: that they are going to find new rainforests.

That is exactly what I was seeing too – when the green beings were intermingling and becoming part of... – was new life coming forth, in that it will be a sign and a testimony of what it was that took place.

I just feel the delight of the Father – thank You, Lord – that He is delighted that, at long last, someone is coming into an agreement for the restoration of all things which has been His divine purpose, that the unfolding of His sovereign plan is going to be a testimony.

Father, we come into agreement now with the establishment of the new rainforests that You are raising up and we thank You that as these testimonies begin to manifest themselves in the earthly realm that it will be conclusive proof that we are working together with You. Thank You that in a place where nothing good can survive and nothing good can live, that You are going to descend with such great power that nobody will be able to refute the fact that it is You.

We just want to confess our belief that You are able to do far above anything we can know or understand or comprehend to fulfil Your divine purpose: to bring to successful completion the good work that You've done. We thank You, Lord, for the de-cloning process that is going on right now amongst all those beings. We thank You that they are going to cease to be linked together, that they are going to cease to function as one, negatively.

I feel like this is the beginning of a dismantling process that the Lord has given us line upon line, the capacity to begin to see the devolution of the cloning and the coming together as one of all of these beings, functioning together as one and being connected as one. I feel like we have future work to do with this yet, that it is something that the Lord wants us to continue to work this process.

Because these beings will be detached from the one that is called Devastation and the deep cloning, their capacity to function as one will cease. There is a lot that the Lord wants us to continue to do, to bring this up before Him and to continue the process of devolution because it is going to be a process.

What has begun here today is going to continue, as long as we stay in agreement.

I know this is a really crazy picture, but the Lord is giving me a picture of a game of solitaire, and all of the kings have been put into position and all the cards are falling in line.

I am going forward in time right now. I'm looking down from a position and what I'm seeing is the whole earth is filled with Your glory. The whole earth is filled with Your glory. We come into agreement with You right now Lord, that the whole earth will be filled with Your glory, that the whole earth will be covered with Your light, the light of Your glory. Thank you Lord.

Your word is true. Your word is perfect. Therefore we say, let it be done unto us, according to your word. Let it be done to the earth, according to Your word. Let it be done in the galaxies. Let it be done in the universe, according to Your word: that all things will be one in You, and You will be one with all things.

What we've done is quite significant and it is part of a bigger picture and strategy that is going to be at work. I do feel some of the tethers have been disconnected, and we're going to see some global financial things begin to shift.

It definitely feels like all these tethers to clones and tethers to control systems are like a dark web. It is a dark financial web that that has been there, but normal people cannot access it, but it has been affecting everybody. I think we are beginning to disrupt – but not just disrupt but restore – and we are going to see the positive preservation and construction start to take place.

I think we're going to start to see evidence in the area of finances and economics of some of the positive changes and exposure of these things.

There were four people involved in this legislative process and each flowed together as the encounter proceeded.

Arise and shine

And here is another transcript of a restoration government ascension.

We were led by a being called Pleiadia to double golden gates that were inscribed with historical events. The gates were opened and we were given access to the ancient pathway of wisdom.

As we were travelling down this path of wisdom, around us were many wonderful brightly coloured notes, lining the hallway of a building that we entered. We entered a round room and over the top of us there was a beautifully constructed dome-like ceiling that had what looked like hand-painted images but right in the middle of it, there was glass in 12 sections.

We were also standing on a round translucent floor divided into 12 different sections, reflecting what was above. The glass that was in the round centre part of the domed ceiling began to spin and open up like the iris of a camera. Many angelic beings were peering down to see what our response was going to be.

There was a huge multi-dimensional shaft of brilliant blue light; and as we stepped into the shaft we were carried up through the ceiling. A golden vortex appeared and we stepped in where 12 lights were coming in from our right and 12 lights were coming in from our left. They came together and joined in a circle and they began to rotate around us in a clockwise fashion.

The Lord said that we have now been joined to the 24 elders. They were rotating around us, beginning to spin very quickly. They spun so fast that their lights were moving together until it looked almost like a solid line.

I feel like it's connected to Isaiah's scroll, as the moment we started to engage, and I started to see how those scriptures in Isaiah, that I've always just interpreted them relating to the earth, but they are heavenly as well. So it says your sons will come from afar, the son shouted for joy at the creation of the earth.

So they're coming from the fires as kings will come, the brightness of your rising will raise the brightness and the kings of the elders, your sons will come from afar, and nations will come to the brightness of your rising, which is cosmic. You will repair the desolation of generations, you'll be called the repairer of the breach, repair what is devastated. And I was seeing a tube with words on it locked in - I think it was not just words but it looked like technology.

I think I felt in the ascension when we were rising it was connected to when Isaiah says, *"Arise and shine, your light has come and the glory of the Lord has come over you."* [Isaiah 60:1 paraphrased].

The kings and sons are also from other dimensions and they are going to be drawn to the brightness of the rising of the sons of God. The brightness of your rising is connected to the formation of the government of God.

We honour the elders and we embrace the elders. The Lord has given me a word for a number of years that the elders are vital to complete the body: we honour the elders; we honour the funnel of light, the glorious light seen upon us.

We call the sons from afar. We just honour those 24 elders and we thank You, Lord, that You brought them to impart to us something from the ancient path of wisdom. Thank You, Lord.

Wow, we just open up our hearts now to receive that which is being imparted by the ancient path of wisdom. I feel like there is almost a crown coming upon us: the crown of government, an expansive corporate crown.

Thank You, Father, for the crown of light, the crown of government and the formation of the crown. We embrace the elders and the sons. We thank You for the frequency of the blood, which is light.

Since we started to engage I felt like the blood frequency – yes it was – blood was just bursting out of us in this encounter. There is a frequency and a sound that is coming out of us into the cosmos, into the heavens, into the heaven of heavens, which is speaking; and it is almost like a beacon of light.

We open our hearts now to receive the maximum. The maximum that can be imparted from the 24 elders from the blood of Your way. We are opening up our hearts: now fill us, Lord.

I feel like a fire in my chest right now. Thank You for the burning flame.

Thank You for the formation of a fuller expression of government into the cosmos, into the galaxies. We bring ourselves now into agreement with the heart of the 24 elders: we open up our hearts, we throw open the doors of our hearts.

We ask you to make impartation from the ancient pathways.

And I'm seeing the Lord gathering many stones from creation, the cosmos, to form in this beautiful structure, and it is reminding me of how the high priests had stones on them; and knowledge is coming back to us, cosmological knowledge, multi-dimensional knowledge, knowledge of the past, present and future, who was, and is, and is to come.

I feel like the Lord is uploading into our DNA the truth, which is setting us free and creation free.

So, Father, I thank you that you are the wisdom that builds the house, the knowledge that fills the house.

We receive 'now' knowledge. Multiple strands of knowledge are absorbed into our DNA. This knowledge is hyper-dimensional quantum knowledge, time and space knowledge, eternity knowledge. Wave, sound, energy, frequency, vibration, that we are built with precious stones. Thank You, Lord, for the knowledge, the covering and the impartation of truth.

Thank You for the multi-dimensional beings, angels and elders. They are also the sons that are coming from afar. Thank You that You're rebuilding us with stones.

The Law of Cosmic Union

I was watching Saturn and I saw three concentric rings of fire around Saturn, but interestingly, now I saw that those rings were on an axis that could be manoeuvred into any position that the planet chose. I saw some beings on the outer ring guarding the ring and I asked the Father, "What do you want me to do about them?"

He said, "Just send them My love." So I started to extend the Father's heart of love to them through me. As I sent them more and more love, I found myself within the planet and I heard the Father say, "Just sit with Me in my peace in this place".

So I completely encapsulated His peace as best I could, extending and projecting His peace into the planet. As I was doing that, I saw that there is a connection with Saturn and the Elementals that function on the earth.

I saw what looked like a light power cable. So, in the old days, I would call it a ley line, but actually, I'm calling it a light power cable, on which the Elementals travel back and forth from Saturn to Earth.

I could see an agenda of plunder, but actually, that had replaced the agenda of replenishment: I could see that the Elementals were originally tasked, along with other beings, to travel back and forth along this line, a power cable, to replenish the earth from Saturn.

So I engaged them, having asked the Father what to say. Father said to remind them. So I engaged them, and I said, "May I remind you that your mandate is for replenishment into the earth? May I remind you that plunder does not feel as good as replenishment?"

As I said that, I got their attention. It was like something sparked for them when I reminded them that replenishment felt more satisfying than plunder. So I said, "You're free to choose, you have another choice. You're free to choose your original design and I encourage you to choose replenishment. I urge you, for your own satisfaction, choose well." And then I felt the Father say "Okay, now stop talking and just release My love into them as beings." So that's what I did and then I was back in the room.

These relationships have got to be restored because it's in our community, isn't it, it's in a community of planets. It makes sense to me that there are elemental forces, you think of them as forces, living forces, where we interact electromagnetically.

Scientists have discovered that without Jupiter and Saturn, Earth would not be able to exist because Jupiter and Saturn are gravity wells. They pull a lot of the materials and cosmic forces in and they act like bouncer planets. So they've said to have an Earth-like planet you also need like a Jupiter and Saturn because they act as guardian planets. And they actually pull a lot of asteroids in that would otherwise hit us. They're very strong gravity wells.

I saw the planet with rings that are able to move on an axis; and as the planet repositions, so do the rings.

Yeah, like, a vibration went out into the cosmos, and it had an impact on the cosmos.

I stopped at the golden double gates and was joined by Time, who pointed out four specific dates inscribed around the golden doors:

1917, 1946, 2015, 2021

Time revealed the significance of those gates was connected to opening portals or gates connected to the earth and the dimension around the earth via the everlasting doors.

As previously noted, in 1917 Aleister Crowley, an occultist, used an ancient ritual called 'The Amalantrah Workings' to open the West gate; and he engaged beings called Lam, who were very similar to the Greys of UFO lore.

In 1946 L. Ron Hubbard and Jack Parsons, a NASA rocket fuel scientist, opened the West gate using the 'Babalonian workings' and many UFO sightings followed, like at Roswell.

In 2015 Jason Westerfield was deceived into trying to open the West gate during an online conference with the web address of openthewesterngate.org. Many gullible believers joined him but the attempt was thwarted by sons assigned by the Father to protect and guard the gate.

This was my journal entry for 7th November 2015:

"Son, the veils between dimensions are being prepared for multi-dimensional incursions. Set the watchmen at the gates to guard, protect and defend. The veils, once removed, will also allow many to travel into the mysteries inter-dimensionally and return with the discoveries for the opening of the Discovery House. In 2021 there will be a legitimate opening of the West gate, where mature sons will be able to access, to bring the light of love and truth of restoration to those dimensions beyond."

The encounters in 2021 were significant steps that facilitated the sons of God to be able to access and use the gateway systems. In 2022, all the Engaging God governmental groups were able to open and engage the West gate.

The four gateways (which are the North, West, East, and South gates) are significant gateways towards the earth and outward. These are not the portals out there in the cosmos but are portals connected to the everlasting doors around the Earth.

"Son, all the dimensions accessible within the 12 constellations do not engage your realm unless everlasting doors are opened, such as the West gate. Most activity between dimensions is coordinated by counterfeit councils and some portals are currently active but many are being awakened and activated. You have a mandate to engage the active portals as before but you will need to cooperate with the angelic orders and guardians to protect those portals that are at risk of activation.

"Son, the pathways of ancient wisdom and knowledge need to be navigated carefully as what they reveal can be used for good or evil.

"Son, come walk with Me."

We walked into a large council room where the guardians, Ambassadors and High Chancellors were in session. The Father took centre stage and the proceedings continued: representatives, in turn, presented dimensional, cosmic and earthly ideas and strategies. They seemed to be making cases for their realms and dimensions. There were representatives of restored fallen angelic and dimensional beings giving evidence and there were non-fallen dimensional beings also.

When everyone had been heard there was a silence and the Father asked for the opinion of the council in regards to the strategies and priorities relating to the activity taking place in this time of transition to the next age. In unison, they all said,

"It is time for the revealing of the forerunners of the sons of God to engage the three spheres and take their places of responsibility."

"Son, what do you think?"

Without actually saying it, I thought "Why are You asking me?"

Then, without thinking, I said, "There needs to be a shield established for each sphere, where all categories of beings are in union, not only for the protection of the spheres but for their restoration. Assign the sons to the spheres that match their destinies to join a council for each sphere, to be strategic in defence and proactive in restoration."

"Son, you have done well. Because you are abiding in the light realm you have become wise beyond your years."

There were others who I felt were kindred spirits who were called to give their opinions and they added other suggestions to the plan, mentioning specific angelic orders to be involved in the process. Protector, Conservation, Preservation, Union, Liberty and Limitless were mentioned, amongst some other dimensional names I did not recognise, except the Servici.

The Father, Son and Spirit were now present and edicts were made and blueprints and mandates were produced. There was a blueprint and mandate for the establishment of people and places of refuge in each of the spheres. A scroll was produced by the Father called The Law of Cosmic Union and it was read out to the council by the Father.

"We hereby authorise a cosmic tripartite union between the sons of God, the council of ages and the dimensional council.

"We authorise the union to take responsibility for establishing and maintaining the three shields for this time of the transition of the ages.

"We assign the guardians, Ambassadors and Chancellors as a privy council to assist with the ordinances between the spheres.

"We authorise the cosmic union to form legions from the three dimensions to be strike forces of restoration.

"We authorise the cosmic union to recruit legions as a defence force for the protection of the spheres.

"We authorise an awakening to the light of love and truth across the dimensions to catalyse creational responsibility.

"We authorise the union of guardians, Elementals and angelic beings for your solar system.

"We authorise the expansion of the earth shield around the planets.

"We authorise the shield to release the sound that would restore the solar system.

"We authorise the shielding of the planets from the sun to allow the planets to reengage with the earth.

"We authorise the establishment of people and places of refuge to be established under the coverings of angelic protection.

"We authorise the jurisdiction to be without limitations."

The Father turned to me and the other sons present and assigned us to the three different spheres: the earth, the cosmic/heavenly and the dimensional. I was assigned, with others, to have dimensional jurisdiction responsible for the dimensional council and shield.

I felt so out of my depth but I was not alone in feeling that way. I drew back to the realm of light and the Father's face, where it was safe and comforting, but I also felt the intentions of the Father's heart form a matrix of light around me. I knew that it is time to grow up and mature in responsibility.

I felt encouraged and motivated for the task ahead but still somewhat overawed, though I did not dwell on it, I just drew closer to the Father's heart and felt His lovingkindness.

"Son, the union between the dimensions is a key in the preparation of the restoration of all things agenda as it is unifying the earth shield with the shields in the other spheres. Union will always command a blessing and when the earth is blessed, so will the other dimensional spheres be, and vice versa. The role of the sons of God is critical to the restoration of all other things as they are destined to provide the government that brings and maintains peace throughout creation.

"The joint councils being established are key to the government of peace being established as the counterfeits thrive on division and conflict. Union is the opposite spirit to division and the conflict it produces; and that weakens the counterfeits' position amongst the spheres as it creates a frequency of coherence that disrupts communication. The union of the three dimensions divides the counterfeits and each act of restoration weakens them, so it is so important to continue this process. With each act of mercy towards the fallen ones, the power of union grows stronger and the frequency of hope increases its effect.

"Son, it is time, during this transition of ages, for the sons of God to have one voice and one frequency; so those who do not yield and surrender to the oracles of Our heart will be removed from their positions of influence. We do not do this lightly, as We have been seeking to deconstruct and transform the false doctrines within their belief systems that oppose restoration, but some have been resistant to the process. Son, continue to reach out to them in the spirit and keep an attitude of lovingkindness towards them; but if they continue to resist and oppose, their influence will begin to wane. Many of them are undertaking fleshly projects, created from their own understanding, as they have lost touch with Our intentions.

"A union between the sons and between the dimensions is the greatest sign of the transition between the ages and there will be more powerful demonstrations. Son, it is time for the sons of God to take their responsibility to join the councils and assemblies of heaven in coheirship. The guardians, Ambassadors and Chancellors have been waiting for the sons to mature so they can take their places in heavenly government. Creation is waiting for the freedom that only the sons can deliver; but only those who have abandoned independence and are free from the path of independent knowledge are able to fulfil their roles. The deception of independence is keeping Our children in bondage so that the union necessary for dimensional freedom is being hindered.

"The law of Cosmic Union must be legislated and enacted and the three shields must function as one if freedom is to be secured. Son those responsibilities are Our sons' and We have left many things for you to do to complete the restoration of all things. Occupying positions on the councils of creation is the birthright and destiny of Our sons but their present vision is too limited to be effective. We are expanding the consciousness of those who are willing to come close enough in the realm of light in perfection to see Our face and feel Our heart.

"Only those who have let go of their own agendas have come to the realm of light and begun to abide here but too many are still leaning to their own understanding. It is time for more radical shaking to take place to free those who are not in the religious systems, as they will be able to let go of their own agendas more easily. Judgment of the religious institutions is continuing and the verdicts will enable justice to shake those systems but those outside the religious systems are beginning to respond to the call to sonship. Religion has obscured who We are and is being rejected by those seeking truth and they will find the truth in love.

The religious and political spirit will fight to keep Our children deceived and in bondage within the institutions. The power of love to reveal the truth is going to awaken those outside of the religious systems more effectively than those within, at first; but as the darkness of deception is illuminated, those inside will also be awakened from their slumber.

As the sons of God begin to occupy the cosmic councils, greater awakenings will occur, as the frequencies of a cosmic union are powerful. The cosmic union will bring dimensional blessing to establish the shields for protection and action and that will bring greater freedom to the three spheres.

What is beginning in the earth shield will be the model that the other spheres will look to, so it is important that it functions in union and oneness. When hearts and minds are in union with Our intentions and purposes, then great blessing will be the result and that will influence creation itself. The cosmic union of heart, mind and purpose will generate frequencies that have great creational power to overcome division, competition, conflict and tribalism with love.

"Union, covenant, peacemaking and family are the key objectives of the cosmic councils and the strategies for those objectives must become a priority. The cosmic union of the physical, spiritual and dimensional in love is the most important agenda for Our sons to embrace and is the most fiercely opposed. Only great focus and perseverance will produce the level of union necessary that will command such blessing, to free creation from its bondage to decay and corruption.

"Union, Liberty and Limitless are your key allies in the process of restoration along with Time, Wealth and Wisdom and Conservation, Preservation and Construction.

"The law of cosmic union has the power to unite the three spheres to one joint cause: and that cause is the restoration and freedom of all creation. The crown of wisdom will be given to all those who will focus on the three and not just the one, as that is the hallmark of true covenant union. The willingness to prioritise others before self is the antidote to the 'I will' agenda that divides and is the crowning wisdom of love."

Restoring the Solar System

Following on from being given the Law of Cosmic Union, there were several encounters with the planets of the solar system, their guardians, Elementals and fallen beings.

In a restoration government ascension, we first received a liquid sapphire infusion of knowledge from the Father in preparation for engaging the planets. The first engagement positively was with Neptune and Pluto, Neptune being a feminine entity which was like a shimmering sapphire blue colour.

We engaged the solar system, specifically Neptune, the water planet. The being associated with it was called Nubulus and was extremely sad. We realised we needed to release light into the planet of Neptune and then engage the being of Neptune to restore the relationship with the Father and with the earth in a renewed marriage union.

We declared the receiving of the positive virtuous grace attributes, but the rejecting of the vice, and saw fire water engulf the planet, revealing a fire stone in the planet's core.

I engaged with the guardians in the council to receive a mandate to establish a shield of light around the solar system, made up of the tri-part union of man, angels and guardians.

We knew that we needed to restore the union between Neptune and the earth but wanted to ensure that nothing would go back in the opposite direction on that connection to pollute it.

The waters of Neptune were designed to have a stabilising effect on the earth and the other planets but it has been twisted to destabilise the solar system.

The earth shield is not just protecting the earth from external interferences but also the cosmos and dimensions from the negative effect of the independent knowledge of the tree of good and evil.

We have a mandate to restore the union of the planets with the earth and discover their original name and purpose, to restore them to their glory by renaming them.

The old assigned names of Roman and Greek gods were a reflection of their fallen identity and need to be restored.

"Son, the solar system, restored to union and harmony, will play a significant role in the restoration of the cosmos as an example of the restoration of the relationship between celestial bodies, man, the angelic and the Elementals.

"Son, the earth shield needs to be expanded to join with others in covering the three dimensional realities that are being restored. This can begin by expanding the earth shield around the planets of your solar system so that they can be restored back to a union of planets.

"Our original intention for all astral bodies and beings was for harmony but with the 'I will' of independence introduced there were many broken relationships. When man chose self over relationship, and chose independence, the Elementals of the solar system became influenced by the fallen beings and separation resulted. The planets became associated with the names of the fallen beings and further lost identity and purpose and became disconnected from the earth and mankind.

"It is time for the relationship and union between planets, guardians, Elementals, angelic and the sons to be restored back to harmony. All the planets were designed to function together in harmony for each to be fruitful in fulfilling their purpose and the whole union being blessed and in balance. The planets need the earth's frequency – and the earth needs the planets to function in harmony – to be at rest and in balance. Engage the Elementals and the guardians and form a union before engaging the fallen beings behind the idolatry associated with the planets.

"The shield, once established around each planet, will isolate them from the influence of each other and the sun, and will make them more open and susceptible to restoration. Engage the Council of Guardians for strategies and mandates for each planet and as each is restored there will be a powerful shift in momentum.

"Son, it is Our pleasure and joy to see the sons of God taking responsibility for their coheirship and government."

I engaged the realm of light, face to face with the Father: the light of His intentions wove around me, conforming me to the frequency of His heart. I felt the intense waves of emotion encapsulating the oracles of restoration for our solar system until I was ready to brood and become the sound of His voice. My resonating frequency energised the grace of the Quantum Lumens to collapse the wave function for the reality of solar union.

"Son, you must not forget the sun itself, as it is the created light of the solar system. The sun and the beings associated with it have been the greatest figures of idolatry that man has worshipped. The sun is the created light and brings physical light and life but it is also the greatest danger to life in the solar system and is able to control and manipulate light because the beings assigned to it are in bondage to corruption. The worship of the sun is the oldest form of religious idolatry that man created and is the most corrupted – and now it is volatile and unstable.

"For all the planets to come into union and harmony it will take many sons in the oneness of heart to shield the planets from the influence of the sun while they are restored. Only when all the planets are restored to union can the sun be restored back to the place of humility, to serve the whole and fulfil its destiny. The central glory of the sun was designed to illuminate the glory of the planets but the sun was deceived into being worshipped for its own glory.

"Son, you will need to engage the Council of the Guardians, Ambassadors and Chancellors with others to form a strategic union to begin this task."

I began to contemplate the shielding and restoration of the sun and realised that this would be a prototype engagement for other systems within our galaxy and others.

"Son, the whole of creation is waiting for the sons to arise and is beginning to awaken to the hope of freedom; and each act of cosmic and dimensional restoration is a catalyst for the light of love to shine with limitless grace and mercy. As the sons of God unify to become oracles of restoration, the awakening to love's frequency is rippling throughout creation in wave after wave of hope. The tri-part cosmic union and the shields of union being formed are providing powerful testimony to the awakening that is creating the environment for many to be turned from darkness to light.

"Son, the momentum is shifting as the sons are arising to take their places of responsibility within the councils and assemblies of heaven for creation."

We have a mandate to restore the union of the planets with the earth and discover their original name and purpose, to restore them to their glory by renaming them. The union of planets was designed to bring harmony and balance to the earth. The Roman and Greek names assigned to the planets were a reflection of their fallen identity as they have become objects of worship and the names need to be restored to reflect their original identity and purpose.

CREATIVE SONSHIP

The Greek god of the sun was Helios but, later, the Roman Apollo became the sun god.

While it is not always obvious, the planets are actually named after Greek gods and goddesses. The Romans worshipped the same gods but gave most of them Roman names, and they named the planets – the Earth is the only exception.

Jupiter, Saturn, Mars, Venus and Mercury were given their names thousands of years ago but the tradition of naming the planets after Greek and Roman gods and goddesses was carried on for the other planets discovered later as well.

Mercury was named after Mercurius, god of commerce, messenger of the gods, and mediator between gods and mortals, corresponding to the Greek god Hermes. Venus is the brightest planet in the sky and was therefore named after the beautiful Roman goddess whose Greek name was Aphrodite. Mars, a fiery, red planet, is named after the Roman god of war, whose Greek counterpart Ares was a hot-tempered god. Jupiter is the largest planet in the solar system and was named after the most powerful of the gods, whose Greek counterpart was Zeus.

Saturn is the second-largest planet and was named after the Roman God of agriculture. In Roman mythology, Saturn was the father of Jupiter. The Greek counterpart was Cronus, who was always in a power struggle with Zeus.

Uranus was discovered by William Herschel in 1781 but was eventually named by Johann Bode after the ancient Greek god of the sky. The name Uranus is a Latinized version of the Greek name Ouranos. Uranus was Cronus's father and the planet has the same blue colouring as the sky.

Neptune was discovered by Johann Galle in 1846. The planet is named after the Roman god of the sea (whose Greek counterpart was Poseidon), probably because it is a bright blue colour.

Pluto was discovered in 1930 and named after the Roman god of the underworld, whose Greek equivalent was Hades. It may no longer be officially considered a planet, but Pluto is the farthest object in the solar system just as Hades, the god of the Underworld, was far removed from everyone else.

The solar system, made up of a union of planets, was designed to be in harmony and balance with the earth. During later explorations of the West gate, it was found that the frequencies of the planets connect through that gate and bless the earth through the everlasting doors. There were originally 4 large crystalline deposits on the earth that received the frequencies from the planets and created energy fields that created a perfect environment for fruitfulness and increase. Subsequent to the fall of man, these crystalline deposits were dissipated throughout the earth's crust and still produce a background energy field. Man has built counterfeit structures perfectly aligned to true north on those original sites as receivers of frequency.

The government groups I engage with have discovered many more truths concerning the planets and how they were designed to relate to the earth. God created a gateway system for travel and communication throughout the universe and dimensions. In a conversation with the Father, He revealed that the original sonship mandate to increase and fill the earth would have continued beyond the earth, so that the moons and some planets of the solar system would have been colonised next as an expansion of God's kingdom government and peace. Travel to other planets and moons were to be accomplished by using the system of wormholes that connect creation.

What follows is a transcript of a restoration government ascension with five people attending and interacting. It is mostly unedited and is a mixture of different people's styles of operating but all remaining in a union of hearts and minds.

We honour the blueprints for the solar system.

We thank you for the Archangel Sandalphon.

[Sandalphon engaged with us in the ascension.]

I pray, Lord, I ask that You would expand our hearts with the knowledge of that blueprint; that we would know things we have never known; that we would see things we have never seen, so we can administer in this hour.

Reveal Your heart for this family of planets and beings, angels and structures that make up our solar system. So, Father we thank You for Sandalphon. Thank You for the blueprint.

I feel like the Lord was pouring in Sapphire liquid into us and it was filling us up with knowledge, wisdom being poured out, Sapphire, like a liquid flowing, Sapphire was being poured into us now, I hear the Lord speaking in it.

That, for what is required of us, He is going to massively expand our consciousness, the way we think, the way we see, the way we talk. It's been superseded by another expansion, again, where the knowledge of the Lord, the knowledge of Christ, the mystery, is filling us. So, Lord, we receive that Sapphire.

The sapphire liquid is being poured into our minds, the spirit of wisdom and understanding of the blueprints and the knowledge of God in creation.

What I'm seeing right now is, we're so human in our culture and our thinking. He's taken us beyond human into language that we've never seen, ways of communicating, ways of thinking that are beyond Earth.

I am seeing a swirling of rainbows in, around and through us, and the cosmos.

I was just instantly in my home in heaven in what I would think of as an angelic conference room – it's just where I meet with them. And this was in a wonderful circular room, lots of white marble, you kind of feel; but I was in there instantly and I was just seeing who was showing up, just kind of asking them, all right, you know, you can come on in; and, you know, my first impression was the planet Pluto, the righteous real of Pluto. I know him by the name Hades, and he was there. Also the righteous real of Neptune, which again I know as a feminine angelic presence, but they were the first ones that came in. They were Pluto and Neptune, so I was just participating with them.

I had some great music going on in the background which was making everything you were saying just sound so epic. It was really awesome.

Thank You, Father, for Pluto; thank You for Neptune, we expand our hearts to include them.

Wow, thank You that it is for man that You've given them as angels. The blueprint that they carry. Thank You. Can you just look at Neptune and say what you're seeing about him at this present moment.

Okay, yes I feel that there's a strong focus there.

I don't know why I saw this, the moment you said to see, I saw like a shimmering huge diamond. And I don't know what the connection is. It almost feels like, you know, like the priests had the stones on them, almost feels like it needs to be put in place again, I don't know. I don't understand that.

I saw like a diamond on a diamond, just a shimmering, Sapphire being. I don't know if I'm seeing Neptune in another form now, or the angel looks like a shimmering thing. I saw a quarter of a diamond shimmering with light and a Sapphire-like being. Yeah, we're seeing right now, but sounds about right. Yeah, I mean Sapphire diamond colours like sapphire blue colours.

But I learned them by jewels when I originally met them, I learned them by the gemstones that they seem to represent, so it wouldn't shock me at all if that's a sapphire and diamond kind of feel of that spiritual being.

This being seems glorious, so it seems very different to the other being, the other that met you and I saw looked really fallen.

This looks incredible, like unreal, like the majesty of the Sapphire, the diamonds, the form of it, it just seems glorious. I think I'm seeing the angelic.

We love you. We love you. Thank you for showing us the multifaceted multi-dimension, multi-reflection, refraction.

Actually, I see him, shining right now in a very prismatic form and I see all of the colours of the seven Spirits beginning to increase as the light is being refracted, and it's like coming from the inside out, it's not from the outside in.

Thank You, Father, I see the reflection of the colours of the light now beginning to hum.

Yeah, they're humming in progressive notes that keep going from lower to higher and lower to higher.

This is weird: I got a word that I've never even heard of before. Nubulus. (not sure of spelling).

I've just looked it up it matches the kind of fallen being and I saw it, the word was Nubulus. It means gloomy, troubled, clouded, sad, melancholy.

That's exactly what that being felt like the first one I saw, and then calling it sad, gloomy, being clouded.

You guys ever heard that word before? Oh yeah, that's so cool, like don't get words normally, that's so cool. Thank you.

I feel like honestly what I'm just saying what I'm sensing of what you're seeing is the pre-Adamic manifestation of what Nubulus was before it fell. And so, with the refraction of all of the light and the glory, and the sound and the humming that's coming off him, I feel like what the Lord wants us to do is just bring Nubulus out of that position of dejection and despair and frustration and disappointment and release him to become the reflection of the light of the issue.

Another meaning is somebody who could take a husband, marriageable, somebody that needs a husband.

And you know, the Lord, our maker, is our husband. So on the one side, it means sad and gloomy; on the other side, it means somebody that needs a husband. Okay. I think it's good to research that as much as I can.

In the sense that, you know, you're talking to them, calling them by name, saying out loud what it is that you're seeing what they look like – I think that's all those positive steps to seeing them the way that God intends them to be.

And when we were doing this, and I was just in my home, and I was asking again, like you, to know Pluto and Neptune, that I know personally, I was just asking them:

Okay, why is this happening? Why now, why are you kind of drawing and close? And I felt like they said, well, you know, the planets are like a cosmic vitamin, you know, that humanity desperately needs. They need to take that vitamin and like they would a mineral, or some other compound or molecule that you take in for your health; but then also it felt like they said, but we're really living out our existence in humanity; just like we're connected to God, we have to be connected to humanity – so there is a kind of a deep existence kind of reason why they want to be revealed.

I think I'd like to just speak over Nubulus new beliefs that it's called married to the Lord, the Lord is your maker, the Lord is your husband. You know, and let's see what happens. Does that resonate?

We thank You for this word, Nubulus, we bless You, Lord, that we recognise this being is sad and gloomy. But we call

CREATIVE SONSHIP

you into your redemptive name, which means marriageable. That you're fit to be married, that the Lord is for you, not against you, and we're really hopeful for you. So we just speak over Nubulus the restoration of his original purpose, the restoration of his original scroll, we speak over him: love, joy, peace, bliss. Let the joy of the Lord become his strength, that he becomes the reflection of Your glory, Lord, that he will shine out. Oh, whoa. Well, thank You, Father, thank You.

I see that the diamond, like a multi-faceted thing, is beginning to spin. And it's just spinning and spinning and it's getting faster and faster and faster; and as it's spinning faster, all of the facets of light that are being reflected are coming together as one huge rainbow refraction of that light. It is spinning over the top of him and it's actually producing blue-white shoots. Thank You, Father, thank You, Father, thank You, Father, Thank You, Lord.

I feel like we're meant to go into the atmosphere of Neptune and release lights: does that resonate? It feels like there's a gloom there, that they need the light: we need to come, arise and shine.

You know, when I spoke, I saw like locks, padlocks, coming off the sphere, because just before you said those are all changed and I didn't know what to say or do. Then when you started to speak, it was like these angelic beings were unlocking this thing; and then I just almost saw the planet, how it's shrouded: it needs light. It needs one of the meanings of Nubulus, as it is kind of shrouded and overcast.

Do you guys want to go into the atmosphere of the planet and release light? Does that resonate? Let's just do that.

The word I was hearing was 'fiery waters' and so there's also something about the fire and the water together for the planet.

Lord, we together, we know we've been called to expand the kingdom and Your government of peace. We hold Neptune in our hearts, and we engage the blueprint of life. That life is meant to come to this planet. We engage with light, the light of life, and we call forth the blueprint of life, that Neptune will be restored, that Neptune will come forth with life and with joy.

This planet is made to be like a glorious sapphire diamond. You are made to be glorious.

We honour you, we release you into your blueprint, hey, into your song, into your sound.

I am seeing the diamond refresh and the action of the light and the reflection of the light just spinning faster and faster and faster. It's like he's just getting smaller and smaller and smaller and smaller to disappear.

Thank You. I can just feel like glory particles being released into the atmosphere of Neptune, into the core of it. I see that life is going to come to their light.

We decree a new blueprint being released to create a new timeline. We decree new structures, angelic structures to be released into the atmosphere. Angel of Neptune, awaken to restoration.

Thank You. I'm almost hearing music like harmonics. I even believe something is going on in the atmosphere. I don't know whether it gets in the aurora, because it's quite far away from the Sun, but it will seem like a roar of new harmonics.

Thank You, Lord, thank You. They're emanating from the restored creature, because the refraction of the light that's coming off is like humming, and the humming is producing a brooding effect over Neptune; thank You, Father,

Have you ever done anything with untethering planets from all the stuff that's been decreed over them, from idolatry stuff and all that incantation stuff? Is there something we could do for next time? And I felt like it was almost reframing it, reframing what it is, and that the negative words that have been framed on it will come off.

Absolutely. I think it's like we take all of the virtue and cast off all of the vice.

You know, all the things that are associated with, like, in the case of Neptune, temper, mental illness, anger, addictiveness and earthquakes, you know, destructive earthquakes.

All of those things were negative, negative connotations, negative words that were spoken about Neptune in particular; so absolutely, it's a great thing to make a practice to take all of the virtue and cast off all the vice.

Yes, we decree a new relationship with Neptune.

As a planet, as an ecosystem in an angelic realm, as a gateway to the old words being broken off in the name of Jesus through the blood and the frequency of life, breaks off corruption and is a higher trading platform than any of the other trading platforms.

A new framework is released that Sandalphon releases the blueprint of Neptune's future and its relationship with us, and the solar system, and the angelic, and the frequencies and the sound.

You are not alone, we see you. We see you, planet Neptune, we see you, angelic beings, we release joy on you, the planet, joy.

Thank You, Lord, it is interesting that it was mentioned fire, water, now seemed like a fiery stone in the core of the planet, like a fire stone from the Lord; thank You Father for that fire.

Thank You. This belongs to You, Lord, we pray for the activation – I don't even know what this means – but the activation of that fire stone, the activation of Your government, and Your glory in Neptune.

I went and engaged with the guardians and went into a council room and there were guardians, chancellors and ambassadors who were there. The Father came and took centre stage and started asking for strategies for the restoration of the cosmic realms.

I feel what we're doing is absolutely right, everything that's been going on is just as I said, you know, separating the virtue from the vice. I feel that while we obviously need to make sure that all of the vice goes but the virtue is preserved.

The planets and the union with the planets have been taken from man and given to others who have abused it and the restoration will restore our union and our connection to the planets in a completely restored way.

It doesn't feel like the names that we know them as were their original names. I believe we're going to get an understanding of the original purpose of all of those planets, and then redefine them in union with us. We are actually involved in participating and protecting this process.

This being was shrinking away – do you feel something is being removed and the right being is being restored? Or is it that the being or the beings shouldn't be there, like is it could you say, some things are not sitting in the right seat, that they don't belong there?

I would say that what I was seeing shrinking away is first the capacity for vice to overcome virtue. Yes. So, not so much the shrinking of the being itself, because the being itself has not been restored.

There is like a connection that has been restored, like a gateway connection, so there's like a flow, like a communication, and a flow between the angelic and Elementals.

You know, it's like when we're engaged in the blueprint like this. I saw that beautiful diamond being.

You know, if you think, is this a system? There's a lot of complexity to it, isn't there? Would it be true to say there's a lot of complexity in the structures of the planet and what's there and how it functions, or is it a simple realm that opens up like a domino effect?

In one sense there are fewer complications because they are no people on it. Yeah. And we create most of the complications within us.

What we've done and what we're authorising and the sort of division and separation there is on earth, we don't want it to go back. Yeah, it's people that create an environment where a lot of negative things can function.

I feel that the word that keeps coming to us is union. There needs to be a union that we come into agreement with, and then that connection gets restored. But we don't want to restore something to actually release bad stuff from the earth into it.

This is why I feel what we need to do is to connect the earth shield. To shield and connect with shields around them. So those are in a union because there isn't anything bad going to come out of the union, it is only going to be positive. Whereas if we reconnect it to the earth at the moment, it creates a risk that can actually go the wrong way into that.

And therefore, I think that's why a shield would be needed. What we're doing is safe, with God, I do think it's a process. Not many things happen instantaneously: I think there's an ongoing process that will open up as we continue.

I've sometimes had encounters where you see what comes as thousands of years in the moment, like, you know, there's a knock-on effect that goes on and on.

And so how do we expand the shield over that?

Well, what I saw and what the Father said was, is that it cannot just be made up of us, just as the earth shield is made up of us and angelic beings and some of the cloud of witnesses.

The shield around the planets needs also to be occupied with the guardians, and with others that we are calling from the cosmos, to come and join us in a union; it feels it needs to be a cosmic union working together.

Well, the Father is saying it is a tri-part union of the sons of God, the Council of angels and also the Guardian council; so there is a sense where what we're doing is together in a union with others for establishing this.

Do you think the reason the Lord is showing us this stuff is because you can't really restore the earth without understanding that it's part of a wider community and ecosystem, in a way, it's a holistic environment?

Yes. All of the dimensions I've engaged and I've engaged like 40 of them, plus another 84 recently. They are most of the ones that are in bondage because of their connection to the earth, and you know the Tower of Babel was a communication device. It communicated things dimensionally which actually have been far worse, then, in those dimensions, as they seem to take on the worst of what was here on earth and then take it to an extreme. And because they have not had sons in their dimensions, they have not had anything to help balance things. So there have been really terrible things on the earth but you also have the covenant people right throughout history who brought a balance.

They have stabilised things with good, and with grace and love and mercy, but they haven't had that in those other dimensions which is why they're reaching out to us now.

They are detecting the frequency of sonship that we are broadcasting and they're reaching out to the sons because they're hearing our sound and they're feeling our frequency, particularly from the earth shield, because it's actually shielding them from the frequencies that are on the earth which are negative. We were not only shielding the earth from wrong things externally, but we're also shielding those things from the earth. And I think that's why shields of light are key because they give a safe place for things to take place, for transformation to take place, and they give us access points. They establish relationships, and unions with others, you know, we don't operate independently.

Part of the problem is man has operated independently, from the wrong source of knowledge.

Today we started with 'we're receiving an infusion of knowledge, sapphire liquid knowledge to help us in this process'. I think that it is the knowledge that joins us in union with others, and it is not independent knowledge. We need to be in coheirship with other spheres and not independent, as that creates a union that brings blessing.

One of the things for me, that I'd like to understand, is you engage these different dimensions and stuff, do you consciously choose to do it? I've never really functioned like that in the spirit – maybe God will give me an infused knowledge but I feel like it's partial, the way I function, it's like I need to explore how you function. So how does one function like that?

Well, for me, I hang out with the Father continually, so I'm continually in that realm of light, face to face in one of my dimensional places of engagement, but I can do that in multiple places. So that gives me a continual sense of the Father's heart. And then in my interactions with the

Father, more recently in that light realm, which is in the realm of perfection, where everything is how it should be, the light forms a matrix of the Father's heart and intentions and conforms me to it. And that's when then I go and engage the places that I have access to or I've seen before.

A lot of those things that I can access are because the Father has initially taken me there. Then, once I have this sense that He's opened this up for me and He's taking me into this realm, that I know I can go back whenever I am aligned with the Father's heart and it is His intention. I do not go just because I can but only when He directs me. So I don't just decide I'd like to go back to that realm, I always do it because I'm connecting to those intentions, the desires and the intentions of the Father's heart and then I just feel led to go; and then I go – because I have done it before, I know how to access it again.

But I always, always, want to be dependent on only doing what I'm seeing the Father doing – or doing what I'm feeling the Father is really conveying in terms of His intention. But I do think it is part of my particular mandate, you know, it's like the dimensional realities are things which I think the Father has prepared me for. And I've gone through a long process of getting to where I know I'm more confident of engaging, but sometimes I don't go into those dimensions, I stand on the event horizon and I impart into it, and I sense what is coming out.

So, when we recently engaged through the portal in Cancer, we engaged a fiery portal; and when we went through this we saw a lot of other dimensional portals connected in groups of Merkabah order. They were all made of different components, different things, colours, like gold, silver, all sorts of different components. I just felt they needed mercy. So, I released the mercy that I have freely received. Having released the mercy, I stood there and I was looking for what came back. And that gives you the clue to the response and what you do next. Because if nothing would come back, I would have known that I needed to impart more mercy into it.

They need to receive our light; they need to see hope, you know, they need an injection of hope and mercy: that was one of the things that I felt. You know, I felt so moved by their need because I felt their deep despair. Mercy just seemed to be my instinctive response to their situation. I then felt there was an echo or there was a response come back; and that then gave me confidence that it was okay and that we've made a good start.

That is really how I do it, you know, and then what will happen, I might not do that for another few weeks, and then all of a sudden I'm engaging the Father and that stirs in me with desire for that place again. And so I go back there, but I have no idea what I'm going to do, you know, no idea at all, most of the time, but then I instinctively do whatever it is I feel it is right to do. And sometimes that will be going into the dimension, sometimes it will actually be connecting with those who become ambassadors from that dimension of what they've received.

I am careful what I do because I don't want to be a mediator for those realms. I want to equip them to function and come into restoration, and therefore they need their own ambassadors because they are races of beings that have been deceived. They need someone who carries the light that brings the truth and starts to illuminate; it's almost like we're mostly only responsible for putting some leaven in there and then the leaven begins to work its way through those realms, those societies, in those areas.

You know, some of it has been pretty direct action because that was what I was led to do, to challenge some of the things that were going on there. Those ambassadors then took that on, so what I do then is just go back and observe.

I sometimes ask the Father, is there anything else that I need to do? And sometimes, there is a no and sometimes there is a yes. The Father does not often tell me what else there is to do at that moment: it is very much when I feel connected, and the Father's heart, that it moves me, then I do something.

I think that's why the Lord asked you in the council what your thoughts were, because you've got the Father's heart and you come from the Father's heart.

I think I've got a lot of work to do. I'm realising that I've got to spend more time in that realm of the Father's heart, and the realm of light and be more proactive. I think I've been a bit passive with some of these things, kind of waiting for them to come to me, rather than me going to them and participating more, and I think I'm not always doing the things I should be doing.

So I think it's a recalibration season. But I do believe I've got a connection to the cosmos and those dimensions as well because the Lord showed me the future where I was dancing in the stars and I was like an energy being, and I looked incredible. I hadn't seen anything like it. So, I know my future is connected there.

One of the things we engaged in one of these meetings, a while ago, was that we went into this Council of Guardians. Three beings, I think it was Limitless, Revelation and Breakthrough angels, came around us and they spun light around us. And they took us up into a pillar of light, and we were transfigured into different forms of energy. So we changed our appearance, we changed our frequency, and we changed into different forms of light, photonic light, protonic light, nano light. I felt connected after that engagement. I could connect more strategically because it felt like I'd been transformed.

Yeah, that's very interesting because in an encounter in the future I was literally an energy being that danced and sparkled and I looked incredible. And I think we're starting to live in our future now, and that's what I'm realising, is that what we do now counts.

If you just think about, you know, how, how much of an effect these planets have in the solar system at large. I mean there is a massive effect and humanity these days has kind of just relegated them to these inanimate objects that one day we'll explore with the satellite. But who really cares, because it's just an inanimate, it doesn't really affect us in any way, you know? But to meet them, I think it is really precious, it's a privilege. I mean, it really is a privilege.

So the only other thing that happened with me, when we were still in the spirit, is that this is like a reoccurring theme for the summer, is that Daniel was there. And that's so fitting because here's the Babylonian astronomy, you know, he was just super encouraging. He was like, "Way to go, guys," like, way to go, realising the importance of the planets and making an effort to, you know, to visualise and to talk to and to relate to and to do it all in a Christ-centred way.

It was like the impression that I was getting from him was, you know, it would have been great if we could have done that, in my day, like, "Here you are, you know, it's your time, this is the time to do it."

It's like a long story coming to its fulfilment, with the planets; I mean there's a lot of myth. There's a lot of history, all surrounding the planets. So to be in the position that we're in, and to be finally like, resolving, you know, that kind of planetary involvement is... it's a big deal, or at least Daniel seemed to think so.

I even feel a difference in the sound of Neptune and I don't know how to describe it: it's just a sense that even the sound of the planet has shifted.

Did you hear me say about I saw like a fire stone too? That make sense to anyone?

Yeah. The word I heard was 'fiery waters'. And so I didn't see it as a stone but I do feel like part of the restoration is this burning, purifying of the planets in that process of restoration.

Yeah, it was like a big fire stone, huge, and it seemed to be in the core of Neptune, and you know, scripture talks about walking on the fire stones doesn't it?

I don't know why I would see him but it was like I think I saw the core of the planet or something.

Every time I've seen inside the planets, they always look like crystals.

To me, the first time I ever saw Mount Zion in an Ian Clayton meeting, it looked like crystal mountains.

Yeah, I mean, when I've engaged the fire stones in the garden of God it's always been about destiny, connecting me deeper to my destiny. And I feel strongly that every planet has a destiny, everything that has been created has a destiny, and maybe each one of them has a stone, which is actually encoded with their destiny at the core of their being.

If I just had to take a guess as to why Neptune was the subject of conversation today, and not another planet, I was thinking, the vice here with Neptune is instability: it is unstable, as are the waters. You know, so the virtue of the righteous real, the opposite of that vice, would be stability, and I was just thinking about how our conversation started, about all of the instability in the world. And it just doesn't seem that surprising that the thing that should be like releasing stability, you know, in the waters, and as a kind of as a governing angelic presence, that that's kind of the one that we've been focused on in this process today.

I was doing this when I was in my home in heaven with you all. Lord, let's have Neptune release stability, especially in our lives, but in general, because the world is unstable at the moment so, yeah.

"Son, come with Me."

We went out into the solar system, but as it was in the beginning, before the fall, and what I saw was mind-blowing.

The earth and the planets were in union, connected by filaments of light and fields of sound frequency in harmonious union. There was no darkness, no separation, and the sound I was feeling was like a musical symphony and light show, where all the coloured fields of gravity and magnetic energy were overlapping concentric circles of pure glory.

I felt the Father's pleasure as He took me to each planet in turn until I saw the sun, which was magnificent and totally different in appearance from what it is now.

"Son, isn't it splendid?" And all I could do was nod in appreciation to what I was witnessing as the whole thing was mesmerising. The sun was calm and peaceful, giving off a light and energy that unified all the planets together with a sense of purpose. Then I saw the Elementals of each planet in their own union with the guardians and the angels, celebrating and rejoicing together.

"Son, now you have seen how it was, you can seek for the restoration of this union by joining with others and engaging the Council of Guardians. Be careful you do not let desire get ahead of wisdom, as this will require many different engagements at different levels to restore everything to how it is intended to be. The spiritual union of the Elementals and angels must precede the physical union of the planets and the sun must be shielded from this activity."

The glory of the union of the planets was replicated throughout the created realms; and all the spheres were once in such a union of light and sound, that they are longing to return to.

"Son, continue to rest in Our love for you and you will go deeper into Our love for all things as you are connected to all things within you, within Us."

All the memories of my encounters with creation flooded back and I felt the connection more intensely, with specific aspects of creation drawing me. I felt the frequency of nature, the solar system, fallen angels, and dimensions activating my desire, drawing me to connect deeper. I opened up my heart to those frequencies and engaged them with my frequency until there was a deeper union of desire for freedom and restoration. I then began to scan the frequencies of each area for more specific connections and felt a strong drawing from specific planets, beings, portals and dimensions.

"Son, your feelings are beginning to become more discerning, so keep your focus and respond to what you feel. The frequencies of sonship that are connecting to creation to bring hope are opening communication lines, so keep your focus to be able to sense their call."

Union of planets

I engaged the realm of light. Waves of emotion radiated from the Father and I felt His desire towards creation, specifically the connection between the earth and the solar system. I engaged the earth shield and focused on the light that constructs it, which is made up of the Quantum Lumens and all the light frequencies of all the beings that are in union.

Limitless, Time and Union began to radiate light around me that focused out into the solar system, illuminating the planets in turn, but focusing on Saturn and Pluto.

The Father said, "The earth was not created to be independent of the union of planets, as the union of planets and those that represent and are responsible for them. Guardians, Elementals and angels were designed to bring balance and harmony. Each planet was created with specific characteristics and functions within the union that the Earth needs and the union is centred around the earth, not the sun, spiritually. There needs to be a restoration of relationship and function within the union of planets but the planets need to be shielded from the sun (which was created to serve the union but has become dominant through its worship). Each planet needs the earth shield to be expanded to enable the fallen beings to be free from the idolatry they have been deceived into receiving. Reconnecting the guardians and the Elementals with the planets will isolate the fallen beings so they can be restored. Each planet needs to be dissociated from the idols and restored to its original function in the union for harmony and balance."

I focused on Saturn, where I saw that the rings were oscillating to produce frequencies that were designed to replenish the earth. The earth shield was producing beams of focused light that were illuminating the planets to awaken them; and the light focused on the furthest, Pluto.

We engaged Pluto, the ice planet that has been downgraded from planet status by scientists, but has a major function within the union. Pluto is the gatekeeper planet for the solar system but that function has been twisted by the association with Hades and the gateway to the underworld.

We engaged Pluto, infusing our light into the planet to melt the ice of the heart-shaped lake we saw, to restore the heart of the planet to be a gatekeeper. Hades' original function as the wealthy one was to be the wealth giver to the solar union but that function has been usurped by the sun, which has drawn worship to itself.

We saw the underworld and the rivers of wealth, health and education that were designed to bring blessing; and the gatekeeper was to oversee the welcome into the blessing of the kingdom.

We released forgiveness to Pluto and Hades to begin the process of their restoration and called for the guardians and the Elementals to reconnect with the planet as we continued to focus on Hades for its restoration.

"Son, continue to focus on the union within the earth shield so you can engage the solar system to unify the planets and restore the system to wholeness. The idolatry and worship that the planets and their representatives have received have promoted their independence from the earth and their failure to fulfil their responsibilities.

The earth is environmentally out of balance because of the broken relationship within and between the planets. The harmony and balance in a union are key in all areas of creation, as it represents who We are as *I am that I am* in the union of *perichoresis*. Restoration, at heart, is the return to the union of all broken and fragmented parts of all creation at all levels and systems.

"Son, prioritise the union of the solar system by engaging each planet in the order as We direct you; and when functions are restored, momentum will build. The outer planets must be engaged first as they are furthest from the influence of the sun and that will create the momentum to engage those planets that are more closely connected to the idolatry of the sun.

"The energy fields generated by the union of the earth shield are powerful and effective but need to be expanded to increase their scope. The union of the three spheres will also enhance the effectiveness of each shield within its own sphere; but the strategic direction will still be needed from the Council of the Guardians. The dimensional portals need to be guarded and protected by the shield, as they have the potential to interfere and disrupt the unions that are being developed."

I engaged the council. The Privy Council assigned for the cosmic union were present as discussions took place and everyone humbled themselves by honouring and preferring one another. It was a precious moment to be part of as it was an indication of how fast things are moving and how far things have shifted. I felt the pleasure of the Father's heart and the deep emotions that are present within the *perichoresis* of *I am that I am*.

"Son, let the light of love and truth guide into all truth by being at rest, face to face, heart to heart and mind to mind." I engaged in the light and was bathed in love in the midst of the matrix of the light of the Father's intentions where I rested in being.

"Son, come with Me."

We began to travel through the solar system: initially beyond the furthest planet, Pluto, and eventually circled the planets one by one. Each planet or celestial body had its own frequency, song and light characteristics and each was so beautiful but I felt its broken or twisted connection to the Father and the earth. I focused my being on connecting and began to feel the groan and pain of disharmony is the deepest longing for a restored relationship.

I have been in several encounters with Neptune, Pluto and Saturn that are the beginning of the process of restoration but there is so much more to do. The planet, Elementals, guardians and fallen beings all need to be connected and restored to a relationship with each other, the sons and the earth.

We began beyond Pluto, where I was surprised to see some other dwarf planets that I had never heard of and as we circled each one, I felt their lostness and isolation.

"Son, these are waiting to become part of the union but Pluto as gatekeeper has excluded them because they refused to follow the rebellion into idolatry and their names and identities have been lost. It is the sons of God who have a responsibility to bring them all into connection with the earth and all the union of planets. There is much to be accomplished but do not be overawed: stay in rest and all will be good."

Planets in the Kuiper belt will also be restored. They were excluded during cosmic conflict and are known as Ceres, Eris, Haumea, Makemake, Sedna, Orcus, Quaoar, Gonggong and Chiron. Eris has been wrongly named after the Greek goddess of strife, indicating its history of conflict.

We moved on to Pluto and as we circled, I began to see Pluto through the Father's eyes and how amazingly beautiful it was and how vital its role is as guardian and gateway planet.

We moved on to circle Neptune and followed the same pattern, where I saw and then connected and felt the deepest desires of the Father's heart for its full restoration. Neptune was breathtakingly beautiful and some of the work to restore it had revealed its destiny and purpose in connection with the earth.

"Son, each planet must be restored to connect with each other, so Pluto to Neptune is the first step and then to Uranus. As we engaged Uranus and began to circle it I saw its many moons and also the almost fluid nature of the surface, like molten ice. The frequency it was giving off was far less intense and it felt almost cold, just like a cool colour, with less emotion, and distant.

Uranus was also rotating very differently than the others, almost like it was out of balance and very disharmonious and disturbed, with vertical rings. There was something very 'off' about what I was sensing but I could not put my finger on what it was.

"Son, there has been much conflict over this planet and it is very disconnected from its original purpose because it was involved in the fall of the watcher angels. Uranus' original function was to connect the earth with the heavens but it became twisted and aligned with the false heaven and throne of the fallen one."

I had much to ponder and learn about the planets and their relationship with the earth that I never even imagined until recently.

We moved on to Saturn and circled the rings, feeling and sensing the oscillation and energy being generated for the replenishment of the earth: it was a beautiful song of life.

"Son, renaming Saturn as Fruitfulness was apt, as it was created with the purpose of replenishment of the life force necessary for abundance and overflow so the earth could be a source of life and creative energy for creation.

"Son, the planets themselves were created to give life to their moons, which were originally designed for habitation, and only Venus and Mercury have no moons yet. There are even more than the 214 moons currently known, that were all originally capable of becoming fruitful through the increase of Our government and peace. There was much that We left for Our sons to complete within the union of planets and then beyond; but independence halted that process and corruption took the place of fruitfulness. Restoration of the union of planets will present the way for a return to the original intention for Our sons to fill the whole solar system with life and abundance.

We continued to circle each planet in order – Jupiter, Mars, Earth, Venus and Mercury – feeling and sensing each frequency and destiny and their disharmony. Lastly, we circled the sun, sensing its violence and turbulence and control over the whole. I felt its anger, but what I was sensing was more the fallen being Apollo's destructive need for worship and adoration that so twisted its original nature and character.

"Son, the union of planets must be shielded from the negative influence of the sun by the light shield of the sons, which has far greater glory. There is so much more for Our sons to know and understand concerning their role in creation, and the union of planets is the place to begin. The tri-part union that is forming between the spheres is what has prepared the way for engaging with your union of planets and this will be a prototype testimony that brings hope to the dimensions.

As I basked in the light radiating from the Father, I soaked it all in until I was in a state of complete rest; and then as the light matrix of the Father's intentions formed around me, I began to be moved. First, my emotions were filled with desire and compassion and then my thoughts were making me aware and focused on one thing only: my whole being became in union with the Father's intentions, and in that oneness, I directed all my energy towards the solar system.

I was joined to the light of the earth shield, aware of the guardians and Elementals of the union of planets, directing my attention to Jupiter. Jupiter is the fifth planet from the Sun and the largest in the Solar System. It is a gas giant with a mass more than two and a half times that of all the other planets in the Solar System combined.

I surrounded that huge planet with my spirit and my consciousness went deep into the core, seeking out the planet's identity, which seemed to be lost, buried under layers of darkness and confusion. I became aware that my probing was being resisted by the fallen being named after Zeus or Jupiter controlling the planet. I pushed harder but the resistance was stronger, so I reached out to the guardians and Elementals and formed a connection.

As I did, I knew that the worship given to Zeus as the head of the gods was a powerful force. The union of oneness that I was in gave me insight that caused me to stop and I became very still until I was able to see the way ahead more clearly. The strategy was simple: to bring all the planets that had already been reached together and engage to awaken Jupiter from its enforced stupor.

The earth shield powered up, energised by the union with the guardians of planets; and that world of light was extended around Jupiter, disconnecting it from the darkness. In the light, we engaged the light at the core and I felt a stirring of consciousness as we gently soaked that presence with the light of truth and love. The sleeping giant awoke and I sensed its memory was returning; and at that moment, all the moons reconnected and were now one, in a union of their own. I felt a sense of relief and rejoicing as all the moons were all reconnected with the guardians and Elementals restored back to their original purpose.

Jupiter, the so-called gas giant, was designed to be the energy and force of harmony within the solar system, where its great mass brought a gravitational balance.

We then turned our attention to the being that we had disconnected and began to engage it with love, releasing harmony and calling forth its identity and purpose. We released forgiveness for all the control and domination that it had exerted and reminded it that it could be restored to bring harmony and balance once again.

There was great resistance and I sensed it really liked the position of dominance, so we continued releasing the light of love that was also filled with the opposite spirit of humility. We released the truth that true authority is to serve, not to dominate and control, and surrounded it with love and light; but it felt like this would need a great deal of patience and perseverance to restore it. The planets themselves are much easier to reach in union with the guardians and Elementals than the fallen beings that have been corrupted by their worship as gods.

"Son, you have discerned well that it will take many in union to restore those who have been the object of such adulation; but with patience and the right strategy it can be accomplished. When the outer planets, those furthest from the control of the sun, are restored, you will be able to focus on those closest and under the greatest influence of darkness."

Multidimensional Reality

"Son, multidimensional reality is what Our children were created for: to be like Us and represent Us to all of creation. All of creation was designed to cooperate in harmony to represent Our manifold nature and is an expression of who We are creatively. Our children were always intended to mature to be all they could possibly be, without limitations and restrictions, within love."

I became acutely aware of where I am in multidimensional realms and positions, sensing both from the Father's intentions and desires and from the portals of the Merkabah within the core of my being. I felt the energy of creative desire pulsating with potential for the restoration of all things and beyond, and the need for a full revelation of immortality.

"It is time for true reality in multidimensional living, so you can fully enjoy the bliss of rest from your labours to just be. I have shielded you from the knowledge of just what your nonlinear being is accomplishing in the spiritual realms, just giving you glimpses. I will take the blinkers off your mind so your consciousness can expand to take in multidimensional reality and truly appreciate your capacity as a mature son of God.

I have learned all things linearly but now can live a nonlinear existence. At that moment I became aware of who I am and what I am doing at a higher level of consciousness in an expanded state of reality.

I am therefore I exist in manifoldness just like my Dad in nonlinear quantum moments of the fulfilment of my destiny.

I am quantumly entangled multidimensionally with the Eternal Now, Cradle of Life, the Sound of Many Waters waterfall, Chamber of Destiny and the Chamber of Creation continually, in just one of many realities.

I am also quantumly entangled multidimensionally with the Eternal Now, Throne of Grace, Judgment Seat, Altar of Fire, fire stones and my Heaven of Heavens throne in another reality set.

I am also quantumly entangled multidimensionally with the Eternal Now, four faces of God within YHVH, Court of the Councils of the Fathers, Court of Kings, Chancellors' Court and my mountain thrones in another quantum moment.

I am also quantumly entangled multidimensionally with the Eternal Now, the Circle of the Deep, 12 High Chancellors' Houses and the Council of 70 in another quantum moment.

I am also quantumly entangled multidimensionally with the Eternal Now, Court of the Upright, the Cloak of Mystery dark cloud, Wisdom's Heights and the consuming fire of love in another quantum moment.

I am also quantumly entangled multidimensionally with the Eternal Now, the beyond beyond dimensional anteroom and many dimensions in another quantum moment.

I am also quantumly entangled multidimensionally with the Eternal Now, Wisdom's Heights, the ancient paths, the four doors and the Earth shield in another quantum moment.

I am also quantumly entangled multidimensionally with the Eternal Now, the Father's garden, the Elementals' seven thrones and creation in another quantum moment.

I am also quantumly entangled multidimensionally with the Eternal Now, my own spirit First Love place, the garden of my heart, Dance Floor, Soaking Room, Bridal Chamber,

Merkabah, Tree of Life, seven energy gates and expanded spirit spheres in another quantum moment.

My heart filled with joy and I sank deeper and blissfully into rest but at the same time was so excited by this revelation that I could hardly contain myself. This was as it was always meant to be, living in *I am that I am* and *I am that I am* living in me.

"Son, see how easy it is to just be! And this is just a glimpse of what it is to be *I am that I am* that you will ascend to when you become an ascended father. Son, learn to become aware of multidimensional reality but always stay at rest, living in love, joy and peace within, balanced by the Tree of Life between spirit, soul and body. As you expand your spirit's boundaries, practise expanding your consciousness to become more aware of the dimensional realities you are mandated to govern in. All you learn to do as a son, made in Our image with creative abilities, will equip you to become an ascended father in the ages to come.

"Son, the true authority of a son is realised through surrender, not service, so abandon yourself totally to just being. Our nature as *I am that I am* is the model and pattern for Our children to follow as sons: just learn to be at rest in who you are. All the doing in the world will not enable you to be; but being who you were created to be will enable all the effective doing from total rest. It is the frequency of rest that creation needs to become still so it can rest from its groaning.

"Son, remember that you are designed to be limitless in unconditional love, grace and mercy, overflowing in lovingkindness. Lovingkindness is the true hallmark of Our nature and that is a new covenant reality, free from all DIY tree law-based knowledge.

"Son, you are slowly learning to see creation through Our loving eyes, so that the oracles of Our heart will be your inspiration. Inspired by lovingkindness, everything is limitless: there are no restrictions, so free your mind from impossibilities and choose a reality that reflects true new covenant unconditional love.

"Son all Our children, along with all created things, were designed to be immortal so they could enjoy limitless union without end. Being deceived into following their own path broke their union with creation: that has created the illusion of separation which continues to keep Our children from their true destiny.

"Ascension was always going to be a process of maturing, following the pathway of the Tree of Life to its conclusion. The deceptive illusion that keeps Our children from their true identity and destiny, living in the futility of their own minds, must be exposed. The full potential of sonship must be realised for creation to be set free and restored to union and harmony."

In that instant, a quantum moment expanded and I remembered all my experiences of creational union and harmony.

"The limitations of a single-dimensional reality must be exposed by the global and cosmic shift and in the expansion of consciousness that is beginning to take place. This awakening to love, and therefore true awareness of who We are, is the goal of this season so Our children can begin to be set free from their bondage and deception. There will continue to be much opposition, both within and without, to the restoration of all things message; but you will begin to find and connect with those who are awakening to reality.

"Son, continue to be at rest so your frequency can resonate across the dimensions. Your whole being has been coming into alignment with the oracles of Our heart and now you can be a dimensional oracle. Your frequency will be joined in union with others who are participating in the earth shield and becoming multidimensional. Different councils are being formed, to facilitate the awakening within different parts of creation, which are all part of a bigger strategy. Pursue the council with the guardians, ambassadors and chancellors, in union with those with who you resonate."

I engaged the Cradle of Life and began to brood over the union and formation of this council and its impact on the restoration of the dimensions. Creative thoughts and intentions of oneness and harmony began to form a picture that was vibrating with desire and energy. As I continued contemplating, I began to vibrate, until I was ready to become the sound of many waters to be able to activate the Quantum Lumens within the Chamber of Creation. I was aware that I was not alone, that others were also part of the creative process who were in such union of heart and mind that they were almost indistinguishable. I released a handshaking frequency of desire to consciously be able to connect with those who are in union and felt multiple energy signatures respond.

"Son, release another blue light call: but now focus this towards the indigo end of the scale of frequencies to connect with those who are awakened."

I released that frequency beacon through my Merkabah portals, dimensionally, as waves of light carrying my desire and intention for union. I sensed the energy of the different people, dimensions of the earth, cosmos, Elementals, angelic realms, heavenly realms and dimensions that were being engaged by the light call; and I opened my heart to them. I knew that I would need to be diligent and vigilant in my desire to connect and that this new blue light call would need to be continually broadcast multidimensionally.

"The multidimensional reality designed for Our sons is being revealed as enlightenment and illumination of truth that will remove the restrictions and limitations which Our children have been in bondage to. The freedom and glory of sonship, demonstrated through an expanded consciousness, will awaken and free creation from its bondage to decay."

I am sure there will be many more discoveries of the heavenly and dimensional realms that are connected to our governmental and creational sonship abilities that will be revealed if we continue the journey to mature sonship.

Journey Reflections

"Son, restoration is a progressive process, as you have experienced in your own journey to enlightenment. Each encounter has multiple layers of revelation that unfold as you mature in character and in the ability to love unconditionally."

I shifted my focus to the realm of light that I abide in and mused and pondered what the Father had just said about my journey. The light of truth that was streaming from the facets of His face was like a data stream of memories that illuminated my mind. Memories of progressive revelation focused my attention as I recalled those precious remembrances of previous encounters that took me deeper into truth.

The fire stone encounters have always been life-changing and are responsible for the many challenges I have faced over the last 13 years. That is where the latter part of my journey began in 2008, with encounters of love that started to reveal the true character and nature of God as love.

That first love encounter was the catalyst for my journey of deconstruction that would later cause so much cognitive dissonance, as my experiences of love challenged my belief about penal substitutional atonement and eventually hell as eternal conscious torment. Those theological doctrines that had programmed me to believe in a God of judgment and wrath, who would consign the majority of creation to eternal torment and separation, were melted away and consumed by love.

Love encounters revealed the oracles of the Father's heart which showed me how limitless and unconditional love is, and therefore by definition who God is. I remembered the encounters, not just as memories of experiences, but I began to relive those precious and life-changing engagements at a level only now possible because of my expanded consciousness towards love – a love so strong that death itself could not defeat it and that is constantly at work to overcome every negative thought and action within everyone at every moment; as I discovered when under the waterfall, a love so powerful that it is unconditional towards all created things, treating all without prejudice. The victim and the victimiser, the abused and abuser, trafficked and trafficker loved equally – a concept that so challenged my idea of justice and fairness – but I soon realised that justice and mercy are synonymous terms to a loving Father.

I remembered how hard it was to accept that all of creation could be restored, including the fallen angels and dimensional beings, but all my objections were consumed one by one in my encounters with the fire of God's love.

- My journey to discover how limitless God's grace is towards all and everything, because love can be nothing but unconditional or it is not love at all.
- My journey to discover how to live loved, love living and live loving; which transformed my understanding and experience of legalism, obedience and works-based performance orientation that had kept me trapped under old covenant law mindsets.
- My journey to find the true rest of love, joy and peace within an expanded consciousness that enabled multidimensional living with exponential energy production. That journey took me through the cosmos, reuniting me with creation itself, where I engaged the harmonious music of the spheres, spaghettified to be at one with creation, experiencing no absence of light in the beginning, and reconnecting with the Elementals.
- My journey to discover true creative reality that I could choose, aligned with the Father's heart, where desires became thoughts and thoughts became sound frequencies that excited the living light grace strings to form reality. I discovered the Cradle of Life, the waterfall of the Sound of Many Waters, the Chamber of Destiny and the Chamber of Creation, and remembered the groan of creation emanating from the black holes.
- My progressive journey to be free from the entanglement to time, where I learned how to expand and contract time, bend time and space, journey in time, expand quantum moments, translate, transrelocate and be multidimensional.
- My journey to discover portals and gateways of spirit, soul and body to eventually experience the Merkabah, dimensional portals, energy gates, energy production within the core of my innermost being.

- My journey to discover the state of being that is my true creational identity within *I am that I am* and to know *I am that I am* is in me.
- My journey to discover the nature of government in love from fire stones to the judgment seat, fiery altar, Holy of Holies, four faces of God, order of Melchizedek, oracles of the Father's heart, Circle of the Deep and the 12 Chancellors' Houses and Thrones.
- My journey beyond beyond continues to expand me, enlighten me, transform and restore me to sonship – and I am sure that there is so much more to come.

Multiple threads of my experiential encounters were intricately woven together to create a wonderful tapestry of my journey to love, enlightenment, sonship and restoration: a wild ride of exploration and progressive revelation full of ups and downs, twists and turns.

I am that I am, fearfully and wonderfully made by the passionate desires and vast and amazing thoughts that my loving Father has about me that enable me to be me.

Creation is waiting and longing for the revealing of the sons of God so it can be set free into the glory of our sonship.

Will you respond and take your place as a son of God?

Are you willing to go through the process of deconstruction it will take to free you from the great deception?

Are you willing to turn from the pathway of independence to find union and oneness within the Tree of Life?

Are you willing to embrace your destiny within the restoration of all things?

Appendices

Appendix 1. 'The day of the Lord' scriptures

So it will happen in that day,
that the Lord will punish the host of heaven on high,
and the kings of the earth on earth.
They will be gathered together
Like prisoners in the dungeon,
and will be confined in prison;
and after many days they will be punished. (Isaiah 24:21-22).

Near is the great day of the Lord,
Near and coming very quickly;
Listen, the day of the Lord!
In it the warrior cries out bitterly.
A day of wrath is that day,
A day of trouble and distress,
A day of destruction and desolation,
A day of darkness and gloom,
A day of clouds and thick darkness,
A day of trumpet and battle cry
Against the fortified cities
And the high corner towers. (Zephaniah 1:14-16).

Behold, the day of the Lord is coming,
Cruel, with fury and burning anger,
To make the land a desolation;
And He will exterminate its sinners from it.
For the stars of heaven and their constellations
Will not flash forth their light;
The sun will be dark when it rises
And the moon will not shed its light.
Thus I will punish the world for its evil

APPENDICES

And the wicked for their iniquity;
I will also put an end to the arrogance of the proud
And abase the haughtiness of the ruthless. (Isaiah 13:9-11).

For that day belongs to the Lord God of hosts,
A day of vengeance, so as to avenge Himself on His foes;
And the sword will devour and be satiated
And drink its fill of their blood;
For there will be a slaughter for the Lord God of hosts,
In the land of the north by the river Euphrates.
(Jeremiah 46:10).

"The increase of his house will depart;
His possessions will flow away in the day of His anger.
This is the wicked man's portion from God,
Even the heritage decreed to him by God." (Job 20:28-29).

A sound of tumult on the mountains,
Like that of many people!
A sound of the uproar of kingdoms,
Of nations gathered together!
The Lord of hosts is mustering the army for battle.
They are coming from a far country,
From the farthest horizons,
The Lord and His instruments of indignation,
To destroy the whole land.
Wail, for the day of the Lord is near!
It will come as destruction from the Almighty. (Isaiah 13:4-6).

In that day the Egyptians will become like women, and they will tremble and be in dread because of the waving of the hand of the Lord of hosts, which He is going to wave over them. The land of Judah will become a terror to Egypt; everyone to whom it is mentioned will be in dread of it, because of the purpose of the Lord of hosts which He is purposing against them. (Isaiah 19:16-17).

"For the day is near,
Even the day of the Lord is near;
It will be a day of clouds,
A time of doom for the nations.
A sword will come upon Egypt,
And anguish will be in Ethiopia;
When the slain fall in Egypt,
They take away her wealth,
And her foundations are torn down." (Ezekiel 30:3-4).

In that day the Lord will punish Leviathan the fleeing serpent, With His fierce and great and mighty sword, Even Leviathan the twisted serpent; And He will kill the dragon who lives in the sea. (Isaiah 27:1).

"Let the nations be aroused
And come up to the valley of Jehoshaphat,
For there I will sit to judge
All the surrounding nations.
Put in the sickle, for the harvest is ripe.
Come, tread, for the wine press is full;
The vats overflow, for their wickedness is great.
Multitudes, multitudes in the valley of decision!
For the day of the Lord is near in the valley of decision."
(Joel 3:12-14).

"Therefore wait for Me," declares the Lord,
"For the day when I rise up as a witness.
Indeed, My decision is to gather nations,
To assemble kingdoms,
To pour out on them My indignation,
All My burning anger;

APPENDICES

*For all the earth will be devoured
By the fire of My zeal."* (Zephaniah 3:8).

... on the day when, according to my gospel, God will judge the secrets of men through Christ Jesus. (Romans 2:16).

Then the kings of the earth and the great men and the commanders and the rich and the strong and every slave and free man hid themselves in the caves and among the rocks of the mountains; and they said to the mountains and to the rocks, "Fall on us and hide us from the presence of Him who sits on the throne, and from the wrath of the Lamb; for the great day of their wrath has come, and who is able to stand?" (Revelation 6:15-17).

*Alas, you who are longing for the day of the Lord,
For what purpose will the day of the Lord be to you?
It will be darkness and not light;
As when a man flees from a lion
And a bear meets him,
Or goes home, leans his hand against the wall
And a snake bites him.
Will not the day of the Lord be darkness instead of light,
Even gloom with no brightness in it?* (Amos 5:18-20).

*For the Lord of hosts will have a day of reckoning
Against everyone who is proud and lofty
And against everyone who is lifted up,
That he may be abased.* (Isaiah 2:12).

*Alas for the day!
For the day of the Lord is near,
And it will come as destruction from the Almighty.* (Joel 1:15).

*Blow a trumpet in Zion,
And sound an alarm on My holy mountain!*

Let all the inhabitants of the land tremble,
For the day of the Lord is coming;
Surely it is near,
A day of darkness and gloom,
A day of clouds and thick darkness.
As the dawn is spread over the mountains,
So there is a great and mighty people;
There has never been anything like it,
Nor will there be again after it
To the years of many generations.
A fire consumes before them
And behind them a flame burns.
The land is like the garden of Eden before them
But a desolate wilderness behind them,
And nothing at all escapes them.
Their appearance is like the appearance of horses;
And like war horses, so they run. (Joel 2:1-4).

"Many will say to Me on that day, 'Lord, Lord, did we not prophesy in Your name, and in Your name cast out demons, and in Your name perform many miracles?' And then I will declare to them, 'I never knew you; depart from Me, you who practice lawlessness.'" (Matthew 7:22-23).

"He who rejects Me and does not receive My sayings, has one who judges him; the word I spoke is what will judge him at the last day." (John 12:48).

But because of your stubbornness and unrepentant heart you are storing up wrath for yourself in the day of wrath and revelation of the righteous judgment of God... (Romans 2:5).

'Alas! for that day is great,
There is none like it;

*And it is the time of Jacob's distress,
But he will be saved from it.*

'It shall come about on that day,' declares the Lord of hosts, 'that I will break his yoke from off their neck and will tear off their bonds; and strangers will no longer make them their slaves. (Jeremiah 30:7-8).

*So rejoice, O sons of Zion,
And be glad in the Lord your God;
For He has given you the early rain for your vindication.
And He has poured down for you the rain,
The early and latter rain as before.
The threshing floors will be full of grain,
And the vats will overflow with the new wine and oil.
Then I will make up to you for the years
That the swarming locust has eaten,
The creeping locust, the stripping locust and the gnawing locust,
My great army which I sent among you.* (Joel 2:23-25).

*Then it will happen on that day that the Lord
Will again recover the second time with His hand
The remnant of His people, who will remain,
From Assyria, Egypt, Pathros, Cush, Elam, Shinar, Hamath,
And from the islands of the sea.* (Isaiah 11:11).

In that day the Lord will start His threshing from the flowing stream of the Euphrates to the brook of Egypt, and you will be gathered up one by one, O sons of Israel. It will come about also in that day that a great trumpet will be blown, and those who were perishing in the land of Assyria and who were scattered in the land of Egypt will come and worship the Lord in the holy mountain at Jerusalem. (Isaiah 27:12-13).

*"In that day," declares the Lord,
"I will assemble the lame
And gather the outcasts,
Even those whom I have afflicted.
I will make the lame a remnant
And the outcasts a strong nation,
And the Lord will reign over them in Mount Zion
From now on and forever."* (Micah 4:6-7).

"And then the sign of the Son of Man will appear in the sky, and then all the tribes of the earth will mourn, and they will see the Son of Man coming on the clouds of the sky with power and great glory. And He will send forth His angels with a great trumpet and they will gather together His elect from the four winds, from one end of the sky to the other." (Matthew 24:30-31)

"Then they will see the Son of Man coming in clouds with great power and glory. And then He will send forth the angels, and will gather together His elect from the four winds, from the farthest end of the earth to the farthest end of heaven." (Mark 13:26-27).

*Shout for joy, O daughter of Zion!
Shout in triumph, O Israel!
Rejoice and exult with all your heart,
O daughter of Jerusalem!
The Lord has taken away His judgments against you,
He has cleared away your enemies.
The King of Israel, the Lord, is in your midst;
You will fear disaster no more.
In that day it will be said to Jerusalem:
"Do not be afraid, O Zion;
Do not let your hands fall limp."* (Zephaniah 3:14-16).

... then the Lord will create over the whole area of Mount Zion and over her assemblies a cloud by day, even smoke, and the brightness of a flaming fire by night; for over all the glory will be a canopy. There will be a shelter to give shade from the heat by day, and refuge and protection from the storm and the rain. (Isaiah 4:5-6).

In that day this song will be sung in the land of Judah:
"We have a strong city;
He sets up walls and ramparts for security." (Isaiah 26:1)

"And it will come about that whoever calls on the name of the Lord
Will be delivered;
For on Mount Zion and in Jerusalem
There will be those who escape,
As the Lord has said,
Even among the survivors whom the Lord calls." (Joel 2:32).

The Lord roars from Zion
And utters His voice from Jerusalem,
And the heavens and the earth tremble.
But the Lord is a refuge for His people
And a stronghold to the sons of Israel.
Then you will know that I am the Lord your God,
Dwelling in Zion, My holy mountain.
So Jerusalem will be holy,
And strangers will pass through it no more.

And in that day
The mountains will drip with sweet wine,
And the hills will flow with milk,
And all the brooks of Judah will flow with water;
And a spring will go out from the house of the Lord
To water the valley of Shittim. (Joel 3:16-18).

*And the Lord their God will save them in that day
As the flock of His people;
For they are as the stones of a crown,
Sparkling in His land.
For what comeliness and beauty will be theirs!
Grain will make the young men flourish, and new wine the
virgins.* (Zechariah 9:16-17).

*It will come about that he who is left in Zion and remains in
Jerusalem will be called holy – everyone who is recorded for
life in Jerusalem. When the Lord has washed away the filth of
the daughters of Zion and purged the bloodshed of Jerusalem
from her midst, by the spirit of judgment and the spirit of
burning...* (Isaiah 4:3-4).

*"In that day you will feel no shame
Because of all your deeds
By which you have rebelled against Me;
For then I will remove from your midst
Your proud, exulting ones,
And you will never again be haughty
On My holy mountain.
But I will leave among you
A humble and lowly people,
And they will take refuge in the name of the Lord.
The remnant of Israel will do no wrong
And tell no lies,
Nor will a deceitful tongue
Be found in their mouths;
For they will feed and lie down
With no one to make them tremble."* (Zephaniah 3:11-13).

*In that day there will be inscribed on the bells of the horses,
"HOLY TO THE LORD." And the cooking pots in the Lord's*

house will be like the bowls before the altar. Every cooking pot in Jerusalem and in Judah will be holy to the Lord of hosts; and all who sacrifice will come and take of them and boil in them. And there will no longer be a Canaanite in the house of the Lord of hosts in that day. (Zechariah 14:20-21).

"For behold, the day is coming, burning like a furnace; and all the arrogant and every evildoer will be chaff; and the day that is coming will set them ablaze," says the Lord of hosts, "so that it will leave them neither root nor branch. But for you who fear My name, the sun of righteousness will rise with healing in its wings; and you will go forth and skip about like calves from the stall." (Malachi 4:1-2).

As for you, tower of the flock,
Hill of the daughter of Zion,
To you it will come –
Even the former dominion will come,
The kingdom of the daughter of Jerusalem." (Micah 4:8).

The remnant of Jacob
Will be among the nations,
Among many peoples
Like a lion among the beasts of the forest,
Like a young lion among flocks of sheep,
Which, if he passes through,
Tramples down and tears,
And there is none to rescue.
Your hand will be lifted up against your adversaries,
And all your enemies will be cut off. (Micah 5:8-9).

And there will no longer be any night; and they will not have need of the light of a lamp nor the light of the sun, because the Lord God will illumine them; and they will reign forever and ever. (Revelation 22:5).

For I am confident of this very thing, that He who began a good work in you will perfect it until the day of Christ Jesus. (Philippians 1:6).

"Now at that time Michael, the great prince who stands guard over the sons of your people, will arise. And there will be a time of distress such as never occurred since there was a nation until that time; and at that time your people, everyone who is found written in the book, will be rescued. Many of those who sleep in the dust of the ground will awake, these to everlasting life, but the others to disgrace and everlasting contempt." (Daniel 12:1-2).

"For this is the will of My Father, that everyone who beholds the Son and believes in Him will have eternal life, and I Myself will raise him up on the last day." (John 6:40).

Martha said to Him, "I know that he will rise again in the resurrection on the last day." (John 11:24).

... who will also confirm you to the end, blameless in the day of our Lord Jesus Christ. (1 Corinthians 1:8).

For this reason I also suffer these things, but I am not ashamed; for I know whom I have believed and I am convinced that He is able to guard what I have entrusted to Him until that day. (2 Timothy 1:12).

... in the future there is laid up for me the crown of righteousness, which the Lord, the righteous Judge, will award to me on that day; and not only to me, but also to all who have loved His appearing. (2 Timothy 4:8).

"Therefore prophesy, son of man, and say to Gog, 'Thus says the Lord God, "On that day when My people Israel are living securely, will you not know it? You will come from your place

out of the remote parts of the north, you and many peoples with you, all of them riding on horses, a great assembly and a mighty army; and you will come up against My people Israel like a cloud to cover the land. It shall come about in the last days that I will bring you against My land, so that the nations may know Me when I am sanctified through you before their eyes, O Gog." (Ezekiel 38:14-16).

For I will gather all the nations against Jerusalem to battle, and the city will be captured, the houses plundered, the women ravished and half of the city exiled, but the rest of the people will not be cut off from the city. (Zechariah 14:2).

"But when you see Jerusalem surrounded by armies, then recognize that her desolation is near." (Luke 21:20).

... and will come out to deceive the nations which are in the four corners of the earth, Gog and Magog, to gather them together for the war; the number of them is like the sand of the seashore. And they came up on the broad plain of the earth and surrounded the camp of the saints and the beloved city, and fire came down from heaven and devoured them. (Revelation 20:8-9)

In that day the Branch of the Lord will be beautiful and glorious, and the fruit of the earth will be the pride and the adornment of the survivors of Israel. (Isaiah 4:2).

Then in that day
The nations will resort to the root of Jesse,
Who will stand as a signal for the peoples;
And His resting place will be glorious. (Isaiah 11:10).

"But they shall serve the Lord their God and David their king, whom I will raise up for them." (Jeremiah 30:9).

Afterward the sons of Israel will return and seek the Lord their God and David their king; and they will come trembling to the Lord and to His goodness in the last days. (Hosea 3:5).

*"In that day I will raise up the fallen booth of David,
And wall up its breaches;
I will also raise up its ruins
And rebuild it as in the days of old..."* (Amos 9:11).

*Rejoice greatly, O daughter of Zion!
Shout in triumph, O daughter of Jerusalem!
Behold, your king is coming to you;
He is just and endowed with salvation,
Humble, and mounted on a donkey,
Even on a colt, the foal of a donkey.* (Zechariah 9:9).

"I will pour out on the house of David and on the inhabitants of Jerusalem, the Spirit of grace and of supplication, so that they will look on Me whom they have pierced; and they will mourn for Him, as one mourns for an only son, and they will weep bitterly over Him like the bitter weeping over a firstborn." (Zechariah 12:10).

For you yourselves know full well that the day of the Lord will come just like a thief in the night. While they are saying, "Peace and safety!" then destruction will come upon them suddenly like labor pains upon a woman with child, and they will not escape. (1 Thessalonians 5:2-3).

"But be sure of this, that if the head of the house had known at what time of the night the thief was coming, he would have been on the alert and would not have allowed his house to be broken into. For this reason you also must be ready; for the Son of Man is coming at an hour when you do not think He will." (Matthew 24:43-44).

"But be sure of this, that if the head of the house had known at what hour the thief was coming, he would not have allowed his house to be broken into. You too, be ready; for the Son of Man is coming at an hour that you do not expect." (Luke 12:39-40).

But of that day or hour no one knows, not even the angels in heaven, nor the Son, but the Father alone. (Mark 13:32).

But the day of the Lord will come like a thief, in which the heavens will pass away with a roar and the elements will be destroyed with intense heat, and the earth and its works will be burned up. (2 Peter 3:10).

But you, brethren, are not in darkness, that the day would overtake you like a thief; for you are all sons of light and sons of day. We are not of night nor of darkness; so then let us not sleep as others do, but let us be alert and sober. (1 Thessalonians 5:4-6).

You have not gone up into the breaches, nor did you build the wall around the house of Israel to stand in the battle on the day of the Lord. (Ezekiel 13:5).

Gather yourselves together, yes, gather,
O nation without shame,
Before the decree takes effect –
The day passes like the chaff –
Before the burning anger of the Lord comes upon you,
Before the day of the Lord's anger comes upon you.
Seek the Lord,
All you humble of the earth
Who have carried out His ordinances;
Seek righteousness, seek humility.

*Perhaps you will be hidden
In the day of the Lord's anger.* (Zephaniah 2:1-3).

"Behold, I am going to send you Elijah the prophet before the coming of the great and terrible day of the Lord." (Malachi 4:5).

Since all these things are to be destroyed in this way, what sort of people ought you to be in holy conduct and godliness, looking for and hastening the coming of the day of God, because of which the heavens will be destroyed by burning, and the elements will melt with intense heat! (2 Peter 3:11-12).

"... so, you too, when you see all these things, recognize that He is near, right at the door." (Matthew 24:33).

"Even so, you too, when you see these things happening, recognize that He is near, right at the door." (Mark 13:29).

"So you also, when you see these things happening, recognize that the kingdom of God is near." (Luke 21:31).

Let no one in any way deceive you, for it will not come unless the apostasy comes first, and the man of lawlessness is revealed, the son of destruction... (2 Thessalonians 2:3).

*"And I will grant wonders in the sky above
And signs on the earth below,
Blood, and fire, and vapor of smoke.
The sun will be turned into darkness
And the moon into blood,
Before the great and glorious day of the Lord shall come."*
(Acts 2:19-20).

*"I will display wonders in the sky and on the earth,
Blood, fire and columns of smoke.
The sun will be turned into darkness
And the moon into blood*

Before the great and awesome day of the Lord comes."
(Joel 2:30-31).

Before them the earth quakes,
The heavens tremble,
The sun and the moon grow dark
And the stars lose their brightness. (Joel 2:10).

"... and there will be great earthquakes, and in various places plagues and famines; and there will be terrors and great signs from heaven." (Luke 21:11).

Its roaring is like a lioness, and it roars like young lions;
It growls as it seizes the prey
And carries it off with no one to deliver it.
And it will growl over it in that day like the roaring of the sea.
If one looks to the land, behold, there is darkness and distress; Even the light is darkened by its clouds. (Isaiah 5:29-30).

'Thus says the Lord God,
"I will also make the hordes of Egypt cease
By the hand of Nebuchadnezzar king of Babylon."'
(Ezekiel 30:10).

"Therefore, I will make you go into exile beyond Damascus," says the Lord, whose name is the God of hosts. (Amos 5:27).

"For then there will be a great tribulation, such as has not occurred since the beginning of the world until now, nor ever will." (Matthew 24:21).

"For those days will be a time of tribulation such as has not occurred since the beginning of the creation which God created until now, and never will." (Mark 13:19).

*And He will lift up a standard for the nations
And assemble the banished ones of Israel,
And will gather the dispersed of Judah
From the four corners of the earth.
Then the jealousy of Ephraim will depart,
And those who harass Judah will be cut off;
Ephraim will not be jealous of Judah,
And Judah will not harass Ephraim.
They will swoop down on the slopes of the Philistines on the west;
Together they will plunder the sons of the east;
They will possess Edom and Moab,
And the sons of Ammon will be subject to them.* (Isaiah 11:12-14).

"'On that day,' declares the Lord of hosts, 'I will take you, Zerubbabel, son of Shealtiel, My servant,' declares the Lord, 'and I will make you like a signet ring, for I have chosen you,' declares the Lord of hosts." (Haggai 2:23).

Now listen, Joshua the high priest, you and your friends who are sitting in front of you – indeed they are men who are a symbol, for behold, I am going to bring in My servant the Branch. (Zechariah 3:8).

Appendix 2. Comparison Charts

Comparison of Jesus' Second Coming
in Matthew 24 and 1 Thessalonians 4:15-17 and 5:1-8

Events occurring during Jesus' Coming	Matthew 24	1 Thessalonians 4 and 5
Jesus returns from heaven	24:30	4:16
With the voice of an Archangel	24:31	4:16
With the trumpet of God	24:31	4:16
Caught up/Gathered together with/to Christ	24:31	4:17
Christ comes as a thief	24:43	5:2
Exact time unknown	24:36	5:1-2
Time of birth pangs	24:8	5:3
Meet the Lord in the clouds	24:30 25:6	4:17
Believers not deceived	24:43	5:4-5
Believers to be watchful	24:42	5:6
Son/Sunlight shining from East to West	24:27, 36, 38	5:4-8
Exhorted to be sober	24:49	5:7

APPENDICES

Comparison of Daniel and Revelation and other NT books re: 67-70 AD when 'the power of the holy people is shattered'.

Events of 67-70 AD	Daniel	Revelation etc.
The leopard, bear, lion, 10 horns	7:4-6, 8	13:1-2, 12:3, 17:3-8
Books were opened	7:10-13	20:12,1:7-17
War against the saints	7:21-27	13:7, 11:15-19;21-22
Transgression filled up	9:24-27	6:9-11,17:4-6, 11:8, 16:6-8
Judgment on Jerusalem	9:24-27	11:8
Seal up vision and prophecy	9:24-27	10:6-7 (2 Peter 3)
Put an end to sin, atone for wickedness and bring righteousness	9:24-27	7:14-17, 21:27, 22:12-14
To anoint the most holy place	9:24-27	21:16-18

APPENDICES

Events of 67-70 AD	Daniel	Revelation etc.
The anointed one cut off, he will end sacrifices and offerings	9:24-27	7:14-17, 21:27, 22:12-14
The end in war, abomination of desolation, power shattered, 3½ years	9:27-27, 12:7	11:1-8, (Luke 21:20, 24-32)
3½ years of tribulation	12:1,7	7:14, 12:14
Dead raised and judged for 3½ years	12:2-3,7	11; 20:5-15 (Acts 24:15)
Daniel told to seal up vision 'until the time of the end' John told *not* to seal up the vision 'for the time is at hand'	12:4,9,13 8:26, 10:14	22:10 (Mark 8:38-9:1) (John 21:18-23)

Appendix 3. Christian Zionism

Reformed theology is in no way Zionist. Many good books and online articles challenge the accepted evangelical view of Christian Zionism, written by very conservative commenters.

If you wish to go deeper into the history of dispensationalism and Christian Zionism, below are some excellent academic works which may be helpful:

Apocalyptic Theopolitics: Dispensationalism, Israel/Palestine, and Ecclesial Enactments of Eschatology A Thesis Submitted for the Degree of Doctor of Philosophy, Faculty of Divinity by Elizabeth Phillips

https://www.repository.cam.ac.uk/bitstream/handle/1810/288883/apocalyptic_theopolotics_combined.pdf

Another academic thesis is *The Promised Land: A Critical Investigation of Evangelical Christian Zionism n Britain and the United States of America since 1800* by Stephen Sizer:

https://eprints.mdx.ac.uk/6403/1/Sizer-promised_land.phd.pdf

A political history of Zionism can be found in another article by Stephen Sizer, *The Road to Balfour: The History of Christian Zionism*

https://balfourproject.org/the-road-to-balfour-the-history-of-christian-zionism-by-stephen-sizer-2/

A good article from a reformed perspective is *Why I am not a Christian Zionist* by Gary M. Burge

https://www.thebanner.org/features/2019/12/why-i-m-not-a-christian-zionist

APPENDICES

Appendix 4. Further Zionist quotes from Israeli Prime Ministers and other politicians[103]

"They are as grasshoppers in our sight." – Prime Minister Yitzhak Shamir

"We say to them *[Palestinian rioters]* from the heights of this mountain and from the perspective of thousands of years of history that they are like grasshoppers compared to us." – Yitzhak Shamir, *New York Times*, April 1, 1988.

"All of the land of Israel is ours." – Prime Minister Yitzhak Shamir.

"We shall use the ultimate force until Palestinians come crawling to us on all fours." – Deputy Prime Minister Rafael Eitan.

"[When we build settlements] Arabs will only be able to scurry around like drugged cockroaches in a bottle." – Deputy Prime Minister Rafael Eitan.

"We shall reduce the Palestinians to a community of woodcutters and waiters." – Prime Minister Yitzhak Rabin, 1960, The Arabs in Israel.

"There is a huge gap between us and our enemies not just in ability but in morality, culture, sanctity of life, and conscience." – President Moshe Katsav, *Jerusalem Post*, May 10, 2001

"There is no such thing as a Palestinian." – Prime Minister Golda Meir, The Sunday Times, June 15, 1969 (later parroted by Newt Gingrich and Rick Santorum).

---

[103] Zionist quotes (and editorial opinions) excerpted from the internet article http://www.thehypertexts.com/Zionist%20Quotes.htm

"It is not as though there was a Palestinian people ... and we came and threw them out and took their country away from them ... they did not exist." – Prime Minister Golda Meir, *The Sunday Times*, June 15, 1969 (also reported in the *Washington Post*, June 16, 1969).

"How can we return the held territories? There is nobody to return them to." – Prime Minister Golda Meir, March 8, 1969.

"Anyone who speaks in favour of bringing the Arab refugees back ... It is better that things are stated clearly and plainly: We shall not let this happen." – Prime Minister Golda Meir.

"There are no two peoples here. There is a Jewish people and an Arab population. There is no Palestinian people, so you don't create a state for an imaginary nation. They only call themselves a people in order to fight the Jews." – Benzion Netanyahu, Maariv interview, April 3, 2009.

Israel's Defence Minister Avigdor Lieberman said in an interview that every Palestinian is a target for the army's snipers, even women and children: "It has to be understood that there are no innocent people in Gaza."

"The Palestinians are like crocodiles, the more you give them meat, they want more." – Ehud Barak, Prime Minister of Israel, August 28, 2000 and reported in the *Jerusalem Post* on August 30, 2000.

"[The Palestinians] are beasts walking on two legs." – Israeli Prime Minister Menachem Begin, speech to the Knesset, quoted in Amnon Kapeliouk, "Begin and the Beasts" in the *New Statesman*, June 25, 1982.

"The Partition of Palestine is illegal. It will never be recognized ... Jerusalem was and will forever be our capital.

Eretz Israel will be restored to the people of Israel. All of it. And for Ever." (Iron Wall p. 25 and Simha Flapan p. 32) Menachem Begin, speaking one day after the UN partition plan was ratified.

"I believed and to this day still believe, in our people's eternal and historic right to this entire land." – Prime Minister Ehud Olmert.

Weitz

"There is no other way than to transfer the Arabs from here to neighbouring countries, all of them." [from his published diary in five volumes, located in the Zionist Archives in Jerusalem.]

"Not one village, not one [Arab] tribe should be left." [ibid].

"If the Arabs leave, the country will become wide and spacious for us [Jews]." [ibid].

"Only after this transfer will the country be able to absorb millions of our [Jewish] brothers." [ibid].

"The transfer of Arabs from the Jewish state [serves two aims]: to diminish the Arab population and release Arab land to Jews." [ibid].

Jabotinsky

"Settlement can thus develop under the protection of a force that is not dependent on the local population, behind an iron wall which they will be powerless to break down." [Ha'aretz Daily, 1923].

"We all [i.e., Zionists of all stripes] demand that there should be an iron wall." ["The Iron Wall" in Razsviet, April 11, 1923].

"And we are all of us, without any exception, demanding day after day that this outside Power [Great Britain], should carry out this task vigorously and with determination." [ibid].

"There is no justice, no law, and no God in heaven, only a single law which decides and supersedes all – [Jewish] settlement [of the land]." [Righteous Victims, p. 108].

"Arabs must make room for Jews. If it was possible to transfer the Baltic peoples, it is also possible to transfer the Palestinians." [*Expulsion of the Palestinians*, p. 29].

"Hitler – odious as he is to us – has given this idea [transfer, ethnic cleansing] a good name in the world. [*One Palestine Complete*, p. 407].

With the two quotes above, Jabotinsky advocated the emulation of Stalin's 1941 ethnic cleansing of the "Baltic peoples" in which over 40,000 Estonians, Latvians and Lithuanians were forcibly transferred and less than half survived, and of Hitler's ethnic cleansing of Jews, Gypsies and other "undesirable" people, which also resulted in a massive death rate, even before the mass killings began. Such massive deportations cannot take place without many unjust, premature deaths, so in effect this was a call for serial murder. – thehypertexts.com: *Zionist Quotes*

"If we desire that Israel should become and remain a Jewish State, we must, first of all, create a Jewish majority [by expelling Arabs.]" [The Ideology of Betar].

"Colonisation carries its own explanation, the only possible explanation, unalterable and as clear as daylight to every ordinary Jew and every ordinary Arab." ["The Iron Wall" in Razsviet, April 11, 1923}.

Bible quotations:

Unless otherwise noted, all scripture quotations are taken from the (NASB®) New American Standard Bible®, Copyright © 1960, 1971, 1977, 1995, 2020 by The Lockman Foundation. Used by permission. All rights reserved. www.lockman.org

Other versions used:

AMP: Scripture taken from the Amplified Bible, Copyright © 2015 by The Lockman Foundation. Used by permission.

AMPC: Scripture taken from the Amplified Bible, Classic Edition. Copyright © 1954, 1958, 1962, 1964, 1965, 1987 by The Lockman Foundation. Used by permission (www.lockman.org).

CEV: Scripture quotations are from the Contemporary English Version Copyright © 1991, 1992, 1995 by American Bible Society. Used by Permission.

KJV: King James Version. This translation is in the Public Domain.

Mirror: The Mirror Bible. Copyright © 2017, 2021 by Francois du Toit. Used by kind permission of the author. All rights reserved.

NIV: Scripture quotations taken from The Holy Bible, New International Version® NIV®. Copyright © 1973, 1978, 1984, 2011 by Biblica, Inc.™. Used by permission. All rights reserved worldwide.

NKJV: Scripture taken from the New King James Version®. Copyright © 1982 by Thomas Nelson. Used by permission. All rights reserved.

NLT: Scripture quotations are taken from the Holy Bible, New Living Translation, copyright ©1996, 2004, 2007, 2013 by Tyndale House Foundation. Used by permission of Tyndale House Publishers, Inc., Carol Stream, Illinois 60188. All rights reserved.

YLT: Bible text is quoted from Young's Literal Translation by Robert Young, published by Baker Book House, Grand Rapids, MI. This translation is in the Public Domain.

Further resources

Books

Mike's previous books, *My Journey Beyond Beyond* (2018) and *The Restoration of All Things* (2021) are available from online and local booksellers. For more details visit our website:

    eg.freedomarc.org/journey
    eg.freedomarc.org/roat

Other resources

Other resources from Mike Parsons and Freedom Apostolic Ministries include:

Engaging God: our self-paced monthly subscription programme for the Joshua Generation. Visit eg.freedomarc.org/subscribe-to-engaging-god

Patreon: an opportunity to partner in taking the message of God's unconditional love, limitless grace and triumphant mercy to all His children. Become a patron at patreon.com/freedomarc to join Mike and other patrons for monthly group Zooms and other benefits.

Mike's YouTube channel: new videos are normally posted daily. View and subscribe at freedomarc.org/youtube

Sons of Issachar blog: short written articles drawn from Mike's teaching and online conversations. Read and subscribe at freedomarc.blog

Social media: follow Freedom ARC at

    freedomarc.org/facebook
    freedomarc.org/twitter
    freedomarc.org/instagram
    freedomarc.org/pinterest